All in One®

Recommended by **Teachers** Trusted by **Toppers**

ENGLISH CORE

Class 11

EVERYTHING YOU NEED TO SCORE

- Detailed Study Material for all the Three Sections
- NCERT & Other Important Questions
- CBQs; Extract Based & SA, LA
- Sample Question Papers

CBSE Exams 2026

Author

Parneet Kaur

arihant

SUCCESS AND NOTHING LESS

AF819701

arihant
SUCCESS AND NOTHING LESS

ARIHANT PRAKASHAN

(School Division Series)

卐 *ADMINISTRATIVE & PRODUCTION OFFICES*

Regd. Office

'Ramchhaya' 4577/15, Agarwal Road, Darya Ganj, New Delhi -110002
Tele: 011- 47630600, 43518550; Fax: 011- 23280316

卐 *Head Office*

Kalindi, TP Nagar, Meerut (UP) - 250002, Tel: 0121-7156203, 7156204

卐 *SALES & SUPPORT OFFICES*

Agra, Ahmedabad, Bengaluru, Bareilly, Chennai, Delhi, Guwahati, Hyderabad, Jaipur, Jhansi, Kolkata, Lucknow, Nagpur & Pune.

PO No : TXT-XX-XXXXXXX-X-XX

Published By Arihant Publications (India) Ltd.

For further information about the books published by Arihant, log on to www.arihantbooks.com or e-mail at info@arihantbooks.com

Follow us on

卐 *PRICE* ₹425.00

PRODUCTION TEAM

Publishing Managers
Mahendra Singh Rawat & Keshav Mohan

Cover Designer
Salman Shaikh

Inner Designer
Ankit Tyagi

Project Head
Manju

Page Layouting
Lalit Chaprana

Proof Readers
Harsh Agarwal, Naina Rajya

Index *cum* Study Planner

Book End Elements

One Book- Endless Features

to Help you Succeed

Summary of the Chapter

In each chapter of the Prose, Poety & Supplementary, Summary of the Chapter & Explanation is given in simple and easy to understand language. It will help the students to understand theme of the chapter easily.

Summary of the Chapter

The Author Remembers his Grandparents

The author recalls his grandmother as being old for the past twenty years. It was hard for him to believe that she had once been young and had a husband.

The author's grandfather's portrait hung on the wall of the drawing room. He wore a big turban and looked at least a hundred years old. One could not imagine him in his youth with his wife and children.

The Author's Grandmother

The thought of the grandmother being young and pretty, was almost revolting to the author. She was short, fat and slightly bent in stature.

The author remembered her moving around the house in spotless white clothes with one hand resting on her waist to balance her stoop and the other hand counting the beads of her rosary.

To the author, she could never have been pretty but she reflected a serene beauty.

The Turning Point in their Relationship

The turning point came in their relationship when they moved to the city to stay with the author's parents. In the city, the author went to an English school in a motor bus and learned subjects that his grandmother did not understand.

Grandmother Distressed and Disturbed

The grandmother was distressed to learn that there was no teaching about God and the scriptures in the school.

Moreover, she was very disturbed at the idea of music lessons being given at the English school. To her, music had immoral associations.

The Common Link of Friendship gets Snapped

The common link of friendship between them broke when the author started going to the University and was given a room of his own. The grandmother accepted her loneliness and spent her time spinning wheel while praying.

Only in the afternoon, she relaxed for a while to feed the sparrows in the verandah.

Word-Meaning

portrait	—	true picture
mantelpiece	—	shelf above a fireplace
fables of the prophets	—	stories of the Sikh Gurus
stoop	—	bent body due to old age
telling the beads	—	counting the beads while chanting prayers
rosary	—	a string of beads used for counting prayers as they are chanted
puckered	—	wrinkled
monotonous	—	unchanging/boring
in a chorus	—	together
courtyard house	—	an open space just outside the
lewd	—	indecent
harlots	—	prostitutes
bedlam	—	confusion
dilapidated	—	falling to pieces
pallor	—	pale colouring of the face
shroud	—	a piece of cloth used to cover a dead body before cremation
crude	—	made in a simple manner

Word Meaning

In each chapter of the Prose, Poetry and Supplementary, Difficult words are given along with their meaning. This will help students to understand difficult word easily.

Formats in Writing Section

In Writing section standard format has been given. This will help students to learn proper format of each writing task.

Format of a Poster

Cyber bullying can affect people's mental health. As the Head Girl of your school, prepare a poster in not more than 50 words to make your fellow students aware of its harms. **Competency Based**

Catchy Title

Cyber bullying is

- Intentionally hurting someone's feelings using information and communication technology.
- It can lead to anxiety, depression and low self-esteem.
- Victims often feel isolated and powerless.

Slogan

STOP CYBER BULLYING : STAND TOGETHER
!!!Stop Being Mean on the Screen!!!

Details about the subject

- ✓ LOG OFF the site where the bullying is happening.
- ✓ BLOCK any messages or e-mails.
- ✓ SAVE the message or e-mail.
- ✓ TELL an adult.

STOP BULLYING

One Book- Endless Features

to Help you Succeed

NCERT Folder

Here, we have covered questions of NCERT Textbook (Intext & Exercise) with their detailed answers in simple and easy language.

NCERT Folder

Notice these Expressions (NCERT Page 3)

Notice these expressions in the text. Infer their meaning from the context.

(a) **'the thought was almost revolting'**

Ans. The thought that the author's grandmother was once young and pretty, raises a doubt in the author's mind. He finds it too hard to believe as he had always seen her in the same old and wrinkled physical condition.

(b) **'an expanse of pure white serenity'**

Ans. It refers to the calm, peaceful and serene character of the author's grandmother. She is compared to the peaceful winter landscape in the mountains. She was always attired in spotless white clothes and had silver hair. She, thus, presented a picture of pure white serenity.

(c) **'a turning-point'**

Ans. It refers to the point where the author's relationship with his grandmother changes drastically after they move to the city-house. The grandmother is unable to accompany the author to school as he travels by motor bus. Neither is she able to help him in his lessons. Although they share the same room, a sort of distance developed in their relationship.

the city and left him with his grandmother. She took utmost care of him right from waking him up in the morning to getting him ready for school.

They were always together and enjoyed an easy companionship.

The second phase was when the author's parents asked them to come to the city. This was the time when the author's relationship with his grandmother began to change. The author went to an English school. She could no longer accompany him nor could she help him in his studies. She continued getting him ready for school and asking him about his studies as they shared the same room. However, she rarely talked to him after learning that he was learning music at school. Slowly, the friendship between them weakened.

The third phase came when the common link of their friendship, snapped when the author moved to the University and was given a room of his own.

His grandmother accepted her seclusion with resignation.

2. Mention three reasons why the author's grandmother was disturbed when he started going to the city school.

SELF ASSESSMENT TEST

Extract based Questions

Read the extract given below and answer the questions that follow.

1. All over the verandah and in her room right up to where she lay dead and stiff wrapped in the red shroud, thousands of sparrows sat scattered on the floor. There was no chirruping. We felt sorry for the birds and my mother fetched some bread for them. She broke it into little crumbs, the way my grandmother used to, and threw it to them. The sparrows took no notice of the bread.

   (i) Why were the birds not chirping?

   This could be because

   (a) they were sad
   (b) they had understood that grandmother was dead
   (c) they understood that no one will feed them
   (d) Both (a) and (b)

   (ii) Complete the following suitably.

   The author's mother's offer of bread crumbs to the sparrows shows ....

   (iii) What was done with the bread crumbs when the sparrows refused to eat them?

Short Answer Type Questions

1. Despite her physical appearance, the grandmother has been called beautiful. Why?
2. "Old, so terribly old that she could not have grown older,...." Explain. Why did the author think so?
3. Mention some instances to show that the grandmother was highly composed and patient.
4. The sparrows ignored the author's mother's generous attempt to feed them. What was the possible reason?
5. "When the people are pious and good, even nature mourns their death." Justify. **Competency Based**

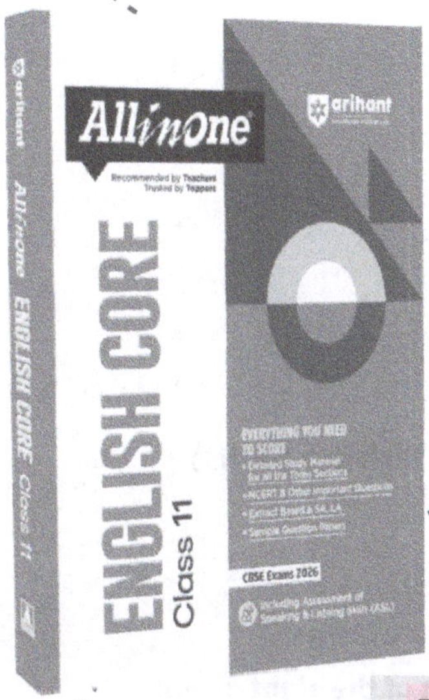

Self Assessment Test

At the end of the chapter, there are unsolved questions for practice and assessment of students. By practising these questions, students can assess their preparation level for the chapter.

Exam Pattern Questions

Each chapter cover all types of questions like MCQs, Extract Based Questions, Short Answer & Long Answer Type Questions.

Exam Pattern Questions

Extract Based Questions

Read the extracts given below and answer the questions that follow.

1. She hobbled about the house in spotless white with one hand resting on her waist to balance her stoop and the other telling the beads of her rosary. Her silver locks were scattered untidily over her pale, puckered face, and her lips constantly moved in inaudible prayer. Yes, she was beautiful. She was like the winter landscape in the mountains, an expanse of pure white serenity breathing peace and contentment.

   (i) Select the option from those given in bracket to fill in the blank.

   The author uses the words 'silver locks' to refer to .... (her eyes/her hair)

   (ii) What is the author's tone in the following sentence?

   "She was like the winter landscape in the mountains, an expense of pure white serenity ...."

   (a) critical
   (b) appreciative
   (c) deductive
   (d) accusatory

   (iii) Why did the grandmother appear like the winter landscape in the mountains?

Ans. (i) her hair

(ii) (b) appreciative

(iii) The grandmother appeared like the winter landscape because she had a divine beauty.

(ii) Complete the following suitably.

The author listened to her prayers because. ....

(iii) What did the author's grandmother do after bathing and dressing him?

Ans. (i) (c) 'I listened because I loved her voice'

(ii) he loved her voice

(iii) The author's grandmother fetched his clean wooden slate, a tiny ink-pot and a red pen to give to him after bathing and dressing him.

3. To her music had lewd associations. It was the monopoly of harlots and beggars and not meant for gentlefolk. She said nothing but her silence meant disapproval. She rarely talked to me after that.

   When I went up to University, I was given a room of my own. The common link of friendship was snapped. My grandmother accepted her seclusion with resignation. She rarely left her spinning-wheel to talk to anyone. From sunrise to sunset she sat by her wheel spinning and reciting prayers.

   (i) Why did the grandmother think that music had 'lewd associations'?

   (ii) In addition to music, what was taught in the author's city school?

   (a) The law of gravity
   (b) Archimedes' Principle
   c The world bein round

Latest Course Structure

Section A (Reading Skills) — 26 Marks

Reading Comprehension through Unseen Passage — **10+8=18 Marks**

1. One unseen passage to assess comprehension, interpretation, analysis, inference and vocabulary. The passage may be factual, descriptive or literary.
2. One unseen **case-based factual** passage with verbal/visual inputs like statistical data, charts etc.to assess comprehension, interpretation, analysis, inference and evaluation.

Note: The combined word limit for both the passages will be 600-750.

Multiple Choice Questions / Objective Type Questions will be asked.

3. Note Making and Summarization based on a passage of approximately 200-250 words.

i. Note Making: **5 Marks**

Title:	1
Numbering and indenting:	1
Key/glossary:	1
Notes:	2

ii. Summary (up to 50 words): **3 Marks**

Content:	2
Expression:	1

Section B (Grammar and Creative Writing Skills) — 23 Marks

Grammar — **7 Marks**

4. Questions on Gap filling (Tenses, Clauses)
5. Questions on re-ordering/transformation of sentences

(Total seven questions to be done out of the eight given).

Creative Writing Skills — **16 Marks**

6. Short Writing Task – Classified Advertisements, up to 50 words. One out of the two given questions to be answered (3 Marks: Format : 1 / Content : 1 / Expression : 1)
7. Short Writing Task – Poster up to 50 words. One out of the two given questions to be answered. (3 marks:Format : 1 / Content : 1 / Expression : 1)
8. Long Writing Task – Speech in 120-150 words based on verbal / visual cues related to contemporary / age-appropriate topic. One out of the two given questions to be answered. (5 Marks: Format: 1 / Content: 2 / Expression: 2)
9. Long Writing Task – Debate based on visual/verbal inputs in 120-150 words, thematically related to contemporary, topical issues. One out of the two given questions to be answered. (5 Marks: Format: 1 / Content: 2 / Expression: 2)

Section C (Literature Text Book and Supplementary Reading Text) 31 Marks

This section will have variety of assessment items including Multiple Choice Questions, Objective Type Questions, Short Answer Type Questions and Long Answer Type Questions to assess comprehension, interpretation, analysis, evaluation and extrapolation beyond the text.

10. One poetry extract out of two, from the book **Hornbill**, to assess comprehension, interpretation, analysis, inference and appreciation. *(3x1=3 Marks)*
11. One prose extract out of two, from the book **Hornbill**, to assess comprehension, interpretation, analysis, evaluation and appreciation. *(3x1=3 Marks)*
12. One prose extract out of two, from the book **Snapshots**, to assess comprehension, interpretation, analysis, inference and appreciation. *(4x1=4 Marks)*
13. Two short answer type questions (one from Prose and one from Poetry, from the book **Hornbill)**, out of four, to be answered in 40-50 words. Questions should elicit inferential responses through critical thinking. *(3x2=6 Marks)*
14. One short answer type question, from the book **Snapshots**, to be answered in 40- 50 words. Questions should elicit inferential responses through critical thinking. One out of two questions to be done. *(3x1=3 Marks)*
15. One long answer type question, from **Prose/Poetry of Hornbill**, to be answered in 120-150 words. Questions can be based on incident / theme / passage / extract / event, as reference points to assess extrapolation beyond and across the text. The question will elicit analytical and evaluative response from the student. Any one out of two questions to be done. *(1x6=6 Marks)*
16. One long answer type question, based on the chapters from the book **Snapshots**, to be answered in 120-150 words, to assess global comprehension and extrapolation beyond the text. Questions to provide analytical and evaluative responses, using incidents, events, themes, as reference points. Any one out of two questions to be done. *(1x6=6 Marks)*

Prescribed Books

1. **Hornbill:** English Reader published by National Council of Education Research and Training, New Delhi
   - The Portrait of a Lady (Prose)
   - "We're Not Afraid to Die… if We Can be Together
   - The Laburnum Top (Poem)
   - Childhood (Poem)
   - Silk Road (Prose)
   - A Photograph (Poem)
   - Discovering Tut: The Saga Continues
   - The Voice of the Rain (Poem)
   - The Adventure
   - Father to Son
2. **Snapshots:** Supplementary Reader published by National Council of Education Research and Training, New Delhi
   - The Summer of the Beautiful White Horse (Prose)
   - Mother's Day (Play)
   - The Tale of Melon City
   - The Address (Prose)
   - Birth (Prose)

Internal Assessment

Assessment of Listening Skills	-	05 marks.
Assessment of Speaking Skills	-	05 marks.
Project Work	-	10 Marks

READING SKILLS

01 CHAPTER

Marking Scheme

In the Class XI examination, two passages carrying a total of 18 marks will be asked from the reading section.

▼ **YOUR STUDY GOALS**

Types of Passages
- **Sample Passages** (Factual, Discursive and Literary Passages)
- Practice Questions
- Self Assessment Test
- **Sample Passages** (Case Based Factual Passages)
- Practice Questions
- Self Assessment Test

Reading Comprehension

Reading Comprehension is defined as the understanding of a passage or a text. Basically, it tests the reader's ability to understand the content as well as style and theme of the passage. In examination, questions on the passage generally appear in a chronological order.

Types of Passages

In the examination, two unseen passages are asked from the following categories

1. The first passage could be of any one of the following types

Factual Passage Focuses on concrete details and objective information about a subject. It provides descriptions, instructions or reports to help the reader form a clear understanding.

Discursive Passage Engages in reasoning and discussion, often presenting various viewpoints or arguments. It aims to guide readers to a conclusion through analysis and interpretation, maintaining a balanced perspective.

Literary Passage Encompasses creative writing forms such as fiction, poetry, or drama. It often evokes emotions and encourages personal reflection through narrative style and artistic expression.

2. The second passage is usually a Case Based factual passage.

Case Based Factual Passages A case based factual passage is based on graphical data or charts.

Types of Questions

In the examination, the students are tested on a variety of questions that assess comprehension, interpretation inference and vocabulary. Both objective and subjective type questions are asked from the passages.

Points to be Kept in Mind while Answering the Questions

- Read each and every line in the passage carefully. Reading the passage twice is always favourable as it helps in better understanding and makes it easier for a student to find answers. If the title of the passage is given, read it first as it gives the central insight of the passage.
- Underline all the difficult words while reading the passage, as you might be tested on these words in the vocabulary questions.
- Always give emphasis on the beginning and end of the passages. These paragraphs often hold the most important information of the passage.
- While answering, be sure that you've clearly understood the question. Answer must be relevant to the question.
- Ensure that you answer the question according to the marks it carries. Subjective questions should be answered in complete sentences.
- Use your own language and modify the answer according to the question. Do not copy exact words from the passage.
- Answers should be based on the given information and inference derived from the information in the passage.
- Make sure that you use the same tense in which the question has been asked.
- In MCQs analyse the questions and options carefully before selecting the correct option because sometimes, the given options are closely related.
- Write the correct question number on answer sheet to avoid mistakes.

Sample Passages

Factual, Discursive & Literary Passages

Read the following passages carefully and answer the questions that follow.

Passage 1 (Factual)

1. Obesity-linked "adult onset" diabetes mellitus is for the first time being reported in children and adolescents in the UK and many other countries. A 1986 landmark study of obesity and television viewing found a clear association between the number of hours of television a child watched and the risk of that child becoming obese or over-weight.
2. In 12 to 17 years old, the prevalence of obesity increase by two percent for every hour of weekly television time. A more recent study found that, while eight percent of children watching one hour or less of television a day were obese, 18 percent of children watching four or more hours were obese.
3. The more children watch television, the more they eat. (By comparison, even reading is a workout, at least in studies that have been done with obese children, perhaps because it engages their minds a bit more emphatically.) Television viewing prompts children to consume more food while they consume less energy, an ideal recipe for adiposity.
4. When children dictate family food choices, as is increasingly the case in the US, entire households are immersed in a miasma of one-dimensional sweet taste that reinforces juvenile preferences. Marketing of soft, sweet and salty foods is good, business and children are the most vulnerable targets.

5. Childhood obesity rates are highest in countries where advertising on children's television programmes is least regulated- in Australia, the US and England. Sweden and Norway maintain a virtual ban on advertising to children and have consistently low levels of childhood obesity. Ireland, Belgium, Italy and Denmark pose restrictions on children's advertising and are pressing the other states of the European Union to do the same.

6. The US and other countries can afford to do no less. Public nutrition campaigns should go beyond vague recommendations to exercise and eat a balanced diet: the link between inactivity, junk food consumption and obesity should be made explicit. The food industry will lobby against these efforts, of course, claiming that they constitute "legislation of food choices".

Questions

Answer the following questions based on the passage above.

(i) According to paragraph 2, which children were found to be obese?

(ii) How is reading a workout? Explain in reference to paragraph 3.

(iii) Choose the correct response from the two options to complete the sentence.

When children dictate family food choices, entire households become ....

(a) immersed in a miasma of one-dimensional sweet taste that reinforces juvenile preferences

(b) immersed in a miasma of two-dimensional sweet taste that reinforces juvenile preferences

(iv) Complete the following suitably.

Children are easy targets for .... in the food production business.

(v) What has been reported for the first time in the UK and other countries?

(a) Television viewing time

(b) Adolescent problems

(c) Diabetes due to obesity among children

(d) Violence among school children

(vi) In which country is childhood obesity rate the highest?

(vii) In the line, 'Sweden and Norway maintain a virtual ban on advertising to children...', what does the phrase 'virtual ban' refer to? (Paragraph 5)

(viii) What has the 1986 landmark study of obesity found?

(a) Relation between teenage and obesity

(b) Relation between teenagers and diabetes

(c) Relation between TV viewing time and obesity

(d) None of the above

(ix) Analyse the passage's suggestion regarding public nutrition campaigns. What will the food industry do in response?

Answers

(i) According to paragraph 2, it was found that 18 per cent of children watching four or more hours of television a day were obese.

(ii) Reading is a workout because it engages children's minds a bit more emphatically.

(iii) (a) immersed in a miasma of one-dimensional sweet taste that reinforces juvenile preferences

(iv) soft, sweet and salty food

(v) (c) Diabetes due to obesity among children

(vi) Childhood obesity rates are highest in Australia, the US and England.

(vii) In the given line, the phrase 'virtual ban' refers to banning advertisements created by computer technology.

(viii) (c) relation between TV viewing time and obesity

(ix) Public nutrition campaigns should go beyond vague recommendations to exercise and eat a balanced diet: the link between inactivity, junk food consumption and obesity should be explicit. The food industry will lobby against these efforts.

Passage 2 (Discursive)

1. For generations, companies have been selling fair skin to young Indian women, promising better marriage and employment prospects. However, over the last few years, men have become a favoured target audience. This followed the realisation that the Indian alpha male, denied a choice in male-specific grooming products, had been using women's fairness creams all along. Until the mid-2000s, deodorants and shaving creams were the only grooming products advertised for men. But India's largest consumer goods companies sensed an opportunity and launched a slew of fairness products for male consumers.

2. In India, as in other parts of the world, light skin is the culturally accepted and endorsed form of beauty and children absorb this message at a young age. According to a 2015 research report by Nielsen, urban Indian men believe that fair skin can improve professional prospects.
3. The cultural pressure to look fair, argues Kiran Khalap, branding expert and founder at communications consultancy Chlorophyll, is something inherent in our society, not manufactured by companies. "And it is certainly not restricted to India: China and Japan have had skin-whitening products for centuries, well before they met Western 'whites'," he said.
4. However, there is a growing awareness among consumers that companies are exploiting their insecurities. Additionally, critics have taken. some of the biggest fairness brands and the celebrities who endorse them, to task for their casual discrimination.
5. Earlier this month, Bollywood actor Abhay Deol took to Facebook to trounce his fellow actors who earn millions from endorsing fairness creams. This comes a few years after actress Nandita Das launched the 'Dark is Beautiful' campaign to encourage Indians to embrace a wider definition of beauty. These efforts are slowly making a difference, increasing awareness and encouraging consumers to take pride in their natural skin tones. That means Indian companies will eventually have to change their approach. "My sense is that brands will wake up to the new reality and you will see propositions reworked around clearer skin (and) glow, rather than pure fairness," Leo Burnett's Sinha said.
6. Rajesh Krishnamurthy, business head for the consumer product division at The Himalaya Drug Company, believes that over time the men's grooming category will evolve to include a wider range of products, including those for normal skin, just like in the women's skin care category. "Companies are increasingly realising that you cannot continue to bullshit consumers anymore; these are educated young men who will question what you sell to them," said Shantanu Deshpande, co-founder and CEO of the male-grooming startup Bombay Shaving Company.

Questions

Answer the following questions based on the passage above.

(i) As men became the targeted audience of fairness products, what was realised?

(ii) Describe what was found in the 2015 research report as per the passage?

(iii) Choose the correct response from the two options to complete the sentence.

The only grooming products advertised for men till the mid-2000s were ....

(a) Shaving creams (b) Fairness creams

(iv) Complete the following suitably.

People, especially women, feel pressured to look fair because ....

(v) According to the author, what is the greatest lesson to be learnt from the above passage?

(a) Men never wanted fairness creams.
(b) Women never wanted fairness creams.
(c) The obsession with fair skin tone is fading away.
(d) The obsession with fair skin tone is increasing rapidly.

(vi) Provide one textual evidence that there have been efforts made to reduce racial discrimination.

(vii) In the line, 'Additionally, critics have taken. some of the biggest fairness brands and the celebrities who endorse them, to task for their casual discrimination', what does the phrase 'take to task' mean? (paragraph 4)

(viii) Which qualities of grooming companies is highlighted in the above passage?

(a) Assistance to their consumers
(b) Shrewdness and money-mindedness
(c) Inclusive treatment of all races
(d) Determination and defensive behaviour to protect themselves

(ix) What does the Rajesh Krishnamurthy believe? Answer in reference to paragraph 6.

Answers

(i) As men became the targeted audience of fairness products, it was realised that they had been using women's fairness creams all this time.

(ii) According to a 2015 research report by Nielsen, urban Indian men believe that fair skin can improve professional prospects.

(iii) (a) Shaving creams

(iv) it is inherent in our society

(v) (c) The obsession with fair skin tone is fading away.

(vi) The passage mentions that campaigns like 'Dark is Beautiful' are slowly making a difference, increasing awareness and encouraging consumers to take pride in their natural skin tones. Thus, as people embrace a wider definition of beauty, racial discrimination is reducing.

(vii) In the given line, the phrase 'take to task' means to reprimand.

(viii) (b) Shrewdness and money-mindedness

(ix) Rajesh Krishnamurthy, business head for the consumer product division at The Himalaya Drug Company, believes that over time the men's grooming category will evolve to include a wider range of products, including those for normal skin, just like in the women's skin care category.

Passage 3 (Literary)

1. We have been brought up to fear insects. We regard them as unnecessary creatures that do more harm than good. Man continuously wages war on them, for they contaminate his food, carry diseases or devour his crops. They sting or bite without provocation, they fly uninvited into our rooms on summer nights, or beat against our lighted windows. We live in dread not only of unpleasant insects such as spiders or wasps but of quite harmless ones as moths. Reading about them increases our understanding without **dispelling** our fears. Knowing that the industrious ants live in a highly organised society does not prevent us from being filled with revulsion when we find hordes of them crawling over a carefully prepared picnic lunch.

2. No matter how much we like honey or how much we have read of the uncanny sense of direction which bees possess, we have a horror of being stung. Most of our fears are unreasonable but they are difficult to erase. At the same time, however, insects are strangely fascinating. We enjoy reading about them, especially when we find that as the Praying Mantis, they lead perfectly horrible lives. We enjoy staring at them, entranced as they go about their business, unaware-we hope-of our presence. Who has not stood in awe at the sight of a spider **pouncing** on a fly or a column of ants triumphantly carrying home an enormous dead beetle? Last summer, I spent many days in the garden watching thousands of ants crawling up the trunk of my prized peach tree. The tree has grown against a warm wall on a sheltered side of the house. I am especially proud of it, not only because it has survived several severe winters, but because it occasionally produces luscious peaches. During the summer I noticed that the leaves of the tree had begun to wither.

3. Clusters of tiny insects called Aphids were to be found on the underside of the leaves. They were visited by a large column of ants which obtained a sort of honey from them.

I immediately embarked on an experiment which, even though it failed to get rid of the ants, kept me fascinated for twenty four hours. I bound the base of the tree with sticky tape, making it impossible for the ants to reach the Aphids. The tape was so sticky that they did not dare to cross it. For a long time, I watched them scurrying around the base of the tree in bewilderment. I even went out at midnight with a torch and noted with satisfaction and surprise that the ants were still swarming around the sticky tape without being able to do anything about it. I got up early next morning to find thc ants were climbing up the wall of the house and then on to the leaves of the tree. I realised sadly that I had been completely defeated by their ingenuity. The ants had been quick to find an answer to my thoroughly unscientific methods.

Questions

Answer the following questions based on the passage above.

(i) What is our approach towards the insects?

(ii) Why does man try to kill insects?

(iii) Choose the correct response from the two options to complete the sentence.

Insects are strangely fascinating. As a consequence, people sometimes ....

(a) collect them and put on display
(b) stare at them

(iv) Complete the following suitably.

During the summer, the author noticed about the leaves that ....

(v) Where were the cluster of tiny insects found? On the

(a) branches
(b) bunch of flowers
(c) underside of the leaves
(d) upper-side of the leaves

(vi) What do you think the writer wants to prove by the experiment he conducted on ants? Provide one textual evidence.

(vii) In the line, 'We enjoy staring at them, entranced as they go about their business...', what does the phrase 'go about business' mean? (paragraph 2)

(viii) What did the narrator see the next morning?
(a) The ants could not cross the tree base
(b) The ants could not reach the Aphids
(c) The ants were climbing up the wall of the house
(d) All of the above

(ix) Why does the writer say that knowing about the insects does not help man to change his attitude toward insects?

Answers

(i) We have been brought up to fear insects. We regard them as unnecessary creatures that do more harm than good.

(ii) Man tries to kill insects as they contaminate the food, carry diseases or devour his crops. They sting or bite without provocation, they fly uninvited into our rooms on summer nights or beat against our lighted windows.

(iii) (b) stare at them

(iv) they had begun to wither

(v) (c) underside of the leaves

(vi) The writer wants to prove that ants are cleverer than man. He says, "I had been completely defeated by their ingenuity."

(vii) In the given line, the phrase 'go about business' means to continue doing one's usual tasks.

(viii) (c) The ants were climbing up the wall of the house

(ix) The writer states the reading about insects increases our understanding without dispelling our fears. Knowing that the industrious ants live in a highly organised society does not prevent us from being filled with revulsion when we find hordes of them crawling over a carefully prepared picnic lunch.

Practice Questions

Factual Passages

Read the following passages carefully and answer the questions that follow.

Passage 1

1. The kingdom of books is as vast as the universe for there is no corner of it which they have left unexplored. There is no dearth of books on any topic, be it as simple as the composition of sodium nitrate or as intricate as the mechanism of a spacecraft. Books report the fruits of our research in various fields of knowledge, and spread our progressive view on matters which are of vital concern to our fellow beings.

2. In fact, no single product of human labour has been as helpful to the advancement of civilisation as books, which are written in all languages of the world and are decoratively placed in bookshelves in our homes and tastefully displayed in bookstall and libraries. If to Keats, works of ancient poets like Homer were realms of gold from which he derived much joy as well as inspiration, to the modern lover of books, the labours of all geniuses, including those of Keats, are mines of inestimable intellectual wealth which he goes on exploring for the sake of his mental and spiritual advancement.

3. There was a time some five centuries back, when books as we know them today did not exist and when there were few people who could read things written on stuff which certainly was not paper. At that time our ancestors used rocks, pillars and parchment with a view to recording and perpetuating their most important thoughts and achievements in the language they then understood.

4. Nowadays, the book-producing machinery gives to the works of every great scientific thinker, poet or philosopher the character of permanence, reproduces in attractive forms old and rare manuscripts and caters to the differing tastes of millions of people for whom book-reading is an extremely pleasant, intellectual exercise. Moreover, the high percentage of literacy, the growth of libraries in towns and villages and the tendency of intellectuals to have their own private collection of useful books, have given birth to a number of big publishing houses with branches

in many parts of the world and publications numbering thousands.

5. In recent years, paperbacks have begun to reveal their attraction for the reading public and although they have not completely thrown into neglect the hard cover markets, they have appealed to people who would not have thought of buying books not so very long ago.
These paperbacks are generally reprints of popular fiction or of established classics or translations from foreign works which are in constant demand at all bookstalls.

Questions

Answer the following questions, based on the passage above.

(i) According to the passage, what is an advantage of paperbacks?

(ii) What has the book producing machinery facilitated?

(iii) Choose the correct response from the two options to complete the sentence.
For the majority of people, book-reading is ....
(a) an enjoyable intellectual exercise
(b) not interesting

(iv) Complete the following sentence.
To the modern lover of books, the labours of all genuises are mines of inestimable intellectual wealth which he goes on exploring for ....

(v) According to the passage, books are helpful. Which of the following presents the purpose of books?
(a) Reporting research results
(b) Spread progressive view on vital matters
(c) Advancement of civilisation
(d) All of the above

(vi) What are popular paperbacks generally reprints of?

(vii) In the line, '...... spread our progressive view on matters which are of vital concern to our fellow beings', what does the phrase 'vital concern' mean? (Paragraph 1)

(viii) Which of the following has contributed to the growth of publishing houses?
(a) High literacy
(b) Growth of libraries
(c) People's desire to have their own collection
(d) All of the above

(ix) What features of book-producing machinery are mentioned in the passage?

Passage 2

1. There's no concept of good or bad food in nutrition science. What matters is the amount of food you consume, something that can be measured in terms of portion or size of serving. Portions and sizes vary from country to country and community to community. Large portions are commonly consumed in the advanced economies while smaller size portions are found mostly in developing economies of Africa and Asia.

2. Incidentally, portion sizes have undergone a considerable change over the years and continue to do so even today. The trend, in general, has been towards consuming larger and larger food portions (expanding waistlines are proof of this). The human mind seems to count the number of portions rather than the portion size. For example, when people say they have only one *chapatti* for lunch or dinner, they rarely discuss its size.

3. Short-term studies have also shown that people eat more when confronted with larger portion sizes. A study at a restaurant setting showed that when pasta was served in different portion sizes on different days, people ate larger amounts on being served larger portions, regardless of the taste. Also, studies show that people do not adjust or eat less in subsequent meals if they have already had larger portions.

4. Technically, a portion means the amount of food you choose to eat at one time – at a restaurant, from a package, or at home. A 'serving' size indicates the calories and nutrients in a certain serving listed under a product's 'nutrition facts' or a single unit or commonly regarded unit of food. The serving size is not the recommended amount to be eaten.

5. Sometimes, the portion size and serving size match; sometimes they don't. For example, one slice of bread equals one serving of bread. But the number of slices you eat would be the number of portions you have eaten, so if you have eaten two slices, you have consumed two portions.

6. So, how do we recognise what's the right amount of food to eat on a regular basis? Learn to recognise standard serving sizes as they help you judge how much you are eating. It may also help to compare serving sizes to common objects.

Questions

Answer the following questions based on the passage above.

(i) What is the recommended amount of food to be eaten?

(ii) What shows that portion sizes are increasing?

(iii) Choose the correct response from the two options to complete the sentence.

When served with larger portion of food, people ....

(a) consume the same amount as always

(b) consume larger amount of food

(iv) Complete the following suitably with reference to paragraph 2.

According to the passage, the problem with the human mind is ....

(v) According to the passage, which of the following statements is true?

(a) Portion sizes are increasing.

(b) Developed economies have larger portions of food.

(c) Portion varies from community to community only.

(d) People do not adjust the size of meals regularly.

(vi) Mention what people do in subsequent meals after they consume large portion sizes for one meal.

(vii) In the line, 'Incidentally, portion sizes have undergone a considerable change over the years...', what does the phrase 'undergone a considerable change' refer to ? (Paragraph 2)

(viii) The write would agree with the given information based on the passage except

(a) Africa and Asia have smaller portions of food.

(b) Larger food portions means larger consumptions.

(c) After larger food portions are consumed people opt for smaller portions.

(d) Portion sizes always match.

(ix) Explain how an individual can judge the right amount of food to be eaten.

Passage 3

1. One of the greatest advances in modern technology has been the invention of computers. They are widely used in industries and in universities. Now, there is hardly any sphere of human life where computers have not been pressed into service of man. We are heading fast towards the day when a computer will be as much part of man's daily life as a telephone or a calculator.

2. Computers are capable of doing extremely complicated work in all branches of learning. They can solve the most complex mathematical problems or put thousands of unrelated facts in order. These machines can be put to varied uses. For instance, they can provide information on the best way to prevent traffic jams. This whole process by which machines can be used to work for us has been called automation. In the future, automation may enable human beings to enjoy more leisure than they do today. The coming of automation is bound to have important social consequences.

3. Some years ago, an expert on automation, Sir Leon Bagrit, pointed out that it was a mistake to believe that these machines could think. There is no possibility that human beings will be "controlled by machines". Though computers are capable of learning from their mistakes and improving on their performance, they need detailed instructions from human beings to operate. They can never, as it were, lead independent lives or "rule the world" by making decisions of their own.

4. Sir Leon said that in future, computers would be developed which would be small enough to carry in the pocket. Ordinary people would then be able to use them to obtain valuable information. Computers could be plugged into a national network and be used like radios. For instance, people going on holiday could be informed about weather conditions. Car drivers can be given alternative routes when there are traffic jams. It will also be possible to make tiny translating machines. This will enable people who do not share a common language to talk to each other without any difficulty or to read foreign publications.

5. It is impossible to assess the importance of a machine of this sort, for many international misunderstandings are caused simply due to our failure to understand each other. Computers will also be used in ordinary public hospitals. By providing a machine with a patient's systems, a doctor will be able to diagnose the nature of his illness. Similarly, machines could be used to keep a check on a patient's health record and keep it up to date. Doctors will, therefore, have immediate access to great many facts which will help them in their work.

Questions

Answer the following questions based on the passage above.

(i) According to paragraph 1, where are computers most widely used?

(ii) How can automation prove to be helpful for humans?

(iii) Choose the correct response from the two options to complete the sentence.

Computers can be used to ....

(a) prescribe a medicine for the patient

(b) diagnose the nature of patient's illness

(iv) Complete the following suitably.

Many international misunderstandings are caused due to our failure to understand ....

(v) Which of the following is correct regarding the use of computers in the field of mathematics?

(a) Computers can solve only certain mathematical problems.

(b) Computers can't solve an mathematical problem

(c) Computers can solve the most complex mathematical problems

(d) Computers can solve only simple mathematical problems.

(vi) Provide one textual evidence that computers may never lead independent lives.

(vii) What does the phrase 'coming of' mean? (Paragraph 2)

(viii) Select the correct option.

(a) There is no possibility that human beings could be on their own with no need of machines.

(b) Human beings are likely to be controlled by machines one day.

(c) There is no possibility that human beings will ever be controlled machines.

(d) Machines can replace humans.

(ix) What does Sir Leon say about computers?

Passage 4

1. A dance which is created or choreographed and performed according to the tenets of the *Natya Shastra* is called a classical dance. The two broad aspects of classical dancing are the *tandava* and the *lasya*. Power and force are typical of the *tandava*; grace and delicacy, of the *lasya*. *Tandava* is associated with Shiva and *lasya* with Parvati. Dance which is pure movement is called *nritta* and dance which is interpretative in nature is called *nritya*. The four main schools of classical dancing in India are Bharatanatyam, Kathakali, Manipuri and Kathak.
2. Bharatanatyam is the oldest and most popular dance form of India. Earlier, it was known by various names. Some called it *Bharatam*, some *Natyam*, some *Desi Attam* and some *Sadir*. The districts of Tanjore and Kanchipuram in Tamil Nadu were the focal points in the development of Bharatanatyam. It was performed as a solo performance by *devadasis* (temple dancers) on all auspicious occasions. Later, kings and rich people lent their patronage to it and it started shedding its purely sacred character.
3. The dancer is directed by the *natuvanar*, who is a musician and, invariably, a teacher. Another musician plays the cymbals. The music for Bharatnatyam is from the Carnatic School of music. The *mridangam* (a drum), played on both sides with the hands, provides the rhythm.
4. The home of Kathakali is Kerala. Kathakali literally means 'story-play'. It combines music, dance, poetry, drama and mime. Its present form has evolved out of older forms such as *Ramanattam* and *Krishnanattam*.
5. Kathakali dance-dramas last from dusk to dawn. The artistes use elaborate costumes; mask like make-up and towering head-dresses. The dancers are all males. Female roles are usually played by boys. There is no stage - a few mats are spread on the ground for the audience to sit on. The only 'stage-lighting' is a brass lamp fed with coconut oil.
6. Two singers provide the vocal music. The *chenda*, a large drum, which is beaten on one side with two slender curved sticks, is an integral part of the Kathakali performance. A metal gong, a pair of cymbals and another drum complete the orchestra. Besides providing the beat, they are also the means by which all the sound-effects are created.

Questions

Answer the following questions based on the passage above.

(i) In which drama form are all the dancers males?

(ii) Where is Bharatanatyam most popular?

(iii) Choose the correct response from the two options to complete the sentence.

The dance which is interpretative in nature is ....

(a) nritta (b) nritya

(iv) Complete the following suitably with reference to the above passage.
The districts of Tanjore and Kanchipuram in Tamil Nadu were …………… .

(v) When did Bharatanatyam start shedding its purely sacred character?
(a) When the devadasis stopped dancing
(b) When it was danced as a solo performance
(c) When kings and the rich patronised it
(d) When they used Carnatic music

(vi) Which two schools of classical dance are described in the passage?

(vii) In the line, 'Later, kings and rich people lent their patronage to it …', what does the phrase 'lent their patronage to it' mean? (Paragraph 2)

(viii) Which of the following statements is true for Kathakali?
(a) Kathakali is performed on drums.
(b) Kathakali performance starts at dusk and ends at dawn.
(c) Kathakali is performed as street plays.
(d) Kathakali is generally based on universal social issues.

(ix) Write a short note on Kathakali dance-dramas.

Passage 5

1. Nothing better sums up the outdoors than the centuries-old human endeavour to scale mighty peaks. Mountaineering involves hiking, climbing or just simply walking, on hilly or mountainous ground, with the help of technical equipment and support. In mountaineering. you will come across different types of terrain-mainly snow, glaciers, ice or just naked rocks. The feats of the likes of Edmund Hilary and George Mallory to mention just two legendary mountaineers, have contributed to making this activity a popular one all around the world, one that has also been known to build a person's character. One has to be physically robust, very fit and display a decent level of athleticism and suppleness of body to climb mountains; training, conditioning and preparation are essential if you are looking to attempt an ascent on a particularly challenging peak. In addition, the mountaineer, often having to withstand extreme climatic conditions, has to display a good degree of mental fortitude to survive and succeed.

2. But in the end, all of this is worth your while-there is no better feeling than being out in the open. In high nature's playground, breathing in the pristine mountain air, as close to the sky as it's humanly possible to be.

3. Mountaineering is as old as the Earth, as old as human life. When it became a passion of the outdoorsy and of the adventurous minded, In the 19th century, many people would climb just for pleasure, for the sheer thrill of conquering peaks near and far. But over time, the sport has split into separate disciplines, each of them calling for varying degrees of skills and preparation. Today, climbers have the comfort of having the most advanced equipment and gear at their disposal. In contrast, men in ancient times had to rely on their feet, their legs, their arms and their hands and their wits to climb mountains. These old climbing techniques are still very much relevant today (as well as being utterly reliable and safe) but the 21st-century mountaineer has the added advantage of depending on hi-tech safety equipment. Closer home, the Himalayan Mountaineering Institute has played a big part in the conquest of the Greater Himalayas. Many of the planet's mountaineering greats have tested their skills, and earned their name, in the Himalayan theatre of dreams, considered the ultimate arena for climbing enthusiasts.

4. Mountaineering demands a lot of your physical fitness, and attempts on the highest peaks can push your body to the limit. Before attempting any climb, make sure you are fit enough to endure amlhing and everything that nature and the elements may throw at you. Remember that mountaineering may be a very exhilarating activity but it is far from being an easy sport! At high altitudes, it is important to give enough time for acclimatisation. And make sure you get a clean bill of health from your doctor before embarking on an expedition.

Questions

Answer the following questions based on the passage above.

(i) According to paragraph 1, what does mountaineering involve?

(ii) How can a person prepare for mountaineering?

(iii) Choose the correct response from the two options to complete the sentence.
In addition to maintaining a strong physical body, a person has to withstand ……………… .
(a) extreme climatic conditions
(b) critique from their peer mountaineers

(iv) Complete the following suitably.

The 21st century mountaineer has the added advantage of............

(v) Two legendary mountaineers who have contributed to make mountaineering popular all around the world are
(a) Edmond Halley and George Mallory
(b) Edmund Hilary and George Mallory
(c) Edmund Hilary and George Mallory
(d) Edmund Hilary and George Miller

(vi) Provide one textual evidence that mountaineering is not a modern practice.

(vii) What does the phrase 'earned their name' mean? (Paragraph 3)

(viii) One of the main institute for climbing enthusiasts is
(a) Mountaineering Institute
(b) Himalayan Mountaineering Institute
(c) Himalayan theatre of dreams
(d) Himalayan Institute

(ix) Contrast the modern way of mountaineering with the one from ancient times. Which of these was more comfortable?

Discursive Passages

Read the following passages carefully and answer the questions that follow.

Passage 1

1. Maharana Pratap ruled over Mewar only for 25 years. However, he accomplished so much grandeur during his reign that his glory surpassed the boundaries of countries and time turning him into an immortal personality. He along with his kingdom became a synonym for valour, sacrifice and patriotism. Mewar had been a leading Rajput kingdom even before Maharana Pratap occupied the throne. Kings of Mewar, with the cooperation of their nobles and subjects, had established such traditions in the kingdom, as augmented their magnificence despite the hurdles of having a smaller area under their command and less population. There did come a few thorny occasions when the flag of the kingdom seemed sliding down. Their flag once again heaved high in the sky thanks to the gallantry and brilliance of the people of Mewar.

2. The destiny of Mewar was good in the sense that barring a few kings, most of the rulers were competent and patriotic. This glorious tradition of the Kingdom almost continued for 1,500 Years since its establishment, right from the reign of Bappa Rawal. In fact only 60 years before Maharana Pratap, Rana Sanga drove the kingdom to the pinnacle of fame. His reputation went beyond Rajasthan and reached Delhi. Two generations before him, Rana Kumbha had given a new stature to the kingdom through victories and developmental work. During his reign, literature and art also progressed extraordinarily. Rana himself was inclined towards writing and his works are read with reverence even today. The ambience of his kingdom was conducive to the creation of high quality work of art and literature. These accomplishments were the outcome of a long standing tradition sustained by several generations.

3. The life of the people of Mewar must have been peaceful and prosperous during the long span of time, otherwise such extraordinary accomplishment in these fields would not have been possible. This is reflected in their art and literature as well as in their loving nature. The ambience of Mewar remains lovely, thanks to the cheerful and liberal character of its people.

4. One may observe astonishing pieces of workmanship not only in the forts and palaces of Mewar but also in public utility buildings. Ruins of many structures which are still standing tall in their grandeur are testimony to the fact that Mewar was not only the land of the brave but also a seat of art and culture. Amidst aggression and bloodshed, literature and art flourished and creative pursuits of literature and artists did not suffer. Imagine, how glorious the period must have been when the Vijaya Stambha is standing high, reflecting how liberal the then administration was which allowed people from other communities and kingdoms to come and carry out construction work.

5. The cycle of time does not remain the same. Whereas, the reign of Rana Sanga was crucial in raising the kingdom to the acme of glory, it also proved to be nemesis. History took a turn. The fortune of Mewar the land of the brave, started waning. Rana tried to save the day with his acumen which was running against the stream and the glorious traditions for sometime.

Questions

Answer the following questions based on the passage above.

(i) According to paragraph 1, what had Kings of Mewar achieved with the cooperation of their nobles and subjects?

(ii) How can we say that Mewar had a good destiny?

(iii) Choose the correct response from the two options to complete the sentence.

Maharana Pratap became immortal because

(a) he ruled Mewar for 25 years.

(b) he added a lot of grandeur to Mewar.

(iv) Complete the following suitably.

Under the reign of .... , the kingdom of Mewar rose to the acme of glory.

(v) What difficulties was Mewar facing?

(a) Lack of cooperation of the nobility

(b) Ancient traditions of the kingdom

(c) Its small area and small population

(d) The poverty of the subjects

(vi) Provide one textual evidence that literature and art flourished in the Kingdom of Mewar. Under whose reign did this happen?

(vii) What does the phrase 'took a turn' mean? (Paragraph 5)

(viii) Why was Mewar lucky?

(a) All of its rulers were competent.

(b) Most of its people were competent.

(c) Most of its rulers were competent.

(d) Only a few of its people were incompetent.

(ix) Give a detailed description of the life of the people of Mewar and its ambience.

Passage 2

1. I was lucky, I found what I loved to do early in life. Woz and I started Apple in my parent's garage when I was 20. We worked hard and in 10 years, Apple had grown into a $ 2 billion company with over 4000 employees. We had just released our finest creation - the Macintosh - a year earlier and I had just turned 30. And then I got fired. How can you get fired from a company you started? Well, as Apple grew, we hired someone, who I thought was very talented, to run the company and for the first year or so things went well. But then eventually we had a falling out. When we did, our Board of Directors sided with him. So at 30 I was out. What had been the focus of my entire adult life was gone and it was devastating.

2. I really didn't know what to do for a few months. I felt that I had let the previous generation of entrepreneurs down - that I had dropped the baton as it was being passed to me. But something slowly began to dawn on me: I still loved what I did. The turn of events at Apple had not changed that one bit. I had been rejected, but I was still in love. And so I decided to start over.

3. I didn't see it then, but it turned out that getting fired from Apple was the best thing that could have ever happened to me. It freed me to enter one of the most creative periods of my life. During the next 5 years, I started a company named NeXT and another company named Pixar. Pixar went on to create the world's first computer Animated Feature Film, Toy Story and is now the most successful animation studio in the world. In a remarkable turn of events, Apple bought NeXT, I returned to Apple and the technology we developed at NeXT is at the heart of Apple's current renaissance.

4. I'm pretty sure none of this would have happened if I hadn't been fired from Apple. It was awful tasting medicine, but I guess the patient needed it. Sometimes, life hits you in the head with a brick. Don't lose faith. I'm convinced that the only thing that kept me going was that I loved what I did. You've got to find what you love.

Questions

Answer the following questions based on the passage above.

(i) According to paragraph 3, interpret the contribution of NeXT.

(ii) What characteristics does the speaker show in the passage?

(iii) Choose the appropriate option from the two options to complete the sentence.

Getting fired from Apple was ....

(a) the worst thing that ever happened to the author

(b) helpful to make him successful again

(iv) Complete the following suitably.
The message that the passage is trying to convey is ....

(v) What can be inferred from the line "But something slowly began to dawn on me"?
(a) He realised he still loved what he did.
(b) He realised he was a public failure.
(c) He realised that he had let down the other entrepreneurs.
(d) He realised he wanted to return to Apple.

(vi) Mention the only thing that kept the author going after getting fired.

(vii) In the line, '... that I had dropped the baton as if it was being passed to me', what does the phrase 'dropped the baton' mean (Paragraph 2)

(viii) What is Pixar credited with?
(a) being the first animation studio
(b) creating the world's first computer animated movie
(c) being a bigger company than Apple
(d) buying Next

(ix) Explain why the author calls getting fired from Apple, the best thing that could ever happen to him?

Passage 3

1. India can really become a tourist's paradise on Earth as we have so much to offer to the visitors. No other country in the world possesses so much variety. The breath-taking beauty of the Himalayas, its valleys and rivers, the numerous wildlife sanctuaries dotted all over the country, our still unspoilt sea beaches, our great temples and caves and historical monuments, our music and dance, our festivals and national celebrations, would attract any tourist in the world. They are all our potential foreign exchange earners.

2. If we wish to earn more from our tourists, we must build up more infrastructure. The Government of India has intensified efforts to build more hotels in the country. Those in the hotel business are allowed to have foreign collaborations. Our hotels must offer such facilities that foreigners love: These are 24-hours service, swimming pools, tennis courts, club houses, massage centres, indoor and outdoor restaurants, playgrounds for children, dance floor with live music in season and so on. These would make for an exciting tour.

3. The government is also providing new and better facilities. If would do us good if certain irritants connected with custom formalities could also be removed.

4. But tourism is everybody's business as all benefit from it. Wealth flows from affluent countries to the less affluent. Within the country itself it moves from the developed areas to the less developed ones. It flows from the rich to the poor, the tourist trade in this country. They can arrange group tours for foreigners on a large scale. Those selling goods to the tourists should not charge them higher rates. Even a humble taxi driver can do something for tourism, if he does not cheat a visitor.

5. So, let us give the tourist the facilities he is used to in his own country. If he goes home irritated and unhappy, he will surely discourage others from visiting our country. We will lose a friend and also some foreign exchange. But if the tourist is satisfied with the facilities offered to him, what he tells his people back home will do publicity for us. Then others would also be tempted to come to our country when we say, "Welcome to India".

Questions

Answer the following questions based on the passage above.

(i) According to paragraph 1, what would attract tourists from all over the world to India?

(ii) What must be done by us to earn more from our tourists? Answer in reference to paragraph 2.

(iii) Choose the correct response from the two options to complete the sentence.
India can become a tourist's paradise ....
(a) by flow of wealth from other countries.
(b) by its rivers, valleys and Himalayas.

(iv) Complete the following suitably.
Wealth flows from affluent countries to the less affluent.
The statement shows ....

(v) What will the tourists do if they go home irritated and unhappy?
(a) Urge others to visit our country
(b) Long-awaited travel to visit our country
(c) Dissuade others from visiting our country
(d) They will only remain mute spectators

(vi) Provide one textual evidence that asserts the role of the government in the field of tourism.

(vii) What does the phrase 'do us good' mean? (Paragraph 3)

(viii) Which agencies can also play an instrumental role in promoting tourism?
- (a) Government agencies
- (b) Private agencies
- (c) Semi-government agencies
- (d) Non-government agencies

(ix) How would it affect us if a tourist returns home with a bad experience?

Passage 4

1. If you're addicted to coffee and doctors warn you to quit the habit, don't worry and keep relishing the beverage, because it's not that bad after all! In fact, according to a new study, the steaming cup of java even beats fruits and vegetables as the primary source of antioxidants. A study by the University of Scranton states that coffee is the number one source of antioxidants in the American diet and both caffeinated and decaf versions appear to provide similar antioxidant levels.
2. "Americans get more of their antioxidants from coffee than any other dietary source. Nothing else comes close to it.", said the study's lead researcher, Dr Joe Vinson, adding that high antioxidant levels in food and beverages don't necessarily translate into levels found in the body. Antioxidants in general have been linked to a number of potential health benefits, including protection against heart disease and cancer but Vinson said that the benefits ultimately depend on how they are absorbed and utilised in the body.
3. The researchers analysed the antioxidant content of more than 100 different food items, including vegetables, fruits, nuts, spices, oils and common beverages. The data was compared to an existing US Department of Agriculture database on the contribution of each type of food item to the average estimated US per capita consumption.
4. The results were surprising. Coffee came out on the top, on the combined basis of both antioxidants per serving size and frequency of consumption. It outranked popular antioxidant sources like tea, milk, chocolate and cranberries.
5. Of all the food and beverages studies, dates actually have the most antioxidants of all based solely on serving size but since dates are not consumed at anywhere near the level of coffee, the drink comes as the top source of antioxidants, Vinson said.
6. Besides keeping you alert and awake, coffee has been linked to an increasing number of potential health benefits, including protection against liver and colon cancer, type 2 diabetes and Parkinson's disease, according to some recently published studies.
7. The researchers, however, advised that one should consume coffee in moderation because it can make you jittery and cause stomach pains.

Questions

Answer the following questions based on the passage above.

(i) Why have dates not made it the top of antioxidant rich foods?

(ii) On what do the benefits of antioxidants depend?

(iii) Choose the correct response from the two options to complete the sentence.

The benefits of consuming coffee are dependent on ....

(a) consumption (b) portion size

(iv) Complete the following suitably with reference to the passage above.

Potential Health benefits of coffee include protection against ....

(v) On what basis does coffee rank as the top source of antioxidants?
- (a) Due to its consumption
- (b) A study by the University of Scranton
- (c) Because it is a primary source
- (d) Due to its potential health benefits

(vi) What will happen if one drank too much coffee? Provide one evidence.

(vii) In the line, 'Coffee came out on the top, on the combined basis', what does the phrase 'came out on the top' mean? (paragraph 4)

(viii) Potential health benefits of antioxidants include ....
- (a) protection against heart disease
- (b) protection against cancer
- (c) Both (a) and (b)
- (d) Neither (a) nor (b)

(ix) Why are dates not considered highest source of antioxidants?

Passage 5

1. It is said that everyone lives by selling something. What you can understand by this statement is that teachers live by selling knowledge, philosophers live by selling wisdom and priests earn their living by selling spiritual comfort. Though it may be possible to measure the value of material goods in terms of money, it is extremely difficult to estimate the true value of the services which people perform for us.
2. There are times when we would willingly give everything we possess to save our lives, yet we might grudge paying a surgeon a high fee for offering us precisely the same service. The conditions of society are such that skills have to be paid for in the same way that goods are paid for at a shop. Everyone has something to sell.
3. Tramps seem to be the only exception to this general rule. Beggars almost sell themselves as human beings to arouse the pity of passers-by. But real tramps are not beggars. They have nothing to sell and require nothing from others. In seeking independence, they do not sacrifice their human dignity. A tramp may ask you for money but he will never ask you to feel sorry for him. He has deliberately chosen to lead the life he leads and is fully aware of the consequences. He may never be sure where his next meal is coming from but he is free from the thousands of anxieties which afflict other people. His few material possessions make it possible for him to move from place to place with ease. By having to sleep in the open, he gets far closer to the world of nature than most of us ever do.
4. He may hunt, beg or steal occasionally to keep himself alive; he may even, in times of real need, do a little work; but he will never sacrifice his freedom.
5. We often speak with contempt for tramps and put them in the same class as beggars. But how many of us can honestly say that we have not felt a little envious of their simple way of life and their freedom from any care in the world?

Questions

Answer the following questions based on the passage above.

(i) What is the advantage of being a tramp?

(ii) Why will a tramp not want you to feel sorry for him?

(iii) Choose the correct option from the two given below.

Even though we might be willing to spend every last penny to save our lives, we ....

(a) might willingly pay a surgeon for service

(b) might despise paying a surgeon for service

(iv) Complete the following suitably.

A tramp doesn't ask people to ....

(v) How is a beggar different from a tramp? It is a because

(a) a beggar sells but tramps don't.

(b) beggars do not travel but tramps are always on the move.

(c) beggars don't know when they will eat their next meal but tramps find a means to earn their meals.

(d) All of the above

(vi) Do you think tramp lives a better life than us? Give reason.

(vii) In the first paragraph, the author mentions people of which profession(s) to be selling their services?

(viii) Which of the following is difficult to judge?

(a) The actual value of services given by people

(b) The actual value of material goods

(c) Both (a) and (b)

(d) The contempt for tramps

(ix) Explain "everyone lives by selling something".

Literary Passages

Passage 1

1. Travel is a bug that was in me when I was born, probably inherited from my father. In 24 years of travelling widely through India, I have been most fascinated by those little islands that dot the Bay of Bengal off the East Coast of India. Yes, I am talking about the Andaman Islands. Andamans somehow seemed almost sinister, with images of being haunted, bleak and scary, until my parents actually returned from a trip to Port Blair and told us about these serene islands. We immediately awaited the first opportunity to take a break and check them out. Finally, the D-Day came and we were all ready. We boarded the aircraft and, to our surprise, found that there were several empty seats.

On enquiry, we learnt that all supplies to the Andamans including newspapers and meat go from the mainland, and so there is always more cargo and less people.

2. Port Blair airport is a small, old airport that was constructed in 1947. On my way to the hotel, I noticed that there are none of the usual auto-rickshaws that noisily wend their way through most Indian towns. There was only one traffic signal in the entire town and the roads were more up and down than level. This was all surprising for a person like me who has lived in the coastal towns of Chennai and Mumbai.
3. The colour of the sea was an unpolluted blue, a colour that I had not seen in any of the beaches in India. It was calm and beautiful. I was thrilled with the fact that we were going to spend 10 entire days there. All we had to do was sit in the open restaurant, look at the sea, enjoy the cool breeze and feel good.
4. The Andaman Islands are a group of several islands, so most of our sightseeing was by boats. There are a total of more than 356 islands there. Even the oldest boatman, Rathnam, had seen only 200 of them. I figured that 10 days was surely not enough to get a full picture of this place, so I started to store every sight, every sound and every smell. The sound and light show at the jail sent a shiver down my spine. (This trip was before the movie 'Kalapani' was released).
5. The realisation that those who fought for our independence had lived, struggled, suffered and even died here, left an impact.

Questions

Answer the following based on the passage above.

(i) How many islands constitute Andaman Islands?

(ii) How does the author describe the scenes at the Andaman islands?

(iii) Choose the correct response from the two options to complete the sentence.

One thing that left a major impact on the author was ....

(a) the serenity of the place
(b) the realisation that freedom fighters had lived, struggled and died there.

(iv) Complete the following suitably.

Since all supplies to the Andamans including newspapers and meat go from the mainland, there is ....

(v) The writer agree with the given statements except.

(a) The narrator liked travelling.
(b) There were no empty seats in the aircraft.
(c) The Port Blair Airport is small.
(d) The Andaman Islands are a group of Islands.

(vi) What was the author's initial impression about the Andaman Islands?

(vii) In the line, 'The sound and light show at the jail sent a shiver down my spine', what does the phrase 'sent a shiver down my spine' mean? (Paragraph 4)

(viii) Where are Andaman Islands located?

(a) In the Arabian Sea (b) In the Bay of Bengal
(c) In the Indian Ocean (d) In the Atlantic Ocean

(ix) What was unique about the Andaman roads?

Passage 2

1. The Lord was the creator of good teachers. It was his sixth day of 'overtime' and he knew that this was a tremendous responsibility, for teachers would touch the lives of so many impressionable young children.

   An Angel appeared to him and said, "You are taking a long time to figure this one out." "Yes," said the Lord, "but have you read the specifications on this order?"
2. **Teacher** Teacher must stand above all students to be at their level. He must be able to do 180 additional things which are not related to their taught subject. Teacher must have to run on coffee. He must be able to communicate as per his vital knowledge to all students daily. Teacher must have more time for others than for himself, besides being **supportive**.
3. "Six pairs of hands,"said the Angel, "that's impossible" "Well," said the Lord," it is not the hands that are the problem. It is the three pairs of eyes that are presenting the most difficulty!"

   The Angel looked incredulous, "Three pairs of eyes...on a standard model?"
4. The Lord nodded his head, "One pair is to see whether a student is doing or not what others have labelled them. The second pair is the pair of eyes which is at the back of the teacher's head to watch what should not be seen, but what must be known. The third pair is the eyes in the front which is only to look at the child and 'act out' in order to **reflect**, "I understand and I still believe in you", without so much as saying a word to the child."

   "Lord," said the Angel," "this is a very large project and I think you should work on it tomorrow."

5. "I can't," said the Lord," "for I have come very close to creating something much like myself. I have one that comes to work when he/she is sick, teaches a class of children that do not want to learn, has a special place in his/her heart for children who are not his/her own, understands the struggles of those who have difficulty and never takes the students for granted."

   The Angel looked closely at the model the Lord was creating.

   "It is too soft-hearted," said the Angel.

6. "Yes,"said the Lord, "but also tough, you cannot imagine what this teacher can endure or do, if necessary." "Can this teacher think?" asked the Angel.

7. "Not only think," said the Lord, "but reason and compromise." The Angel came closer to have a better look at the model and ran his finger over the teacher's cheek.

8. "Well, Lord," said the Angel, Your job looks fine but there is a leak. I told you that you were putting too much into this model. You cannot imagine the stress that will be placed upon the teacher." The Lord moved in closer and lifted the drop of moisture from the teacher's cheek. It shone and glistened in the light.

   "It is not a leak," He said, "It is a tear."

9. "A tear? What is that?" asked the Angel, "What is a tear for?" The Lord replied with great thought, "For the joy and pride of watching what a child accomplishes even it's the smallest task to do. It is done for the loneliness of children who have a hard time to fit into the compassionate feelings of their parents. This has been done when a teacher had to leave the class and to say good bye to his students and get ready to welcome a new class."

10. "My, "said the Angel," The tear thing is a great idea...You are a genius!"

    The Lord looked sombre, "I didn't put it there."

Questions

Answer the following questions based on the passage above.

(i) When did God create teachers? Why is this creation a tremendous responsibility?

(ii) What are the specifications for a teacher?

(iii) Choose the correct response from the two options to complete the sentence.

A teacher must be able to .... in addition to teaching their subject.

(a) make coffee for themselves

(b) do 180 additional things which aren't related to their subject

(iv) Complete the following suitably.

According to God, a teacher's special qualities consist of ....

(v) What can a teacher do in addition to thinking?

(a) Reprimand (b) Reason

(c) Compromise (d) Both (b) and (c)

(vi) What is the teacher's tear for? Give one point.

(vii) Why does a teacher need three pairs of eyes?

(viii) What did the Angel think that the teacher's tear was?

(a) Tear

(b) Water droplet

(c) Leak

(d) All of the above

(ix) Describe how did God envision 'creating a good teacher'.

Passage 3

1. Lucie, a student from the United States, has just arrived at Charles de Gaulle in Paris, the airport that greets a million visitors to Paris everyday. Paris, finally. It's always been a dream of Lucie to live in the city of light, the city of fine arts, of the Latin Quarter, of wine and, who knows, the city of a little love story perhaps. She plans to study in France for one year, to get her degree in Computer Science at the University of Versailles St. Quentin-en-Yvelines. It's the university that offered her a **scholarship** to study. Plus, her friend Josephine studies there so that Lucie can live with her in a small apartment.

2. She takes the RER train which brings her straight to the St. Lazare Station at the city center. After arriving there, she looks for Versailles. She boards the train and soon it's heading into a black tunnel towards Versailles. Lucie is a little **disappointed** because she has to stay in Versailles when she'd like to live in Paris. But, she tells herself that Versailles is only a few minutes by train from the big city of Paris and, moreover, there are several attractions in Versailles.

3. The train exits the tunnel and, while passing the big city, she sees a large cemetery, the Eiffel Tower and Montmartre with the Sacre Coeur Cathedral nearby. A few moments later she arrives at the Versailles Station.

4. She has arrived. This is her destination. In front of her is the grand Chateau of Versailles where Lucie 14th, the Sun king, had parties and lived the high life with his mistresses. To the right is the avenue St. Cloud where the apartment that she'll live in with Josephine is located. She is tired but joyful. She starts looking for the address of the apartment. "All alone in a new country, knowing no one, future I'm ready!" Lucie says to herself. Lucie has arrived at the Versailles train station.

5. She has already seen the Chateau of Versailles but she wants to come back later for a more in-depth visit. But, she walks along avenue St. Loud first to find her apartment. She finds the address in front of the police station in a little brick house. She sets her bags down in front of the gate of the little pathway that leads to the sidewalk of the house. She rings the yellow doorbell next to 'Josephine Gerard'. Her friend, Josephine, whom she met on the web, opens the door. Josephine gives her two kisses. Shocked Lucie asks why she did that. That's how it's done in France.

6. Girls give each other two kisses, guys give two kisses to girls and guys shake each other's hands. We do all this to say hello, Josephine says. 'Come with me', she says. "I'll show you the apartment. It's small but it's our own little place." Silently, Lucie follows her. She looks at the apartment's entryway in awe. She can't believe her eyes when she enters the hallway and sees the walls are painted red, completely red. The floors are wood, beautiful and possible oak. The ceiling is painted black.

7. On the left is an iron table with the telephone on it. She goes on and to the left is a bathroom which is across from Josephine's room. A little farther, to the right, is Lucie's room. She puts all of her things in the corner, jumps into the bed and stretches her arms and legs. "Finally at my own place", she says to herself.

Questions

Answer the following questions based on the passage above.

(i) What are the two reasons for Lucie to take admission to the University of Versailles?

(ii) How does Lucie console herself about living in Versailles? What is her sorrow?

(iii) Choose the correct response from the two options to complete the sentence.

Lucie was pursuing a degree in Computer Science at the University of Versailles that offered her ....

(a) a scholarship to study

(b) a small apartment to study and live in

(iv) Complete the following suitably.

Lucie is ready for the ....

(v) How do people say, 'hello' in France?

(a) Girls say 'hello' in France by giving each other two kisses

(b) Guys say 'hello' in France by giving girls two kisses

(c) Guys say 'hello' in France by shaking each other's hands

(d) All of the above

(vi) Why does Lucie say, 'Finally, at my own place' according to you?

(vii) How is the phrase 'who knows' used in Paragraph 1?

(viii) What has Paris been called in the above passage?

(a) City of light
(b) City of fine arts
(c) City of love
(d) Both (a) and (b)

(ix) Describe the apartment in which Lucie goes to stay, right from the entry in your own words.

Passage 4

1. Archimedes with his lever, desired a place to stand that he might move the world of matter. [William Lloyd] Garrison with his paper, having found a place for his feet, demonstrated speedily his ability to push from its solid base the world of mind. His plan was very simple, *viz.*, to reveal slavery as it then existed in its naked enormity, to the conscience of the North, to be "as harsh as truth and as uncompromising as justice." And so, week after week, he packed in the columns of the Liberator facts, the most damning facts, against slaveholders, their cruelty and tyranny. He painted the woes of the slaves as if he, too, had been a slave. For the first time the masters found a man who rebuked them as not before had they been rebuked. Others may have equivocated, but this man called things by their proper names, a spade, a spade and sin, sin. Others may have contented themselves with denunciations of the sins and with excuses for the sinner, as a creature of circumstances, the victim of ancestral

transgressions but this man offered no excuses for the slave-holding sinner. Him and his sin he denounced in language which the Eternal puts only into the mouths of his prophets.

2. It was, as he had said, "On this subject I do not wish to think, or speak, or write, with moderation." The strength and resources of his mother-tongue seemed to him wholly inadequate for his needs, to express the transcendent wickedness of slave-holding. All the harsh, the stern, the terrible and tremendous energies of the English speech he drew upon and launched at slaveholders. Amid all of this excess of the enthusiast there was the method of a calculating mind. He aimed to kindle a conflagration because he had icebergs to melt. "The public shall not be imposed upon," he replied to one of his critics, "and men and things shall be called by their right names. I retract nothing, I blot out nothing. My language is exactly such as suits me; it will displease many, I know; to displease them is my intention."

3. He was philosopher enough to see that he could reach the national conscience only by exciting the national anger. It was not popular rage, which he feared but popular apathy. If he could goad the people to anger on the subject of slavery, he would soon be rid of their apathy. And so week after week, he piled every sort of combustible material, which he was able to collect on board the Liberator and lighting it all, sent the fiery messenger blazing among the icebergs of the Union.

4. Slaveholders were robbers, murderers, oppressors; they were guilty of all the sins. At the same moment that the reformer denied their right of property in the slave, he attacked their character also, held them up in their relation of masters to the reprobation of the nation and of mankind as monsters of injustice and inhumanity. The tone which he held toward them, steadily, without shadow of change, was the tone of a righteous man toward the workers of iniquity. The indifference, the apathy, the pro-slavery sympathy and prejudice of the free States rendered the people of the North hardly less culpable.

Questions

Answer the following questions based on the above passage.

(i) How were slaveholders seen by Garrison?

(ii) Why was Garrison's tone called a tone of a righteous man?

(iii) Complete the sentence by choosing an appropriate option out of the two given below.

According to the passage, Garrison's language was so strong because ....

(a) He had been a slave himself and wrote from experience.

(b) He saw himself as a sort of Prophet and his language was given to him by God.

(iv) Complete the following suitably.

In his writings, Garrison offered no excuses for ....

(v) What made William Lloyd Garrison different from other abolitionists?

(a) He went onto Southern plantations and freed slaves.

(b) He worked in Congress to pass abolitionist legislation.

(c) He didn't make any excuses in his writings and exposed the truth.

(d) He operated an underground railroad to help slaves escape to the North.

(vi) Mention what can be said about the works of Garrison.

(vii) What does the phrase 'goad the people mean'?

(viii) All of the following statements are true about Garrison's intentions, EXCEPT

(a) He hoped that people would ignore his writings and keep owning slaves.

(b) He wanted to provoke the national anger.

(c) He attacked the character of the slave-owners, showing them to be monsters.

(d) He wanted people to react so that they wouldn't be apathetic any more.

(ix) Draw an inference about the statement.

'Garrision's views of the people in North' from the passage.

Passage 5

1. Curious as it may sound, I have always felt I am an Indian by accident. Let me explain why I say this. I was born in Bhagalpur. This ought to make me a Bihari. But I am not one because my mother was a Bengali whose family had settled in Bihar. Within weeks of being born I came to Calcutta, where I spent all my growing up years. My school was founded by a Frenchman, a soldier of fortune. And though I scored far better marks in Bengali and Hindi there, the only language I learnt was English. How and why I have no clue, since we all spoke Bengali at home. My first English article appeared in the Statesman when I was 13. Soon, I published my first book of poems, again in English. I dropped out of college.
2. I wrote more books till the desire to change the world (yes, in those days we actually thought we could) brought me to what was then Bombay, to be a journalist.
3. Mumbai is where I have lived for most of my life. In between, for what seemed like six long years, I also lived in Lutyens' Delhi. In a charming bungalow just opposite the BJP office on Ashoka Road, eating subsidised meals in Parliament and representing Maharashtra's interests on a Shiv Sena ticket. So, am I a Mumbaikar? Or a Bengali from Calcutta?
4. A Bihari? Or a born again Anglophile like Nirad C Chaudhari? I have no clue. Most Indians are like me, put together by accident. That's the magic of being a migrant in your own land, trying to discover your many identities.
5. My mother's maiden name seemed to suggest that someone in her family in the past had Muslim connection though her first name was Hindu (or Bengali, depending on how you see it). The only place of worship I ever saw her visit was the St. Paul's Cathedral on New Year's eve more out of convention than faith. My father was born a Hindu and his family home was in Kalighat. His father remarried and chucked them out. My father, his mother and two sisters found themselves on the street trying to fend for themselves, when a passing Jesuit took pity on them. He gave them shelter in Bishnupur where he ran a school.
6. The freedom struggle brought my parents together. They married and we three brothers were born. Never did it once strike me what my religion was, which state I belonged to, what my language ought to be, which culture I should fight for.
7. My adolescent years were spent in protesting against the Russians invading Czechoslovakia and the Americans in Vietnam. My Bengali DNA I guess, if you look around you, you will find many people like me who, in the midst of their many identities, accidentally chanced upon their Indianness. Each of them will swear by their regional culture, the language they speak, the faith they follow or (like me) do not. And, as they wander through all these, and discover themselves, they also discover the magic of being Indian.

Questions

Answer the following questions based on the passage above.

(i) Why does the author say that he is an Indian by accident?

(ii) Which quality in himself does the author attribute to his Bengali DNA?

(iii) Choose the correct response from the two options to complete the sentence.

The author's first English article was published when ………………. .

(a) he was 13 years old (b) he was 30 years old

(iv) Complete the following suitably.

The author's desire 'to change the world' brought him ………………… .

(v) Which was the only language that the author learnt at his school?

(a) Bengali
(b) Hindi
(c) English
(d) All of the above

(vi) What similarity does the author seem to have with Nirad C. Chaudhuri as mentioned in the passage?

(vii) What did the passing Jesuit on road do to the author's family?

(viii) What never occurred to the author of the above passage?

(a) What his religion was
(b) Which state he belonged to
(c) What his language should be
(d) All of the above

(ix) Write, in your own words, how the author discovers the magic of being Indian.

Answers

Factual Passages

Passage 1

(i) According to the passage, paperbacks appeal to people who would not have bought books otherwise.
(ii) The book producing mechanism has facilitated in providing permanence to the words of scientist, philosophers and thinkers.
(iii) (a) an enjoyable intellectual exercise

(iv) for the sake of his mental and spiritual advancement
(v) (d) All of the above
(vi) Popular paperbacks are generally reprints of popular fictions.
(vii) In the given line, the phrase 'vital concern' means something that is necessary.
(viii) (d) All of the above
(ix) The passage states that the book producing machinery gives permanence to the works of thinkers, poets and philosophers, and books provides intellectual exercise to readers.

Passage 2

(i) As per the amount of food to be eaten, it is recommended that it is to be decided by the individual.
(ii) The expanding waistlines of people shows that the portion size is increasing.
(iii) (b) consume larger amount of food
(iv) that it does not consider portion sizc
(v) (b) Developed economies have larger portions of food
(vi) People do not eat less in subsequent meals after they have consumed large portion sizes for one meal.
(vii) In the given line, the phrase 'undergone a considerable change' refers to the difference in portion size over the years.
(viii) (d) Portion sizes always match.
(ix) The passage states that to judge the right amount of food to be eaten, an individual must recognise the standard serving size to understand how much he/she is eating.

Passage 3

(i) According to paragraph 1, computers are widely used in industries and universities.
(ii) Automation can prove to be helpful for humans as it may help them enjoy more leisure than they do now.
(iii) (b) Diagnose the nature of patient's illness
(iv) each other
(v) (c) Computers can solve the most complex mathematical problems
(vi) The passage mentions that computers need detailed instructions from human beings to operate even though they are capable of learning from their mistakes and improving on their performance.
(vii) The phrase 'coming of' means to happen as a result of something.
(viii) (c) There is no possibility that human beings will ever be controlled machines.
(ix) Sir Leon says that, in future, small computers will be developed. Ordinary people would then be able to use them to obtain valuable information.

Passage 4

(i) In the Kathakali drama form, all the dancers are males.
(ii) Bharatanatyam is most popular in Tanjore and Kanchipuram.
(iii) (b) nritya
(iv) the focal points in the development of Bharatnatyam.
(v) (c) When kings and the rich patronised it
(vi) The two schools of classical dance described in the passage are Bharatanatyam and Kathakali.
(vii) In the given line, the phrase 'lent their patronage to it' means supported it and gave money to it.
(viii) (b) Kathakali performance starts at dusk and ends at dawn.
(ix) Kathakali dance-dramas last from dusk to dawn. The artistes use elaborate costumes, mask-like make-up and towering head-dresses. In these dramas, all dancers are males.

Passage 5

(i) According to paragraph 1, mountaineering involves hiking, climbing or just simply walking on hilly or mountainous ground with the help of technical equipment and support.
(ii) A person can prepare for mountaineering by building a robust body, being very fit and by displaying a decent level of athleticism and suppleness of body.
(iii) (a) extreme climatic conditions
(iv) depending on hi-tech safety equipment
(v) (c) Edmund Hilary and George Mallory
(vi) The statement 'Mountaineering is as old as the earth, as old as human life' proves that mountaineering has been in practice for a long time and isn't a modern thing.
(vii) The phrase 'earned their name' means that someone has successfully gained a specific reputation or title through their actions or achievements.
(viii) (b) Himalayan Mountaineering Institute

(ix) The modern way of mountaineering provides the comfort of having the most advanced equipment and gear at climbers' disposal. In contrast, men in ancient times had to rely on their feet, their legs, their arms, hands and wits while climbing.

Discursive Passages

Passage 1

(i) According to paragraph 1, Kings of Mewar, with the cooperation of their nobles and subjects, had established traditions that augmented their magnificence even when they had smaller areas under their command.

(ii) The destiny of Mewar can be said to be good as most of its rules were competent and patriotic. This glorious tradition of the Kingdom almost continued for 1,500 years since its establishment.

(iii) (b) He added a lot of grandeur to Mewar.

(iv) Rana Sanga

(v) (c) Its small area and small population.

(vi) During the reign of Rana Kumbha, literature and art flourished in the Kingdom of Mewar. The ambience of his kingdom was conducive to the creation of high-quality work of art and literature.

(vii) The phrase 'took a turn' means to change in condition or quality, especially quickly or suddenly.

(viii) (b) Most of its people were competent.

(ix) The life of the people of Mewar must have been peaceful and prosperous during the long span of time; otherwise, such extraordinary accomplishment in the field of arts and literature would not have been possible. The ambience of Mewar remains lovely as well.

Passage 2

(i) The contribution of NeXT is that the technology developed at NeXT is central to Apple's success.

(ii) The speaker of the given passage shows strength of character and mental resilience in the times of sufferings.

(iii) (b) helpful to make him successful again

(iv) that one should always do what one loves

(v) (a) He realised he still loved what he did.

(vi) The only thing that kept the author from going after getting fired is that he loved what he did.

(vii) In the given line, the phrase 'dropped the baton' means 'not living upto expectations'.

(viii) (b) creating the word's first computer animated movie

(ix) The narrator/author calls getting fired from Apple as one of the best things that could ever happen to him because it was after that he created NeXT and Pixar which brought him several accolades.

Passage 3

(i) According to paragraph 1, the breath-taking beauty of the Himalayas, its valleys and rivers, the numerous wildlife sanctuaries dotted all over the country, our still unspoilt sea beaches, our great temples and caves and historical monuments, our music and dance, our festivals and national celebrations, would attract any tourist in the world.

(ii) We must build up more infrastructure to earn more from our tourists.

(iii) (b) By its rivers, valleys and Himalayas.

(iv) proper distribution of wealth

(v) (c) Dissuade others from visiting our country

(vi) The statement 'The Government of India has intensified efforts to build more hotels in the country' asserts the role of the government in the field of tourism.

(vii) The phrase 'do us good' means to have a positive effect on someone.

(viii) (a) Government agencies

(ix) If a tourist returns home with a bad experience, he is sure to dissuade others from visiting our country. As a consequence, the tourism sector will suffer a financial loss and we will lose some foreign exchange.

Passage 4

(i) Dates have not made it to the top of antioxidant rich foods due to their low consumption.

(ii) The benefits of antioxidants depend on the way they are absorbed and utilised in the body.

(iii) (a) consumption

(iv) type 2 diabetes, Parkinson's disease, liver and colon cancer

(v) (b) A study by the University of Scranton

(vi) If one drank too much coffee, he/she may feel jittery or experience stomach pain.

(vii) In the given line, the phrase 'came out on the top' means to be in the best or most successful position.

(viii) (c) Both (a) and (b)

(ix) Dates are not considered highest source of antioxidants as they are not consumed anywhere in a quantity near to coffee.

Passage 5

(i) The advantage of being a tramp is that you are free from the worries which burden other humans.

(ii) A tramp will not want you to feel sorry for him because he had made the choice to become a tramp.

(iii) (b) might despise paying a surgeon for service

(iv) feel sorry for them

(v) (a) A beggar sells but tramps don't.

(vi) Yes, I think that a tramp lives a better life than us. A tramp is not anxious. He/she is independent, possesses human dignity and lives closer to nature.

(vii) In the first paragraph, the author mentions teachers, philosophers and priests to be selling their services.

(viii) (a) The actual value of services given by people

(ix) The statement means that our society is such that we pay for every service that we get. Teachers get paid by selling their knowledge, philosophers sell their wisdom, priest sell spirituality and surgeons sell their medical knowledge to get paid.

Literary Passages

Passage 1

(i) The Andaman Islands constitutes more than 356 Islands.

(ii) The author describes the scenes at Andaman islands as calm and beautiful. The occan was unpolluted and the region was very peaceful.

(iii) (b) the realisation that freedom fighters had lived, struggled and died there.

(iv) always more cargo and less people.

(v) (b) There were no empty seats in the aircraft.

(vi) The author's initial impression about the Andaman Islands was that they were sinister, haunted and scary.

(vii) In the given line, the phrase 'sent a shiver down my spine' means to feel very frightened.

(viii) (b) In the Bay of Bengal

(ix) According to the author of the passage, Andaman roads were unique because unilke the chaos of the many traffic signals on the straight roads of Chennai and Mumbai, Andaman only had one traffic signal. Its roads went up and down and there was no noise or chaos of auto-rickshaws.

Passage 2

(i) God created teachers on the sixth day of his 'overtime'. This creation is a tremendous responsibility because teachers touch the lives of many impressionable children.

(ii) The specifications for a teacher are

- He/she must stand above all students to be at their level.
- He/she must be able to communicate as per his/her vital knowledge to all students daily.
- He/she must have more time for others than for himself/herself.

(iii) (b) do 180 additional things which aren't related to their subject

(iv) being soft-hearted and caring as well as very tough when it comes to disciplining the child

(v) (d) Both (b) and (c)

(vi) The teacher's tear is for the joy and pride of watching what a child accomplishes even if it's the smallest task to do.

(vii) A teacher needs three pairs of eyes because one pair is to see whether a student is doing or not what others have labelled them. The second pair which is at the back of the teacher's head is to watch what should not be seen but what must be known. The third pair is the eyes in the front which is only to look at the child and 'act out' in order to reflect 'I understand and I still believe in you' without saying a word to the child.

(viii) (c) Leak

(ix) According to God's vision, a good teacher must have additional pair of hands and eyes to carry out additional things besides teaching. An ideal teacher will be very committed to his/her work, motivating the unwilling learners and treating his/her class children well. He/she should understand the problems of children from their perspectives and find out a solution to each problem.

Passage 3

(i) Lucie took admission to the University of Versailles for the following reasons:

- The University offered her a scholarship to study Computer Science and get a degree.
- Her friend Josephine studies there and Lucie can share the apartment where she stays.

(ii) Lucie consoles herself by saying that Versailles has several attractions, besides being only a few minutes away by train from Paris. Her sorrow is that she has to live in Versailles instead of Paris where she would have liked to stay.

(iii) (a) a scholarship to study

(iv) future, all alone in a new country

(v) (d) All of the above

(vi) Lucie says these words to herself because she is much relieved to have finally reached where she is going to live for the next one year. It was her dream to live in Paris which has been fulfilled now.

(vii) The phrase 'who knows' is used in paragraph 1 to express uncertainty or doubt about a particular situation, idea or outcome.

(viii) (d) Both (a) and (b)

(ix) On entering, the hallway was painted red on the walls and black on the roof. The floor was wooden. On the left was the telephone on a table and, further on, a bathroom. On the right are two rooms with Josephine's room being the first and Lucie's room the second one.

Passage 4

(i) Garrison saw slaveholders as robbers, murderers and oppressors who are guilty of all sins.
(ii) Garrison's tone is called a tone of a righteous man as he was raising his voice and writing for the just cause of anti-slavery.
(iii) (b) He saw himself as a sort of Prophet and his language was given to him by God.
(iv) the slave-holding sinner
(v) (c) He didn't make any excuses in his writings and exposed the truth.
(vi) It can be said about Garrison's works that he writes as if he too had been a slave.
(vii) The phrase 'good the people' means to make the people react.
(viii) (a) He hoped that people would ignore his writings and keep owning slaves.
(ix) It can be inferred from the statement from the passage that Garrison felt that people in the North were partially responsible because they were indifferent to the plight of the slaves.

Passage 5

(i) The author says that he is an Indian by accident because he has many identities because of his connection with many cultures within India.
(ii) The quality in himself that the author attributes to his Bengali DNA is protesting against happenings that do not concern him in the least.
(iii) (a) he was 13 years old
(iv) to what was then known as Bombay
(v) (c) English
(vi) The author seems to have the similarity with Nirad C. Chaudhuri of being a migrant in his own land who is trying to discover himself through his many identities.
(vii) The passing Jesuit on the road took pity on the author's family when they were wandering on the roads and gave them shelter in Bishnupur where he ran a school.
(viii) (d) All of the above
(ix) The author discovers the magic of being Indian after wandering through his many identities. These include his regional culture, the languages he speaks, the faith he follows and the state to which he belongs. He discovers this by accident after going through the various identities, just like many other Indians.

SELF ASSESSMENT TEST

Passage 1

1. When another old cave is discovered in the South of France, it is not usually news. Rather, it is an ordinary event. Such discoveries are so frequent these days that hardly anybody pays heed to them. However, when the Lascaux cave complex was discovered in 1940, the world was amazed. Painted directly on its walls were hundreds of scenes showing how people lived thousands of years ago. The scenes show people hunting animals, such as bison or wild cats. Other images depict birds and, most noticeably, horses, which appear in more than 300 wall images, by far outnumbering all other animals.
2. Early artists drawing these animals accomplished a monumental and difficult task. They did not limit themselves to the easily accessible walls but carried their painting materials to spaces that required climbing steep walls or crawling into narrow passages in the Lascaux complex. Unfortunately, the paintings have been exposed to the destructive action of water and temperature changes, which easily wear the images away. Because the Lascaux caves have many entrances, air movement has also damaged the images inside.
3. Although they are not out in the open air, where natural light would have destroyed them long ago, many of the images have deteriorated and are barely recognisable. To prevent further damage, the site was closed to tourists in 1963, 23 years after it was discovered.

Questions

Answer the following questions based on the passage above.

(i) Which animals are shown getting hunted by humans on the wall scenes?

(ii) For what reasons were the Lascaux caves closed?

(iii) Complete the sentence by choosing an appropriate option.

According to the passage, no damage has been caused to the paintings by ....

(a) temperature changes (b) light

(iv) Complete the following suitably.

Although the paintings are not in the open air, where they would have been destroyed by natural light, many images have ....

(v) Based on the passage, what is probably true about the south of France?

(a) It is home to rare animals.
(b) It is known for horse-racing events.
(c) It has a large number of caves.
(d) It has attracted many famous artists.

(vi) Why was painting inside the Lascaux complex a difficult task? Provide textual evidence.

(vii) What does the phrase 'pays heed to' in the passage mean?

(viii) Select the most suitable title which best summarises the main idea of the passage.

(a) Wild Animals in Art
(b) Hidden Prehistoric Paintings
(c) Exploring Caves Respectfully
(d) Determining the Age of French Caves

(ix) List what the passage says happened at the Lascaux caves in 1963.

Passage 2

1. One of the most devastating periods in European history came during the fourteenth century, with the epidemic of bubonic plague, also known as the 'Great Plague' and later dubbed the 'Black Death.' At the time of its first pandemic, the bubonic plague was a terrifying disease, killing indiscriminately and leaving cities and towns devastated in its wake. It appeared to spread just by touching clothes and people who seemed healthy one day might be dead the next. Faced with such a mysterious and horrifying illness, many believed that this was a divine punishment for their sins.

2. The true cause of the plague wasn't discovered until its most recent outbreak, which began in 1855 in China and didn't officially end until 1959. Researchers in Hong Kong at the end of the 19th century discovered that the disease is caused by the bacteria 'Yersinia pestis'. Several years later, Chinese doctors noticed that rats showed similar plague symptoms to humans and that the victims often had fleabites. This was the key to unraveling the mystery of the plague, which is transmitted by rat fleas. Modern sanitary practices and medicine have greatly subdued the impact of the bubonic plague, but have never completely eliminated it. Today, there are still incidences of it in sub-Saharan Africa and there have been confirmed cases in the United States, Vietnam, Mongolia, China and India as well.
3. The Black Death first came to Europe by way of Asia, when the Genoese trading port of Kaffa was laid siege to by Kipchak Khan Janibeg's army in the fall of 1346. The plague destroyed the army and also spread to the besieged town, and when in the spring the Genoese took to their ships and fled, they carried the disease with them to Constantinople. From there, it spread far and wide into Europe and Northern Africa, hitting hub cities such as Marseilles, Alexandria, Florence, Venice and Paris.
4. In order to escape its horrors people fled from plague-stricken areas, bringing the disease with them to the countryside or other cities via fleas that were on their clothes or belongings. They would then infect the new city's house rat population and kill it off. After the rodents had been killed off, the fleas would turn to humans as a source of blood, transmitting the disease in turn to them. Once bitten by a plague-carrying flea, the disease typically takes three to five days to incubate before a person shows symptoms, and then another three to five days before it kills the person.
5. More so than by individual humans, the plague was transferred from place to place by boat, which travelled much faster and farther than people on foot or horseback. Rats and fleas on board the vessel would infect the local populations wherever they docked. As the disease spread, its effects were felt not only by its victims and their families, but by the population at large. Because of the elevated number of deaths, there were great shortages of labour, especially in agriculture, causing food shortages across Europe.
6. There are conflicting conjectures about the number of people killed by the Black Death, varying from 30 percent of Europe's population at the most conservative, to up to 60 percent. Since the population is estimated to have been approximately 80 million before the epidemic started, this means that somewhere between 25 and 53 million people died from the plague. In many cases whole families and communities were wiped out. The population did not recover its pre-plague numbers until the start of the 16th century.

Questions

Answer the following questions based on the passage above.

(i) Can we say that we have eradicated the Bubonic plague? Give reason for your answer.

(ii) How was the cause of the Bubonic plague detected?

(iii) Choose the correct option.

It can be inferred from Paragraph 3 that ....

(a) the Black Death was an epidemic in Asia
(b) the plague killed everyone in Kaffa

(iv) Complete the following suitably.

The Primary manner in which the plague spread was ....

(v) Why does the author mention that many believed this was a divine punishment for their sins?

(a) To show how religious people were at that time
(b) To compare past reactions to disease with current reactions
(c) To show how little people understood the plague
(d) To explain why the disease spread so rapidly

(vi) What can be inferred about modern cases of the Bubonic plague?

(vii) To whom does the word 'they' in the Paragraph 3 of the passage refer to?

(viii) According to the passage, why was the plague felt by the population at large?

(a) People's family members were dying.
(b) People were migrating away.
(c) There wasn't enough food for everyone.
(d) People had to stay in their homes.

(ix) Describe the effects of the Bubonic plague.

Passage 3

1. Why is it that there are very few women players in our orchestras? If one could reply flatly - sex discrimination: they don't want women in orchestras - that would be a definite answer. But one can't say that. As a matter of fact there are, if not many, a few women playing today in symphony orchestras. Nevertheless, it is true that male orchestral players are in an overwhelming majority. Why is that? I'm afraid, there is no one answer.
2. There are physical reasons why women don't perform well on certain instruments. The average woman is not likely to possess sufficient lung power and sheer muscular strength to play the tuba just as an average woman's hands are not likely to be large enough to finger a double bass satisfactorily. But what about the other instruments?
3. I think social and family pressures have been very strong in keeping women out of orchestras. Think of the prejudice that existed half a century ago against the so-called 'nice' girls going on stage. The stage has won out for the simple reason that it had to have women to play feminine roles in plays and operas, and was willing to offer a young woman more money than she could make in any other profession. Moreover, on stage, she was appearing as an individual, as a centre of attraction. This was gratifying to both her and her family. To this day, while the average parents are reconciled to seeing their daughter become an opera singer or concert artist, they don't like the idea of seeing her submerging her personality to become the member of a chorus of the orchestra.
4. Another reason why we have so few women orchestral musicians is that so few of them play wind instruments well enough. They don't play well enough because they haven't had the proper training; and the reason for that lies in the history of orchestral music. You will find that famous European families of bassoon players or clarinet players taught their sons to play the family instrument. Their sons; but never their daughters. If they had any other pupils, those were also boys; not girls. And to this day, while women vote, hold public office and practise many other professions without shocking our sensibilities, in this particular field, the orchestra, our attitude towards women still remains the same.

Questions

Answer the following questions based on the passage above.

(i) What is our attitude towards women in the context of the passage?

(ii) What does the given passage highlight?

(iii) Parents support their daughters working on the stage more than that in an orchestra because ....
- (a) they do not want to be shocked
- (b) she is not submerging her personality on the stage

(iv) Women do not play wind instruments well because ....
- (a) famous musicians taught only their sons to play these instruments
- (b) they haven't been trained properly
- (c) the attitude is negative towards women playing such instruments
- (d) they don't have enough muscle or lung power

(v) Why are very few women playing today in symphony orchestras? Because ....
- (a) there is sex discrimination
- (b) they don't possess sufficient lung power
- (c) they don't possess sheer muscular strength
- (d) there is no one answer

(vi) Why women could not play tuba? Provide textual evidence.

(vii) What does the phrase 'centre of attraction' mean (Paragraph 3)

(viii) All of the statements highlight the problem of lack of women in orchestra, EXCEPT
- (a) Women are considered weaker than men.
- (b) The musical instruments suit more to the males.
- (c) Girls were not trained to play musical instruments.
- (d) People liked women on stage acting as individuals.

(ix) Why do more women play roles on the stage than playing in orchestra?

Passage 4

1. The oceans are so vast and deep that until recently, it was widely assumed that no matter how much trash and chemicals humans dumped into them, the effects would be negligible. Proponents of dumping in the oceans even had a catchphrase: "The solution to pollution is dilution."
2. Today, we need look no further than the New Jersey-size dead zone that forms each summer in the Mississippi River Delta or the thousand-mile-wide swath of decomposing plastic in the Northern Pacific Ocean to see that this 'dilution policy has helped place a once flourishing ocean ecosystem on the brink of collapse.
3. There is evidence that the oceans have suffered at the hands of mankind for millennia, as far back as Roman times. But recent studies show that degradation, particularly of shoreline areas, has accelerated dramatically in the past three centuries as industrial discharge and runoff from farms and coastal cities has increased.
4. Pollution is the introduction of harmful contaminants that are outside the norm for a given ecosystem. Common man-made pollutants that reach the ocean include pesticides, herbicides, chemical fertilizers, detergents, oil, sewage, plastics and other solids. Many of these pollutants collect at the ocean's depths, where they are consumed by small marine organisms and introduced into the global food chain. Scientists are even discovering that pharmaceuticals ingested by humans but not fully processed by our bodies are eventually ending up in the fish we eat.
5. Many ocean pollutants are released into the environment far upstream from coastlines. Nitrogen-rich fertilizers applied by farmers inland, for example, end up in local streams, rivers, and groundwater and are eventually deposited in estuaries, bays, and deltas. These excess nutrients can spawn massive blooms of algae that rob the water of oxygen, leaving areas where little or no marine life can exist. Scientists have counted some 400 such dead zones around the world.
6. Solid wastes like bags, foam, and other items dumped into the oceans from land or by ships at sea are frequently consumed, with often fatal effects, by marine mammals, fish, and birds that mistake it for food. In certain regions, ocean currents corral trillions of decomposing plastic items and other trash into gigantic, swirling garbage patches.
7. Pollution is not always physical. In large bodies of water, sound waves can carry undiminished for miles. The increased presence of loud or persistent sounds from ships, sonar devices, oil rigs and even from natural sources like earthquakes can disrupt the migration, communication, hunting and reproduction patterns of many marine animals, particularly aquatic mammals like whales and dolphins. (421 Words)

Questions

Answer the following questions based on the passage above.

(i) According to Paragraph 1, what was assumed about the oceans?

(ii) What has happened in the past three centuries?

(iii) Choose the correct response from the two options to complete the sentence.

Pollution is the introduction of harmful contaminants that ....

(a) are natural parts of a particular ecosystem
(b) are not natural parts of a particular ecosystem

(iv) Complete the following suitably.

The dead zone in the Mississippi River Delta has brought ....

(v) According to the author, what is the greatest lesson being taught by the above passage?

(a) Trash dumped into the ocean is fatal to the marine organisms.
(b) Pollution is not only physically manifested.
(c) Human beings are not responsible for the pollution of large water bodies.
(d) Both (a) and (b)

(vi) Provide one textual evidence that proves that aquatic organisms have consumed man-made pollutants.

(vii) What does the phrase 'on the brink of' mean? (Paragraph 2)

(viii) What has increased in the past 300 years?

(a) Trading of ocean valuable
(b) Killing of aquatic life
(c) Degradation of shoreline areas
(d) None of the above

(ix) Explain how excess nutrients can create dead zones around the world.

Passage 5

1. I have said this much because it is my wish that the principles which have guided me in the composition of these memoirs may be understood. I am aware that they will not please every reader; that is a success to which I cannot pretend. Some merit, however, may be allowed to me on account of the labour I have undergone. It has neither been of a slight nor an agreeable kind. I made it a rule to read everything that has been written respecting Napoleon, and I have had to decipher many of his autographed documents, though no longer so familiar with his scrawl as formerly. I say decipher, because a real cipher might often be much more readily understood than the handwriting of Napoleon. My own notes, too, which were often very hastily made, in the hand I wrote in my youth, have sometimes also much embarrassed me.

2. My long and intimate connection with Bonaparte from boyhood, as well as my close relations with him when he was General, Consul and Emperor, enabled me to see and appreciate all that was projected and all that was done during that considerable and momentous period of time. I not only had the opportunity of being present at the conception and the execution of the extraordinary deeds of one of the ablest men nature ever formed, but notwithstanding an almost unceasing application to business, I found means to employ the few moments of leisure which Bonaparte left at my disposal in making notes, collecting documents and in recording for history the facts respecting which the truth could otherwise with difficulty be ascertained; and more particularly in collecting those ideas, often profound, brilliant and striking, but always remarkable, to which Bonaparte gave expression in the overflowing frankness of confidential intimacy.

3. The knowledge that I possessed much important information has exposed me to many inquiries and wherever I have resided since my retirement from public affairs, much of my time has been spent in replying to questions. The wish to be acquainted with the minutest details of the life of a famous man is very natural; and the observation on my replies by those who heard them always was, "You should publish your memoirs"!

Questions

Answer the following questions based on the passage above.

(i) Regarding his memoirs, what does the narrator says that he is aware of?

(ii) What does the narrator claim to know that others don't?

(iii) Complete the sentence by choosing the correct option.
The author was known to Napoleon Bonaparte since ....
(a) boyhood
(b) Bonaparte became consul and emperor

(iv) Complete the following suitably.
According to the author, his hastily made notes have ....

(v) Why is the author embarrassed as stated in Paragraph 1?
(a) Napoleon's handwriting was unreadable.
(b) The author's handwriting was very poor in his youth.
(c) He cannot please every reader.
(d) None of the above

(vi) What is the essential purpose of writing the given passage?

(vii) What does the phrase 'on account of' mean in Paragraph 1?

(viii) What advantage did the narrator have for being close to Bonaparte as an Emperor and General?
(a) He enjoyed all luxuries.
(b) He could witness all the historical decisions being taken.
(c) He got a lot of money.
(d) None of the above

(ix) Comment on the use of the word 'decipher' with respect to Napolean's handwriting.

Passage 6

On Women's Rights to Vote (1873)

1. "Fellow people in this here world": I stand before you tonight under indictment for the alleged crime of having voted at the last presidential election, without having a lawful right to vote. It shall be my work this evening to prove to you that me thus, voting, I not only committed no crime, but instead, simply exercised my citizen's rights, guaranteed to me and all United States citizens by the National Constitution, beyond the power of any state to deny.
2. The preamble of the Federal Constitution says: "We, the people of the United States, in order to form a more perfect union, establish justice, insure domestic tranquillity, provide for the common defence, promote the general welfare, and secure the blessings of liberty to ourselves and our posterity, do ordain and establish this Constitution for the United States of America."
3. It was we, the people; not we, the white male citizens; nor yet we, the male citizens; but we, the whole people, who formed the Union. And we formed it, not to give the blessings of liberty, but to secure them; not to the half of ourselves and the half of our posterity, but to the whole people - women as well as men. And it is a downright mockery to talk to women of their enjoyment of the blessings of liberty while they are denied the use of the only means of securing them provided by this democratic-republican government - the ballot.
4. For any state to make sex a qualification that must ever result in the disfranchisement of one entire half of the people, is to pass a bill of attainder, or, an ex post facto law, and is therefore a violation of the supreme law of the land. By it the blessings of liberty are forever withheld from women and their female posterity.
5. To them this government has no just powers derived from the consent of the governed. To them this government is not a democracy. It is not a republic. It is an odious aristocracy; a hateful oligarchy of sex; the most hateful aristocracy ever established on the face of the globe; an oligarchy of wealth, where the rich govern the poor. An oligarchy of learning, where the educated govern the ignorant, or even an oligarchy of race, where the Saxon rules the African, might be endured; but this oligarchy of sex, which makes father, brothers, husband, sons, the oligarchs over the mother and sisters, the wife and daughters, of every household - which ordains all men sovereigns, all women subjects, carries dissension, discord, and rebellion into every home of the nation. Webster, Worcester and Bouvier all define a citizen to be a person in the United States, entitled to vote and hold office.
6. The only question left to be settled now is: Are women persons? And I hardly believe any of our opponents will have the hardihood to say they are not. Being persons, then, women are citizens; and no state has a right to make any law or to enforce any old law, that shall abridge their privileges or immunities. Hence, "every discrimination against women in the constitutions and laws of the several states is today null and void."

Questions

Answer the following questions based on the above passage.

(i) In the last sentence of the passage, what does the writer mean by 'null and void'?

(ii) How does the author claim 'women's position in the right to vote' as per the last paragraph?

(iii) Choose the correct response from the two options to complete the sentence.

The union was formed by the people to ....

(a) to give the blessings of liberty

(b) secure the blessings of liberty

(iv) Complete the following suitably.

To women, the government that restricts their rights and liberty is ....

(v) Which of the following is true about the speaker's interpretation of the Federal Constitution?

(a) The Constitution was formed to secure liberty to half of the citizens of the U.S.A.

(b) The Constitution was designed to protect the rights and liberty of all the citizens of the U.S.A. and not just men.

(c) It is unfair to suggest that women can enjoy their liberty when they don't even have the right to vote.

(d) Can't say

(vi) How do Webster, Worcester and Bouvier define a citizen?

(vii) What does the phrase 'exercised my citizen's rights' mean?

(viii) Which of the following statements best expresses the main idea of what the speaker wants to communicate in the first paragraph?
(a) She wants to explain that she was under indictment for the alleged crime of having voted in the election as she had no lawful right to vote as women.
(b) She wants to prove that by voting she had simply exercised her citizen's rights and had not committed a crime.
(c) She wanted to outline the rights that she was entitled to as a citizen which were guaranteed by the National Constitution.
(d) Can't say

(ix) Why does the author call the government 'a hateful oligarchy of sex'?

Sample Passages

Case Based Factual Passages

Read the following passage carefully and answer the questions that follow.

Passage 1

1. Present-day India owes an immeasurable debt of gratitude to the vision, tact, diplomacy and pragmatic approach of Sardar Vallabhbhai Patel, the indomitable man who integrated 562 princely states with the Union of India and prevented the Balkanisation of the newly-independent country.
2. Back in 1947, India had finally gained a hard-fought independence but it had come with besetting problems - partition, communal riots and a refugee crisis. Add to that crippling resource constraint, fledgling institutions and an ill-equipped colonial machinery and it's not difficult to understand why India's new government found the integration of more than 500 princely states a tough nut to crack.

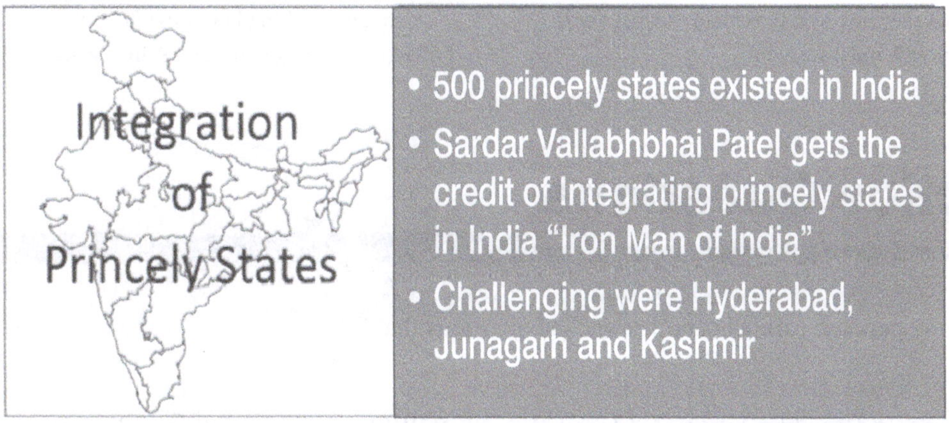

3. The Indian Independence Act of 1947, (based on the Mountbatten Plan) provided for the lapse of paramountcy of the British Crown over the Indian states. It also gave each of these rulers the option to accede to the newly born dominions India or Pakistan or continue as an independent sovereign state.
4. By 15th August, 1947, the process of integration of Princely States was almost complete except for a few, who held out. Some simply delayed signing the Instrument of Accession - like Piploda, a small state in central India that did not accede to India until March 1948.
5. The biggest problems, however, arose with Jodhpur, which tried to negotiate better deals with Pakistan, with Junagadh, which actually did accede to Pakistan and with Hyderabad and Kashmir, both of which declared that they intended to remain independent.
6. Realising the need to get these 500-odd chiefdoms to accede to India before the day of independence, Patel and VP Menon began using all the tricks in the bag - including the use of both force and friendly advice - to achieve their integration with the Indian dominion.

Questions

Answer the following questions based on the passage above.

(i) Complete the sentence.

The state which did not accede to India until March 1948 was ....

(ii) What is the common thing between Mysore, Hyderabad and Benaras?

(a) They acceded to Pakistan
(b) They decided to remain independent
(c) They were Princely States at the time of independence.
(d) None of the above

(iii) What problem was faced with the integration of the states of Hyderabad and Kashmir?

(iv) Classify the following sentences as 'fact' or 'opinion'.

Sentence 1 500 princely states existed in India.

Sentence 2 Sardar Vallabhbhai Patel gets the credit of integrating the princely states in India.

(v) Complete the given sentence by selecting the most appropriate option.

The method used by Sardar Patel for the unification of India was ....

(a) Force (b) Friendly advice
(c) Both (a) and (b) (d) Neither (a) nor (b)

(vi) Which Princely States caused the most trouble?

(vii) What do you think would have happened if Sardar Patel did not unite India?

(viii) What was the biggest contribution of Sardar Patel?

(a) He fought for the independence of India.
(b) He was the first Home Minister of India.
(c) He merged the 562 Princely States with India.
(d) He prevented partition of India.

Answers

(i) Piploda

(ii) (c) They were Princely States at the time of Independence.

(iii) The problem with the integration of Hyderabad and Kashmir is that both Hyderabad and Kashmir had declared that they intended to remain independent.

(iv) Both sentences 1 and 2 are facts.

(v) (c) Both (a) and (b)

(vi) The Princely States of Junagarh, Jodhpur and Hyderabad caused the most trouble.

(vii) If Sardar Patel did not unite India, India as we know today wouldn't have existed.

(viii) (c) He merged the 562 Princely States with India.

Practice Questions

Read the following passages carefully and answer the questions that follow.

Passage 1

1. In the contemporary world, where technology has become an integral part of our lives, previously complex tasks have become much easier and seamless. This is especially true in the case of education. Technology has transformed learning and has improved educational offerings in a major way. India, standing at a high adult illiteracy rate of 30% had been struggling to disseminate education, especially in remote areas with poor connectivity. However the availability of economical smart phones, computers, and the internet is making education cheaper and more easily accessible. As a result, people in tier 2 and tier 3 cities are experiencing high-quality learning.

2. With cloud computing and e-learning, we can now learn on the go. This has made home learning and distance learning much more effective and has given rise to the concept of online courses. Online courses range from basic to professional degree courses, which anyone from students to working professionals can enroll in.

3. With the rise of digital media, the concept of books is no more restricted to bundles of paper bound in covers. The advent of e-book has upturned the scenario and there is almost no limit to how many books one can own and access on the go. They are cheaper, interactive, eco-friendly and easy to store.

4. Technological applications have facilitated a shift in the mode of instruction from one way to two way and multi way learning. Tech-based learning modules are making room for active student participation. More teachers are engaging im webinars, live online classrooms, etc. This is also giving rise to peer-to-peer learning in the context of schools as well as in preparation for competitive exams.
5. Numerous Artificial Intelligence (AI) applications are facilitating the customisation of education through simple tools. This is making it possible for teachers to personalise learning for each and every student. They are customising lessons to fit every individual's pace and learning style.
6. Technology is widening the scope of creativity in learning and boosting student engagement. Newer applications of Augmented Reality (AR) and Virtual Reality (VR) are revolutionising how knowledge is shared and absorbed. With gamification of difficult concepts, students are now experiencing the fun element in learning. As technology continues to unfold it's offerings in the sector, it is enabling a movement in basic as well as technical literacy in the country.

Questions

Answer the following questions based on the passage above.

(i) Complete the following suitably.

Technology had transformed our lives by ....

(ii) Cloud Computing and e-learning have given rise to
(a) eco friendly reading habits
(b) online courses
(c) personalised learning
(d) All of the above

(iii) Explain how the advent of technology has transformed learning.

(iv) Classify the following sentences as 'fact' or 'opinion'.

Statement 1 With cloud computing and e-learning, we can learn on the go.

Statement 2 Technology is widening the scope of creativity in learning and boosting student engagement.

(v) Pick the option that lists statements that are not True according to the passage.
(a) People in tier 2 and tier 3 cities are experiencing high quality learning.
(b) Adult illiteracy could be reduced through technology based education.
(c) E-books are costlier than bundles of paper bound in covers.
(d) With rise in digital media, classrooms have become more collaborative.

(vi) What does 'gamification' mean?

(vii) What was not possible when the technological advancements were not as they are in their current form?

(viii) What is true about personalised learning?
(a) It aims to customise learning for each student's strength, skills and interests
(b) It aims to assess every student on a few rigid parameters
(c) It is only possible through e-learning
(d) Technology has caused it's downfall

Passage 2

India is likely to continue for several decades as a country with the largest share of rural population in the world. Rural labour and the sources of their employment are not only predominantly informal but also not very productive in nature and often spread across several activities. Though estimates of visible unemployment are very low, under-employment is widely prevalent. Rural employment, which was for a long time considered as equal to employment in agriculture, is no longer true. During the last two decades there have been rapid changes in the structure of rural employment, and rural non-farm employment has been growing at a faster pace and there are significant changes within the structure of non-farm employment.

Notwithstanding these changes there is persistence of certain characteristics of unorganised informal rural labour, such as dependence on multiple activities for work, segmentation by gender and social groups, seasonal nature of work and work which is temporary and vulnerable to low levels of earnings and high levels of persisting poverty.

Distribution of Occupation of 200 Males of a Village in Uttar Pradesh

Occupation	Number
Farmers	02
Government service, clerks	44
Lawyers	03
Newspapers and presses	05
No occupation	25
Not recorded	08
Students	68
Teachers	11
Trade and commerce	23
Other	08

Questions

Answer the following questions based on the passage above.

(i) Complete the following suitably.
India predominantly consists of ....

(ii) What is a prediction being made about India in the above passage?
(a) It has the largest urban population.
(b) It has the smallest urban population.
(c) It has the largest rural population.
(d) It has the smallest rural population.

(iii) What can we say about the rural employment of this village? List two things.

(iv) Classify the following sentences as 'fact' or 'opinion'.
Statement 1 44 men worked in government service in a village of UP.
Statement 2 68 men in a village of UP are students.

(v) The least number of men in the village are involved in which field?
(a) Education (b) Agriculture
(c) Government service (d) Publishing

(vi) There is a significant number of unemployed people. What appropriate conclusion can be drawn from this fact?

(vii) What peculiar conclusion can we draw from studying the chart?

(viii) Which statement is incorrect?
(a) Sources of employment of rural labour are not very productive.
(b) Rural employment means employment in agriculture only.
(c) Underemployment in rural labour is widely prevalent.
(d) Rural non-farm employment has been growing at a faster pace.

Passage 3

1. A tornado is a violent rotating column of air extending from a thunderstorm to the ground. The most violent tornadoes are capable of tremendous destruction with wind speeds of up to 300 mph. They can destroy large buildings, uproot trees and hurl vehicles hundreds of yards. They can also drive straw into trees. Damage paths can be in excess of one mile wide to 50 miles long. Most tornadoes form from thunderstorms. A change in wind direction and an increase in wind speed with increasing height creates an invisible, horizontal spinning effect in the lower atmosphere.
Rising air within the updraft tilts the rotating air from horizontal to vertical. An area of rotation, 2-6 miles wide, now extends through much of the storm. Most strong and violent tornadoes form within this area of strong rotation.

2. Several conditions are required for the development of tornadoes and the thunderstorm clouds with which most tornadoes are associated. Abundant low level moisture is necessary to contribute to the development of a thunderstorm and a 'trigger' (perhaps a cold front or other low level zone of converging winds) is needed to lift the moist air aloft. Once the air begins to rise and becomes saturated, it will continue rising to great heights to produce a thunderstorm cloud, if the atmosphere is unstable. An unstable atmosphere is one where the temperature decreases rapidly with height.
Atmospheric instability can also occur when dry air overlays moist air near the Earth's surface. Finally,

tornadoes usually form in areas where winds at all levels of the atmosphere are not only strong, but also turn with height in a clockwise or veering direction.

3. Tornadoes can appear as a traditional funnel shape or in a slender rope-like form. Some have a churning, smoky look to them, and other contain 'multiple vortices', which are small, individual tornadoes rotating around a common centre. Even others may be nearly invisible, with only swirling dust or debris at ground levels as the only indication of the tornado's presence.

Classification	Wind Speed	Damage
F0	40–72 mph	Mild
F1	73–112 mph	Moderate
F2	113–157 mph	Significant
F3	158–206 mph	Severe
F4	207–260 mph	Devastating
F5	261–318 mph	Incredible
F6	319–379 mph	Inconceivable

The Fujita-Pearson Tornado Intensity Scale

Questions

Answer the following questions based on the passage above.

(i) Complete the following suitably.

The major cause for the development of thunderstorms is ....

(ii) What can the range of damage path of tornadoes be?

(a) 2-3 miles (b) 1-50 miles
(c) 3-7 miles (d) 10-15 miles

(iii) What are the causes of unstable atmosphere?

(iv) Classify the following sentences as 'fact' and 'fiction'.

Statement 1 A tornado is a violent rotating column of air.

Statement 2 Tornado can appear to have a cyclonic shape.

(v) Which one of the following words is the antonym of the word 'invisible' given in paragraph 3?

(a) Veering (b) Swirling
(c) Saturated (d) Apparent

(vi) A tornado with a wind speed of 143 mph would be assigned which classification?

(vii) A district reports winds speed ranging about 215 mph. What damaging effect will the tornado have?

(viii) What shape can a tornado have?

(a) Funnel shape
(b) Slender rope-like form
(c) Cyclonic shape
(d) Both (a) and (b)

Passage 4

1. About 75 million people above 60, in India, suffer from some chronic disease, shows the first part (2017-18) of the world's largest study on the aged the Longitudinal Ageing Study in India (LASI) released by the Health Ministry. While 27% of the elderly have multi-morbidities, around 40% have issues related to mental health, said the report that aims to provide a base for national and state level programmes and policies for the elderly population.

2. In 2011 census, the 60+ accounted for 8,6% of India's population, accounting for 103 million elderly people. Growing at around 3% annually, the number of elderly age population will rise to 319 million in 2050.

3. The LASI, Wave 1, covered a baseline sample of 72,250 individuals aged 45 and above and their spouses. This included 31,464 people aged 60 and above 6,749 aged 75 and above from all states and Union Territories, excluding Sikkim.

4. The survey used bio-markers based on direct health examinations to estimate the prevalence of chronic health conditions, including hypertension, visual impairment, overweight or obesity or under nutrition and chronic respiratory diseases. Around three quarters of those 60 and above who were diagnosed with chronic conditions have been treated for hypertension (77%), chronic heart disease (74%), diabetes (83%), chronic lung disease (72%) and cancer (75%).

More than half the elderly have been treated for stroke (58%) and bone or joint diseases (56%) whereas the treatment rate for neurological and psychiatric disease is 41%.

5. The treatment rate for all chronic health conditions is higher among the elderly in urban areas. The overall hospitalisation rate was 7% for adults aged 45 and above. In the 12 months prior to the survey, the hospitalisation rate increased from 6% among adults in the 45-49 age group to 8% among those 60 and above and 9% among 70 and above.

6. The survey also showed that about one fifth of those 60 and above, are receiving pension and an additional 3% are expected to receive it. A large proportion (78%) are neither receiving nor expected to receive pension.

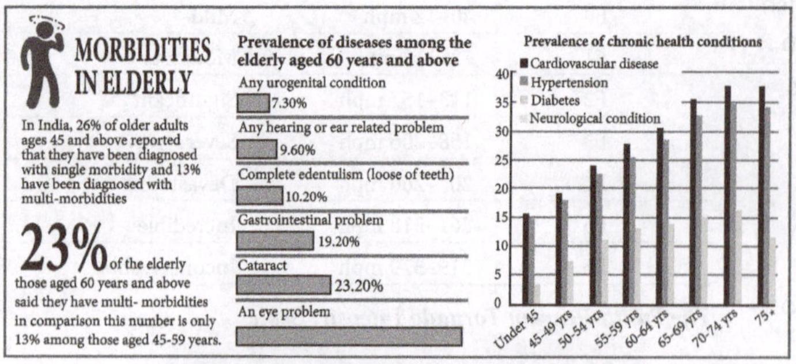

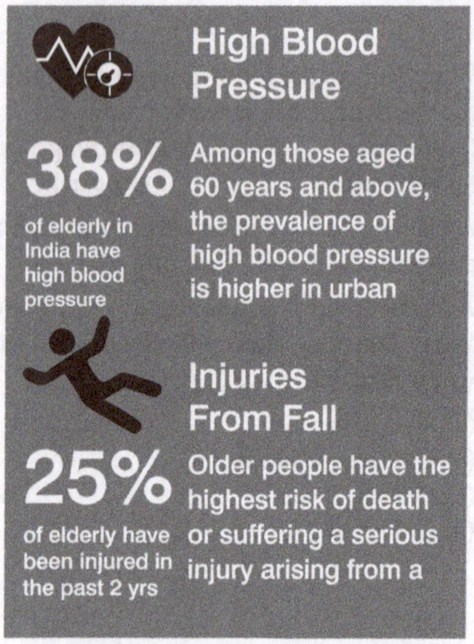

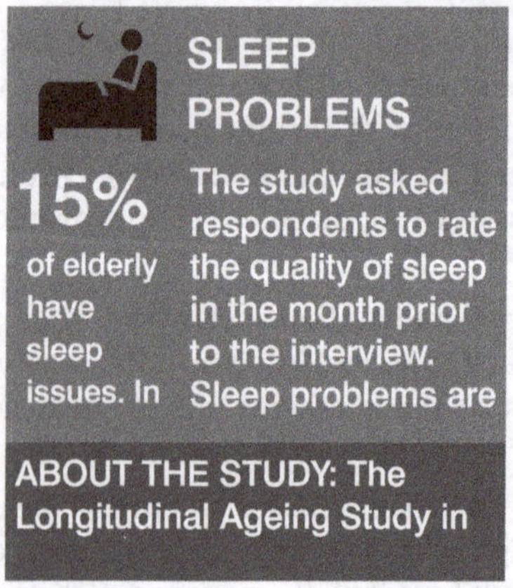

Answer the following questions based on the passage above.

(i) Complete the following suitably.
The world's largest study on the aged shows ……………… .

(ii) What statement is not true according to the 2011 Census?
(a) 60+ aged accounted for 8.6% of India's total population.
(b) The number of such people would rise to 319 million in 2050
(c) The growth rate of elderly population is around 3%
(d) The elderly population will surpass the youth population by 2050.

(iii) Explain what the LASI survey used the bio-markers to do.

(iv) Classify the following sentences as 'fact' or 'opinion'.

Statement 1 The treatment rate for all chronic health conditions is higher among the elderly in urban areas.

Statement 2 In 2011 census, the 60+ accounted for 8.6% of India's population accounting for 103 million elderly people.

(v) How many of those who are 60 and above are currently receiving the pension currently?
(a) 3/4
(b) 1/5
(c) All are receiving
(d) None of the above

(vi) What is the purpose of the LASI?

(vii) 15% of elderly have sleep issues according to the above passage. Define sleep issues.

(viii) From the graph, what are the two most prevalent diseases among the 60+?
(a) Cataract and other eye problems
(b) Hearing and other ear problems
(c) Gastro and intestinal problems
(d) Loss of teeth and bone problems

Passage 5

1. A survey was conducted on student preferences with respect to the most popular means of communication among them. Surprisingly, the students didn't seem much interested in traditional means of communication. Only 7% were interested in writing letters to their friends or kins as compared to those who preferred e-mails.

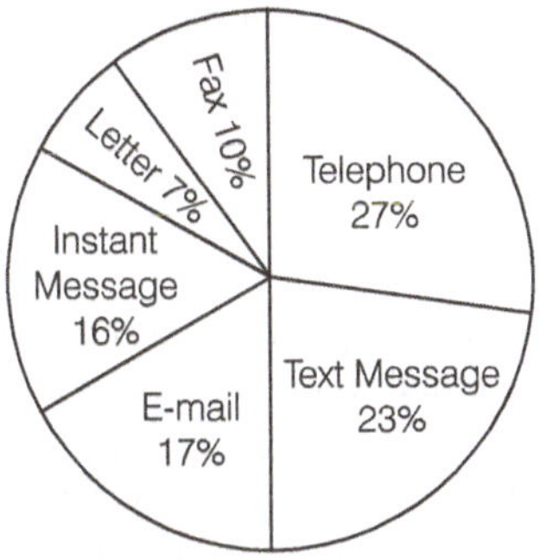

2. However, the chief competition is between users of Instant Messenger and those of telephone lines. The users of fax line as a medium of communication are only marginal. There are supporters of text messaging also.

   Overall, the survey had a mixed response from the students.

3. The students have indicated that they out of the choices given in the survey questionnaire, they have indicated the most preferred option. But, most of the students are of the view that video calling needs to be mentioned in the questionnaire as it is the most effective and most popular means of communication.

   Further, voice messages are the second most preferred means of communication.

Questions

Answer the following questions based on the passage above.

(i) Complete the following suitably.

In the introduction, it is suggested that students didn't seem much interested in ....

(ii) Which means of communication is liked by more than one-fourth of the students?

(a) Telephone (b) Text message
(c) E-mail (d) Fax

(iii) List two means of communication between which there was a proper competition.

(iv) Classify the following sentences as 'fact' or 'opinion'.

Statement 1 The users of fax line as a medium of communication are only marginal.

Statement 2 There are supporters of text messaging also.

(v) What is the overall response of the students to the survey?

(a) Biased (b) Unbiased
(c) Mixed (d) None of these

(vi) According to the survey, what were 7% of students interested in?

(vii) What was the topic on which the survey was conducted? Explain.

(viii) What is the correct order of the median of communication in decreasing order of preference?

(a) Voice message, Text message, Instant Messenger, Fax
(b) Text Message, Instant Messenger, Voice message fax
(c) Instant Messenger, Fax Voice message, Text message
(d) Text message, Instant Messenger, Fax, Voice Message

Passage 6

1. Human life changes constantly over time. Mobile phones were previously seen only among few high-class and were considered as something lavish. Then slowly, even the average or the common men on the street, like or vegetable vendor, could be seen having a cell-phone. In the world today, even young and school going kids are found busily chatting away on their mobile phones. Now kids as young as seven and eight too have started a mobile phone. Welcome to the new age world!

2. Studies recommend that mobile phones should only be given to children above sixteen years of age. Children below the age of sixteen should not be given mobile phones since their brain is too sensitive to withstand the effects of radiation. Since the tissues in the brain and body are still developing, these radiations can cause cell damage. To the absorption of radiation, children can have severe health issues. Although adults also get affected by these raditions it will be more severe in children because of increased

absorption of these radiation levels. Experts also think there is a link between childhood cancer and mobile phone usage among children.

3. A survey was conducted to get the views of the parents and teachers as to whether the children below sixteen years of age should be given mobiles or not was conducted. The responses received were formulated into a pie diagram under.

Whether students should be given mobiles or not

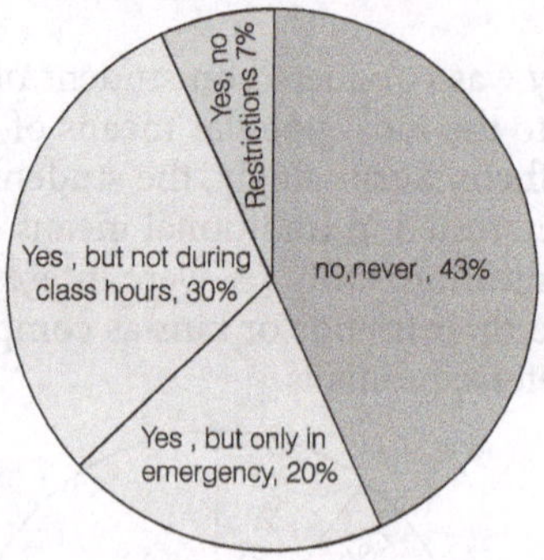

Questions

Answer the following questions based on the passage above.

(i) Complete the following suitably.
Mobile phones were previously seen only among
....

(ii) Which of these diseases are linked to mobile phone usage?
(a) Childhood obesity
(b) Childhood retardation
(c) Childhood cancer
(d) All of these

(iii) List two ways in which mobile phones are used today that present a contrast with their use previously.

(iv) Classify the following sentences as 'fact' or 'opinion'.
Statement 1 Experts also think there is a link between childhood cancer and mobile phone usage among children.
Statement 2 Human life changes constantly over time.

(v) What percentage of parents and teachers are against giving mobile phones to students in any situation?
(a) 7%
(b) 20%
(c) 30%
(d) 43%

(vi) Why should children under the age of sixteen not be given mobile phones?

(vii) How can radiation from mobile phones cause cell damage among children?

(viii) Which of these categories is represented by this pictorial representation?

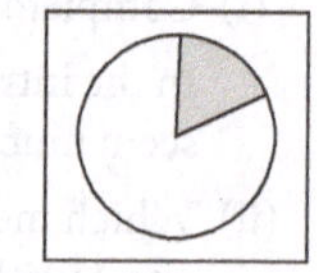

(a) Yes, no restrictions
(b) Yes, but not during class hours
(c) Yes, but only in emergency
(d) No, never

Passage 7

1. Over the last five years, more companies have been actively looking for intern profiles, according to a 2018-19 survey by an online internship and training platform. This survey reveals that India had 80% more internship applications - with 2.2 million applications received in 2018 compared to 1.27 million in the year before. The trend was partly due to more industries looking to have fresh minds and ideas on existing projects for better productivity. What was originally seen as a Western concept, getting an internship before plunging into the job market, is fast gaining momentum at Indian workplaces.

2. According to the survey data, India's National Capital Region has been the top provider of internships, with a total of 35% internship opportunities, followed by Mumbai and Bengaluru at 20% and 15%, respectively. This includes opportunities in startups, MNCs and even government entities. The survey also revealed popular fields to find internships in (Fig 1).

Internship Trends 2018
Popular fields to find internship in
Source : Internshala

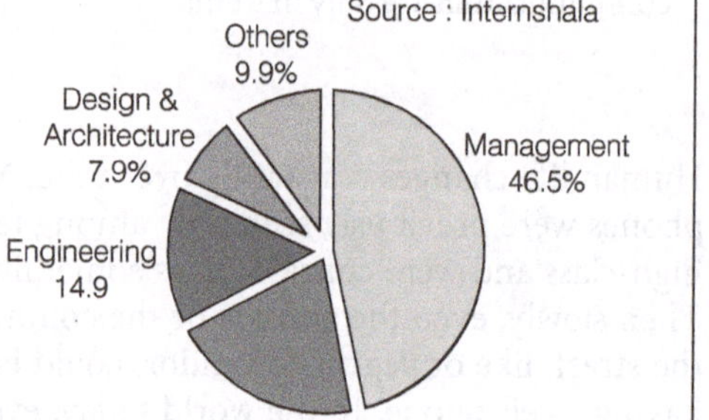

3. There has been growing awareness among the students about the intern profiles sought by hiring companies that often look for people with real-time experience in management than B-school masters.

4. The stipend has been an important factor influencing the choice of internships.

   The survey data reveals that the average stipend offered to interns was recorded as ₹ 7000 while the maximum stipend went up to ₹ 85,000.

5. According to statistics, a greater number of people considered virtual internships than in-office internships.

   Virtual internships got three times more applications than in-office, since a large chunk of students were the ones already enrolled in various courses, or preferred working from home.

6. Internship portals have sprung up in the last three to four years and many of them already report healthy traffic per month. Reports suggest that on an average, an internship portal company has around 200,000-plus students and some 8,000 companies registered on it. It gets around two lakh visits online every month.

7. The Managing Director of a leading executive search firm says that though these web platforms are working as an effective bridge between the industry and students, most established companies are still reluctant to take too many interns on board for obvious reasons.

Questions

Answer the following questions based on the passage above.

(i) Complete the following suitably.

The phrase 'healthy traffic' has been used in the passage ....

(ii) Select the central idea of the paragraph likely to precede Paragraph 1.

(a) Process of registering for internships
(b) Knowing more about internships
(c) Do's and Don'ts for an internship interview
(d) Startups and internships

(iii) State a reason for an increase in internship applications.

(iv) Identify the word from the second last passage which highlights the growth of internship portals.

(v) Select the option that displays the true statement with reference to Fig 1.

(a) Internships in engineering and management are the top two favourites.
(b) Design and architecture internships are significantly more popular than others.
(c) Internships in media and others have nearly equal popularity percentage.
(d) Management internships' popularity is more than twice that for media.

(vi) Why is virtual internship preferred?

(vii) Why do you think companies do not prefer taking many interns?

(viii) The survey statistics mention the average stipend, indicating that

(a) 50% interns were offered ₹ 85,000.
(b) 7,000 was the lowest and ₹ 85,000 was the highest.
(c) most interns were offered around ₹ 7,000.
(d) no intern was offered more than ₹ 7,000.

Passage 8

1. Festivals are synonymous with celebration, ceremony and joy. However, festivals bring to fore the flip side of celebrations - pollution of air, water, soil and noise. This led to the need of assessing the awareness level among people about ecological pollution during festivals. So, a study was conducted by scholars of an esteemed university in India. This study was titled *'Awareness Towards Impact of Festivals on Ecology.'*

2. There were two main objectives of the study. The first one was to assess the awareness level among people about ecological protection during festivities. Exploring solutions to bring awareness about celebrating festivals without harming ecology was the second objective. The method used to collect data was a simple questionnaire containing 6 questions, shared with 50 respondents across four selected districts of a state in the Southern region of India.

3. The research began by understanding the socio-economic conditions of the respondents before sharing the questionnaire. Once the responses were received, the data collected was tabulated (Table 1), for analysis.

4. The study recommended the imposition of strict rules and regulations as opposed to a total ban on all festive activities which have a drastic impact on our environment. The researchers believed that such measures would help in harnessing some ill-effects that add to the growing pollution and suggested further studies be taken up across the country to assess awareness about ecological degradation.

5. The observations made in the study pointed to the environmental groups and eco-clubs fighting a losing battle due to city traffic issues, disposal of plastics, garbage dumping and all sorts of ecological degradation. The researchers stressed that the need of the hour is increasing awareness among people to reduce ecological pollution which can be facilitated by celebrating all festivals in an eco-friendly manner.

Questions

Answer the following questions based on the passage above.

(i) Complete the following suitably.
The eco-clubs are losing the battle because …………… .

(ii) According to the study, what percentage of people do not enjoy bursting crackers?
(a) More than half people (b) Less than half people
(c) Entirety of the population (d) Only adults

(iii) Comment on the significance of the second objective of the study with reference to lines 7-12.

(iv) Even though a larger number of people say 'no' to bursting crackers than those who say 'yes', festival pollution persists. How does evidence from table 1 support this statement?

(v) According to the passage, festival is synonymous with …………… .
(a) celebration (b) ceremony
(c) joy (d) All of these

(vi) What was the objective of the study mentioned in the passage?

(vii) Justify the researchers' recommendation for limiting the drastic impact of festival pollution on the environment with reference to lines 16-21.

(viii) Which of the following was not recommended by the study?
(a) Imposition of strict rules
(b) A total ban on festive activities
(c) Punishment for the violators of the regulations
(d) Both (a) and (c)

Passage 9

1. Graduates in India feel let down by the education system's failure to equip them with the skills needed to become a success at work. A recent study from Hindustan Times drew conclusions about the state of the Indian Education System and its effect on employability and career success amongst recent graduates, with the youth feeling that their education did not significantly contribute to them landing their first jobs.
2. Young people are feeling out of their depth during the first few years of employment, crediting a deficit of industry links, lack of practical experience and inadequate career counselling at universities for the shortcomings in employability following graduation.
3. Aimed at assessing the efficacy of India's education system, the survey connected with 1,680 young professionals, men and women aged between 21 and 27. Those surveyed have been employed for three years or less, pursuing new-age careers - digital entertainment, advertsising and media, retail, e-commerce, social media, and start-ups - in the six base metro areas: Mumbai, Delhi, Kolkata, Bengaluru, Hyderabad and Chennai.
4. Only 26 per cent of those surveyed felt their education contributed highly to their interpersonal management skills - a key trait needed for interviews and employment. A problem with the relevance and timeliness of university curricula was also highlighted with respondents saying their college and university syllabus are not updated regularly.
5. An overwhelming majority of graduates felt that they lacked the necessary practical experience, and blamed the deficiency on inadequate industry-academia linkages. A historical focus on rote learning still prevalent in much of India's educational system can lead to graduates attaining good grades but failing to pick up the skills needed for innovation or out-of-the-box thinking that is so vital in today's workplace. Where some may lack in skills, however, they make up for in character with 26 per cent feeling they secured jobs through the sheer power of their personalities.
6. A case was also made for self-development and taking it upon oneself to bridge the gap inadequate education has left, with 24 per cent of respondents believing personal initiatives to improve their skills paid off when it came to landing a job.
7. Despite the negative outcome of the survey, founder of global learning company XSEED Ashish Rajpal told Hindustan Times the future isn't all bleak if the system can be overhauled at primary school level. By encouraging children at a young age to engage with the world around them, they learn more practical real-world experience and bolster their communication skills and confidence to boot.

Questions

Answer the following questions based on the passage above.

(i) Complete the sentence appropriately.
Ashish Rajpal finds a solution in a primary school level as ....

(ii) Select the option that displays one of the skills relevant to the present-day employment.
(a) Innovation (b) Communication
(c) Collaboration (d) All of these

(iii) Do you think the researchers of the study aimed to highlight the changes required in the Indian education system by pointing out the problems youth face in getting jobs?

(iv) Classify the following as 'fact' or 'opinion'.

Sentence 1 Only 26 per cent of those surveyed felt their education contributed highly to their interpersonal management skills...

Sentence 2 An overwhelming majority of graduates felt that they lacked the necessary practical experience, and blamed the deficiency on inadequate industry-academia linkages.

(v) Complete the given sentence appropriately with one/two words.
Apart from education, ... plays an important role in employability.
(a) personality (b) family values
(c) luck (d) references

(vi) Self Development was also promoted to bridge the gap inadequate education has left. Give a reason for such a claim.

(vii) Based on the reading of the text, state a point to challenge the given statement.

By focusing on industry links, practical experience and career counselling, individuals will be wasting their resources and fall back in their studies.

(viii) Complete the given sentence by selecting the most appropriate option. Indian youngsters find that the education system ....
(a) provides wholesome factual knowledge
(b) does not have any role in employability
(c) does not promote professional skills
(d) is the best system in the world

Passage 10

1. Tourism, for millennia, has been a perpetual industry. Though initially unorganised and highly chaotic, it retained a place in each nook of history. The present tourism scenario in India is on the rise, with destinations grabbing eyeballs globally and domestically. Being the youngest nation in the world, it's no wonder that the aggregate of 'millennials' spends more time and money on travel than previous generations. This could be huge for the economy of various states that rely majorly on tourism, if only it were sustainable.
2. Unsustainability prevails throughout the country, in states with higher domestic tourist inflow than foreign. The Dev Bhoomi is a prime example. No matter how popular, Uttarakhand tourism is loop-holed through and through.
3. Approx. 80% of tourists arrive to complete the infrastructure of the Dham Yatra. Such unchecked tourism puts immense pressure on natural and infrastructure facilities. The extreme shortage of accommodation in correspondence with thriving footfalls has led to the construction of illegal buildings, the majority of which exist on riverbanks. With an increasing number of tourists coming in through private vehicles to save "transportation money", pollution levels are rising, increasing temperatures in return. With unlawful construction and pollution on riverbanks, the Ganges could cause direct harm to local species in Rishikesh and Haridwar.
4. Around 10,000 hilly areas are being convened for the construction of roads alone. We know roads are basic infrastructure but the Forest Conservation Act requires a project developer to plant trees in a non-forest/degraded forest area equal to or twice the trees, it's clearing respectively, to compensate which does not happen.
5. The India State of Forest Report illustrates how Uttarakhand is losing its forest cover, which has indirect development through tourism, at its core. The government and private tour operators may think they can deny allegations but the charts speak for themselves.
6. We, as consumers of the tourism industry, hold the power to cause a massive stir in this context. According to research conducted, Uttarakhand's mass tourism comprises people between 25-35 years of age, with higher education, out with either family or friends and enough average income to contribute to the local economy.

7. Regardless of what the figures say, if we look forward to sustainable tourism being the target market, it leaves little choice to the rest of the hierarchy. Consciously making efforts to be responsible tourists and thinking of how to provide for the local community/environment in a way - tiny or big, could act as a catalyst in obliterating this ruckus due to ignorance. After all, there can only ever be seven deadly sins and wanderlust isn't one of them.

Questions

Answer the following questions based on the passage above.

(i) Complete the sentence appropriately.
The Forest Conservation Act vouches for ....

(ii) Select the appropriate option to fill in the blank.
From paragraph 1, we can infer that .... is the main cause for putting pressure on infrastructural and natural resources.
(a) unchecked tourism (b) illegal construction
(c) pollution (d) increasing temperatures

(iii) List any two reasons to explain why unsustainability prevails in the Dev Bhoomi.

(iv) Infer one consequence, based on your understanding of the passage, that highlights the result of the pressures of a large number of tourists.

(v) Complete the following analogy correctly with a word/phrase from the passage.
Movie : Viewers : : Product : ....
(a) Serivce (b) Consumers
(c) Operators (d) Millennia

(vi) What do the tourist statistics show in the region of Uttarakhand?

(vii) What does the India State of Forest Report illustrate regarding Uttarakhand?

(viii) Based on your understanding of the passage, choose the option that lists the result of the pressures of a large number of tourists.
(a) Illegal infrastructural constructions, Rise in pollution
(b) Higher education, Deforestation
(c) Higher education, Rise in pollution
(d) None of the above

Passage 11

1. Social media addiction is an emerging health problem in India, especially among the young population. Nowadays, irrespective of their socioeconomic background, adolescents have greater exposure to electronic gadgets like smartphones at a much younger age. The introduction of internet and the launch of low-cost data packages in 2016/2017 has put India on the global map for large-scale consumption of mobile data with active social media users going up to 197 million (14% of the population).

2. For adolescents, phone-based communication is an important way to maintain their social relationships. The use of social media websites then is one of the most common activities that has become an integral part of their day-to-day lives. Hence, making them more prone to social media overuse or addiction which may have a deleterious effect on the physical, and psychological health. Hence, it became important to study the pattern of social media usage and associated physical and mental health issues among Pre-University (PU) college students as they are the vulnerable group.

3. A cross-sectional study was conducted in Government and Private PU colleges situated in Urban Bengaluru city, Karnataka, India, during July to December 2016. The objectives of the study were to assess and compare the prevalence of social media addiction in different organisations, to assess the health problems related to social media usage, and to assess the various factors associated with social media addiction.

4. A total of 1870 study participants were recruited from both Government and Private PU colleges. Each participant was administered a pretest and semi-structured questionnaire as the study tool. They were asked to answer about the non-academic usage of social media. Scale comprised 10 questions, each given a score ranging from 0 to 4 (0-never, 1-seldom, 2-occasionally, 3-often, and 4-always), with a minimum score of 0 and a maximum score of 40. Participants were classified based on the scores as: Normal (<12), mild addiction (13-20), moderate addiction (21-32) and severe addiction (^{3}33). Distribution of Study Subjects According to Grading of Social Media Addiction*

Questions

Answer the following questions based on the passage above.

(i) Complete the sentence based on the following statement.

It was assumed that private college students will be more prone to social media addiction.

This was because of their ....

(ii) What did the study tool used in the survey comprise of?

(a) Yes-no questions
(b) A scale-based questionnaire
(c) Some physical and IQ based tests
(d) Both (b) and (c)

(iii) What, according to you, makes the adolescents susceptible to social media overuse?

(iv) Classify the following sentences as 'fact' or 'opinion'.

Statement 1 Social media addiction is an emerging health problem in India, especially among the young population.

Statement 2 A cross-sectional study was conducted in Government and Private PU colleges situated in Urban Bengaluru city, Karnataka, India, during July to December 2016.

(v) Complete the sentence by selecting the most appropriate option.

The students were classified into .... categories based on their ....

(a) three, scores
(b) four, scores
(c) five, addiction
(d) four, usage

(vi) Give one reason for the rise in active social media users in India.

(vii) Based on the reading of the text, state a point to challenge the given statement.

Higher social status and purchasing capacity is directly linked to Social Media Addiction.

(viii) Which of the following was not an objective for the study?

(a) To assess the health problems associated with social media usage
(b) To assess and compare the prevalence of social media in a particular organisation
(c) To assess the various factors related to social media usage
(d) To assess and compare the prevalence of social media in different organisations

Passage 12

1. J.K. Rowling-A Journey The story of Joanne Kathleen Rowling's near magical rise to fame is almost as well known as the Characters She Creates. Rowling was constantly writing and telling stories to her younger sister Dianne. "The first story I ever wrote down was about a rabbit called Rabbit." Rowling said in an interview. "He got the measles and was visited by his friends including a giant bee called Miss Bee. And ever since Rabbit and Miss Bee, I have always wanted to be a writer, though I rarely told anyone so."

2. However, my parents, both of whom come from impoverished backgrounds and neither of whom had been to college, took the view that my overactive imagination was an amusing personal quirk that would never pay a mortgage or secure a pension art. A writer from the age of six, with two unpublished novels in the drawer, she was stuck on a train when Harry walked into her mind fully formed. She spent the next five years constructing the plots of seven books, one for every year of his secondary school life.

3. Rowling says she started writing the first book, Harry Potter and the Sorcerer's Stone, in Portugal, where she was teaching English. At first, nobody wanted to publish Harry Potter. She was told that plot was too complex. Refusing to compromise, she found a publisher. In 1997 Rowling received her first royalty cheque.

4. By book three, she had sky rocketed to the top of the publishing world. A row of zeroes appeared on the author's bank balance and her life was turned upside down. Day and night she had journalists knocking on the unanswered door of her flat. Rowling's quality control has become legendary, as her obsession with accuracy. She's thrilled with Stephen Fry's taped version of the books and outraged

that an Italian dust jacket showed Harry minus his glasses. "Don't they understand that the glasses are the clue to his vulnerability."

Questions

Answer the following questions based on the passage above.

(i) Complete the sentence appropriately.

Harry's glasses are important because ....

(ii) Rowling was .... when the idea of Harry Potter book came to her mind.

(a) a college student (b) in a train
(c) 6 years old (d) watching TV

(iii) What was the drawback of achieving fame?

(iv) Why was Rowling outraged with the Italian dust jacket?

(v) What was Rowling's profession when she wrote the first Harry Potter book?

(a) Writer (b) Editor
(c) Publisher (d) Teacher

(vi) According to the graph, how many years did it take Rowling to become very successful?

(vii) Explain J.K. Rowling's 'near magical rise to fame'. Answer in about 40 words.

(viii) What does the passage tell us about Rowling's parents?

(a) They were dead.
(b) They were very rich.
(c) They were very poor.
(d) They wanted her to become a writer.

Passage 13

1. India's average temperature has already increased by around 0.7 degrees Celsius during the 1901-2018 period due to Greenhouse gas emissions and by the end of 2100 it is expected to rise by approximately 4.4 degrees Celsius warns the first-ever climate change assessment report by the Indian government.
2. The report Assessment of Climate Change over the Indian Region prepared by the Union Ministry of Earth Sciences (MoES) warned that the rapid changes in the temperature would mean increasing stress on India's "natural ecosystems, agricultural output and freshwater resources, while also causing escalating damage to infrastructure." This ultimately means a serious impact on the country's biodiversity, food, water, energy security and public health.
3. It said that several regions in India are global biodiversity hotspots with numerous endemic species of plants and animals and with the "climate changing more rapidly than usual, they may face increasing threats on account of these changes."
4. The MoES report cautioned that by the end of 2100, the "frequency of summer (April-June) heat waves over India is projected to be 3 to 4 times higher" and the "average duration of heat-wave events is also projected to approximately double." According to the report, the Sea Surface Temperature (SST) of the tropical Indian Ocean has also risen by one degree Celsius, on average, during 1951-2015.
5. The rise in temperature is playing havoc with India's rainfall which is significant for India's agriculture sector. The report noted that the summer monsoon precipitation (June to September) over India has declined by around six per cent from 1951 to 2015, with notable decreases over the Indo-Gangetic Plains and the Western Ghats. It stressed that the overall decrease of seasonal summer monsoon rainfall during the last 6-7 decades has led to an increased propensity for droughts in India.
6. "In particular, areas over Central India, South-West coast, Southern peninsula and North-Eastern India have experienced more than two droughts per decade. The area affected by drought has also increased by 1.3 per cent per decade over the same period.

Climate model projections indicate a high likelihood of an increase in the frequency, intensity and area under drought conditions in India by the end of the twenty-first century," said the MoES report.

Questions

Answer the following questions based on the passage above.

(i) Complete the following sentence appropriately:

As per reports, an overall decrease in seasonal summer monsoon rainfall has led to ....

(ii) What does rapid changes in the temperature mean?

(a) Increased stress on India's natural ecosystems
(b) Increased stress on India's agricultural output
(c) Increased stress on India's freshwater resources
(d) All of the above

(iii) Infer 3 reasons for the following, based on information in paragraph 1.

India's average temperature has already increased by around 0.7 degrees Celsius during the 1901-2018 period.

(iv) What will be the titles of the paragraphs 1-3 appropriately.

(v) Select the correct option to fill in the blank and complete the following analogy.

Rainfall :Monsoon : : .... : Summer

(a) Heat wave (b) Temperature
(c) Endemic (d) Drought

(vi) List any one point how the temperature rise will affect the summer heat waves.

(vii) List any two social and economic impacts of climate change.

(viii) Select the appropriate option to fill in the blanks.

From paragraph 5 we can infer that the .... in temperature has wreaked havoc on the rainfall pattern. The overall .... of seasonal summer monsoon rainfall during the last 6-7 decades has led to an increased tendency of droughts.

(a) rise, decrease (b) sufficient, elaborate
(c) decrease, rise (d) elaborate, sufficient

Passage 14

1. A new poll of global experts by the Thomson Reuters Foundation suggests that India is perceived as the most dangerous country for women. India's rise to the top place is driven by the perception about rising sexual violence in the country, Thomson Reuters Foundation reported. But a Mint analysis of data from Demographic and Health Surveys (DHS) conducted across developing nations of the world shows that the incidence of sexual violence reported by women is lower in India than in most other countries for which such data is available.

2. According to the data provided by the DHS, the incidence of such violence against women has declined over time. Of the 43 countries for which recent data on sexual violence is available, India ranks 32 when it comes to the share of women, aged 15-49, who experienced such violence in their lifetime.

3. From the details given above, there seems to arise a dissonance between the perception about India, as recorded by the Thomson Reuters Foundation poll of around 550 global experts, and the actual experiences of millions of women across the world, as recorded by the DHS surveys. While it is possible that the DHS surveys underestimate the true extent of sexual violence faced by women, there is little reason to believe that the bias, if it indeed exists, is higher for India than for other countries. While the risk of sexual violence in India is undeniable, India does not seem to be the most dangerous place when it comes to the risk of sexual violence.

Not the most dangerous place
The incidence of sexual violence is lower in India compared to several other developing nations

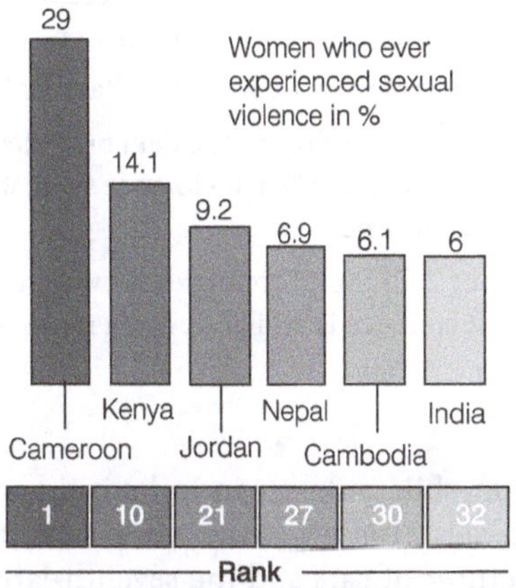

Countries for which DHS data is available for 2010 and later have been considered here.

4. The nature of sexual violence women face, however, has a unique dimension in India. Chances that the perpetrator of sexual violence is known to the victim are among the highest. Most offenders tend to be partners of the victims.

The high share of known offenders might also partly explain why most sexual assaults go unreported in the country. As pointed out, 99% of sexual assaults in the country go unreported. Even if one excludes marital rape, 85% of sexual assaults go unreported.

5. The silver lining in the data is that the actual incidence of sexual violence, as recorded by NFHS (the DHS of India), has declined over the past decade even as the reporting of sexual assaults has risen.

Questions

Answer the following questions based on the passage above.

(i) Complete the sentence based on the following statement.

According to the Thomson Reuters Foundation, India is the most dangerous country for women because of ………………… .

(ii) What does the passage try to claim?

(a) India is not the most dangerous country for women.
(b) The surveys often take incorrect data.
(c) India has been subduing the patriarchal structure.
(d) There are discrepancies in various surveys regarding women's health.

(iii) As a reader whose data would you accept as more accurate? Give reasons for your answer.

(iv) Classify the following sentences as 'fact' or 'opinion'.

Statement 1 According to the data provided by the DHS, the incidence of such violence against women has declined over time.

Statement 2 Of the 43 countries for which recent data on sexual violence is available, India ranks 32 when it comes to the share of women, aged 15-49, who experienced such violence in their lifetime.

(v) The countries that participate in the DHS are

(a) third world countries.
(b) developed countries.
(c) developing countries.
(d) Asian countries.

(vi) The nature of sexual violence women face, however, has a unique dimension in India. Give a reason for such a claim.

(vii) Based on the reading of the text, state a point which challenges the given statement.

In the modern world, people are still not reporting sexual assaults as the numbers have been increasing.

(viii) Complete the given sentence by selecting the most appropriate option.

The case of known offenders explains the ……….. .

(a) rising nature of sexual violence
(b) unreported nature of cases of violence
(c) dissonance between data and reality
(d) unfearful attitude of offenders

Passage 15

1. The automobile industry in India is the world's fourth-largest. India was the world's fourth-largest manufacturer of cars and the seventh-largest manufacturer of commercial vehicles in 2019. The Indian automotive industry (including component manufacturing) is expected to reach 16.16-18.18 trillion (US $ 251.4-282.8 billion) by 2026. The industry attracted Foreign Direct Investment (FDI) worth US $ 24.21 billion from April 2000 to March 2020 according to the data released by the Department for Promotion of Industry and Internal Trade (DPIIT).

2. Two-wheelers and passenger vehicles dominate the domestic Indian auto market. Passenger car sales are dominated by small and mid-sized cars. Two-wheelers and passenger cars accounted for 80.8 per cent and 12.9 per cent market share, respectively, accounting for a combined sale of over 21.55 million vehicles in FY20. The CAGR during FYI 6-FY20 is 1.29 per cent.

3. The government aims to develop India as global manufacturing and Research and Development (R & D) hub. It has set up National Automotive Testing and R and D Infrastructure Project (NATRiP) centres as well as National Automotive Board to act as a facilitator between the government and the industry. Under (NATRiP), five testing and research centres have been established in the country since 2015. NATRiPs proposal for "Grant-In-Aid for test facility infrastructure for Electric Vehicle (EV) performance Certification from NATRIP Implementation Society" under FAME (Faster Adoption and Manufacturing of (Hybrid) and Electric Vehicles in India) scheme was approved by Project Implementation and Sanctioning Committee (PISC) on 3rd January, 2019.

4. The Indian Government has also set up an ambitious target of having only EVs sold in the country. The Ministry of Heavy Industries, Government of India, has shortlisted 11 cities in the

country for the introduction of EVs in their public transport system under the FAME scheme. The first phase of the scheme was extended toMarch 2019 while in February 2019, the government approved the FAME-II scheme with a fund requirement of Rs 10,000 crore (US $ 1.39 billion) for FY20-22. Under Union Budget 2019-20, government announced providing an additional income tax deduction of Z 1.5 lakh (US $ 2146) on the interest paid on the loans taken to purchase EVs.

5. EV sales, excluding e-rickshaws, in India witnessed a growth of 20 per cent and reached 1.56 lakh units in FY20 driven by two-wheelers. The Government of India expects the automobile sector to attract US $ 8-10 billion in local and foreign investment by 2023.

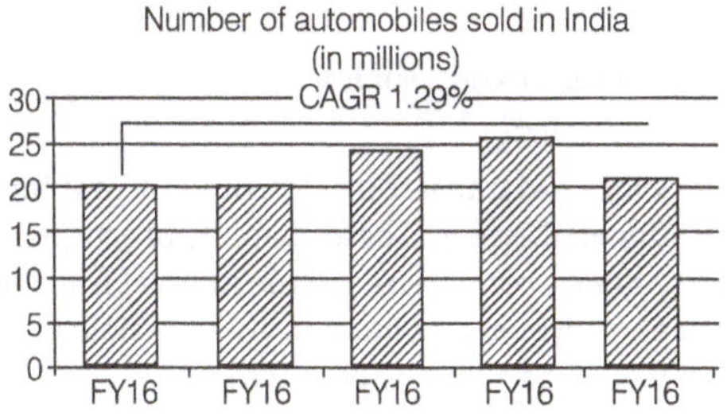

Questions

Answer the following questions based on the passage above.

(i) Complete the sentence appropriately.
Paragraph 4 focuses on the ambitious target of having ....

(ii) Fill in the blanks by selecting the correct option.
According to the passage, ... vehicles dominate the Indian markets.
(a) two-wheelers
(b) auto-Rickshaws
(c) passenger vehicles
(d) Both (a) and (c)

(iii) What does the Indian Government want to establish?

(iv) What does the Department for Promotion of Industry and Internal Trade highlight?

(v) Complete the following analogy correctly with a word/phrase from the passage.
Kitchen : Cooking : : Factory : ....
(a) Operating (b) Sanctioning
(c) Manufacturing (d) Implementation

(vi) From the passage above, in which field does the government of India want to grow?

(vii) What was the NATRiP's proposal?

(viii) Based on your understanding of the passage, choose the option that lists the initiatives taken by the government to promote the automobile industry.
(a) Established NATRiP and a NAB
(b) Set up 5 testing and research centres.
(c) Introduction of EVs in their public transport.
(d) All of the above

Answers

Passage 1

(i) making it easier and seamless
(ii) (b) online courses
(iii) Technology has transformed learning and has improved educational offerings. The availability of economical smart phones, computers and the internet is making education cheaper and more easily accessible for everyone, especially in remote areas.
(iv) **Statement 1** opinion; **Statement 2** fact
(v) (c) E-books are costlier than bundles of paper bound in covers.
(vi) Gamification means application of game design elements and game principles in non game contexts.
(vii) E-learning and online courses and education, use of AR and VR in education and webinars were not possible when the technological advancements were not as they are in their current form
(viii) (a) It aims to customise learning for each student's strength, skills and interests

Passage 2

(i) rural population
(ii) (c) It has the largest rural population.
(iii) The following can be said about the rural employment of this village
 (i) People are following a variety of occupations.
 (ii) Agriculture is the least popular occupation.
(iv) **Statements** 1 and 2 are facts.
(v) (b) Agriculture
(vi) From the given fact, it can be concluded that there is scarcity of work opportunities in the village.
(vii) After studying the chart, it can be concluded that despite being a village, country farmers are the least in the region.
(viii) (b) Rural employment means employment in agriculture only.

Passage 3

(i) abundant low level moisture
(ii) (b) 1-50 miles
(iii) The causes of unstable atmosphere are
 (a) dry air overlays moist air near Earth's surface
 (b) rapidly decreasing temperature with height
(iv) **Statement 1** is fact; **Statement 2** is fiction.
(v) (d) Apparent
(vi) A tornado with a wind speed of 143 mph would be registered under F2 classification.
(vii) The tornado with wind speed ranging about 215 mph would have a devastating effect.
(viii) (d) Both (a) and (b)

Passage 4

(i) that about 75 million Indians above 60 years of age suffer from some chronic disease
(ii) (d) the elderly population will surpass the youth population by 2050.
(iii) The LASI survey used bio-markers based on direct health examinations to estimate the prevalence of chronic health conditions including hypertension, visual impairment, obesity or under nutrition and chronic respiratory diseases.
(iv) **Statement 1** opinion; **Statement 2** fact
(v) (b) 1/5
(vi) The purpose of the LASI is to provide a base for government policies for the elderly population.
(vii) Sleep issues are defined as the difficulty in falling or staying asleep or sleep that is non-restorative. It, further, leads to significant daytime impairment.
(viii) (a) Cataract and other eye problems

Passage 5

(i) traditional means of communication
(ii) (a) Telephone
(iii) The two means of communication between which there was a proper competition are
 1. Instant messenger 2. Telephone
(iv) **Statements** 1 and 2 are facts.
(v) (c) Mixed
(vi) According to the survey, 7% of students were interested in writing letters to their friends or kins as compared to those who preferred e-mails.
(vii) The survey presented in the given passage was conducted on the means of communication. There are six means of communication mentioned in the passage : fax, letter, instant messenger, e-mail, text message and telephone.
(viii) (a) Voice message, Text message, Instant Messenger, Fax

Passage 6

(i) few high-class people and were considered as lavish
(ii) (c) Childhood cancer
(iii) Two ways in which mobile phones are used today that present a contrast with their use previously are

1. Common men being able to access it
2. Young kids and school going children chatting on mobile phones

(iv) **Statement 1** opinion; **Statement 2** fact

(v) (d) 43%

(vi) Children under the age of sixteen should not be given mobile phones because their brain is too sensitive to withstand the effects of radiation.

(vii) Radiation from mobile phones cause cell damage among children as the tissues in the brain and body of a child are stull developing. As a result of absorption of radiation, children can have severe health issues.

(viii) (c) Yes, but only in emergency

Passage 7

(i) to highlight the increasing number of visitors on the internships portal per month.

(ii) (b) Knowing more about internships

(iii) There has been a rise/increase in internship applications because more and more companies today are looking for fresh minds and ideas for better productivity.

(iv) Sprung up

(v) (d) Management internships' popularity is more than twice that for media.

(vi) Virtual internships are preferred because most of the applicants are students who are enrolled in various courses and so, prefer working from home.

(vii) I believe that companies do not prefer taking many interns because too many interns would reduce the number of people with expertise. The lack of expertise and effective training would then reduce productivity.

(viii) (c) most interns were offered around ₹ 7,000.

Passage 8

(i) of city traffic issue, plastic disposal and garbage dumping

(ii) (b) less than half people

(iii) The passage mentions exploration of solutions to bring about awareness about celebrating festivals without harming the environment as the second objective of the study. It is significant because we need to know what steps can be taken to deal with the issue and what should be avoided to fix the problem of increase in pollution during festivals.

(iv) The table states that a large percentage of people abuse environmental resources to celebrate festivals. As a result, they fail to see its effect on the environment.

(v) (d) All of these

(vi) The objective of the study mentioned in the passage is to assess how much people knew about ecological protection during festivals and to find ways to bring awareness to people about celebrating festival without harming ecology.

(vii) The researchers' recommendation suggests bringing strict rules to ensure a decrease in pollution during festivals. It is much better than the alternative which is to impose a complete ban as it will not only make the people aware about the problems but also increase the chance of a revolt against the ban. Hence, strict rules along with some freedom are a better option.

(viii) (b) A total ban on festive activities

Passage 9

(i) if children are given practical exposure since very early age, they develop communication skills and confidence easily.

(ii) (d) All of these

(iii) Yes, I believe that the researchers of the study aimed to highlight the changes required in the Indian education system. By pointing out the problems youth face in getting jobs, the study guides the education system about the aspects which needs to be modified and updated.

(iv) **Statement 1** Fact; **Statement 2** Opinion

(v) (a) personality

(vi) Self Development was also promoted to bridge the gap inadequate education has left because many respondents in the survey found that personal initiatives to improve their skills paid off when it came to getting a job.

(vii) The given statement is incorrect because while theoretical knowledge gained in studies is important, without industry links, practical experience and proper guidance, they become ineffective. By focusing on industry links, practical experience and career counselling, individuals will not be wasting their resources but will be preparing themselves for the future.

(viii) (c) does not promote professional skills

Passage 10

(i) plantation of trees in a non-forest/degraded forest area equal to or twice the trees it's clearing

(ii) (a) unchecked tourism

(iii) The two reasons that leads to unsustainability in Dev Bhoomi are

I. unchecked number of tourists causing stress on infrastructure.

II. self-transportation causes pollution, which leads to rise in temperature.

(iv) The influx of a large number of tourists and the urgency to accommodate them, puts pressure on the infrastructure of that place, leading to several illegal constructions in the area.

(v) (b) Consumers

(vi) The tourist statistics showed that in Uttarakhand, domestic footfall is much greater than international footfall.

(vii) The India State of Forest Report illustrates how Uttarakhand is losing its forest cover, which has indirect development through tourism, at its core. The government and private tour operators may think they can deny allegations but the charts speak for themselves.

(viii) (a) Illegal infrastructural constructions, Rise in pollution

Passage 11

(i) higher social status and purchasing capacity

(ii) (b) A scale-based questionnaire

(iii) Adolescents use phone-based communication as an important way to maintain their social relationships. Therefore, social media websites are used by them and have become an integral part of their lines. This makes them susceptible to social media overuse.

(iv) **Statement 1** opinion; **Statement 2** fact

(v) (b) four, scores

(vi) The launch of low-cost data packages in 2016/17 has led to the rise of active social media users in India.

(vii) The given statement is untrue as the data revealed by the survey indicates that despite higher social status and purchasing capacity of private PU students, there is not much difference between government and Private PU college students as far as social Media relevance is concerned.

(viii) (b) To assess and compare the prevalence of social media in a particular organisation

Passage 12

(i) they are a clue to his vulnerability

(ii) (b) in a train

(iii) The drawback of achieving fame was constant disturbance of journalists knocking at her door day and night for interviews.

(iv) Rowling was outraged with the Italian dust jacket because it showed Harry without his glasses.

(v) (d) Teacher

(vi) According to the graph, it took Rowling seven years to become very successful.

(vii) J.K. Rowling's 'near magical rise to fame' refers to the fact that no one believed in her work at first but when she finally published the Harry Potter book series, she achieved true fame and skyrocketed to the top of the publishing world.

(viii) (c) They were very poor.

Passage 13

(i) an increased tendency for droughts

(ii) (d) All of the above

(iii) The three reasons are as follows

1. Greenhouse gas emission,
2. Destruction of the natural ecosystems
3. Over-exploitation of natural resources are the reasons for the rising in temperature of around 0.7 degrees Celsius during the 1901-2018 period.

(iv) The titles will be

- Effect of greenhouse gases,
- Loss of biodiversity
- Stress on ecosystems

(v) (a) Heat wave

(vi) The rise in temperature will increase the frequency and duration of the heat waves.

(vii) The two social and economic impacts of climate change:

1. Less capacity to work
2. Increase in carpooling

(viii) (a) Rise, decrease

Passage 14

(i) rising cases of sexual violence

(ii) (a) India is not the most dangerous country for women.

(iii) As a reader, I would find the data produced by the DHS to be more accurate as it covers the real experiences of millions of women across the world. In opposition, Thomas Reuters covers the data received from experts.

(iv) **Statements** 1 and 2 are facts.

(v) (c) developing countries.

(vi) It is true that the nature of sexual violence women face has a unique dimension in India. This is so because, in India, the perpetrator of sexual violence is known to the victim.

(vii) The given statement is incorrect because in the present world, more and more women are reporting sexual assaults as a result of which the actual incidents of assaults have decreased.

(viii) (b) unreported nature of cases of violence

Passage 15

(i) only the EVs being sold in the country

(ii) (d) Both (a) and (c)

(iii) The Indian Government wants to establish the following

1. National Automotive Testing and R&D Infrastructure Project centres
2. National Automotive Board

(iv) The Department for Promotion of Industry and Internal Trade highlights that India had received a considerable amount of FDI.

(v) (c) Manufacturing

(vi) As per the passage, the Government of India wants to grow in R&D, i.e. Research and Development.

(vii) The NATRIP's proposal is to provide Aid for test facility infrastructure for Electric Vehicle (EV) performance certification.

(viii) (d) All of the above

SELF ASSESSMENT TEST

Passage 1

1. With the enormous amount of information potentially available to travellers, the Internet constitutes an important platform for information exchange between the consumer and industry suppliers (e.g., hotels, transportation sectors, attractions), intermediaries (e.g., travel agents), controllers (e.g. governments and administrative bodies), as well as many non-profit organisations such as destination marketing organisations.
2. Different technological interfaces, such as search engines, online travel booking sites and websites of destination marketing organisations facilitate the information exchange between online travellers and the so-called 'online tourism domain'. Particularly, it has been argued that understanding the nature of the online tourism domain, i.e. the composition of online tourism related information potentially available to travellers, provides an important stepping-stone for the development of successful marketing programmes and better information systems in tourism.
3. The relation between social interaction, communication media and content can provide various supplementary advantages. It is more convenient and efficient way of spreading information compared to traditional media and thus, more and more companies are utilising it as a marketing channel. Furthermore, through media visibility, companies are able to create more approachable image and possibly bring awareness among new customers as well as retain existing consumer relationships.

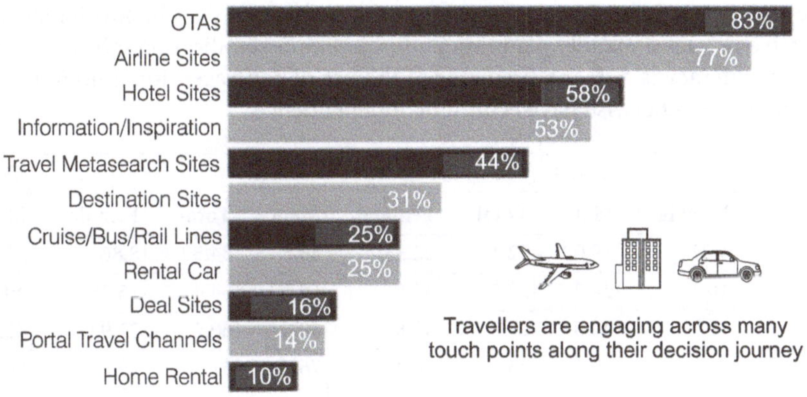

Travel Buyer Reach

4. It's no wonder destinations, airlines, hotels and most travel marketers are embracing social networks such as Pinterest but also photo/video applications such as Instagram and Vine, as part of their storytelling toolkit, reaching out to growing crowds of travellers.

Questions

Answer the following questions based on the passage above.

(i) Complete the following analogy.

Search engines, online travel booking sites and websites of destination marketing organisations facilitate the ....

(ii) What creates a more approachable image and brings awareness among new customers?

(a) Media visibility
(b) The review system
(c) The content view system
(d) The system of interaction and communication

(iii) Who are the controllers in the field of tourism?

(iv) Classify the following sentences as 'fact' or 'opinion'.

Statement 1 Companies are able to create a more approachable image through media visibility.

Statement 2 Better services will benefit the tourism sector.

(v) According to the given data graph, which marketing field shows the greatest influence of tourists?

(a) Travel Metasearch sites
(b) Portal travel channels
(c) Online travel agencies
(d) Airline sites

(vi) How can social interaction provide various supplementary advantages?

(vii) What can online tourism domain be understood as?

(viii) What does the given passage focus on?

(a) The increasing role of social media in tourism
(b) The increasing demand of tourism
(c) The need to boost tourism in India
(d) None of these

Passage 2

1. Literacy and level of education are basic indicators of the level of development achieved by a society. Spread of literacy is generally associated with important traits of modern civilisation such as modernisation, urbanisation, industrialisation, communication and commerce. Literacy forms an important input in overall development of individuals enabling them to comprehend their social, political and cultural environment better and respond to it appropriately. Higher levels of education and literacy lead to a greater awareness and also contributes in improvement of economic and social conditions. It acts as a catalyst for social upliftment enhancing the returns on investment made in almost every aspect of development effort, be it population control, health, hygiene, environmental degradation control or employment of weaker sections of the society.
2. Literacy in India is a key for socio-economic progress. Despite government programmes, India's literacy rate increased only 'sluggishly'. There is a wide gender disparity in the literacy rate in India: effective literacy rates (age 7 and above) in 2011 were 82.14% for men and 65.46% for women. The low female literacy rate has a dramatically negative impact on family planning and population stabilisation efforts in India. Studies have indicated that female literacy is a strong predictor of the use of contraception among married Indian couples, even when women do not otherwise have economic independence.

YEAR	RURAL			URBAN			TOTAL		
	Female	Male	Total	Female	Male	Total	Female	Male	Total
1951	4.87	19.02	12.1	22.33	45.6	34.59	8.86	27.15	18.32
1961	10.1	34.3	22.5	40.5	66	54.4	15.35	40.4	28.31
1971	15.5	48.6	27.9	48.8	69.8	60.2	21.97	45.96	34.45
1981	21.7	49.6	36	56.3	76.7	67.2	29.76	56.38	43.57
1991	30.17	56.96	36	64.05	81.09	67.2	39.29	64.13	52.21
2001	46.7	71.4	59.4	73.2	86.7	80.3	53.67	75.26	64.83
2011	58.75	78.57	67.8	79.92	89.67	84.1	65.46	82.14	74.04
% increase in 2011 over 2001	26%	10%	14%	9%	3%	5%	22%	9%	14%

Questions

Answer the following questions based on the passage above.

(i) Complete the following suitably.

The low female literacy rate in India has a negative impact on ....

(ii) What is spread of literacy associated with?

(a) Modernisation
(b) Urbanisation and industrialisation
(c) Commerce and communication
(d) All of these

(iii) How does literacy form an important input in the overall development of individuals?

(iv) Classify the following as 'evidence' or 'prediction'.

Statement 1 Literacy in India is a key for socio-economic progress.

Statement 2 Female literacy rate will increases in the future.

(v) The maximum percentage increase from 2001 to 2011 was in the literacy rate of ....

(a) rural male (b) rural female

(c) urban male (d) urban male

(vi) What is the difference between male literacy rate and female literacy rate as per Census 2011?

(vii) How does female literacy affect population control?

(viii) Select the most appropriate title for the above passage.

(a) Changes in Indian Literacy Rate (b) Women Literacy Rate

(c) Men literacy Rate (d) Literacy in India

Passage 3

1. Adivasi is the collective term for the Tribes of India, who are considered to be the indigenous people of India, prior to the Dravidians and Indo-Aryans. It refers to "any of various ethnic groups considered to be the original inhabitants of the Indian subcontinent." It is a modern Sanskrit word specifically coined for that purpose in the 1930s by political activists and recognised by the Supreme Court of India. In Hindi, Adivasi means 'Original Inhabitants,' from adi 'beginning, origin'; and vasin 'dweller' (itself from vas 'to dwell'), thus literally meaning 'original inhabitant'. The Constitution of India grouped these ethnic groups together "as targets for social and economic development. Since that time, the Adivasi of India have been known officially as Scheduled Tribes."

2. Tribal communities in India are the least educationally developed. First generation learners have to face social, psychological and cultural barriers to get education. This has been one of the reason for poor performance of tribal students in schools. Poor literacy rate since independence has resulted in absence of tribals in academia and higher education. Most tribes are concentrated in heavily forested areas that combine inaccessibility with limited political or economic significance. Historically, the economy of most tribes was subsistence agriculture or hunting and gathering. Tribal members traded with outsiders for the few necessities they lacked, such as salt and iron.

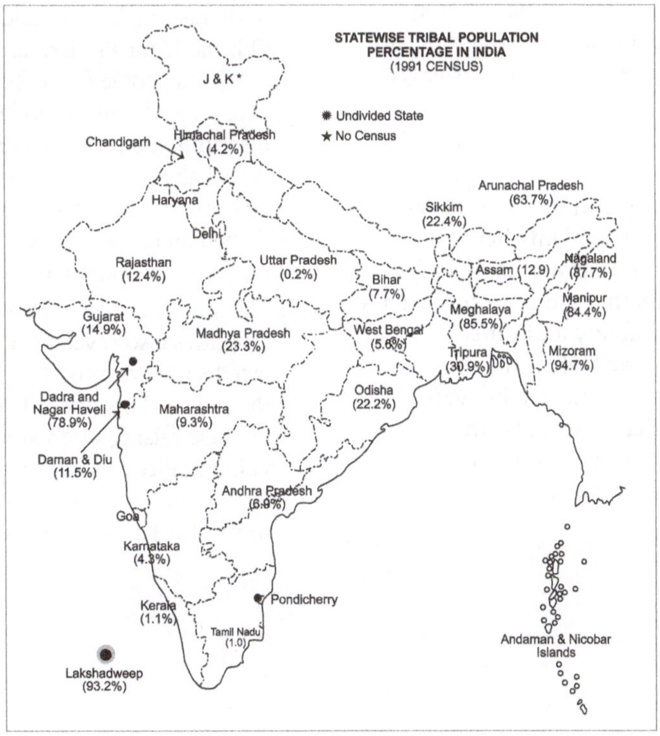

Questions

Answer the following questions based on the passage above.

(i) Complete the following suitably.
Constitution of India focuses on scheduled tribes as ....

(ii) Select the option that displays what the economy of tribal people consists of.
(a) Trade and commerce
(b) Subsistence agriculture and hunting
(c) Cash crops
(d) None of the above

(iii) What is the cause of the absence of tribals from higher education?

(iv) Classify the following sentences as 'evidence' and 'prediction'.
Statement 1 Adivasi means original inhabitants.
Statement 2 Meghalaya is projected to noon have the highest Adivasi population.

(v) Maximum % of tribal population is in the state of ....
(a) Mizoram (b) Meghalaya
(c) Manipur (d) Nagaland

(vi) From where has the term 'Adivasi' been taken?

(vii) Minimum percentage of tribal population is in which state?

(viii) What is known about who the adivasis are through the passage?
(a) Dravidians (b) Aryans
(c) Indigenous people prior to Indo-Aryans and Dravidians
(d) Successors of Indus Valley Civilisation people

Passage 4

1. India is one of the few former colonies of the world that has progressed so far as to become the second-fastest growing economy in the world, along with being projected as a future superpower. Socially, however, India's progress has not been as steep and stark. Its society continues to remain in the tight grip of patriarchy and caste – two dominant features that continue to determine how far one can go socially, economically and politically. However, unlike patriarchy that is finally being challenged, caste still remains that dirty laundry in modern India which no one likes to acknowledge publicly.
2. Through a Video Volunteers survey conducted by its Community Correspondents with 490 people from the SC/ST community in nine states, it was recorded that 64% of the respondents have experienced discrimination or atrocities in some form. The survey confirms that there is no space for us to assume that untouchability and other discriminatory practices ended when the Constitution abolished it as a practice in 1950 through Article 17. In order to actualise the intention of the law, it is necessary for law enforcement and social sensitisation to work concurrently.
3. The survey was rolled out to relay to a wider audience that caste-hierarchy and discrimination continue to fuel inequality in Indian society. When the SC/ST Act was enacted and amended, it was done in order to slowly eliminate the roadblocks placed in front of the communities to support them in leading an equal and dignified life as citizens of India.
4. The survey in Bihar, Jharkhand, Chhattisgarh, Maharashtra, Jammu and Kashmir, West Bengal, Odisha, Uttar Pradesh and Madhya Pradesh reveals that 45% people from the SC/ST communities have experienced untouchability – the crassest form of discrimination. The survey also reveals that 15% faced verbal abuse, 12% had experienced physical violence, 10% were denied access to public places, 7% were denied an economic opportunity, and 1% had been raped or had experienced other forms of sexual assault.
5. The survey on caste-based discrimination and atrocities also reveals that only 21% of those who had faced some form of discrimination filed a report with the police. This doesn't come as a shocking revelation because raising one's voice corresponds to vulnerability to social boycott, physical violence, or losing one's source of income. The top-tier position in most organisations are held by 'upper-caste' men,

which can place people from 'lower-castes' and women in a disempowered position.

6. Of the small number of people who did report going to the police, 63% said that the response of the police was not helpful. Just as both the formal and informal sector is dominated by 'upper-caste' men who mostly lack sensitisation, one of the building blocks of a democracy, the police too is dominated by 'upper-caste' men, and they may refuse to support a person from the SC or ST communities.

Questions

Answer the following questions based on the passage above.

(i) Complete the following suitably.
Two factors that determine the social, economic and political growth of a country are ....

(ii) What shows the progress of India?
(a) It being the second largest economy.
(b) It being projected as a future super power.
(c) Its growth towards a society free from any injustice.
(d) Both (a) and (b)

(iii) Why was the SC/ST Act amended?

(iv) Classify the following as 'suggestion' or 'law'.

Statement 1 It is necessary for law enforcement and social sensitiation to work concurrently in order to actualise the intention of the law.

Statement 2 The Indian Constitution abolished untouchability as a practice in 1950 through Article 17.

(v) What revelations were made by the survey report, according to the passage?
(a) Caste still remains that dirty laundry in modern India.
(b) Only 21% of the people facing discrimination filed a report with the police.
(c) 63% of the people who filed a report of discrimination said that the police was not helpful.
(d) All of the above

(vi) According to the passage, what fuels inequality in India?

(vii) Why do people who have faced discrimination refuse to raise their voice?

(viii) What does the passage seem to highlight?
(a) Problems related to caste in India.
(b) How the growth of the country is hindered.
(c) The apathy of modern India towards gender discrimination.
(d) The corruption of the law-enforcers.

Passage 5

1. India is home to 18 per cent of the global population but has only 4 per cent of the global water resources. Its per capita water availability is around 1,100 cubic meter (m3), well below the internationally recognised threshold of water stress of 1,700 m^3 per person, and dangerously close to the threshold for water scarcity of 1,000 m3 per person.

2. Paradoxically, India is also the largest net exporter of virtual water (the amount of water required to produce the products that India exports) and has one of the most water-intense economies. Despite looming water scarcity, India is one of the largest water users per unit of GDP suggesting that the way in which India manages its water resources accounts for much of its water woes. The problem lies with the government capacities which are lacking in improving water management, while policies and incentives often favor inefficient and unproductive use of water. This coupled with weak or absent institutions (e.g. for water regulation) and poor data collection and assessment results in the increasing state of water woes in the country.

3. When it comes to improving water service delivery, India can learn from Brazil, Colombia, Mozambique and New South Wales (Australia). We don't even have to go overseas to see good examples of water resources management. The Maharashtra Water Resources Regulatory Authority, established under a World Bank project, is putting in place policies, regulations, institutions and incentives that promote more efficient and more productive use of water. Efforts to establish effective authorities are also underway in other states, and Maharashtra is disseminating the lessons learned from its experience.

4. Further, the World Bank's Country Partnership Framework for India recognises the importance of the efficient use of natural resources, including water, in support of the country's ambitious growth targets. Several World Bank projects support India's efforts in the water sector. Through the National Mission for Clean Ganga, the World Bank is helping the Government of India build institutional capacity for the management and clean-up of the Ganga and investing to reduce pollution.

5. Another World Bank project, the Dam Rehabilitation and Improvement Project, has improved the safety and performance of 223 dams in the country. The National Hydrology Project is providing significant support to strengthen capacities, improve data monitoring and analysis, and laying the foundations for benchmarking and performance-based water management. There are many more such projects that aid an efficient water management system.

Questions

Answer the following questions based on the passage above.

(i) Complete the sentence appropriately.
The World Bank's Country Partnership Framework for India recognises water as ....

(ii) What is virtual water?
(a) Water that is used during production of a product.
(b) The amount of rainfall in a region.
(c) The total capacity of the water bodies present within the country.
(d) The distance covered in water for export of products.

(iii) Why are the water woes in the country ever on rise?

(iv) What does the author mean by 'water-intense economies'?

(v) Complete the following correctly with a word/ phrase from the passage.
The writer of the given passage blames .... for the country's water woes.
(a) government (b) common people
(c) lack of implementation (d) Both (a) and (b)

(vi) State one example which proves the statement.
The way in which India manages its water resources accounts for much of its water woes.

(vii) What is the National Mission for clean Ganga?

(viii) How does the Maharashtra Water Resources Regulatory Authority serve as an example for the nation?
(a) By putting in place policies, regulations, institutions and incentives that promote more efficient use of water.
(b) By limiting the use of water to certain hours of the day.
(c) By putting strict enforcement of laws against those who pollute or waste potable water.
(d) All of the above

02

CHAPTER

Note-Making and Summarisation

Note-making basically involves noting the main points of whatever is being read or heard. It is a complex activity that combines several skills and thus, requires good practice.

Marking Scheme

In the Class XI examination, a passage on which the student has to make notes and a summary is given.

Types of Questions

(i) **Making Notes of the Given Passage** This carries 5 marks split up into 2 marks for the actual notes, 1 mark for the title, 1 mark for numbering and indenting and 1 mark for key/glossary. We always use title, heading, sub-headings and abbreviations while answering this question.

(ii) **Write a Summary of the Given Passage** The summary carries 3 marks, 2 marks for content and 1 mark for expression. It should be grammatically correct and cover all the important points given in the notes. Word limit of the summary should be up to 50 words.

Points to be Kept in Mind while Answering the Questions

The following points will help you in making good notes

- Read the passage quickly but carefully. Try to understand main points and supporting details.
- Underline the keywords as you read.
- Notes should be in points and in an appropriate format.
- Organise your ideas into main heading, sub-headings and sub-sub-headings (if possible).
- Abbreviations and a symbols are freely used. Remember to give atleast 5-6 abbreviations in the glossary.
- Give title to your notes. Avoid a long sentence for title.
- While making a summary, ensure that your summary does not exceed 1/3 of the length of the original text.
- The summary should contain only the main ideas and the supporting details.
- Refer back to the original piece of writing to ensure that your summary is a true reflection of the writer's ideas.

Uses of Abbreviations in Note-Making

Use of abbreviations are recommended while making notes as they help in writing the information briefly. *The following are some of the ways in which you can make abbreviations.*

(1) First few letters of the word are enough to remember what the abbreviation stands for.

For example

- imp for 'important'
- info for 'information'
- eval for 'evaluation'

(2) Remove all (or most of) the vowels from the word and use just the key consonants bunched together.

For example

- mngmt for 'management'
- mkt for 'market'
- mktng for 'marketing'
- dvpt for 'development'

Some Common Abbreviations

Abbreviations	*Words*	*Abbreviations*	*Words*
+	Positive, Plus	e.g.	for example
–	Minus, Negative	ie	that is
=	equals, is the same as,	w/o	without
≠	does not equal, is not the same as	etc.	etcetera
≈	is approximately equal to	♂♀	male / female
<	is less than, is smaller than	Viz	namely
>	is greater than, is larger than	Asap	as soon as possible
↑	increase, rise, growth	Mr.	Mister
↓	decrease, fall, shrinkage	Mrs.	Mistress
&	and	Dr.	Doctor
*	special, important, notable	Govt.	Government
/	per, each		

Sample Passages

Read the following passages carefully and answer the questions that follow.

Passage 1

What actually is a robot? When different persons have different concepts of robots, the only way of deciding what really is a robot is to look for a definition of the term robot.

The dictionary meaning of a robot is that it is an automatic apparatus or device that performs functions ordinarily ascribed to human beings or operates with what appears to be almost-human intelligence. It is interesting to observe that this meaning does not give a human shape to the robot. In order to dramatise the fact that the robot does the work of a human being, a human shape is given to the robot in science-fiction stories and movies. The human shape is irrelevant as far as the functions of the robot are concerned.

The Robot Institute of America, which is an association of several robot manufacturers gives the following definition of an industrial robot.

"An industrial robot is a reprogrammable, multifunctional manipulator designed to move material, parts, tools or specialised devices through variable programmed motions for the performance of a variety of tasks."

The key word in this definition is 'reprogrammable'. This means that a robot is capable of being reprogrammed. This feature is the one that distinguishes it from a fixed automation. A fixed automation is designed to do one, and only one, specific task. If the specifications of the tasks change even slightly, the fixed automation becomes incapable of performing the task it was designed to perform according to one fixed specification. However, a robot can be reprogrammed to perform even when the specifications are changed drastically. The original programme is simply erased and the new programme takes care of the changed tasks.

The characteristic that a robot can be reprogrammed to handle a variety of tasks makes the robot a flexible device. Because of the flexibility offered by robots, manufacturing systems which use robots are called Flexible Manufacturing Systems (FMS).

Karel Capek was responsible for introducing the word robot. Sir Isaac Asimov is the one who coined the word robotics. According to Asimov, robotics is the science of dealing with robots. Hence robotics involves a scientific study of robots. The study includes design, selection of materials of proper quality for the components, fabrication, study of various motors required for moving the components, design of electronic circuits, computers and computer programming, and control of robots. Since robots and robotics are still in the developing stages, a considerable amount of research is required and is being pursued.

Questions

(a) On the basis of your reading of the above passage, make notes on it using headings and sub-headings. Use recognisable abbreviations wherever necessary. Supply an appropriate title to it.

(b) Write a summary of the above passage in up to 50 words.

Answers

(a) Title Robots and Robotics-Introduction

<u>Notes</u>

1. Robot Definition

1.1 Dict meaning

1.1.1 auto apparatus

1.1.2 performs funcs ascribed to humans

1.1.3 human shape irrelevant for functioning

1.2 RIA defines robot

1.2.1 reprogrammable - different from fixed automation

1.2.2 flexible– used in FMS

2. Robotics

2.1 Karel Capek introduced word robot

2.2 Isaac Asimov defined Robotics - science dealing with robots

2.3 study includes steps:

design → selection of mtrl → fabrication → motor selection → EC design → Computers and comp progmg → Robot ctrl

Key to Abbreviations

Abbreviations	*Words*
dict	dictionary
auto	automatic
funcs	functions
RIA	Robot Institute of America
FMS	Flexible Manufacturing Systems
mtrl	material
EC	electronic circuits
comp progmg	computer programming
ctrl	control

***(b)* Summary**

A robot is a flexible reprogrammable automatic device that works just like human beings and operates with almost man-like intelligence. The scientific study of robots is referred to as robotics. It includes design, selection of proper materials, design of electronic circuits, computers and computer programming and controls.

Passage 2

Information is power. It is predictable, therefore, that those in authority will seek to manipulate others through the control of data. However, all information in a democratic society should be freely available unless there are specific, well-formulated reasons for withholding it in the interest of security.

The Freedom Of Information (FOI) functions at a number of different levels- in itself, for the fulfillment of all other rights and as an underpinning of democracy. Information held by public bodies is not only for the benefit of officials, politicians or other designated people associated with the organisation, but also for the public as a whole. Unless there are good reasons for withholding such information, all interested parties should be able to access it. More importantly, freedom of information is a key component of transparent and accountable government. It plays a key role in enabling citizens to see what is going on within government and in exposing corruption and mismanagement. Transparent and open government is also essential if voters are to be able to assess the performance of elected officials and if individuals are to exercise their democratic rights effectively, for example, through timely protests against new policies or by using their vote against candidates who have indulged in undemocratic activity.

Freedom of expression and access to information is a fundamental right and must be held as a cornerstone of democracy. In its absence, government can and often does, behave with impunity. It is argued, however, that it is not an absolute right - the International Covenant on Civil and Political Rights (ICCPR) for instance, specifies certain permissible constraints. One of these is the right of the state to withhold information "for the protection of national security or of public order or of public health and morals". This is irascibly vague and provides many loopholes for governments to use this wording as a basis for restricting information that is inconsistent with their ambitions.

The public's right to know is an intrinsic part of informed public debate, which has traditionally been dependent on the freedom to receive and impart information without government interference. However, it may also be argued that this does not mean a right to receive any type of information from the government. It is of paramount importance that any restrictions on information or expression regarding security matters must designate in law only the specific and narrow categories of information absolutely necessary to protect a legitimate national security concern.

Along these lines, in a seminal judgement in 1982, the Supreme Court held that, "The concept of an open Government is the direct emanation from the right to know, which seems to be implicit in the right of free speech and expression...disclosure of information in regard to the functioning of government must be the rule and secrecy an exception, justified only where the strictest requirement of public interest so demands".

Questions

(a) On the basis of your reading of the above passage, make notes on it using headings and sub-headings. Use recognisable abbreviations wherever necessary. Supply an appropriate title to it.

(b) Write a summary of the above passage in up to 50 words.

Answers

(a) Title Freedom of Information (FOI)

Notes

1. **Information**
   1.1 pwr
   1.2 access : officials, politicians, public
   1.3 should be freely avlbl
2. **Importance**
   2.1 fulfill rights
   2.2 supports dmcrcy
3. **Functions**
   3.1 transparent and accessible govt
   3.2 citizens aware of the workings of govt
   3.3 expsg crptn and msmng
4. **Freedom of Expression and Freedom of Information**
   4.1 infmd dbt
   4.2 fndmntl but not abslt
   4.3 in public interest
   4.4 withhold if NS affected
   4.5 SC judgement supports

Key to Abbreviations

Abbreviations	*Words*
pwr	power
avlbl	available
dmcrcy	democracy
govt	government
expsg	exposing
crptn	corruption
msmng	mismanagement
infmd	informed
dbt	debate
fndmntl	fundamental
abslt	absolute
NS	National Security
SC	Supreme Court

(b) Summary

Freedom Of Information (FOI) is essentially important for the fulfillment of public rights and as a support for democracy. Information is power and thus, its access must not be limited to officials or politicians; rather, it should include the public too. Its function is to assure a transparent and accountable government, inform the public about the workings within the government and expose corruption and mismanagement.

Freedom of expression and access to information are imperative for an informed public debate. They are fundamental but not absolute rights, with restrictions for information of national security or with potential to incite violence, as supported by a Supreme Court judgement.

Practice Questions

Read the following passages carefully and answer the questions that follow.

Passage 1

The Mayan civilisation of Mexico and Central America is one of the ancient world's most fascinating, prolific and mysterious civilisations. They left their mark on the region's culture, architecture, cuisine and language – and left an indelible impression on the imagination of the modern world. Who were they? How were they able to build such an impressive civilisation of towering temples and sophisticated artwork in the middle of the harsh rainforests of Meso-America? And why did they vanish?

The earliest Mayans lived along the Pacific coast of what is now Guatemala and can be dated to about 1800 BC; by 1000 BC they were also living in Guatemala's southern lowlands. The period from about 1800 BC to about AD 250 is referred to as the Pre-classic, a time when the early Mayans lived as farmers in small villages along rivers and other bodies of water, hunting game, tending gardens and making use of the abundant natural foods found in the region's marshes and seasonal swamps. In time, strong rulers began wielding power over these communities and the Mayan culture grew in complexity. Cities rose from the forest floor, boasting of stone temples with stuccoed and painted facades created at the behest of elite rulers. People in the new power centres communicated over long distances and traders using the same routes carried luxury goods such as cacao beans, jade ornaments, quetzal feathers and jaguar pelts.

The Classic period, AD 250-900, is the time of the civilisation's greatest glory and of the greatest depths of political intrigue between rival cities. During these centuries, the Mayans erected countless stelae, stone monuments inscribed with portraits and hieroglyphs that recorded dynastic histories – the births, marriages and conquests of the ruling families. There were dozens of important regional capitals at the time and among the most important were Tikal in Guatemala and its fierce rival Calakmul in Mexico, Palenque in southern Mexico, Caracol in Belize and Copan in Honduras. The Classic period is known for artistic and intellectual splendour. The Mayans developed a complex religious and ritual system that considered rulers divine beings and called for blood sacrifices. They also grasped the numerical notion of zero, created agricultural timetables and sophisticated calendars to track the heavens, and made beautiful polychrome pottery as well as exquisite ornaments, murals and carved decorations.

But the Classic Mayans were also known for their rancorous political fighting and for being extremely bellicose – warfare was always on the horizon. One by one, the cities in the southern Mayan lowlands fell to each other, their downfall often recorded on stelae in the conquering city. By AD 900, most of the important Classic period cities had collapsed and their remaining populations had scattered into the surrounding forests. The last date recorded on stelae that archaeologists have found so far is from AD 909 in Tonina, in southern Mexico. Among the factors that help explain why the civilisation collapsed were the endemic warfare, overpopulation, degradation of the environment and drastic climate change and drought. While the cities and ceremonial centres to the Southern lowlands were being reclaimed by the jungle, the Mayans living to the North were gaining prominence, rising to amazing heights during the post-classic period (AD 900-1502), wonderful and wealthy cities in Mexico's Yucatan Peninsula flourished, most famous among them being Chichen ltza. Yet it too fell victim to political infighting and by AD 1200 had collapsed.

The Mayans never truly disappeared. Centuries after the major cities were abandoned, small groups of Mayans continued to live in the area. It was they who met and resisted the Spanish conquistadors after the first contact in 1502. And today, more than six million Mayans live in Mexico, Guatemala and Belize, speaking 28 languages and blending ancient and modern ways.

Questions

(a) On the basis of your reading of the above passage, make notes on it using headings and sub-headings. Use recognisable abbreviations wherever necessary. Supply an appropriate title to it.

(b) Write a summary of the above passage in up to 50 words.

Passage 2

You may never want to fly kites to keep away evil spirits, as the Chinese have done for centuries or to make rain, as the Tibetans did, but some more modern and western uses may tempt you to try experimenting yourself along similar lines. Ancient and medieval Chinese sources describe kites being used for measuring distances, testing the wind, lifting men, signalling and communication for military operations. The earliest known Chinese kites were flat (not bowed) and often rectangular. Later, tailless kites incorporated a stabilising bowline. Kites were decorated with mythological motifs and legendary figures; some were fitted with strings and whistles to make musical sounds while flying. From China, kites were introduced to Cambodia, India, Japan, Korea and the Western world.

The most widespread use of kites in modern times has been for meteorological investigations. Everybody knows about how Benjamin Franklin, the great American scholar and statesman, sent a kite up in 1752 during a thunderstorm to prove that lightning was caused by electricity. He produced sparks at ground level from a key hung on the wet line as the current flowed down it.

A second investigator repeated Franklin's experiment shortly afterwards and was killed. By sending up instruments on kites, it has been possible to make readings of air pressure, temperature, speed, direction and humidity. Although thermometers had been sent up long before, it was not until 1894 that a self-reading thermometer, a thermograph, was sent up by a kite. The army, navy and air force have used kites in various ways for decades. Another Korean version of the invention of the kite tells how a general used one to carry a line across a stream. This line then formed the basis of a bridge. Lines are still occasionally flown from point to point in this way using kites. At sea, kites have often been used to carry a line to distressed ships in rough weather.

Questions

(a) On the basis of your reading of the given passage, make notes on it using headings and sub-headings. Use recognisable abbreviations wherever necessary. Supply an appropriate title to it.

(b) Write a summary of the above passage in up to 50 words.

Passage 3

Cloud computing is a type of Internet-based computing that provides shared computer processing resources and data to computers and other devices on demand. It is a model for enabling ubiquitous, on-demand access to a shared pool of configurable computing resources (e.g. computer networks, servers, storage, applications and services) which can be rapidly provisioned and released with minimal management effort. Cloud computing and storage solutions provide users and enterprises with various capabilities to store and process their data in third-party data centres that may be located far from the user-ranging in distance from across a city to across the world. Cloud computing relies on sharing of resources to achieve coherence and economy of scale, similar to a utility (like the electricity grid) over an electricity network.

As a metaphor for the Internet, 'the cloud' is a familiar cliché, but when combined with 'computing', the meaning gets bigger and fuzzier. Cloud computing encompasses any subscription based or pay per use service that, in real time over the Internet, extends IT's existing capabilities.

In a cloud computing system, there's a significant workload shift. Local computers no longer have to do all the heavy lifting when it comes to running applications. The network of computers that make up the cloud handles them instead. Hardware and software demands on the user's side decrease. The only thing the user's computer needs to be able to run is the cloud computing system's interface software, which can be as simple as a Web browser, and the cloud's network takes care of the rest.

The goal of cloud computing is to apply traditional supercomputing or high-performance computing power, normally used by military and research facilities, to perform tens of trillions of computations per second, in consumer-oriented applications such as financial portfolios, to deliver personalised information, to provide data storage or to power large, immersive computer games. As the foundation of cloud computing is the broader concept of converged infrastructure and shared services. Companies can scale up as computing needs increase and then scale down again as demands decrease. In 2013, it was reported that cloud computing had become a highly demanded service or utility due to the advantages of high computing power, cheap cost of services, high performance, scalability, accessibility as well as availability.

Questions

(a) On the basis of your reading of the given passage, make notes on it using headings and sub-headings. Use recognisable abbreviations wherever necessary. Supply an appropriate title to it.

(b) Write a summary of the given passage in up to 50 words.

Passage 4

The effects of plastic bags on the environment are really quite devastating because there is no disposal method that will really help eliminate the problem. While reusing them is the first step, most people don't do it, because most of them are not durable enough to survive multiple use.

The biggest problem with them is that once they have been soiled, they end up in the trash, which then ends up in the landfill or is burned. Either solution is very poor for the environment. Burning emits toxic gases that harm the atmosphere while landfills hold them indefinitely as part of the plastic waste problem throughout the globe.

One of the greatest problems is that an estimated 300 million plastic bags end up in the Atlantic Ocean alone. These bags are very dangerous for sea life, especially those of the mammal variety. Any hunting mammal can easily mistake the size, shape and texture of the plastic bag for a meal and find its airway cut off. Needless deaths from plastic bags are increasing every year.

The indefinite period of time that it takes for the average plastic bag to break down can be literally hundreds of years. Every bag that ends up in the woodlands of the country threatens the natural progression of wildlife. Because the breakdown rate is so slow, the chances that the bag will harmlessly go away are extremely slim. Throughout the world plastic bags are responsible for suffocation and deaths of woodland animals as well as inhibiting soil nutrients. The land litter that is made up of plastic bags has the potential to kill over and over again. It has been estimated that one bag has the potential to unintentionally kill one animal per every three months due to unintentional digestion or inhalation.

While it's a noble thought to place the plastic bags in the recycling bin every week, studies have proven that there are very few recycling plants that actually recycle them. Most municipalities either burn them or send them off to the landfill after sorting. This is because it can be expensive to recycle this type of plastic. It doesn't melt down easily and is often not fit to be reused in its original form.

Questions

(a) On the basis of your reading of the given passage, make notes on it using headings and sub-headings. Use recognisable abbreviations wherever necessary. Supply an appropriate title to it.

(b) Write a summary of the above passage in up to 50 words.

Passage 5

The work of the heart can never be interrupted. The reason is that the heart's job is to keep oxygen rich blood flowing through the body. All the body's cells need a constant supply of oxygen, especially those in the brain. The brain cells live only for four to five minutes after their oxygen is cut off and then, brain death occurs, leading to the entire body dying.

The heart is a specialised muscle that serves as a pump. This pump is divided into four chambers, two called atria and two called ventricles, connected by tiny doors called valves. The chambers work to keep the blood flowing round the body in a circle with a detour to the lungs to purify the blood by removing carbon dioxide from it and adding oxygen to it.

At the end of each circuit, veins carry the blood to the right atrium, the first of the four chambers. Two-fifths of the oxygen by then is used up and it is on its way back to the lungs to pick up a fresh supply and to give up the carbon dioxide it has accumulated. From the right atrium the blood flows through the tricuspid valve into the second chamber, the right ventricle. The right ventricle contracts when it is filled, pushing the blood through the pulmonary artery, which leads to the lungs. In the lungs, the blood gives up its carbon dioxide and picks up fresh oxygen. Then it travels to the third chamber, the left atrium. When this chamber is filled, it forces the blood through the mitral valve to the left ventricle. From here, it is pushed into a big blood vessel called aorta, the main artery and sent round the body through the various arteries.

Heart diseases can result from any damage to the heart muscle, the valves or the 'natural pacemaker' of the heart. Electrical impulses from the heart muscle cause our heart to beat (contract). This electrical signal begins in the Sino-Atrial (SA) node, located at the top of the heart's upper-right chamber (the right atrium). The SA node is sometimes called the heart's 'natural pacemaker'.

Questions

(a) On the basis of your reading of the above passage, make notes on it using headings and sub-headings. Use recognisable abbreviations wherever necessary. Supply an appropriate title to it.

(b) Write a summary of the above passage in up to 50 words.

Passage 6

The Maasai tribe live on the wide plains in southern and northern Kenya and northern Tanzania. They are among the best known local populations due to their residence near the many game parks of the African Great Lakes, as well as their distinctive customs and dress. The Maasai were famous fighters. They used to raid the neighbouring tribes and carry away their cattle. All the other tribes were afraid of them because of their skills in war.

The Maasai are handsome people, tall and slim with light brown skins, straight noses and long hair. They do not belong completely to the Negro race. They belong mostly to the same race as the people of ancient Egypt. The ancient Egyptians probably looked like the Maasais of today.

The Maasais live in a very beautiful part of Africa. It consists of miles of rolling grassland, on which you can find thorny bushes and here and there a rocky hill. The people move from one place to another according to the seasons, looking for the grasses and other plants on which their cattle can graze. They have no permanent home. When they want to settle in a place for some time, they build a kind of camp called a 'Manyatta', where a few families live for a few weeks or months. Then they move on again, taking their few belongings with them, and burning the old 'Manyatta' to the ground.

To make a hut, they take a number of long thin wooden poles and plant them in a circle. Then each pole is bent into a shape of a 'U' and its other end is also planted in the earth. Now the framework for the hut is ready.

Next, the space between the poles is filled with leaves, and small branches of tree and mud. Then the outside of earth hut is covered or plastered with cow-dung, which quickly becomes hard in the Sun. An opening is left for the door but there are no windows. The hut is about 5 feet high, so that grown-up men cannot stand up straight inside his hut.

Questions

(a) On the basis of your reading of the above passage, make notes on it using headings and sub-headings. Use recognisable abbreviations wherever necessary. Supply an appropriate title to it.

(b) Write a summary of the above passage in up to 50 words.

Passage 7

After creating the world's fastest mode of transport, the French are now returning to something much more simple, the bicycle (Velo in French). On 15th July, 2007, 10,000 public bicycles were made available to the residents of Paris, in a new experiment on urban transport.

The basic principle is that nobody owns the cycle, but everybody can borrow one. For €29 and a deposit of €150, one can subscribe to a year's access to the cycles. Cycle-stands have been created outside every metro station in the city. With a magnetic card in hand, one can simply help oneself to a cycle, use it to ride up to one's destination and park it at the nearest cycle-stand.

It took three years of negotiations before the experiment was put into place, but one week before the launch, nearly 8000 Parisians had signed up for a subscription. The city expects to have nearly 2,00,000 by the end of the year.

In the last seven years, Paris has doubled its cycle tracks to 371 km at present.

This emerging new trend has quite a serious impact on urban planning, as rules are changed to suit a growing population of cyclists. Instead of the motor-car, in some places the cyclists have priority, allowing them to use one-way streets and even ignore traffic lights.

Finally, it comes down to a personal choice that the French are making. Cycling is good for one's health; according to some studies, half an hour of cycling per day can significantly elongate one's lifespan, reducing stress and hypertension. It is also an efficient tool of weight control. On the other hand, a cycle is a non-polluting form of transport, using no fuel and creating no emissions. Until a few years ago, only 1-5% of Parisians used cycles on a regular basis. Now more of the urban French population is turning to a mode of transport very common in rural France.

Questions

(a) On the basis of your reading of the above passage, make notes on it using headings and sub-headings. Use recognisable abbreviations wherever necessary. Supply an appropriate title to it.

(b) Write a summary of the above passage in up to 50 words.

Passage 8

Fasting, in some form or the other, is part of every religion. In Islam, it is called 'Roza'. The Arabic equivalent of 'roza' is sawm. Sawm literally means abstinence, i.e. to refrain from doing something. The ninth month of the Hijri calendar, i.e. Ramzan has been especially chosen for fasting. Fasting during the month of Ramzan is obligatory for every Muslim, except when he has a genuine reason not to do so.

In every human being, there are two faculties to take into consideration: one is desire and the other is reason. In all matters, the individual has to decide whether to follow his desire or his reason. The great merit in fasting is that it trains us to refrain from following our desires and instead always to bow to reason. That is the spirit of sawm.

Self-control, far from being a negative or passive action, has great value in human behaviour. In life, there are more than 50 per cent of occasions when one should refrain from action and less than 50 per cent of occasions when one should take action. This is the formula for success for both individuals and society.

Self-control is integral to social ethics. If you live alone on an island, there is no need for any control, as the absence of others leaves you free to do whatever you want to do. However, when you are living in a society, you have to give leeway to others. This is what every person on the road does when he drives a car: he either keeps to the left (or to the right depending upon which country he is in) so that he gives way to other cars and can carry on his journey without accidents.

This principle is applicable to the entire life of an individual. It entails giving others the chance to live their lives while living one's own life.

Questions

(a) On the basis of your reading of the above passage, make notes on it using headings and sub-headings. Use recognisable abbreviations wherever necessary. Supply an appropriate title to it.

(b) Write a summary of the above passage in up to 50 words.

Passage 9

Just a few years ago, we witnessed how a national project, the India-based Neutrino Observatory (INO), which is to study fundamental particles called neutrinos, was subject to a barrage of questions from environmentalists, politicians and others ever since it was cleared. The project, which involves the construction of an underground laboratory, was initially to be located in the Nilgiris but later, on grounds that it was too close to tiger habitat, was moved to a cavern under a rocky mountain in the Bodi West Hills region of Theni district, about 110 Kilometres West of Madurai in Tamil Nadu. The already much-delayed and important physics project needs to be explained.

India has been among the pioneers in neutrino research, the first of such laboratories having been established in the 1960s. We led neutrino research when our physicists used a gold mine at Kolar in Karnataka to set-up what was then the world's deepest underground laboratory. This was called the Kolar Gold Field Lab. In 1965, it enabled researchers to detect atmospheric neutrinos. In 1992, when the mine became uneconomical, the laboratory was shut down. With that, we lost our advantage in understanding the most mysterious particle in the universe. INO may now reclaim this advantage and our global leadership.

Neutrinos, first proposed by Swiss Scientist Wolfgang Pauli in 1930, are the second most widely occurring particle in the universe, only second to photons, the particles which make up light.

In fact, neutrinos are so abundant among us that every second, there are more than 100 trillion of them passing right through each of us - we never even notice them.

This is the reason why INO needs to be built deep into the earth - 1300 metres into the earth. At this depth, it would be able to keep itself away from all the trillions of neutrinos produced in the atmosphere and which would otherwise choke an over-the-ground neutrino detector.

Neutrinos have been in the universe literally since forever, being almost 14 billion years old - as much as the universe itself.

Questions

(a) On the basis of your reading of the above passage, make notes on it using headings and sub-headings. Use recognisable abbreviations wherever necessary. Supply an appropriate title to it.

(b) Write a summary of the above passage in up to 50 words.

Passage 10

Fashion is a force - a powerful force of constantly altering patterns of change and growth. Its constant movement affects the fate of the designers and manufacturers who distribute it, and of course, the lives of the consumers, who follow what it dictates. All of its facts taken together add up to a multimillion dollar industry. Fashion today means mega bucks. Fashion is also a science. Surprising, isn't it? However, it is well known that it involves known facts and basic principles and its actions and reactions can be predicted, as these are based on those facts and principles. Fashion is one of those distinct and unique trades that is highly dependent on the environment and the changes that are continuously taking place in it. These have to be understood by the designers if they want to become successful.

For one to make it to the top in the fashion business and stay there, one has to continue to discover and innovate to fulfill the needs and wants of the customers. For this, most of the top designers such as Yves Saint Laurent, Karl Lagerfeld, Liz Claiborne, etc. all rely upon their creativity backed by years of invaluable experience. In this line of work, instinct and intuition play a very major role besides the knowledge of past successes and failures.

There were changes in Western dressing that followed the dictates of the designers and the fashionable elite trend-setters. These were the fashion world's drainpipes in the 60s, the popular safaris in the 70s, the denims in the 80s and the ethnic wear that has caught on these days.

Questions

(a) On the basis of your reading of the above passage, make notes on it using headings and sub-headings. Use recognisable abbreviations wherever necessary. Supply an appropriate title to it.

(b) Write a summary of the above passage in up to 50 words.

Passage 11

Unemployment is a serious problem in our country. If millions of people are without any jobs, its effect is very bad. A man without any employment is a burden on others. If he has got to maintain a family, the situation is worse. Such unemployed persons are reduced to poverty. It demoralises them and they are forced to do undesirable things. They may commit crimes. They may create trouble and spread discontent. In fact, they are a source of danger to society and the state.

The causes of unemployment are mainly the rapid growth of population, the prevailing system and under-development of industry and trade. The population of India is growing very rapidly. It is very difficult to get jobs for all who are in need of it. The British Government had introduced a system of education in this country for carrying on administration only. It is being continued in free India also with very slight changes. The system of education prepares most young men to be clerks. But neither the government nor private firms can absorb all the educated unemployed persons in their offices for clerical work. Industry and trade have not yet properly developed.

Cottage industries in the villages have been ruined owing to the establishment of large mills and factories in towns. Consequently, many artisans have been thrown out of employment.

There has been great pressure on agricultural land because of the growth of population; consequently, many cultivators have got no land for cultivation.
All these are mainly responsible for this acute problem of unemployment.

Questions

(a) On the basis of your reading of the above passage, make notes on it using headings and sub-headings. Use recognisable abbreviations wherever necessary. Supply an appropriate title to it.

(b) Write a summary of the above passage in up to 50 words.

Passage 12

Depression is a common problem of modern times. Both the rich and poor suffer from it. According to the World Health Organisation, by the year 2020, depression will become the second leading cause of disease in the world. Many solutions have been prescribed for the problem of depression but most have proved to be ineffective as a complete cure. They may offer temporary relief but fail to resolve the problem permanently.

Meditation is often advised to treat this problem of depression. But meditation focuses on the heart and modern science has established that the heart is merely an organ that pumps blood, whereas many kinds of depression stem from the mind. It is the mind that controls the heart and not vice-versa. In many cases, depression is non-physical and the heart is physical. How can a physical organ resolve a non-physical problem?

We also often hear about physical techniques to counter depression. But the reach of physical techniques is confined to the body and does not extend to the mind.

Many kinds of depression are the result of non-acceptance of reality. The real solution to this problem is the acceptance of reality. While non-acceptance creates the problem, acceptance of reality will solve it.

Our world is one of freedom, competition, challenge and clash of interests. This nature of human life is bound to create problems. No one is exempt from this process. This being so, to de-stress, learn the art of stress management rather than trying to eliminate the stress.

A person may become sad upon facing a loss in business or feeling discriminated against at work. He may give in to anxiety and frustration if he suffers a loss in an election, his love marriage turns into a problem or if he is offended by criticism.

In all such cases, a person becomes negative because of being unaware of the real cause. He attributes the cause to another person and holds this person responsible for his difficulties. He fails to realise that all these are due to the law of nature.

Questions

(a) On the basis of your reading of the above passage, make notes on it using headings and sub-headings. Use recognisable abbreviations wherever necessary. Supply an appropriate title to it.

(b) Write a summary of the above passage in up to 50 words.

Passage 13

In Indian homes, the floor of the house is always the best maintained element, cleaned twice a day and wiped down to a sparkling state. In front of the threshold of the home, the floor often is decorated with Rangoli and other ritual diagrams. This is true in rural as well as in many urban homes in metropolitan cities. When building a new home, people spend as much money per square foot for a beautiful floor as they would spend on the entire structure. Yet, this pride and obsession for a clean floor suddenly vanishes as we step out into the street: the floor of the city.

In Delhi, where 80 per cent of the people are pedestrians in some stage of their commuting, least attention is paid to pedestrian paths. Delhi's sidewalks are too narrow, very poorly maintained and full of potholes, poles, junction boxes and dangerous electrical installations, not to speak of the garbage dumps that stink and stare at the pedestrian. Ashram Chowk is a good case in point where thousands of pedestrians change direction from the Mathura Road radial to the Ring Road. A flyover facilitates the automobiles while the pedestrian is orphaned by the investment-hungry authorities. One corner of Ashram Chowk has a ridiculous imitation wood sculpture with an apology of a fountain and across the same chowk, you have the open mouthed, massive garbage dump right on the pedestrian path, in full exhibition for the benefit of the public. These symbols of poor taste and abject apathy are then connected by narrow, dangerous and often waterlogged footpaths for the hapless pedestrians to negotiate. In the night, street lighting in the central median lights up the carriageway for cars and leaves the pedestrian areas in darkness.

Questions

(a) On the basis of your reading of the above passage, make notes on it using headings and sub-headings. Use recognisable abbreviations wherever necessary. Supply an appropriate title to it.

(b) Write a summary of the above passage in up to 50 words.

Passage 14

India is surrounded by water bodies on three sides, yet we face water shortage every year! Consider this - the per capita water availability in India was 3450 cu m in 1951. By 2025, the annual per capita availability of water is expected to fall drastically from the current 1800 cu m per person to between 1200 and 1500 cu m.

Mumbai's demand for water was 7950 MLD (million litres per day) in 2011. The supply was only around 3100 MLD - a substantial shortfall, but the city receives only 2500 MLD, the balance being lost on account of leakages and pilferage. Delhi Jal Board is able to supply only around 650 million gallons of water per day against the demand of 750 million gallons. According to a World Bank study of 27 Asian cities with population of over one million, Kolkata is the fourth worst performing metro in terms of hours of water availability per day.

The quality of available water is also fast deteriorating. In 1982, it was reported that 70 percent of all available water in India was polluted. The situation is much worse today. Overextraction of ground water has led to salt water intrusion into coastal aquifers. It has also resulted in problems of excessive fluoride, iron, arsenic and salinity in water, which is currently affecting about 44 million people in India. Ground water is facing an equally serious threat from contamination by industrial effluents and faecal matter, as well as pesticides and fertilisers from farm run-offs.

Unless priority is given quickly to creating an infrastructure to assure availability of water, there may soon be no water to meet the agricultural, domestic and industrial needs of a population that will has tripled in 50 years to one and a quarter billion. Water management is therefore a major challenge for town planners, builders and architects today, not just in terms of availability of water, but most importantly its quality.

As water shortage increases, alternate sources of water supply are gaining importance. These include sewage recycling, rainwater harvesting, generating water from humidity in the atmosphere etc. Water recycling is a simple, effective and economical solution to conserve water so that more fresh water is available for uses such as drinking, bathing, cooking and laundry.

Questions

(a) On the basis of your reading of the above passage, make notes on it using headings and sub-headings. Use recognisable abbreviations wherever necessary. Supply an appropriate title to it.

(b) Write a summary of the above passage in up to 50 words.

Passage 15

There is nothing more frustrating than when you sit down at your table to study with the most sincere of intentions and instead of being able to finish the task at hand, you find your thoughts wandering. However, there are certain techniques that you can use to enhance your concentration. "Your concentration level depends on a number of factors," says Samuel Ghosh, a social counsellor. "In order to develop your concentration span, it is necessary to examine various facts of your physical and internal environment," she adds.

She disagrees with the notion that people can concentrate or study in an environment with distractions like a loud television, blaring music etc. Also do not place your study table or desk in front of a window. "While there is no cure for a mind that wants to wander, one should try and provide as little stimulus as possible. Looking out of a window when you are trying to concentrate will invariably send your mind on a tangent," says Ghosh.

The second important thing, she says, is to establish goals for oneself instead of setting a general target and then trying to accomplish what you can in a haphazard fashion. It is very important to decide what you have to finish in a given span of time. The human mind recognises fixed goals and targets and appreciates schedules more than random thoughts. Once your thoughts and goals are in line, a focused system will follow.

She recommends that you divide your schedule into study and recreation hours. When you study, choose a mix of subjects that you enjoy and dislike and save the former for the last so that you have something to look forward to. For instance, if you enjoy verbal skill tests more than mathematical problems, then finish Maths first. Not only will you find yourself working harder, you will have a sense of achievement when you wind up.

Questions

(a) On the basis of your reading of the above passage, make notes on it using headings and sub-headings. Use recognisable abbreviations wherever necessary. Supply an appropriate title to it.

(b) Write a summary of the above passage in up to 50 words.

Answers

Passage 1

(a) Title The Mystery Behind Mayan Civilisation

Notes

1. Questions Regarding Mysteries
- 1.1 who were they?
- 1.2 how did they create impressive civilisation?
- 1.3 why disappeared?

2. The Classic Period (AD 250-900) : Glory
- 2.1 pltcl conspiracies
- 2.2 countless monuments
  - 2.2.1 recorded dynastic histories
- 2.3 many regional capitals came up
- 2.4 complex religious & ritual system
- 2.5 excellence in maths
- 2.6 notion of zero
- 2.7 made agricultural timetables
- 2.8 beautiful art & craft

3. The Post-Classic period (AD 900-1502) : Downfall
- 3.1 most important cities collapsed
- 3.2 reasons
  - 3.2.1 endemic warfare
  - 3.2.2 overpopulation
  - 3.2.3 degradation of envrmt
- 3.3 Northern Mayans survived
- 3.4 resisted Spanish conquistadors
- 3.5 now live in Mexico, Guatemala & Belize

Key to Abbreviations

Abbreviations	Words
1. comn	communication
2. dvlpd	developed
3. pltcl	political
4. &	and
5. maths	mathematics
6. envrmt	environment

(b) Summary

The Mayan civilisations of Mexico and Central America is one of the mysterious civilisations. They reached the peak of their glory during the Classic period (AD 250 - 900), which saw magnificence in architecture, intellectual excellence including mathematics, along with a rise in complex religious systems and rituals. Subsequently, their downfall occurred due to endemic warfare, overpopulation and environmental degradation. The remnant Mayans still live in Mexico, Guatemala & Belize.

Passage 2

(a) Title Kites and their History

Notes

1. History of Flying Kites
- 1.1 Chinese used them for various purposes
- 1.2 Tibetans used them for making rain
- 1.3 Intrdcd to rest of the world from China

2. Modern Uses of Flying Kites
- 2.1 for mtrlgl invstgtns
- 2.2 started with Benjamin Franklin's famous expt

3. Used for
- 3.1 msrg air pressure, temperature, humidity
- 3.2 msrg wind speed and direction
- 3.3 military purposes
- 3.4 carry a line

Key to Abbreviations

Abbreviations	Words
1. intrdcd	introduced
2. mtrlgl	meteorological
3. invstgtns	investigations
4. expt	experiment
5. msrg	measuring

(b) **Summary**

In ancient times, kites in China and Tibet were thought to bring rain and keep evil spirits away. The Chinese also used them for other purposes and introduced them to the rest of the world. Benjamin Franklin discovered that electricity produced lightning by flying a kite. Kites are presently used for measuring various atmospheric parameters like air pressure, temperature, wind speed, direction, etc. Kites are also used for carrying lines.

Passage 3

(a) **Title** Cloud Computing

Notes

1. **Definition and Meaning of Cloud Computing**
   - 1.1 servers ntwkd to centralise data storage, access computer services or rscs
   - 1.2 sharing cmptg rscs
   - 1.3 Internet-base cmptg
2. **Goal of Cloud Computing**
   - 2.1 apply tdnl supercomputing or high pfmc cmptg power to perform trillions of computations p/s
   - 2.2 deliver prsnld info in consumer-oriented apps
   - 2.3 provide data storage
   - 2.4 power large, immersive computer games
   - 2.5 converge infra and shared services

Key to Abbreviations

Abbreviations	*Words*
1. ntwkd	networked
2. rscs	resources
3. cmptg	computing
4. tdnl	traditional
5. pfmc	performance
6. p/s	per second
7. prsnld	personalised
8. info	information
9. apps	applications
10. infra	infrastructure

(b) **Summary**

In cloud computing, large groups of remote servers are networked to allow centralised data storage. It is basically internet-based computing and relies on sharing computing resources. Its goal is to apply traditional supercomputing or high performance computing power to perform trillions of computations per second. It can also power consumer-oriented applications. It is based on the broader concept of converged infrastructure and shared services.

Passage 4

(a) **Title** Harmful Effects of Plastic Bags

Notes

1. **Plastic Bags Harmful for Environment**
   - 1.1 no effective disposal method
     - 1.1.1 trashed in lfls and held indefinitely
     - 1.1.2 burned but emit harmful gases
   - 1.2 reuse not practical
   - 1.3 millions of plastic bags end in Atlantic Ocean
     - 1.3.1 harmful for sea life, particularly mammals
       - 1.3.1.1 cuts off airway, causing death
       - 1.3.1.2 adversely affects envtl balance
     - 1.3.2 burned but emit harmful gases
   - 1.4 on land, breakdown period is centuries
     - 1.4.1 suffocate forest animals
     - 1.4.2 inhibit soil nutrients
2. **Recycling Impractical**
   - 2.1 few rclg plants actually work cuz
     - 2.2.1 operation expensive
     - 2.2.2 products cannot be used as earlier
   - 2.2 most bags dumped in lfls
   - 2.3 cause land pltn

Key to Abbreviations

Abbreviations	*Words*
1. lfls	landfills
2. envtl	environmental
3. rclg	recycling
4. cuz	because
5. pltn	pollution

(b) **Summary**

Plastic bags are harmful for the environment because there is no effective disposal method for them and their reuse is impractical. A large number of plastic bags which ultimately land in the Atlantic Ocean become harmful for sea life, particularly mammals, causing their death and creating an environmental imbalance in the sea.

If dumped on land, they not only cause land pollution but also suffocate forest animals and inhibit soil nutrients. Their recycling is impractical because few recycling plants actually work as they are uneconomic.

Passage 5

(a) Title How the Heart Works

Notes

1. **Functions of Heart**
   - 1.1 vital for living
     - 1.1.1 never stop wrkg
   - 1.2 supplies oxygen rich blood to diff parts of body
2. **Structure of Heart**
   - 2.1 divided into 4 chambers connected by vlvs
   - 2.2 blood purified in lungs
   - 2.3 arteries carry pure blood to diff parts of body
3. **Causes of Heart Disease**
   - 3.1 weak heart mscls
   - 3.2 def vlvs
   - 3.3 def 'natural pacemaker'

Key to Abbreviations

Abbreviations	*Words*
1. wrkg	working
2. diff	different
3. vlvs	valves
4. def	defective
5. mscls	muscles

(b) Summary

The heart is a vital organ of the body which never stops working. It supplies oxygen-rich blood to all parts of the body. It is divided into four chambers inter-connected by valves. Blood is purified and arteries carry it to different parts of the body. Heart disease has various causes such as weak heart muscles, defective valves or a defective natural pacemaker.

Passage 6

(a) Title The Maasai Tribe - Life and History

Notes

1. **Maasai Tribe- Famous Fighters**
   - 1.1 live in Kenya & northern Tanzania
   - 1.2 carried away cattle of nbrg tribes
2. **Maasais Handsome People**
   - 2.1 tall & slim with light brown skins
   - 2.2 straight noses & long hair
   - 2.3 don't blg to Negro grps
   - 2.4 blg to people of ancient Egypt
3. **Maasais are Nomadic Cattle Herders**
   - 3.1 move from place to place looking for grass for cattle
   - 3.2 build 'Manyatta' - a camp
   - 3.3 use wdn poles to build huts
     - 3.3.1 plant U shaped wdn poles in circle on earth
     - 3.3.2 fill frmwk with leaves, branches & mud
     - 3.3.3 plaster outside with cow-dung
     - 3.3.4 opening kept for door - no windows

Key to Abbreviations

Abbreviations	*Words*
1. &	and
2. nbrg	neighbouring
3. blg	belong
4. grps	groups
5. wdn	wooden
6. frmwk	framework

(b) Summary

The Maasai tribe live in Kenya and Northern Tanzania. They were famous fighters and attacked other tribes for cattle. They are handsome people and belong mostly to the same race as that of ancient Egypt and not to the Negro race. They move from place to place looking for grass for their cattle.

Passage 7

(a) Title Revival of Cycling in France

Notes

1. **French Experiment in Urban Transport**
   - 1.1 public bicycles hired to Parisians
   - 1.2 can xchg bicycles at cycle stands at metro stations
   - 1.3 popular
     - 1.3.1 8000 signed up before launch
     - 1.3.2 lakh expected by year end
     - 1.3.3 cycle tracks doubled
2. **Impact of Experiment**
   - 2.1 road rules changed
   - 2.2 cycles given priority in some places
   - 2.3 will improve health
     - 2.3.1 ↑ lifespan
     - 2.3.2 ↓ stress
     - 2.3.3 control weight
     - 2.3.4 non-pltg
   - 2.4 reduces pltn

Key to Abbreviations

Abbreviations	*Words*
1. xchg	exchange
2. ↑	increase
3. ↓	reduce
4. pltg	polluting
5. pltn	pollution

(b) Summary

Cycling has been revived as a mode of transport in France. Public bicycles are hired to Parisians, which can be exchanged at various cycle stands, making the experiment popular. Its impact is that road rules have been changed to give cycles priority in some places. It will improve health, increase lifespan, reduce stress and control weight of people, besides reducing pollution.

Passage 8

(a) Title Traditional Culture of Self-restraint

Notes

1. **Fasting**
   - 1.1 roza in Islam
   - 1.2 refrain from doing smth
   - 1.3 Ramzan, ninth month of Hijri clnd
   - 1.4 oblgtry for every Muslim
   - 1.5 train to refrain from folwg our desires, how to reason
   - 1.6 worship - for God
   - 1.7 observed in right spirit - make individual pious and responsible
2. **Self-control: Need and Importance**
   - 2.1 great value in human behaviour
   - 2.2 formula for success for indvls and society
   - 2.3 integral to social ethics

Key to Abbreviations

Abbreviations	*Words*
1. smth	something
2. clnd	calendar
3. oblgtry	obligatory
4. folwg	following
5. indvls	individuals

(b) Summary

Fasting is known as 'Roza' in Islam, which means to refrain from doing something. It is worship of God. Fasting basically teaches self-control, which is observed as a formula for success for individuals and society. Self-control is vital to social ethics. It holds great value in human life.

Passage 9

(a) Title Race for the Neutrino

Notes

1. **India-based Neutrino Observatory**
   - 1.1 subject of questions from envlsts & others
   - 1.2 involves cnstrn of underground lab
   - 1.3 initially to be located in Nilgiris
   - 1.4 later moved to Bodi West Hills in Tamil Nadu
2. **India's Position in Research**
   - 2.1 pioneer
   - 2.2 1st lab estd in 1960s
   - 2.3 Kolar in Karnataka: world's deepest underground lab
     - 2.3.1 enabled detection of atmospheric neutrinos
     - 2.3.2 lab shut down in 1992
3. **Understanding Neutrinos**
   - 3.1 1st proposed by Swiss Scientist Wolfgang Pauli
   - 3.2 2nd most widely occurring particle
   - 3.3 labs to be built deep into earth
   - 3.4 in atmosphere, detector would choke

Key to Abbreviations

Abbreviations	*Words*
1. envlsts	environmentalists
2. &	and
3. cnstrn	construction
4. lab	laboratory
5. 1st	first
6. estd	established
7. 2nd	second

(b) Summary

India-based Neutrino Observatory (INO) was subject to questions from many groups. It involved construction of an underground laboratory, which was supposed to be located in the Nilgiris, but was later moved to Bodi West Hills in Tamil Nadu. India had been among the pioneers in neutrino research and the first lab was set up in 1960 but was shut down in 1992. Understanding neutrinos has become essential due to their wide occurrence.

Passage 10

(a) **Title** Fashion - A Life Force

Notes

1. **Constantly Altering Patterns Affect**
   - 1.1 dsnrs
   - 1.2 mfrs
   - 1.3 lives of consumers
2. **Fashion means Multimillion Dollar Industry**
3. **Fashion - A Science**
   - 3.1 facts & basic principles
   - 3.2 action & reaction predicted
   - 3.3 dependent on envt
4. **Fashion - Discover & Innovate**
   - 4.1 cntnu to fulfill needs & wants
   - 4.2 instinct & intuition play major role
5. **Fashion - Western Dressing**
   - 5.1 trend setters
     - 5.1.1 drnp in 60s
     - 5.1.2 safaris in 70s
     - 5.1.3 denims in 80s
     - 5.1.4 ethnic wears today

Key to Abbreviations

Abbreviations	Words
1. dsnrs	designers
2. mfrs	manufacturers
3. envt	environment
4. &	and
5. cntnu	continue
6. drnp	drainpipes

(b) **Summary**

Fashion is a force which keeps changing and affecting all related people. It is a science as it is based on facts and principles. To remain on top in this business, designers have to continually innovate and discover to fulfill people's needs. Western dressing gave us drainpipes, safaris and denims but now ethnic wears are fashionable.

Passage 11

(a) **Title** Unemployment: A Serious Problem

Notes

1. **Consequence of Unemployment**
   - 1.1 poverty
   - 1.2 low morale
   - 1.3 high crime rate
   - 1.4 discontent
2. **Causes of Unemployment**
   - 2.1 rapid growth of ppltn
   - 2.2 prevailing system of edu
     - 2.2.1 prepares young people to be clerks
   - 2.3 underdevelopment of indty & trade

Key to Abbreviations

Abbreviations	Words
1. ppltn	population
2. edu	education
3. indty	industry
4. &	and

(b) **Summary**

The consequences of unemployment, a serious problem in India, are poverty, low morale, high crime rate and discontent among the population. The causes of unemployment are rapid growth of population, the prevailing system of education which prepares young people to be clerks and the underdevelopment of industry and trade.

Passage 12

(a) **Title** Depression: Accept It, Tackle It

Notes

1. **Depression**
   - 1.1 common prblm of modern times
   - 1.2 acc to WHO, will soon become second leading disease
   - 1.3 prescribed soln
     - 1.3.1 offer temporary relief
   - 1.4 no permanent cure
2. **Kinds of Depression and its Cure**
   - 2.1 non-acceptance of reality
     - 2.1.1 soln - acceptance of reality
   - 2.2 clash of interests
     - 2.2.1 soln - learn stress mgmt
3. **Causes of Stress / Depression**
   - 3.1 atrbt to another person cause of prblm
   - 3.2 fail to realise law of nature

Key to Abbreviations

Abbreviations	Words
1. prblm	problem
2. acc	according
3. WHO	World Health Organisation
4. soln	solution
5. mgmt	management
6. atrbt	attribute

(b) Summary

According to the World Health Organisation, depression is expected to become the second leading cause of disease in the world. Prescribed solutions offer temporary relief but offer no permanent solution. The cause is non-acceptance of reality or clash of interests. Solutions are acceptance of reality and learning to manage stress.

Passage 13

(a) Title Delhi's Neglected Pedestrians

Notes

1. **Floors in Indian homes**
    - 1.1 well mntnd
    - 1.2 clnd twice a day
    - 1.3 decorated
    - 1.4 home buyers invest on good floors
    - 1.5 streets neglected in cmprsn
2. **Delhi's Pedestrian Sidewalks**
    - 2.1 most people use them for some time
    - 2.2 sdwks poorly made and cltrd due to
        - 2.2.1 potholes
        - 2.2.2 dangerous electrical installations
        - 2.2.3 garbage dumps
        - 2.2.4 being too narrow
        - 2.2.5 waterlogging

Key to Abbreviations

Abbreviations	*Words*
1. mntnd	maintained
2. clnd	cleaned
3. cmprsn	comparison
4. sdwks	sidewalks
5. cltrd	cluttered

(b) Summary

Floors in Indian homes are well maintained and decorated. Home buyers invest on good floors but in comparison, the Indian streets are neglected.

Delhi's pedestrian sidewalks, used by most people, are poorly made and cluttered with large garbage dumped on them. These paths are often too narrow and waterlogged.

Passage 14

(a) Title Tackling Water Scarcity

Notes

1. **Water Availability Status**
    - 1.1 per capita in India: 3450 cu m (1951) reduced to1800 cu m (today) and will reduce to 1200-1500 cu m (2025)
    - 1.2 Mumbai's dmd more than triple of supply
    - 1.3 Delhi's dmd is 15% more than supply
    - 1.4 Kolkata 4th worst performing metro in Asia for water supply
2. **Quality of Available Water**
    - 2.1 groundwater constantly dtrtg
        - 2.1.1 salt water intrusion into coastal aquifers
        - 2.1.2 excessive fluoride, arsenic, iron and salinity
        - 2.1.3 polluted by
            - industrial effluents
            - faecal matter
            - pesticides & fertilisers from farm run-offs
3. **How to Handle the Problems**
    - 3.1 water mgmt major problem
    - 3.2 promote alternate sources
        - 3.2.1 sewage recycling
        - 3.2.2 rainwater harvesting
        - 3.2.3 water gnrtn from atmospheric humidity
    - 3.3 effective and economical solution to conserve water

Key to Abbreviations

Abbreviations	*Words*
1. dmd	demand
2. dtrtg	deteriorating
3. mgmt	management
4. &	and
5. gnrtn	generation

(b) Summary

Water availability in India is falling steadily, particularly in the metros. The quality of available water is also deteriorating, with 70 per cent of water being polluted due to salinity and excessive presence of fluorides, iron and arsenic. Groundwater is contaminated by industrial effluents, faecal matter and agricultural run-offs.

Passage 15

(a) **Title** Concentration Techniques

Notes

1. Enhance your Concentration
- 1.1 avoid wdrg thoughts
- 1.2 idfy phsl & int env
- 1.3 create focus
- 1.4 plan study hrs time and lctn

2. Avoid
- 2.1 distractive env
- 2.2 study near window
- 2.3 actvtg > two senses

3. Setting Goals
- 3.1 fix goals & targets
- 3.2 divide schedule
- 3.3 attempt dfclt tasks first

Key to Abbreviations

Abbreviations	*Words*
1. wdrg	wandering
2. idfy	identify
3. phsl	physical
4. &	and
5. int	internal
6. env	environment
7. hrs	hours
8. lctn	location
9. actvtg	activating
10. >	more than
11. dfclt	difficult

(b) **Summary**

It is very frustrating to lose concentration while working. Certain techniques can definitely help to build up concentration. First, the physical and internal environment should be conducive for focused thinking. Avoid noisy areas and other distractions such that not more than two of your senses are active at any time. Second, establish definite goals and accomplish them, thus establishing a focused system. Plan, divide and prioritise your schedule.

SELF ASSESSMENT TEST

Passage 1

1. How does television affect our lives? It can be very helpful to people who carefully choose the shows that they watch television can increase our knowledge of the outside world; there are high quality programmes that help us understand many fields of study, science, medicine, the arts and so on. Moreover, television benefits very old people who can't often leave the house, as well as patients in hospital. It also offers non-native speakers the advantage of daily informal language practice. They can increase their vocabulary and practice listening.
2. On the other hand, there are several serious disadvantages to television. Of course, it provides us with a pleasant way to relax and spend our free time, but in some countries, people watch television for an average of six hours or more a day. Many children stare at a television screen for more hours each day than they do at anything else, including studying and sleeping.
3. Recent studies show that after only thirty seconds of watching television, a person's brain 'relaxes' the same way that it does just before the person falls asleep. Another effect of television on the human brain is that it seems to cause poor concentration. Children who view a lot of television can often concentrate on a subject for only fifteen to twenty minutes. They can pay attention only for the amount of time between commercials.
4. Another disadvantage is that television often causes people to become dissatisfied with their own lives. Real life does not seem as exciting to these people as the lives of actors on the screen. To many people television becomes more real than reality and their own lives boring.

   Also many people get upset or depressed when they can't solve problems in real life as quickly as television actors seem to.
5. Before a child is fourteen years old, he or she views eleven thousand murders on the screen. He or she begins to believe that there is nothing strange about fights, killings and other kinds of violence. Many studies show that people become more violent after certain watching programmes. They may even do the things that they saw in a violent show.

Questions

1. On the basis of your reading of the above passage, make notes on it, using headings and sub-headings. Use recognisable abbreviations (wherever necessary- minimum 4) and a format you consider suitable. Also supply an appropriate title to it.
2. Write a summary of the above passage in about 50 words.

Passage 2

1. Delhi's citizens leave and want to get to their destination as fast they can. No one wants to linger on the road, no leisure walks, no one looks a stranger in the eye. It is on the pedestrian path that citizens encounter head on the poor public management and the excuse called multiplicity of authorities. One agency makes the road, another digs it up to lay cables, third one comes after months to clear up the mess and the cycle of unaccountability goes on. Meanwhile crores are spent in reparing the carriageway for vehicles and in construction of the flyovers without a care for the pedestrian below. Solution offered is to make an expensive underpass or an ugly foot overbridge, ostensibly for facilitating the pedestrian, while in reality they only facilitate the car to move faster at the expense of the pedestrian. Take Kashmiri gate, ITO, Ashram Chowk, AIIMS or Dhaula Kuan, at all these important, pedestrian crossover points, the story is the same. They have pulled the sidewalk from the pedestrian's feet.
2. In modern cities across the world, the pedestrian is king. The floor of the city is designed and maintained as an inclusive environment, helping the physically challenged, the old and the infirm children and the ordinary citizens to move joyful

across the city, Delhi aspires to be world class city. Hopefully the authorities would look once again at the floor of Delhi.

3. The pleasure of strolling on the road is deeply connected to our sense of citizenship and sense of belonging. Pride in the city grows only on a well designed floor of the city.

Questions

1. On the basis of your reading of the above passage, make-notes using heading and sub-heading. Also use recognised abbreviations wherever necessary (minimum 4) and a format you consider suitable. Also supply an appropriate title to it.
2. Write a summary of the above passage in about 50 words.

Passage 3

1. Corruption in one form or another, is a worldwide phenomenon. But everyone admits that corruption is something ugly, immoral and detestable. Unfortunately, in our country, corruption has become a part of life. It has entered the very roots of the Indian society.
2. Corruption is prevailing at all levels- economic, social, administrative, moral and spiritual. During the past few years, the images of the country has been defaced beyond redemption. A large number of scams, involving top politicians, administrators and VVIPs have come to light. These scams, most of them unearthed by the Central Bureau of Investigation, involve huge sums running into thousands of crores. They have shaken the entire conscience of the country to the bones.
3. The root cause of corruption is red tape or delay. Persons found guilty should be punished severely. Exemplary punishments should be given to corrupt officials, national character should be improved.
4. Social and spiritual organisations can give a healthy education to the public. Persons of strong character should be employed. The government employees must be told to withstand any temptation while discharging their duties. Such officials as lay down noble standards of honesty and efficiency, should be encouraged and honoured at public functions. Dishonest public servants should not only be dismissed, but should also be publicly flogged and put behind the bars. The education system of the country should be re-oriented to inculcate a spirit of honesty amongst the people.

   All ministers and public servants should be made to declare their assets. The vigilance department should keep a constant eye on the corrupt officers and other public servants.
5. Corruption at any level, is bad. The government should launch a vigorous campaign against this social evil. Charity, however, must begin at home.

Questions

(a) On the basis of your reading of the above passage make, notes on it, using headings and sub-headings. Use recognisable abbreviations (wherever necessary- minimum 4) and a format you consider suitable. Also supply an appropriate title to it.

(b) Write a summary of the above passage in about 50 words.

Passage 4

1. Conversation is indeed the most easily teachable of all arts. All you need to do in order to become a good conversationalist is to find a subject that interests you and your listeners. There are, for example, numberless hobbies to talk about. But the important thing is that you must talk about other fellow's hobby rather than your own. Therein lies the secret of your popularity. Talk to your friends about the things that interest them, and you will get a reputation for good fellowship, charming wit and a brilliant mind. There is nothing that pleases people so much as your interest in their interest.
2. It is just as important to know what subjects to avoid and what subjects to select for good conversation. If you don't want to be set down as a wet blanket or a bore, be careful to avoid certain unpleasant subjects. Avoid talking about yourself, unless you are asked to do so. People are interested in their own problems not in yours. Sickness or death bores everybody. The only one who willingly

listens to such talk is the doctor, but he gets paid for it.

3. To be a good conversationalist you must know not only what to say, but how also to say it. Be mentally quick and witty. But don't hurt others with your wit. Finally try to avoid mannerism in your conversation. Don't bite your lips or click your tongue, or roll your eyes or use your hands excessively as you speak.
4. Don't be like that Frenchman who said, "How can I talk if you hold my hand?"

Questions

1. On the basis of your reading of the above passage make notes on it, using headings and sub-headings. Use recognisable abbreviations (wherever necessary- minimum 4) and a format you consider suitable. Also supply an appropriate title to it.
2. Write a summary of the above passage in about 50 words.

Passage 5

1. A good business letter is one that gets results. The best way to get results is to develop a letter that, in its appearance, style and content, conveys information efficiently. To perform this function, a business letter should be concise, clear and courteous.
2. The business letter must be concise: don't waste words. Little introduction or preliminary chat is necessary. Get to the point, make the point, and leave it. It is safe to assume that your letter is being read by a very busy person with all kinds of papers to deal with. Re-read and revise your message until the words and sentences you have used are precise. This takes time, but is a necessary part of a good business letter. A short business letter that makes its point quickly has much more impact on a reader than a long-winded, rambling exercise in creative writing. This does not mean that there is no place for style and even, on occasion, humour in the business letter. While it conveys a message in its contents, the letter also provides the reader with an impression of you, its author- the medium is part of the message.
3. The business letter must be clear. You should have a very firm idea of what you want to say and you should let the reader know it. Use the structure of the letter-the paragraphs, topic sentences, introduction and conclusion-to guide the reader point by point from your thesis, through your reasoning, to your conclusion. Paragraph often, to break up the page and to lend an air of organisation to the letter. Use an accepted business-letter format. Re-read what you have written from the point of view of someone who is seeing it for the first time, and be sure that all explanations are adequate, all information provided (including reference numbers dates and other identification). A clear message, clearly delivered, is the essence of business communication.
4. The business letter must be courteous. Sarcasm and insults are ineffective and can often work against you. If you are sure you are right, point that out as politely as possible, explain why you are right and outline what the reader is expected to do about it. Another form of courtesy is taking care in your writing and typing of the business letter. Grammatical and spelling errors (even if you call them typing errors) tell a reader that you don't think enough of him or can lower the reader's opinion of your personality faster than anything you say, no matter how idiotic. There are excuses for ignorance; there are no excuses for sloppiness.
5. The business letter is your custom-made representative. It speaks for you and is a permanent record of your message. It can pay big dividends on the time you invest in giving it a concise message, a clear structure and a courteous tone.

Questions

1. On the basis of your reading of the above passage make notes on it, using headings and sub-headings. Use recognisable abbreviations (wherever necessary- minimum 4) and a format you consider suitable. Also supply an appropriate title to it.
2. Write a summary of the above passage in about 50 words.

Passage 6

1. Good decoration reflects the personality of the people who live in the home. It should, first of all, be distinctive, just as each person is distinctive. A home should have unity not only within each room but also throughout the house. Rooms should, to some degree, harmonize with each other. The colour and styling of each room, particularly, should fit into the colour and styling of the rooms which run out of it.
2. Attractive home furnishings set the stage for pleasant living. If they are an expression of yourself, you will have a feeling of satisfaction every time you enter your home, and friends will share your enjoyment.
3. However, furnishings and surroundings expressive of just the right note of restfulness, gay informality, or elegant simplicity are not often assembled by accident. Even enthusiasm alone is not enough. For most home decorators, it takes poring over plans, trying colour schemes, finding ingenious ways to make the best of what you have and shopping around to search out just the right purchases at prices you can afford to pay. But there is keen pleasure in striving for the perfect result and great satisfaction in achieving it.
4. A successful house and successful rooms will depend upon the proper relationship of each element in it to the others and to the whole. Therefore, in selecting each piece it is well to consider the background, the usage, the draperies, the floor covering, the upholstering materials, the woods, shapes, colour scheme and the 'feeling' you prefer for the room.
5. Work and plan to enjoy your house. Limit the expenditures of time, effort and money to the extent of your abilities, so that just running the house doesn't dominate your life. Elegance and delicate things may be a drain you can afford only in a limited way.

   If you can't afford outside help, select a house and furnishings that require less care. Plan your activities so that tumult and upset are limited to a few rooms-an activity room or a bedroom or a corner of the dining room.

Questions

1. On the basis of your reading of the above passage make notes on it, using headings and sub-headings. Use recognisable abbreviations (wherever necessary- minimum 4) and a format you consider suitable. Also supply an appropriate title to it.
2. Write a summary of the above passage in about 50 words.

Creative Writing Skills & Grammar

01 CHAPTER

Writing : Short Composition

An advertisement refers to a public notice or an announcement communicating about goods, services, ideas, buying and selling of properties, vehicles, etc. It is done through the means of telephone, newspapers, magazines, radio, television and internet.

Advertisements are of two types

A. Classified Advertisements

B. Commercial or Display Advertisements in Class XI, question from only classified advertisements are asked.

Marking Scheme

Format	1 Mark
Content	2 Marks
Expression	1 Mark

(Accuracy of Spelling and Grammar)

Advertisements

Classified Advertisements

The purpose of a classified advertisment is to convey more while paying less. They are brief as the advertiser is charged per word or per column.

The characteristics of classified advertisements are

1. They are categorised according to different classes and subject matter.
2. They are brief, economical and occupy less space.
3. They are composed of short phrases and words.
4. The language is simple, concise and formal.

Points to be Kept in Mind while Writing an Advertisements

- Advertisements should always be drafted in such a way that they attract the readers to go through them.
- They should always be meaningful and interesting so that they can attract the attention of the readers.
- They should always have simple and effective language.
- They should always be brief and to the point.
- The name of the advertiser and the advertised product or service should be properly highlighted.

TIP To develop expertise in drafting classified advertisements, students are advised to read classified advertisement columns of leading newspapers.

Type 1 Situations (Vacant/Wanted)

Details Required

- *Give heading 'Wanted', 'Required' or 'Situation Vacant' (as appropriate).*
- *Write the name of the organisation/ company, in the case of 'Situation Vacant'.*
- *Indicate the post and number of vacancies.*
- *State the essential qualifications and experience.*
- *Give preferences such as age limit and gender of the candidate (if applicable).*
- *Other preferences/ details like pay and perks, mode of applying, etc. are optional and may be included where relevant.*
- *Contact address and phone number of the advertiser is optional.*

Format of Situation Vacant/Wanted

1. Arun Gupta of M-3 Kamal Apartments, Shimla, has a very good knowledge of tourist places in Shimla. He wants to work as a tourist guide. Draft a suitable advertisement in 50 words for publication in the Tours and Travels Section of a local newspaper.

Ans.

Situation Wanted — Heading

Seeking a job as a Tourist Guide with Tours and Travels companies in Shimla area. I am well acquainted with the hills and historical places around Shimla. I am well versed in English, Hindi and Punjabi. Tours and Travels companies may contact Arun Gupta, M-3, Kamal Apartments, Shimla or call 98682XXXXX. — Content details

Solved Examples

2. You are General Manager of Orient Export House, Tri Nagar, Delhi. You want to appoint a Stenographer/ PA for your company. Draft an advertisement about the same in 50 words.

Ans.

Situation Vacant

Wanted a smart, confident PA/ Stenographer for a leading export house. Qualification—graduate, age 20-35 years, typing speed 40 wpm, shorthand 100 wpm. Computer and MS-Office literacy essential. Salary negotiable. Apply with complete bio-data within two weeks to General Manager, Orient Export House, Tri Nagar, Delhi-110061.
Tel. No. 011-27345XX

3. You are Ravi/Ria Sharma of 29, XYZ Villa, Chennai. You want to teach Chemistry in a private school. Draft a suitable advertisement in 50 words for publication in a local newspaper.

Ans.

Situation Wanted

Looking for a job in one of the private schools. I did my Post Graduation in Chemistry from IGU (Indira Gandhi University). I have 5-year experience, excellent communication skills and a pleasing personality. Available for interview on any working day.
Contact: 999XXXXXXX (Ravi Sharma); 29, XYZ Villa, Chennai.

Type 2 Sale/Purchase (Property)

Details Required

- *Begin with 'For Sale/ Purchase' or 'Available/ Wanted'*
- *Brief physical description*
- *Fittings and fixtures (optional)*
- *Type of property under consideration (Plot/ Residential / Commercial/ Industrial)*
- *Contact name, phone number/ address/e-mail*
- *Financial aspects/cost (optional)*
- *Area (sq m) and location, size, number of rooms, floors / flat / bungalow, etc.*
- *Location and surroundings*
- *Facilities - power connection, parking, proximity to business/ shopping area*

Format of Sale/Purchase (Property)

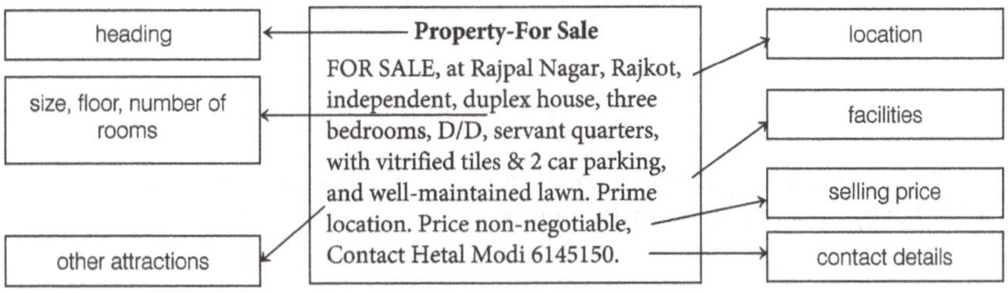

Solved Examples

1. You plan to sell your flat. Draft a suitable advertisement in 50 words to be published in the classified columns of a local daily giving all necessary details of the flat.

Ans.

FLAT for SALE

At Mukherjee Nagar, DDA Flat, SFS-II, Ground floor, Two bedrooms, D/D with full interiors for sale. Car parking available. East/ park facing. Reasonable price. Contact AB Singh 011-2723XXXX

2. You are General Manager of PNT Company, NOIDA, which requires to purchase posh bungalows as guest houses. Draft an advertisement in 50 words to be published in the classified columns of 'The Tribune'.

Ans.

BUNGALOWS WANTED

Wanted high end bungalows in various posh locations in South Delhi to be run as guest houses. Uninterrupted water and electricity supply is a must. Nearby market and other facilities are preferred. Owners please contact with lowest rates, terms and conditions, etc. to General Manager, PNT Company, Noida.
Phone No. 0120- 42242XX
e-mail : divyansh174@gmail.com

Type 2B Sale/Purchase (Vehicle)

Details Required

- *Start with 'Sale / Purchase' or 'Available / Wanted'*
- *Model/Year of manufacturing*
- *Features/ accessories fitted*
- *Ownership details (optional)*
- *Insurance details (optional)*
- *Type/ make of vehicle*
- *Colour*
- *Mileage and condition, new or second hand*
- *Kilometres run/ done/price expected*
- *Contact address/ e-mail/ phone number*

Format of Sale/Purchase (Vehicle)

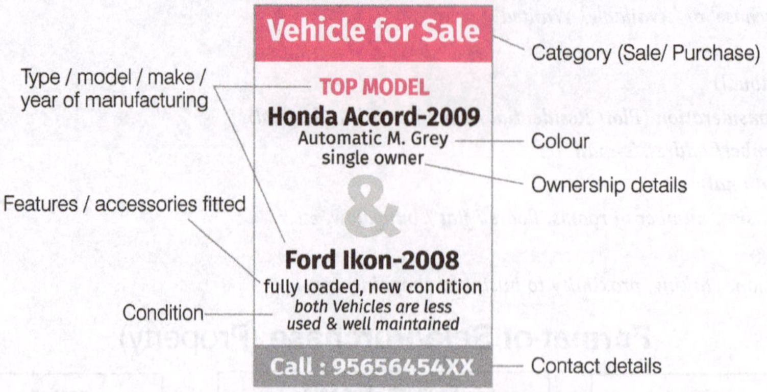

Solved Examples

1. You want to sell your old car as you are planning to buy a new one. Draft a suitable advertisement in 50 words to be published in a local daily under the classified columns.

Ans.

Vehicle for Sale

Available Ford Ikon 2004, 1300CC, silver colour, travelled 49000 kms only, Chandigarh registration, sparingly used, fitted with alloy wheels and latest Panasonic music system with CD Player, 1000 watts amplifier, woofer and speaker, giving 15 Kmpl petrol with AC, leather upholstery, beige interior, sunroof, good condition, fully insured. No dealers please.
Contact Srishanth Jha: 97112702XX

2. You plan to sell your motorcycle. Draft a suitable advertisement in 50 words to be published in the classified column of the 'Hindustan Times', Delhi. Invent all necessary details.

Ans.

Motorcycle for Sale

Available a yellow Hero Karisma with disk brakes, double speed engine, 180cc, alloy wheels, digital meter, tail brake lights, 50 km/h, sparingly used, fully insured, good condition. Sale price negotiable.
Contact Shravan Kumar: 78124679XX

Type 2C Sale/Purchase (Household/Office Goods)

Details Required

- *Start with 'Sale / Purchase' or 'Available / Wanted'*
- *Product brand, model, year of manufacture*
- *Duration used/ period of usage/ when purchased*
- *Price offered/ expected (optional)*
- *Contact address / e-mail / phone number*
- *Name/ Type of household/ office item*
- *Product features*
- *Condition*
- *Specify material (in case of furniture)*

Format of Sale/Purchase (Household / Office goods)

HOUSEHOLD GOODS FOR SALE — Category (Sale / Purchase)

Name / types of items / details — **Sofa set, dining table, double bed, fridge, TV and other household goods** *for sale*

Sunday 24th July, 20XX at
House no 567, Sector 43, Noida. — Contact address
Come, inspect and buy 9 AM to 5 PM.

CONTACT: Sandeep Makhija 98754XXXXX — Phone number

Solved Examples

1. You are going abroad. You want to sell your household items. Draft an advertisement in not more than 50 words to be published in a local daily. You are Aman/Amna living at 432, East of Kailash, New Delhi.

Ans.

FOR SALE

Available a LG LED TV 70 inches, Samsung refrigerator 360lt, HITACHI 5 star AC 1.5 ton, dishwasher, IFB Microwave, Durian 5 seater leather Sofa set for inmediate Sale. All items are in good and working condition, prices negotiable. Owner going abroad. Interested parties may Contact Aman/Amna, East of Kailash, 432, New Delhi, Ph.No. 9871XXXXXX

2. You are moving to a new city with your family. Draft an advertisement in 50 words for disposing items of furniture and electrical equipment to be published in a local newspaper.

Ans.

For Sale - Household Items

Available 6 seater sofa, teakwood, in excellent condition with dunlop seats, glass centre table, two LG AC's, LG Microwave, Samsung fridge, dining table with four chairs, two double beds. Reasonable sale offer, owner moving to new city.
Contact Brijesh Saini 99944422XX

Type 3 To Let

Details Required

- *Give heading 'To Let' or 'Available' or other suitable phrase*
- *Details of accommodation — number of bedrooms, size of rooms, bathrooms, etc.*
- *Location and surroundings*
- *Brief description of the accommodation*
- *Facilities — water/electricity supply, park facing, proximity to market, school, etc.*
- *Fixtures and fittings (if any)*
- *Preference of tenants—small family, company lease, etc.*
- *Rent expected, agreement required, other terms*
- *Contact address/ e-mail/ phone number*

Format of To Let

Solved Examples

1. You want to let out a house. Draft an advertisement in 50 words to this effect for publication in a newspaper giving location of the building, nature of accommodation, rent expected, etc.

Ans.

TO LET

Available newly built marbled house in Sector 22, Gurgaon on lease. Ground Floor 2 rooms, one covered verandah, attached bathroom, kitchen. First Floor 2 rooms, verandah, attached bathroom, modular kitchen. Walking distance from the local market. East/ park facing. 24×7 water, electricity and security. For bank/ company lease, single executives/ working ladies.

Contact Shekhar Yadav, 98141770XX

2. A US based NRI wants to let out his three bedroom independent floor in Green Park, New Delhi. Draft an advertisement in 50 words for publication in the classified columns of a local daily. Provide suitable details.

Ans.

TO LET

A 3BHK independent floor in Green Park, New Delhi available on a 2 years lease. Park facing with all modern amenities. Well-ventilated and modern construction. 24-hour water supply, power back-up, lift facility, strong security, fully furnished, parking space. Owner US based NRI.

Contact Milind Oberoi : 998899XXXX

Type 4 Missing (Persons and Pets)

Details Required

- *Give heading 'Missing'*
- *Contact address / e-mail / phone number*
- *Date and place (since when / from where missing)*
- *Indicate reward, if any*

Person

- *Name, age, complexion, height and build*
- *Brief physical description*
- *Health and mental condition*
- *Clothes and other identifying features*
- *Photo (optional)*

Pet

- *Brief physical description*
- *Name, breed, age, colour of fur/skin. etc.*
- *Identifying features*
- *Answers to what name, etc.*

Format of Missing (Persons and Pets)

Your brother has been missing from his home for the last two days. Draft an advertisement for a newspaper providing necessary details and offer of a reward to informer.

> **PERSON MISSING**
>
> Deepak Kumar, 14 years, 5'3" fair complexion, average built, wearing black striped shirt and blue jeans, injury scar over left eye brow, missing since 1st April, 20XX from Nand Nagri Delhi. Informer will be duly rewarded. Contact: SHO Nand Nagri Police station or call at 9999XXXXXX.

Solved Examples

1. You are AP Raman of 22/14 Arabi Tank Lane, Trichy, Tamil Nadu. Your grandmother, Chennamo is missing from your home for the last 5 days. Draft a suitable advertisement in 50 words with all details to be published in a local daily in the classified column.

Ans.

> **MISSING**
>
> Woman named Chennamo aged 80 years from Orakalam, since 14th January, 20XX. She is about 5' 5", dark complexion, speaks only Tamil. She was wearing light green saree and slippers. She has a big scar on her forehead. Anyone who finds her will be suitably rewarded. Kindly Contact AP Raman, 22/14 Arabi Tank Lane, Trichy, Tamil Nadu, 81245678XX.

2. Your cat is missing since the last two days. Draft an advertisement in 50 words to be published in the missing column of classified advertisements in 'The Tribune'.

Ans.

> **MISSING**
>
> Missing a beautiful tabby cat named Tessa, white and brown fur, 1-year-old, healthy since 4th March, 20XX from Khan Market. If found, please contact Saravjeet Kaur, House No. 83, Lajpat Nagar, Delhi.
> Phone number 011-267628XX.

Type 5 Lost and Found

- *Give heading 'Lost' or 'Found'*
- *When and where lost/found*
- *Specify the items*
- *Reward, if any*
- *Brief description*
- *Contact address/e-mail/phone number*

Format of Lost and Found

LOST — Heading

I lost allotment letter of my flat

No. 9999 of Kalypso J P Greens, Noida. — Item details/description

Mob: 999999XXXX — Contact details

Email: lost_found@gmail.com

Sanjay Kumar

Solved Examples

1. Mr. Aggarwal lost his passport while travelling in the Metro on the yellow line from Model Town to Rajiv Chowk Metro Station. Draft an advertisement in 50 words to be published in the Lost and Found Section of the classified columns of 'Hindustan Times'.

Ans.

LOST

An Indian passport bearing No. A330007 in the name of Satish Aggarwal along with an Air France ticket to Paris got lost on 17th February, on Metro route from Model Town to Rajiv Chowk at approximately 10 AM. Finder contact Satish Aggarwal, House No. 243, Model Town, New Delhi. Phone- 97112402XX. Suitable reward promised.

2. You have found a briefcase in a bus to Ajmer. Draft an advertisement in 50 words to be published in the 'Lost and Found' column of the newspaper.

Ans.

FOUND

A black American Tourister briefcase was found while travelling by a bus from Delhi to Ajmer on 19th March, 20XX, contains documents and driving licence. Will be returned to the owner after the particulars and details of the content are given. Please contact Swaraj Singh, 99222348XX.

Type 6 Tours and Travel

Details Required

- *Give heading 'Package Available' or other suitable phrase*
- *Specify destinations, duration, etc.*
- *Indicate the cost and special discount, if any*
- *State the name of the travel agency*
- *Details of package - food/ boarding/ lodging/ sight-seeing, etc.*
- *Contact address/ e-mail/ phone number*

Format of Tours and Travel

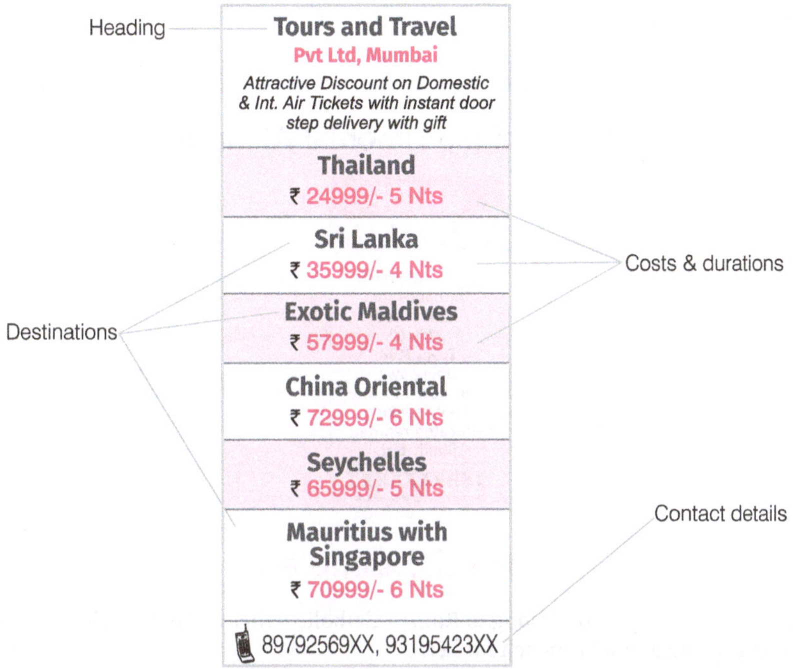

Solved Examples

1. You are the proprietor of Shatabdi Travels and have organised a 3 nights/ 4 days package for Singapore. Draft the advertisement in 50 words to be published in a national daily to draw people to it.

Ans.

TOURS AND TRAVEL

Attractive package available for Singapore, 3 nights/ 4 days, breakfast and dinner, stay at 4 star hotels, inclusive of sight-seeing and transfers, ₹ 49,999 per person. Special Diwali discount for bookings before 10th November. Contact Shatabdi Travels, N-24, Outer Circle, Connaught Place, New Delhi.

Phone 98122567XX, 011-225672XX

2. Your uncle has just established a tours and travels company and needs a classified advertisement to popularise it. Draft an advertisement giving all necessary details.

Ans.

TOURS AND TRAVEL

Holidays Tours & Travel, India's most trusted name in domestic and overseas travel. Contact for air tickets, tour packages, hotel, resort and cab booking. Book online and avail 20% discount on hotel room tarrifs anywhere in India. Try once, trust forever. Special pilgrimage packages available. Visit our website www.holidays.com or call toll free number 1800-444-XXXX.

Type 7 Matrimonial Alliance

Details Required

- *Give heading 'Wanted', 'Required', 'Available', etc.*
- *Give personal details such as*
  Looks and appearance
  Age, height, complexion
  Educational/ professional qualifications
  Family background, community, etc.
- *State your preferences, if any*
- *Contact address/ phone number/ PO box number/ e-mail*

Format of Matrimonial Alliance

Solved Examples

1. Your sister Suji is of marriageable age. You belong to Roman Catholic Religion. On behalf of your parents draft a suitable advertisement inviting a suitable match for her.

Ans.

BRIDEGROOM WANTED

The family of Suji, 23/5'8", Roman Catholic, slim, cultured, smart, radiologist working in a super specialty hospital in New Delhi seeks compatible match, preferably 26/6', fair complexioned, doctor, IAS, IFS officer with strong Christian values. Write with full particulars to Post Box XXXX, Times of India, New Delhi-01.

2. Draft a suitable matrimonial advertisement in 50 words for your well-educated and well settled divorcee friend.

Ans.

BRIDE WANTED

Suitable match for a 31 years, Iyer boy. Issueless divorcee after three months of marriage. 170 cm, wheatish complexion, lean, modest, M Tech, IT literate, well settled, only child of a well-to-do harmonious family. Requires a smart, educated girl from a good family. Simple early marriage. Caste no bar. Contact Box No. 8484, The Indian Express, New Delhi.

Type 8 Obituary/Remembrance

Details Required

- *Photograph and name of deceased*
- *Message from family/company*
- *Names of persons giving obituary with their relationship to the deceased*
- *Date and cause of death*
- *Background/accomplishments/a tribute to his/her work*
- *Details of any special ceremony being held*

Format of Obituary/Remembrance

Name of deceased	**In Loving Memory** of Late Vidya Wati W/o Late S Hari Singh Kumar	Photo — Photograph
Message from family	*We all miss you in every moment of our life & cherish your memories.*	
Names of persons giving advertisement and relationship with deceased	*Remembered by* *Inderjeet Singh, Jagjeet Singh* *Transport Group of Companies*	

Solved Examples

1. Draft a suitable advertisement in 50 words announcing the death of your uncle to be published in a newspaper in the 'Obituary' column.

Ans.

OBITUARY

With profound grief and sorrow we regret to inform the untimely demise of our beloved uncle Mr. Harinder Prakash on 7th June, 20XX. The Uthala/ Chautha ceremony for the departed soul will be held on 11th June, 20XX at Arya Samaj Mandir, Usha Nagar, Delhi from 3 pm to 5 pm.

Grief stricken: Family and friends of deceased

2. Draft an advertisement in 50 words announcing the death of your childhood friend Shweta to be published in the 'Obituary' column.

Ans.

IN LOVING MEMORY OF SHWETA

We mourn the passing of our beloved childhood friend, Shweta who left us on 05/04/20XX. Her kindness, laughter and cherished memories will forever remain in our hearts.

A memorial service will be held on 09/04/20XX at 198, JL Villa, Gandhinagar.

Rest in peace, dear friend. You will be missed.

Type 9 Appeal

Details Required

- *Give heading 'Appeal' or 'Help Required' (optional)*
- *Reason for appeal*
- *Specify the help required*
- *Contact address and phone number*
- *Specify the nature of the appeal*
- *Give brief description of the problem/ issue*
- *Donations to be sent where / to whom, if required*
- *Inserted by (name / designation)*

Format of Appeal

APPEAL FOR IDENTIFICATION — Heading

General public is hereby informed that unidentified dead body of a male Age : about 30 years, — Nature of and reason of appeal

Brief description — Height : **5'8"**, Complexion: wheatish, Build: Strong
Identification: **BBD tatto on right forearm**, Wearing: **Blue colour T-Shirt & grey colour pant** has been found on road side near flyover, Dilshad Garden Metro Station, Delhi.

Any person having any information or clue about this dead body may kindly inform the following.

Inserted by — **INSPECTOR**

Contact details — Dilshad Garden Metro Station, Delhi
Phone : 011-2929346XX

Photo

Solved Examples

1. The Delhi Police have recovered the body of a young boy from an old, dilapidated office building near Nehru Place, New Delhi. They have no proof of the victim's identity. The police want to issue an advertisement in the local newspaper asking for identification. Draft an advertisement in 50 words.

Ans.

APPEAL FOR IDENTIFICATION

General public is hereby informed that an unidentified dead body of a young boy, Age 14 to 16 years, height 5'3", round face, wheatish complexion, thin built, wearing navy blue t-shirt and black colour pants has been found from an old, dilapidated office building near Nehru Place, New Delhi. Victim bore injury marks on forehead and arms. Any person having any clue about the deceased may kindly inform SHO, Nehru Place Police Station.
Tel. 011-210121XX.

2. Draft an appeal in 50 words to be published in a newspaper, inviting suitable donors to offer a kidney to save the life of a young man whose kidneys are damaged beyond repair.

Ans.

APPEAL

Help required for a handsome, promising young man, blood group B, lying on death bed in AIIMS, New Delhi. Both his kidneys are damaged beyond repair. You can save his life and earn the gratitude of his family by donating one of your kidneys. Donors please contact the Director of the Institute.
Phone 98110-373XX.

Type 10 Educational

Details Required

- *Give heading*
- *Name of the institution*
- *Courses offered, duration*
- *Eligibility criteria*
- *Facilities*
- *Fee structure (optional)*
- *Job prospects after completion/ placement facilities/ features of training*
- *Incentive and discount offered*
- *Last date for registration*
- *Contact address/ e-mail/ website/ phone number*

Format of Educational

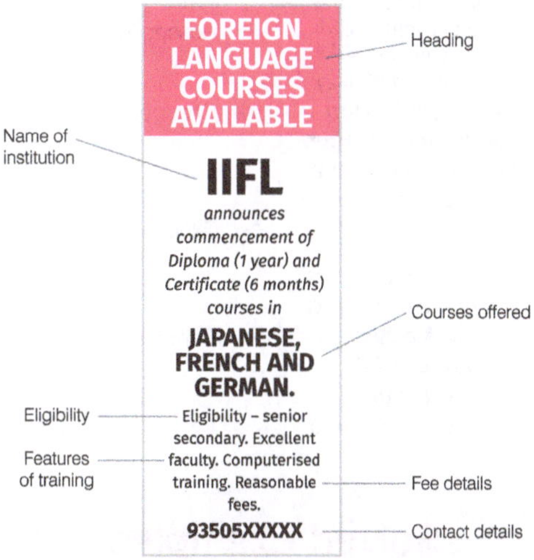

Solved Examples

1. You want to launch a tuition center from Class X to XII. Draft a classified advertisement with all relevant details.

Ans.

TUITION

Available online/Skype/ home based tutor for all the subjects for Classes X to XII CBSE/ ICSE. One to one personalised coaching with special emphasis on concept formation, higher order thinking, application and problem solving. Regular tests and feedback. Hourly classes -three days a week. Affordable fee. For bright future, register now. Visit careerwise.com or call toll free number-1800-256-XXXX24X7 from anywhere in India.

2. Draft a classified advertisement in 50 words for your institution which is accredited for running 'O' Level Courses. Give details of minimum qualification, fees, etc.

Ans.

DOEACC 'O' LEVEL COMPUTER COURSE AVAILABLE

Sarvodaya Computer Institute runs 1-year Foundation Level Course in Computer Applications equivalent to DOEACC 'O' Level. Our Accreditation No is O14XX. Minimum eligibility as per DOEACC norms. Fees reasonable & payable in installments. For other details, contact Reception Phone 011– 2829XXXX or Malay Saran on Phone 92106XXXXX.

Type 11 Change of Information

Details Required

- *Heading*
- *Father's name/ Husband's name (if applicable)*
- *Reason for change*
- *Present name/ address/ other information*
- *Changed Name/ address/ other information*
- *Calling attention of the public, relatives and friends*

Format of Change of Information

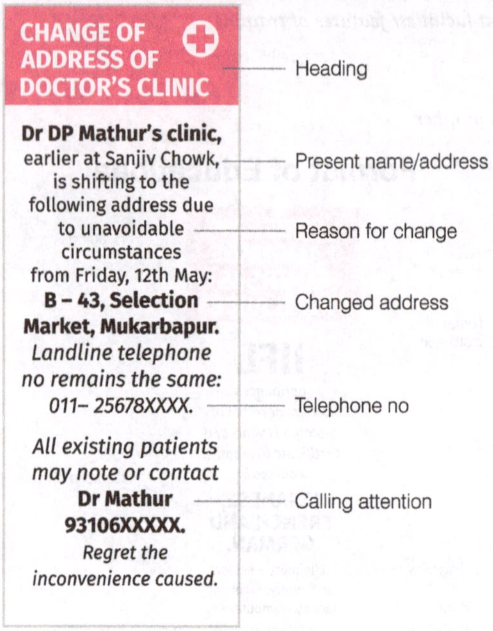

Solved Examples

1. You, as Vasu Sharma, need to change your name and address due to your marriage. Draft an advertisement in 50 words to declare the change.

Ans.

CHANGE OF NAME
I, Vasu Sharma, daughter of Ramkishan Sharma resident of 31, Park Avenue, 63 Street, Kolkata, hereby declare that I have changed my name to Vasu Arora after my marriage to Vineet Arora, son of Pankaj Arora of House No. 211, Karol Bagh, New Delhi. All concerned are requested to note and to address me by my new name.

2. Draft a classified advertisement in 50 words for your company, Shraddha Distributors, which has shifted their administrative office. You are Jagdish Sareen, MD of the company.

Ans.

CHANGE OF OFFICE ADDRESS
Shraddha Distributors, a distributor for Kolkata biscuits Ltd, has shifted its administrative office from First floor, 43, Park Road to Ground Floor, 75A, Park Road wef 23rd June, 20XX. Our Telephone No. remains the same 033 – 2624XXXX. All dealers are requested to note. Jagdish Sareen, Managing Director, Shraddha Distributors.

ADVERTISEMENTS FOR PRACTICE

1. AK International School is looking for a receptionist for the school. Write an advertisement in 50 words on behalf of the Administrative Officer in the classified columns of the local newspaper giving necessary details.

Ans.

SITUATION VACANT

Wanted a friendly and organised receptionist. Responsibilities include greeting visitors, handling phone calls, and assisting with administrative tasks.
Requirements: excellent communication skills and proficiency in MS Office. Salary negotiable.
Interested candidates should send their resume to admin@akinternationalschool.com by 10th March, 20XX.
Tel. No. 011-2586XXX

2. Santa Public School in Delhi requires cricket and hockey coaches. Draft a suitable advertisement in 50 words for the 'Situations Vacant' column of the 'Daily Herald', stating your requirements regarding age, qualification, experience, etc. You are the Principal of the school.

Ans.

SITUATION VACANT

Santa Public School, Delhi is seeking experienced Cricket and Hockey Coaches. Applicants should be 25-40 years old with a degree in Physical Education or Sports Science. Minimum 3 years of coaching experience required. Strong leadership and communication skills essential.
Send your resume to principal@santapublicschool.com by 23rd November, 20XX.

3. You are Krishna/Tisha, Secretary, Greenland Enterprises Enterprises Ltd, Delhi-110006. Draft an advertisement in 50 words to be published in a local daily under the classified columns for the vacant posts of one accountant and two office assistants. **Competency Based**

Ans.

SITUATION VACANT

One accountant and two office assistants required for a renowned firm. Minimum qualification: Bachelor's degree in Commerce and work experience of atleast one year. Remuneration—best in the industry. Interested candidates can send their CVs by courier/speed post to Greenland Enterprises Ltd, 4436/16, Daryaganj, Delhi-110006.
Contact Krishna, Secretary, Mobile No. 98111XXXXX

4. Maria Agnes, House No. 196, Mapusa, Goa, wishes to sell her house as she is migrating to USA. Draft an advertisement in 50 words for her to be published in the 'For Sale/Property' section of a daily newspaper.

Ans.

HOUSE FOR SALE

A House located at House No. 196, Mapusa is available for sale. Ideal for families, this spacious property features 3 bedrooms, a garden, and convenient amenities. Reasonable price. Selling due to migration to the USA.
Interested buyers, please contact Maria Agnes at 89765XXXXX.

5. You wish to open a showroom for 'Adidas' and are looking for a suitable place to purchase. Draft an advertisement in 50 words for it to be published in 'The Tribune', New Delhi, under classified columns, giving all relevant details.

Competency Based

Ans.

WANTED: SHOWROOM SPACE FOR ADIDAS

Looking to purchase a showroom space for Adidas in a high-traffic area of New Delhi. Minimum 1,000 sq. ft. preferred with good visibility and access. Immediate purchase ready!
Interested property owners, please contact 011-2516XXX for further details.

6. You wish to buy a second-hand owner driven car in good condition. Draft an advertisement in 50 words for the same in 'The Indian Express' under the classified column, giving your preferences.

Competency Based

Ans.

REQUIRED SMALL CAR

Required a second-hand owner driven small car in good condition. Preferred makes Maruti/ Hyundai/ Ford. Must be Delhi registered. Contact with best price, Alok Mohapatra, Flat 304, SKS Society, Sector 29, Gurgaon.
Phone 098123XXXXX

7. You are Mayank. You are leaving for Germany to pursue an engineering course and so you wish to sell your high definition motion gaming console with built-in 85 exciting real action wireless games. Draft a suitable advertisement in 50 words for publication in 'Hindustan Times' advertising the sale of the gaming system, giving features and relevant details.

Competency Based

Ans.

FOR SALE: HIGH-DEFINITION MOTION GAMING CONSOLE ??

Selling a gaming console with 85 exciting real-action wireless games due to a move to Germany.

Features

- High-definition graphics
- Motion sensor technology
- Includes all original accessories

Price: ₹15,000 (negotiable).

Contact: 95826XXXXX for further details.

Don't miss out!

8. You are the Regional Manager of Lakshmi Bank, Mumbai. As your bank is introducing a 24-hours banking facility for its customers, some ATM machines are being installed in certain localities. Draft an advertisement in 50 words to be published in the classified columns of a newspaper for suitable premises on rent to be used as ATM centres for the company.

Competency Based

Ans.

WANTED

Lakshmi Bank, Mumbai is seeking suitable premises on rent for 24-hour ATM installations.

Ideal locations: high footfall areas, shopping complexes, or near residential communities.

Minimum space required: 100 sq. ft.

Contact: 0XX-2536XXXX for further details and proposals.

9. You own a commercial flat suitable for an office/ bank. You wish to rent it out. Draft an advertisement in 50 words to be published in 'The Times of India', (New Delhi) under the classified columns.

Ans.

TO LET

Spacious commercial flat available for rent, ideal for offices or banks. Located in Bangalore. Area: 1,200 sq. ft. Amenities: 24/7 security, ample parking, and easy access to public transport.

Contact: 0XX-526XXXX for inquiries and viewing.

10. You are Advocate TL Gupta. You are looking for an independent shop in Gurgaon on a reasonable rent for your office. Draft a suitable advertisement in 50 words to be published in a local newspaper.

Ans.

REQUIRED SHOP ON RENT

Independent shop required in Gurgaon main road for lawyer's office, reasonable rent. Contact TL Gupta on 098765XXXXX or e-mail details on tig456@gmail.com.

11. You had visited the International Trade Fair that was very crowded and your 6-year-old son got lost in the crowd. He has been missing since then. Draft an advertisement in 50 words to be published in the newspaper.

Ans.

MISSING

BOY MISSING! Divesh Sharma, 6 years, 3'4" tall, fair, slim built, wearing a blue t-shirt and jeans went missing at the International Trade Fair.

If you have any information, please contact us immediately at 8965XXXXXX.

12. Shivangi Mittal has lost her original school certificates while travelling on the Delhi Metro from Vishvidyalaya to Green Park. Draft an advertisement in 50 words to be published in the 'Lost and Found' column of a national daily. **Competency Based**

Ans.

LOST

Original school certificates including Class 10th Marksheet, Transfer Certificate and Class 12th Marksheet was lost while traveling on the Delhi Metro from Vishwavidyalaya to Green Park.

If found, please contact Shivangi Mittal at 95865XXXXX.

Suitable reward promised.

13. While travelling in a bus you found some certificates, a wallet and some jewellery in a bag. You found no contact details of the owner in the bag. Draft an advertisement to be published in a local newspaper.

Ans.

LOST AND FOUND

Found a bag with some certificates, a wallet and some jewellery items on 21st Jan. in Central Park, Rohini. Whosoever has lost it may claim the same by providing authentic proof of ownership. In case of no claim within a week, the bag will be submitted to Mayapuri police station. Contact: Sanchay at 9999XXXXXX.

14. You have found a book in the name of Sakshi Thakur lying on a table in a coffee shop. Draft a suitable advertisement in 50 words to be published in the 'Lost and Found' column of a national daily.

Ans.

FOUND

A book titled 'The Fellowship of the Ring' by J. R. R. Tolkien was found lying on a table in Third Wave Boosters Coffee Café. It belongs to Sakshi Thakur.

If this is yours, please contact 9335XXXXXX to claim it.

15. You are the General Manager of Dream Travels. Draft a suitable advertisement in 50 words for the classified columns because the holiday season is approaching and lots of people will like to go on guided tours. **Competency Based**

Ans.

EXPLORE WITH DREAM TRAVELS!

The holiday season is here! Join our exciting guided tours to breathtaking destinations. Choose from various family packages, adventure trips and cultural experiences. Book now for exclusive discounts and early bird offers.
Contact us at 011-2536XXXX or visit www.dreamtravels.in.
Make unforgettable memories this season!

16. You are the proprietor of Happy Travels and have organised a 20 day tour of Europe for ₹ 2,10,000 inclusive of two meals a day. Draft an advertisement in 50 words to be published in a national daily.

Ans.

EXPLORE EUROPE WITH HAPPY TRAVELS!

Join our 20-day unforgettable tour of Europe for just ₹ 2,10,000! Enjoy two meals a day while visiting iconic landmarks, rich cultures and stunning landscapes. Limited spots available!
Contact us at 9858XXXXXX or visit www.happytravels.com to book your adventure today!
Don't miss out!

17. First Flight Travels, Shop No. 62, Upper Basement, Pacific Mall, Subhash Nagar, New Delhi offers its patrons cheapest air tickets for any destination by an airline on booking two months in advance. Draft a suitable advertisement in 50 words.

Ans.

FLY SMART WITH FIRST FLIGHT TRAVELS!

Book your air tickets at unbeatable prices!
Visit us at Shop No. 62, Upper Basement, Pacific Mall, Subhash Nagar, New Delhi. Enjoy the cheapest fares to any destination when you book two months in advance.
Contact us at 011-2395XXXX for more details!

18. A 26-year-old highly qualified software engineer seeks suitable alliance with an educated bride. Draft a suitable matrimonial advertisement in 50 words for a match for him to be published in the classified columns of a newspaper.

Ans.

BRIDE WANTED

26-year-old highly qualified software engineer seeks an educated bride. Based in Noida, he values family, ambition and shared interests. Looking for a partner with a positive outlook and strong values.
Interested families may contact 89532XXXXX or email at xyz555@gmail.com.

19. Draft a matrimonial advertisement in 50 words on behalf of your neighbour who is seeking a suitable match for his physically handicapped daughter. **Competency Based**

Ans.

GROOM WANTED

Seeking a suitable match for our daughter, a kind and resilient physically handicapped girl, aged 28 years. She is well-educated and values family and compassion. Looking for a caring and understanding partner.
Interested families may contact 89537XXXXX.

20. You are Raj Kumar, a divorcee aged 55 years, residing in Dubai as an NRI and want to return to India. Draft a suitable advertisement in 50 words for a match for you in 'The Times of India' under the classified column. **Competency Based**

Ans.

BRIDE WANTED

NRI Divorcee, 55. Hindu, good looking, slim, wheatish complexion, well settled businessman, planning to settle in India, internationally travelled, Caste no bar.
Contact: rajkumar51@hotmail.com

21. Your five year old nephew was abducted while playing in the society compound. His abduction resulted in his untimely death. Draft an advertisement in 50 words expressing your profound grief and sorrow.

Ans.

OBITUARY

With profound grief, we announce the tragic loss of our dear nephew, Akshay who was taken from us far too soon. His joyful spirit and laughter will forever be in our hearts.

We seek justice and remember him with love.

Rest in peace, sweet boy.

22. After fighting against cervical cancer for the last two years, your neighbour's wife passed away yesterday. Draft a classified advertisement in 50 words to be published under 'Obituary' column of the newspaper.

Ans.

IN LOVING MEMORY OF SAMIKSHA GUPTA

We mourn the passing of our beloved neighbour, Samiksha Gupta who bravely fought cervical cancer for two years. She left us on 22/02/20XX. Her strength, kindness and spirit will be deeply missed.

A memorial service will be held on 26/02/20XX at Bhole Baba Mandir, Umeshnagar.

Rest in peace.

23. SKY is the main activity centre of a charitable trust 'Foundation for Spastic and Mentally Handicapped Persons'. It helps and guides parents/ guardians of children with special needs. It tries to improve the quality of life of disabled children wherever possible. Draft an appeal in 50 words to be published in a newspaper on their behalf asking for donations to their cause. **Competency Based**

Ans.

APPEAL FOR DONATIONS

SKY, a project of the Foundation for Spastic and Mentally Handicapped Persons, seeks your generous donations to enhance the quality of life for children with special needs. Your contributions will help provide essential resources and support for their families.

Together, we can make a difference! Thank you!

Contact: 8953XXXXXX for further details.

24. You are Rajan/Rajat, residing at 30A, Munirka. Your friend had to undergo an operation for which he needs rupees two laks. Some generous people have donated some money but that is not sufficient. Draft an appeal which will be published in a local daily to generate money for the operation. Do not exceed 50 words.

Ans.

APPEAL

DONATE GENEROUSLY TO SAVE A PRECIOUS LIFE

It is earnestly appealed to kind people of the society that one Mr. Sunderram aged 35, father of two small kids is on his last legs since he cannot afford money amounting Rs. Two lakhs for his heart transplantation/kidney failure. Some donors have contributed but the amount is quite insufficient Please help by sending a part of your hard-earned money immediately at the following address:

Medical Superintendent

ESCORT HOSPITAL

25. Thalassemia is a disorder caused by the weakening and destruction of red blood cells. The body requires monthly transfusion of blood in people having this disorder. Draft an advertisement in 50 words appealing to the general public to come forward and donate blood to help such people.

Ans.

DONATE BLOOD, SAVE LIVES!

Thalassemia affects many individuals who require monthly blood transfusions for survival. Your donation can make a vital difference in their lives. We urge the community to come forward and donate blood.

Together, let's bring hope and health to those in need.

Contact: 9572XXXXXX for details.

26. You have recently started a coaching centre for yoga at Rajaji Nagar, Bengaluru. Draft an advertisement in 50 words to be published under the classified columns of 'The Deccan Herald'.

Ans.

JOIN OUR YOGA COACHING CENTRE!

Discover the benefits of yoga at our newly opened coaching centre in Rajaji Nagar, Bengaluru. Classes for all levels, led by certified instructors. Improve flexibility, strength and mindfulness.

Enrol now for a free trial class!

Contact: 0XX-2953XXXX or visit www.yogaccac.com.

Transform your health today!

27. Draft a classified advertisement in 50 words announcing crash courses for the preparation of IELTS and TOEFL.

Ans.

EDUCATIONAL

Era Institute offers crash courses for the preparation of IELTS and TOEFL. High scores guaranteed. Highly trained and experienced faculty. Small batches of 10 students. Scholarships available. Completely air conditioned and wi-fi enabled campus. Fees - INR 7999. Last date: 6th June 20XX.

Contact: Era Institute Phone 011-727472XX

28. You have been asked to draft a classified advertisement in 50 words offering cookery classes for various age groups. Also provide details regarding cuisine, total cost, duration, etc.

Ans.

JOIN OUR COOKERY CLASSES!

Learn to cook a variety of cuisines including Indian, Italian and Chinese for all age groups.

- Duration: 4 weeks (2 classes/week).
- Total cost: ₹ 4,000, including all materials.
- Classes held at CookIt, Anant Nagar, Gujrat

Register now to secure your spot!

Contact: 0XX-2956XXXX

29. You wish to get your family name added to your particulars on your passport after getting married for which you need to get a public notice published in a newspaper. Draft a suitable advertisement in 50 words declaring the change of your name.

Ans.

CHANGE OF NAME

I, Kritika Gupta, residing at 158, Saket, Kolkata hereby declare my intention to add my family name, Sahni, to my passport following my marriage.

I shall be henceforth known as Kritika Gupta Sahni for all purposes.

Thank you!

30. You have changed your name from 'Kulwant Singh Talwandi' to 'Kulwant Talwandi' through an affidavit. Inform the general public about the changed name by drafting a classified advertisement in 50 words to be published in a local newspaper.

Ans.

CHANGE OF NAME

I, Kulwant Singh Talwandi s/o Jagir Singh Talwandi, have changed my name to Kulwant Talwandi by affidavit sworn before the Notary Public, Janakpuri, New Delhi on 24th May, 20XX. Henceforth, I shall be known as Kulwant Talwandi for all purposes.

SELF ASSESSMENT TEST

1. You are HR Manager of Elephenta Software Services. You require software engineers familiar with ERP Software Oracle with minimum 5 years' experience. Draft a suitable classified newspaper advertisement in 50 words for the same.
2. You want to purchase a 400 sq m or larger plot in Gomti Nagar, Lucknow, for building a bungalow. Draft a classified advertisement in 50 words to be published in a local daily giving your requirements.
3. You are interested in selling your Maruti Eeco Van which has run 10,000 km and is 3 years old. Draft a suitable classified advertisement in 50 words to be published in the 'Vehicle for Sale' column of a local newspaper giving all details.
4. You have changed your job and are leaving the city. You want to sell all your furniture, refrigerator, car, air conditioner, etc., before moving. Draft a suitable classified advertisement in 50 words to be published in a local newspaper for the same.
5. Your company, Sarvan Constructions Ltd, requires large flats on rent in Metro cities to serve as guest houses for your touring staff. The flats should preferably be furnished. As Administrative Manager of your company, draft a suitable classified advertisement in 50 words to be published in newspapers in Metro cities.
6. Your pet dog, a black Pomeranian answering to the name 'Pommy', has been lost outside the compound of your housing society and is not traceable for the last 3 days. Draft a suitable classified advertisement in 50 words to be published in a local newspaper, offering a reward. **Competency Based**
7. You have changed your surname due to getting remarried after being widowed. Inform all concerned by drafting a suitable classified advertisement in 50 words to be published in the 'Change of Name' column of a local newspaper. You are Parul Shreshtha (new name). **Competency Based**
8. You have lost your wallet containing a large amount of cash and some identification documents while travelling in a bus from Lucknow to Etawah. Draft a classified advertisement in 50 words to be published in the 'Lost & Found' columns of The 'Times of India', Lucknow edition, offering a reward for its recovery.
9. You are the proprietor of Anil Tours, a travel agency specialising in pilgrimages. Design a suitable classified advertisement in 50 words to be published in the 'Tours & Travel' columns of a local newspaper. Give some details of the packages offered.
10. Draft a matrimonial advertisement in 50 words to be published in the classified advertisement section of newspapers for the marriage of your sister. State her age, height, weight, qualifications and any other features you feel should be mentioned. Specify what you are looking for as the ideal husband for her.
11. Draft an Obituary notice in 50 words to be published in the classified columns of a local newspaper for your father who died yesterday. Give details of the last rites ceremonies proposed.
12. Issue an appeal in 50 words for organ donation to be published in the classified columns of a local newspaper on behalf of the NGO 'Society for Helping the Poor'. Specify that all organs donated will be used for helping only the weaker sections of society.
13. Your institution is running coaching classes for candidates attempting the NEET examination. Draft an advertisement in 50 words to be published in the classified advertisement section of newspaper giving the various courses offered.
14. You are the Creative Director of an advertising agency. Draft an attractive commercial advertisement in 50 words on behalf of Safal Vajradanti Toothpaste giving a visual and stating the advantages that this brand has over others. **Competency Based**
15. Draft a commercial advertisement in 50 words for advertising the feature film 'Antony ki Arpita' featuring famous stars. Give a visual and at least 3 attractive features of the film.

02
CHAPTER

Posters

A poster is essentially a type of advertisement to make people aware about a social issues or an event. Prepared while keeping a specific audience in mind, a poster is a captivating, attractive and persuasive means of communication for a larger audience.

Marking Scheme

Format	1 Mark
Content	2 Marks
Expression	1 Mark
(Accuracy of Spelling and Grammar)	

Points to be Kept in Mind

- A poster is designed to be put up at a public place so it should be designed in such a way that it **catches the attention** of the passers by.
- A poster should have **big/ bold/ capital letters** because it is read by people from a distance.
- A poster should not have any **extra** or **irrelevant matter**.
- A poster can be made more catchy by using **phrases, slogans** and **attractive language.**
- A poster should always be put in a rectangular box.

Format of a Poster

Cyber bullying can affect people's mental health. As the Head Girl of your school, prepare a poster in not more than 50 words to make your fellow students aware of its harms. **Competency Based**

→ Catchy Title

Cyber bullying is
- Intentionally hurting someone's feelings using information and communication technology.
- It can lead to anxiety, depression and low self-esteem.
- Victims often feel isolated and powerless.

Slogan ← **STOP CYBER BULLYING : STAND TOGETHER**

!!!Stop Being Mean on the Screen!!!

✓ LOG OFF the site where the bullying is happening.
✓ BLOCK any messages or e-mails.
✓ SAVE the message or e-mail.
✓ TELL an adult.

STOP BULLYING

Details about the subject

POSTERS FOR PRACTICE

1. You are Vinayak/Revati from the Green School, Thoothukudi. You read an article about the proposed garbage segregation programme in the neighbourhood, which is set to begin from next week. You decide to make a poster telling your neighbourhood about the programme and the value of garbage segregation. Draft a poster in 50 words to be put in your neighbourhood.

Ans.

Garbage Segregation Drive on 5th November 20XX,
11:30 a.m. onwards at District Park, Near XYZ

Recycle More, Pollute Less

You can easily recycle 75% of all your waste. Place your waste in the correct bin to increase recycling, support a social cause and protect the environment.

Segregating Waste at Source

Increases ▲	**Reduces ▼**
Recycling	Pollution
Composting	Litter
Resource recovery	Toxic landfills
Environmental sustainability	Costs
Support for a social cause	Diseases

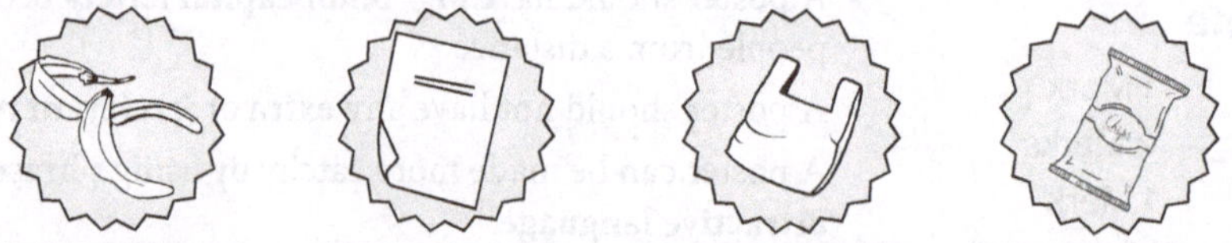

Organic
Left over food, Fruit peels, Leaves & twigs, Floor sweepings, Flowers, Soil & sand and Hair

Paper
White paper, Notebooks & covers, Small pieces of papers, Newspapers, Coloured papers, Cardboard, Chart paper, Tetra pack, Paper cups

Plastic
Plastic bags, Juice, Soft drinks & water bottles, Milk packets, Pens & refills, Scales, Glue stick & bottles, Paint pallets & bowls, Broken sharpners, Broken dusters.

Mixed
Dirty or wet waste, Food packaging, Sweet chocolate & biscuit wrappers, Pencil shavings. Erasers, Crayons, Thermocol, Broken shoes & slippers, Cloth.

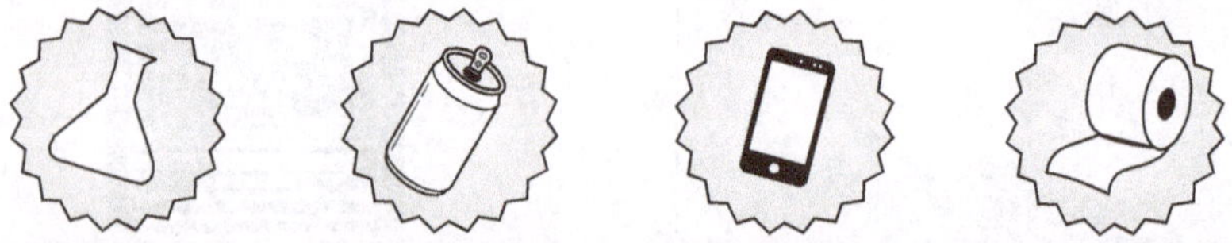

Glass
Glass jars, Dettol bottles, Pipettes, Test tubes, Lab bottles, Drinking glasses, Ink bottles.

Metal
Aluminium foil cans, Paper clips, Thumb tasks, Metal bottles, Caps, Metal accessories, broken hole punchers, Broken staplers

E-waste
Printer cartridges, Mouse, Computer monitors, Laptops, Mobile phones.

Sanitary
Used tissue papers, Soiled toilet papers, Sanitary pads, Diapers

2. An anti-alcohol campaign will be organised in your college next week. Prepare a poster in not more than 50 words for the same.

Ans.

SAY NO TO ALCOHOL
SAY IT NOW!

Addiction leads to:

- Ruined Health
- Ruined Family Life
- Ruined Self
- Finally....painful death

Join De-addication Camp Today.......!

Regain health Control and happiness

3. Incidents of road-rage are increasing day by day. Draft a poster in 50 words on behalf of Delhi Traffic Police providing Road Safety Tips.

Ans.

PRESCRIPTION

from Delhi Traffic Police

- ✓ Always drive in your lane.
- ✓ Never jump a traffic signal.
- ✓ Never exceed the prescribed speed limit.
- ✓ Never drive after drinking.
- ✓ Park only at authorised parking space.
- ✓ Never use mobile while driving.

REMEMBER !
ROAD SAFETY IS NO JOKE
Follow safety tips, enjoy safe driving

Delhi Traffic Police wishes you safe and accident free driving on the roads

TRAFFIC POLICE DELHI
We Want You Safe

DELHI TRAFFIC POLICE

Call 24 Hours Traffic Helpline at 23378XX Fax 26190XX
e-mail : dcpdlh@satyam.net.in
Website : www.delhipolice.nic.in, www.delhitrafficpolice.nic.in

4. You are a professional poster designer who has been asked to design a poster for recruitment of soldiers in the Indian Army, to be put up at prominent places in a district where a recruitment camp is to be held. Draft a poster in not more than 50 words giving details of the recruitment camp. **Competency Based**

Ans.

JOIN INDIAN ARMY

Where Life is a Passion

Join the Indian Army and be the man among men!
Recruitment Camp at Rajputana Rifles Headquarters, Kota
Cantt on 24th July, 20XX from 8 a.m.
Issued by : Indian Army

5. Fireworks and crackers are known to create pollution during festivals. As an environmentalist, design a poster in about 50 words to create awareness of their ill effects.

Ans.

SAY NO TO CRACKERS

DEEPAWALI IS A FESTIVAL OF LIGHTS AND ELATION

LETS'S NOT MAKE IT A FESTIVAL OF POLLUTION

- CAUSE EXTREME NOISE POLLUTION
- CAN SCARE ANIMALS
- MAY CAUSE FIRE ACCIDENTS
- CAUSE AIR POLLUTION
- ARE DETRIMENTAL TO HEALTH IN MANY WAYS

Let's not damage our mother nature with the toxic smoke of crackers.
LET THERE BE NO CRACKERS AND ONLY LIGHT ON DIWALI NIGHT

6. You are the Secretary of your colony. Design a poster in not more than 50 words for the 'Cleanliness Drive' being organised by the colony.

Ans.

Cleanliness Begins at Home

Let's Make Our Colony a Clean and Neat Place to Live; Join us for a

CLEANLINESS DRIVE

on 1st March, 20XX
Assemble at Japanese Park, Rohini, Sector 11 at 10:00 a.m.

We pledge to –

- Remove Filth
- Plant More Trees
- Put More Dustbins on the Roads

7. Draft an attractive poster in not more than 50 words for 'Save Trees, Save Earth' Campaign.

Ans.

Let's Bequeath

A greener environment to our future generation!

It takes 10-15 years for a tree to fully mature...

& Less than an hour to cut it down!!

Let's Save Trees & Save Earth

- Saving trees will save lives
- Plant more & more trees

More than 7 Billion lives!
Our Earth Save it for Posterity
Issued by Green Earth Foundation, New Delh.

8. You are Secretary, Social Service League of your school. Design a poster in not more than 50 words to be displayed in your colony and in a local hospital premises inspiring people to make a pledge to donate eyes and other organs of their bodies.

Competency Based

Ans.

Donate Organs, Donate Life

Organ Donation Camp
on 23rd April, 20XX at Anand Hospital

Benefits of Organ Donation

- It saves a life of an ailing person
- A great opportunity to help others
- One organ donor can save upto 8 lives
- A rewarding and positive experience

Issued by Social Service League XYZ School
For further details, Contact Anand Hospital

SELF ASSESSMENT TEST

1. Repeated floods in various flood-prone areas in India have resulted in unprecedented damage and destruction to both life and property. Educating people on the need for donations, prepare a poster in not more than 50 words.
2. Design a poster in not more than 50 words to highlight the correct way of e-waste disposal. **Competency Based**
3. Design a poster in not more than 50 words for your school library on the value of books and good reading habits. You may use slogans.
4. Design a poster in not more than 50 words on 'World Health Day'. Mention benefits of physical activities.
5. Prepare a thought-provoking poster in not more than 50 words on the topic 'Stop Child Abuse'. Use catchy slogans and visuals.
6. A women's safety week is being organised by Delhi Police to create awareness among women about the ways to stay safe and details of the helpline numbers are available for them to seek help in case of an emergency. Design a poster for the event. **Competency Based**
7. You are making an effort to spread the message of Communal Harmony. Design an attractive poster in not more than 50 words to be displayed in the school campus. **Competency Based**
8. Department of Science and Technology, Government of India is organising a science exhibition in your school. Design an attractive poster in not more than 50 words announcing the event and inviting the general public to visit it.
9. Design a poster in not more than 50 words emphasising the ill effects of binging on fast food.
10. Design a poster in not more than 50 words urging people to adopt a pet. **Competency Based**
11. You are Gaurav, the Secretary of the Science Club of Avinash Public School, Rewari. Your school is organising an Exhibition on the cultural variety of India. Draft a poster in not more than 50 words to bring awareness among the school students about the importance of culture.
12. Design a poster in not more than 50 words on 'Clean Yamuna Campaign'.
13. You are the Publicity Manager of ABC TV Channel. Your channel is organising a 'Talent Hunt Show' of college students to be telecast on your channel. Design a suitable poster in not more than 50 words giving necessary details.
14. Draft a poster in not more than 50 words on behalf of the local police advising the public to be wary of pickpockets in buses and bag snatchers on the roads. Suggest the precautions to be taken.
15. Draft a poster in not more than 50 words for announcing the Annual Fete of your school, asking for participation of groups of students interested. Invent the necessary details.

03 CHAPTER

Very Long Compositions

A speech is an effective way of communicating a message to a large audience. It is one of the ways of spreading awareness regarding social issues or giving information regarding other important issues.

As a form of writing, a speech is similar to an article except that it begins with a formal address to the audience, is more conversational in tone and concludes with a 'Thank you'.

Marking Scheme

Format 1 Mark
Proper Address to the audience

Organisation of Ideas 1 Mark
(Coherence and relevance of ideas and style)

Content 2 Marks
(Introduction causes, effects and suggestions)

Expression 1 Mark
(Accuracy of spelling and grammar)

Speech

Components of a Speech

Introduction It begins with greeting the chief guest/principal/teachers and other listeners. It may include a striking statement, short anecdote, a saying or anything else which will immediately make the audience interested. Then, the topic of the speech is announced along with the occasion, if required.

Elaboration of the topic It will include a sequence of ideas to build up to the summing up and conclusion. You may include examples, evidence or data to support the ideas. You can paint verbal pictures and dramatise or personalise the information.

Summing up Summarise the most important points in your speech but do not repeat them.

Conclusion Depending on the purpose of your speech, conclude with a call for an action, an appeal, a warning, a request and an expression of thanks.

Points to be Kept in Mind

- A speech should begin with a **catchy introduction** in the form of an **anecdote, quotation, statistical data** or a **thought provoking question.**
- A speech must reflect the **speaker's clarity of thought, accuracy of facts** and **a balanced view** through a comparison and contrast with other viewpoints.
- A speech may also give reference to newspaper reports, posters, advertisements or other stimuli.
- The main part of the speech should be restricted to the word limit of **120-150 words.**

Format of a Speech

Write a speech in not more than 120-150 words on the topic 'Unity in Diversity'. Use the clues given below.

- Rich tapestry of cultures
- Diversity is our identity
- Strength in unity
- Unique perspective and experience
- Working together

Unity in Diversity

Heading or Title (optional - not to be spoken)
The title of the speech should be apt, precise and exact.

Respected Principal, honourable teachers and my dear friends. Good morning. Today, I would like to share my views on the topic 'Unity in Diversity'.

Formal address

Our world is a rich tapestry of cultures, languages and traditions. Each of us brings unique perspectives and experiences that contribute to our collective strength. In our country, diversity is not just a fact; it's our identity. It teaches us tolerance, understanding and respect for one another. Embracing our differences fosters harmony and helps break down barriers, allowing us to work together towards common goals.

In unity, we find strength. Together, we can promote inclusivity and create a society where everyone feels valued and heard. We can celebrate our uniqueness while remembering that we are all part of one human family. Whether through festivals, art, or simply sharing stories, we can build connections that transcend our differences.

Remember, our diversity is our greatest asset!

Content

Expression
- Grammar, vocabulary and spelling
- Coherence, relevance of ideas and style

Thank you!

Formal thanks to audience

PRACTICE QUESTIONS

1. Write a speech, in about 120-150 words, on the 'Importance of Education' to be delivered during your school assembly. Use the following clues.
- Foundation of our future
- Develops critical thinking
- Learn from experiences and grow as individuals
- Making positive impact on the world

Ans. Respected Principal, honourable teachers and my dear friends. Good morning. Today, I, would like to share my views on the topic 'Importance of Education'.

Education is the foundation of our future. It provides us with the knowledge and skills that we need to succeed in life. It helps us understand the world around us and make informed decisions. Education also helps us develop critical thinking skills and problem-solving abilities.

Moreover, education is not just about obtaining a degree or a certificate. It's a lifelong process that never ends. Education helps us learn from our experiences and grow as individuals. It opens doors to new opportunities and helps us achieve our dreams. It empowers us to make a positive impact on our community and the world.

I urge everyone to prioritise education in their lives. Whether it's pursuing a formal education or learning through other means, we must never stop learning. Education is the key to a brighter future and we must invest in it today to reap the benefits tomorrow.

Thank you!

2. Draft a speech in about 120-150 words on the topic 'Advantages of Nuclear Power'. Use the clues given below.
- Development of the medical sector
- Improvement in surveillance capacity
- Increased production in agricultural field
- Electrical supply

Ans. Respected Principal, worthy teachers and my dear friends. It is a matter of great privilege for me to get an opportunity to share my views on the 'Advantages of Nuclear Power'.

Atomic energy and technology possesses a vast potential to improve the quality of life. It's a gift to mankind for fulfilling many of its needs. With the advent of the technology of nuclear power, there is a commendable increase in the development of the medical sector. A complex disease like cancer, leprosy, etc. can be treated using nuclear power technology. This has saved many lives in an easy and less complex manner.

In the field of agriculture and industry, production has increased with the use of nuclear technology. It has helped this sector to progress and prosper a lot. If we talk about defence, the surveillance capacity has improved a lot with the use of this technology.

Now, we have more weapons and devices which operate on this technology. Thus, nuclear power is safeguarding the nation. In the field of basic amenities, this technology works in the form of reverse osmosis which purifies water and spares us from the bad effects of unsafe water. The most important contribution of nuclear technology is electricity. The electricity supply has increased drastically with the advent of nuclear power reactors.

In a nutshell, nuclear power has changed our lives for the better. Similarly, there are some things which need to be taken care of in this regard. It should not be used to harm life and people in wars. It should serve mankind.

Thank you!

3. Keeping good personal and public hygiene can play a crucial role in mitigating the spread of deadly viral diseases. Write a speech in 120-150 words on how it can be implemented in our personal and social lives. You are Naman/Nidhi Gupta.

Ans. Respected Principal, honourable teachers and my dear friends. Good morning.

Today, I, Naman Gupta, would like to emphasise the importance of personal and public hygiene in preventing the spread of deadly viral diseases. Maintaining good hygiene is not just a personal responsibility; it's a collective effort that benefits our entire community.

At a personal level, simple practices such as regular handwashing with soap, using hand sanitisers and wearing masks in crowded places can significantly reduce the risk of infections. It's vital to cover our mouths when coughing or sneezing and to avoid touching our faces.

On a social level, we can promote hygiene by encouraging awareness campaigns in schools and communities. Organising workshops on proper sanitation, providing accessible handwashing facilities and ensuring clean public spaces are crucial steps we can take together.

By adopting these practices in our daily lives, we not only protect ourselves but also safeguard the health of those around us.

Thank you!

4. You are Nisha/Nishant. As Secretary of the Literary Club of your school, you have been asked to deliver a speech on the importance of reading. The following histogram clearly states how irrelevant reading has become for the present generation. Taking ideas from the histogram along with your own ideas, write the speech in about 120-150 words. **Competency Based**

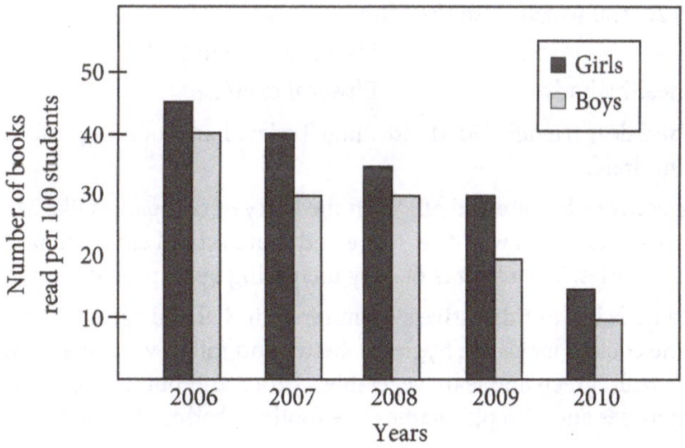

Ans. The famous writer Anthony Trollope once said, "The habit of reading is the only enjoyment in which there is no alloy; it lasts when all other pleasures fade." But sadly, today's teenagers are busy pursuing more ephemeral pleasures.

Good morning Principal, teachers and dear friends. Today, I, Nisha, Secretary of the Literary Club, stand before you to speak about the importance of reading.

Reading improves awareness, vocabulary and knowledge. Unfortunately, there has been a steady decline in reading habits. The advent of technology with television, Internet, mobile phones, I-pads, etc. and today's fast-paced life have led to a sharp decline in the reading population. Reading is crucial for an all-round development. Students who read well do better in all aspects of schooling and beyond. As the world becomes more complex, reading is increasingly important for children trying to find their place in it.

Thank you!

5. A survey was conducted by students of Sacred Heart Convent School regarding the importance of examinations. Given below are their findings. **Competency Based**

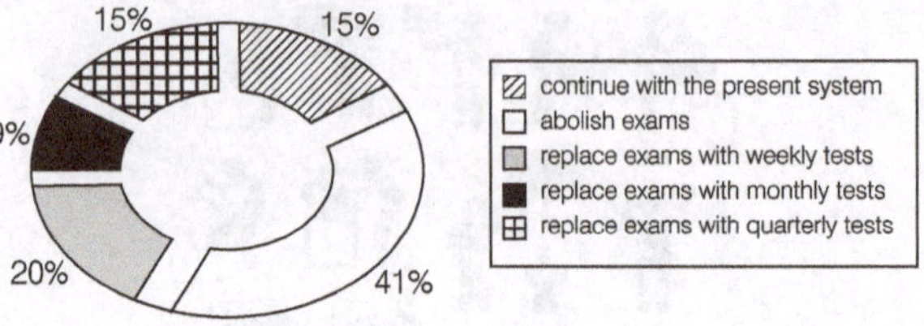

Based on the above information and your own ideas, write a speech in about 120-150 words on the topic 'Examinations Should Be Abolished'. You are Kartik/Kritika Mehra.

Ans. Respected Principal, honourable teachers and my dear friends. Good morning. Today, I, Kritika Mehra, would like to share my views on the topic 'Examinations Should Be Abolished'.

While exams have traditionally been seen as a measure of knowledge, they often create immense pressure and anxiety among students. This stress can hinder true learning and creativity. Examinations promote rote memorisation rather than critical thinking. Many students excel in understanding concepts but struggle in exam settings, leading to unjust evaluations of their abilities.

During a survey recently conducted by students of Sacred Heart Convent School, it was discovered that 20% of the students wanted to replace exams with weekly tests, 9% with monthly tests and 15% with quarterly tests. And, while 15% of the students wished to continue with the present system, 41% wanted to do away with exams completely. This evidence proves students' unhappiness with examinations.

In place of exams, what we can do is adopt continuous assessment methods that encourage a deeper understanding of subjects. Project work, presentations and group activities can provide a more holistic evaluation of a student's capabilities. Let us advocate for an educational system that values learning over testing.

Thank you!

6. You have to write a speech to be delivered in the Inter School Speech Competition on the topic 'Obesity Among School Children'. Draft a speech in 120-150 words. Use the following clues.

- Fast food chains
- Harm to human body
- Nutrients required for a healthy body
- Physical exercises

Ans. Respected Principal, teachers and dear friends. Good morning! Today, I am standing before you to express my views on the topic 'Obesity among school children'.

Obesity has become a cause of concern for one and all. With the entry of companies like McDonalds, Dominos, Pizza Huts, etc., the concept of fast food has spread like a wild fire. More and more school children have taken to chocolates and soft drinks without worrying about calories. The result is obesity increasing by leaps and bounds among school children.

'Junk food' appeals to our taste buds but our digestive system repels it. Oil and extra fat harm our liver. We put on flesh and increase our weight. Fresh home cooked meals are hygienic, better and full of vitamins. Minerals can be easily digested. Our food should consist of coarse cereals, green and leafy vegetables, fruits, and pulses, etc. To keep ourselves agile, energetic and robust, we must do physical exercises and also play games like football, badminton, kabbaddi, volleyball, etc.

By eating healthy food and doing regular physical activities, not only will our body be healthy and toned but also our minds would remain active. I hope you all will give some consideration to my suggestion and try to instill it in your daily routine.

Thank you!

7. The number of vehicles has increased in your city during the last five years, polluting the environment with poisonous emission. Many people have started complaining about problems related to lungs. Using the information given in the graph below and your own ideas, write a speech, in about 120-150 words, to be delivered on a topic 'World Environment Day'.

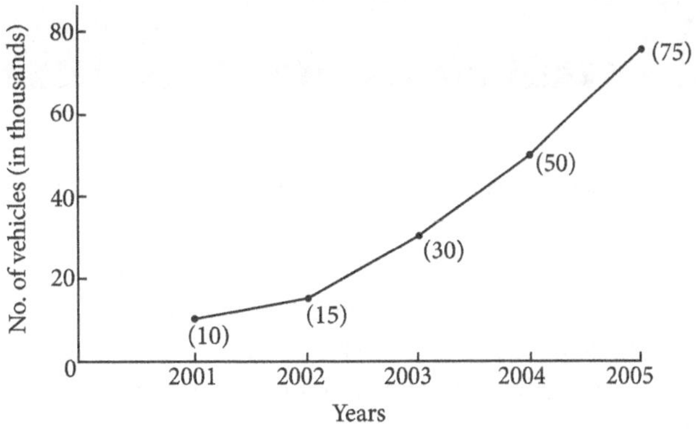

Ans. Respected Principal, honourable teachers and my dear friends. Good morning.

Today, on World Environment Day, we confront a pressing issue: the alarming increase in vehicle emissions in our city. Over the past couple of decades, the number of vehicles has surged, leading to heightened air pollution. This has dire consequences for our health with rising cases of respiratory problems among our citizens. In 2001, there were only ten thousand vehicles on the streets. This number saw an astounding increase reaching seventy-five thousand in 2005.

We must take action. It's time to promote public transport, cycling and walking in order to reduce our reliance on personal vehicles. Additionally, we should advocate for cleaner technologies and support policies that encourage electric vehicles.

Let's work together to create a cleaner, healthier environment for ourselves and future generations. Remember, every small effort counts.

Thank you!

8. The increasing amount of time spent playing indoor games has been a major cause for decreasing outdoor appearance of children. With this concern, write a speech to be delivered in the morning assembly in 120-150 words. You are Parag/Pragati. Use the following clues. **Competency Based**

- Modern gadgets
- Internet Surfing
- Indoor games make us isolated
- Outdoor games keep healthy

Ans. Respected Principal Sir, honourable teachers and my dear friends. Good morning. I am Parag of Class XI A. Today, I want to share my views on the topic 'Indoor games *vs.* Outdoor games'.

Modern gadgets like computers, gaming consoles, video games and mobile phones have made us crazy as well as lazy. In our spare time, we can be seen either surfing the internet or sending SMS on mobile phones. We have forgotten games like hide and seek, cricket and football, all of which make us physically active and alert.

Outdoor games strengthen our physique and help us to remain healthy. When we play outdoor games we grow enthusiastic, we agree and disagree and fight. We make more friends, which broadens our social circle. On one hand, when we play alone on computers, we are damaging our eyes, polluting our minds and turning into couch potatoes which is not good for our health. Outdoor games inculcate values like team work, coherency and zest for living. On the other hand, playing indoor games makes us isolated and self-centred. Considering all these, it can be said that while outdoor games carry joys in their basket, indoor games do not in any way. So, we should adopt outdoor games and come out to play them more often.

Thank you!

SELF ASSESSMENT TEST

1. The Tourism Industry in India is a fast-growing sector. Write a speech in 120-150 words on the growth of this sector. Use the following clues.

- Arrival of foreign tourists
- 'Incredible India' campaign
- Employment potential
- Multiple policies adopted

2. You have to speak on 'How to Avoid Being Cyber Bullied?' Prepare your speech to be delivered at the Inter-School Declamation contest being organised as a part of the annual cultural festival of your school. You are Darpan/Deepika. (120-150 words). Use the following clues.

Competency Based

- Be mindful
- Don't engage with negativity
- Seek support
- Treat everyone with respect

3. Write a speech to be given in the morning assembly of your school on the topic 'Evil of Casteism in Our Country' in 120-150 words.

4. You have been chosen for representing your school at the regional level Inter-School Debate Contest. Prepare a speech in 120-150 words for the same on the topic "Newspapers Ought to Contain More News and Fewer Advertisements". Use the following clues.

Competency Based

- Purpose of newspaperDiluting the credibility of news source
- Upholding journalistic integrity
- Informative content

5. In the modern fast paced urban world, more and more people are moving to countryside. Add to this the fact that homestays, farmhouses, etc. are increasingly becoming popular. Recently you have read an article about this increasing movement of urban settlers. Write a speech on the same in 120-150 words.

Competency Based

Clues

- Free from rat race
- Escape
- Focus on personal satisfaction

6. Despite rising taxes and increasing restrictions against tobacco use, there are still approximately 250 million smokers in India and the number is going up. Prepare a speech in 120-150 words on the topic 'Quit Smoking, Not Life' for a group of young smokers urging them to quit smoking.

Clues

- Rise in use of tobacco
- Harmful for both body and environment
- Multiple health problems
- Benefits of quiting smoking

7. The success of any business or consumer product in today's world depends in part on the target market's ability to distinguish one product from another. Branding helps consumers to ultimately identify a product from those of the competition. Write a speech for the morning assembly on the topic 'Brand Names Cost More But is the Quality Better'. You are Suresh/Smita. (120-150 words) Use the following clues. **Competency Based**

- Relying of marketing and reputation
- Importance of research and reviews
- Quality indicators

8. Road accidents are a common sight. Further, people are often seen shouting at and threatening the people who have annoyed them in other ways. Even overtaking them quite legally can enrage them. Write a speech on the topic 'Road Rage' in 120-150 words. Use the image given below.

9. Narcotics Control Bureau is organising a declamation contest in your school as part of its observance of International Day against Drug Abuse and Illicit Trafficking. Write a speech in 120-150 words on the topic 'Youth and Drug Abuse' by using the image given below.

10. On the occasion of National Consumer's Day, you have to speak on the topic 'Consumer Rights and their Protection'. Draft the speech in 120-150 words. Use the following clues.

- Fundamental Rights
- Integral to educate ourselves
- Enforcing laws
- Awareness and education

11. The Delhi Government has banned the use of polythene and plastic bags as they are non-biodegradable and harmful to every living being and the environment. But people are still using them for carrying things. Write a speech, to be delivered in the morning assembly, on the topic 'Say No to Polythene Bags' in 120-150 words.

12. India is a country of festivals. There is a series of festivals which are celebrated throughout the year. They reflect our culture and bring us closer. Based on the visuals given below, write a speech in 120-150 words to be delivered in your school's morning assembly on this topic. You are Kiran, Class XI A.

13. You are participating in an Inter-School Declamation contest and the topic chosen is 'Keep Your Town Clean'. Basing your ideas on the picture given below, write a speech in 120-150 words to be delivered in this contest. You are Prateek/Pragati.

14. The Internet has become essential in our life today. Some browse for many hours at a stretch everyday. However, we know that excess of anything is bad. So by doing this, they not only waste their time but spoil their health also. Write a speech to be delivered in an Inter-Class Declamation Contest in 120-150 words on the topic 'The Harms of Excessive Internet Browsing'.

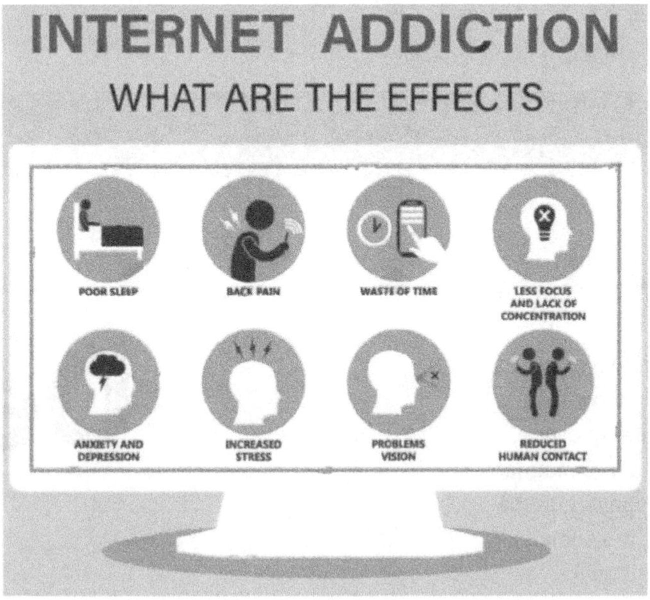

15. High buildings, the Metro train, shopping malls, big parks, wide roads etc attract people to live in metro cities. However, traffic jams, pollution, crime and insecurity disappoint them. Basing your ideas on the picture given below, write a speech in 120-150 words to be delivered in the morning assembly on the topic 'Disadvantages of Living in a Big City'.

Competency Based

04 CHAPTER

Debate

Debate is a contest between two speakers or two groups of speakers to show their skills and abilities in an argument over a topic. It is essentially a persuasive manner of speaking with the aim of converting the view of another person or of the audience, to one's own point of view. A speaker either speaks for or against the issue being discussed.

Marking Scheme

Format 1 Mark
Address to the speakers
Organisation of Ideas 1 Mark
(Coherence and relevance of ideas and style)
Content 2 Marks
(Introduction causes, effects and suggestions)
Expression 1 Mark
(Accuracy of spelling and grammar)

Points to be Kept in Mind while Writing Debate

- Debate should always have a good introduction to grab the audience's attention and garner interest in the topic.
- Prepare the debate properly by considering both positive and negative aspects of the topic.
- Address the jury and the audience properly.
- Make your stand very clear from the very beginning.
- Highlight the main points of your argument emphatically.
- While developing points, substantiate them with relevant examples,
statistics, etc.
- State your own opinion or view in the concluding lines with a powerful statement to emphasise your stand on the issue.
- Throughout the debate, stick to your viewpoint either in favour or against.
- Include rhetorical questions, which can make your opponents consider the validity of your point while it undermines their point.

Format of a Debate

Write a debate in about 120-150 words either for or against the motion 'Crime-based TV Serials Lead to a Reduction in Crime'.

For the Motion

Honourable Principal, jury members, teachers and my dear friends. A very good morning to all.

Today, I stand here to express my views in favour of the motion 'Crime-based TV Serials Lead to a Reduction in Crime'. It is commonly accepted that television is considered a powerful tool for education and awareness. It the content of crimes shows such as Crime Patrol or CID can lead the way to an ideal crime less society. This is because crime dramas often highlight the consequences of illegal activities, showcasing the repercussions faced by criminals. This portrayal can deter potential offenders by illustrating the harsh realities of crime, such as arrest, imprisonment and loss of reputation.

Furthermore, these serials frequently emphasise the importance of law enforcement and community vigilance. By depicting police work and justice being served, they encourage viewers to respect the law and report suspicious activities. In addition, crime-based shows can stimulate discussions about societal issues, prompting viewers to reflect on the factors contributing to crime, such as poverty and lack of education. This awareness can lead to community initiatives aimed at addressing these root causes.

In conclusion, crime-based TV serials can indeed contribute to a reduction in crime by educating and influencing public attitudes.

Thank you!

Formal address
A debate begins with a formal address to the chief guest, other eminent people and the audience.

Content

Expression
(a) Grammatical accuracy appropriate words and spelling
(b) Coherence and relevance of ideas and style

Formal thanks
At the end of the debate, the speaker formally thanks the audience for their cooperation and listening to him/her.

Against the Motion

Honourable Principal, jury members, teachers and my dear friends. A very good morning to all.

Today, I stand here to express my views against the motion 'Crime-based TV Serials Lead to a Reduction in Crime'. In fact, these shows can have the opposite effect. Such dramas often glamorise illegal activities, portraying criminals as clever and heroic. This can desensitise viewers to the realities of crime and may even inspire some to emulate these behaviours, believing they can evade consequences.

Moreover, these serials frequently depict exaggerated violence and sensationalism, which can skew public perception of crime. Instead of understanding the complexities of criminal behaviour, viewers may develop irrational fears or biases, leading to misinformed beliefs about safety in their communities. Additionally, focusing on crime in media can create a culture of fear, causing individuals to distrust one another and erode community cohesion.

In conclusion, rather than reducing crime, crime-based TV serials can glorify it, distort reality and negatively impact societal attitudes.

Thank you!

Formal address
A debate begins with a formal address to the chief guest, other eminent people and the audience.

Content

Expression
(a) Grammatical accuracy appropriate words and spelling
(b) Coherence and relevance of ideas and style

Formal thanks
At the end of the debate, the speaker formally thanks the audience for their cooperation and listening to him/her.

PRACTICE QUESTIONS

1. Consumerism is increasing day-by-day. Luxuries of yesterday have become necessities of today. The result is that the more we want the more miserable we become. Write a debate in 120-150 words on "The only way to minimise human suffering and pain is to control our needs". You are Navtej/Navita. Use the following clues. **Competency Based**

- The different world of the past
- The material world's control on us
- Different needs for different people
- Fulfillment is the key

Ans.

For the Motion

Honourable Judges, my worthy opponents and dear students. Today I, Navtej of Class XI, will speak in favour of the motion 'The only way to minimise human suffering and pain is to control our needs'.

I am sure all of you watch TV programmes regularly, particularly entertainment programmes, serials and telecasts of cricket matches on various TV channels. You will find it hard to believe that just 25 years ago there was only one TV channel to watch, i.e., Doordarshan. Even then, having a TV set was a luxury and not a necessity, like it is nowadays. If we are prevented from watching TV by our parents even for a few days, like during exam time, most of us become miserable. However, our ancestors did not face any such misery. Their needs were minimum and items like a TV, fridge, etc., were just considered as luxury. This clearly points to the fact that we must learn to control our needs. Our need becomes greed which then becomes an obstacle in our lives. In greed, the material world controls us and we join a rat-race which puts us through immense physical and mental stresses. We all know that excessive desires and needs have always been considered immoral and a violation of divine law.

Thus, we all must control our needs and desires to live our life without any suffering and pain.

Thank you!

Against the Motion

Respected Principal, members of the Jury, teachers and my dear opponents. Good morning to you all. Today I, Navita, take the opportunity to express my disagreement with this view.

Scientifically stating, all human beings are born with defined needs which are different for each and every individual. These needs grow and develop with time and age. A small child always has small and meagre needs but a grown up has a much larger and different set of needs.

With this knowledge, the concept of controlling our needs and desires seem to be flawed. Fulfillment is the key here. Pain and suffering that humans face is because of the lack of satisfaction and fulfillment. If we focus on fulfillment, we can easily remove the obstacle that hurt us. Finding joy in simple things, and happiness and peace is the main aim of human life. Controlling needs then may make a person mentally sick and disgusted which would have physical impacts. Thus, instead of controlling our needs, we must find ways to satisfy them and march towards a happy and fulfilled life.

Thank you!

2. Migration from villages to cities has led to the spread of urban slums. People living in these slums lead a miserable life. Economic disparity leads to the problems of law and order. Write a debate in 120-150 words on "Solution to the problem of misery in the urban slums lies in creating jobs in the villages". You are Navtej/Navita. Use the following clues.

- Problems of law and order
- Lack of prosperity
- Unskilled people
- Multiple miseries unsolved

Ans.

For the Motion

Honourable Judges, my worthy opponents and dear students. Today I, Navita of Class XI, will speak in favour of the motion 'Solution to the problem of misery in the urban slums lies in creating jobs in the villages'. People living in cities are aware that every city has slum areas in which the poor, mostly migrated from nearby rural areas, are leading a miserable existence, doing odd jobs to earn a living. Due to their condition, they sometimes create problems of law and order. We should understand why people migrate to cities, even though they are forced to lead a life of misery there. The reason is that rural areas do not provide adequate avenues for employment or alternate sources of livelihood. The rural people feel that they can earn better in cities, leading to their migration. Thus, if jobs are created in the villages by setting up more agro-based industries or some other self-employment opportunities people can lead a reasonable livelihood there and will have no reason to migrate to cities.

Consequently, slums will not expand and more people will not lead impoverished lives in urban slums.
This will also lead to prosperity in villages and may ultimately give rise to reverse migration, i.e., slum dwellers going back to their villages to lead a more satisfactory life! I'm sure this is possible with adequate planning by our state and central governments.

Thank you!

Against the Motion

Respected Principal, members of the Jury, teachers and my dear opponents. Good morning to you all. Today I, Navtej, take the opportunity to express my disagreement with this view. While creating job is essential for the growth and development of the country, it is not the primary step that would ensure that the problem at hand will be solved.
The slums and villages of the country have a lot of people who are jobless and aimless because they are unskilled. Hence, the first priority should be providing them with the basic necessities of life as well as making them skilled to get a job. Once they are mentally and physically healthy as well as skilled, they can easily find jobs and end the miseries of their life. Focusing directly on jobs can easily take away the financial stress but the other miseries faced by them are left unresolved. Hence, other problems must be given first priority and then proper jobs as well as good salary will make them come out of their problems forever.

Thank you!

3. Write a debate in 120-150 words either for or against the motion: 'Participation in sports is a mere wastage of time'.

Ans.

For the Motion

Respected Judges, honourable opponents and friends, I, Rajani, will speak for the motion 'Participation in sports is a mere wastage of time'.
First, I will raise the point regarding the length of the career of a sportsperson. Most sportspersons retire by the age of 35 to 40 years, whereas other persons can have a career normally stretching to the age of 60 or 65. After retirement, a sportsperson finds it difficult to get a suitable job to make ends meet. The majority of sportspersons in India are neglected after they retire. There are many examples of sportspersons living in poverty in their old age.
Second, particularly in physical sports, there are chances of injuries, which may cause permanent bodily harm or reduce their efficiency. This may shorten the career of many sportspersons too.
My third point is regarding the time consumed in practising, participating in competitions, maintaining physical fitness, etc. All these consume a large amount of time; thus, reducing a sportsperson's social life significantly. What it amounts to is that many sacrifices have to be made for a sportsperson to be successful even if the person is talented.
Summing up, we can understand that participation in sports is really a wastage of time, which cannot lead to a productive career.

Thank you!

Against the Motion

Respected Judges, honourable opponents and friends, I, Ram, will speak against the motion 'Participation in sports is a mere wastage of time'.
Sports has become a viable career option today. With the government launching schemes like 'Khelo India' and others to identify sports talent at the primary school level, any child who is talented will be trained effectively using government funds to develop their talent. Talent for a particular sport can be recognised at this age and developed accordingly. Then, it is the duty of the child's parents to allow the child adequate time for practising and participating in competitions. There are many cases of sportspersons being successful and gaining recognition at a local, national or international platform's. Even if a child is not found talented in a particular sport, participation in sports is definitely not a mere wastage of time because it keeps one mentally and physically fit. Regular participation in sports develops the body and keeps the child physically fit. It also develops a competitive attitude, besides developing other qualities like leadership, cooperation and a sportsman's spirit. Thus, sports develops a person in every sense.
In addition, even a moderately successful sportsperson gets to travel abroad for training or competition and meet sportspersons of other countries, thus developing their personality in an all-round manner. Thus, we can conclude that participation in sports is not a mere wastage of time.

Thank you!

4. Write a debate on the topic 'Evaluation is the key to testing one's academic knowledge and not intelligence' in about 120-150 words. You can use the following clues to form your arguments. Competency Based

- Does not reflect potential
- Focuses on factual details
- Examination has particular pattern
- Examination checks level of learning
- Role of intelligence
- Scholarships

Ans.

For the Motion

Evaluation is the key to testing one's academic knowledge and not intelligence.

Good morning to one and all present here. We all know that evaluations or pen-paper examinations have been accepted by everyone as one of the best ways to tests a student's knowledge, understanding and learning. But does it test the practical skills or a student's presence of mind?

The answer is no. Hence, I stand in favour of the motion that School examinations do not test intelligence. While success in school examinations may reflect the knowledge and hard-work of a student, it may not necessarily reflect their intelligence or their potential. It only tests, the factual knowledge that the student learn from books and in classes.

We all agree that each individual is unique in their own way and there is not one particular pattern of defining intelligence. The school examinations, however, do have a particular pattern and those who fit the mould tend to succeed in it. History is full of examples of individuals who didn't particularly fit in the pattern of school or examinations but went on to become great individuals in their fields. Look at the great Mathematician, Srinivasa Ramanujan or Albert Einstein. It would not have been possible for either of them to be considered as intelligent had they been judged based on their examination results only. It was only when they were allowed to think freely instead of being restricted by the education system that they could achieve their true potential.

Thus, I strongly believe that examinations do not test the true measure of a student.

Thankyou!

Against the Motion

Evaluation is an essential criterion that tells us the level of learning possessed by a child.

Good morning to one and all present here. We all learn a variety of subjects in our school. But do we check if the child has understood and learnt the basic ideas or concepts that are crucial to life. The answer is examinations. Therefore I stand against the motion that 'school examinations do not test intelligence.'

While I agree that examination does not completely test a student's intelligence, I disagree that intelligence and examination have no relation. We know that some students work really hard and do not often get the best results, while some can get top results by working less than others. This kind of a situation shows us that intelligence does have a role in examination.

It is also important to take into consideration that many universities and schools provide scholarships as well as admission on the basis of the examination results.

Further, examinations can be extremely helpful for teachers to assess the students, and find out who are able to understand the subject and who need more help to improve.

Examinations are important in this regard as they help the students to test how much they learnt from what was taught to them. This can reflect the knowledge, dedication and work put in by a student to their studies and acts as a crucial indicator of their general level of intelligence. Thus, good examination result is a reward that a student receives in return for their effort and speaks volumes about their intelligence.

Thank you!

5. Academic excellence is a pursuit that lies at the core of education, reflecting the highest standards of achievement and performance in academics. Write a debate in about 120-150 words for or against the topic "Academic excellence is the only requirement for a successful career". Use the following clues. Competency Based

- Providing basic knowledge
- Preparing students for future competition
- Admission to best universities
- Education fails to impart life skills
- Creative thinking

Ans.

For the Motion

Honourable Principal, jury members, teachers and my dear friends. A very good morning to all. Today, I stand here in favour of the motion 'Academic excellence is the only requirement for a successful career'.

The education system in the primary years is designed so as to provide basic knowledge to each subject and help the youth of today in choosing their subject of interest for its deeper study in higher classes. This part of education can only be provided effectively through universities, which plays a key role in the development of society and the nation. In fact, information cannot be converted into knowledge without education.

Excellence in academics prepares students for the competition ahead and teaches them to work hard in all aspects of life. Academic qualifications indicate that the person who possesses them has got the necessary knowledge required. Conversely, imagine a new world

order in education where people don't study beyond school but join their business or look for jobs straight after school, with no higher qualifications which certify their worth. Then, how would employers choose the candidate with requisite skills?
Further, academic excellence will ensure admission to the best universities for higher education which provide exposure to a variety of knowledge; thus, giving an excellent start to the student's career.

Thank you!

Against the Motion

Honourable Principal, jury members, teachers and my dear friends. A very good morning to all. Today, I stand against the motion 'Academic excellence is the only requirement for a successful career'.
Education today fails to impart necessary life skills and polish the personality of an individual. For these, students have to attend specialised workshops or training sessions. Education will surely give you an overview of a subject but it fails to provide an overview of how the world works. It does not ensure mastery of skills and competencies. It tells people what to think instead of how to think. The end result is that society now has just robots who have switched their minds off only to believe what is being taught.
Many successful college dropouts have proved that prosperity does not depend upon academic qualifications but upon opportunities provided by entrepreneurs who may not necessarily be highly educated. Successful entrepreneurs even benefit from not having academic qualifications because going to college and taking examinations forces people to learn and think like millions of other graduates.
Thus, academic excellence is in no way the only requirement for a successful career.

Thank you!

6. Write a debate in about 120-150 words either for or against the topic 'Junk food should be banned'.

Ans.

For the Motion

Honourable Principal, jury members, teachers and my dear friends. A very good morning to all.
Wise people, including our parents, have often been quoted to say that health is wealth. Thus, I stand, for the motion 'Junk food should be banned'. Junk food is an umbrella term that refers to highly processed and calorie-dense foods that are low in nutritional value. These foods often contain high levels of unhealthy ingredients such as sugar, salt, unhealthy fats and artificial additives. The short-term effects of consuming these foods include energy spikes and crashes, bloating, constipation and dehydration. Various scientific studies and researches have associated junk food with lifelong illnesses including obesity, diabetes, heart disease, hypertension and even nutritional deficiencies.
If you are a reasonable individual, then you will be aware of the fact that all living beings eat food to gain energy and to cultivate a strong body. Unfortunately, youngsters cannot be trusted to make the right decisions for themselves. Hence, it is essential that the decision to stop partaking in this particular form of poison be taken for them. Considering the significant risk to the health and wellbeing of humans as individuals and as a society, I support the complete ban of all non-nutritious junk food in a vision to create a healthier society.

Thank you!

Against the Motion

Honourable Principal, jury members, teachers and my dear friends. A very good morning to all. Today, I stand here against the motion 'Junk food should be banned'.
While it may not be nutritious and conducive to a healthy lifestyle, for many people, consumption of junk food is the only choice. The rushed lifestyle of the modern world does not allow people the time to carefully choose ingredients according to their nutritional value and cook it. Many people only have the time to cook two-minute noodles before rushing off to work.
In today's world, healthier food options are also more expensive and, thus, unaffordable to many. It is an ironic fact but one that the common people cannot do anything about. Although it is imperative that we cultivate good eating habits, the ability to have a nutritious meal is not a necessity; it is a luxury. Organic and chemical-free food available in the market is much costlier than the junk food and difficult to access.
As of present, thus, it is unwise to ban junk food as it would leave many people hungry.
Thank you!

7. Write a debate in about 120-150 words either for or against the topic 'Technology has made us overly dependent on its existence'.

Ans.

For the Motion

Honourable Principal, jury members, teachers and my dear friends. A very good morning to all.

Today, I stand in favour of the motion 'Technology has made us overly dependent on its existence'. While technology undoubtedly offers numerous benefits, it has also created a significant reliance that affects our daily lives and interactions.

First, consider how we communicate. With the rise of smartphones and social media, many people have shifted from face-to-face conversations to digital interactions, leading to a decline in meaningful personal connections. This dependence can hinder our social skills and emotional well-being. Moreover, our reliance on technology extends to basic tasks. We often turn to GPS for navigation instead of using maps or our sense of direction and many people struggle with mental arithmetic due to calculators and apps. This diminishes our critical thinking and problem-solving abilities.

Lastly, technology has made us vulnerable. Cybersecurity threats and system failures can disrupt our lives significantly. Therefore, while technology is a valuable tool, our excessive dependence on it poses serious challenges.

Thank you!

Against the Motion

Honourable Principal, jury members, teachers and my dear friends. A very good morning to all.

Today, I stand against the motion 'Technology has made us overly dependent on its existence'. Technology has empowered us, enhancing our capabilities and improving our quality of life.

First, technology has revolutionised communication, allowing us to connect with others instantly across the globe. This fosters relationships, collaboration and cultural exchange, enriching our lives in ways that were once unimaginable. Furthermore, technology enhances our productivity. Tools like project management software and automation enable us to work more efficiently, freeing up time for creativity and innovation. Rather than making us dependent, technology allows us to focus on higher-level tasks. Additionally, technology has improved access to information and education. Online learning platforms provide opportunities for individuals to gain knowledge and skills, breaking down barriers and promoting lifelong learning.

In conclusion, rather than viewing technology as a crutch, we should recognise it as a powerful ally that enables growth, connection and progress in our lives.

Thank you!

8. Write a debate in about 120-150 words either for or against the topic 'All girls or all boys school provide a better learning environment than co-educational schools'. Competency Based

Ans.

For the Motion

Honourable Principal, jury members, teachers and my dear friends. A very good morning to all. Today, I stand in favour of the motion 'All girls or all boys school provide a better learning environment than co-educational schools'.

It has been noted that an all-girls or all-boys school can provide a more structured learning environment for both girls and boys, respectively. Boys and girls differ in the way they act, how they learn and their interests and abilities. They need an educational environment tailored to meet their unique needs.

In general, boys are more physically active, assertive and comfortable learning in a more chaotic environment than girls. Girls are able to sit still and prefer a quiet, focused and orderly classroom. In all-girls or all-boys schools, the curriculum and course provide advanced work in areas of the children's greatest interests and natural abilities.

Moreover, single-sex schools encourage children to take risks in expressing themselves as they learn without the fear of embarrassing themselves in front of the opposite sex. In the secondary and senior secondary classes, single-sex schools remove the distraction of the opposite sex, allowing students to focus more seriously on their school work.

Thus, all girls and all boys schools provide a better learning environment.

Thank you!

Against the Motion

Honourable Principal, jury members, teachers and my dear friends. A very good morning to all. Today, I stand against the motion 'All girls or all boys school provide a better learning environment than co-educational schools'.

Co-education and its benefits for long has been a topic of debate in our country. The modes of education do not vary as per the sex of the students. Thus, education cannot be divided on the lines of sex. When it comes to schools, there are many more important issues than having same sex schools.

When girls sit along with boys in the same classroom, it helps develop a cordial relation among students and instils in them a spirit of sportsmanship, confidence, mutual harmony and brotherhood. Moreover, co-ed schools offer a diverse curriculum that is available to all students de-emphasising gender-linked stereotypes related to course work. Today is an age where men and women work together and compete with each other in offices, homes, etc.; thus, co-education teaches and prepares them to interact with the opposite sex in the future.

Thank you!

SELF ASSESSMENT TEST

1. You are Ram/ Rajani. Write a debate either for or against the motion: 'Hard work, and not only good luck helps us to achieve success in life'. (120-150 words) Use the clues given below. **Competency Based**

- Relentless effort
- Fosters a sense of accomplishment
- Significant role of luck
- Builds resilience and character
- Increases confidence
- Supportive environment

2. The policy of reservation of seats for admission to the professional courses is good for the deprived sections of society. Write a debate in 120-150 words either for or against the motion.

Clues

- Exploitation of lower class
- Deprived of opportunities
- Brain drain
- Article 46 of the Indian Constitution
- Principle of equality

3. 'Our large population is not a cause of poverty but an asset, a resource.' Write a debate in 120-150 words either for or against the motion.

4. 'Brain drain is not a bane for a developing country like India'. Write a debate in 120-150 words either for or against the motion. **Competency Based**

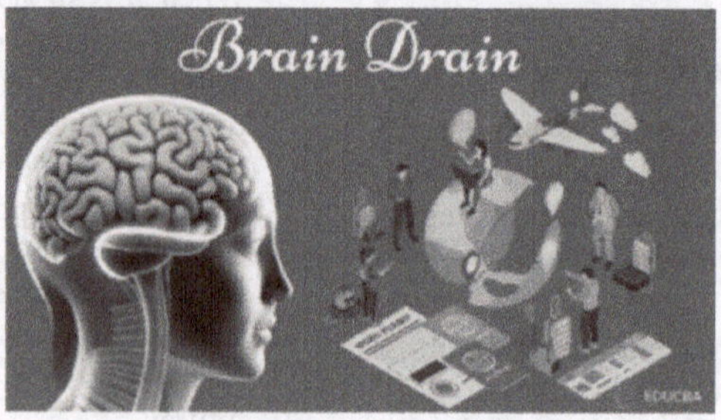

5. 'The Internet cannot replace a classroom teacher'. Write a debate in 120-150 words either for or against the motion.

6. 'Rising prices can be controlled only by the government'. Write a debate in 120-150 words either for or against the motion.

7. 'The policy of no detention till Class VIII is not in the interest of students'. Write a debate in 120-150 words either in favour of or against the motion. Use the clues given below.

- Essential skills and knowledge
- Undermining motivation
- Frustration and disengagement
- Reducing anxiety and pressure
- Supportive atmosphere
- Fostering a love for learning
- Stigma of failure

8. 'The government has banned the use of animals in the laboratories for the purpose of dissection'. Write a debate in 120-150 words either for or against this decision. **Competency Based**

9. Some people feel that electronic media (TV news) will bring about the end of print media (newspapers). What are your views on the issue? Write a debate in 120-150 words either for or against this view. Use the given clues.

- Use of visuals on TV
- Not enough news for 24 hours telecast
- Become repetitive and dull
- Print media-time tested
- Editorial comments
- Authentic and fast
- May fabricate news
- Even scandals become news
- Analysed, verified news
- Cater to all interests

10. A number of your classmates (especially those from science and commerce streams) bunk their classes in order to attend coaching centres. Write a debate in 120-150 words on 'Tuition at coaching centres is not essential'. Use the given clues.

- School teachers better equipped
- Philanthropic approach
- No infrastructure
- Schools should reorient their teaching process
- Infrastructure much better at schools
- Coaching centres - money minting machines
- Competition oriented education

11. Write a debate in about 120-150 words either for or against the motion 'College education should be free'. **Competency Based**

12. Are celebs responsible for the products they endorse? Taking a cue from the headlines given below and using your own ideas, write a debate for or against the topic. (about 120-150 words) **Competency Based**

- Amitabh Bachchan steps back from promoting Pepsi after a school girl questions the health impact of the drink.
- Brief ban on Maggi noodles causes trouble for its celebrity Brand ambassadors.

13. Write a debate in about 120-150 words either for or against the motion 'Climate changes are caused by human activities'.

14. Write a debate in about 120-150 words either for or against the motion 'Nuclear energy is a viable solution to energy needs'.

15. Write a debate in about 120-150 words either for or against the motion 'Children's opinion should be considered on matters concerning them'. Use the clues given below. **Competency Based**

- Crucial for development
- Leads to better outcomes
- Limited experience
- Adults have a guiding role
- Valuable perspectives
- Importance of civic participation
- Heavily influenced

01

CHAPTER

Tenses

Tense is defined as the form of verb that gives the relation between Time and Action. As such, tense gives the time when the action is done.

YOUR STUDY GOALS

Classification of Tenses

- Present Tense
- Past Tense
- Future Tense
- Exam Pattern Questions

There are three phases of time

(i) **Present** (now)

(ii) **Past** (passed)

(iii) **Future** (yet to come)

Let's consider the sentences given below

(a) My father goes to the gym. (Present)

(b) My father went to the gym. (Past)

(c) My father will go to the gym. (Future)

We can observe that each sentence given above has a different meaning. The reason is that each sentence has a different form of verb. These different forms of verbs are called tenses.

Classification of Tenses

On the basis of time, there are three tenses

(i) Present Tense (ii) Past Tense

(iii) Future Tense

Each tense has four forms. Study the chart given below to understand more about all tenses and their forms.

TENSE

- **Present**
  - Indefinite
  - Continuous
  - Perfect
  - Perfect Continuous
- **Past**
  - Indefinite
  - Continuous
  - Perfect
  - Perfect Continuous
- **Future**
  - Indefinite
  - Continuous
  - Perfect
  - Perfect Continuous

Present Tense

Present Indefinite Tense

(Also Called Simple Present Tense)

This tense is used in the following ways

(i) To express habitual action, habit or custom.

e.g. • Alex plays tennis every morning with his little brother.
• I like to read a book every day.

(ii) To talk about a general or universal truth.

e.g. • Ice is the frozen form of water.
• Laughter is the best medicine.

(iii) To indicate a future event which is part of a plan or arrangement.

e.g. • The first class of this session convenes tomorrow.
• The exhibition begins next week.

(iv) To introduce quotations with the verb 'says'.

e.g. • Einstein says, "Failure is success in progress".
• Churchill says, "Solitary trees, if they grow at all, grow strong."

(v) Vivid narration, as a substitute for the simple past.

e.g. • He eats a lot but he is hungry always.

(vi) Exclamatory sentences that begin with here or there.

e.g. • Here it is!
• There he sat!

(vii) Time clauses and conditional clauses in place of simple future.

e.g. • If it rains tomorrow, we'll go to the cinema.
• If I pass my exams, I will go on vacation.

〉Rules for Affirmative Sentences

- Singular subject + first form of verb + s/es + ...
- Plural subject + first form of verb + ...

e.g. • Rhea goes to the market to shop for grocery.
• My friend, Gracy, and I go to St. Thomas School.

〉Rules for Negative Sentences

- Singular subject + does not + first form of verb + ...
- Plural subject + do not + first form of verb + ...

e.g. • It doesn't smell very delicious in the kitchen.
• I do not go for a walk.

〉Rules for Interrogative Sentences

- Do/does + subject + first form of verb + ...?
- Question word + do/does + subject + first form of verb + ...?

e.g. • Do the girls play hockey?
• Does it rain daily?

Present Continuous Tense

This tense is used in the following ways

(i) To describe an action in progress and the continuity of the action.

e.g. • He is writing in his book.
• She is pacing left to right in the middle of the room.

(ii) An action that is not happening at the time of speaking but is in progress.

e.g. • Online shopping is growing in popularity nowadays.

(iii) An action that has been pre-arranged to take place in the near future.

e.g. • I am going tot he metting after work.
• Pallavi is planning a lunch for next week.

(iv) Persistent and undesirable habit, especially with adverbs like always, continually, constantly.

e.g. • He is continually walking around.
• You are always running late.

〉Rules for Affirmative Sentences

- Singular subject + is/am + first form of verb + ing +.......
- Plural subject + are + first form of verb + ing +.......
- I + am + first form of verb + ing +.......

e.g. • Mark is making lunch right now.
• Pallavi is talking on the phone at the moment.

〉Rules for Negative Sentences

- Singular subject + is + not + first form of verb + ing +.......
- Plural subject + are + not + first form of verb + ing +.......
- I + am + not + first form of verb + ing +.......

e.g. • The kids are not leaving at six'o clock.
• She is not going to speak at the conference this evening.

〉Rules for Interrogative Sentences

- Is/are/am + subject + first form of verb + ing + ...?
- Question word + is/are/am + subject + first form of verb + ing + ... ?

e.g. • What are you training to become?
• Are you washing the clothes that you will wear in the evening.

Present Perfect Tense

This tense is used in the following ways

(*i*) To express an action that has recently been completed.

e.g. • He has just entered the restaurant.

• They have completed the tournament.

(*ii*) To describe an action whose time is not given.

e.g. • The hens have laid plenty of eggs.

• Have you prepared anything for the Talent Show?

(*iii*) To describe past events whose effects still exist.

e.g. • You have grown since the last time I saw you.

(*iv*) To describe actions that started in the past and are continuing until now and possibly into the future.

e.g. • I have already met him.

(*v*) To show how a past situation relates to the present.

e.g. • Sara has worked in Florida for a long time and is coming home for the holidays.

› Rules for Affirmative Sentences

- Singular subject + has + third form of verb + ...
- Plural subject + have + third form of verb + ...

e.g. • My mother has helped me in my research.

• My sister has lost the key to her almirah.

• I have seen that movie.

› Rules for Negative Sentences

- Singular subject + has + not + third form of verb + ...
- Plural subject + have + not + third form of verb + ...

e.g. • I have not seen him in the past nine years.

• Alia has not cleaned the room.

› Rules for Interrogative Sentences

- Has/have + subject + third form of verb +.....?
- Question word + has/have + subject + third form of verb + ... ?

e.g. • Have you prepared the lunch for my journey?

• Have you even been to London?

Present Perfect Continuous Tense

This tense is used in the following ways

(*i*) To describe an action that began in the past and is still continuing.

e.g. • They have been working on the Itihas Project for a week.

• Harry has been trying to learn French for two weeks and is now done.

(*ii*) To express an action already completed, but whose effect is still continuing.

e.g. • Every summer vacation, we have been going to the hill station.

• He has been working in this garage for eight years.

› Rules for Affirmative Sentences

- Singular subject + has + been + first form of verb + ing + ... + for/since +......
- Plural subject + have + been + first form of verb + ing + ... + for/since +......

e.g. • She has been working on this project for a week.

• They have been working as doctors for two years.

› Rules for Negative Sentences

- Singular subject + has + not + been + first form of verb + ing + ... + for/since +......
- Plural subject + have + not + been + first form of verb + ing + ... + for/since +......

e.g. • The mechanic has not been repairing our refrigerator.

• They haven't been resting as they should have, after the accident.

› Rules for Interrogative Sentences

- Have/has + subject + been + first form of verb + ing + ... + since/for +.....?
- Question word + has/have + subject + been + first form of verb + ing + since/for + ...?

e.g. • Has he been playing PUBG since last evening?

• Have you been reading The Lord of the Rings?

Check Point 1

1 Fill in the blanks with the correct form of present tense from those given in brackets.

(a) I am attempting the Civil Services exam coming up, so I .... (am/is) studying hard these days.

(b) My grandmother .... (carries/carrying) a walking stick when she goes out for a walk.

(c) Shashi isn't at home. She .... (is/are) out shopping with our father.

(d) Can you speak louder please, I .... (am not/cannot) hear you.

(e) My widower uncle often .... (coming/comes) to our house for lunch on Sundays.

(f) Since he changed his job, he .... (found/has found) more time to relax and enjoy his hobby.

(g) I feel proud of my team as it .... (performed/has performed) very well.

(h) Look! They .... (gossip and while away/are gossiping and whiling away) their time.

(i) An apple a day .... (keeps/is keeping) the doctor away.

(j) By profession, an artist .... (creates/is creating) a picture whereas an author .... (writes/is writing) a book.

2 Fill in the blanks in the telephonic conversation given below with the correct present tense form of the verb given in brackets.

Sameer Savita! How (a) .... (be) you? This is Sameer.

Savita Ahhh...Sameer! I (b) .... (be) fine. How are you?

Sameer I'm great, thanks.

Savita That (c) .... (be) good. So, what's up?

Sameer Well, I (d) .... (has) a problem for you to solve.

Savita Sure, just say it.

Sameer My motorcycle (e) .... (be) defective. I (f) .... (try) to repair it for days. I (g) .... (not, know) what is wrong with it. I (h) .... (no, can, fix) it.

Past Tense

Past Indefinite Tense
(also called Simple Past Tense)

This tense is used in the following ways

(i) To indicate an action that happened in the past and to report completed actions. It is used often in recounts and narratives.

e.g. • My father lived in California for the entirely of last year.

• We met yesterday around 7 p.m.

(ii) To indicate past habits or repeated events that are now over.

e.g. • During the summer holidays this year, I woke very late in the morning.

• I always came late when I used to go to school.

(iii) The habitual past can also be expressed by using 'used to'.

e.g. • They used to talk to each other every day.

• Claire used to hunt monsters before becoming a cop.

(iv) Sometimes this tense is used without an adverb of time. In such cases, the time may be either implied or indicated by the context.

e.g. • We drank a whole bottle of pepsi each.

(v) To indicate another action which happened in the middle of a longer action.

e.g. • I ate the last cookie while my sister Niharika was looking for it in the kitchen cabinet.

〉Rules for Affirmative Sentences

- Subject + second form of verb +......

e.g. • She spoke good English to the interviewer.

• They reached the venue of the seminar before its commencement.

〉Rules for Negative Sentences

- Subject + did not + first form of verb +......

e.g. • You didn't write to me last week.

• We didn't do a lot of shopping at the mall.

〉Rules for Interrogative Sentences

- Did + subject + first form of verb + ... ?
- Question word + did + subject + first form of verb +........?

e.g. • Did they watch the movie on Friday?

• Why did you choose Loki as your favourite character from the Avenger series?

Past Continuous Tense

This tense is used in the following ways

(i) To indicate an action that was happening at some time in the past. The time of action may or may not be indicated.

e.g. • They were planning to go to the library.

(ii) Used with *always*, *continually* etc for persistent habits in the past.

e.g. • My dog, Miracle, was always barking at the neighbour's kid.

(iii) The past continuous is also used for an action that was going on during a given period or at a period of time in the past.

e.g. • My brothers were playing football while I was working on my science project.

〉Rules for Affirmative Sentences

- Singular subject + was + first form of verb + ing +.....
- Plural subject + were + first form of verb + ing +.....

e.g. • Shreya was buying the new iPhone.

• He was doing a great job.

› **Rules for Negative Sentences**

- Singular subject + was + not + first form of verb + ing +.....
- Plural subject + were + not + first form of verb + ing +.....

e.g. • My television wasn't working properly all day yesterday.
• They weren't speaking in English today.

› **Rules for Interrogative Sentences**

- Was/were + subject + first form of verb + ing +......?
- Question word + was/were + subject + first form of verb + ing +.....?

e.g. • Was he learning anything in the tuition classes?
• What was he doing in his room last evening?

Past Perfect Tense

This tense is used in the following ways

(i) To indicate an action that was completed before a definite time or before another action that took place in the past.

e.g. • The movie had finished by the time that my cousins arrived.

(ii) It indicates desires in the past that have not been fulfilled.

e.g. • I wish I had pursued my dream of becoming a singer.

(iii) It expresses those conditions of the past that were impossible to fulfill.

e.g. • If you had invested in shares, you would have become very rich by now.

› **Rules for Affirmative Sentences**

- Subject + had + third form of verb + ...

e.g. • I had known how to solve all the problems.

› **Rules for Negative Sentences**

- Subject + had + not + third form of verb + ...

e.g. • They hadn't cut the tree last week.

› **Rules for Interrogative Sentences**

- Had + subject + third form of verb + ... ?

e.g. • Had they been married when I was born?
• Had the woman cried till the morning?

Past Perfect Continuous Tense

This tense is used in the following way

It indicates an action which began in the past and continued up to a certain point of time in the past.

e.g. • When her husband came home in the evening, she had been cleaning the house for hours.
• When they called, I had been working on the science project.

› **Rules for Affirmative Sentences**

- Subject + had been + first form of verb +ing + ... + since/for +.....

e.g. • They had been waiting for ten minutes.
• Anna had been trying to repair her car.

› **Rules for Negative Sentences**

- Subject + had + not + been + first form of verb + ing + ... + since/for +......

e.g. • I had not been cooking any meal when Anant came to my home.

› **Rules for Interrogative Sentences**

- Had + subject + been + first form of verb + ing + ... + since/for + ...?
- Question word + had + subject + been + first form of verb + ing + ...since/for+..... ?

e.g. • Had Akshat been working on the computer all day long?

Check Point 2

1 Fill in the blanks with the correct form of past tense by selecting from the options given in brackets.

(a) The other employees had already left the office but Kanika .... (still worked/was still working) there.

(b) A small boy .... (fell/was falling) from the train when it was moving at full speed.

(c) We saw a bus fall into a ditch when we .... (went/were going) to Mussoorie.

(d) Anita .... (burnt/was burning) her finger while she was cooking.

(e) While I .... (waited/was waiting) for my bus Rachita was running after hers.

(f) The farmer sold the crop after he .... (harvested/had harvested) it.

(g) Indians .... (had fought/fought) a long struggle before they .... (had attained/attained) independence.

(h) The train .... (departed/had departed) before we reached the station.

2 Fill in the blanks with the correct form of past tense of the verbs given in brackets.

(a) Binod ...... (bring up) by his father because his mother died when he was a baby.

(b) Ramesh, who .... (work) in Kolkata for 10 years, is now seriously ill.

(c) I once .... (hear) Honey Singh singing live on the stage.

(d) Majid, my best friend, ... (stay) in Kanpur for the last five years.

(e) Kritika .... (break) her left ankle bone while she .... (dance) at the party.

(f) Tailor Master, are the clothes I .... (give) for stitching ready yet?

(g) Parveen .... (not/write) a letter to me since last year.

(h) Mummy, tell Papa that his phone .... (ring) while he .... (have) his bath.

Future Tense

Future Indefinite Tense (also called Simple Future Tense)

This tense is used in the following ways

(i) To say what we believe or think will happen in future.

e.g. • Sonal will arrive for the meeting a little late.
• They believe they will win the match.

(ii) Things which we cannot control and are factual.

e.g. • January 26th, 2025 will be India's 78th Republic Day.

(iii) To indicate an instant decision.

e.g. • I will eat my breakfast in a minute.

› Rules for Affirmative Sentences

- You/He/She/It/They (Second and Third Person Pronouns) + will + first form of verb + ...
- I/We (First Person Pronouns) + shall + first form of verb + ...

e.g. • They will be victorious in today's game.
• He will sleep till late this weekend.

› Rules for Negative Sentences

- You/He/She/It/They (Second and Third Person Pronouns) + will + not + first form of verb + ...
- I/We (First Person Pronouns) + shall + not + first form of verb + ...

e.g. • I will not go to my grandparent's home during vacations.
• You will not reach on time if you delay.

› Rules for Interrogative Sentences

- Will/shall + subject + first form of verb +......?
- Question word + will/shall + subject + first form of verb + ...?

e.g. • Will your mother retire next year?
• Will you send her the invitation through e-mail?

Future Continuous Tense

This tense is used in the following ways

(i) To indicate an action that will occur in the normal course.

e.g. • The baby will be sleeping in the afternoon.
• She will be talking to him tomorrow.

(ii) To indicate an action that will be in progress at a given point of time in the future.

e.g. • Won't we be cleaning the kitchen tomorrow in the afternoon?
• She will be watching the news at eight.

› Rules for Affirmative Sentences

- You/He/She/It/They (Second and Third Person Pronouns) + will + be + first form of verb + ing + ...
- I/We (First Person Pronouns) + shall + be + first form of verb + ing + ...

e.g. • Rahil will be studying at the library tonight.
• Suman will be singing in the Talent Show.

› Rules for Negative Sentences

- You/He/She/It/They (Second and Third Person Pronouns) + will + not + be + first form of verb + ing + ...
- I/We (First Person Pronouns) + shall + not + be + first form of verb + ing + ...

e.g. • Trent will not be playing football in college.
• Abhay won't be going to his office tomorrow.

› Rules for Interrogative Sentences

- Will/shall + subject + be + first form of verb + ing + ...?
- Question word + will/shall + subject + be + first form of verb + ing +.....?

e.g. • What will you be doing when I arrive?
• Will it be raining all day tomorrow?

Future Perfect Tense

This tense is used to describe an action which will be completed at some point of time in the future.

e.g.
- By next week, we will have earned lots of money.
- They will have their dinner by then.

Rules for Affirmative Sentences

- You/He/She/It/They (Second and Third Person Pronouns) + will + have + third form of verb + ...
- I/We (First Person Pronouns) + shall + have + third form of verb + ...

e.g.
- Arya will have married George by then.
- I will have finished my assignment by next week.

Rules for Negative Sentences

- You/He/She/It/They (Second and Third Person Pronouns) + will + not + have + third form of verb + ...
- I/We (First Person Pronouns) + shall + not + have + third form of verb + ...

e.g.
- You will not have finished your report by this time tomorrow.
- My mother will not have prepared breakfast by the time my father wakes up.

Rules for Interrogative Sentences

- Will/shall + subject + have + third form of verb +......?
- Question word + will/shall + subject + have + third form of verb ......?

e.g.
- Will he have gotten his wallet by then?
- Will the concert have started by 10 p.m.?

Future Perfect Continuous Tense

This tense is used in the following way

It describes an action that will be in progress over a period of time that will end in the future.

e.g.
- At 4 o'clock, we will have been waiting you for one hour.

Rules for Affirmative Sentences

- You/He/She/It/They (Second and Third Person Pronouns) + will + have + been + first form of verb + ing + ...
- I/We (First Person Pronouns) + shall + have + been + first form of verb + ing + ...

e.g.
- He will have been reading a newspaper this time tomorrow.

Rules for Negative Sentences

- You/He/She/It/They (Second and Third Person Pronouns) + will + not + have + been + first form of verb + ing + ...
- I/We (First Person Pronouns) + shall + not + have + been + first form of verb + ing + ...

e.g.
- I will not have been shopping on Wednesday.
- She will not have been seeing Sakshi because she is very angry.

Rules for Interrogative Sentences

- Will/shall + subject + have + been + first form of verb + ing + ...?
- Question word + will/ shall + subject + have + been + first form of verb + ing + ...?

e.g.
- How long will you have been learning French for, in April of 2022?
- Will you have been making a cake in the kitchen?

Check Point 3

1 Fill in the blanks with the correct form of future tense of the verbs given in brackets.

(a) Now Nikhil .... (want) to move to a bigger city for a better job.

(b) The famous Dr. Prahlad .... (operate) on my uncle tomorrow to remove his tumour.

(c) Sarla's mother .... (stay) in a rented house after her divorce gets through.

(d) Prodipta .... (win) the wrestling bout against Vijay this evening, I'm sure.

(e) I think Ranjan .... (start) his journey tomorrow.

(f) Our Maths teacher .... (correct) the exam papers by Sunday.

(g) I think Anil .... (certainly/get) good marks in the Social Science test.

(h) By 7 p.m., Sameera .... (finish) her homework.

2 Fill in the blanks with the correct form of future tense by selecting from the options given in brackets.

(a) The train ...... (will have left/will leave) from Rajkot by 10 p.m..

(b) My grandfather will .... (have arrived/be arriving) at home by now.

(c) The entertainment programme .... (will have ended/will end) by now.

(d) I think that tomorrow Ramita .... (is starting/will start) on her new project.

(e) My class teacher .... (probably assigning/will probably assign) a lot of homework for the summer holidays.

(f) The building contractor .... (will finishing /will have finished) my new house by next month.

(g) I will .... (be completing/have completed) this task at this time tomorrow.

(h) I .... (will be passing/will have passed) my MBA by the time you return from abroad.

3 Fill in the blanks with the correct form of the verb (mixed tenses) given in brackets.

One day a husband and wife (a) ...... (drive) to the countryside to visit their friends when they realised they needed to stop for petrol. The man was filling up the car when he (b) ...... (see) a penguin standing by the petrol pump. He (c) ...... (think) it was very strange and when he went to the cashier to pay, he asked, "Why is there a penguin standing next to the pump?"

The cashier replied, "I don't know. It has been there all morning."

Exam Pattern Questions

Objective Type Questions

1. Gap Filling

Fill in the blanks with the correct options.

1. **In 1619, the first African slaves .... in Virginia, USA and by 1790, their numbers .... nearly 700,000.** **Competency Based**

(a) were arriving/have been reaching
(b) arrived/had reached
(c) have arrived/were reaching
(d) were going to arrive/reach

2. **We .... a lovely view of the Bosphorus and the bridges over it while the plane .... over Istanbul.**

(a) are getting/flies (b) had got/is flying
(c) got/was flying (d) get/has flown

3. **When they .... in Sydney Harbour, they .... nonstop for three months.**

(a) anchor/will have been sailing
(b) were anchoring/sailed
(c) have anchored/were sailing
(d) are anchoring/have been sailing

4. **According to the new schedule the whole team has accepted, we .... every Monday and Wednesday next term, but I'm sure we .... back to our normal routine of once a week before long.** **Competency Based**

(a) had trained/revert (b) train/have reverted
(c) are training/reverted (d) are going to train/will revert

5. **The prospector ran into town in excitement because, at last, he .... some gold at the site which he .... for months.**

(a) was finding/was panning
(b) will find/is going to pan
(c) will have found/has panned
(d) had found/had been panning

6. **I know that you .... bored with working at the Post Office by this time next year and .... for a more interesting job.**

(a) have become/will have looked
(b) will have become/will be looking
(c) had found/had been panning
(d) found/will have panned

7. **Listen! The coach .... the strengths of our opponents because our team .... against them before.** **Competency Based**

(a) has explained/weren't playing
(b) explains/won't play
(c) is explaining/hasn't played
(d) will explain/hadn't been playing

8. **When I .... the alterations to the company accounts, I was left in no doubt that the accountant .... money from the firm.**

(a) saw/had been stealing
(b) am seeing/has stolen
(c) was seeing/was stealing
(d) have seen/will have stolen

9. **According to the doctor, this time next week, I .... around as normal and the cut on my foot .... completely.**

(a) am walking/healed
(b) will be walking/will have healed
(c) walked/was healing
(d) have been walking/heals

10. **Over recent years, many skilled craftsmen and women .... their jobs in the pottery trade in the UK, but gradually English porcelain .... its reputation.** Competency Based

(a) will have lost/will regain
(b) had been losing/has regained
(c) are losing/regained
(d) have lost/is regaining

11. **Radioactive pollution of water .... but is of grave concern for water pollution and human health.**

(a) have newly emerged (b) had newly emerged
(c) is newly emerging (d) newly emerged

12. **I .... that time wasn't fixed like concrete but in fact .... fluid as sand, or water.**

(a) have forgotten, is
(b) have been forgetting, had been
(c) had forgotten, was
(d) had been forgetting, had been

13. **Their plane .... at 4 p.m. at the London airport.**

(a) shall be landing (b) was landing
(c) is landing (d) will be landing

14. **He .... all that the criminal speaks right from his entry.**

(a) shall have been recording
(b) will have been recording
(c) been recording
(d) have been recording

15. **The tiger .... away before the hunter .... the forest.**

(a) run, reached (b) had run, reached
(c) ran, reach (d) had run, reach

Directions (Q. Nos. 16-18) *Complete the following passage by filling in the blanks by choosing the appropriate words from the options.* Competency Based

'Atticus said to Jem one day, "I'd rather you shot at tin cans in the backyard, but I know ......(16)...... after birds. Shoot all the blue jays you want, if you can hit 'em, but remember it's a sin to kill a mockingbird." That was the only time I ever heard Atticus say it was a sin to do something, and I asked Miss Maudie about it. "Your father's right," she said. "Mockingbirds don't do one thing except make music for us to enjoy. They ......(17)...... eat up people's gardens, don't nest in corn cribs, they don't do one thing but ......(18)...... their hearts out for us. That's why it's a sin to kill a mockingbird.'

16. (a) you went (b) you'll go
(c) you go (d) you had been gone

17. (a) didn't (b) hadn't
(c) haven't (d) don't

18. (a) sang (b) sung
(c) sings (d) sing

2. Transformation of Sentences

Change the tense of the following sentences as directed without changing their meaning.

1. **Change into Simple Present Tense.**

Anand was breathing oxygen from the cylinder.

(a) Anand breathe oxygen from the cylinder.
(b) Anand breathes oxygen from the cylinder.
(c) Anand is breathing oxygen from the cylinder.
(d) Anand took a breath of oxygen from the cylinder.

2. **Change into Simple Past Tense.**

But I have taken my revenge at last.

(a) But I had taken my revenge at last.
(b) But I taken my revenge at last.
(c) But I took my revenge at last.
(d) But I have my revenge at last.

3. **Change into Future Perfect Continuous Tense.**

I had been working for Anil.

(a) I will have worked for Anil.
(b) I will work for Anil.
(c) I will be working for Anil.
(d) I will have been working for Anil.

4. **Change into Past Continuous Tense.**

Dingko Singh had inspired many youngsters in Manipur.

(a) Dingko Singh did inspiring many youngsters in Manipur.
(b) Dingko Singh had been inspiring many youngsters in Manipur.
(c) Dingko Singh was being inspired many youngsters in Manipur.
(d) Dingko Singh was inspiring many youngsters in Manipur.

5. **Change into Simple Future Tense.**

What are we doing?

(a) What shall we be doing?
(b) What shall we have been doing?
(c) What shall we do?
(d) What shall be done?

6. **Change into Present Perfect Tense.**

She had an eager interest in athletics.

(a) She had have an eager interest in athletics.
(b) She had had an eager interest in athletics.
(c) She has an eager interest in athletics.
(d) She has had an eager interest in athletics.

7. Change into Past Perfect Tense.

The chairs were being arranged.

(a) The chairs had arranged.

(b) The chairs had been arranged.

(c) The chairs were arranged.

(d) The chairs had had arranged.

8. Change into Simple Future Tense.

He was kidnapped by an extremist militia.

(a) He will be kidnapped by an extremist militia.

(b) He will have been kidnapped by an extremist militia.

(c) He will be kidnapping by an extremist militia.

(d) He will kidnapped by an extremist militia.

9. Change into Present Continuous Tense. **Competency Based**

Will you train your child to be a boxer as well?

(a) Are you training your child to be a boxer as well?

(b) Were you training your child to be a boxer as well?

(c) Will you have been training your child to be a boxer as well?

(d) Are you being trained your child to be a boxer as well?

10. Change into Future Perfect Tense.

I had a cup of coffee in the morning.

(a) I will have had a cup of coffee in the morning.

(b) I will have a cup of coffee in the morning.

(c) I shall be having a cup of coffee in the morning.

(d) I will had a cup of coffee in the morning.

Subjective Type Questions

1. Gap Filling

***Directions** (1-6) Fill in the blanks with the correct form of verb given in the brackets to complete the passage.*

The first half of the 20th century was dominated by the two World Wars. The wars resulted in unprecedented numbers of casualties. Eight and a half million people are believed ....(1)....... (die) fighting in the First World War of 1914-1918. During the Second World War as many as 60 million ......(2)....... (kill) in Asia and the Pacific. From all the total number of casualties, half ....(3)......... (to be) civilians.

I met Sherlock Holmes by chance. It seems strange to me that such random occurrences may have such an impact on the direction of one's life, but that is precisely what happened that day in London. I ......(4)...... (return) to the city in 1879 after a bullet wound in my shoulder had ended my career as an army surgeon. My pension barely ......(5)...... (covered) the expense of keeping a room at a hotel, and my health was too fragile for me to find work as a doctor.

I was having a drink at the Criterion Bar and considering how to find cheaper lodgings when someone tapped me on the shoulder. I turned to see young Stamford, who ......(6)...... (assist) me when I was a doctor at St. Bartholomew's Hospital.'

***Directions** (7-15) Fill in the blanks with the correct form of verb given in the brackets.*

7. After she .... (fail) to turn up for our appointment for the third time, I ....(refuse) to meet her again.

8. Since I took part in my first debating match, I .... (be) a member of the debating club, which I .... (attend) most weekends.

9. By the first half of the 19th century, potato .... (become) the staple food in the Ireland. In 1854, a disease .... (strike), which resulted in widespread starvation.

10. The origins of domestic poultry .... (to be) uncertain, but experts believe that some breeds are descended from the Indian jungle-fowl, which still ....(exist) in India today. **Competency Based**

11. Shadow puppets .... (originate) in China and .... (spread) as far as Turkey and Greece today.

12. I took a deep breath and .... to the old brag of my heart. (listen)

13. My mother .... the best pasta for dinner yesterday. (make)

14. She had waited all her life for something, and it .... her when it found her. (kill)

15. The Samyukta Kisan Morcha leadership .... the farmers' protests after the repeal of farm laws. (withdraw)

2. Transformation of Sentences

Change the tense of the following sentences as directed without changing their meaning.

1. Change into Present Perfect Tense.

I have been working here since I graduated school.

2. Change into Past Indefinite Tense.

He hadn't washed his car this morning.

3. Change into Future Perfect Continuous Tense.

Be 2021, we will have waited in Morocco for 2 years.

4. Change into Past Perfect Continuous Tense.

I have been working on my laptop for the past hour.

5. Change into Present Indefinite Tense.

They will leave the classroom in a short period of time.

6. Change into Future Perfect Tense.

The Sun will not be rising till 4 o'clock.

7. Change into Present Continuous Tense.

We will be planning a surprise party for Rishabh.

8. Change into Past Perfect Tense.

He went to the coffee shop before she arrived.

9. Change into Future Continuous Tense.

Mishti will run in the race next week.

10. Change into Past Continuous Tense.

Had she been reading a book when they came?

Answers

Check Point 1

1. (a) am (b) carries
(c) is (d) cannot
(e) comes (f) has found
(g) has performed (h) are gossiping and whiling away
(i) keeps (j) creates, writes
2. (a) are (b) am
(c) is (d) have
(e) is (f) have been trying
(g) do not know (h) cannot fix

Check Point 2

1. (a) was still working (b) fell
(c) were going (d) burnt
(e) was waiting (f) had harvested
(g) had fought, attained (h) had departed
2. (a) was brought up (b) had been working
(c) heard (d) has been staying
(e) broke, was dancing (f) had given
(g) has not written (h) rang, was having

Check Point 3

1. (a) will want (b) will operate
(c) will stay (d) will win
(e) will start (f) will have corrected
(g) will certainly get (h) will have finished
2. (a) will have left (b) have arrived
(c) will have ended (d) will start
(e) will probably assign (f) will have finished
(g) be completing (h) will have passed
3. (a) were driving (b) saw
(c) thought

Answers to Exam Practice

Objective Type Questions

1. Gap Filling

1. (b) arrived / had reached
2. (c) got/was flying
3. (a) anchor/will have been sailing
4. (d) are going to train/will revert
5. (d) had found/had been panning
6. (b) will have become/will be looking
7. (c) is explaining/hasn't played
8. (a) saw/had been stealing
9. (b) will be walking/will have healed
10. (d) have lost/is regaining
11. (c) is newly emerging
12. (c) had forgotten, was
13. (d) will be landing
14. (b) will have been recording
15. (b) had run, reached
16. (b) you'll go
17. (d) don't
18. (d) sing

2. Transformation of Sentences

1. (b) Anand breathes oxygen from the cylinder.
2. (c) But I took my revenge at last.
3. (d) I will have been working for Anil.
4. (d) Dingko Singh was inspiring many youngsters in Manipur.
5. (c) What shall we do?
6. (c) She has an eager interest in athletics.
7. (b) The chairs had been arranged.
8. (a) He will be kidnapped by an extremist militia.
9. (a) Are you training your child to be a boxer as well?
10. (a) I will have had a cup of coffee in the morning.

Subjective Type Questions

1. Gap Filling

1. to have died
2. were killed
3. were
4. had returned
5. covered
6. had assisted
7. had failed, refused
8. have been, attend
9. had become, struck
10. are, exists
11. originated, have spread
12. listened
13. made
14. had killed
15. has withdrawn

2. Transformation of Sentences

1. I have worked here since I graduated school.
2. He didn't wash his car this morning.
3. By 2021, we will have been waiting in Morocco for 2 years.
4. I had been working on my laptop for the past hour.
5. They left the classroom a short period of time ago.
6. The Sun will not have risen by 4 o'clock.
7. We are planning a surprise party for Rishabh.
8. He had gone to the coffee shop when she arrived.
9. Mishti will be running in the race next week.
10. Was she reading a book when they came?

02

CHAPTER

A clause is a group of related words containing a subject and a verb. It is a larger word group than a phrase and includes a little more information.

▼ **YOUR STUDY GOALS**

- Independent Clause
- Dependent Clause

Clauses

Types of Clauses

There are two types of clauses

1. Independent Clause (Main/Principal Clause)

Independent clause is the main/principal clause in a sentence. It can stand alone and thus, can be called a sentence. It does not start with subordinate conjunctions such as **when, which** or **if.**

The main properties of an independent clause are

- It contains a subject.
- It contains an action.
- It expresses a complete thought.

e.g.
- I am going to the planetarium.
  (Here, 'I' is the subject and 'am going' is the action.)
- The food has become stale.
  (Here, 'The food' is the subject and 'has become' is the action.)

2. Dependent Clause (Subordinate Clause)

A dependent clause is a subordinate clause. It cannot stand alone as a sentence and requires an independent clause to be meaningful.

Dependent clauses are further divided into three kinds

Kinds of Dependent Clause

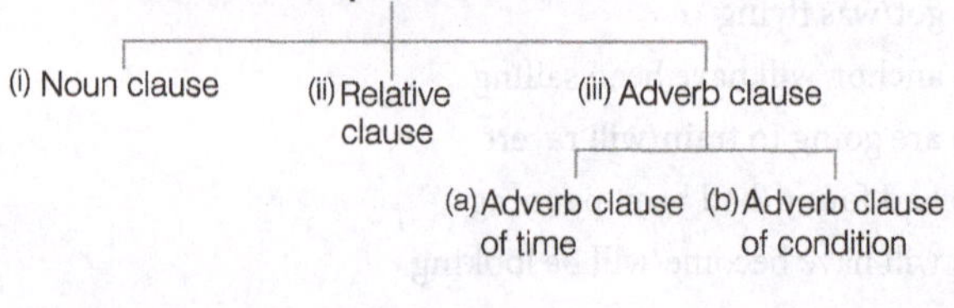

(i) Noun Clause

A noun clause is a dependent clause that acts as a noun in a sentence. It begins with words such as *how, that, what, whatever, when, where, whether, which, whichever, who, whoever, whom, whomever and why.* These words generally come before the subject and the verb of the noun clause.

e.g.
- *When he will make full recovery* is uncertain.
- One can never understand the meaning in *what he does.*
- They are confident *that they will win the prize for the Best Band of 2021.*

(ii) Relative Clause

Relative clauses are dependent clauses introduced by a relative pronoun such as *(that, which, whichever, who, whoever, whom, whomever, whose and of which).* Relative clauses add extra information to a sentence by defining a noun. Relative clauses are also called **adjective clauses.** *The introductory words used for various categories of nouns are*

For people	*who, whose* or *what*
For things	*which* or *that*
For places	*where*
For times	*when*
For possession	*whose*

e.g.
- The woman *you met yesterday* is my wife.
- The boy *who came to play with my little brother* is my friend.
- The house *which was empty for so long* has soon recently been inhabited.

Check Point 1

1 Complete each sentence with a properly formed noun clause by selecting from the options given. **Competency Based**

(a) Ravi asked me ...... (where was his wallet/where his wallet was).

(b) I don't know ...... (how many children he has/how many children does he have).

(c) (How close we are/How close are we) ...... is not important.

(d) (What did she say/What she said) ...... was sad.

(e) We are not responsible for ...... (what our children say/what do our children say).

2 Complete each sentence with what or that. In this question, what is used for noun clauses and that is used for relative clauses.

(a) ...... he said is not important.

(b) The book ...... I'm reading is very interesting.

(c) The world needs more people ...... help animals to survive.

(d) Many of the people ...... saw that movie were disappointed.

(e) Do you believe ...... he told us? Yes, I think he was telling the truth.

(iii) Adverb Clause

An adverb clause (also called adverbial clause) is a word or expression in a sentence that functions as an adverb. It adds extra information about the time, place, manner, etc. to a sentence and modifies the verb.

The adverbial clause may come before or after the main clause. When it comes before the main clause, a **comma is used** to separate the two clauses. When it comes after the main clause, no comma is necessary.

e.g.
- *Once they saw the car coming*, the birds flew away from the road.
- *Although she has a business degree*, she is working as a retail clerk.
- We must make reservations **before we go to the restaurant**.
- You have to go to bed now **whether you like it or not.**

Types of Adverb Clause

The two commonly used adverb clauses are

(a) **Adverb Clause of Time** We use adverb clause of time to tell the time when an action takes place.

Subordinating Conjunctions used with these clauses are **when, whenever, anytime, before, after, till, until, while, since, just as, as soon as, as often as, now that, as long as,** etc.

e.g.
- I was not at home *when he came to see me.*
- *As soon as she finished that project*, she started working on the next.

(b) **Adverb Clause of Condition** We use adverb clause of condition to tell the condition under which an action takes place or someone does something.

Subordinating Conjunctions used with these clauses are **if, even if, whether, if.....not, unless, supposing that, provided that, in the condition that, as long as that,** etc.

e.g. • You will be shot *unless you give me the keys of the locker.*
• *Should you meet my brother*, tell him that I have gone to the railway station.

Check Point 2

1 Complete each adverb clause below with the correct conjunctions by selecting them from the options given.

(a) (So that/After) ...... he saw the way the animals were treated, he stopped eating meat.

(b) (After/Although) ...... he worked very hard, his boss did not give him a raise.

(c) (So that/Because) ... you have no money, I'll pay for you.

(d) I said goodbye to all my local friends (because/before) ...... I moved to Mumbai.

(e) I will show you how to prepare this sweet dish (so that/because) ...... you can prepare it for your family.

(f) (Before/Since) ...... he discovered this website, he couldn't speak English.

(g) I'm going to ask someone else (before/since) ...... you obviously don't know the answer.

(h) (Unless/After) ...... they saw him turning the corner, they knew that he was going to win the race.

2 Complete the combined single sentence given below the two sentences by choosing the correct reduced adverb clause from the options given in brackets.

(a) They played basketball for two hours. Later, they went home.
...... (After playing basketball/Playing basketball) for two hours, they went home.

(b) I was reading your essay. I noticed a lot of mistakes.
...... (Before reading your essay/While reading your essay), I noticed a lot of mistakes.

(c) I didn't want to miss my train. I set my alarm clock for 6 AM.
...... (Not wanting to miss my train/While not wanting to miss my train), I set my alarm clock for 6 AM.

(d) You came here. Before that, you were sad.
...... (Before coming here/While coming here), you were sad.

(e) She returned from work. She noticed that the front door was open.
...... (Upon returning from work/While returning from work), she noticed that the front door was open.

(f) He is a perfectionist. He noticed all the flaws.
...... (Being a perfectionist/Since being a perfectionist), he noticed all the flaws.

Clauses at a Glance

Clauses	Definition	Begins with	Example
Noun Clause	• that functions as a noun. • answers the question 'what' to the main verb	**Connectives** like who, whose, whom, when, where, which, what, why, how, that, if and whether	• Nisha told me **that she was feeling unwell.** • Your success depends on how **you prepare yourself.**
Relative Clause/Adjective Clause	• describes a noun or pronoun.	**Relative Pronouns** like who, whose, whom, that, which, whichever, whoever, of which	• They work in a factory **whose owner is cruel.** • This is the girl **whose mother has been appointed as Director.**
Adverb Clause	• it tells you something about how the action was done. **Adverb Clause of Time** tells the time when the action takes place.	**Subordinating Conjunctions** like when, whenever, anytime, before, after, till, until, while, since, just as, as soon as, as often as, now that, as long as	• **As soon as he saw his mother**, he began to weep. • The world will always be the same **as long as men are men.**
	Adverb Clause of Condition tells the condition under which the action happens or someone does something.	**Subordinating Conjunctions** like if, whether, as long as, unless, provided that, supposing that, in that condition	• **If it rains** we shall stay home. • I won't pay it **unless he sends me the bill again.**

Exam Pattern Questions

Objective Type Questions

1. Gap Filling

Fill in the blanks in the following sentences by choosing the correct option.

1. Listen to .... your brother says.
(a) when (b) how (c) what (d) why

2. My friend admitted .... he was guilty.
(a) that (b) as (c) when (d) whenever

3. Suman found ...... she had passed the test.
(a) when (b) that (c) if (d) as

4. You may do .... you like.
(a) how (b) what (c) since (d) unless

5. She has a book .... she can give to you.
(a) which (b) what (c) when (d) as

6. My friend has a bowl .... is made of silver.
(a) that (b) who
(c) which (d) Both (a) and (c)

7. Your action is such .... cannot be pardoned.
(a) that (b) because (c) as (d) since

8. .... you recommended him, I appointed him.
(a) Since (b) If (c) When (d) Though

9. .... I know, she is dullard.
(a) Since (b) So far as
(c) Although (d) Because

10. She works hard, ... she may get a scholarship.
(a) so that (b) as
(c) such that (d) when

11. Do you understand .... the email contains?
(a) what (b) if (c) how (d) unitl

12. She will never forget the day .... the accident occurred.
(a) before (b) when (c) while (d) unless

13. My sister was playing with our dad .... I was in the kitchen helping mom.
(a) where (b) while
(c) who (d) None of these

14. The boy is standing .... far away .... he cannot be seen without binoculars.
(a) so, that (b) such, that
(c) in case, that (d) where, there

15. She wants to find out .... the party is today or not.
(a) either (b) whether (c) why (d) when

2. Sentence Reordering

Rearrange the parts of the sentence in correct order.

1. P : so much noise
Q : you make
R : cannot work
S : that I
(a) QSPR (b) QPSR (c) RSQP (d) RPSQ

2. P : as though
Q : he were
R : mad
S : he acts
(a) SPQR (b) SRQP (c) PQRS (d) PRSQ

3. P : wherever you
Q : like to sit
R : you may
S : sit
(a) RPSQ (b) SPQR (c) RQSP (d) RSPQ

4. P : the money
Q : that you gave
R : was spent
S : me
(a) PSRQ (b) PRSQ (c) PQSR (d) RSPQ

5. P : she ran away
Q : because she
R : afraid
S : was
(a) PSQR (b) PQSR (c) RQSP (d) RSPQ

6. P : send me a telegram
Q : in case you
R : train
S : miss the
(a) PQRS (b) PSRQ (c) SRQP (d) QSRP

7. P : who built
Q : I know
R : the house
S : the man
(a) QSRP (b) PQRS (c) QSPR (d) PRQS

8. P : endured
Q : must be
R : cannot be cured
S : what
(a) PQRS (b) PSQR (c) SPQR (d) SRQP

9. P : the gallery
Q : which holds only

R : one thousand people
S : was crowded
(a) PQRS (b) SRQP (c) SQRP (d) PRQS

10. P : requires?
Q : can you
R : what he
S : tell me
(a) QSPR (b) QSRP (c) PRSQ (d) RSPQ

11. P : how he
Q : I can
R : tell you
S : stole your watch
(a) PQRS (b) SRQP (c) SPQR (d) QRPS

12. P : a mystery
Q : why he
R : place is
S : left the
(a) PQRS (b) SRQP (c) QRSP (d) QSRP

13. P : is just a matter of
Q : geting your account opened
R : providing certain details and
S : funding your account
(a) QPRS (b) SPRQ
(c) PRSQ (d) RSPQ

14. P : Kalamkari is a type of
Q : States of Andhra Pradesh and Telangana
R : hand-painted or block-printed cotton
S : textile, produced in the Indian
(a) PSRQ (b) QRSP
(c) SQPR (d) PRSQ

15. P : the whole idea of
Q : majority and minority
R : in India
S : is irrelevant and inappropriate
(a) PRQS (b) PQRS
(c) SRQP (d) PQSR

Subjective Type Questions

Fill in the blanks with correct connecting words to complete the sentences with clauses.

1. She runs fast .... she missed the train.
2. .... I had finished my homework, I went to bed.
3. We played cricket to pass time .... the bus came.
4. Always lock your car .... you leave it.
5. Let's cross the bridge .... we come to it.
6. We'll keep on driving .... there's still daylight.
7. Shikha has changed a lot .... I last saw her.
8. He'll keep the book for me ..... I, come back.
9. A baby starts crying ...... it is born.
10. .... you have time, you should call him.
11. I am going to play with the toy …… was a gift from my grandfather.
12. …… he won the game or not is still unknown.
13. She brushed her hair …… she saw her reflection.
14. We haven't seen our class teacher …… the morning assembly.
15. Do you recognise the woman …… was on the TV last night.

Answers

Answers to Check Points

Check Point 1

1. (a) where his wallet was (b) how many children he has
   (c) How close we are (d) What she said
   (e) what our children say
2. (a) What (b) that (c) that
   (d) that (e) what

Check Point 2

1. (a) After (b) Although
   (c) Because (d) before
   (e) so that (f) Before
   (g) since (h) After
2. (a) After playing basketball
   (b) While reading your essay
   (c) Not wanting to miss my train
   (d) Before coming here
   (e) Upon returning from work
   (f) Being a perfectionist

Answers to Exam Practice

Objective Type Questions (MCQ)

Gap Filling

1. (c) what
2. (a) that
3. (b) that
4. (b) what
5. (a) which
6. (d) Both (a) and (c)
7. (a) that
8. (a) Since
9. (b) So far as
10. (a) so that
11. (a) what
12. (b) when
13. (b) while
14. (a) so, that
15. (b) whether

Sentence Reordering

1. (b) QPSR
2. (a) SPQR
3. (d) RSPQ
4. (c) PQSR
5. (b) PQSR
6. (d) QSRP
7. (c) QSPR
8. (d) SRQP
9. (a) PQRS
10. (b) QSRP
11. (d) QRPS
12. (d) QSRP
13. (a) QPRS
14. (d) PRSQ
15. (b) PQRS

Gap Filling

1. yet
2. After
3. until
4. whenever
5. when
6. while
7. since
8. till
9. as soon as
10. when
11. which/that
12. Whether
13. as soon as
14. since
15. who

03

CHAPTER

Transformation of sentences is the process by which a sentence in particular form is transferred to another without altering its meaning.

YOUR STUDY GOALS

- Active and Passive Voice
- Reported speech
- Adjective — Degree of Comparison
- Types of Sentence

Transformation of Sentences

Basis of Transforming Sentences

We transform sentences on various basis

- Voice
- Reported speech
- Adjectives-Degrees of comparison
- Type of sentences

All of these transformations follow certain rules which are discussed below

Active and Passive Voice

We know in **Active Voice,** the subject is the doer of the action.

In **Passive voice,** the action is done by the subject.

Changing Active Voice into Passive Voice

1. The subject of the verb in the active voice becomes the object in the passive voice sentences.

   For example

   Kanika is cleaning the house. (Active)

   The house is being cleaned by **Kanika.** (Passive)

2. The third form of the verb, (the past participle form of the verb) is used in the passive voice.

   For example

   Kanishk **buys** a pen every week. (Active)

   A pen is **bought** by Kanishk every week. (Passive)

3. Auxiliary verb 'be' (am, is are, was, were) is added before the past participle according to the tense of the verb.

   For example

   The postman delivered the letters on time. (Active)

   The letters **were** delivered by the postman on time. (Passive)

4. Generally, 'by' is used before the object of the passive voice sentences.

   For example

   The teachers are attending a meeting. (Active)

   A meeting is being attended **by** the teachers. (Passive)

5. Certain verbs take fixed prepositions after them instead of 'by'. Some of these verbs are: known to, surprised by/at, contained in, annoyed with/at, etc.

   For example

   The child's irrelevant pleadings annoyed his parents. (Active)

   His parents were **annoyed at** him for his irrelevant pleadings. (Passive)

6. The pronouns are changed into objective case while changing into passive voice.

   For example

   I water my plants everyday. (Active)

   My plants are watered by **me** everyday. (Passive)

7. If the subject of the sentence is not known, we can drop the subject in to the passive voice.

   For example

   Someone has sent me a bouquet of flowers. (Active)

   A bouquet of flowers has been sent to me. (Passive)

8. When a sentence in active voice has a modal auxiliary (can, could, may, might, etc.), the modal verb does not change its form.

For example

Shaurya **can** cook many international cuisines. (Active)

Many international cuisines **can be** cooked by Shaurya. (Passive)

Changing Interrogative Sentences into Passive Voice

When an interrogative sentence is changed into passive voice, the sentence remains in the question form and further changes are done in the following manner.

1. The question words such as what, why, when, where, which and how do not change and remain at the starting position of the sentence.

   For example

   What did you buy? (Active)

   What was bought by you? (Passive)

> **Note** 'Who' is converted to 'By whom' in passive voice.
>
> **For example**
>
> Who told you about tomorrow's holiday? (Active)
>
> **By whom** were you told about tomorrow's holiday? (Passive)

2. (i) The questions that start with helping verbs do/ does/ did are changed into be verbs (is, am, are, was, were) in the passive voice.

   For example

   Do they perform fine arts? (Active)

   Are fine arts performed by them? (Passive)

   (ii) The questions that start with helping verbs has/ have are changed into has been/ have been in the passive voice.

   For example

   Have they won the match? (Active)

   Has the match **been** won by them? (Passive)

   (iii) When the questions start with modal auxiliaries, the modal verbs do not change their forms and remain at the starting position of the sentence in the passive voice.

   For example

   Can you sing a song?

   Can a song **be** sung by you?

Changing Imperative Sentences into Passive Voice

1. Subject is usually not mentioned in imperative sentences. Thus, they can be changed into passive voice in the following manner:

   For example

   Do not harm the animals. (Active)

   The animals **should not be** harmed. (Passive)

   OR

   Let the animals not be harmed. (Passive)

   OR

   You are advised not to harm the animals. (Passive)

2. If the sentence starts with 'Let', change it into passive voice in the following manner.

   For example

   Let him feed the dog. (Active)

   Let the dog **be** fed by him. (Passive)

Check Point 1

1 **Change the following sentences in active/ passive voice into passive/ active voice.**

(i) Will schemes for unemployed graduates have been made by the government? **Competency Based**
   (a) Will the government have made schemes for unemployed graduates?
   (b) Will the schemes have made for unemployed graduates by government?
   (c) Will the government have been making schemes for unemployed graduates?
   (d) Have the government made schemes for unemployed graduates?

(ii) Let it be carried home.
   (a) It should be carried home.
   (b) You are ordered to carry it home.
   (c) Carry it home.
   (d) Carry it home at once.

(iii) What has been thrown by her?
   (a) What was she thrown?
   (b) What she thrown?
   (c) What have she thrown?
   (d) What has she thrown?

(iv) Why is milk not being drunk by him?
   (a) Why not he is drinking milk?
   (b) Why is not he drinking milk?
   (c) Why is he not drinking milk?
   (d) Why was not he drinking milk?

(v) The report was mislaid.
   (a) Somebody mislaid the report.
   (b) The report was mislaid by someone.
   (c) Somebody mislaids the report.
   (d) Somebody mislead the report.

2 **Change the following sentences in active/ passive voice into passive/ active voice.**

(i) A father ought to earn the bread.
(ii) I need to submit my homework.
(iii) Have the lands been cultivated by the farmers?
(iv) I will send money to my parents in the village.
(v) He was not being teased by us.

Reported Speech

Basic Rules of Speech and Conversion

We know

In **direct speech**, the exact words of the speakers are used.

In **indirect speech**, the words are told to someone else.

Note Reporting verb is the verb placed outside the inverted commas in direct speech.

Rules for Changing Simple Direct Speech into Indirect Speech

Rules	Direct Speech	Indirect Speech
Remove separating comma, inverted commas and use the connector 'that'.	He said, "I do not like pasta."	He said that he did not like pasta.
When there is an object in Reporting verb, change 'said to' into 'told' and 'says to' into 'tells'.	• He said to me, "You have been a great help." • He says to me, "My teacher is highly educated."	• He told me that I had been a great help. • He tells me that his teacher is highly educated.
When there is no object in Reporting verb, 'said' and 'says' remain the same.	Sheeba said, "I work in an MNC." Kamya says, "I will go to the party."	Sheeba said that she worked in an MNC. Kamya says that she will go to the party.

Changes in Reported Speech when Reporting Verb is in Past Tense

Change of Verb Forms	Change of Pronouns	Time, Place Expressions and Other Changes
is, am, are — was, were	1st person → according to the subject	now — then
has, have — had	2nd person → according to the object	ago — before

$V_1 - V_2$	3rd person → unchanged	today — that day
did — had + IIIrd form of the verb	2nd person → changed to 3rd person if the reporting verb has no object	last night—the previous night or the night before
was, were — had been		next week — the following week
will — would		here — there
shall — should		
can — could		this — that

Tensewise Conversion of Direct into Indirect Speech

Present Tense

Simple Present Changes to Simple Past

Direct Speech	Indirect Speech
(i) Ashi said, "Govind sings bollywood songs."	Ashi said that Govind sang bollywood songs.
(ii) Mohit said to Neetu, "You look very nice in this dress."	Mohit told Neetu that she looked very nice in that dress.

Exception If the reported speech is a universal truth or a general fact, then its 'tense' does not change.

Direct Speech	Indirect Speech
(i) My father said, "The Earth is round."	My father said that the Earth is round.
(ii) Our teacher said to us, "Respecting elders is a virtue."	Our teacher told us that respecting elders is a virtue.

Present Continuous Changes to Past Continuous

Direct Speech	Indirect Speech
(i) I said to her, "You are doing a good job."	I told her that she was doing a good job.
(ii) Bhakti said, "I am looking for a good novel to read now."	Bhakti said that she was looking for a good novel to read then.

Present Perfect Changes to Past Perfect

Direct Speech	Indirect Speech
(i) I said, "I have watched this movie earlier."	I said that I had watched that movie earlier.
(ii) Raman said to Ishita, "You have done it wonderfully."	Raman told Ishita that she had done it wonderfully.

Present Perfect Continuous Changes to Past Perfect Continuous

Direct Speech	Indirect Speech
(i) Aunt said, "Women have been tolerating a lot for years."	Aunt said that women had been tolerating a lot for years.
(ii) Bunty said to Shipra, "I have been working on this project for two years."	Bunty told Shipra that he had been working on that project for two years.

Past Tense

Simple Past Changes to Past Perfect

Direct Speech	Indirect Speech
(i) "We got here yesterday", said Manu.	Manu said that they had got there the previous day.
(ii) Ketan said to mother, "You made my day with such a delicious meal."	Ketan told mother that she had made his day with such a delicious meal.

Past Continuous Changes to Past Perfect Continuous

Direct Speech	Indirect Speech
(i) Ninad said, "I was playing football in the morning."	Ninad said that he had been playing football in the morning.
(ii) My father said to me, "India was living in peace before the British came."	My father told me that India had been living in peace before the British had come.

Past Perfect remains Past Perfect

Direct Speech	Indirect Speech
(i) She said, "I had finished my job before 5 pm."	She said that she had finished her job before 5 pm.
(ii) Madhavi said to Manish, "You had borrowed a suitcase from me."	Madhavi told Manish that he had borrowed a suitcase from her.

Future Tense

Simple Future (Shall/Will) Changes to (Should/Would)

Direct Speech	Indirect Speech
(i) Anurag said, "I will give India a very nice movie next year."	Anurag said that he would give India a very nice movie the coming year.

Direct Speech	Indirect Speech
(ii) Shaina said to Survi, "You shall perform the role of the princess."	Shaina told Survi that she would perform the role of the princess.

Future Continuous (Shall be/Will be) **Changes to** (Should be/Would be)

Direct Speech	Indirect Speech
(i) Mann said, "You shall be following my orders."	Mann said that he/she/they should be following his orders.
(ii) Father said, "I will be joining you all at the airport."	Father said that he would be joining us all at the airport.

Future Perfect (Shall/Will + have) **Changes to** (Would + have)

Direct Speech	Indirect Speech
(i) He said, "I will have completed my MBA by next year."	He said that he would have completed his MBA by the coming year.
(ii) Gurmeet said to Manpreet, "I will have taught you good spoken English by next month."	Gurmeet told Manpreet that he would have taught her good spoken English by the next month.

Rules for Changing Interrogative Sentences into Indirect Speech

Interrogative sentences are of two types

(i) Yes-No type questions or verbal questions

(ii) Wh-type questions

Yes-No Type Questions

When the reported speech is a yes-no type question. Further, the reporting verb is changed from 'says' and 'said' to 'asks' and 'asked', respectively. The conjunction 'if' or 'whether' is used and the interrogative sentence (or question) is converted into an assertive sentence.

The other changes (tense, pronouns, etc.) are made as usual.

Direct Speech	Indirect Speech
(i) I said to Mayur, "Do you like mangoes?"	I asked Mayur if he liked mangoes.
(ii) Rohan said to his brother "Are you coming with me?"	Rohan asked his brother whether he was going with him.

Wh-Type Questions

No conjunction is used as the Wh-word itself works as a conjunction to join the reporting verb with the reported speech. All other changes are made in the same manner as the yes-no type questions.

Direct Speech	Indirect Speech
(i) The man said to the boy, "Where did you come from?"	The man asked the boy where he had come from.
(ii) Anup said to me, "Which movie do you like the most?"	Anup asked me which movie I liked the most.
(iii) Harsh said to his mother, "Who was the first man to travel to the space?"	Harsh asked his mother who the first man to travel to the space had been.
(iv) I said to her, "How long will you stay here?"	I asked her how long she would stay **here**.

Rules for Changing Imperative Sentences into Indirect Speech

Depending upon the type of imperative sentence (i.e. order, suggestion, advice, request, etc.), the reporting verb is changed into ordered, suggested, advised, requested, etc. Further, the preposition 'to' is used in place of conjunction after the reporting verb.

- In case of negative imperative sentences (such as don't play there), 'to' is put after 'not' that follows reporting verb.
- In case of sentences beginning with 'Let's', the reporting verb is changed to proposed or suggested.

Direct Speech	Indirect Speech
(i) The teacher said to the students, "Quickly settle down and open your books."	The teacher ordered the students to settle down quickly and open their books.
(ii) Rati said to Mani, "Please, pass the salt and pepper."	Rati requested Mani to pass the salt and pepper.
(iii) Pari said to her friend, "Take proper rest."	Pari advised her friend to take proper rest.
(iv) I said to my sister, "Let's go for a movie tonight."	I suggested my sister that we should go for a movie that night.

Rules for Changing Exclamatory Sentences into Indirect Speech

- We replace the reporting verb with 'exclaimed with joy,' 'exclaimed with sorrow', 'exclaimed with surprise', etc. according to the sense of the reported speech.
- The conjunction 'that' is used.

Direct Speech	Indirect Speech
(i) Ritu said, "Wow! That's beautiful".	Ritu exclaimed with joy that it was beautiful.
(ii) He said, "Alas! His heartbeats have stopped."	He exclaimed with sorrow that his heartbeats had stopped.
(iii) She said, "Oops! The power is cut."	She exclaimed that the power was cut.

Check Point 2

1 **Change the given sentences into indirect speech and choose the correct option.**

(i) Sushma said to Asmita, "Where are you going?"
  (a) Sushma asked Asmita where she is going.
  (b) Sushma asked Asmita where was she going.
  (c) Sushma asked Asmita where she was going.
  (d) Sushma asked Asmita where had she been going.

(ii) She said to me, "The Charlatan will be breaking into the safe."
  (a) She told me that the Charlatan would be breaking into the safe.
  (b) She said to me that the Charlatan will be breaking in the safe.
  (c) She said to me that the Charlatan can be breaking into the safe.
  (d) She said to me that the Charlatan is breaking into the safe.

(iii) The kids yelled in a loud voice, "We love our family."
  (a) The kids yelled in a loud voice that they loved our family.
  (b) The kids were shouting loudly that they loved their family.
  (c) The kids yelled in a loud voice that they loved their family.
  (d) The kids yelled loudly that they love our family.

(iv) I said to Amit, "I am not participating in the annual function."
  (a) I said Amit that I was not participating in the annual function.
  (b) I told Amit that he was not participating in the annual function.
  (c) I told Amit that I was not participating in the annual function.
  (d) I told to Amit that I was not participating in the annual function.

(v) The father said to Apoorva, "Change the dress."
  (a) The father ordered Apoorva to change the dress.
  (b) The father requested Apoorva to change the dress.
  (c) The father urged Apoorva to change the dress.
  (d) The father asked Apoorva to change the dress.

2 **Change the given sentences into indirect speech.**

(i) He said, "Let us move to the party."
(ii) The police said, "No one was in this room."
(iii) He said to us, "Can we have some tea?"
(iv) The union leader said, "Let's show the management that we are always together."
(v) Sarita said, "You shall not miss the chance to study."

Adjectives - Degree of Comparison

Change of Degree

There are three degrees of adjectives.

Positive degree just states the quality of nouns without any comparison.

Comparative degree compares the same quality between two nouns.

Superlative degree compares the same quality of a noun with all others. It indicates the highest degree of quality.

Herein, it is important to note that by using different structures, we can use the degree of comparisons for different purposes. To understand it clearly, look at the following transformations.

Superlative Degree to Positive and Comparative Degree

When we use superlative degree, we mean to say that it has the highest degree of that particular quality among all the objects being compared. This means 'no other' object has that quality to the same degree.

We can also use the positive or the comparative degrees of adjectives to show the highest degree of a quality.

To transform superlative degree into positive degree, we use 'No other'. In comparative degree we use 'all other' or 'any other'. e.g.

(i) **Superlative Degree** Hardik is **the strongest** player of our team.

Positive Degree **No other player** of our team is **as strong as** Hardik.
↑ (Singular noun with 'no other')

Comparative Degree Hardik is **stronger than any other** player of our team.
↑ (Singular noun with 'any other') ↑ (The sentence begins with the same entity as

Or

Hardik is stronger than **all other players** of our team.
↑ (Plural noun with 'all other')

(ii) **Superlative Degree** Mumbai is **the most expensive** place to live in Maharashtra.

Positive Degree No other place in Maharashtra is as expensive to live in as Mumbai.

Comparative Degree Mumbai is **more expensive than** any other place to live in Maharashtra.

Positive to Comparative and Vice-Versa

We often use positive degree to make comparisons. In these cases we use the structure as + positive degree + as.

For example

Ram is as tall as shyam.

If we change this sentence to comparative degree, we use 'not' before the comparative degree of adjective.

For example

Shyam is not taller than Ram.

Note When the positive and the comparative degree are used to compare only two things or persons (like the above sentences), they cannot be transformed into superlative degree.

Check Point 3

1 **Change the given sentences as directed and choose the correct option.**

(i) English is as tough as French. (Use: tougher)

(a) French is tougher than English.
(b) French is not tougher than English.
(c) English is tougher than French.
(d) French is not tough.

(ii) Akhilesh Yadav is the youngest Chief Minister in India. (Use: younger)

(a) Akhilesh Yadav is younger than most other Chief Ministers in India.
(b) Akhilesh Yadav is younger than any other Chief Ministers in India.
(c) Akhilesh Yadav is younger than all other Chief Ministers in India.
(d) None of the above

(iii) Diamond is the costliest non-metal. (Use: costly)

(a) No other non-metal is as costly as diamond.
(b) Other non-metals are costly than diamond.
(c) No other non-metal is costly as diamond.
(d) Other non-metals are not costly as diamond.

(iv) Iodine is the most lustrous non-metal. (Use: as lustrous as)

(a) No other non-metal is as lustrous as iodine.
(b) No other metal is as lustrous as iodine.
(c) Some other non-metals are as lustrous as iodine.
(d) Other metals are as lustrous as iodine.

(v) Groundnuts are as good as cashewnuts. (Use: better)

(a) Groundnuts are better as cashewnuts.
(b) Cashewnuts are not better than groundnuts.
(c) Cashewnuts are better than groundnuts.
(d) All of the above

2 **Change the given sentences as directed.**

(i) Shakespeare is the most famous of all writers in English.
(Begin: No......)

(ii) Iron is more useful than any other metal.
(Begin: Iron..............)

(iii) I earn as much money as Ram.
(Begin Ram.............)

(iv) China is larger than India. (Use: large)

(v) Air is lighter than water. (Use: as....... as)

Types of Sentences

We know that sentences can be divided into various kinds on the basis of their use and the presence of dependent clauses.

On the basis of their uses, sentences can be

- **Assertive sentences** which include positive or negative statements.
- **Interrogative sentences** which ask questions.
- **Imperative sentences** which express order, suggestion, request, etc.
- **Exclamatory sentences** which express extreme emotions.

On the basis of the presence of dependent clause, sentences can be

- **Simple sentence** are independent or main clauses.
- **Complex sentences** contain one independent and at least one dependent clause.
- **Compound sentences** contain more than one independent clauses joined by a comma, semicolon or conjunction.

Now, lets study how we transform sentences into various kinds.

Interchanging Affirmative and Negative Sentences

Rule 1 Use antonyms in the sentence along with negative words like **'not'**, **'no'**, **'never'**, etc.

For example

- He is a **bad** man. (Affirmative)
  He is **not** a **good** man. (Negative)
- Prajjwal is **always punctual** to school. (Affirmative)
  Prajjwal is **never late** to school. (Negative)

Rule 2 When the positive sentences contain words like **only, everyone, everything,** etc., it is replaced with words like **none but** (for person), **nothing but** (for thing), etc.

For example

- **Only** you can solve this question. (Affirmative)
  None but you can solve this question. (Negative)
- I watch **only** horror movies. (Affirmative)
  I watch **nothing but** horror movies. (Negative)

Interchanging Assertive and Interrogative Sentences

Rule 1 If the question is not seeking an answer, change affirmative question into a negative sentence and vice-versa.

For example

- **Was** there a notebook on the table? (Positive Interrogative)
  There **wasn't** a notebook on the table. (Negative)
- **Weren't** you calling me? (Negative Interrogative)
  You **were** calling me. (Affirmative)

Rule 2 If the question is seeking an answer, use phrases like **'I wonder', 'I want to know'** or **'I would like to know'** in the assertive sentence.

For example

- What will he think of the gift I gave? (Interrogative)
  I wonder what he will think of the gift I gave. (Assertive)
- Which is your favourite book? (Interrogative)
  I would like to know your favourite book. (Assertive)

Interchanging Assertive and Exclamatory Sentences

Rule 1 When changing an exclamatory sentence into an assertive sentence, words like **'very', 'great', 'extremely'**, etc. are added.

For example

- How beautiful this monument is! (Exclamatory)
  This is a **very** beautiful monument. (Assertive)
- What a happy day this is! (Exclamatory)
  This is an **extremely** happy day. (Assertive)

Rule 2 Words expressing strong emotions like **'Hurrah!', 'Alas!'**, etc. in an exclamatory sentence are replaced by similar emotions in an assertive sentence.

For example

- **Hurrah!** We won the match.
  It is a matter of joy that we won the watch. (Assertive)
- **Alas!** I lost my phone.
  It is a matter of sorrow that I lost my phone. (Assertive)

Interchanging Simple and Compound Sentences

Rule 1 Convert the participle phrase present in the simple sentence into a clause by using a coordinating conjunction.

For example

- **Going home**, she had dinner. (Simple)
  She went home **and** had dinner. (Compound)
- **Being guilty**, he ran away and hid. (Simple)
  He was guilty **so** he ran away and hid. (Compound)

Rule 2 Use infinitives in place of conjunctions to convert a compound to a simple sentence.

For example

- He brought some flowers **and** gave them to his wife. (Compound)
  He brought some flowers **to give** to his wife. (Simple)

Interchanging Simple and Complex Sentences

Rule 1 Convert the adjective word or phrase present in the simple sentence into a subordinating clause by using a subordinating conjunction.

For example

- He was wearing a blue shirt. (Simple)
  He was wearing a shirt **which** was blue. (Complex)
- Dr. APJ Abdul Kalam, the Former President of India, was also a scientist. (Simple)
  Dr. APJ Abdul Kalam, **who** was the Former President of India, was also a scientist. (Complex)

Rule 2 Convert the participle phrase in the simple sentence to adverb clause by using an adverb.

For example

- Locking the door, I went to work (Simple)
  I went to work **after** locking the door. (Complex)

Rule 3 Use **'so...that'** in a complex sentence when changing from simple sentences containing **'to'** or **'too...to'**.

For example

- We drink water **to** survive. (Simple)
  We drink water **so that** we can survive. (Complex)
- He is **too** short **to** reach the shelf. (Simple)
  He is **so** short **that** he cannot reach the shelf. (Complex)

Interchanging Compound and Complex Sentences

Rule Convert either of the independent clauses in a compound sentence into a dependent clause and replace the coordinating conjunction with the subordinating conjunction.

For example

- You should hurry **or** you will miss the chance. (Compound)
  If you don't hurry, you will miss the chance. (Complex)
- The teacher entered the classroom **and** the students opened their books. (Compound)
  When the teacher entered the classroom, the students opened their books. (Complex)

Check Point 4

1 Change the given sentences as directed and choose the correct option.

(i) He arrived in school on time even though he stopped for a bit on the way.
Change into simple sentence.
(a) In spite stopping for a bit on the way, he arrived in school on time.
(b) Stopping for a bit on the way, he arrived in school on time.
(c) Despite of stopping for a bit on the way, he arrived in school on time.
(d) All of the above

(ii) The old woman was too slow to catch the bus.
Change into complex sentence.
(a) The old woman was so slow that she could not catch the bus.
(b) The old woman was so fast that she could not catch the bus.
(c) The old woman was so slow that she could catch the bus.
(d) The old woman was so fast that she could not catch the bus.

(iii) He will issue the cheque only when he hears from the head office.
Change into simple sentence.
(a) On hearing from the head office only he issue the cheque.
(b) On hearing from the head office only he will issue the cheque.
(c) On hearing from the head office only will he issue the cheque.
(d) On hearing from the head office he will only issue the cheque.

(iv) He was very intelligent and knowledgeable.
Change into exclamatory sentence.
(a) How intelligent and knowledgeable he is!
(b) How intelligent and knowledgeable he was!
(c) What intelligent and knowledgeable he was!
(d) What intelligent and knowledgeable he is!

(v) As soon as I heard the noise, I rushed to the spot.
Change into compound sentence.
(a) I heard the noise or rushed to the spot immediately.
(b) I heard the noise for rushed to the spot immediately.
(c) I heard the noise but rushed to the spot immediately.
(d) I heard the noise and rushed to the spot immediately.

2 Change the given sentences as directed.

(i) Doesn't my father read newspaper every morning? Change into assertive sentence.
(ii) He took off his clothes and jumped into the river. Change into simple sentence.
(iii) Nobody was absent in my class yesterday. Change into affirmative sentence.
(iv) That boy who is very tall is my best friend. Change into simple sentence.
(v) Alas! We have lost the debate competition. Change into assertive sentence.

Exam Pattern Questions

Objective Type Questions

Directions (Q. Nos. 1-20) Transform the following sentences as directed without changing their meaning.

1. "What time does the train arrive?" she asked.
Change into indirect speech.
(a) She said what time the train arrived.
(b) She asked what time the train had arrived.
(c) She asked what time the train arrived.
(d) She told what time the train does arrive.

2. The policeman said to the boy, "Where do you live?"
Change into indirect speech.
(a) The policeman asked the boy where he had lived.
(b) The policeman told the boy where he did lived.
(c) The policeman asked the boy where he lived.
(d) The policeman said to the boy where he do lived.

3. People expect that the Queen will appoint a new Prime Minister later today. **Competency Based**
Change into passive voice.
(a) A new Prime Minister was expected to be appointed later today.
(b) It will be expected that the Queen will appoint a new Prime Minister later today.
(c) The Queen is expected to appoint a new Prime Minister later today.
(d) It is expected Queen will appoint a new Prime Minister today.

4. Police are investigating a Russian citizen who was scrutinised for ties to Trump. **Competency Based**
Change into passive voice.
(a) A Russian citizen who was scrutinised for ties to Trump is being investigated.
(b) A Russian citizen was scrutinised for ties to Trump is being investigated.
(c) A Russian citizen who has been scrutinised for ties to Trump is being investigated by police.
(d) A Russian citizen who is scrutinised for ties to Trump is being investigated.

5. I have never worn a more ill-fitting suit.
(**End** worn)
(a) This is the more ill-fitted suit I have ever worn.
(b) This is the ill-fitted suit I have never worn.
(c) This is the most ill-fitted suit I have ever worn.
(d) This is the most ill-fitted suit I have never worn.

6. Anil is too fast a runner not to come first in the race.
(**Begin** Anil is so ....)
(a) Anil is so faster a runner, he came first in the race.
(b) Anil is so faster a runner that he came first in the race.
(c) Anil is so fast a runner that he came first in the race.
(d) Anil is so fastest a runner that he came first in the race.

7. They have accused Prince Charles of conflict of interest.
Change into passive voice.
(a) Prince Charles is been accused of conflict of interest by them.
(b) Prince Charles was accused of conflict of interest.
(c) Prince Charles have been accused of conflict of interest.
(d) Prince Charles has been accused of conflict of interest.

8. He always lacks faith before any important task.
Change into negative sentence.
(a) He always has faith before any important task.
(b) He has faith before any important task.
(c) He never has faith before any important task.
(d) He never not has faith before any important task.

9. The teacher said to the student, "Do not make a noise."
Change into indirect speech.
(a) The teacher enquired the student to not make a noise.
(b) The teacher requested the student to not make a noise.
(c) The teacher pleaded the student not to make a noise.
(d) The teacher ordered the student not to make a noise.

10. Didn't Nelson Mandela fight against apartheid?
Change into assertive sentence.
(a) Nelson Mandela fights against apartheid.
(b) Nelson Mandela fought against apartheid.
(c) Nelson Mandela fought with apartheid.
(d) Nelson Mandela fights with apartheid.

11. A judge has given a suspended sentence to an Oxford student for stabbing her boyfriend.
Change into passive voice.
(a) An Oxford student have been given a suspended sentence for stabbing her boyfriend.
(b) An Oxford student has been given a suspended sentence for stabbing her boyfriend.

(c) A suspended sentence had been given to an Oxford student for stabbing her boyfriend.
(d) A suspended sentence was given to an Oxford student for stabbing her boyfriend by a judge.

12. Besides being a teacher, he is a social worker.
Change into compound sentence.
(a) He was a teacher and a social worker.
(b) He was a teacher or a social worker.
(c) He was a teacher for a social worker.
(d) He was a teacher but a social worker.

13. Mobile phones are better than pagers.
(**Use** good)
(a) Pagers are not as good as mobile phones.
(b) Pagers are as good as mobile phones.
(c) Pagers are not good as mobile phones.
(d) Pagers are good as mobile phones.

14. He wanted to win the prize so he worked hard.
Change into complex sentence.
(a) When he wanted to win the prize, he worked hard.
(b) If he wanted to win the prize, he worked hard.
(c) Since he wanted to win the prize, he worked hard.
(d) Unless he wanted to win the prize, he worked hard.

15. Ganesha is the wisest among all Gods.
(**Begin** No other.....)
(a) No other God is wise as Ganesha.
(b) No other God is as wise as Ganesha.
(c) No other Ganesha is as wise as God.
(d) No other Ganesha is wise as God.

16. They are going to allow the contaminated blood scandal victims to sue the government.
Change into passive voice.
(a) The contaminated blood scandal victims are allowed to sue the government.
(b) The contaminated blood scandal victims will be soon allowed to sue the government.
(c) The contaminated blood scandal victims are going to allow to sue the government.
(d) The contaminated blood scandal victims are going to be allowed to sue the government.

17. Grapes are as lovely as Jumblums.
(**Begin** Jumblums)
(a) Jumblums are not lovelier than grapes.
(b) Jumblums are lovelier than grapes.
(c) Jumblums are lovely than grapes.
(d) Jumblums are not lovely than grapes.

18. How cleverly she tells her story!
Change into assertive sentence.
(a) She tell her story extremely cleverly.
(b) She tells her story extremely cleverly.
(c) She told her story extremely cleverly.
(d) She tells her story cleverly.

19. His writes in a way which is illegible.
Change into simple sentence.
(a) He write in an illegible way.
(b) He writes in an illegible way.
(c) He writes in a legible way.
(d) He doesn't write in a legible way.

20. Shardha said, "Keep quiet and listen to my words."
Change into indirect speech.
(a) Shardha urged her to keep quiet and listen to her words.
(b) Shardha urged them to keep quiet and listen to their words.
(c) Shardha urged them to keep quiet and listen to her words.
(d) Shardha urged her to keep quiet and listen to their words.

Subjective Type Questions

Directions (Q. Nos. 1-15) Transform the following sentences as directed without changing their meaning.

1. James is not as intelligent as Mark.
(**Use** 'more intelligent')

2. Saree is the most graceful dress.
(**Begin** No other dress..................)

3. She said, "Keep this room open."
Change into indirect speech.

4. They have proposed a six-month minimum sentence for repeat acid offences.
Change into passive voice.

5. Hurrah! We won the match.
Change into assertive sentence.

6. Dr. APJ Abdul Kalam, the Former President of India, was also a scientist.
Change into complex sentence.

7. She asked him what he had decided to do.
Change into direct speech.

8. Everybody knows that typhoid is curable.
Change into compound sentence.

9. Africa is hotter than any other continent in the world. (Use hottest)
10. A burglar who murdered a former navy officer has been jailed for 27 years.
Change into active voice.
11. He brought some flowers and gave them to his wife.
Change into simple sentence.
12. Going home, she had dinner.
Change into compound sentence.
13. Had he not been warned by his parents before he did the crime?
Change into active voice.
14. The officer said to him, "'You will be dismissed if you do not attend the office in time."
Change into indirect speech.
15. I wonder what he will think of the gift I gave.
Change into interrogative sentence.

Answers

Check Point 1

1. (i) (a), (ii) (c), (iii) (d), (iv) (c), (v) (a)
2. (i) The bread ought to be earned by a father.
(ii) My homework needs to be submitted by me.
(iii) Have the farmers cultivated the lands?
(iv) The money will be sent to my parents in the village by me.
(v) We were not teasing him.

Check Point 2

1. (i) (c), (ii) (a), (iii) (b), (iv) (c), (v) (c)
2. (i) He proposed that they should move to the party.
(ii) The police said that no one was in that room.
(iii) He asked us if we can have some tea.
(iv) The union leader urged the empolyees to show the management that they were always together.
(v) Sarita told me not to miss the chance to study.

Check Point 3

1. (i) (b), (ii) (c), (iii) (a), (iv) (a), (v) (b)
2. (i) No other writer in English is as famous as Shakespeare.
(ii) Iron is the most useful of all metals.
(iii) Ram does not earn more money than I do.
(iv) India is not as large as China.
(v) Water is not as light as air.

Check Point 4

I. (i) (b), (ii) (a), (iii) (c), (iv) (b), (v) (d)
2. (i) My father reads newspaper every morning.
(ii) He took off his clothes to jump in the river.
(iii) Everyone was present in my class yesterday.
(iv) That very tall boy is my best friend.
(v) It is a matter of sorrow that we have lost the debate competition.

Objective Type Answers

1. (c) She asked what time the train arrived.
2. (c) The policeman asked the boy where he lived.
3. (c) The Queen is expected to appoint a new Prime Minister later today.
4. (c) A Russian citizen who has been scrutinised for ties to Trump is being investigated by police.
5. (c) This is the most ill-fitted suit I have ever worn.
6. (c) Anil is so fast a runner that he came first in the race.
7. (d) Prince Charles has been accused of conflict of interest.
8. (c) He never has faith before any important task.
9. (d) The teacher ordered the student not to make a noise.
10. (b) Nelson Mandela fought against apartheid.

11. (b) An Oxford student has been given a suspended sentence for stabbing her boyfriend.
12. (a) He was a teacher and a social worker.
13. (a) Pagers are not as good as mobile phones.
14. (c) Since he wanted to win the prize, he worked hard.
15. (b) No other God is as wise as Ganesha.
16. (d) The contaminated blood scandal victims are going to be allowed to sue the government.
17. (a) Jumblums are not lovelier than grapes.
18. (b) She tells her story extremely cleverly.
19. (b) He writes in an illegible way.
20. (c) Shardha urged them to keep quiet and listen to her words.

Subjective Type Answers

1. Mark is more intelligent than James.
2. No other dress is as graceful as saree.
3. She ordered to keep that room open.
4. A six-month minimum sentence has been proposed for repeat acid offences.
5. It is a matter of joy that we won the match.
6. Dr. APJ Abdul Kalam, who was the Former President of India, was also a scientist.
7. "'What have you decided to do?" she asked him.
8. Typhoid is curable and everybody knows this.
9. Africa is the hottest continent in the world.
10. A judge has jailed a burglar who murdered a former navy officer for 27 years.
11. He brought some flowers to give to his wife.
12. She went home and had dinner.
13. Had his parents not warned him before he did the crime?
14. The officer warned him that he would be dismissed if he did not attend the office in time.
15. What will he think of the gift I gave?

Integrated Grammar Exercises

CATEGORY I Gap Filling

Direction *(Q. Nos. 1-10) Fill in the blanks with the correct option.*

1. **The Mughals .... the Battle of Panipat that .... place in 1761.**

(a) won, took (b) wins, taking
(c) win, took (d) win, take

2. **Nupur .... since morning.**

(a) has been singing (b) has singing
(c) has been sings (d) have sung

3. **I was .... a memento by my boss.** **Competency Based**

(a) give (b) been given
(c) giving (d) given

4. **I will come home when I .... my work.** **Competency Based**

(a) finished (b) finishes
(c) finish (d) should finish

5. **A stapler is a thing .... you use to attach papers together.**

(a) which (b) where
(c) who (d) whose

6. **Hiroshima is the place .... the first atomic bomb was dropped.**

(a) whose (b) which
(c) where (d) when

7. **You .... wear a uniform in school.** **Competency Based**

(a) are suppose to (b) are supposed to
(c) were supposed in (d) are suppose

8. **I will come tonight. I .... my homework by then.** **Competency Based**

(a) will have finish
(b) will having finished
(c) will have finished
(d) will finished

9. **Aditya Aggarwal is the person .... I am meeting after a long time.**

(a) which (b) whose
(c) who (d) when

10. **Comrades, you all .... about the strange dream that I .... last night.**

(a) heard, had (b) will heard, has
(c) have heard, had (d) hear, has

Direction *(Q. Nos. 1-5) Fill in the blanks.*

1. **When I was living in London, a strange thing .... (happen) to me.**

2. **Sunday is the day .... most countries respect as the day of rest in the week.**

3. **I cannot remember .... happened that night.**

4. **Tony .... (live) in Manhattan now but he .... (go) home to Brooklyn at least twice a year.** **Competency Based**

5. **The man sitting next to me on the plane was nervous because he .... (fly) before.** **Competency Based**

Direction *(Q. Nos. 1-5) Fill in the blanks with the help of the words given in the bracket.*

Economic development of country is ......(1)....... (relate) to their industrial growth. In a developing country like India, Small Scale Industries ..... (2) ..... (play) a significant role in economic development of the country. They are a vital segment of Indian economy in terms of their contribution towards country's industrial production, exports employment and creation of an entrepreneurial base. These industries by and large .... (3) .... (represent) a stage in economic transition from traditional to modern technology. Small industry plays a very important role in widening the base of entrepreneurship. The development of small industries .... (4) .... (offer) an easy and effective means of achieving broad based ownership of industry, the diffusion of enterprise and initiative in the industrial field. Given their importance, the Government policy framework right from the First plan......(5)....... (highlight) the need for the development of SSI sector keeping in view its strategic importance in the overall economic development of India.

CATEGORY II Sentence Reordering

Direction *(Q. Nos. 1-10) The questions given below consist of certain phrases. Rearrange these phrases to form a meaningful sentence.*

1. The managing director (1)/ in listening to her (2)/ was not interested (3)/ explanation about why profits were lessening (4)

(a) 1234 (b) 1243 (c) 1324 (d) 2341

2. Supported by soft term loans (1)/ to supply the raw material worth ₹ 5 lakh (2)/ the dealer has agreed (3)/ with a very low rate of interest (4)

(a) 3214 (b) 4213 (c) 1432 (d) 2134

3. when meat (1)/ the food poisoning occurred (2)/added in the food preparations (3)/ of low quality was (4)

(a) 3214 (b) 2341 (c) 1423 (d) 2143

4. for thousands of years(1)/famous symbols of ancient civilizations(2)/ Monuments have been created(3)/ and they are often the most durable and(4)

(a) 3142 (b) 1234 (c) 2143 (d) 4321

5. She saw her opportunity (1)/ to make amends (2)/ when he came to her home (3)/ to borrow some sugar (4)

(a) 2341 (b) 1234 (c) 2314 (d) 1423

6. The CEO (1)/ of making the right decision (2)/ was not scared (3) /despite a loss in profits (4)

(a) 1234 (b) 1243 (c) 1324 (d) 2341

7. Half its beauty and usefulness (1)/ knowledge would lose (2)/ without hard toil (3)/ if we could acquire it (4)

(a) 3241 (b) 2143 (c) 3421 (d) 4312

8. Containing memorable letters of Churchill(1)/ Recently a book(2)/ has been published(3)/ by a reputed publisher(4)

(a) 2134 (b) 1234 (c) 2314 (d) 2314

9. We can give him (1)/ and let him do nothing (2)/ to lock up a man (3)/ is one ofthe cruelest punishments (4)

(a) 1432 (b) 3241 (c) 2431 (d) 4312

10. The mutterings of (1)/ As lightning accompanies thunder(2)/ so was mingled with in my character(3)/ my wrath a flash of humour (4)

(a) 2314 (b) 2413
(c) 1342 (d) 2134

CATEGORY III Transformation of Sentences

Direction *(Q. Nos. 1-15) Transform the following sentences without changing their meaning as directed in the question.*

1. Change into future continuous tense.
She ran as fast as she could.
(a) She will be running as fast as she could.
(b) She will have been running as fast as she could.
(c) She am running as fast as she can.
(d) She will run as fast as she could.

2. Change into past perfect tense.
The visitor is spoiled for choice.
(a) The visitor had spoiled for choice.
(b) The visitor had been spoiled for choice.
(c) The visitor had been spoilt for choice.
(d) The visitor has spoiled for choice.

3. Change into present perfect tense.
A new breed of jellyfish is recently discovered by the biologists. Competency Based
(a) A new breed of jellyfish have been recently discovered by the biologists.
(b) The biologists have recently discovered a new breed of jellyfish.
(c) The biologists will have recently discovered a new breed of jellyfish.
(d) The biologists had recently discovered a new breed of jellyfish.

4. Change into past perfect continuous tense.
He was bathing in the rain since morning.
(a) He had being bathed in the rain since morning.
(b) He had been bathing in the rain since morning.
(c) He had being bathing in the rain since morning.
(d) He has been bathing in the rain since morning.

5. Change into simple future tense.
How long had you been studying Turkish?
(a) How long you study Turkish?
(b) How long will you have studied Turkish?
(c) How long will you study Turkish?
(d) How long will you study Turkish?

6. Change into future continuous tense.
I am leaving for London tomorrow after my meeting with the traders. Competency Based
(a) I would be leaving for London tomorrow after my meeting with the traders.
(b) I will have been leaving for London tomorrow after my meeting with the traders.
(c) I will leaving for London tomorrow after my meeting with the traders.
(d) I will be leaving for London tomorrow after my meeting with the traders.

7. Change into simple past tense.

Gunjan had studied very hard last year.

(a) Gunjan study very hard last year.
(b) Gunjan studies very hard last year.
(c) Gunjan has studied very hard last year.
(d) Gunjan studied very hard last year.

8. Was there a notebook on the table?

Change into assertive sentence.

(a) There was a notebook on the table.
(b) There is a notebook on the table.
(c) There isn't a notebook on the table.
(d) There wasn't a notebook on the table.

9. He must work hard or he will fail.

(Transform into Simple sentence)

(a) He must work hard that he could avoid failure.
(b) He must work hard to avoid failure.
(c) He must work hard and he avoided failure
(d) None of the above

10. I boarded a running train.

(Change into complex sentence)

(a) I boarded a train that was running.
(b) I boarded the train and it was running.
(c) I running to boarded a bus.
(d) I boarded a train when running.

11. This is a very beautiful monument.

Change into exclamatory sentence.

(a) What beautiful this monument is!
(b) What beautiful this monument was!
(c) How beautiful this monument is!
(d) How beautiful this monument was!

12. The Pyramids of Egypt are the greatest architecture.

(Rewrite using positive degree of adjective) **Competency Based**

(a) No other architecture is great as the Pyramids of Egypt.
(b) No other architecture is as great as the Pyramids of Egypt.
(c) None other architecture is as great as the Pyramids of Egypt.
(d) Any other architecture is great as the Pyramids of Egypt.

13. He tried hard to breathe. **Competency Based**

Change into complex sentence.

(a) He tried hard so he could breathe.
(b) He tried hard so that he could breathe.
(c) He tried hard to he could breathe.
(d) He tried hard that he could breathe.

14. Mr. Sinha is the most successful businessman of his town. **Competency Based**

(Rewrite using positive degree of adjective)

(a) No other businessman of his town is successful as Mr. Sinha.
(b) No other businessman of his town is as successful as Mr. Sinha.
(c) None other businessman of his town is as successful as Mr. Sinha.
(d) Any other businessman of his town is successful as Mr. Sinha.

15. Do it or you will regret it. **Competency Based**

(Transform into complex sentence)

(a) You do not do it for your regret it.
(b) If you do not do it, you will regret it.
(c) You do not do it to regret it.
(d) Unless you do not do it, you will not regret it.

Direction *(Q. Nos. 1-10) Transform the following sentences without changing their meaning as directed in the question.*

1. Change into future perfect continuous tense.
By 2021, we will have lived in Morocco for 2 years.

2. Change into past perfect continuous tense.
I have been working on my laptop for the past hour.

3. Change into present indefinite tense.
They will leave the classroom in a short period of time.

4. Change into future perfect tense.
The Sun will not be rising till 4 o'clock.

5. Change into present continuous tense.
We will be planning a surprise party for Rishabh.

6. Change into past perfect tense.
He went to the coffee shop before she arrived.

7. Supriya is the smartest girl in the class.
(Rewrite using comparative degree of adjective)

8. In spite of having breakfast, he is hungry.
Change into complex sentence. **Competency Based**

9. Rashi missed the conference yesterday.
Change into negative sentence.

10. When the teacher entered the classroom, the students opened their books. **Competency Based**
Change into compound sentence.

Answers

Category I Gap Filling

1. (a) won, took
2. (a) has been singing
3. (d) given
4. (c) finish
5. (a) which
6. (c) where
7. (b) are supposed to
8. (c) will have finished
9. (c) who
10. (c) have heard, had

Fill in the blanks

1. happened
2. when
3. what
4. lives, goes
5. hasn't flown

Fill in the blanks

1. related
2. play
3. represent
4. offers
5. has highlighted

Category II Sentence Reordering

1. (c) 1324
2. (a) 3214
3. (d) 2143
4. (a) 3142
5. (b) 1234
6. (c) 1324
7. (a) 3241
8. (a) 2134
9. (b) 3241
10. (a) 2314

Category III Transofrmation of Sentences

1. (a) She will be running as fast as she could.
2. (b) The visitor had been spoiled for choice.
3. (b) The biologists have recently discovered a new breed of jellyfish.
4. (b) He had been bathing in the rain since morning.
5. (b) How long will you have studied Turkish?
6. (d) I will be leaving for London tomorrow after my meeting with the traders.
7. (d) Gunjan studied very hard last year.
8. (d) There wasn't a notebook on the table.
9. (b) He must work hard to avoid failure.
10. (a) I boarded a train that was running.
11. (c) How beautiful this monument is!
12. (b) No other architecture is as great as the Pyramids of Egypt.
13. (b) He tried hard so that he could breathe.
14. (b) No other businessman of his town is as successful as Mr. Sinha.
15. (b) If you do not do it, you will regret it.

Transformation of Sentences

1. By 2021, we will have been living in Morocco for 2 years.
2. I had been working on my laptop for the past hour.
3. They left the classroom a short period of time ago.
4. The Sun will not have risen by 4 o'clock.
5. We are planning a surprise party for Rishabh.
6. He had gone to the coffee shop when she arrived.
7. Supriya is smarter than any other girl in the class.
8. He had breakfast but he was still hungry.
9. Rashi did not attend the conference yesterday.
10. The teacher entered the classroom and the students opened their books.

LITERATURE TEXTBOOKS

01

The Portrait of a Lady

About the Author

Khushwant Singh (1915–2014) was a prolific and renowned author. Along with his prominent writing career, he also served as a lawyer, diplomat, and politician. However, he was more recognised for his writing, with works such as 'Train to Pakistan' (1956), 'Delhi: A Novel' (1990), 'The Company of Women' (1999), 'Truth, Love, and a Little Malice' (2002), 'The Good, The Bad, and the Ridiculous' (2013), and others. In 1974, he was awarded the Padma Bhushan, one of India's highest civilian honours. His writing continues to resonate with readers, exploring themes of identity, history, and social dynamics. Singh's fearless approach to addressing controversial subjects and his ability to connect with readers through his writing style have made him an influential figure in Indian literature.

▼ YOUR STUDY GOALS

- Chapter Sketch
- About the Characters
- Summary of the Chapter

▼ YOUR PRACTICE GOAL

- NCERT Folder
- Extract Based Questions
- Short Answer Type Questions
- Long Answer Type Questions

Chapter Sketch

'The Portrait of a Lady' is part of an autobiography by Khushwant Singh. In this story, the author draws a pen portrait of his grandmother. He beautifully unfolds their relationship and how it undergoes several changes. In other words, the story is a loving tribute from a grandson to his grandmother. It is a realistic account of how grandparents give all their time, attention and love to their grandchildren.

About the Characters

Khushwant Singh, the author He recounts his childhood days and his relationship with his grandmother.

Grandmother Khushwant Singh's grandmother is described as an extremely religious person. She was a very kind lady. She was short, fat and slightly bent. Her face was wrinkled and she was always dressed in spotless white clothes. In the village, she took care of the author's needs when he was a child. She is also an animal lover.

Summary of the Chapter

The Author Remembers his Grandparents

The author recalls his grandmother as being old for the past twenty years. It was hard for him to believe that she had once been young and had a husband.

The author's grandfather's portrait hung on the wall of the drawing room. He wore a big turban and looked at least a hundred years old. One could not imagine him in his youth with his wife and children.

The Author's Grandmother

The thought of the grandmother being young and pretty, was almost revolting to the author. She was short, fat and slightly bent in stature.

The author remembered her moving around the house in spotless white clothes with one hand resting on her waist to balance her stoop and the other hand counting the beads of her rosary.

To the author, she could never have been pretty but she reflected a serene beauty.

The Author's Childhood with his Grandmother

The author and his grandmother were good friends. His parents left him to stay with her when they moved to the city. In the village, his grandmother took care of all his needs. She used to wake him up in the morning and get him ready for school.

She would fetch his wooden slate, take an earthen inkpot and a red pen, tie them in a bundle and hand it to author. They would have a thick, stale chapatti with a little butter and sugar spread on it for breakfast and then, leave for school. The author's grandmother always accompanied him to the school as it was attached to the temple.

The Author at School

The priest taught children the alphabet and the morning prayer. They would sing the alphabet or the prayer in a chorus. Meanwhile, the grandmother would read scriptures in the adjoining temple. On their way back, they would feed stale chapattis to the dogs.

The Turning Point in their Relationship

The turning point came in their relationship when they moved to the city to stay with the author's parents. In the city, the author went to an English school in a motor bus and learned subjects that his grandmother did not understand.

Grandmother Distressed and Disturbed

The grandmother was distressed to learn that there was no teaching about God and the scriptures in the school.

Moreover, she was very disturbed at the idea of music lessons being given at the English school. To her, music had immoral associations.

The Common Link of Friendship gets Snapped

The common link of friendship between them broke when the author started going to the University and was given a room of his own. The grandmother accepted her loneliness and spent her time spinning wheel while praying.

Only in the afternoon, she relaxed for a while to feed the sparrows in the verandah.

The Author Leaves for Higher Studies

The author decided to go abroad for higher studies for five years. He was sure that his grandmother would be upset at his departure but she was not even sentimental. She came to the railway station to see him off. Silently, she kissed his forehead. The author thought that perhaps it was the last sign of physical contact between them.

The Grandmother Celebrates the Author's Return and Falls Sick

When he returned after five years, the author found his grandmother at the station. Even that day, the happiest moment for her was feeding the sparrows. However, something strange happened to her in the evening.

For the first time ever, she did not pray. Instead, she collected the women of the neighbourhood, got an old drum and started singing songs of the homecoming of warriors. Her family tried to persuade her to stop to avoid overstraining herself but she didn't listen. She fell ill the next morning.

The Grandmother's Death

The grandmother was diagnosed with a mild fever by the doctor but she insisted that her end was near. She told everyone that she would spend her last moments praying.

After a short while, her lips stopped moving. She died a peaceful death.

The Sparrows Mourn her Death

When people came to take away the grandmother's body, they saw that a lot of sparrows had silently surrounded her body. When the author's mother offered the sparrows some bread, they refused to eat. They quietly flew away after the grandmother's body was carried away for the last rites.

Word-Meaning

portrait	—	true picture	courtyard house	—	an open space just outside the house
mantelpiece	—	shelf above a fireplace	lewd	—	indecent
fables of the prophets	—	stories of the Sikh Gurus	harlots	—	prostitutes
stoop	—	bent body due to old age	bedlam	—	confusion
telling the beads	—	counting the beads while chanting prayers	dilapidated	—	falling to pieces
rosary	—	a string of beads used for counting prayers as they are chanted	pallor	—	pale colouring of the face
puckered	—	wrinkled	shroud	—	a piece of cloth used to cover a dead body before cremation
monotonous	—	unchanging/boring	crude	—	made in a simple manner
in a chorus	—	together			

Important Themes of the Chapter

Nostalgia The author lovingly remembers the days he spent with his grandmother. He feels nostalgic about the time.

Family and Relationships The story centers around the notion of familial relationships and how they change over time.

Change The story is filled with instances of change. Both the characters and their relationship go through multiple changes throughout their life.

Generation Gap The story deals with the changing relationship between the youth and the elderly.

Separation and Reunion The story asserts that separating and reuniting with people is a permanent and vital part of life.

NCERT Folder

Notice these Expressions (NCERT Page 3)

Notice these expressions in the text. Infer their meaning from the context.

(a) **'the thought was almost revolting'**

Ans. The thought that the author's grandmother was once young and pretty, raises a doubt in the author's mind. He finds it too hard to believe as he had always seen her in the same old and wrinkled physical condition.

(b) **'an expanse of pure white serenity'**

Ans. It refers to the calm, peaceful and serene character of the author's grandmother. She is compared to the peaceful winter landscape in the mountains. She was always attired in spotless white clothes and had silver hair. She, thus, presented a picture of pure white serenity.

(c) **'a turning-point'**

Ans. It refers to the point where the author's relationship with his grandmother changes drastically after they move to the city-house. The grandmother is unable to accompany the author to school as he travels by motor bus. Neither is she able to help him in his lessons. Although they share the same room, a sort of distance developed in their relationship.

(d) **'accepted her seclusion with resignation'**

Ans. This shows the author's grandmother's passive submission to her secluded life after she gradually loses touch with her grandson. When the author was given a room of his own, the common link of friendship between the two was snapped. However, the grandmother accepted her fate without complaint.

(e) **'a veritable bedlam of chirpings'**

Ans. It refers to the noise, confusion and chaos caused by the chirping of the sparrows that scattered and perched around the author's grandmother.

(f) **'frivolous rebukes'**

Ans. It refers to the grandmother's casual and light-hearted rebukes to the sparrows.

(g) **'the sagging skins of the dilapidated drum'**

Ans. It points to the shabby and deteriorated condition of the drum.

Understanding the Text (NCERT Page 6-7)

1. Mention the three phases of the author's relationship with his grandmother before he left the country to study abroad.

Ans. **The first phase** of the author's relationship with his grandmother was when the author's parents went to live in the city and left him with his grandmother. She took utmost care of him right from waking him up in the morning to getting him ready for school.
They were always together and enjoyed an easy companionship.

The second phase was when the author's parents asked them to come to the city. This was the time when the author's relationship with his grandmother began to change. The author went to an English school. She could no longer accompany him nor could she help him in his studies. She continued getting him ready for school and asking him about his studies as they shared the same room. However, she rarely talked to him after learning that he was learning music at school. Slowly, the friendship between them weakened.

The third phase came when the common link of their friendship, snapped when the author moved to the University and was given a room of his own.
His grandmother accepted her seclusion with resignation.

2. Mention three reasons why the author's grandmother was disturbed when he started going to the city school.

Ans. *The author's grandmother was disturbed when he started going to the city school because*

(i) She could not accompany him to school as he went in the school bus. This broke her connection with the author and disturbed her.

(ii) In the English school, she could not help him with his lessons in English and Science because she knew neither. Further, she had no faith in what was being taught there.

(iii) She was unhappy that there was no teaching about God and scriptures in the school. Instead, music was being taught which, to her, had indecent associations. This disturbed her the most.

3. Mention three ways in which the author's grandmother spent her days after he grew up.

Ans. *The three ways in which the author's grandmother spent her days after he grew up are*

(i) She now spent most of her time at her spinning wheel, spinning thread.

(ii) While spinning, she continued reciting her prayers, rarely leaving her spinning to talk to anyone.

(ii) During the afternoons, she relaxed for a while to feed the sparrows. While she sat in the verandah breaking the bread into little bits, hundreds of little birds collected round her. It used to be the happiest half-hour of the day for her.

4. Mention the odd way in which the author's grandmother behaved just before she died.

Ans. Just before the day the grandmother died, a change came over her. She did not pray. She rather collected the women of the neighbourhood, took an old drum and started singing. Next morning, she was taken ill due to overstraining. The doctor said it was a mild fever and will go away but the grandmother thought differently.

She told everyone that her end was near and she would spend the last few living moments in prayer. She laid peacefully in bed praying and, soon, her lips stopped moving. She passed away peacefully.

5. Mention the way in which the sparrows expressed their sorrow when the author's grandmother died.

Ans. In the evening, when the author and his family members went to grandmother's room to take her for the last rites, they saw thousands of sparrows sitting scattered on the floor near her. They were silent. The author's mother offered them some bread but the sparrows took no notice. After the grandmother's body was taken away, the sparrows flew away quietly. Thus, the sparrows mourned her death and paid a silent tribute to the grandmother.

Talking about the Text (NCERT Page 7)

Talk to your partner about the following

1. The author's grandmother was a religious person. What are the different ways in which we come to know this?

Ans. The author's grandmother was a truly religious lady. She hobbled about the house in her spotless white clothes, always counting the beads of her rosary and reciting prayers. When the author was in the village with her, he would always find her saying morning prayers while she bathed him and dressed him in the hope that her grandson would learn them by heart.

The grandmother would always go to the village school with her grandson because the school was attached to the temple. There, while the children were taught, the grandmother would sit inside the temple and read scriptures.

Later, when they moved to the city and the author got busy in his education, she started devoting her time to prayers. He always found her lips moving in silent prayer and her hands counting the beads of her rosary. She was doing the same when she went to receive him at the station when he came back. Even the moments of her life were spent in praying rather than talking to her family members.

All these instances show that the author's grandmother was a religious person.

2. Describe the changing relationship between the author and his grandmother. Did their feelings for each other change?

Ans. Several constantly changing circumstances affected the relationship between the author and his grandmother. In the village, the author and his grandmother spent most of their time together. She used to get him ready for school, accompany him to the school and help him in his studies. But, moving to the city proved to be a turning point in their friendship.

They still shared the same room but the grandmother could no longer accompany him to school or help him in his studies.

The gap in their relationship further widened when the author went to the University and was given a room of his own. She accepted her loneliness and gave more time to praying.

However, their feelings for each other never changed. The author still respected her and she loved him. She went to the station to see him off when he was going abroad for higher studies. Further, when he returned from abroad after five years, she celebrated his homecoming by singing songs and beating the drum.

3. Would you agree that the author's grandmother was a person strong in character? If yes, give instances to show this.

Ans. Yes, it is true that the author's grandmother had a very strong personality. She was a highly religious and conservative lady who hated modern views and ways. She had very strong personal likes and dislikes. Being a religious person and a widow, she could be seen hobbling about the house in a spotless white dress, counting and reciting the beads of her rosary.

She had certain rigid ideas about life. She liked the village school as it was attached to the temple and children were taught prayers and about God.

She hated the English school in the city for various reasons. However when she came to know about the music lessons there, she rarely talked to the author. Moreover, when the author was leaving for abroad, she showed no emotion and was not even sentimental.

She was a strong and determined character as she led her own kind of life and never compromised with her principles. She loved the narrator deeply but never showed her sentiments or emotions.

Even when she knew that she was dying, her strength of character did not allow her to show any sorrow or regret. All this shows that the grandmother was strong in character.

4. **Have you known someone like the author's grandmother? Do you feel the same sense of loss with regard to someone whom you have loved and lost?**

Ans. Yes, I have known someone like the author's grandmother. It was my own grandmother. She was old but not as old as the author's grandmother. She didn't wear white either. She was also fat and hobbled around the house. But, she had a very strong voice. She was very religious and fasted a lot.

I was very close to her and we shared a very strong bond. I had seen her taking care of my small needs. She loved me unconditionally.

She was one of my closest friends and we also had secrets. If someone scolded me, I would run straight to her and she would hug me. The sweetest gesture of her was hiding food from others so that I could eat them.

After she died, her death left a void in my life which I have been unable to fill. Even now as I write about her, I have tears in my eyes. I miss her presence a lot. I will always cherish the moments that I shared with her.

Talking about Language (NCERT Page 7)

1. **Which language do you think the author and his grandmother used while talking to each other?**

Ans. The author and his grandmother lived in a village and belonged to a Punjabi Sikh family. Therefore, they must have used their mother tongue, Punjabi, to converse with each other.

2. **Which language do you use to talk to elderly relatives in your family?**

Ans. Do it yourself.

3. **How would you say 'a dilapidated drum' in your language?**

Ans. Do it yourself.

4. **Can you think of a song or a poem in your language that talks of homecoming?**

Ans. Do it yourself.

Working with Words (NCERT Page 7)

I. *Notice the following uses of the word 'tell' in the text.*

1. Her fingers were busy telling the beads of her rosary.
2. I would tell her English words and little things of Western Science and learning.
3. At her age one could never tell.
4. She told us that her end was near.

Given below are four different senses of the word 'tell'. Match the meanings to the uses listed above.

1. make something known to someone in spoken or written words
2. count while reciting
3. be sure
4. give information to somebody

II. *Notice the different senses of the word 'take'.*

1. to *take to* something: to begin to do something as a habit
2. *to take ill*: to suddenly become ill

Locate these phrases in the text and notice the way they are used.

III. **The word 'hobble' means to walk with difficulty because the legs and feet are in bad condition.**

Tick the words in the box below that also refer to a manner of walking.

haggle	shuffle	stride	ride	waddle
wriggle	paddle	swagger	trudge	slog

Answers

I.
1. Her fingers were busy *telling the beads* of her rosary — count while reciting
2. I would *tell her* English words and little things of Western Science and learning — give information to somebody
3. At her age *one could never tell* — be sure
4. She *told us* that her end was near — make something known to someone in spoken or written words

II. *The instances where these phrases have been used in the story are given below*

1. "She took to feeding sparrows in the courtyard of our city house" — The grandmother began to feed the sparrows as a habit when they shifted to the city.
2. "The next morning she was taken ill" — It refers to the author's grandmother's sudden illness.

III. The words that also refer to a manner of walking are

shuffle stride waddle
swagger trudge slog

Thing to Do (NCERT Page 9)

Talk with your family members about elderly people who you have been intimately connected with and who are not there with you now. Write a short description of someone you liked a lot.

Ans. Do it yourself.

Exam Pattern Questions

Extract Based Questions

Read the extracts given below and answer the questions that follow.

1. **She hobbled about the house in spotless white with one hand resting on her waist to balance her stoop and the other telling the beads of her rosary. Her silver locks were scattered untidily over her pale, puckered face, and her lips constantly moved in inaudible prayer. Yes, she was beautiful. She was like the winter landscape in the mountains, an expanse of pure white serenity breathing peace and contentment.**

(i) **Select the option from those given in bracket to fill in the blank.**

The author uses the words 'silver locks' to refer to .... (her eyes/her hair)

(ii) **What is the author's tone in the following sentence?**

"She was like the winter landscape in the mountains, an expense of pure white serenity ...."

(a) critical (b) appreciative
(c) deductive (d) accusatory

(iii) **Why did the grandmother appear like the winter landscape in the mountains?**

Ans. (i) her hair
(ii) (b) appreciative
(iii) The grandmother appeared like the winter landscape because she had a divine beauty.

2. **My parents left me with her when they went to live in the city and we were constantly together. She used to wake me up in the morning and get me ready for school. She said her morning prayer in a monotonous sing-song while she bathed and dressed me in the hope that I would listen and get to know it by heart; I listened because I loved her voice but never bothered to learn it.**

Competency Based

(i) **Select the textual option that is closest to indicating a sense of adoration.**

(a) 'My parents left me with her'
(b) '... she bathed and dressed me in the hope that I would listen'
(c) 'I listened because I loved her voice'
(d) All of the above

(ii) **Complete the following suitably.**

The author listened to her prayers because. ....

(iii) **What did the author's grandmother do after bathing and dressing him?**

Ans. (i) (c) 'I listened because I loved her voice'
(ii) he loved her voice
(iii) The author's grandmother fetched his clean wooden slate, a tiny ink-pot and a red pen to give to him after bathing and dressing him.

3. **To her music had lewd associations. It was the monopoly of harlots and beggars and not meant for gentlefolk. She said nothing but her silence meant disapproval. She rarely talked to me after that.**

When I went up to University, I was given a room of my own. The common link of friendship was snapped. My grandmother accepted her seclusion with resignation. She rarely left her spinning-wheel to talk to anyone. From sunrise to sunset she sat by her wheel spinning and reciting prayers.

(i) **Why did the grandmother think that music had 'lewd associations'?**

(ii) **In addition to music, what was taught in the author's city school?**

(a) The law of gravity
(b) Archimedes' Principle
(c) The world being round
(d) All of the above

(iii) **Which emotion did the grandmother express regarding music lessons in the author's new school?**

(a) Admiration (b) Disapproval
(c) Awestruck (d) Thoughtful

(iv) **Select the correct option from those given in brackets to fill in the blank.**

The author's admission to the University led to his grandmother becoming .... (isolated /annoyed).

(v) **Complete the following suitably.**

The relationship between the author and his grandmother weakened because ....

(vi) **What did the grandmother do throughout the day?**

Ans. (i) The grandmother thought that music had 'lewd associations' because it was not meant for gentlefolk. According to her, it was the monopoly of harlots and beggars.

(ii) (d) All of the above

(iii) (b) Disapproval

(iv) isolated

(v) the author went up to the University

(vi) The grandmother would spend all day spinning and reciting prayers. Only in the afternoon, she relaxed for a while to feed the sparrows.

Short Answer Type Questions

1. Explain the sentence - "As for my grandmother being young and pretty, the thought was almost revolting".

Ans. The narrator's grandmother was terribly old and wrinkled. She had stayed like this for the past twenty years. People had said that she was once young and pretty but the very idea was revolting and unbelievable to the author.

2. Give the description of the author's grandfather.

Ans. The portrait of Khushwant Singh's grandfather was hung above the mantelpiece. He wore a big turban and loosely-fitted clothes. His long white beard covered a major part of his chest. He looked a hundred years old. To the author, he did not look like the sort of person who would have a wife or children; he looked as if he could only have lots and lots of grandchildren.

3. Describe the author's grandmother. Was she young and pretty once?

Ans. The author's grandmother was short, fat and slightly bent in stature. Her silvery white hair was scattered over her wrinkled face.

The author remembers her hobbling around the house in spotless white clothes with one hand resting on her waist to balance her stoop and the other busy in counting beads. It was difficult for the author to believe that once she too was young and pretty as he had always known her as an old woman.

4. Elucidate the phrase 'not pretty but beautiful' with reference to the chapter.

Ans. To the author, the grandmother was not pretty but beautiful. She was beautiful in a peaceful way. He remembered her counting the beads of her rosary untiringly. Her silver locks lay scattered untidily over her pale, puckered face and her lips constantly moved in an inaudible prayer. She was like the winter landscape in the mountains, serene and content.

5. Interpret the use of metaphor by Khushwant Singh as he compares his grandmother to the 'winter landscape in the mountains'.

Ans. The author brings out the inner beauty of the grandmother by comparing her to the winter landscape in the mountains. This comparison shows her calmness and serenity.

Moreover, like the winter, the grandmother too was going through the last stage of her life. Just as the mountains are covered with snow and appear white, the old lady with her white clothes, white hair and pale skin appeared the same. Through the comparison, the author brings out the serenity and peacefulness of the grandmother.

6. Give details about the narrator's education and school in the village.

Ans. The author would take a wooden slate plastered with yellow chalk, a tiny earthen ink-pot and a red pen to the school. His school was located right next to a temple. He was taught in his school by the priest. In addition to the alphabet, he learned the morning prayer. The children would sit on either side of the verandah singing the alphabet or the prayer in a chorus.

7. The grandmother herself was not formally educated but was serious about the author's education. Identify instances from the text that support the above statement.

Ans. The grandmother was quite serious about the author's education. She woke him up in the morning and got him ready for school. She washed his wooden slate. She plastered it with yellow chalk. She tied his earthen ink-pot and reed pen into a bundle. She took him to school and waited for him in the temple reading scriptures.

Even in the city, she showed interest in his studies. However, when she learnt what was being taught there, she became distressed.

8. Bring out the contrast between the school education in the village and in the city.

Ans. The education in the village school was vastly different from the education in the city school. In the village, the school was next to a temple and the priest himself was the teacher. He taught them the alphabet and the morning prayer. However, in the city school, there was no teaching of God or the scriptures. English and science along with music were taught in the city school.

9. Explain the grandmother's reaction to discovering that music was taught in the school.

Ans. The grandmother thought that music was associated with indecent professions. She thought that it should not be taught to decent and gentle people like her grandson. That is why she was disturbed when she came to know that the narrator was being taught music in the English school in the city.

10. "I was sure my grandmother would be upset." What was the author sure about? Was he right?

Ans. When the author decided to go to abroad for further studies, he was sure that his grandmother would be upset. But she was not sentimental. She went to bid him goodbye at the railway station. However, she didn't talk or show any emotion. She was lost in prayer and was counting her beads.

11. Identify the instance of last physical contact between them. Why did the author think, so?

Ans. When the author was going abroad for five years for higher studies, the grandmother went to see him off at the railway station. He could tell that she was still reciting prayers. The grandmother then kissed his forehead lovingly. That kiss seemed to the author as the last sign of physical contact between them. He perhaps thought that the grandmother, being old, might not survive for five years.

12. The grandmother's farewell and reception of her grandson were very touching. Comment.

Ans. When the author went abroad, the grandmother came to the station to see him off. She was not sentimental and was silently praying and counting her beads. She kissed her grandson's forehead as a goodbye gesture.

When he returned after five years, she expressed her joy by collecting the women of the neighbourhood and singing for hours about the homecoming of warriors. For the first time, she missed her prayers.

13. Even though the narrator and his grandmother lose their friendship, she is not alone. Mention where she finds new companionship and with whom. How did she feel about it? **Competency Based**

Ans. After the author went to the University, the grandmother accepted her seclusion. However, she was not alone. She finds new companionship in a few sparrows. She sits in the verandah and feeds them bits of bread as they perch all around her. Some perch on her legs, some on shoulders and some even on her head. She would smile and spent the happiest half-hour of the day with them.

14. The contract between the city and the village is quite apparent in the lesson.
How does this contrast impact the grandmother's characteristics?
(Hint: Focus on the grandmother's actions with respect to animals) **Competency Based**

Ans. It is true to say that the contrast between the city and the village impacts how we percieve the grandmother. First, in both the contrasting scenario's, we find the grandmother to be extremely religious.

Second, this contrast points out the love the grandmother has for animals. In the village, she used to feed the dogs. In the city, where she couldn't find dogs, the grandmother fed sparrows. The simple act of feeding animals or birds indicates the grandmother's kindness.

15. The distance between the author and his grandmother becomes unavoidable. Elaborate on this statement focusing on the theme of separation. **Competency Based**

Ans. It is true to say that the distance between the author and his grandmother became unavoidable in the city. The relationship and bond between the grandson-grand mother duo developed in the village where grandmother was responsible for taking care of the narrator's needs. She was involved in every aspect of the narrator's life.

In contrast, there came a gap in the city as the grandmother could not be much involved in her grandson's education. While she was involved, it was only partial. As time passed, this gap widened perhaps because the narrator's life revolved around other things. Later, the bond deteriorated as the narrator got his own room and went abroad.

The gap which was created and separation that happened was inevitable as their lives changed and the author developed his own interests.

16. What factors were largely instrumental in shaping the author's personality? [Refer to the grandmother's role]

Ans. The grandmother played a key role in her grandson's life from his childhood. She is the one who took care of him from sunrise to sunset. She indirectly taught him how a person should live a religious life with God, scriptures and values as guides. That is why the author was more attached to his grandmother.

17. How does the grandmother's routine change when the narrator's family moves to the city?

Ans. The grandmother's routine undergoes a significant transformation as she adapts to the urban environment. No longer surrounded by village dogs, she redirects her nurturing instincts towards feeding sparrows, symbolising her resilience and capacity to find solace amid change. Her adjustment reflects the fluid nature of life and the ability to find meaning and purpose in new surroundings.

18. How does the narrator's pursuit of Western education affect his relationship with his grandmother?

Ans. The narrator's pursuit of Western education symbolises the broader clash between tradition and modernity in Indian society. As he embraces new ideas and ways of thinking, a rift gradually emerges between him and his grandmother, who steadfastly clings to her traditional beliefs. Their once-close relationship becomes strained as they struggle to reconcile their differing worldviews, highlighting the challenges of generational and cultural divides.

19. How does the narrator perceive his grandmother's passing?

Ans. For the narrator, his grandmother's passing represents the culmination of a life well-lived, characterised by devotion, resilience, and unwavering faith. Her peaceful departure underscores the cyclical nature of existence and the inevitable mortality, prompting the narrator to reflect on the transient nature of human life and the enduring legacy of love and tradition.

20. What role does the setting play in shaping the narrative of 'The Portrait of a Lady'?

Ans. The rural setting serves as a backdrop against which the timeless themes of family, tradition, and cultural identity unfold. The village landscape's simplicity and closeness to nature highlight the grandmother's deep connection to her surroundings and her rootedness in tradition. As the narrative shifts to the urban environment, the clash between tradition and modernity becomes more pronounced, reflecting the broader societal changes sweeping across India during the period.

Long Answer Type Questions

1. Describe the author's grandmother's life in the village in contrast with the kind of the life she led in the city, highlighting her values. **Competency Based**

Ans. The author's grandmother had been living in the village for a very long time. As a result, she had a fixed routine. She got up early in the morning. After that she used to wake up her grandson and get him ready for school. Later, she accompanied him to the school. She sat in the temple reading the scriptures. Thus, she practised all her values of being pious and dutiful.

In contrast, the city life and its culture did not suit her. Now, she could no more accompany her grandson to his school. Neither could she help him in his lessons. Thus, she could not practise the values of the life in which she believed properly. When the author went to the university, he was given a room of his own. This made the grandmother even more lonely. However, she accepted her loneliness and devoted her time in spinning the wheel, feeding the sparrows and praying, thus, continuing to practise some of her values.

2. "All over the verandah and in her room right up to where she lay dead and stiff wrapped in the red shroud, thousands of sparrows sat scattered on the floor. There was no chirruping.... The sparrows took no notice of the bread. When we carried my grandmother's corpse off, they flew away quietly."

Animals recognise and value a relationship established with human beings. Explain this, keeping in mind the relationship established by Khushwant Singh's grandmother with animals. **Competency Based**

Ans. Animals are said to have no intelligence but they do have feelings and it is out of feeling, concern or love for a human being that they let themselves be domesticated. They recognise relationships and bond well with humans. The relationship between Khushwant Singh's grandmother and the dogs as well as the sparrows is just one of them.

The grandmother was a very kind-hearted lady. She loved feeding the animals. In the village, she used to carry stale chapattis with her and, on her way back from school, feed the stray dogs. The dogs loved the grandmother and developed a bond between them.

In the city, there were no street dogs, so the grandmother took to feeding sparrows. The sparrows gathered around her and she threw little crumbs of bread to them. These sparrows sat on her head, legs and shoulders. It was their way of showing affection to her. When she died, they came in huge numbers to mourn her death.

This shows that animals recognise and value relationships established with human beings. It also shows that they are more compassionate, more affectionate and more dependable than most human beings.

3. After the death of his grandmother, Khushwant Singh decides to write a character sketch of her, reflecting on her values and her relationship with him from his childhood until her death. Imagine yourself to be Khushwant Singh and express these thoughts.
You may begin like this
My grandmother was a symbol of ....

Ans. My grandmother was a symbol of love, care and affection as well as a strong character with traditionally religious beliefs. She loved me immensely. She was not physically attractive, but had an inwardly spiritual beauty. In the village she was actively involved in my life but when we shifted to the city, the bond of friendship was first weakened and finally broken when I went abroad for higher studies. Yet, she always presented a picture of peace and contentment. Her love for animals was reflected in the way she fed the dogs and sparrows. She did not like the English school but never interfered in my education. She accepted every decision of mine regarding my life in a calm and composed manner. Even in death, she achieved peace and contentment.

4. Discuss the advantages and disadvantages of the joint family system. What values do you think children learn from their grandparents?

Ans. 'The Portrait of a Lady' gives us a picture of human relationships in a joint family. It is a realistic account of how grandparents give all their time, attention and love to their grandchildren. Grandparents play an important role in inculcating good manners and values in the children. The children imitate their grandparents in a positive way and learn to be good individuals. They learn important human values such as love, compassion and respect from them.

Grandparents also imbibe religious and spiritual values in children. Children, thus, learn to love and respect God and all creation. They also learn about customs and traditions from their grandparents. Many children can even sing religious songs and recite prayers. All this has a very positive effect on their character development.

Grandparents share their life experiences with children in order to help them handle different situations. Children, thus, face adverse situations with a positive attitude and learn to take challenges in their stride. They also learn to be competitive in a positive light.

Further, grandparents guide children from time to time to follow the right path in life and respect their parents. Thus, the children become not only good human beings but also good citizens.

5. The chapter 'The Portrait of a Lady' displays the sad reality of old age. Old people face loneliness and seclusion. Imagine yourself to be a high school teacher who has to give a speech on the topic 'Pain of Old Age' in the school assembly. Write this address in 120-150 words, elaborating on the importance of respecting old people.

You may begin like this.

Good morning, students! Growing old is inevitable. One who is ....

Ans. **Pain of Old Age**

Good morning Students! Growing old is inevitable. One who is born will get old someday and energy and exuberance of youth will eventually be replaced by the loneliness and sadness of old age. As one's body gets old, the day-to-day tasks become tedious and tiresome. One starts to become dependent on others.

This leads to emotional insecurity and finally gives mental trauma to the old as they feel unwanted. They develop the thought of being a burden on others and hence, try to remain away from others. Hence, in such situations, it becomes the duty of their relatives to give them due respect.

Our elders dedicate their whole lives in providing us with a better life. We should take care of them at a time when they need us the most. However, such care has become a thing of the past. People nowadays send their elderly relatives into old age homes where they experience a life of loneliness.

What would have happened if they had treated us the same way? We cannot belittle their importance in our lives. It would be a shameful thing if we do not care for them in their old age.

Thank you!

6. The grandson in 'The Portrait of a Lady' emerges as a complex and multifaceted character whose journey of self-discovery and cultural exploration resonates with themes of identity, belonging, and the search for meaning in a changing world. Comment.

Competency Based

Ans. The grandson, who also serves as the narrator in 'The Portrait of a Lady' by Khushwant Singh, emerges as a complex and multifaceted character whose journey of self-discovery and cultural exploration resonates with themes of identity, belonging and the search for meaning in a changing world.

The grandson is naturally curious about the world around him, especially as he navigates the contrasting values of traditional Indian culture and modern Western influences. As he pursues his education, and experiences life beyond his rural upbringing, he demonstrates ambition and determination to explore new opportunities and broaden his horizons.

Despite his evolving worldview, the grandson maintains a sense of compassion and empathy towards his grandmother, recognising the depth of their bond and the importance of familial connections. He navigates the complexities of family dynamics and societal expectations, he demonstrates resilience in adapting to new environments and confronting challenges with courage and determination.

Through his experiences and interactions, the grandson catalyses moments of reflection and transformation within himself and among those around him. His journey reflects broader themes of generational divide, cultural identity and the pursuit of personal fulfillment.

SELF ASSESSMENT TEST

Extract based Questions

Read the extract given below and answer the questions that follow.

1. All over the verandah and in her room right up to where she lay dead and stiff wrapped in the red shroud, thousands of sparrows sat scattered on the floor. There was no chirruping. We felt sorry for the birds and my mother fetched some bread for them. She broke it into little crumbs, the way my grandmother used to, and threw it to them. The sparrows took no notice of the bread.

(i) Why were the birds not chirping?

This could be because

(a) they were sad

(b) they had understood that grandmother was dead

(c) they understood that no one will feed them

(d) Both (a) and (b)

(ii) Complete the following suitably.

The author's mother's offer of bread crumbs to the sparrows shows ....

(iii) What was done with the bread crumbs when the sparrows refused to eat them?

Short Answer Type Questions

1. Despite her physical appearance, the grandmother has been called beautiful. Why?

2. "Old, so terribly old that she could not have grown older,...." Explain. Why did the author think so?

3. Mention some instances to show that the grandmother was highly composed and patient.

4. The sparrows ignored the author's mother's generous attempt to feed them. What was the possible reason?

5. "When the people are pious and good, even nature mourns their death." Justify. **Competency Based**

Long Answer Type Questions

1. The grandmother herself was not formally educated but was serious about the author's education. How does the text support this? What values does the grandmother display through her seriousness towards education? **Competency Based**

2. Gradually, the author and the grandmother saw less of each other and their friendship was broken. Was the distancing in the relationship deliberate or due to the demand of the situation?

3. Give a character sketch of Khushwant Singh's grandmother.

02

About the Authors

Gordon Cook and **Alan East** are well-known authors of adventure and survival stories for children. Their books feature themes of bravery, resilience, and the human spirit's ability to triumph in difficult situations.

YOUR STUDY GOALS

- Chapter Sketch
- About the Characters
- Summary of the Chapter

YOUR PRACTICE GOAL

- NCERT Folder
- Extract Based Questions
- Short Answer Type Questions
- Long Answer Type Questions

"We're Not Afraid to Die...if We Can All Be Together"

Chapter Sketch

The chapter revolves around a part of the round-the-world voyage undertaken by the narrator and his family in a sailboat. It describes their thrilling journey across the sea and their close encounter with death and their possible attempt to save their lives during their voyage.

About the Characters

The narrator He is a 37-year-old businessman who wants to duplicate the round-the-world journey made by Captain James Cook 200 years earlier. He spends a long time improving his sea skills and finally begins his journey with his wife Mary, six-year-old son Jonathan and seven-year-old daughter Suzanne.

Mary She is the narrator's wife. She supports her husband's dream and improves her sea skills. She joins her husband on their planned three-year voyage.

Larry Vigil An American who joins the narrator and Mary at Cape Town to help them tackle one of the world's roughest seas.

Herb Seigler A Swiss who also joins them at Cape Town to help them cross the southern Indian Ocean.

Suzanne The narrator's seven-year-old daughter who displays immense courage throughout their voyage.

Jonathan The narrator's six-year-old son who shows immense strength and optimism even in difficult times.

Summary of the Chapter

The Voyage Begins

In July 1976, the narrator, a 37-year-old businessman, his wife Mary, 6-year-old son Jonathan and 7-year-old daughter Suzanne started their sea voyage from Plymouth, England. They wanted to go round-the-world on a long sea journey just as Captain James Cook had done 200 years earlier. The narrator and his wife had spent 16 years preparing for this voyage, improving their marine skills. Their boat *Wavewalker* was a 23 metre, 30 ton boat that was professionally built and tested in the roughest weather.

The first part of their planned journey passed pleasantly. Then, they took two crewmen—the American Larry Vigil and the Swiss Herb Seigler-before heading East from Cape Town to help them cross the Southern Indian Ocean.

The First Problem

On the second day out of Cape Town, they encountered strong winds and high waves of upto 15 metres. Despite the bad weather, they celebrated Christmas Day wonderfully. New Year's Day saw no improvement in the weather; in fact, it only worsened with time.

On 2nd January, the waves were gigantic. The boat moved to the top of each wave. To minimise the damage to the ship, they dropped the storm jib and lashed a heavy rope in a loop across the stern. Then, they prepared themselves for the worst.

Disaster Strikes

The first indication of disaster came at about 6 pm. The wind stopped and the sky immediately grew dark. The narrator thought that he saw a cloud coming towards them, which he realised was actually the biggest wave that he had ever seen.

The wave hit the boat and a tremendous explosion shook the deck. Water poured in and the narrator's head smashed against the steering wheel. He was suddenly thrown into the sea. Immediately after, his head popped out of the water. He saw that the boat had almost capsized. Suddenly, a wave hurled it upright and the narrator was thrown onto the boat. Somehow, he managed to find the wheel, lined up the stern for the next wave and hung on.

Frantic Survival Attempts

The narrator dared not abandon the wheel to investigate the flooding. Suddenly, Mary came and informed him that the boat was sinking. He handed the wheel to her and crawled towards the hatch. Larry and Herb were pumping the water out. The whole starboard side had bulged inwards and the boat had been damaged.

The narrator somehow managed to reach the children. Sue had a big bump on her head to which he did not pay much attention. Then, he found a hammer, screws and canvas. Somehow, he managed to stretch the canvas and secure waterproof hatch covers across the gaping holes which reduced the water coming into the boat. Now, they started pumping out the water with handpumps.

However, this also brought trouble as their handpump stopped working and the electric handpump short circuited. Suddenly, the narrator remembered that they had another electric handpump. He took it out and they spent the entire night. Pumping, steering and working the radio.

However, there was no response to their Mayday calls. She's injury now had worsened but she did not tell anyone as she did not want to worry them.

Situation on 3rd January

On the morning of 3rd January, the pumps had reduced the amount of water on board. The narrator knew that there was another hole on the boat and found that the boat's main ribs were heavily damaged. He knew that they had survived for 15 hours since the wave hit the *Wavewalker* but the boat was not strong enough to take them to Australia.

Pinpricks in the Vast Ocean

The narrator checked his charts and calculated that the only hope for them was if they could reach Ile Amsterdam. However, the weather started deteriorating again and, by the dawn on 5th January, their situation had become desperate.

The narrator went to assure the children that they were going to make it. Jon said that they were not afraid of dying if they can all be together. This gave the narrator hope and a reason to fight the sea. However, later in the evening, as more water came into the boat, they felt defeated again. On 6th January, the weather improved. While he was at work, Sue came to him and gave him a card. The narrator was filled with optimism.

Ile Amsterdam

At about 6 pm, the narrator woke up to discover that the island was just in front of them. He rushed out to the deck and saw the island. It was Ile Amsterdam, a piece of volcanic rock with little vegetation. When his feet touched land the next day, he thought of the cheerfulness and optimism of all the people on the boat which made them pass through the worst stress.

Word-Meaning

set sail	—	started a sea voyage
in the wake of	—	following
honing	—	improving
seafaring skills	—	knowledge of navigation, handling a sailboat and its equipment etc
wooden-hulled beauty	—	beautiful boat made of wood
fitting it out	—	furnishing it
leg	—	part
Swiss from	—	Switzerland
out of	—	after starting from
gales	—	extremely strong winds
atrocious	—	very unpleasant
storm jib	—	small sail used at the time of a storm
knots	—	nautical miles per hour
lashed	—	fastened
mooring	—	used for tying the boat to a fixed object
stern	—	back part
life-raft drill	—	practising how to climb into a lifeboat if the main boat sinks
lifelines	—	ropes fixed around the bodies of persons to prevent drowning
oilskins	—	waterproof clothing
life jackets	—	jackets without sleeves which can be filled with air to help persons to float in the sea
impending	—	approaching
ominous silence	—	quietness just before some dangerous happening
aft of	—	behind
breaking crest	—	top of wave overturning
ride over	—	go above
torrent	—	large amount
overboard	—	into the sea
popped out	—	came out suddenly
capsizing	—	overturning
strayed past	—	came through
taut	—	tightly
guard rails	—	rails on the outside of the deck of the boat
sailed	—	was thrown
boom	—	long pole to which the bottom of a sail is attached
rag doll	—	very light object
lined up	—	straightened
hung on	—	held the boat tightly
hatch	—	door leading below the deck
scrambled	—	ran
like madmen	—	very hard
timbers	—	wood planks
starboard	—	right side
bulged	—	swelled
sloshed	—	moved noisily
bunk	—	sleeping berth
bashed	—	broken
taking	—	drawing in
stream	—	fall like a stream
block up	—	get stuck
short-circuited	—	became electrically defective
wrenched	—	removed and thrown from where they were fixed
forestay sail	—	big front sail
dighies	—	small open boats used for emergencies
anchor	—	heavy metal object used to keep the ship fixed in one place
chartroom	—	room in the boat where maps are kept
out-pipe	—	drainage pipe
working	—	transmitting messages on
Mayday calls	—	distress messages sent over the radio
made more of	—	highlighted
waterline	—	the level of the boat in water
rib frames	—	wooden pieces forming the frame of the boat
keel	—	long wood / steel piece fixed vertically at the bottom of the boat to keep it vertical
rigging	—	ropes that balance the mast of the boat
sextant	—	instrument measuring angles and distances used for calculating position of a boat
tousled head	—	head with hair not arranged

Important Themes of the Chapter

Strong Familial Bond The story shows the strength of the family bond and how it can help people overcome any hurdle.

Bravery The narrator's children, Sue and John, exhibit extraordinary bravery in the time of crisis.

Resilience Even though they face obstacles repeatedly, the narrator and his family show immense strength and resilience.

Optimism and Courage The story encourages people to stay optimistic and not lose hope in the face of challenges.

NCERT Folder

Notice these Expressions (NCERT Page 13)

Notice these expressions in the text. Infer their meaning from the context.

1. 'honing our seafaring skills'

Ans. It refers to the efforts made by the narrator and his wife to perfect and sharpen their knowledge of navigation, handling of the boat and equipment, other sea skills.

2. 'ominous silence'

Ans. It refers to the silence that prevailed just before an impending danger. The peace and quiet suggest that something bad is going to happen.

3. 'Mayday calls'

Ans. They are radio-telephonic calls which are given by aircrafts or ships stuck in disastrous situations. They are distress calls made to secure help from other ships nearby.

4. 'pinpricks in the vast ocean'

Ans. This phrase refers to tiny islands in a vast ocean. They are so small that they appear like tiny pinheads on a map of the vast ocean.

5. 'a tousled head'

Ans. It refers to hair in disarray or the disarranged hair of the author's son. His hair was all messed up and uncombed.

Understanding the Text (NCERT Page 18)

1. List the steps taken by the captain
(i) to protect the ship when rough weather began.
(ii) to check the flooding of water in the ship.

Ans. (i) In order to protect the ship from rough weather, the captain decided to slow it down. So, he dropped the storm jib and lashed a heavy mooring rope in a loop across the stern. Then, they double-fastened everything, and went through their life-raft drill, attached lifelines and donned oilskins as well as life jackets.

(ii) To check the flooding in the ship, the captain made some repairs and stretched waterproof oilskins in the openings. He secured waterproof hatch covers across the gaping holes which diverted the water to the side. When the two handpumps were jammed and the electric pump short-circuited, he found another electric pump, connected it to an out-pipe and managed to pump out the water.

2. Describe the mental condition of the voyagers on 4th and 5th January.

Ans. On 4th January, the mental condition of the voyagers was vacillating between hope and despair. After 36 hours of continuous pumping, they had pumped much of the water out. But, they had to keep pace with the water still coming in. However, their respite was only short-lived. The storm started building up and the situation became worse again. However, when the narrator went to comfort his children, Jon asked innocently if they were 'going to die' but added that he did not mind dying as long as all the family members were together. This statement boosted the narrator's morale and he became resolute to fight the sea. Those were critical moments for all of them. Mary and the narrator sat together holding each other's hands. They were scared and felt that their end was very near.

3. Describe the shifts in the narration of the events as indicated in the three sections of the text. Give a subtitle to each section.

Ans. The text has been divided into three sections. They are

Section 1: Disaster Strikes

This part describes the narrator's desire to go sailing around the world, the preparations they made, the start of their journey and the coming storm. The family celebrates a wonderful Christmas. However, by the New Year, the sea becomes rough and, the next evening, an enormous wave wrecks the ship and injures the narrator and his family members.

Section 2: Survival Attempts and Searching for Land

This section describes the frantic efforts to save the boat from flooding and the display of heroism by all in the face of disaster. Near the end of this section, the efforts of the narrator to navigate to some nearby islands for safety are mentioned which the narrator terms as 'pinpricks in the vast ocean'.

Section 3: Triumph of the Spirit

This part describes the triumph of the spirit and seamanship of the narrator as they reach the island safely. Fittingly, the narrator is given the title of 'The Best Daddy and The Best Captain' by his son.

Talking about the Text (NCERT Page 18)

Discuss the following questions with your partner.

1. What difference did you notice between the reaction of the adults and the children when faced with danger?

Ans. We find a huge difference in the reactions given by the adults and the children in the face of danger. When the adults faced the danger, they became anxious and searched for ways to battle it. Later, when the motion of the boat brought more and more water in all hope was lost. Both Mary and the narrator sat holding hands as they felt the end was very near.

In contrast, the childre showed great courage and did not lose hope. When Sue hurt herself, she did not worry others about her injury. When the narrator went in to comfort them, Jon said that they weren't afraid to die if they could all be together. Sue also gave a card to the narrator that she made with the message of hope.

Thus, the children showed greater positivity than their parents. Hence, we can say that the children were more optimistic than the adults.

2. How does the story suggest that optimism helps to endure 'the direst stress'?

Ans. It is true to say that optimism helps to endure 'the direct stress'. This is clearly presented in the story wherein all the six people present on the boat lose complete hope or show any weakness.

When the waves were high, the hopeful crew slowed the ship down, fastened everything with a mooring rope and went through the life-raft drill. When the storm struck their ship, the captain was almost killed and the ship was nearly a wreck. However, he held onto the wheel. Water was getting into the ship but Larry and Herb kept pumping it like madmen. This shows that they were not willing to give in to danger and were ready to fight it.

Even the little girl, she was so brave that she didn't worry her parents about her injuries. The little boy, an epitome of courage, said that he was not afraid of dying. All this gave the captain a new hope and a will to fight.

As a result, the narrator checked, calculated and sailed to their only chance of survival, a 65 kilometre wide island in the ocean. They were optimistic about finding the small island. Finally, they were able to set foot on land and survive. Their optimism paid off. All this shows that optimism was the key to their survival. It helped them endure the direst stress.

3. What lessons do we learn from such hazardous experiences when we are face-to-face with death?

Ans. Experience wherein we are face-to-face with death teach us that courage, perseverance and tolerance can achieve what seems to be insurmountable odds. They teach us how to react in the most difficult situations. They make us learn to never lose hope and find reasons to stay optimistic in the face of adversity. We learn to try our best to stay calm and composed.

We also understand the importance of unity and teamwork and how to utilise our common sense, skill and efforts to avert any catastrophe. Further, we learn to be very careful and cautious in our actions when facing such hazardous experiences.

4. Why do you think people undertake such adventurous expeditions in spite of the risks involved?

Ans. The world is full of all sorts of people. Most of them like to lead a risk-free and peaceful life but there are a few among us who believe that, if we want to live life to the fullest, we have to go beyond the day-to-day routine. They don't hesitate even to undertake dangerous expeditions. If that were not the case, a lot of mysteries, places and events would not be known to the world.

Such expeditions are risky but still people go on them without caring for death or disasters. For people who undertake such daring risk, life is a battle which can be won only after fighting for it rather than sitting relaxed and carefree. The history of mankind shows that our progress owes much to such brave and fearless people.

Thinking about Language (NCERT Page 18-19)

1. We have come across words like 'gale' and 'storm' in the account. Here are two more words for 'storm': typhoon, cyclone. How many words does your language have for 'storm'?

Ans. In Hindi, 'storm' is known as *'aandhi'*, *'toofan'*, *'jhanjavat'* and *'chakravat'*.

2. Here are the terms for different kinds of vessels: yatch, boat, canoe, ship, steamer, schooner. Think of similar terms in your language.

Ans. *'Naav'*, *'Nauka'*, *'Pot'*, *'Jahaaz'* and *'Kashti'* are some of the words used in Hindi for the word 'boat'.

3. 'Catamaran' is a kind of a boat. Do you know which Indian language this word is derived from? Check the dictionary.

Ans. The word 'Catamaran' is derived from the Tamil word *'Kattumaram'*, which means 'tied wood'.

Catamaran is a name applied to any craft having twin hulls. Originally, it denoted a form of sailing and paddling raft employed on the coasts of India.

4. Have you heard any boatmen's songs? What kind of emotions do these songs usually express?

Ans. Yes, I have heard some boatmen's songs. They usually express love and nostalgia. Boatmen sing these songs to curb their longing and express their love.

Working with Words (NCERT Page 19)

1. The following words used in the text as ship terminology are also commonly used in another sense. In what contexts would you use the other meaning?

knot	stern	boom	hatch	anchor

Ans. (a) **knot**

(i) in a rope / string / ribbon: a joint made by tying together two pieces of rope / string / ribbon, etc.
e.g. Tying a knot while wearing a tie.

(ii) (verb) way of tying two ropes / strings.
e.g. knot together two ropes

(iii) a tangled mass.
e.g. many ropes / strings jumbled together which are hard to separate

(iv) a tight group of people.
e.g. A knot of people surrounded the politician.

(v) tight feeling or tenseness.
e.g. I could feel a knot of fear in my throat.

(vi) a lump in a tree trunk.
e.g. The old tree had many knots on its trunk.

(vii) a dark round patch in a plank of wood.
e.g. The wooden plank was of poor quality due to having too many knots.

(viii) lump in the outer surface of the body.
e.g. The old man had many knots on his face and back.

(b) **Stern**

(i) serious and usually disapproving.
e.g. The teacher gave the student a stern look.

(ii) strict.
e.g. The father gave a stern warning to his son.

(c) **boom**

(i) (*noun*) a large increase in something.
e.g. A population boom occurred after the war ended.

(ii) (*noun*) a deep loud sound.
e.g. the boom of the cannons could be heard far away.

(iii) (*noun/adjective*) long pole for a microphone / the microphone fixed on a long pole.
e.g. The boom mike could be stretched right across the stage.

(iv) (*verb*) making a loud sound.
e.g. A voice suddenly boomed out of the darkness.

(d) **hatch**

(i) (*verb*) to come out of an egg.
e.g. The chicken takes many days to hatch from an egg.

(ii) (*verb*) to create a plan.
e.g. The thieves took a long time to hatch a plan for robbing the bank.

(iii) (*noun*) opening in a wall between two rooms.
e.g. The kitchen had a serving hatch to the dining room.

(e) **anchor**

(i) (*noun*) person or thing giving a feeling of safety.
e.g. The grandfather was the anchor of the family in all the crises they faced.

(ii) (*noun*) co-ordinator of a programme.
e.g. Satish is the anchor of this popular TV programme.

(iii) (*verb*) fix firmly in position.
e.g. The athlete anchored his foot on the starting block.

(iv) (*verb*) base on some subject.
e.g. Premchand's stories are anchored in real life.

2. The following three compound words end in ship. What does each of them mean?

airship	flagship	lightship

Ans. (a) **airship** A large aircraft without wings, filled in its balloon with a gas which is lighter than air. It is driven by an engine.

(b) **flagship**

(i) (*noun*) The main ship in a fleet which also carries the navy's flag.
e.g. The flagship carried the tricolour.

(ii) (*adjective*) The most important product / service / programme that an organisation owns or produces.
e.g. The flagship programme of BBC TV is its World News.

(c) **lightship** A small ship with a powerful light that stays at a fixed point at sea to warn other ships to stay away because of some danger.

3. **The following are the meanings listed in the dictionary against the phrase 'take on'. In which meaning is it used in the third paragraph of the account:**

take on sth : to begin to have a particular quality or appearance; to assume sth

take sb on : to employ sb; to engage sb; to accept sb as one's opponent in a game, contest or conflict

take sb/sth : on to decide to do sth; to allow sth/sb to enter e.g. a bus, plane or ship; to take sth/sb on board

Ans. In the third paragraph, in the lines "...... we took on two crewmen to help us tackle ...... roughest seas......", the phrase 'take on' means 'to employ' or 'to engage'.

Things to Do (NCERT Page 19-20)

1. **Given is a picture of a yacht. Label the parts of the yacht using the terms given in the box.**

bow	cabin	rudder	cockpit
stern	boom	mainsail	mast

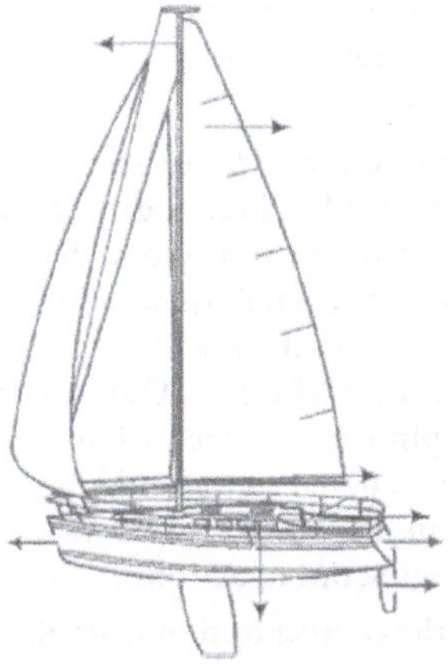

Ans.

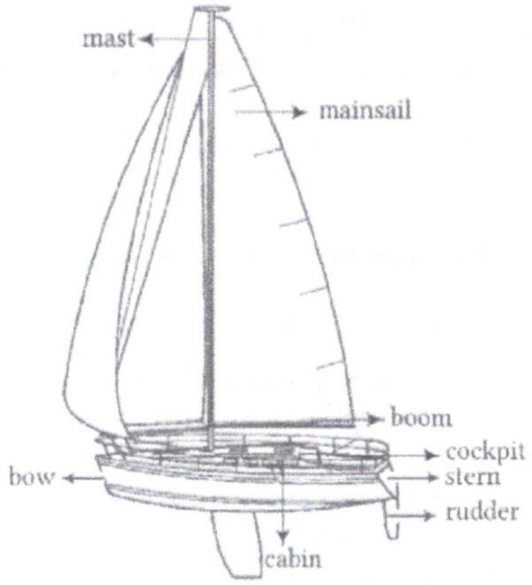

2. **Here is some information downloaded from the Internet on Ile Amsterdam. You can view images of the isle if you go online.**

Location	South Indian Ocean, between southernmost parts of Australia and South Africa
Latitude and longitude	37 92 S, 77 67 E
Sovereignty	France
Political status notes	Part of French Southern and Antarctic Lands
Population	35
Census notes	Meteorological station staff
Land area in square kilometres	86

Ans. Do it yourself.

3. **Locate Ile Amsterdam on the world map.**

Ans. Do it yourself.

Exam Pattern Questions

Extract Based Questions

Read the extracts given below and answer the questions that follow.

1. There, before heading east, we took on two crewmen — American Larry Vigil and Swiss Herb Seigler — to help us tackle one of the world's roughest seas, the southern Indian Ocean. On our second day out of Cape Town, we began to encounter strong gales. For the next few weeks, they blew continuously. Gales did not worry me; but the size of the waves was alarming — up to 15 metres, as high as our main mast.

(i) Which part of the journey was pleasant for the narrator and his family?

(ii) Complete the following suitably.

The narrator and his family hired two extra crewmen to ....

(iii) What was the narrator worried about?

(a) The strong winds
(b) The size of the waves
(c) The experience of his new crewmen
(d) The problems in the mast of the ship

Ans. (i) The journey from England to Cape Town was the only part that was pleasant for the narrator and his family.

(ii) help them tackle the Southern Indian Ocean.

(iii) (b) The size of the waves

2. At dawn on January 2nd, the waves were gigantic. We were sailing with only a small storm jib and were still making eight knots. As the ship rose to the top of each wave we could see endless enormous seas rolling towards us, and the screaming of the wind and spray was painful to the ears. To slow the boat down, we dropped the storm jib and lashed a heavy mooring rope in a loop across the stern.

(i) What had happened to Sue when the narrator went to check on the children?

(ii) Complete the following suitably.

The crew of the Wavewalker decided to reach Ile Amsterdam to ....

(iii) Select the textual option that is closest to indicating a sense of panic.

(a) We were sailing with only a small storm jib...
(b) At dawn on January 2nd, the waves were gigantic.
(c) ...the screaming of the wind and spray was painful to the ears.
(d) ...lashed a heavy mooring rope in a loop across the stern.

Ans. (i) When the narrator went to check on the children, he found out that Sue's head was hurt and it had a bump.

(ii) save everyone and the ship

(iii) (c) ...the screaming of the wind and spray was painful to the ears.

3. We had survived for 15 hours since the wave hit, but Wavewalker wouldn't hold together long enough for us to reach Australia. I checked our charts and calculated that there were two small islands a few hundred kilometres to the East. One of them, Ile Amsterdam, was a French scientific base. Our only hope was to reach these pinpricks in the vast ocean. But unless the wind and seas abated so we could hoist sail, our chances would be slim indeed. The great wave had put our auxilliary engine out of action.

(i) Select the correct option from those given in brackets to fill in the blank.

On seeing the charts, the narrator felt more .... (hopeful/hopeless) than before about their survival.

(ii) Why were their chances slim even after finding the island on the charts?

(iii) What did the narrator mean by 'pinpricks in the vast ocean'?

(a) Their boat was very small.
(b) The islands were very small.
(c) They were very small.
(d) All of the above

Ans. (i) hopeful

(ii) (c) Their chances were slim even after finding the island on the charts because they could not hoist sail unless the wind and seas abated. Their engine was out of action too.

(iii) (b) The islands were very small.

Short Answer Type Questions

1. The narrator and his wife show great patience and perseverance before they start the journey. Comment. **Competency Based**

Ans. It is true to say that the narrator and his wife show great patience and perseverance before they start the journey. The narrator and his wife wanted to 'duplicate' the round-the-world voyage made 200 years ago by Captain James Cook. So, they started making their preparations 16 years ago. First of all, they got a boat especially designed and professionally built for this purpose. They tested it for months in the roughest weather. They spent all their leisure time in strengthening their seafaring skills in British waters. They were both mentally and physically prepared to undertake their exceptionally long and challenging sea voyage.

2. Describe the boat Wavewalker.

Ans. In order to undertake the journey around the world, the narrator and his wife got a boat built professionally. The boat, named *Wavewalker*, was a 23 metre, 30 ton wooden-hulled sailboat. They had spent months fitting it out and testing it in the roughest weather they could find.

3. Explain why they took two crewmen alongwith them?

Ans. Before heading East from Cape Town, they took on two crewmen who were experienced seamen. They were Larry Vigil, an American and Herb Seigler, a Swiss. The narrator took this step because he knew that they would require help to tackle one of the world's roughest seas - the Southern Indian Ocean.

4. Explain how the voyagers celebrated their Christmas and where.

Ans. On Christmas Day, the voyagers were 3500 kms East of Cape Town in the southern Indian Ocean. Though the sea was rough, they enjoyed a wonderful holiday. They celebrated Christmas singing carols complete with a Christmas tree. They expected the weather to improve but it didn't.

5. Mention the weather on the morning of 2nd January and explain how it affected their boat.

Ans. On New Year's Day, the weather saw no improvement and was very bad. On 2nd January, it got even worse. The waves were gigantic. They were sailing with only a small storm jib but still were going pretty fast. As the ship rose to the top of each wave they could see the endless, enormous sea rolling towards them. The wind seemed to be howling.

6. Identify the first indication of the 'impending disaster' that ultimately struck them on January 2nd.

Ans. The first indication of the impending disaster came at about 6 pm on January 2nd. An ominous silence prevailed all around. The wind dropped. The sky immediately grew dark. Then, came a growing roar. A huge vertical wave, almost twice the height of the other waves, came roaring towards the ship. These were the indications of the coming disaster.

7. Analyse the consequences of the 'tremendous explosion'.

Ans. The gigantic wave hit the boat and a tremendous explosion shook the deck. A torrent of green and white water broke over the ship.

The narrator's head smashed against the wheel and he was flung overboard. He was almost dead and the whole ship was reduced to a wreck.

Others were also hurt in the process. Then, the frantic efforts to save the boat and everybody's life began.

8. Interpret the narrator's acceptance of his 'approaching death'.

Ans. The narrator saw a torrent of green and white water breaking over the ship. His head had smashed into the wheel. He felt himself flying overboard and sinking below the waves.

He was losing consciousness. He accepted his approaching death without murmuring. He felt quite peaceful even when death was approaching and *Wavewalker* was near capsizing.

9. "I had no time to worry about bumped heads", says the narrator. What problem do you think deserved his immediate attention?

Ans. The problem that deserved immediate attention was the repair of the starboard side, which had bashed open; with every wave, it was letting water enter the boat. If he did not make some repairs, the boat would have surely sunk and they would have drowned.

10. Explain what you understand by Mayday calls. Why was the ship getting no replies to its Mayday calls?

Ans. Mayday calls are distress signals sent through the radio by ships facing trouble in the sea. They are made to get help from other ships passing nearby.

The boat *Wavewalker* was not getting replies to its Mayday calls because the boat had reached a remote part of the sea where other ships did not go.

11. Identify an instance where Sue showed immense courage in the face of trouble.

Ans. Sue had been injured badly when the wave had hit the ship. Her head had swollen alarmingly. She had two black eyes and she had also showed to her parents a deep cut on her arm. When asked why she had not complained about her injuries earlier, she replied that she had not wanted to worry her parents when they were trying to save them all.

12. Identify an instance of utter hopelessness in the story and analyse the situation that led to it.

Ans. The situation which made them feel that "the end was very near" was when black clouds began building up behind their boat, within an hour the wind increased to 40 knots and the waves were getting higher. The weather continued to deteriorate throughout the night, and by dawn on January 5th, the motion of the boat brought more and more water in through the broken planks. Thus, they felt that the boat would sink and they would all die.

13. Interpret Jonathan's views about his father. Give reasons to support his views. **Competency Based**

Ans. Jonathan called the narrator 'the best daddy and the best captain in the world' because they had reached the island Ile Amsterdam. His son was expressing his relief and gratitude towards his father due to the narrator's devotion to save them all from death as well as his seafaring skills. He was the 'best daddy' because his devotion to them helped them survive the storm with his efforts to keep the boat afloat. He was the 'best captain' because he had correctly enabled them to steer to the island so that they survived.

14. Describe Ile Amsterdam. How did its inhabitants behave with the newcomers?

Ans. Ile Amsterdam was a French scientific base. It was 'a bleak piece of volcanic rock'. It had little vegetation but still it appeared to be 'the most beautiful island in the world'. The boat anchored offshore for the night. The next morning all 28 inhabitants of the island cheered them and helped them ashore.

15. Analyse the narrator's thoughts on landing at Ile Amsterdam.

Ans. On landing at Ile Amsterdam, the narrator's thoughts were full of Larry and Herb, his crew members who remained cheerful and optimistic throughout the hardships they had faced. He thought of his wife who stayed at the wheel for all those crucial hours. He also thought of his daughter, who had been so brave all through the ordeal and had not bothered about her head injury.

16. Justify the title of the story: "We're Not Afraid to Die..."

Ans. "We're Not Afraid to Die...if We Can All Be Together" is the story of rare courage and perseverance that was shown by the narrator, his crewmen, his wife and children. Everybody confronted the disaster with patience, courage and determination. Even the children showed courage.

They did not give up hope even till the last moment. The narrator made all possible attempts to save their lives. Like his father, Jon reacted very bravely that they were not afraid to die, if they died together. Hence, the title is apt and logically justified.

17. How did Gordon Cook's leadership and problem-solving skills contribute to the family's survival? **Competency Based**

Ans. Gordon Cook's leadership and problem-solving skills were instrumental in the family's survival. He remained calm under extreme pressure, assessed the situation pragmatically and devised innovative solutions to address the challenges they faced. His ability to make tough decisions, such as rigging makeshift repairs and navigating without proper equipment, ensured the family's continued safety and eventual rescue.

18. How did the family's ordeal strengthen their bonds and perspective on life?

Ans. The family's harrowing ordeal forged an unbreakable bond among its members. They faced death together and emerged stronger as a unit. The experience deepened their appreciation for life, resilience and the importance of cherishing each moment with loved ones. It taught them the value of courage, love, and unwavering faith in the face of adversity.

Long Answer Type Questions

1. After reaching the island, the narrator writes his thoughts highlighting the tremendous courage and forbearance shown by his two children during the struggle to keep the boat from sinking.

You may begin like this:

My children, Suzanne and Jonathan, showed tremendous courage ....

Ans. My children, Suzanne and Jonathan, showed tremendous courage and forbearance during the gruesome struggle being faced by their parents and the crewmen to keep the boat from sinking. Sue had been injured badly when the big wave hit the boat. Her head had swollen alarmingly and both her eyes were hurt. She also had a deep cut on her arm. But she did not complain about her injuries as she did not want to worry her parents when we were trying to save us all.

When I went and tried to comfort the children, my son, Jonathan, asked me if we were going to die. When he was assured that we would all survive, he told me that they were not afraid of dying if they could all be together.

Moreover, Sue had patience and power enough to draw the caricatures of her parents with a message of hope and gratitude to us. The children, thus, exhibited extraordinary patience, courage and tolerance.

2. Both the narrator of 'We're not Afraid to Die...' and Howard Carter from the chapter 'Discovering Tut: The Saga Continues' made great discoveries. The narrator found an island in a challenging situation while Carter found the tomb of Tutankhamun after years of futile searching.

As a part of the research, compare and contrast the challenges faced by the two and their response/s in about 120-150 words.

[Clue: Include the similarities and differences in the challenge they faced - their feelings - determination to overcome hurdles - success] **Competency Based**

Ans. Both the narrator of 'We're not Afraid to Die...' and Howard Carter from the chapter 'Discovering Tut: The Saga Continues' made great discoveries. And, both of them faced challenges on their journey.

The narrator's undertaking to replicate Captain James Cook's voyage was challenging as they were to sail in some of the roughest seas of the world. So, they exposed themselves to rigorous training before commencing the journey. Even in the direst of circumstances, the narrator did not give up hope and utilised all his seafaring skills to protect the ship from sinking and to pump out water.

Similarly, Carter faced many problems when he reached the mummy of King Tut. The resins used to embalm the mummy had hardened, making it difficult to take the body out of the solid gold coffin. So, he decided to place the mummy in the scorching heat to loosen the raisins. When even the Sun didn't melt it, he decided to remove the solid resins using a chisel and hammer in order to free the King's remains from the coffin. This damaged the King's mummy and brought shame to Carter's name eventually.

In conclusion, though both the narrator and Carter faced different challenges on their journey. While the narrator found success at the end of it, Carter faced humiliation.

3. The prose selection, 'We're Not Afraid to Die ...... if We Can All Be Together' brings out the importance of having confidence and making optimum use of our potential. Imagine yourself to be a motivational speaker who has to address high school students. Write this address in 120-150 words elaborating on occurrences from the text to inspire your audience to challenge the hurdles of life.

You may begin like this.

Good morning, students! It is said that "the hurdles of life can ....

Ans. Good morning students! It is said that the hurdles of life can be challenged if we have confidence to make optimum use of our potential. The statement holds true in the light of the story 'We're Not Afraid to Die......'. The narrator along with his wife, children and two crewmen overcame the worst situations and defeated death by fighting the adverse situations which cropped up during their voyage. When the big wave hit the boat, it was severely damaged and the narrator was badly injured. However, he did not pay attention to it and held on to the wheel. Both Larry and Herb kept pumping out water and did not stop.

Even the children had confidence in their father and they hoped to survive. They also showed great courage. Jon said that they were not afraid to die if they are all together. Sue made a card to thank her parents. The entire incident, thus, was a great example of unity and trust that they had on each other. Thus, it can be concluded that by staying optimistic like the children and making the best use of your potential like the narrator, one can fight adversities and be a winner.

Thank you!

4. The reaction of the crew and children gives us an insight into the human mind and how it can help us to survive any disaster. Discuss.

Ans. The reaction of the crew and children gives us an insight into the human mind. The crew reacted to the danger with a fighting spirit and optimism. Their undaunted efforts helped them to survive the disaster. On the other hand, the children showed amazing maturity and resilience in the face of disaster. They remained strong and composed. Despite serious injuries, both of the children displayed courage and patience.

Adopting a courageous attitude in times of difficulties motivates one to face the upheavals of life courageously. It is rightly said "Cowards die many times before their death; the valiant face death only once", and when the valiant do die, they die a hero's death. The story inspires us to maintain our calm in a crisis. Stress and panic only worsen the situation. If we accept difficulties as a way of life and face them with a brave front, they soon fade away. By being positive and not losing faith in ourselves, we can survive any disaster.

5. Discuss the role of teamwork and determination in the Cook family's survival narrative.

Ans. Teamwork and determination were central to the Cook family's survival narrative during their ordeal at sea. Despite overwhelming challenges, the family worked cohesively, leveraging their strengths to confront the crisis. Each family member contributed to the collective effort, from Gordon's leadership and navigation skills to Mary's support and assistance in managing the situation.

Larry and Herb, the crew members, played vital roles in aiding the family during the crisis. Their determination to overcome adversity and persevere through the storm reflected their unwavering resolve to survive. Together, they faced the relentless elements, repaired critical damage to the vessel, and maintained hope amidst uncertainty. Through their collaborative efforts and unwavering determination, the Cook family exemplified the power of unity and resilience in the face of adversity.

6. Mary emerges as a resilient, compassionate, and courageous individual who plays a pivotal role in guiding her family through the challenges of their arduous journey. Her unwavering support, resourcefulness, and unwavering commitment to her family epitomise the strength of the human spirit in the face of adversity. Comment.

Ans. It is true to say that Mary emerges as a resilient, compassionate, and courageous individual who plays a pivotal role in guiding her family through the challenges of their arduous journey. Her unwavering support, resourcefulness, and unwavering commitment to her family epitomise the strength of the human spirit in the face of adversity.

Mary, the narrator's wife, is portrayed as a dedicated and supportive partner to the narrator throughout the ordeal at sea. Despite the challenging circumstances, she stands by her husband's side, offering him encouragement, assistance, and unwavering support in navigating the crisis.

As a mother, Mary demonstrates a deep sense of care and protection towards her children, Jonathan and Suzanne. She remains composed even in the face of danger, prioritising the safety and well-being of her family above all else.

Mary exhibits resilience and resourcefulness when coping with the challenges of the sea voyage. She adapts to the changing circumstances, actively participates in the efforts to address the crisis and remains calm under pressure, contributing to the family's collective resilience and survival. Her compassion and empathy shine through her interactions with her family and crew members. She offers comfort and reassurance to her children during moments of fear and uncertainty, demonstrating her ability to provide emotional support, and stability amidst chaos.

Despite the overwhelming odds stacked against them, Mary displays determination and courage in confronting the dangers at sea. She remains steadfast in her resolve to overcome adversity, drawing strength from her familial bonds and unwavering commitment to her loved ones.

SELF ASSESSMENT TEST

Extract Based Questions

Read the extract given below and answer the questions that follow.

1. I checked and rechecked my calculations. We had lost our main compass and I was using a spare which had not been corrected for magnetic variation. I made an allowance for this and another estimate of the influence of the westerly currents which flow through this part of the Indian Ocean.

About 2 p.m., I went on deck and asked Larry to steer a course of 185 degrees. If we were lucky, I told him with a conviction I did not feel, he could expect to see the island at about 5 p.m.

(i) What is the reason that the author was not convinced about finding the island?

(a) He did not think that he was a good captain.
(b) He was not sure about the skills of his crewmen.
(c) He was using an inaccurate compass.
(d) He did not think that the island could be found.

(ii) Who was Larry and what was he doing on the deck?

(ii) Complete the following suitably.

The narrator was using the spare compass because ....

Short Answer Type Questions

1. When did the narrator set sail for the round-the-world voyage and how did it pass in the beginning?

2. In what way did the *Wavewalker* escape capsising? How did the captain steady it?

3. What problems were caused due to the handpumps? How were they resolved?

4. The chances of the voyagers' survival after the big wave hit them was very bleak. Comment.

5. Ile Amsterdam was a piece of volcanic rock. Why is it called the most beautiful island in the world?

6. Explain why the captain changed the plan to reach Australia.

Long Answer Type Questions

1. What do we learn from such a terrible and hazardous experience as described in 'We're not afraid to die...'? Give your opinion.

2. It is rightly said that life is either a daring adventure or nothing. Write your views on the statement. Also, talk about how adventures make life worth living in reference to the story.

3. The story 'We're not Afraid to Die.....' is a story of human endurance, bravery and courage in the face of adversity. Discuss.

03

About the Author

A.R. Williams is a young author who developed a love for reading at a very young age. His works have appeared in Heroic Fantasy Quarterly, Three Crow Press, and Every Day Fiction. He crafted stories of imagination in science fiction and fantasy genres. Williams received an honourable mention in the fourth quarter of the Writers of the Future Contest in 2010.

YOUR STUDY GOALS

- Chapter Sketch
- About the Characters
- Summary of the Chapter

YOUR PRACTICE GOAL

- NCERT Folder
- Extract Based Questions
- Short Answer Type Questions
- Long Answer Type Questions

Discovering Tut : The Saga Continues

Chapter Sketch

The story deals with the mysteries and various theories regarding the life and death of the youngest ruler of ancient Egypt -Tutankhamun. His tomb was discovered in 1922 by the famous archaeologist Howard Carter. Since then, his mummy has been subjected to an X-ray and later, a CT scan. These investigations have answered a lot of questions and offered new clues about his life and death.

About the Characters

King Tut The last heir of a powerful family that had ruled Egypt and its empire for centuries. His preserved body was the first to be scanned.

Howard Carter The British archaeologist who in 1922 discovered King Tut's tomb. His search caused great damage to the King's preserved body.

Zahi Hawass The Secretary General of Egypt's Supreme Council of Antiquities. He scanned King Tut's mummy for an accurate forensic reconstruction.

Amenhotep III King Tut's father or grandfather, was a powerful ruler who ruled for almost four decades.

Amenhotep IV He promoted the worship of Aten and changed his name to Akhenaten. He outraged the country by attacking Amun, a major God, by smashing his images and closing his temples.

Summary of the Chapter

Death of King Tut

King Tut-a teenager-was the last heir of a powerful family that had ruled Egypt and its empire for centuries. He was buried and had been forgotten over the years. But, after the discovery of his tomb in 1922, the modern world wondered about the cause of his untimely death. He was brought out of his tomb and a CT scan was done recently to ascertain the reason of his death.

The Mummy of King Tut

At 6 pm on 5th January, 2005, the world's most famous mummy was taken out of its burial tomb. As the mummy of King Tut was being put into a scanner for performing a CT scan, the atmosphere became windy and dark clouds covered the stars. King Tut's tomb lies 26 feet underground in the ancient Egyptian cemetery known as the 'Valley of the Kings'. Tourists from around the world came to visit the tomb to pay their respects. They gazed at the murals on the walls of the burial chamber and looked at King Tut's gilded face on the lid of his outer coffin. Some visitors feared that the pharaoh's curse would befall those who disturbed him.

Howard Carter and his Discoveries

Howard Carter was a British archaeologist who, in 1922, discovered King Tut's tomb. He was buried with gilded treasures and everyday items as per the belief of the time. Zahi Hawass, Secretary General of Egypt's Supreme Council of Antiquities, explained that the mummy was in a very bad condition because of what Howard Carter did to it. Howard Carter found King Tut's body in three nested coffins. In the first coffin, he found a shroud decorated with garlands of willow and olive leaves, wild celery, lotus petals and cornflowers which indicated that the burial took place in March or April. When he finally reached the mummy, he found that the ritual resins had hardened, cementing King Tut to the bottom of the coffin.

Howard Carter tried to loosen the resins by putting the mummy outside in the sun for several hours. However, nothing happened. He reported that the tough material had to be cut from under the limbs and trunk to free the King's remains. To separate King Tut from his ornaments, Howard Carter's men removed the mummy's head and cut off nearly every major joint; then, they reassembled the remains of the body on a layer of sand in a wooden box with padding.

King Tut's Mummy X-Rayed

Archaeology has changed since then focusing less on treasures and more on the fascinating details of life and mysteries of death. In 1968, an anatomy professor X-rayed the mummy and revealed that King Tut's chest that his breast bone and front ribs were missing.

King Tut's Ancestors

King Tut's death was a big event as it meant the end of the royal dynasty. King Tut's father or grandfather, Amenhotep III, was a powerful King, who ruled for almost four decades. Amenhotep IV succeeded him. He was a very strange king. He promoted the worship of Aten, the sun disk, and changed his name to Akhenaten. He attacked a major god 'Amun' by breaking his images and closing down his temples.

Ray Johnson, Director of the University of Chicago's research centre in Luxor, called this King very odd. He said it must have been a terrible time for the people because the family that had ruled for centuries was coming to an end. After Akhenaten's death, Smenkhkare, a mysterious ruler, ruled for a brief period and departed with hardly any sign. It was then that a very young King Tutankhaten took over the throne. The boy soon changed his name to Tutankhamun. He oversaw revival of the old ways.

The CT Scan

King Tut's mummy was the first to be CT scanned to ascertain the secret of his death. On the night of the scan, workmen carried him from the tomb and rose it on a hydraulic lift into a trailer that held the scanner.

The CT scan showed an astonishing image of King Tut and his entire body very clearly. Zahi Hawass was relieved that nothing had seriously gone wrong. As the technicians left the trailer, they saw the star constellation which the ancient Egyptians knew as the soul of Osiris, the God of the afterlife. They felt as if the God was watching over the boy king.

Word-Meaning

saga	—	long story of a series of happenings
forensic reconstruction	—	process of reconstruction of the face and body based on the information in the CT scan
pharaoh	—	Egyptian king
murals	—	paintings on the wall
gilded	—	thinly covered with gold
antiquities	—	very old objects
archaeologist	—	a scientist who studies ancient objects dug up from the ground
board games	—	games like chess
linen	—	a fabric cloth made from flax used to make high quality clothes
cases	—	boxes
nested	—	fitted one inside another
shroud	—	cover of the dead body
willow	—	soft wood
wild celery	—	a wild plant
cornflowers	—	bluish-purple flowers of a wild plant
resins	—	a sticky flammable organic substance, insoluble in water
collars	—	necklaces
amulets	—	ornaments worn round the neck or arm or waist (Taaveez) to keep away the evil
adornments	—	items used for decoration and make-up
tomography	—	a technique for displaying a representation of a cross section using X-Rays or ultrasound
cross section	—	parts seen when an object is cut in the middle
pallbearers	—	those who carry coffins

Important Themes of the Chapter

The excerpt explores ancient history and the mysteries surrounding figures like King Tutankhamun. Several sub-themes emerge.

Archaeological Discovery and Exploration Howard Carter's discovery of Tutankhamun's tomb in 1922 is significant in archaeological history. The excerpt details the process of uncovering Tutankhamun's remains and the subsequent scientific examination, highlighting the evolving techniques and technologies used in archaeological research.

Mystery and Intrigue The excerpt delves into the mysteries surrounding Tutankhamun's life and death and the events of ancient Egypt's Eighteenth Dynasty. Speculation about the circumstances of Tutankhamun's demise, the brief reigns of other pharaohs, and the religious and political upheavals add intrigue to the narrative.

Legacy and Cultural Significance Tutankhamun's legacy reverberates throughout history, as evidenced by the global fascination with ancient Egypt and its rulers. The meticulous preservation of Tutankhamun's tomb treasures reflects the cultural significance of royal burials and the belief in an afterlife.

Technological Advancement and Scientific Inquiry Modern medical technology, such as CT scanning, highlights the importance of scientific inquiry in unravelling historical mysteries. The application of computed tomography allows researchers to gain new insights into Tutankhamun's life and death, demonstrating the intersection of archaeology and cutting-edge scientific methods.

NCERT Folder

Notice these Expressions (NCERT Page 22)

Notice these expressions in the text. Infer their meaning from the context.

(a) **'forensic reconstruction'**

Ans. It refers to rebuilding the facts about life and death by putting back together the evidence to examine a scene/event scientifically.
The reconstruction of King Tut's mummy was done to find solutions to the mysteries surrounding his death.

(b) **'funerary treasures'**

Ans. It refers to the valuables and treasures which were buried along with the pharaoh in the pyramid.

(c) **'scudded across'**

Ans. It refers to moving swiftly from one place to another. It is used in the chapter to describe the movement of the dark-bellied clouds.

(d) **'casket grey'**

Ans. It refers to ash coloured clouds that hid the stars.

(e) **'resurrection'**

Ans. It refers to rebirth or revival after death.

(f) **'circumvented'**

Ans. Outsmarted or outwitted. The thieves would have easily bypassed the guards with artfulness and ripped the mummy apart to remove the gold.

(g) **'computed tomography'**

Ans. It refers to CT scan that provides the X-ray image of a body in cross section. It is used for diagnostic purposes.

(h) **'eerie detail'**

Ans. It refers to details relating to the supernatural.

Understanding the Text (NCERT Page 28)

1. Give reasons for the following

(i) **King Tut's body has been subjected to repeated scrutiny.**

Ans. King Tut's body has been subjected to repeated scrutiny because, right from the time of the discovery of his tomb in 1922 by Howard Carter, the modern world has been curious to find out what happened to King Tut. No one knows how the boy king lived and died. His unexpected death has been obscured in mystery with murder being the most extreme possibility.

(ii) **Howard Carter's investigation was resented.**

Ans. Howard Carter's investigation was resented because he destroyed the original state of the mummy. His men cut off the mummy's head and severed almost every major joint of the body to raise King Tut from the coffin. They, then, reassembled the remains on a layer of sand in a wooden box and put the body back.

(iii) **Howard Carter had to chisel away the solidified resins to raise the King's remains.**

Ans. Howard Carter had to chisel away the solidified resins to raise the King's remains because the ritual resins had hardened, cementing King Tut to the bottom of his solid gold coffin.

(iv) **King Tut's body was buried along with gilded treasures.**

Ans. Tut's body was buried with gilded treasures because ancient Egyptians believed in the afterlife and wanted to ensure that the deceased had everything they needed for their journey into eternity. Gold was considered a symbol of eternity and was believed to guarantee resurrection in the afterlife.

(v) **The boy king changed his name from Tutankhaten to Tutankhamun.**

Ans. The boy changed his name from Tutankhaten to Tutankhamun perhaps because he wanted the restoration of the old ways. His ancestor, Amenhotep IV, had shocked the country and created unrest by attacking a major God 'Amun'.
The boy tried to establish the old faith by renaming himself as Tutankhamun which means 'living image of Amun'.

2. (i) **List the deeds that led Ray Johnson to describe Akhenaten as 'wacky'.**

Ans. Ray Johnson described Akhenaten as 'wacky' because what he did was nothing less than crazy in those times. He promoted the worship of Aten, the sun disk, changed his own name and moved the religious capital from the old city of Thebes to the new city of Akhetaten, now known as Amarna. He further attacked a major God 'Amun' by smashing his images and closing his temples. His reign was a horrible time.

(ii) **What were the results of the CT scan?**

Ans. The CT machine scanned the mummy from head to toe and created 1700 digital X-ray images in cross-section. It scan showed King Tut's neck vertebrae as clearly as in an anatomy class. Other images revealed a hand, several views of the rib cage and a transection of the skull, indicating that there was nothing unnatural in his death.

(iii) List the advances in technology that have improved forensic analysis.

Ans. Advances in technology have improved forensic analysis significantly. Today, diagnostic imaging can be done by Computed Tomography or CT.

In CT scan, hundreds of X-rays in cross-section are put together like slices of bread to create a three-dimensional virtual picture of the body. The scanners can scan even an intricate structure by scanning it in thin slices.

(iv) Explain the statement, "King Tut is one of the first mummies to be scanned - in death, as in life ..."

Ans. King Tut was the last ruler of a powerful family that had ruled Egypt for centuries. He ascended to the throne when he was not even a teenager. At a very young age, he contributed tremendously in restoring the past glory and old ways of Egypt. However, he died very early under mysterious circumstances in his teenage. Since the discovery of his tomb in 1922, the modern world has speculated a lot about him. His mummy was the first one to undergo a CT scan. Hence, in life as in death, he has gained the attention of all.

Talking about the Text (NCERT Page 28)

Discuss the following in groups of two pairs, each pair in a group taking opposite points of view.

1. Scientific intervention is necessary to unearth buried mysteries.

Ans. For If we think history has any relevance in our life, we must get to the truth. There are so many mysteries which remain unsolved. For example, we know very little about the Indus Valley Civilisation. Where the seals remain undeciphered. Without scientific intervention, their meaning will remain unknown.

Against We need to know the past because history is relevant to our lives. But sometimes, we take it too far. King Tut's mummy has been repeatedly investigated but in spite of spending much money, nothing new has been revealed about why King Tut died so young. We must utilise our resources to help the living rather than just investigating the dead.

2. Advance technology gives us conclusive evidence of past events.

Ans. For Today, technology is so advanced that we can reconstruct the past. For example, we know how Pompeii was destroyed. So now, we have reconstructed the whole city. We know precisely how the people lived.

Against It is incorrect to say that advance technology gives us conclusive evidence of past events. King Tut's body was CT-scanned. What can it tell us about how he died? If he was murdered, who murdered him and why? A CT scan might give some idea about how he died but it cannot give conclusive evidence.

3. Traditions, rituals and funerary practices must be respected.

Ans. For People who buried their dead with rituals and funerary practices showed reverence for their dead. They wanted them to lie in peace, undisturbed. We must respect their sentiments.

Against Traditions, customs and funerary practices of the past may encourage superstition. They may also hamper the development of society and affect unity. In fact, they could lead to violence and friction between people belonging to different cultures.

4. Knowledge about the past is useful to complete our knowledge of the world we live in.

Ans. For The past acts as a mirror to our mistakes and teaches us many lessons. In fact, the present is the outcome of the past. It helps us understand the progress of the events down the ages. It builds a good foundation for our present and future.

Against We must live in the present. The past is infinite and should be left as it is. It should not be searched again and again. Instead of looking at the past, we must focus on the present and build a better future.

Thinking about Language (NCERT Page 29)

Read the following piece of information from the Encyclopaedia of Language by David Crystal.

Egyptian is now extinct: its history dates from before the third millennium BC, preserved in many hieroglyphic inscriptions and papyrus manuscripts. Around the second century AD, it developed into a language known as Coptic.

Coptic may still have been used as late as the early nineteenth century and is still used as a religious language by Monophysite Christians in Egypt.

1. What do you think are the reasons for the extinction of languages?

Ans. *Some of the reasons for the extinction of languages are*

(a) Migration of people to other lands.

(b) Absence of written script along with prevalence of oral tradition.

(c) Globalisation, as it has led to the use of only dominant languages.

(d) Social status of a language.

(e) Lack of inter generational transmission.

2. Do you think it is important to preserve languages?

Ans. Yes, I think it is important to preserve languages as they are responsible for development of the culture of the community. It helps in preservation of one's heritage and traditions. Our language defines our identity. One can differentiate between the people speaking the same language by their dialect or the way they talk. A language represents a whole cultural history.

3. In what ways do you think we could help prevent the extinction of languages and dialects?

Ans. *We could help prevent the extinction of languages and dialects by*

(a) Transferring the vocabulary and dialects of the language to the next generation.

(b) Documenting the language and preserving information about native literature and linguistics of the language.

(c) Encouraging younger generations to speak the language as they grow.

(d) New technologies such as 'podcasts' can be used to preserve the spoken versions of languages.

(e) Teaching the languages in college and universities and encouraging students to specialise in the same.

Working with Words (NCERT Page 29)

1. Given below are some interesting combinations of words. Explain why they have been used together.

(i) ghostly dust devils	**(ii) desert sky**
(iii) stunning artefacts	**(iv) funerary treasures**
(v) scientific detachment	**(vi) dark-bellied clouds**
(vii) casket grey	**(viii) eternal brilliance**
(ix) ritual resins	**(x) virtual body**

Ans. (i) **Ghostly dust devils** 'Ghostly' describes the eerie or supernatural quality of the dust devils, implying that they appear otherworldly or mysterious. 'Dust devils' are whirlwinds or mini-tornadoes formed of dust, typically in desert areas. The combination creates a vivid image of swirling, spectral phenomena.

(ii) **Desert sky** 'Desert' indicates the location or context, suggesting an arid, open environment. 'Sky' refers to the expanse of the atmosphere above. Together, they evoke the vast, often clear or hazy expanse of sky typical of desert landscapes.

(iii) **Stunning artefacts** 'Stunning' conveys the impressive, breathtaking quality of the artefacts, suggesting they are visually striking or remarkable. 'Artefacts' refers to objects of historical, cultural, or artistic significance. The combination emphasises the beauty and impact of the objects being described.

(iv) **Funerary treasures** 'Funerary' relates to funeral rites or ceremonies, suggesting these treasures are associated with burial or the afterlife. 'Treasures' implies that the objects hold significant monetary, cultural, or symbolic value to the deceased or their culture.

(v) **Scientific detachment** 'Scientific' pertains to the methodology or approach of science, implying objectivity, analysis, and systematic inquiry.
'Detachment' suggests a sense of emotional or personal separation, indicating a dispassionate or objective viewpoint. The combination describes an impartial and analytical approach to study or observation.

(vi) **Dark-bellied clouds** 'Dark-bellied' describes the underside or lower part of the clouds, suggesting they are heavy with moisture and potentially laden with precipitation. 'Clouds' refers to masses of water vapour visible in the atmosphere.

The combination emphasises the colour and density of the clouds, possibly indicating an impending storm or change in weather.

(vii) **Casket grey** 'Casket' refers to a coffin or burial container. 'Grey' describes the colour of the sky, suggesting a sombre, overcast atmosphere often associated with funerals or mourning.

(viii) **Eternal brilliance** 'Eternal' suggests something everlasting or timeless. 'Brilliance' refers to brightness, radiance, or exceptional quality. Together, they imply a perpetual, dazzling quality, often associated with precious metals or divine attributes.

(ix) **Ritual resins** 'Ritual' indicates that the resins are used in religious or ceremonial contexts, implying symbolic significance. 'Resins' are sticky substances often extracted from plants and used for various purposes. Together they are associated them embalming or preservation rituals.

(x) **Virtual body** 'Virtual' denotes something that exists in essence or effect but not actuality, often referring to simulations or digital representations. 'Body' refers to the physical form of a living organism. The combination suggests a digital representation of a physical body.

2. Here are some commonly used medical terms. Find out their meanings.

CT scan	MRI	tomography
autopsy	dialysis	ECG
post mortem	angiography	biopsy

Ans. CT Scan A CT scan makes use of computer-processed combinations of many X-ray images taken from different angles to produce cross-sectional (tomography) images (virtual 'slices') of specific areas of a scanned object, allowing the user to see inside the object without cutting.

MRI Magnetic Resonance Imaging (MRI) is a diagnostic technique that uses magnetic fields and radio waves to produce a detailed image of the body's soft tissue and bones.

Tomography A method of producing a three - dimensional image of the internal structures of a solid object (like the human body) by the observation and recording of the differences in the effects on the passage of waves of energy hitting those structures.

Autopsy An examination of a body after death to determine the cause of death or the character and extent of changes produced by disease.

Dialysis The purification of blood by separating the waste products from it to replace the normal function of kidneys.

ECG An Electrocardiogram (EKG or ECG) is a test that checks for problems with the electrical activity of the heart. It shows the heart's electrical activity as line tracings on paper.

Post mortem (also called post mortem examination) An examination of a dead body to determine the cause of death.

Angiography A procedure performed to view blood vessels after injecting them with a dye that outlines them on an X-ray. This technique can be used to look at arteries in many areas of the body, including the brain, neck (carotids), heart, chest, pulmonary circuit, kidneys, gastrointestinal area and limbs.

Biopsy A medical procedure during which a small sample of tissue is removed from a part of a body. The sample of tissue is then examined under the microscope to look for abnormal cells.

Things to Do (NCERT Page 29-30)

1. The constellation Orion is associated with the legend of Osiris, the god of the afterlife. Find out the astronomical descriptions and legends associated with the following.

(i) Ursa Major *(Saptarishi mandala)*

(ii) Polaris *(Dhruva tara)*

(iii) Pegasus *(Winged horse)*

(iv) Sirius *(Dog star)*

(v) Gemini *(Mithuna)*

Ans. (i) **Ursa Major** *(Saptarishi mandala)* Ursa Major is a constellation visible throughout the year in the Northern Hemisphere. It consists of seven stars which form the well-known Big-Dipper. Its name means Great Bear in Latin, and is associated with the Legend of Callisto.

According to Sanskrit mythology, it is a group of seven sages (*Saptarishi*) which moves around the constant star *Dhruva tara* known as Polaris.

(ii) **Polaris** *Dhruva tara* Polaris, also known as the North Star, is a bright star close to the North celestial pole. It remains nearly stationary in the night sky as a reliable reference point for determining direction, especially in the northern hemisphere.

In Hindu scriptures, Polaris is associated with the legend of Dhruva, a young prince who meditated intensely to gain Lord Vishnu's blessings. Impressed by Dhruva's devotion, Lord Vishnu granted him a place in the heavens as the Pole Star (Dhruva tara), which remains fixed and unchanging amidst the movement of the other stars.

(iii) **Pegasus** (*Winged Horse*) Pegasus is a large constellation in the northern sky, representing a winged horse from Greek mythology.

In Greek mythology, Pegasus is the offspring of the sea God Poseidon and Medusa. According to legend, Pegasus was born from the severed head of Medusa when the hero Perseus killed her.

(iv) **Sirius** (*Dog Star*) Sirius, also known as the Dog Star, is the brightest star in the night sky. It is located in the constellation Canis Major and is visible from both hemispheres.

In ancient Egyptian mythology, Sirius was associated with the goddess Isis and was considered a symbol of rebirth and fertility. The appearance of Sirius in the sky was also linked to the annual flooding of the Nile River, which played a crucial role in Egyptian agriculture and civilisation.

(v) **Gemini** (*Mithuna*) Gemini is one of the twelve zodiac constellations representing the twins Castor and Pollux from Greek mythology.

In Hindu texts, Gemini is associated with the twins Ashwini Kumaras, who are considered celestial physicians in Hindu cosmology. They are depicted as horse-headed twins and are believed to be the physicians of the gods, possessing the ability to heal and cure diseases.

2. Some of the leaves and flowers mentions in the passage for adorning the dead are willow, olive, celery, lotus, cornflower. Which of these are common in our country?

Ans. Willow, olive, lotus and cornflower are common in our country.

3. Name some leaves and flowers that are used as adornments in our country.

Ans. Roses, lotus, *mehendi*, marigolds, *champa* and *chameli* flowers and the leaves of mango, *peepal*, banana and *tulsi* are used as adornments in our country.

Exam Pattern Questions

Extract Based Questions

Read the extracts given below and answer the questions that follow.

1. **Since the discovery of his tomb in 1922, the modern world has speculated about what happened to him, with murder being the most extreme possibility. Now, leaving his tomb for the first time in almost 80 years, Tut has undergone a CT scan that offers new clues about his life and death — and provides precise data for an accurate forensic reconstruction of the boyish pharaoh.**

(i) Why was CT scan performed on Tut's Mummy?

(a) To know about his life and death

(b) To know about his age

(c) To know about his internal structure

(d) Both (a) and (b)

(ii) Complete the following suitably.

The CT scan done on King Tut is integral because ....

(iii) What was the cemetery of Tut called?

Ans. (i) (a) To know about his life and death

(ii) it revealed that his breast bone and front ribs were missing

(iii) The cemetery of Tut was called the 'Valley of the Kings'.

2. **They remain the richest royal collection ever found and have become part of the pharaoh's legend. Stunning artefacts in gold, their eternal brilliance meant to guarantee resurrection, caused a sensation at the time of the discovery — and still get the most attention. But Tut was also buried with everyday things he'd want in the afterlife: board games, a bronze razor, linen undergarments, cases of food and wine.**

(i) What does the following line from the extract showcase?

But Tut was also buried with everyday things he'd want in the afterlife: board games, a bronze razor, linen undergarments, cases of food and wine.

(a) Confusion

(b) Affirmation

(c) Superstition

(d) Universal belief

(ii) Identify the artefacts mentioned in the extract which were buried with King Tut's body that can be categorised as everyday things.

(iii) Complete the following suitably.

King Tut was buried with everyday things because ....

Ans. (i) (c) Superstition

(ii) Board games, a bronze razor, linen undergarments, cases of food and wine.

(iii) it was believed that he would need them in the afterlife

3. **Once they had finished, they reassembled the remains on a layer of sand in a wooden box with padding that concealed the damage, the bed where Tut now rests.**

Archaeology has changed substantially in the intervening decades, focusing less on treasure and more on the fascinating details of life and intriguing mysteries of death.

It also uses more sophisticated tools, including medical technology. In 1968, more than 40 years after Carter's discovery, an anatomy professor X-rayed the mummy and revealed a startling fact: beneath the resin that cakes his chest, his breast-bone and front ribs are missing.

(i) What had Carter's men done to separate Tut from his adornments?

(ii) How has archaeology changed over the decades?

(a) It is fascinated with the details of life.

(b) It hopes to solve the mysteries of death.

(c) It uses more sophisticated tools now.

(d) All of the above

(iii) Complete the following suitably.

About Tut's mummy, an anatomy professor made the startling discovery that ....

Ans. (i) Carter's men removed the mummy's head and severed nearly every major joint to separate Tut from his adornments.

(ii) (c) It uses more sophisticated tools now.

(iii) his breast-bone and front ribs were missing

Short Answer Type Questions

1. Describe the atmosphere when King Tut's body was scanned.

Ans. As King Tut's body was taken from his resting place in the ancient Egyptian cemetery known as the Valley of the Kings, an angry wind stirred up ghostly dust devils. Dark-bellied clouds had moved across the desert sky all day and covered the stars in grey colour.

But when the CT scan was over, the wind had stopped and the winter air lay still. The clouds were gone and the Orion constellation of stars was clearly visible.

2. Explain the significance of the date 5th January, 2005, in Tutankhamun's saga.

Ans. 5th January, 2005 is a significant date in Tutankhamun's saga because, on this day, the world's most famous mummy gilded from head to toe was CT scanned in order to probe the remaining mysteries of this little understood young ruler who had died more than 3300 years ago.

3. Give a proof of Tut's mummy's popularity.

Ans. King Tut's mummy was so popular that tourists from around the world queued up all afternoon and descended into the narrowed rock-cut tomb to pay their homage to King Tut.

They watched the murals on the walls of the burial chamber. Some visitors read from guidebooks while others stood silently peering at King Tut's gilded face.

4. Identify the superstition that had prevailed about Tutankhamun. Did Howard Carter believe this?

Ans. The superstition of the pharaoh's curse – death misfortune falling upon those who disturbed him – had prevailed about Tutankhamun. The Egyptians thus never tried going near King Tut's tomb and feared it be disastrous. It could invite the pharaoh's curse.

Howard Carter did not believe this because he thought it was just a superstition to keep thieves away from the tomb and from the enormous wealth buried with the little pharaoh.

5. Carter was absolutely wrong in cutting King Tut's body into pieces. Analyse. Competency Based

Ans. Carter was absolutely wrong in cutting King Tut's body into pieces. He damaged the mummy to a great extent and destroyed the natural state of the mummy. Moreover, he did not use scientific methods while excavating King Tut's mummy, resulting in immense disfiguration of the body. This prevented other scientific investigators from trying to find out the reasons for King Tut's death at an early age.

6. What conclusion did Hawass draw about Carter's discovery?

Ans. Zahi Hawass, Secretary General of Egypt's Supreme Council of Antiquities, bent over the mummy and watched it carefully. He discovered that the mummy was in a very bad condition because Howard Carter cut the body into many pieces as it was stuck to the bottom of the coffin due to the ritual resins becoming hardened. So, Zahi Hawass held Howard Carter responsible for the bad condition of the mummy.

7. Mention the materialistic aspect that became part of the pharaoh's legend.

Ans. The wealth with which King Tut was buried remains the richest royal collection ever found and this has become a part of the pharaoh's legend. The wealth basically contains different stunning artefacts of gold. Tut was also buried with everyday things such as board games, bronze razor, linen undergarments and cases of food and wine.

8. Explain the significance of the gold in the artefacts found in Tut's tomb.

Ans. Tutankhamun was an extremely wealthy pharaoh. When he died, he was buried with numerous artefacts like pieces of jewellery such as precious collars, inlaid necklaces and bracelets, rings, amulets, etc. Even the inner coffin and mask were made of pure gold. It was believed that the eternal glitter and brilliance of the precious gold will ensure the rising of King Tut.

9. Howard Carter ran into trouble when he finally reached the mummy. Give reasons.

Ans. When Howard Carter finally reached the mummy, he ran into trouble because he could not raise the mummy out of the coffin. The ritual resins had hardened, cementing King Tut's body to the bottom of his solid gold coffin. No amount of force could pull it out.

10. Identify an instance to prove that the burial of King Tut took place in March or April.

Ans. After months of carefully recording the pharaoh's funerary treasures, Howard Carter began investigating the three nested coffins. When he opened the first coffin, he found a shroud adorned with garlands of willow and olive leaves, wild celery, lotus petals and cornflowers. It was a faded evidence of a burial that took place in March or April because these plants would only be available in Egypt during this period of the year.

11. What efforts did Howard Carter make to separate King Tut's mummy from its solid gold bottom?

Ans. When Howard Carter discovered King Tut's tomb and his mummy in 1922, he found that the ritual resins had hardened and thus cemented the mummy to the bottom of his solid gold coffin. So, he put the mummy in the blazing sunshine to loosen the resins. When nothing melted, they decided to chisel away the resins before removing the King Tut's remains.

12. Identify the startling fact was revealed by a professor of anatomy about King Tut.

Ans. In 1968, more than 40 years after Howard Carter's discovery of King Tut's tomb, a professor of anatomy X-rayed King Tut's mummy. The professor revealed an astonishing fact that beneath the resin that layered his chest, his breast-bone and front ribs were missing.

13. Years later, two questions still linger about King Tut's life. Identify them. Competency Based

Ans. The two questions that still linger about King Tut are how he died and how old he was at the time of his death. He was the last ruler of his dynasty and his funeral marked the end of the dynasty. However, the particulars of his passing away and its aftermath are still unclear.

14. King Tut's demise was a big event, even by royal standards. Analyse.

Ans. King Tut's demise was a big event, even by royal standards because he was the last ruler in his dynasty. This funeral was the end of a dynasty that ruled Egypt for centuries. Moreover, he died unexpectedly at a very young age.

15. Describe King Tut and his family.

Ans. King Tut was the last ruler of a powerful family that ruled Egypt for centuries. He was quite young when he sat on the throne. He ruled for about 9 years.

King Tut died unexpectedly in his early youth which gave rise to many doubts and speculations. He was laid to rest laden with his possessions and forgotten.

Amenhotep III, King Tut's father or grandfather, ruled for almost 40 years. His son Amenhotep IV succeeded him and changed his name to Akhenaten, which meant 'servant of the Aten'. He shifted his religious capital from the old city of Thebes to Akhetaten. He further shocked the country by attacking Amun, a major God. Then, a mysterious ruler, Smenkhkare, ruled briefly. After him, Tutankhaten took the throne.

16. King Tut's reign was an era of restoration. Justify the statement with reference to the chapter.

Ans. King Tut was named Tutankhaten at the time of his birth. On succeeding to the Egyptian throne after Akhenaten, King Tut brought about a restoration of the old customs. First, he changed his name to Tutankhamun in reverence of the old god Amun. Second, he oversaw the restoration and reopening of old temples, shrines and idols.

17. Explain why King Tut's mummy had to undergo a CT scan?

Ans. King Tut's mummy had earned worldwide fame for the riches it was buried with. Moreover, there arose a great controversy regarding the manner of his death and his age at the time of death. As a result, King Tut's body was CT scanned to examine the medical mysteries about his life and death.

18. "Curse of the pharaoh", joked a guard nervously. What is the curse and why did the guard say so?

Ans. The curse of the pharaoh states that death or misfortune would fall upon those who disturbed him. When King Tut's mummy was carried to be scanned, one of the fans of the CT scan machine stopped working due to sand getting into it. That is why the guard jokingly remarked that it was the curse of the pharaoh.

19. How did Tutankhamun's burial reflect ancient Egyptian religious beliefs? Competency Based

Ans. Tutankhamun's elaborate burial rituals and rich offerings reflected the profound religious beliefs of ancient Egypt, particularly concerning the afterlife and the preservation of the soul.

His tomb, filled with treasures and provisions for the journey to eternity, epitomised the Egyptians' fervent belief in immortality and divine judgement.

20. What symbolic significance does the constellation Orion hold in relation to Tutankhamun's burial site?

Ans. The constellation Orion holds symbolic significance in relation to Tutankhamun's burial site. In ancient Egyptian mythology, Orion was associated with Osiris, the God of the afterlife and rebirth. Osiris was believed to judge the souls of the deceased and oversee their journey to the afterlife. The constellation's presence above Tutankhamun's tomb suggests a connection between the pharaoh's burial and the soul's journey into the afterlife. It signifies the belief in the continuation of life after death and the hope for resurrection. The ancient Egyptians carefully aligned their burial sites and rituals with celestial bodies, reflecting their deep spiritual beliefs and reverence for the cosmos.

Long Answer Type Questions

1. In 1922, King Tut's tomb was discovered. On returning home, Howard Carter writes his thoughts about the fact that much of the treasure buried in the tomb had already been stolen. Materialistic attitude of man does not allow even the dead to sleep in peace. Will there be any end to this attitude? Imagine yourself to be Howard Carter and express these thoughts.

You may begin like this Competency Based

Man can go to any extent for a handful of gold. In King Tut's time ....

Ans. Man can go to any extent for a handful of gold. In King Tut's time, the royals were fabulously wealthy and they believed that they could take their riches with them. King Tut's mummy was thus buried with a lot of gold and other items of daily use in the belief that the dead pharaoh would need those things in the afterlife. It was a matter of faith.

When King Tut's tomb was discovered, much of the treasure had already been looted. Ethics and morals are not understood by thieves. Their goal in life is to acquire as much wealth as possible by any means. This materialistic attitude will never end but only increase day by day.

2. Imagine a conversation between King Tut and Khushwant Singh's grandmother from the chapter 'The Portrait of a Lady' which takes place after their deaths. They speak about their lives, things that happened after their deaths and the things they wished could happen differently. **Competency Based**

You may begin the conversation like this King Tut: Greetings, dear Khushwant Singh's grandmother! It's quite a remarkable encounter, isn't it? Tell me, how has life been for you after our respective departures?

Ans. **King Tut** 'Greetings, dear Khushwant Singh's grandmother! It's quite a remarkable encounter, isn't it? Tell me, how has life been for you after our respective departures?

Khushwant Singh's grandmother Ah, King Tut, what an honour to converse with you! Life after death has been filled with intriguing experiences. I've witnessed the changing world and the lives of my descendants. How about you? What have you observed in the realm beyond?

King Tut Fascinating, isn't it? I've seen the marvels of modern civilisation unfold from advancements in technology to the exploration of distant lands. Yet, I do wonder if there were things we wished could have been different during our time on Earth. Are there any regrets you carry, my dear friend?

Khushwant Singh's grandmother Indeed, King Tut. If only I had spoken up more, shared my wisdom and pursued my passions without hesitation. I also wish I had spent more time with loved ones and cherished every moment. How about you? Are there aspects of your life that you wish could have unfolded differently?

King Tut Absolutely, my friend. I wish I had ruled with more compassion and fairness, fostering unity among my people. I also long for the opportunity to explore the world beyond Egypt's borders to witness the wonders of different cultures. Alas, time has its limits and we must make the most of the moments we are given.

Khushwant Singh's grandmother Wise words, King Tut. It's a reminder for all of us, both in life and beyond, to embrace each day and strive to make a positive impact. Our stories may have ended but our legacies live on. Let us cherish the memories we've created and inspire others to live their lives to the fullest.

King Tut Indeed. Let us continue to inspire and guide those who come after us, even from the realms beyond. Our lives may have been different but our shared desire for a meaningful existence unites us. Thank you for this enlightening conversation, Khushwant Singh's grandmother.

Khushwant Singh's Grandmother The pleasure is all mine, King Tut. May our spirits find solace in knowing that our stories continue to resonate through the ages. Farewell, dear friend, until we meet again in the realm of eternal existence.

3. What do you understand by the statement, "Archaeology has changed substantially ...."? Discuss with reference to the chapter 'Discovering Tut: The Saga Continues.' What do you learn from modern archaeology?

Ans. During the last few decades, archaeology has undergone a revolutionary change. It is not what it used to be. It has transformed with time. Earlier it was more about gilded treasures and forgotten fortunes.

But now, the focus is not on the treasure.

Today, archaeology focuses on the fascinating details of peoples' lives and the mysteries behind their deaths. Now, archaeologists are more interested in other relevant details, like in the case of King Tut's mummy.

Archaeologists are more interested to know about the facts of his life - how he lived and how he died.

Also, archaeology uses more sophisticated tools like CT scan machines. It also employs forensic methods and X-ray technology.

Such scientific implements were not available to the archaeologists of earlier years. Hence, they were not able to discover most of the facts about their searches.

4. The chapter 'Discovering Tut : The Saga Continues' shows the importance of understanding our past through archaeological and historical sites and monuments.

Imagine yourself to be an archaeologist who has to address high school students. Write this address in 120-150 words highlighting the vandalism and neglect faced by the historical monuments in our country and encouraging the students to preserve our national wealth.

You may begin like this

Good morning, students!

India has an extraordinarily vast and diverse pool of ....

Ans. Good morning, students! India has an extraordinarily vast and diverse pool of cultural heritage and ancient monuments which reminds us of the golden historic era of over a thousand years. They carry a special and a well deserved respect in the eyes of Indians. However, it is unfortunate that most of these monuments are damaged and are falling to pieces due to thievery and neglect.

We should try to preserve out national wealth. We should prevent others from scribbling on walls. Regular cleanliness drives should be carried out in order to maintain historical monuments. As students, we can also volunteer by being a part of the 'Adopt a Heritage' initiative. Moreover, we should help in spreading awareness about these monuments and their importance. In today's competitive world, we have to preserve the monuments and showcase them to the next generation as the achievements of our ancestors.

Thank you!

SELF ASSESSMENT TEST

Extract based Questions

Read the extract given below and answer the questions that follow.

1. When he finally reached the mummy, though, he ran into trouble. The ritual resins had hardened, cementing Tut to the bottom of his solid gold coffin. "No amount of legitimate force could move them," Carter wrote later. "What was to be done?" The sun can beat down like a hammer this far south in Egypt, and Carter tried to use it to loosen the resins. For several hours he set the mummy outside in blazing sunshine that heated it to 149 degrees Fahrenheit. Nothing budged.

(i) What was the reason behind placing the Mummy under the Sun?

(a) Due to negative atmosphere inside the Tomb. (b) Carter hoped that resin would melt.

(c) There was darkness inside the Tomb. (d) Carter wanted to disinfect the Mummy.

(ii) Select the correct option from those given in brackets to fill in the blank.

Howard Carter had struggled so much to find the mummy; however, when he discovered it, he felt .... (disappointed/exhilarated) because the ritual resins had hardened.

(iii) Complete the following suitably.

The trouble face by Carter was that ....

Short Answer Type Questions

1. What, according to AR Williams, were the thoughts of the visitors who stood silently near King Tut's tomb?

2. Opening the first gilded coffin, Howard Carter reached a conclusion. What conclusion did he reach? How did his speculation work?

3. Howard Carter's justification for ruining King Tut's mummy is skewed. Do you agree? Give reason.

4. How can a CT scan prove more effective than X-rays?

5. Why was the era of Amenhotep IV called 'the strangest period in the history of Egypt'?

6. Describe the main features of the Egyptian rulers that you find mentioned in the lesson.

Long Answer Type Questions

1. 'Discovering Tut' is an account of the archaeologists' attempts to unveil the mystery that surrounded the death of King Tut. Being aware of the past is an important quality of any culture or nation. Write a short article on the need to be aware of one's heritage.

2. After reading the chapter, you realise that the funerary practice of the Egyptians was somewhat exaggerated as they buried their kings with all kinds of ornaments and items of daily use. Though traditions and rituals must be respected, some superstitious beliefs should be discarded. Discuss.

04

The Adventure

About the Author

Jayant Vishnu Narlikar (1938- Present) is an Indian astrophysicist and professor at the Inter-University Centre for Astronomy and Astrophysics (IUCAA). He is best known for developing the conformal gravity theory, known as Hoyle -Narlikar theory, along with Sir Fred Hoyle. Besides scientific papers and books and popular science literature, Narlikar has written science fiction, novels, and short stories in English, Hindi, and Marathi. He is also the consultant for the Science and Mathematics textbooks of NCERT.

▼ YOUR STUDY GOALS

- Chapter Sketch
- About the Characters
- Summary of the Chapter

▼ YOUR PRACTICE GOAL

- NCERT Folder
- Extract Based Questions
- Short Answer Type Questions
- Long Answer Type Questions

Chapter Sketch

This is an extract from the later half of the story 'The Adventure' by Jayant Narlikar. It is a science fiction story in which two theories, the Catastrophe theory and the lack of determinism in Quantum theory are explained. It presents the imaginary set of events which would have occurred in the life of a professor of history if the result of a battle which was fought more than 200 years earlier had been different.

About the Characters

Professor Gangadharpant Gaitonde He is an eminent professor of history working in Pune. He has a catastrophic accident which causes him to transition to a parallel world for 60 hours.

Rajendra Deshpande He is a mathematical and scientific expert who tries to rationalise Professor Gaitonde's experience by applying the Catastrophe theory and the lack of determinism in Quantum theory.

Khan Sahib He sat beside Gaitonde in the train. He was going to Peshawar for business. Through him, Gaitonde learnt a lot about this parallel world.

Context of the Story (Not the Part of Text)

Professor Gangadharpant Gaitonde was an eminent historian and a leading public figure in Pune. He had just completed his 999th occasion for presiding at a function. He had decided that his thousandth appearance on the stage would be for history. That occasion was to come two weeks later at a seminar devoted to the Third Battle of Panipat.

While he was walking home, a truck on the road hit him. When he regained consciousness, he had entered to a parallel world (although he was not aware of this). He decided to go to Bombay because his son was working in a British company there. So, he boards a train. The chapter starts from here.

Summary of the Chapter

Gaitonde's Journey to Bombay

When Gaitonde had to get a permit to visit Bombay, he was told that Bombay was a British territory while the rest of India was independent. On the journey in a first class compartment of the Jijamata Express, he sat beside Khan Sahib, who would be going on to Peshawar from Delhi on business. Then, he realised that there had been no partition of India (in this parallel world).

On the route, the train stopped only at Lonavala, Karjat and the border town of Sarhad where the permits were checked. It did not stop at Kalyan and finally terminated at the Victoria Terminus in Bombay. While going through Bombay's suburbs, he observed that the carriages of the local trains had the British flag painted on them.

Gaitonde Fails to Find his Son

Gaitonde had planned to meet his son and then, go to a big library to solve the mystery of his transition. When Gaitonde stepped out of the railway station, he saw 'East India House, headquarters of The East India Company written on a building. Further, he found various British companies and buildings on the road. He visited his son's office to meet him but found that no such person worked there. This made Gaitonde realise that he had really made the transition to a parallel world.

Gaitonde Finds the Information he Needed

Gaitonde visited the Town Hall building in which the library of the Asiatic Society was located. There he found the five books on Indian history which he had written. On going through the fifth volume, he found that the result of the Third Battle of Panipat in 1761 was different from what he knew.

It said that the Marathas had won the battle whereas, in his reality, they had lost it. From here onwards, the history of India changed.

The Changed History

In this new history, India never went under British rule. The Marathas did not allow the East India Company to expand its influence in India.

He found confirmation in a Marathi journal about how exactly the Marathas had won the battle. It stated that a bullet just brushed past Vishwasrao's ear. Gaitonde, in the real world, had written that Vishwasrao had been killed by a bullet in the battle.

Gaitonde Returns to the Real World

After taking a meal, Gaitonde went for a stroll to the Azad Maidan. There was a lecture going on there. When Gaitonde saw a vacant presidential chair on the stage, he went and sat on it. The audience reacted by strongly protesting against Gaitonde's act.

The reason was that, in this world, the people were only interested in what the speaker was saying and had abolished the custom of having a chairman long ago. The chair kept on the platform was only symbolic. The audience pelted him with tomatoes, eggs and other objects as they did not want any remarks from him and, later, swarmed on to the stage to remove him.

During the commotion, Gaitonde disappeared. He had returned to the real world as he was found on the Azad Maidan the next morning with his clothes torn.

Rajendra Deshpande's Explanation

Gaitonde narrated his adventure to his friend Rajendra Deshpande. Deshpande tried to explain what had happened by stating how the Catastrophe Theory and the lack of determinism in Quantum theory applied to his adventure.

Rajendra felt that Gaitonde had imagined things because he was thinking of the catastrophe theory and its implications on history when the truck hit him. In reply, Gaitonde showed him the torn-off page of the History book from the other world in which Vishwasrao escaped death.

Rajendra Deshpande explained that he had come to the conclusion that there could be many 'different worlds existing at different points of time'. They could all have a different history. Professor Gaitonde had been to another parallel world.

Gaitonde Refuses to Chair any More Seminars

When Rajendra suggested that Gaitonde could recount his adventure at the thousandth seminar he was presiding over after a few days, Gaitonde told him that he had already declined the invitation. Gaitonde stated that he had already made his thousandth address in the Azad Maidan and did not want to chair any more seminars.

Word-Meaning

ghat section	—	section of railway track in the Western Ghats, i.e. the hilly region
roared through	—	passed through with a roaring sound without stopping
Anglo-Indian	—	An Indian of English descent or of mixed English and Indian parentage
ventured	—	dared to ask
central	—	Bombay Central railway station
been wound up	—	stopped its operations
blow-by-blow account	—	detailed description
morale booster	—	event that improved their confidence and raised their morale
from the sidelines	—	but not taking part in it
relegated to	—	assigned to a lower rank or position
political acumen	—	political shrewdness with keen insight
pockets	—	areas
de facto	—	existing
astute	—	marked by practical intelligence
Shahenshah	—	ruler
rubber-stamp	—	formally approve
doctored accounts	—	narratives changed so as to deceive
after his heart	—	to his liking
throng	—	crowd
pandal	—	temporary structure
gave vent to	—	expressed his feelings and ideas
valiantly	—	courageously
dumbfounded	—	greatly surprised
Bakhar	—	form of historical narrative written in Marathi prose
food for thought	—	something that requires serious consideration
catastrophic	—	sudden happening causing damage and/or suffering
take issue	—	disagree
ignoramus	—	ignorant

Important Themes of the Chapter

Historical Significance of Events The story explores the profound impact of a specific historical event, such as the Battle of Panipat, on shaping history. It highlights how pivotal moments in the past can have far-reaching consequences and influence the development of societies and civilisations.

Interdisciplinary Exploration The chapter emphasises the interconnectedness of different fields of study through Professor Gaitonde's journey of investigating historical events and engaging with scientific theories like catastrophe theory and quantum mechanics. It highlights the importance of interdisciplinary approaches in understanding complex phenomena and unravelling mysteries.

Alternate Realities and Parallel Worlds The concept of divergent historical timelines and parallel worlds is central to the narrative. The story explores the possibility of multiple realities coexisting simultaneously and the profound implications of individuals traversing between different versions of history. This theme prompts reflection on the nature of reality and the fluidity of historical narratives.

Identity and Self-Discovery As Professor Gaitonde grapples with discovering alternate realities and confronts the mystery of his own experiences, the story delves into themes of identity, self-discovery, and existential inquiry. It explores how encountering divergent versions of history challenges one's sense of self, perception of reality, and understanding of personal and collective identity.

NCERT Folder

Notice these Expressions (NCERT Page 45)

All the expressions have been explained in the 'Word Meanings' given above.

Understanding the Text (NCERT Page 54-55)

I. Tick the statements that are true.

1. The story is an account of real events.
2. The story hinges on a particular historical event.
3. Rajendra Deshpande was a historian.
4. The places mentioned in the story are all imaginary.
5. The story tries to relate history to science.

Ans. Only statements 2 and 5 are true. The other statements are false.

II. Briefly explain the following statements from the text.

1. **'You neither travelled to the past nor the future. You were in the present experiencing a different world.'**
2. **'You have passed through a fantastic experience: or more correctly, a catastrophic experience.'**
3. **Gangadharpant could not help comparing the country he knew with what he was witnessing around him.**
4. **'The lack of determinism in Quantum Theory!'**
5. **'You need some interaction to cause a transition.'**

Ans. 1. This statement was made by Rajendra Deshpande to explain Professor Gaitonde's. It meant that Gaitonde had made a transition from one world to another and has come back again. Thus, he was able to experience two worlds, one at a time. He did not travel either to the past or the future. He was physically present in the real world and mentally experiencing another world for two days.

2. This statement was made by Rajendra Deshpande to Professor Gaitonde. It meant that Gaitonde had passed through a strange experience of living successively in two worlds, one in which he was now and the other in which he had spent the last two days.

3. Professor Gaitonde knew the India in which the power of the Peshwas declined and the British colonised the country. However, the India he had seen during the two days was completely different. This country had not been colonised by the British. Instead, it was self-dependent and enjoyed self-respect. He compared the two different situations of the country.

4. This means that, if a bullet is fired from a gun in a given direction at a given speed, one will know where it will be at any time after this but such an assertion cannot be made for an electron where Quantum Theory applies. When an electron is fired from a source, it may be here, there or anywhere else. This is called the lack of determinism in Quantum Theory. This theory asserts that reality is never one-sided. Alternative worlds may exist at the same time.

5. Professor Gaitonde made a transition which, according to Rajendra Deshpande, had happened because of the interaction happening in the professor's mind at the time of his collision.

   When the collision took place, Gaitonde was thinking about the Catastrophe Theory and its role in the history. He was probably wondering about the Third Battle of Panipat and its consequences. The interaction in his brain acted as a trigger to cause the transition.

Talking about the Text (NCERT Page 55)

1. **Discuss the following statements in groups of two pairs, each pair in a group taking opposite points of view.**

(i) **A single event may change the course of the history of a nation.**

(ii) **Reality is what is directly experienced through the senses.**

(iii) **The methods of inquiry of history, science and philosophy are similar.**

Ans. (i) **For** A single event can profoundly impact a nation's history. History is replete with examples of pivotal moments-such as the invasion of India, the bombing of the World Trade Centre, or World War I and II — that fundamentally altered the trajectory of entire nations. These events catalysed political, social, and economic changes that reverberated for generations, shaping the destiny of societies in profound ways.

Against While significant events can serve as catalysts for change, attributing the entire course of history to a single event oversimplifies the complex dynamics at play. Many interconnected factors shape history, including socioeconomic conditions, cultural norms and geopolitical tensions. While a single event may serve as a tipping point or trigger for broader shifts, it is often the culmination of underlying trends and circumstances that determine the direction of a nation's history.

(ii) **For** Reality, by definition, captures the world as perceived through our senses. Our sensory experiences of sight, sound, touch, taste and smell provide us with direct access to the physical environment around us. This sensory input forms the basis of our understanding of reality and shapes our interactions with the world. Without sensory perception, our conception of reality would be incomplete and lacking in immediacy.

Against While sensory experience offers valuable insights into the physical world, it represents only one aspect of reality. Reality extends beyond sensory perception, including abstract concepts as well as subjective experiences. For example, emotions, thoughts and beliefs are integral parts of reality and are not directly perceptible through the senses. Furthermore, phenomena like dreams, hallucinations and illusions demonstrate that sensory perception can be deceiving and may not always accurately reflect reality. Therefore, defining reality solely based on sensory experience overlooks its multifaceted nature.

(iii) **For** The methods of inquiry in history, science and philosophy share fundamental similarities in their approach to seeking knowledge and understanding. Each discipline employs critical thinking, systematic analysis, and logical reasoning to investigate phenomena. Interdisciplinary approaches often demonstrate the interconnectedness of these fields, showcasing their shared methodologies and objectives.

Against While there may be some overlap in their methodologies, history, science, and philosophy have distinct objectives and hence, different approaches to inquiry. History relies heavily on archival research, literary resources and interpretation of past events to reconstruct narratives and understand human societies. On the other hand, science emphasises observation, experimentation and hypothesis testing to uncover natural laws and explain physical phenomena. Through conceptual analysis and logical arguments, philosophy explores fundamental questions about existence, knowledge, ethics, and reality. While interdisciplinary collaboration is valuable, it is essential to recognise each discipline's unique methods and goals.

2. **(i) The story is called 'The Adventure'. Compare it with the adventure described in 'We Are Not Afraid to Die...'**

(ii) Why do you think Professor Gaitonde decided never to preside over meetings again?

Ans. (i) The underlying theme of both the stories 'The Adventure' and 'We Are Not Afraid to Die' is the same. However, the application of the theme to the events is different in both.

One deals with the adventure in a real-life situation and the other one is about the adventure that was mentally experienced. In the story 'We Are Not Afraid to Die', the characters take a hazardous sea voyage, overcome the odds and survive. The dangers they faced were very real.

In the story 'The Adventure', the protagonist (Gaitonde) does not embark upon an actual adventurous journey. His collision with the truck triggers his mind to travel to a world which is different from the world that he lives in.

(ii) Professor Gaitonde had recently had a harrowing experience in the parallel world which was contrary to the conventions in the normal world. In his real world, a lecture session always has a chairperson. However, in the world of his experience, he was pelted with various objects because he tried to occupy the Chairperson's chair. Due to this attack by the public, Gaitonde realised that such a speech would not be welcomed at the seminar and so, decided to never preside over such meetings again.

Thinking about Language (NCERT Page 55)

1. In which language do you think Gangadharpant and Khan Sahib talked to each other? Which language did Gangadharpant use to talk to the English receptionist?

Ans. Gangadharpant and Khan Sahib would have talked in Hindi or another Indian language, as both of them are educated and speaking fluently to each other. Gangadharpant must have used English to talk to the English receptionist.

2. In which language do you think *Bhausahebanchi Bakhar* was written?

Ans. *Bhausahebanchi Bakhar* was written in the Marathi language as the words are Marathi words and *Bakhar* is a form of historical narrative written in Marathi prose.

3. There is mention of three communities in the story: the Marathas, the Mughals, the Anglo-Indians. Which language do you think they used within their communities and while speaking to the other groups?

Ans. Within their communities, the Marathas would have spoken in Marathi, the Mughals in Urdu or Persian and the Anglo-Indians in English. While speaking to the other groups, they would have used the services of interpreters who were fluent in both languages to translate what was said into the language of the listener.

4. Do you think that the ruled always adopt the language of the ruler?

Ans. No, the adoption of the ruler's language by the ruled can vary depending on several factors, including the policies of the ruling power, the level of cultural exchange between the ruler and the ruled, and the existing linguistic diversity within the region. While some communities may adopt the ruler's language for practical reasons such as administration, trade, or social mobility, others may resist linguistic assimilation due to cultural pride, identity preservation, or political resistance. Therefore, it is not necessarily a universal rule that the ruled always adopt the language of the ruler, as complex historical, social, and political factors influence language dynamics.

Working with Words (NCERT Page 55-56)

I. Tick the item that is closest in meaning to the following phrases.

1. to take issue with

   (i) to accept (ii) to discuss

   (iii) to disagree (iv) to add

Ans. (iii) to disagree

2. to give vent to

   (i) to express (ii) to emphasise

   (iii) suppress (iv) dismiss

Ans. (i) to express

3. to stand on one's feet

   (i) to be physically strong (ii) to be independent

   (iii) to stand erect (iv) to be successful

Ans. (ii) to be independent

4. to be wound up

   (i) to become active (ii) to stop operating

   (iii) to be transformed (iv) to be destroyed

Ans. (ii) to stop operating

5. to meet one's match

   (i) to meet a partner who has similar tastes

   (ii) to meet an opponent

   (iii) to meet someone who is equally able as oneself

   (iv) to meet defeat

Ans. (iii) to meet someone who is equally able as oneself

II. Distinguish between the following pairs of sentences.

1. (i) He was *visibly* moved.

   (ii) He was *visually* impaired.

Ans. Sentence (i) means that the concerned person's behaviour was obviously or clearly affected. Sentence (ii) means that the concerned person's sight was affected, i.e., he was partially or fully blind.

2. (i) Green and black stripes were used *alternately*.

   (ii) Green stripes could be used or *alternatively* black ones.

Ans. Sentence (i) means that green and black stripes were used one after the other. Sentence (ii) means that either green stripes could be used or black ones.

3. (i) The team played the two matches *successfully*.

   (ii) The team played two matches *successively*.

Ans. Sentence (i) means that the team played two matches with success, i.e., they won both the matches. Sentence (ii) means that the team played two matches one after another.

4. (i) The librarian spoke *respectfully* to the learned scholar.

   (ii) You will find the historian and the scientist in the archaeology and natural science sections of the museum, *respectively*.

Ans. Sentence (i) means that the librarian spoke with respect to the learned scholar. Sentence (ii) means that one will find the historian in the archaeology section and the scientist in the natural science section of the museum.

Noticing Form (NCERT Page 57)

The story deals with unreal and hypothetical conditions. Some of the sentences used to express this notion are given below.

1. If I fire a bullet from a gun in a given direction at a given speed, I know where it will be at a later time.
2. If I knew the answer I would solve a great problem.
3. If he himself were dead in this world, what guarantee had he that his son would be alive!
4. What course would history have taken if the battle had gone the other way?

   Notice that in an unreal condition, it is clearly expected that the condition will not be fulfilled.

Ans. Do it yourself.

Things to Do (NCERT Page 57-58)

I. Read the following passage on the Catastrophe Theory downloaded from the Internet.

Originated by the French mathematician, Rene Thom, in the 1960s, catastrophe theory is a special branch of dynamical systems theory. It studies and classifies phenomena characterised by sudden shifts in behaviour arising from small changes in circumstances.

Catastrophes are bifurcations between different equilibria, or fixed point attractors. Due to their restricted nature, catastrophes can be classified on the basis of how many control parameters are being simultaneously varied. For example, if there are two controls, then one finds the most common type, called a 'cusp' catastrophe. If, however, there are more than five controls, there is no classification.

Catastrophe theory has been applied to a number of different phenomena, such as the stability of ships at sea and their capsising, bridge collapse, and, with some less convincing success, the fight-or-flight behaviour of animals and prison riots.

II. Look up the Internet or an encyclopaedia for information on the following theories.

(i) Quantum theory (ii) Theory of relativity

(iii) Big Bang theory (iv) Theory of evolution

Ans. Do it yourself.

Exam Pattern Questions

Extract Based Questions

Read the extracts given below and answer the questions that follow.

1. **"Greater Bombay Metropolitan Railway," explained Khan Sahib. "See the tiny Union Jack painted on each carriage? A gentle reminder that we are in British territory." The train began to slow down beyond Dadar and stopped only at its destination, Victoria Terminus. The station looked remarkably neat and clean. The staff was mostly made up of Anglo-Indians and Parsees along with a handful of British officers.**

(i) According to Khan Sahib, how could one tell if they were in the British territory?

(ii) Select the correct option from those given in bracket to fill in the blank.

The train is moving towards its last station which is .... (Dadar/Victoria Terminus).

(iii) Complete the following suitably.

When he got out of the station, Gaitonde saw the letters .... on a building.

Ans. (i) According to Khan Sahib, each carriage had a tiny Union Jack painted on it and it was a gentle reminder that they were in British territory.

(ii) Victoria Terminus

(iii) East India House Headquarters of East India Company

2. **The twentieth century brought about further changes inspired by the West. India moved towards a democracy. By then, the Peshwas had lost their enterprise and they were gradually replaced by democratically elected bodies. The Sultanate at Delhi survived even this transition, largely because it wielded no real influence. The Shahenshah of Delhi was no more than a figurehead to rubber-stamp the 'recommendations' made by the central parliament.**

As he read on, Gangadharpant began to appreciate the India he had seen. It was a country that had not been subjected to slavery for the white man; it had learnt to stand on its feet and knew what self-respect was.

(i) Complete the following suitably.

India was moving towards a democracy by the twentieth century because ....

(ii) Explain why the Delhi Sultanate survived this transition?

(iii) What does the following line from the extract showcase?

It was a country that had not been subjected to slavery for the white man; it had learnt to stand on its feet and knew what self-respect was.

(a) Expectation **(b) Appreciation**
(c) Understanding **(d) Criticism**

Ans. (i) the Peshwas had lost their enterprise and they were gradually replaced by democratically elected bodies.

(ii) The Delhi Sultanate survived this transition because it wielded no real influence.

(iii) (b) Appreciation

3. **Rajendra motioned him to silence and started pacing the room, obviously under great mental strain. Finally, he turned around and said, "Professor Gaitonde, I will try to rationalise your experience on the basis of two scientific theories as known today. Whether I succeed or not in convincing you of the facts, only you can judge — for you have indeed passed through a fantastic experience: or, more correctly, a catastrophic experience!"**

(i) Select the textual option that is closest to indicating a sense of confusion.

(a) Rajendra motioned him to silence and started pacing the room...

(b) I will try to rationalise your experience...

(c) Whether I succeed or not in convincing you of the facts...

(d) None of the above

(ii) Complete the following suitably.

Rajendra tried to rationalise Gaitonde's experience ....

(iii) What is the 'catastrophic experience' mentioned in the above extract?

Ans. (i) (d) None of the above

(ii) on the basis of two scientific theories

(iii) The 'catastrophic experience' mentioned in the given extract is Professor Gaitonde's transition to a parallel world and his return.

Short Answer Type Questions

1. **Professor Gangadharpant Gaitonde was planning to find out how the 'present state of affairs' had been reached? Explain.**

Ans. Professor Gangadharpant Gaitonde had been mystified to realise that Bombay was a British territory whereas the rest of India was independent. He planned to find out how the 'present state of affairs' had been reached by visiting a big library in Bombay and going through History books on the subject. Then, he would go back to Pune and consult Rajendra Deshpande to help him understand what had happened.

2. Explain why a permit was required to enter Bombay for the passengers in the train. Competency Based

Ans. In the parallel world, Bombay is shown as a British territory while the areas surrounding it are Indian territory. In a normal situation, a passport and a visa are required to enter another country's territory. Here, it has been assumed that only a permit is required due to the frequent journeys Indian citizens make to Bombay.

3. Which expression did the contrasting image of East India House evoke in Gaitonde and why?

Ans. Gaitonde was shocked to see East India House just outside the Victoria Terminus railway station. In his reality, the East India Company had stopped its operations in India after the events of 1857 according to the History books. This made Gaitonde conclude that, in this world, India's history was different from what he knew.

4. Write the names of buildings that Gaitonde saw while walking along Hornby Road which made it look as if he was on a typical high street in an English town.

Ans. The names of buildings which Gaitonde saw while walking along Hornby Road were Boots and Woolworth departmental stores, imposing offices of Lloyds, Barclays and other British banks and the Forbes building. These English names made it appear to Gaitonde as if he was in an English town.

5. Describe the conclusion drawn by Gaitonde after visiting the forbes office.

Ans. In the world that Gangadharpant knew, Vinay Gaitonde, his son, worked in the Forbes building in Bombay. However, when Gangadharpant enquired with the English receptionist in the building about his son, the receptionist informed him after checking the telephone extension list, the staff list and employees list in other branches of Forbes that no such person worked there. Thus, Gangadharpant concluded that in this world his son did not exist.

6. Identify the instance from history discovered by Gaitonde which stood in contrast with what he knew.

Ans. In the fifth book which he himself had written, Gaitonde found the exact event which resulted differently from what he knew. This was the Third Battle of Panipat in 1761 about which the history book mentioned that the Maratha forces had defeated the invader Ahmed Shah Abdali. However, Gaitonde had known that the Marathas had lost this battle.

7. Give reason why the East India Company stopped its expansion in this parallel world.

Ans. With the victory of the Marathas in the Third Battle of Panipat, their supremacy in northern India was established. When the East India Company observed this, it temporarily shelved its expansionist programme.

8. The practical intelligence of the Peshwa rulers benefitted their nation. Elucidate. Competency Based

Ans. The Peshwa rulers had the practical intelligence to understand the significance of the technological age starting in Europe. So, they set up their own scientific and technological centres using the aid and expertise offered by the East India Company to make the local centres self-sufficient.

9. Explain how India became a democracy during the twentieth century in this parallel world. Competency Based

Ans. By the time of the twentieth century, the Peshwas had lost their resourcefulness. Also, the Delhi Sultanate did not actually have any power or influence. It was just to 'rubber stamp' the recommendations made by the government. Thus, inspired by changes occurring in the West, India moved to becoming a democracy.

10. The fifth book Gaitonde read lacked certain information so he had to read another book. Identify the book and also mention how that information was significant.

Ans. The fifth history book Gaitonde was reading did not give details of the Third Battle of Panipat to enable Gaitonde to understand how the Marathas had won that battle; thus, making Gaitonde's investigations incomplete. The *Bhausahebanchi Bakhar*, a form of historical narrative written in Marathi prose, gave him the answer to how the Marathas had won this battle.

11. Identify the instance as mentioned in Bhausahebanchi Bakhar that was different from what happened in Gaitonde's world.

Ans. *Bhausahebanchi Bakhar*, the document that Gaitonde read, mentioned that during the battle, a bullet brushed past Vishwasrao's ear. He could easily have been killed if he was just a fraction of an inch towards the path of the bullet. Then, the Marathas would have lost the battle. In his world, Vishwasrao had been killed by a bullet and the Marathas lost the battle.

12. Identify the peculiar thing about the event going on at Azad Maidan.

Ans. When Gaitonde reached Azad Maidan, he saw many people moving towards a *pandal* where a lecture was going on. However, what was peculiar about it was that the presidential chair on the platform was unoccupied although the speaker was speaking. Gaitonde felt that this chair was kept vacant for him.

13. Explain the audience's reaction to Gaitonde sitting on the presidential chair. Give reason.

Ans. The audience reacted by strongly protesting against Gaitonde sitting on the presidential chair. The reason was that, in this world, the people had become sick of hearing long introductions, vote of thanks and remarks of the person on the chair. They were only interested in what the speaker was saying and had abolished the custom of having a chairman long ago. The chair kept on the platform was only symbolic.

14. Point the evidence that Gaitonde showed to Deshpande to convince him that he was speaking the truth about his experiences in another world.

Ans. The evidence Gaitonde showed to Deshpande to convince him that he was speaking the truth about his experiences in another world was a page torn out of the *Bhausahebanchi Bakhar* which mentioned that the bullet missed Vishwasrao although, in the actual book which Gaitonde had written, Vishwasrao was hit by the bullet.

15. Identify the instances Rajendra Deshpande used to illustrate his contention that reality may not be unique. Competency Based

Ans. Rajendra Deshpande used the examples of atoms and sub-atomic particles to illustrate his contention that reality may not be unique. He said that, if an electron is fired from a source, we cannot predict exactly the location of the electron after a specified period of time. This is explained in the Quantum Theory as 'lack of determinism'.

16. How did Gaitonde's experience in the parallel world influence his decision in his world?

Ans. Professor Gaitonde did not make his presidential address at the seminar he had been invited to chair. He conveyed his regrets to the organisers of the seminar. The reason was that, due to his experience in the parallel world, he had realised that such a speech would not be welcomed at the seminar.

17. What implications did Gangadharpant's experience hold for understanding reality? Competency Based

Ans. Gangadharpant's experience challenged his perception of reality, forcing him to consider the existence of multiple parallel worlds and the unpredictable nature of historical outcomes. It prompted him to reassess the boundaries of reality and the role of individual consciousness in experiencing different realities.

18. How does the portrayal of Bombay, particularly Victoria Terminus and East India House, challenge Professor Gaitonde's understanding of history? Competency Based

Ans. The portrayal of Bombay, notably Victoria Terminus and East India House, challenges Professor Gaitonde's understanding of history by presenting a reality that contradicts established historical narratives. East India Company headquarters' continued existence and prominence defies historical accounts suggesting its dissolution after 1857. Similarly, the pristine condition of Victoria Terminus, staffed predominantly by Anglo-Indians and Parsees, contradicts the expected post-independence transformation of institutions.

These discrepancies force Professor Gaitonde to question the accuracy of his historical knowledge and consider alternative timelines or divergent historical events that led to the development of this alternate reality.

19. Explore the role of catastrophic events in triggering transitions between alternate worlds, such as the collision and Professor Gaitonde's contemplation of the catastrophe theory. Competency Based

Ans. Catastrophic events are pivotal in triggering transitions between alternate worlds in the narrative. For instance, Professor Gaitonde's collision acts as a catalyst for his journey into an alternate reality. Furthermore, his contemplation of the catastrophe theory, particularly its implications for historical events like the Battle of Panipat, fuels his transition between worlds. This suggests that moments of upheaval or intense contemplation can serve as points of divergence, leading individuals to experience different realities.

Long Answer Type Questions

1. What shocks did Gangadharpant Gaitonde get in the Bombay of the parallel world?

Ans. Gangadharpant Gaitonde got a lot of shocks in Bombay of the parallel world. First was that the East India Company still existed and was flourishing. The second shock was the sign of British rule everywhere in Bombay from the suburban railway carriages having a British flag painted on them to the British road names and building names.

The third shock came when he found that nobody with his son's name worked in the company in which he had been working in the real world. Gaitonde got another shock when, in the library of the Asiatic Society, he read a history book written by him which described the Third Battle of Panipat ending in a different way from what he had actually written in his book in the real world.

The final shock, which enabled him to return to the real world, came when he tried to chair a seminar at the Azad Maidan. He was vociferously opposed by the audience but, when he stood his ground, the audience stormed the stage. He was concussed in the melee and found himself in the real world when he regained consciousness.

2. What method did Professor Gaitonde adopt to find the information he wanted in the library of the Asiatic Society? Did he find the required information? Competency Based

Ans. The method that Professor Gaitonde adopted to find the information he wanted in the library of the Asiatic Society was to go through reliable history books. As he had himself written the history of India in five volumes in his world, he felt them to be a reliable source. He did not find any difference from what he knew in the first four volumes which covered India's history up to the death of Aurangzeb.

However, in the fifth volume, he found that the Third Battle of Panipat was described differently from what he had actually written. Thus, he understood that the result of the battle was different. From that point onwards, the history of India in the parallel world was different from that of his world. This explained all that he had witnessed in Pune and Bombay during the last few hours. However, he still could not find an explanation for the reason of his transition to a parallel world with a different history.

He resolved to return to Pune and ask Rajendra Deshpande, a mathematical and scientific expert, to solve this mystery for him provided that Rajendra Deshpande existed in this parallel world.

3. How did Rajendra Deshpande initially explain Professor Gaitonde's experience? Was Gaitonde convinced with the explanation? How did Rajendra change his explanation based on the new evidence given by Gaitonde?

Ans. Rajendra Deshpande initially explained Professor Gaitonde's experience as imagination because he may have been thinking about the Third Battle of Panipat at the time the truck hit him. However, Gaitonde was not convinced with the explanation as his adventure was too real to be imagined.

Further, he had evidence to prove this. He showed Rajendra the torn off page of the *Bhausahebanchi Bakhar* in which the description of the Third Battle of Panipat was different from what he had actually written. At first, Rajendra was puzzled by this new evidence. But, after further discussion with Gaitonde, Rajendra explained that he had come to the conclusion that there could be many 'different worlds existing at different points of time'. They could all have different histories. Professor Gaitonde had been to another parallel world. The time was the present but its history was quite different. This explanation was more likely to be correct due to the application of the Quantum Theory to Gaitonde's experience.

4. In the chapter 'The Adventure', the author has discussed a transition and its different possibilities. Imagine you are a scientist who has to give a speech explaining what the author has been trying to tell through the story to school students.

You may begin like this

Good morning, students!

In the story 'The Adventure', the author has ....

Ans. Good morning, students! In the story 'The Adventure', the author has tried to explain two theories of Science—the Catastrophe Theory and the lack of determinism in Quantum Theory—through an imaginary set of events which occurred in the life of a professor of history. The author wanted to show what would have happened if the Marathas had won the Third Battle of Panipat.

India (in 1986, when this story was written) would be different from the India which we know due to the catastrophe of the Marathas losing the Third Battle of Panipat. Our lifestyle would not have been that much influenced by the West, there would have been no partition of the country and so on. The author has tried to show how a single but small turning point in history would have resulted in a completely different set of events later on. From what we know at present about the Quantum Theory, it can only be applied to sub-atomic particles and not to discrete objects.

Thus, it cannot explain what happened to Gaitonde. Even the Catastrophe Theory only tries to explain the behaviour of various systems when they undergo catastrophic stress. It cannot explain the transition to a parallel world. Thus, we can conclude that it is not possible for such a transition to occur.

Thank you!

5. Imagine that you have been asked to write a newpaper article about the experience and adventure of professor Gaitonde. Write the article presenting this adventure reflects Gaitonde's character.

Ans. **The Adventures of Professor Gaitonde** Shaking the world of history, the eminent and popular historian Professor Gaitonde had a collision with a truck which led him to 'supposedly' transition into another world. It is suggested that at the time he was thinking of the Catastrophe Theory and its implications. So, when he regained consciousness, he found himself in another world which looked totally different from the one that he knew. However, he was resolute enough to try and figure out what was happening. That is why he journeyed to Bombay.

He, as we all know, was very knowledgeable about Indian history as he had written a set of five books on it. However, he seems to be quite vain as he prided himself on his eloquence by speaking as a Chairman at various seminars. This vanity was punctured after the hostile reception he received in the parallel world when he tried to chair a seminar at the Azad Maidan in Bombay. He also displayed persistence to know the truth of his adventure when he questioned his friend Rajendra Deshpande about the explanation that Rajendra gave him about his transition.

All in all, Gaitonde was a vain but persistent historian who was thorough in his subject as well as reasoning power. He also had some scientific knowledge because he understood the Quantum the Theory and its implications.

6. The chapter 'The Adventure' takes the reader deep into the mathematical and scientific world of theories and possibilities.
Imagine yourself to be a quantum scientist who has to give a speech about the character Rajendra Deshpande and his role in the story to high shcool students. Write this address in 120-150 words based on your understanding of Rajendra Deshpande from the incidents in the story.
You may begin like this
Good morning, students!
Rajendra Deshpande was a mathematical and scientific expert who ....

Ans. Good morning, students!
Rajendra Deshpande was a mathematical and scientific expert who tried to rationalise Professor Gaitonde's experience by applying the Catastrophe Theory and the lack of determinism in Quantum Theory. He understood both the theories very well and was able to apply them to Gaitonde's adventure.

This shows his knowledge and expertise in his field of work. In addition, he displayed an attitude of loyalty towards his friend, Professor Gaitonde, because he believed his story completely despite the story being totally bizarre. He displayed analytical power by being initially able to analyse Gaitonde's story as a figment of his imagination. But, when Gaitonde showed evidence that he had really been to a parallel world, Rajendra displayed flexibility by changing his explanation based on his mathematical and scientific knowledge.

Thus, Rajendra Deshpande was a rational-thinking mathematical and scientific expert in his profession who was loyal to his friend, had analytical power and was flexible enough to modify his explanation based on new evidence.

Thank you!

7. Discuss Professor Gaitonde's realisation about the strength and self-reliance of India he encountered in the alternate history, contrasting it with the colonial subjugation in his familiar world. Competency Based

Ans. In the alternate history, Professor Gaitonde realises that India has not experienced colonial subjugation to the extent he is familiar with it. He encounters a nation that stands on its own feet, displaying strength and self-reliance. This contrasts starkly with the colonial domination he knows, where India endured centuries of exploitation and oppression under British rule.

Witnessing India's independence from foreign control prompts Professor Gaitonde to appreciate the resilience and autonomy of this alternate reality. It highlights the potential for a different trajectory in Indian history-where the nation develops on its terms, free from external interference and exploitation.

8. How does the story address reality and the possibility of multiple parallel worlds, drawing from scientific theories and historical speculation?

Ans. The story addresses reality by incorporating scientific theories, such as quantum mechanics, to suggest the existence of multiple parallel worlds. Drawing from historical speculation and scientific principles, it presents a narrative where the protagonist, Professor Gaitonde, experiences a transition between different realities.

Through Rajendra's explanation, the story explores the concept of divergent timelines, where historical events lead to bifurcations, resulting in distinct parallel worlds. This blending of scientific theories with historical speculation challenges traditional notions of reality, suggesting that the universe may contain multiple coexisting realities. It prompts readers to contemplate the interconnectedness of time and history and the potential for divergent paths in human experience.

SELF ASSESSMENT TEST

Extract Based Questions

Read the extract given below and answer the questions that follow.

1. The Maratha army was facing Abdali's troops on the field of Panipat. There was no great disparity between the latter's troops and the opposing forces. Their armour was comparable. So, a lot depended on the leadership and the morale of the troops. The juncture at which Vishwasrao, the son of and heir to the Peshwa, was killed proved to be the turning point. As history has it, his uncle, Bhausaheb, rushed into the melee and was never seen again. Whether he was killed in battle or survived is not known.

(i) Upon which of the following factors was battle dependent?

(a) Leadership
(b) Morale of the troops
(c) Use of nuclear weapons
(d) Both (a) and (b)

(ii) What proved to be a turning point in the battle?

(iii) Complete the following suitably.

According to the extract, Bhausaheb ....

Short Answer Type Questions

1. What was Gaitonde's plan for his visit to Bombay?

2. What was peculiar about the suburban trains in Bombay?

3. When Gaitonde saw East India House, what did he think and then resolve to do?

4. How did **Vishwasrao** and **Madhavrao** curb the ambitions of the East India Company?

5. Gaitonde was attracted to the vacant presidential chair at the Azad Maidan. What does this show about his character?

6. How did Rajendra explain to Gaitonde that reality may not be unique?

Long Answer Type Questions

1. What was the purpose of Professor Gaitonde's visit to Bombay? Was his purpose fulfilled? Why or why not?

2. 'The Adventure' has been placed in science fiction genre. Find instances from the story that justify this statement.

05

Silk Road

About the Author

Nick Middleton (1960-present) is an award-winning geographer, writer, TV presenter, environmental scientist and a university lecturer. His curiosity about how planet Earth works and how people interact with it was fuelled from an early age by his family's world atlas, The Adventures of Tintin and Willard Price's novels. Now, he works and communicates on a wide variety of environmental issues and travel topics for a broad range of audiences. Nick is the author of seven travel books, including the bestseller, Going to Extremes. 'Extremes Along the Silk Road' is about the author's journey across the Silk Road, one of the most inhospitable places on Earth.

▼ YOUR STUDY GOALS

- Chapter Sketch
- About the Characters
- Summary of the Chapter

▼ YOUR PRACTICE GOAL

- NCERT Folder
- Extract Based Questions
- Short Answer Type Questions
- Long Answer Type Questions

Chapter Sketch

This chapter is part of a travelogue about the author's journey along the ancient trade route called the 'Silk Road'. This account of the Silk Road, with its contrasts and exotic details describes the challenges and hardships faced by the author while journeying to Mount Kailash on a pilgrimage.

About the Characters

The Author He is a Professor of Geography at the Oxford University and an environmental consultant.

Tsetan He is the owner of the car hired by the author for the journey as well as a tourist guide.

Daniel He is an interpreter from Lhasa who travelled for some distance with the author.

Norbu He is a Tibetan working at an academy in Beijing who wants to carry out the pilgrimage to Mount Kailash.

Lhamo She is the lady who had provided the author accommodation at Ravu

Summary of the Chapter

Departure from Ravu

The author left Ravu along with Daniel and Tsetan. Before leaving, Lhamo gave the author a gift of a long-sleeved sheepskin coat as they were going to Mount Kailash. Tsetan knew a short cut to reach the mountain. He said the journey would be smooth if there was no snow.

As they passed through the hills, they saw individual *drokbas* (nomad shepherds) looking after their flocks. They were wearing thick woollen clothes. They would stop and stare at their car, sometimes waving to them as they passed.

Encounter with Tibetan Mastiffs

As they passed the nomad's tents, they saw some Tibetan mastiffs. Whenever a car came close to their tents, they would bark furiously and fearlessly. They would chase the car for some distance and then, go back. In earlier days, Tibetan mastiffs became popular in China's imperial courts as hunting dogs. They were brought along the Silk Road as a tax payment from Tibet.

Journey Becomes Difficult

As they climbed, the turns became sharper and more difficult. The author started getting a severe headache. Suddenly, snow started falling and blocked the route. Daniel and the author got out of the car to reduce its load on sharp bends. They were at a height of 5210 metres above sea level.

When they reached a height of 5515 metres, Tsetan had to open the lid of the petrol tank to release the evaporated fuel.

Reaching HOR

By late afternoon, they had reached the small town of Hor on the shore of Lake Manasarovar which was on the old trade route between Lhasa and Kashmir. From there, Daniel returned to Lhasa while Tsetan got the flat tyre of the car repaired there. Hor was a grim, miserable place. There was no vegetation whatsoever, and the place no longer appeared holy.

By 10.30 PM, they had reached Darchen where they found a guesthouse to stay in The author had a troubled and sleepless night. His nostrils were blocked and he was not able to get enough air into his lungs.

The Author's Illness

The next day, Tsetan took the author to the Darchen Medical College. The doctor told him it was just the cold and the altitude which were giving him trouble. The doctor gave him some medicine and that night, the author was able to sleep well.

Tsetan left the author in Darchen and returned to Lhasa. He did not mind if the author would die in Darchen. He was a good Buddhist and believed in life after death. However, he was worried that the author's death could affect his business.

The Author Meets Norbu

Like Hor, Darchen was dusty and a lot of rubbish could be seen all around. The town appeared to be sparsely populated.

The author had come there because he wanted to reach Mount Kailash to do *kora* and get a feel of what a pilgrimage was like.

However, he didn't want to do it alone. He was looking for someone who could speak or understand English when he meet Norbu.

Norbu was a plump Tibetan, working in Beijing at the Chinese Academy of Social Sciences. He introduced himself to the author. He was also there to do *kora* although he was not a religious person. So, both of them decided to do *kora* together.

Word-Meaning

French loaves	thin loaf of French bread commonly made from basic lean dough
ducking back	quickly going inside
kora	pilgrimage (in Tibetan language)
drokba	nomad shepherd (here it means "You look like a nomad shepherd.")
Changtang	plateau in Western Tibet
gazelles	small antelopes
kyang	wild asses
pall	cloud
en masse	together
manoeuvres	exercises involving a large number of animals
billowed	swelled out and went
mastiff	large and strong breed of dog
tribute	payment for tax
meanders	winding curves or bends of the river
daubed	spread on the surface
hunks	large pieces
snorted	made a loud sound by forcing breath through a nostril
exited	came out of
swathe	long strip
petered out	gradually came to an end
negotiated	went around
four wheel drive	having a transmission system to provide power directly to all four wheels
lurching	moving unsteadily
cairn of rocks	pile of stones marking a special place
festooned	ornamentally decorated
careered down	descended
salt flats	areas of flat land covered with a layer of salt
brackish	slightly salty
vestiges	remains
a hive of activity	full of people working hard
as smooth as my bald head	totally worn out
grim	bleak or dreary
refuse	rubbish
cosmology	ancient history
headwaters	streams forming the source
striking distance	a distance from which it can be easily reached
draught	current of air
spread the grease around on	cleaned
solitary confinement	loneliness
hallowed	holy
prone	inclined
kicking around	passing time aimlessly
power	breathing
disappearing into the land of nod	going to fall asleep
put my finger on	pinpoint
paraphernalia	dress identifying his profession
screws of paper	small paper packets
derelict	run down
pool	game similar to billiards
supremely incongruous	totally out of place
babbled	flowed with a babbling sound
cavernous	like a cave
struck up	started
escaped from the library	removed themselves from academic work
tempered	weakened
envisaged	thought of
yaks	Tibetan ox
prostrating	stretching, and lying down with face down

Important Themes of the Chapter

Resilience The article captures the physical and mental struggles of journeying in the high altitudes of Tibet.

Spirituality The article reflects on the significance of spiritual pilgrimages highlighting the contrast between the harshness of the environment and the traveller's inner journey.

Nature's beauty and unpredictability In giving the description of the journey, the article captures the beauty of the mountain and valley, and also the unpredictable incidents that the travellers come upon.

NCERT Folder

Notice these Expressions (NCERT Page 59)

All the expressions have been explained in the 'Word Meanings' given above.

Understanding the Text (NCERT Page 67)

I. Give reasons for the following statements.

1. The article has been titled 'Silk Road'.

Ans. The 'Silk Road' refers to a network of overland routes linking Europe with Asia. This had been the trade route followed by the Europeans since ancient times who had a passion for silk, horses and exotic fauna and flora of the East. It is a link between the East and the West.

The author Nick Middleton, in his travelogue, follows the footsteps of Alexander the Great and Marco Polo, and travels along this Silk Road, focusing on its untainted beauty as well as the challenges it pose. Hence, the article has been titled 'Silk Road'.

2. Tibetan mastiffs were popular in China's imperial courts.

Ans. Tibetan mastiffs were popular in China's imperial courts. Tibetan mastiffs were known for their loyalty, strength, and fierce nature. These qualities made them highly valued in China's imperial courts, where they were often given as gifts and used as guard dogs.

3. The author's experience at Hor was in stark contrast to earlier accounts of the place.

Ans. According to the earlier accounts, the town, named Hor on the shore of Lake Manasarovar, abounded in natural beauty. A Japanese monk who had arrived there in 1900 was so moved by the sanctity of the lake that he burst into tears. A couple of years later, the hallowed waters had a similar effect on another traveller. However, now it was a grim and miserable place. There was no vegetation whatsoever. Only dust and rocks remained liberally scattered with years of accumulated rubbish left by tourists.

4. The author was disappointed with Darchen.

Ans. The author was disappointed with Darchen because it differed from his imagined lively town. Instead, he found it dull and empty, lacking the energy and excitement he had anticipated. Further, his illness also impacts his view of the place.

5. The author thought that his positive thinking strategy worked well after all.

Ans. Despite the challenges and disappointments during the journey, the author's positive thinking helped him remain optimistic and appreciate his unique experiences. This mindset allowed him to find value in the journey, even when things did not go as planned. We can also say that it helped him find a companion for his kora.

II. Briefly comment on

1. The purpose of the author's journey to Mount Kailash.

Ans. The purpose of the author's journey through the Silk Road to Mount Kailash was to complete the *kora*, which is a sacred religious ritual according to Hindu and Buddhist tradition.

2. The author's physical condition in Darchen.

Ans. The author was not physically well when he reached Darchen. His sinuses were blocked due to the cold wind at Hor and he was not able to sleep well at night. The next day, Tsetan took him to the Darchen Medical College and the doctor there gave him some medicine that gave him some relief.

3. The author's meeting with Norbu.

Ans. The author met Norbu, a fellow traveller and scholar who shared his interest in Mount Kailash. His presence increases the author's optimism for doing the *kora*. Further, Norbu, being overweight and not physically fit, made the author realise that the pilgrimage was more about the spiritual journey than the physical one.

4. Tsetan's support to the author during the journey.

Ans. Tsetan was a good and efficient driver. He drove the car very carefully. During the journey, he spoke to the author giving information about the places they were visiting. He was also very caring. At Darchen, when he found that the author was not well, he took him to the medical college and got medicine for him. He was also a good and devout Buddhist.

5. "As a Buddhist, he told me, he knew that it didn't really matter if I passed away, but he thought it would be bad for business."

Ans. This statement reflects Tsetan's practical approach to life. While his Buddhist beliefs made him see death as a natural part of life, he also recognised the practical consequences of a tourist dying on the trip, which would negatively affect his reputation and business.

Talking about the Text (NCERT Page 67)

Discuss in groups of four.

1. The sensitive behaviour of hill-folk.

Ans. The hill folks in the story show a lot of sensitivity, especially towards the visitors. For example, the Tibetan mastiffs are very protective of their territory. They run towards the vehicle to scare it away, showing their strong sense of duty and guardianship. Further, the way they react when they see the car is interesting, too.

They pause and sometimes wave, but their sheep move away from the vehicle, showing they are cautious and respectful of their animals' safety. The hill folks are also careful about their environment. For instance, people living in high-altitude areas know the harsh conditions and manage their resources carefully. They live in harmony with their surroundings and adapt to the challenges of their environment. Their sensitivity isn't just about protecting their land and animals and being aware of visitors' needs. For instance, Lhamo gives the author a sheepskin coat to help with the cold, which shows their thoughtfulness and kindness towards guests.

2. The reasons why people willingly undergo the travails of difficult journeys.

Ans. People often undertake challenging journeys for various reasons. A major reason could be personal growth. The experience of overcoming difficulties can be enriching. It helps people learn more about themselves and develop resilience. Some people are however motivated by adventure and the desire to explore new places. The thrill of discovering unknown lands and cultures can be a strong driving force. They seek the excitement and unique experiences that come with travelling. Religious or spiritual reasons also play a significant role. Many people go on difficult journeys as part of a pilgrimage or spiritual quest. They believe that enduring hardships will bring them closer to their spiritual goals or provide a sense of fulfillment.

People might undertake challenging journeys to achieve specific goals or missions. Whether it's for research, to fulfill a personal dream, or to meet important objectives, the challenges faced are seen as necessary steps toward achieving something significant.

3. The accounts of exotic places in legends and the reality.

Ans. The accounts of exotic places in legends often differs from the reality. Legends about exotic places often make them sound magical and perfect. For example, many old stories describe places like Mount Kailash with reverence and mysticism. The legends usually focus on these places' spiritual and mystical aspects, making them seem almost otherworldly. In reality, these places can be very different from what legends describe. For example, the author's experience at Hor was quite disappointing compared to the historical reverence for Lake Manasarovar. The town was dusty and full of refuse, contrasting with the sacred and beautiful image in legends. Legends can create high expectations, sometimes leading to disappointment when visiting these places.

Thinking about Language (NCERT Page 67-68)

1. Notice the kind of English Tsetan uses while talking to the author. How do you think he picked it up?

Ans. Tsetan must have picked up some English through his interactions with tourists.

2. What do the following utterances indicate?

(i) "I told her, through Daniel ..."

Ans. It indicates that the listener was not able to understand English so Daniel translated what the speaker said in English into the Tibetan language.

(ii) "It's a cold," he said finally through Tsetan.

Ans. The doctor spoke in Tibetan language, which Tsetan translated into English for the author.

3. Guess the meaning of the following words. In which language are these words found?

kora	*drokba*	*kyang*

Ans. *Kora* means pilgrimage.
Drokba means nomads.
Kyang means wild ass.
These words are found in the Tibetan language.

Working with Words (NCERT Page 68)

1. The narrative has many phrases to describe the scenic beauty of the mountainside like :
A flawless half-moon floated in a perfect blue sky.
Scan the text to locate other such picturesque phrases.

Ans. (i) ....the river was wide and mostly clogged with ice, brilliant white and glinting in the sunshine.

(ii) It was marked by a large cairn of rocks festooned with silk scarves and ragged prayer flags.

2. Explain the use of the adjectives in the following phrases.

(i) shaggy monsters (ii) brackish lakes
(iii) rickety table (iv) hairpin bend
(v) rudimentary general stores

Ans. (i) Shaggy means hairy and unkempt.
(ii) Brackish means slightly salty.
(iii) Rickety means wobbly or shaky.
(iv) Hairpin means very sharp; shaped like a hairpin.
(v) Rudimentary means simple or basic.

Noticing Form (NCERT Page 68)

1. The account has only a few passive voice sentences. Locate them. In what way does the use of active voice contribute to the style of the narrative?

Ans. Some passive voice sentences are

1. The slope was steep and studded with major rocks...
2. It was marked by a large cairn of rocks.
3. The plateau is pockmarked with....

Passive voice is used only when the object is to be stressed. Passive voice is mainly used in reporting events. Active voice is more realistic and direct, thus contributing a more lively style to the narrative.

2. Notice this construction: Tsetan was eager to have them fixed. Write five sentences with a similar structure.

Ans. The sentences are

1. Savita was keen to get her cycle repaired.
2. Ravi was impatient to visit the exhibition.
3. Jagdish was itching to get started on his journey.
4. Malati was anxious to have her way in the argument.
5. Beena was fervently wishing to clear her exams.

Things to Do (NCERT Page 68)

"The Plateau is pockmarked with salt flats and brackish lakes, vestiges of the Tethys Ocean which bordered Tibet before the continental collision that lifted it skyward."

Given below is an extract from an account of the Tethys Ocean downloaded from the Internet. Go online, key in Tethys Ocean in Google search and you will find exhaustive information on this geological event.

You can also consult an encyclopaedia.

Today, India, Indonesia and the Indian Ocean cover the area once occupied by the Tethys Ocean. Turkey, Iraq, and Tibet sit on the land once known as Cimmeria. Most of the floor of the Tethys Ocean disappeared under Cimmeria and Laurasia. We only know that Tethys existed because geologists like Suess have found fossils of ocean creatures in rocks in the Himalayas. So, we know those rocks were underwater, before the Indian continental shelf began pushing upward as it smashed into Cimmeria. We can see similar geologic evidence in Europe, where the movement of Africa raised the Alps.

Ans. Do it yourself.

Exam Pattern Questions

Extract Based Questions

Read the extracts given below and answer the questions that follow.

1. A FLAWLESS half-moon floated in a perfect blue sky on the morning we said our goodbyes. Extended banks of cloud like long French loaves glowed pink as the Sun emerged to splash the distant mountain tops with a rose-tinted blush. Now that we were leaving Ravu, Lhamo said she wanted to give me a farewell present. One evening I'd told her through Daniel that I was heading towards Mount Kailash to complete the kora, and she'd said that I ought to get some warmer clothes.

(i) Complete the following suitably.

The extract suggests that the Sun gives the mountain tops a ....

(ii) What did Lhamo give them as they were leaving?

(a) Food for the travel (b) Warm clothes
(c) Offerings for the kora (d) All of the above

(iii) Why did the author travel to Mount Kailash?

Ans. (i) pink colour blush

(ii) (b) Warm clothes

(iii) The author travelled to Mount Kailash in order to complete Kora- a form of meditation performed by Buddhist believers.

2. Further on, where the plains became more stony than grassy, a great herd of wild ass came into view. Tsetan told us we were approaching them long before they appeared. "Kyang," he said, pointing towards a far-off pall of dust. When we drew near, I could see the herd galloping en masse, wheeling and turning in tight formation as if they were practising manoeuvres on some predetermined course. Plumes of dust billowed into the crisp, clean air.

(i) What did Tsetan tell them?

(a) The plains were becoming greener
(b) The plains were becoming stonier
(c) A herd of wild donkeys were coming into the view
(d) A herd of wild donkeys were moving away from them

(ii) What are 'drokbas'?

(iii) What did the Tibetan doctor give to the author when he was unwell?

Ans. (i) (c) A herd of wild donkeys were coming into the view

(ii) 'Drokbas' are the hill tribe people (sheperds) that the author witnesses tending their flocks.

(iii) The Tibetan doctor gave a five-day course medicine in a brown envelope to the author.

3. **I checked my watch again as we continued to climb in the bright sunshine. We crept past 5,400 metres and my head began to throb horribly. I took gulps from my water bottle, which is supposed to help a rapid ascent.**

We finally reached the top of the pass at 5,515 metres. It was marked by a large cairn of rocks festooned with white silk scarves and ragged prayer flags. We all took a turn round the cairn, in a clockwise direction as is the tradition, and Tsetan checked the tyres on his vehicle. He stopped at the petrol tank and partially unscrewed the top, which emitted a loud hiss. The lower atmospheric pressure was allowing the fuel to expand. It sounded dangerous to me. "Maybe, sir," Tsetan laughed "but no smoking."

(i) Complete the following suitably.
The narrator's head began to ache because ....

(ii) What did they find at the pass of 5,515 metres?

(iii) What did they eat when they stopped for lunch and where?

Ans. (i) of the rapid ascend to 5,400 metres

(ii) The pass of 5,515 metres was marked by by a large cairn of rocks festooned with white silk scarves and ragged prayer flags.

(iii) They ate hot noodles for lunch inside a long canvas tent, part of a workcamp erected beside a dry salt lake.

Short Answer Type Questions

1. **Giving farewell present is a significant part of hospitality. How has this custom been upheld by Lhamo in 'Silk Road'?**

Ans. The farewell present given by Lhamo to the author when he told her that he was going to Mount Kailash was a long-sleeved sheepskin coat that shepherds normally wore. She felt that the coat would protect him from the cold weather on the mountain.

2. **Snow plays a significant role in this story. Explain its role as a hurdle in 'Silk Road'.** Competency Based

Ans. It is rightly said that snow plays a significant role in the story 'Silk Road'. It not only adds an aesthetic quality of the landscape but also becomes a means of hurdle in the journey undertaken by the author. The presence of snow impacts the time it would take the author to reach his destination. It also adds an aspect of danger and adventure in the story.

3. **While crossing the rocky wilderness, they saw drokbas. Write a short note on them.**

Ans. While crossing the rocky wilderness, the author and his companions. saw solitary *drokbas* (shepherds) - both men and women, well wrapped in sheepskin coats - who were tending their flocks. They would pause and stare at their car, sometimes waving as they passed.

4. **Describe the Tibetan mastiff's reaction when they approached.**

Ans. The Tibetan mastiff dogs would cock their great big heads when they became aware of their approach and would fix them in their sights. As they drew nearer, they would explode into action, speeding directly towards them like a bullet from a gun and nearly as fast.

5. **Why the plateau on the top of the mountain was pockmarked with salt flats?** Competency Based

Ans. The plateau was pockmarked with salt flats on the top of the mountain as the plateau had been a part of the Tethys Ocean before the great continental collision. After the collision, the plateau was formed above the sea water, leaving the residue of salt.

6. **The place of salt flats was a hive of activity. Explain.**

Ans. This place was a hive of activity. Men were working with pickaxes and shovels, walking back and forth in their long sheepskin coats and salt-encrusted boots, carrying loads of salt mined from the flats.

7. **Describe the author's troubles at Darchen.**

Ans. The author was troubled by a bad cold at Darchen. He was unable to go to sleep at night as his nostrils were blocked. When he was just dozing off, he woke up suddenly. He felt his chest becoming very heavy as he was not able to breathe in enough oxygen.

8. **Write a short note on Norbu.**

Ans. Norbu was Tibetan but he worked in Beijing at the Chinese Academy of Social Sciences, in the Institute of Ethnic Literature. He had come to Darchen to do the *kora* of Mount Kailash, just like the author.

9. **Give reasons for Norbu's arrival to Kailash.**

Ans. Norbu had been writing academic papers about the Kailash *kora* and its importance in various works of Buddhist literature for many years, but he had actually never done it himself. Hence, he was there to do *kora*.

10. **Norbu was an ideal companion for the author. Analyse.**

Ans. Norbu was an ideal companion for the author as both were academicians who had come away from their academic work. Both were not devout believers and they did not intend to prostrate themselves all round the mountain like other pilgrims.

11. **What is the significance of the Tibetan mastiffs mentioned in the travelogue, and how do they contribute to the atmosphere of the journey?** Competency Based

Ans. Tibetan mastiffs are large, powerful dogs known for their fierce loyalty and protective nature. These dogs are tied up during the day but let loose at night to guard the area. The travelogue mentions them as part of the journey, adding a sense of tension and adventure. Their presence highlights the remote and rugged nature of the region, where such powerful animals are needed for protection. Further, their mention emphasises the wild and untamed environment through which the author travels, making it clear that the path to Mount Kailash is physically demanding and filled with the unexpected.

12. **How does the author's interaction with the local people, like Lhamo and Norbu, reflect the cultural setting of the region?** Competency Based

Ans. The author's interaction with local people like Lhamo and Norbu provides insight into the region's unique cultural setting. Lhamo, a Tibetan woman, welcomes the author warmly and offers hospitality, a significant part of Tibetan culture. A Tibetan scholar, Norbu shares his knowledge and deep spiritual connection to Mount Kailash, showing the mountain's importance in the local belief system. These interactions highlight the Tibetan people's kindness, spirituality, and strong cultural traditions. Through these meaningful encounters, the author learns about the region's customs, beliefs, and way of life, which enrich his journey and give him a deeper understanding of the local culture.

13. **How does the author's experience at Darchen Medical College contribute to the narrative?**

Ans. The author's experience at Darchen Medical College adds a critical layer to the narrative. When the author starts feeling the effects of high altitude, such as breathlessness and dizziness, he visits the college for treatment. The medical staff there provided him with a simple yet effective remedy that helped him feel better. This visit not only highlighted the physical challenges of his journey but also showed the local medical practices and the care provided in such remote areas. This adds depth to the travelogue by showing a glimpse of everyday life and healthcare in the region.

Long Answer Type Questions

1. **On returning home, Nick Middleton writes his thoughts reflecting on how his experience of Hor was a stark contrast to the accounts he had read of the earlier travellers. Imagine yourself to be Nick Middleton and express these thoughts.**

You may begin like this

Hor was a small town in the back on the main East-West highway that...

Ans. Hor was a small town in the back on the main East-West highway that followed the old trade route from Lhasa to Kashmir. I found the place very grim and miserable. There was no vegetation whatsoever, just dust and rocks, liberally scattered with years of accumulated rubbish left behind by tourists.

The town sat on the shore of lake Manasarovar, Tibet's holiest stretch of water. Ancient Hindu and Buddhist scriptures tell that Lake Manasarovar was the source of four great Indian rivers: Indus, Ganges, Sutlej and Brahmaputra. In truth, only the Sutlej flows from the lake, but the headwaters of the others all rise nearby on the slopes of Mount Kailash.

My experience in Hor came as a stark contrast to accounts I had read of earlier travellers' first encounters with Lake Manasarovar. Ekai Kawaguchi, a Japanese monk who had arrived there in 1900, was so moved by the sanctity of the lake that he burst into tears. Similarly, in 1902, Sven Hedin from Sweden was also moved by the vision of the lake. However, now you could only find open-air dumps of rubbish in the town.

2. **The chapter 'Silk Road' portrays Nick Middleton as an adventurous but at heart more a meticulous academic than a daredevil. Imagine yourself to be a professor of geography who has to address university students.**

Write this address in 120-150 words based on your reading of the story and taking incidents from it.

You may begin like this

Good morning, students!
Oxford professor and travel writer, Nick Middleton, is truly an adventurer, but...... Competency Based

Ans. Good morning students!

Oxford professor and travel writer, Nick Middleton is truly an adventurer but at heart he is more a meticulous academic than a daredevil adventurer. He is an environmental consultant who has written many articles in journals, magazines and newspapers as well as 16 books. Nick Middleton teaches geography at Oxford University and is a fellow of St. Anne's College. His main research interest is in the nature and human use of deserts and their margins.

While his journey on the silk road seems to have spiritual connotation, throughout the journey we get a glimpse of his knowledge. We see him talking about his knowledge of history through mention of Tibetan mastiff. We see him comparing what he had read about the various places with the reality of the situation.

Thus, throughout his journey, he compared and contrasted what he and learned with his experiences showing him as a meticulous academician.

Thank you!

3. How does the journey through the Silk Road reflect the spiritual and personal growth of the author?

Ans. The journey through the Silk Road represents the author's physical and spiritual path. As he travels, he encounters harsh landscapes, high altitudes, and challenging conditions that test his endurance. These physical challenges mirror his inner journey, where he seeks a deeper understanding of himself and the world around him.

The sacred destination of Mount Kailash is not just a goal but a symbol of spiritual growth. Meeting people like Tsetan and Lhamo helps the author learn about Tibetan culture, spirituality, and the significance of the places he visits. The journey ultimately leads to personal growth as the author gains new perspectives and a deeper appreciation for the Silk Road's spiritual significance.

4. What role does the natural environment, such as the cold desert and mountain terrain, play in shaping the experience and mood of the travelogue?

Ans. The natural environment, including the cold desert and mountain terrain, plays a crucial role in shaping the experience and mood of the travelogue. The harsh, barren landscape reflects the author's challenges on his journey, adding a sense of isolation and struggle. The cold desert's vast emptiness and the towering mountains create a backdrop of awe and reverence, emphasising the spiritual nature of the journey.

The extreme conditions, such as freezing temperatures and thin air, heighten the sense of adventure and danger, making the journey more intense and memorable. The environment tests the author's physical endurance and deepens his connection to the spiritual significance of the sacred places he visits along the Silk Road.

SELF ASSESSMENT TEST

Extract Based Questions

Read the extract given below and answer the questions that follow.

1. The snow didn't look too deep to me, but the danger wasn't its depth, Daniel said, so much as its icy top layer. "If we slip off, the car could turn over," he suggested, as we saw Tsetan grab handfuls of dirt and fling them across the frozen surface. We both pitched in and, when the snow was spread with soil, Daniel and I stayed out of the vehicle to lighten Tsetan's load. He backed up and drove towards the dirty snow, eased the car on to its icy surface and slowly drove its length without apparent difficulty.

(i) What was the danger as a result of the snow?

(a) It's depth
(b) They could slip off on it
(c) Their car could turn over
(d) Both (b) and (c)

(ii) Identify the phrase from the passage that allows the reader to infer the reason why the author and Daniel also contributed in covering the snow with soil along with Tsetan.

(iii) Complete the following suitably.

to cross the frozen track, Tsetan, Daniel and the author ....

Short Answer Type Questions

1. How does the author describe the atmosphere and the sky when they were leaving Ravu?

2. Why did the travellers decide to take a short cut which made them get off the main road?

3. What did the river clogged with ice indicate to the travellers?

4. What were the reasons for the author's illness which kept him awake during the first night at Darchen?

5. Explain how the author deals with the physical difficulties of high altitude and the extreme conditions during the trip.

6. Discuss the contrast between the author's expectations and the reality he encounters in Hor.

Long Answer Type Questions

1. What steps did the travellers take to negotiate the snow on the road during the shortcut they took to reach Hor?

2. You are a news writer for a newspaper. After reading Nick Middletion's story 'The Silk Road', you were very disappointed about how the environment near lake Marsarovar and at Darchen has been neglected by the authorities. Write an article in 120-150 words describing the poor conditions in these regions and suggest some steps they should have taken to ensure that it did not deteriorate.

You may begin like this

Travelling to lake Mansarovar and Darchen has become so challenging that ......

01

A Photograph

About the Poet

Shirley Toulson (1924-1998) was a distinguished English poet, renowned for her introspective poetry. Born in Henley-on-Thames, England, Toulson developed a deep love for literature and language from an early age. Toulson's poetic voice was influenced by a myriad of factors, including her upbringing in a literary household, her experiences as a mother and wife, her profound connection to nature and her observations of human experiences. Toulson crafted verses that resonated with readers on a profound everyday level.

YOUR STUDY GOALS

- Central Idea of the Poem
- Explanation of the Poem

YOUR PRACTICE GOAL

- NCERT Folder
- Extract Based Questions
- Short Answer Type Questions
- Long Answer Type Questions

Central Idea of the Poem

Shirley Toulson's poem 'A Photograph' is a tribute to her mother. The poem describes three stages in the passage of time. In the first stage, the photograph shows the poet's mother standing at the beach enjoying her holiday with her two girl cousins.

The second stage takes us twenty or thirty years forward. The mother would laugh at the way she and her cousins were dressed up for the beach holiday.

In the third stage, the poet remembers the dead mother with a heavy heart. The photograph revives a nostalgic feeling in the poet.

Explanation of the Poem

Stanza 1

"The cardboard shows me how it was
When the two girl cousins went paddling,
Each one holding one of my mother's hands,
And she the big girl — some twelve years or so."

Exp. An old photograph of the poet's mother which was pasted on cardboard makes the poet recall the old memories of her mother's childhood. The photograph is a depiction of her mother's enjoyable moments at a sea-beach with her two cousins who were younger to her. They were walking in shallow water with bare feet near the beach. The mother was standing in the middle and holding hands of her two cousins on either sides. The poet's mother was twelve years old then. The given lines show that the photograph was very old but the poet has kept it very carefully as it reminded her of sweet memories of her mother's childhood. It also indicates how enjoyable her mother's childhood was.

Stanza 2

"All three stood still to smile through their hair
At the uncle with the camera. A sweet face,
My mother's, that was before I was born.
And the sea, which appears to have changed less,
Washed their terribly transient feet."

Exp. The photograph shows that all three girls - the poet's mother and her two cousins - stood still and smiled at the camera while their uncle clicked their photograph at the beach.

Their hair was flying over their smiling faces. They were happy and enjoying it all. The mother looked very pretty in the photograph taken a long time ago.

The stanza shows that things have changed. The poet's mother grew up, got older and died. The only thing that has remained unchanged is the sea which was washing the feet of all three girls.

The mention of the word 'transient' indicates the ever changing lives of human beings as well as the shortness of their stay on this world in contrast to the permanence of nature.

Stanza 3

"Some twenty - thirty - years later
She'd laugh at the snapshot. "See Betty
And Dolly," she'd say, "and look how they
Dressed us for the beach." The sea holiday
Was her past, mine is her laughter. Both wry
With the laboured ease of loss."

Exp. Even 20-30 years later, the poet's mother would look at the photograph and laugh nostalgically remembering the happy memories of her past. She would look at the photograph and comment on the dresses worn by Dolly, Betty and herself.

Sea holiday was her mother's past and her mother's laughter has now become a thing of the past for the poet as her mother is dead.

The poet still remembers how her mother would laugh at the photograph, remembering the sea-holiday with a fondness and a sense of loss because that time would never come back.

Stanza 4

"Now she's been dead nearly as many years
As that girl lived. And of this circumstance
There is nothing to say at all.
Its silence silences."

Exp. The poet recalls that it has been nearly twelve years since her mother died. The poet is consumed with grief but is left with no words to express her loss and pain. The poet is totally absorbed in memories of her dead mother. The poet can feel the grief but is unable to express it through words. The silence caused by death makes the atmosphere gloomy where no one is able to utter words.

Word-Meaning

terribly	—	extremely
transient	—	temporary, lasting only for a short time
wry	—	disgusted

Literary devices used in the Poem

- **Allusion** *Stanza 1, Line 1* 'The cardboard' [It refers to the photograph of her teenage mother]
- **Alliteration** *Stanza 2, Line 5* 'stood still to smile' [repetition of the initial letter 's']
  Stanza 2, Line 9 'terribly transient' [repetition of the initial letter 't']
  Stanza 4, Line 19 'silence silences' [repetition of the initial letter 's']
- **Transferred Epithet** *Stanza 2, Line 9* 'transient feet' [It refers to human feet but is used to describe the lack of permanence of human life]
- **Oxymoron** Stanza 3, Line 15 'laboured ease' [laboured means with great difficulty and ease means comfortably]
- **Personification** Stanza 4, Line 19 'Its silence silences' ['It' is used to refer to the situation and has been given the human quality of silence.]

NCERT Folder

A. Find Out

1. Infer the meanings of the following words from the context

- **Paddling**
- **Transient**

Now, look up the dictionary to see if your inference is right.

Ans **Paddling** wading in the water in bare feet

Transient temporary

Dictionary	**Meanings**
• **Paddling**	walking through shallow water in bare feet
• **Transient**	for only a short time

B. Think it Out (NCERT Page 12)

1. What does the word 'cardboard' denote in the poem? Why has this word been used?

Ans. The word 'cardboard' in the poem refers to the photograph of the poet's mother enjoying a sea-holiday with her two cousins when she was twelve years old. The cardboard stands for the frame that supports and holds the photograph. It signifies that life is transient and what remains is memory captured in a piece of paper.

2. What has the camera captured?

Ans. The camera has captured some happy childhood moments of the poet's mother's life when she had gone for a sea holiday with her two cousins, Dolly and Betty. The girls were paddling in the water and enjoying the moment. The photograph clicked by the mother's uncle shows the girls' innocent smiles while their hair was flying all over their faces.

3. What has not changed over the years? Does this suggest something to you?

Ans. Time has moved on but what has not changed over the years is the sea. Sea, a symbol of nature, is immortal.

It appears to be the same today as it looked in the old photograph. This suggests the permanence or immortality of nature. It also brings out the transient nature of man when compared to nature and its objects. The pretty faces and the feet of the three girls are 'terribly transient' or mortal when compared to the unchangeable and immortal sea.

4. The poet's mother laughed at the snapshot. What did this laugh indicate?

Ans. The poet's mother was a girl of around twelve years of age when the photograph was taken. Hence, the poet's mother laughed in nostalgia at the snapshot that was taken years ago. She also laughed at the way all of them were dressed for the beach as she thought that, they looked funny. This laugh indicated that the poet's mother enjoyed remembering her childhood days, when she was young and free from the tensions and worries of adult life.

5. What is the meaning of the line 'Both wry with the laboured ease of loss'?

Ans. The context of the above lines is the mother's recollection of her childhood days and the poet's recollection of her mother's laughing face.

The mother had fond memories of her past but there was a sense of loss of the carefree childhood days. The poet's loss referred to here is the loss of her mother as she is dead.

The memories in each case were beautiful but painful to recall.

6. What does 'this circumstance' refer to?

Ans. 'This circumstance' refers to the death of the poet's mother. Whenever she sees the photograph of her mother, she becomes sad as it brings sad nostalgic feelings. She gets lost in the old sweet memories of the past. But, she can't do anything about it now. So, she maintains silence and this silence leads to a deeper pall (cover) of silence.

7. The three stanzas depict three different phases. What are they?

Ans. *Shirley Toulson's 'A Photograph' describes three phases in time.*

(i) In the first phase, the poet's mother is described as a twelve-year-old girl with a sweet and innocent smile. She is standing at the beach enjoying a holiday with her two cousins — Dolly and Betty. This was the phase before the poet's birth.

(ii) In the second phase, the poet's mother's middle age is described where she is laughing at her own snapshot. Perhaps, the girls were looking quite funny in the beach clothes.

(iii) The third phase describes the poet's feelings for her mother who has died many years ago. This is the current phase. The photograph revives nostalgic feelings in her and it leads to a deeper silence.

Exam Pattern Questions

Extract Based Questions

Read the extracts given below and answer the questions that follow.

1. **"The cardboard shows me how it was**
When the two girl cousins went paddling,
Each one holding one of my mother's hands,
And she the big girl – some twelve years or so."

(i) **Read the Assertion and Reason below with reference to the above stanza.**

Assertion (A) Each cousin held the poet's mother's hand.
Reason (R) The poet's mother was the big girl.

Choose the correct option regarding their relationship.
(a) Both A and R are true, and R is the correct explanation for A.
(b) Both A and R are true, but R is not the correct explanation for A.
(c) A is true, but R is false.
(d) A is false, but R is true.

(ii) **What does the cardboard refer to here?**

(iii) **Complete the following suitably.**

The poet is looking at the photograph and talking about the past because ....

Ans. (i) (a) Both A and R are true and R is the correct explanation for A.
(ii) The 'cardboard' refers to the photograph of the poet's mother. She is enjoying with her cousins at the beach.
(iii) she is missing her mother and feeling nostalgic

2. **"All three stood still to smile through their hair**
At the uncle with the camera. A sweet face,
My mother's, that was before I was born.
And the sea, which appears to have changed less,
Washed their terribly transient feet."

(i) **What does the poet indicate by the use of the phrase 'smile through their hair'?**
(a) It was a windy day.
(b) The girls were having fun.
(c) The faces of the girls were covered with their hair.
(d) All of the above

(ii) **Why did the poet use the word 'transient'?**

(iii) **Complete the following suitably.**

The poet's mother stands in contrast with the sea because ....

Ans. (i) (d) All of the above
(ii) The poet used the word 'transient' to indicate the ever changing lives of the human being, which stands in contrast to the permanence of the sea, which doesn't change.
(iii) her life is short and temporary while the sea is immortal.

3. **"Some twenty-thirty-years later**
She'd laugh at the snapshot. "See Betty
And Dolly," she'd say, "and look how they
Dressed us for the beach." The sea holiday
Was her past, mine is her laughter. Both wry
With the laboured ease of loss."

(i) **How did the poet's mother feel about the photograph?**

(ii) **How long has it been since the poet's mother's death?**

(iii) **Select the correct option from the bracket. The poet's action of looking at the photograph show her .... (nostalgic/enthusiastic) emotion.**

Ans. (i) The poet's mother felt a sense of fondness as well as a sense of loss for a time that she enjoyed, which will never come back.
(ii) The poet recalls that it has been nearly twelve years since her mother's death.
(iii) nostalgic

4. **Now she's been dead nearly as many years**
As that girl lived, And of this circumstance
There is nothing to say at all
Its silence silences.

(i) **Read the assertion and the reason below, with reference to the given extract.**

Assertion (A) The poet has not grieved her mother's death properly.

Reason (R) The poet is speechless due to the loss of her mother.

Choose the correct option regarding their relationship.

(a) Both A and R are true, and R is the correct explanation for A.

(b) Both A and R are true, but R is not the correct explanation for A.

(c) A is true, but R is false.

(d) A is false, but R is true.

(ii) Select the correct option from the bracket.

That girl in the lines refer to .... (Dolly/poet's mother)

(iii) Comment on the tone of the given lines.

Ans. (i) (b) Both the A and the R are true, but the R is not the correct explanation of the A.

(ii) poet's mother

(iii) The tone of the given lines is gloomy and nostalgic. There is a subdued sadness and acceptance of the passage of time and the inevitability of loss. The tone also carries a touch of reverence for the memory of the poet's mother and the enduring power of the photograph to evoke emotions.

Short Answer Type Questions

1. Give instances to prove that the poet's mother had a pleasant childhood. Competency Based

Ans. The childhood of the poet's mother must have been filled with fun and happiness. This is clear from the snapshot of the sea holiday. They are enjoying their holiday.

The poet's mother laughs when looking at the snapshot even after many years have passed since the sea holiday. All this shows us that it was a very pleasant childhood.

2. Explain how the poet has expressed her bond with her mother?

Ans. The poet expresses bond with her mother by describing an old photograph of her mother. Her description of the photograph gives the readers an insight into her strong relationship with her mother. She remembers not only the when, where and with whom the photograph was taken but also how her mother felt about it. She remembers how happy her mother would become when looking at the photograph.

3. Interpret the use of visual imagery by the poet in the poem 'A Photograph'. Competency Based

Ans. The poet creates a clear visual image by describing the details of the photograph. The poet's mother's two cousins held onto her hand and went for paddling when her mother's uncle captured the moment. This helps the reader visualise the scene from the past. Also, this creates a sense of nostalgia for both the poet and the readers.

4. Explain why the sea is referred to as something that is unchanging?

Ans. The poet depicts the sea as something that is unchanging to present a contrast between the mortality of human beings and the immortality of the sea. She expresses that, even though her mother grew old and is now gone, the sea remains and always shall remain unchanged.

5. Identify instances of nostalgia in the poem 'A Photograph'.

Ans. There are two instances of nostalgia in the poem. The first is of the poet's mother who fondly remembers the sea holiday. The second is of the poet who remembers her mother and how she laughed while looking at the photo. Both the instances carry an aspect joy of reminiscing the memory while suggesting a pain due to the loss.

6. 'Memories hold a deep value for human beings.' Explain what the poet remembered and said about her mother. Competency Based

Ans. The poet remarks that her mother had a sweet face, smiling and caring for her cousins who were younger to her. The poet also says that her mother used to enjoy these sea holidays, and would laugh heartily, later on when she saw the photograph.

7. Explain how the poets react to her past. Why has she not mentioned anything about her mother's death?

Ans. The poet remembers with sadness her mother's laughter which she cannot hear anymore. The poet is full of a sense of loss and does not mention about her mother's death as it may bring more gloom to her and make her speechless.

8. Briefly comment on the structure of the poem.

Ans. The poem 'A Photograph' can be categorised as a lyric poem. It is a brief, emotionally charged work expressing the poet's feelings and reflections through three stanzas, each with varying line lengths. The lack of a traditional rhyme scheme or meter allows the poet to convey a natural and conversational tone, which suits the reflective nature of the poem. The absence of a strict structure contributes to the poem's sense of openness and contemplation.

9. The poem comprises two powerful symbols. What are they? Competency Based

Ans. The poem comprises two powerful symbols – the photograph and the sea. The photograph itself is a powerful symbol. It represents a frozen moment in time, a captured memory that transcends the limitations of the present. It serves as a bridge between the past and the present, a tangible reminder of people and moments that have passed away. The sea symbolises the relentless passage of time and the enduring nature of the natural world. It appears unchanged in the photograph, highlighting the transient nature of human life and experiences in contrast to the timeless sea.

Long Answer Type Questions

1. The poet has paid a tribute to her mother. Similar instances can be seen in 'The Portrait of a Lady'. This made you think that writing about a loved one is much better than building their statues or drawing their portraits. You decide to write an article for the school magazine expressing your opinion about why writing about a deceased loved one is the ideal way to remember them.

You may begin like this **Competency Based**

Many writers have paid tributes to their loved ones ....

Ans. **Writing About Loved Ones**

by XYZ

Many writers have paid tributes to their loved ones through beautiful writing. Khushwant Singh gave an adorable description about his grandmother through his story. Shirley Toulson remembered her mother through her heart-touching poem.

In my opinion, writing about a loved one is much better than building their statues or drawing their portraits. One can never tell the true personality of a person just by looking at their sculptures or portraits. One can never know about the amazing time someone has spent with them. That magic can only be created by words.

Words stand the passage of time whereas sculptures or portraits may get damaged by it. Hence, words are the best way by which anyone can pay a tribute to one's loved ones.

2. A moment of happiness prepares a person to face the troubles of future. Comment in the light of the poem 'A Photograph' by Shirley Toulson.

Ans. Our life is a mixture of happy as well as adverse times. We must learn to move on with the help of those happy memories which provided us with so much enjoyment and happiness. As life is not a bed of roses, everyone at one stage or another is likely to face difficulties.

At the time of difficulties, happy moments can give us solace and fill us with positivity which is required during difficult times. Happy moments will certainly provide us with a hope that, as happy moments are short-lived, so are difficult times. One must learn to cope with the situation. The memories of happy times can provide us a cushion to bear difficulties with patience and peace.

3. 'A Photograph' is a reflective and poignant poem that explores the power of a photograph to evoke memories and emotions. Keeping this statement in mind, comment on the themes present in the poem.

Ans. 'A Photograph' is a reflective and poignant poem that explores the power of a photograph to evoke memories and emotions. In doing so, it touches upon various themes which are as follows

Memory and Nostalgia The poem revolves around memory and nostalgia. The photograph is a powerful trigger for memories, transporting the poet back to the moment it captures. The poet reflects on the past with a sense of longing and wistfulness, highlighting the enduring impact of memories on our lives.

Time and Transience The photograph captures a specific moment in the past, contrasting it with the present.

The poem acknowledges the transience of life and the inevitability of ageing and loss, as the poet's mother has been dead for many years.

Loss and Acceptance The theme of loss is prevalent in the poem, both in terms of the loss of the past and the loss of the poet's mother.

The poem conveys a sense of acceptance regarding the passing of time and the inevitability of death. It explores how memories can be both a source of comfort and a reminder of what has been lost.

Emotion and Sentiment Emotion and sentiment are at the poem's core. The poet's emotional response to the photograph and her mother's laughter is evident throughout the poem. It explores the depth of human emotions, from the sweetness of memories to the melancholy of loss.

SELF ASSESSMENT TEST

Extract Based Questions

Read the extract given below and answer the questions that follow.

1. "The sea holiday
Was her past, mine is her laughter. Both wry
With the laboured ease of loss."

(i) Read the Assertion (A) and the Reason (R) below with reference to the given extract.

Assertion (A) The sea holiday in the photograph depicts the poet's childhood.

Reason (R) The poet's mother's laughter is the poet's present.

Choose the correct option regarding their relationship.

(a) Both A and R are true, and R is the correct explanation for A.
(b) Both A and R are true, but R is not the correct explanation for A.
(c) A is true, but R is false.
(d) A is false, but R is true.

(ii) "The sea holiday was her past, mine is her laughter". What does this line indicate?

(iii) Which poetic device has been used in the phrase 'laboured ease'? Define it.

Short Answer Type Questions

1. How has the photograph been preserved?

2. Did the mother enjoy her childhood? How do we know?

3. Describe the big girl as shown in the photograph.

4. Explain what happened to the poet's mother. How do we know?

5. Shirley Toulson has brought out her grief beautifully. Explain.

Long Answer Type Questions

1. The poet Shirley Toulson experienced the harsh reality and pain of losing a loved one and she beautifully expresses it in the poem. You wish to include a cameo of her in your upcoming blog post. As part of the research, describe her experience from your understanding of the poem in 120-150 words.

[**Clue** Include the various stages described by Toulson in the poem 'A Photograph'.]

2. The poem 'A Photograph' describes the pain of losing and missing one's mother.

Imagine yourself to be a psychologist who has to address the university students. Write this address in 120-150 words elaborating on the role of the mother in forming the personality of a child.

You may begin like this

Good morning, Students!

02

About the Poet

James Hughes

Edward James Hughes OM OBE FRSL (1930–1998) was an English poet, translator, and children's writer. Critics rank him as one of the best poets of his generation and one of the twentieth century's greatest writers. He was appointed Poet Laureate in 1984 and held the office until his death. Ted Hughes wrote frequently of animal life, of nature, the elemental force of non-human life and the inner turbulence of modern man. His themes express the powerful, often violent energies and the divided nature of modern man.

YOUR STUDY GOALS

- Central Idea of the Poem
- Explanation of the Poem

YOUR PRACTICE GOAL

- NCERT Folder
- Extract Based Questions
- Short Answer Type Questions
- Long Answer Type Questions

The Laburnum Top

Central Idea of the Poem

'The Laburnum Top' is a beautiful poem which describes how the visit of a goldfinch changes the Laburnum tree.

The Laburnum tree symbolises the pattern of our life in general which is usually dull and inanimate. The goldfinch breaks the usual pattern and makes it lively. Without the goldfinch, the Laburnum tree is just like another tree. In other words, it is the attitude of a person towards life that makes life meaningful and worth living.

Explanation of the Poem

Stanza 1

The Laburnum top is silent, quite still
In the afternoon yellow September sunlight,
A few leaves yellowing, all its seeds fallen.

Exp. The poet describes a beautiful sunny autumn in the month of September. The Laburnum tree is silent and still. It is laden with yellow leaves and flowers and its seeds have fallen.

This stanza presents the Laburnum tree as being lifeless and dull. It is silent and still with hardly any activity on it.

Stanza 2

Till the goldfinch comes, with a twitching chirrup,
A suddenness, a startlement, at a branch end.
Then sleek as a lizard, and alert, and abrupt,
She enters the thickness, and a machine starts up
Of chitterings, and a tremor of wings, and trillings-
The whole tree trembles and thrills.
It is the engine of her family.
She stokes it full, then flirts out to a branch-end
Showing her barred face identity mask.

Exp. Just then, a goldfinch alights on the Laburnum tree making short, high-pitched sounds. The goldfinch has her nest in the tree and her chicks are resting in the nest. On the mother's return, a sudden movement stirs the tree. Her little ones are excited on her arrival and start chirruping. The cautious mother enters the tree with great care so that no predator can come to know that her babies are housed in the nest.

The poet has compared the alert, abrupt and sleek movement of the goldfinch with that of a lizard. The goldfinch has been called the engine of her family. Just as the engine starts up the machine, her arrival in the nest has suddenly started up the silent machine (tree), i.e. the young ones have started chittering and making noise.

By feeding her young ones, she has added fuel to the machine and, as a result, the chicks now have the energy to be active and make noise.

After feeding her chicks, the goldfinch flies up and rests on the end of a branch of the tree, her identity concealed behind the yellow flowers and yellowing leaves.

Stanza 3

Then with eerie delicate whistle-chirrup whisperings
She launches away, towards the infinite
And the Laburnum subsides to empty.

Exp. After some time, the goldfinch makes a strange short, high-pitched sound. Then, she flies away towards the infinite sky. The Laburnum tree becomes silent again. The poet has shown that it is only the coming of the goldfinch that makes the tree alive. Her departure brings the poem as well the tree back to the beginning as the tree seems to become the same as before.

Word-Meaning

Laburnum top	—	top part of the Laburnum tree
goldfinch	—	a small, yellow bird
twitching	—	a small, often involuntary movement of the body
chirrup	—	the sound made by a bird
startlement	—	amazement
tremor	—	shaking
trilling	—	to sing a series of quickly repeated high notes
trembles and thrills	—	shakes violently
the engine of her family	—	the goldfinch
stokes	—	adds fuel (here the goldfinch is feeding her chicks)
flirts	—	moves abruptly or jerkily with light steps
eerie	—	strange in a frightening or mysterious way
infinite	—	the sky
subsides to empty	—	becomes silent, just as earlier

Literary devices used in the Poem

- **Simile** *Stanza 2, Line 6* 'sleek as a lizard' [comparison between the two using 'as']
- **Metaphor** *Stanza 2, Line 10* 'engine of her family' [engine represents the goldfinch and machine represents the nest]
- **Alliteration** *Stanza 1, Line 2* 'September sunlight' [repetition of the initial letter 's']
  Stanza 2, Line 5 'A suddenness, a startlement' [repetition of the initial letter 's']
  Stanza 2, Line 6 'alert and abrupt' [repetition of the initial letter 'a']
  Stanza 2, Line 9 'tree trembles' [repetition of the initial letter 't']
- **Onomatopoeia** *Stanza 2* 'chirrup', 'chitterings', 'trillings' and 'whistle-chirrup' [words formed from sounds similar to them]
- **Transferred Epithet** *Stanza 2, Line 12* 'her barred face identity mask' [the shadow of the flowers on her face looks like she is wearing a mask that has bars on it]

NCERT Folder

Find Out (NCERT Page 32)

1. What laburnum is called in your language.

Ans. In Hindi, a laburnum tree is called the *amaltaas* tree.

2. Which local bird is like the goldfinch.

Ans. The local bird similar to the goldfinch is the Indian Lutino Ringneck.

Think it Out (NCERT Page 32)

1. What do you notice about the beginning and the ending of the poem?

Ans. The beginning and the ending of the poem present a similarity that the Laburnum tree is still and silent on both occasions.

2. To what is the bird's movement compared? What is the basis for the comparison?

Ans. The bird's (goldfinch's) movement is compared to that of a lizard. The basis of the comparison is that the goldfinch's movement is sudden and abrupt which is quite similar to the movement of a lizard.

3. Why is the image of the engine evoked by the poet?

Ans. The poet evokes the image of the engine as it is the source of energy for a machine. The poet compares the bird with an engine as she is the source of energy for the nest where the chicks are resting.

4. What do you like the most about the poem?

Ans. I like the description of the Laburnum tree laden with yellow flowers. Apart from this, I also like the arrival of the goldfinch which changes the silent tree into one full of noise and activity.

5. What does the phrase 'her barred face identity mask' mean?

Ans. The Laburnum tree has flowers that fall like bars and when the bird sits behind the flowers, the shadow of the flowers on her face looks like she is wearing a mask that has bars on it. Thus, 'barred' is actually an adjective for the flowers and has been transferred and applied to the bird.

Exam Pattern Questions

Extract Based Questions

Read the extracts given below and answer the questions that follow.

1. The Laburnum top is silent, quite still
In the afternoon yellow September sunlight,
A few leaves yellowing, all its seeds fallen.
Till the goldfinch cames, with a twitching chirrup,
A suddenness, a startlement, at a branch end.

(i) Read the Assertion (A) and the Reason (R) below with reference to the given extract.

Assertion (A) The laburnum tree's seeds have fallen and its leaves are yellow.

Reason (R) It is the afternoon time of the day.

Choose the correct option regarding their relationship.

(a) Both A and R are true, and R is the correct explanation for A.
(b) Both A and R are true, but R is not the correct explanation for A.
(c) A is true, but R is false.
(d) A is false, but R is true.

(ii) Which characteristic is associated with the Laburnum Top in the above stanza?

(a) Peaceful (b) Quiet
(c) Dying (d) Beautiful

(iii) Select the correct option from those given in brackets to fill in the blank.

The yellow colour of the leaves of the laburnum tree and its fallen seeds suggest that it was the .... (autumn/spring) season.

Ans. (i) (b) Both A and R are true, but R is not the correct explanation for A.
(ii) (b) Quiet
(iii) autumn

2. Then sleek as a lizard, and alert, and abrupt,
She enters the thickness, and a machine starts up
Of chitterings and a tremor of wings, and trilling
The whole tree trembles and thrills.

(i) What does the imagery of 'tree trembles and thrills' primarily represent?

(a) The tree dances when she comes.
(b) The tree experiences fear and shock.
(c) The tree seems to stir up.
(d) The tree feels shock and dies.

(ii) Who is making the chittering sounds when the goldfinch arrives?

(iii) What is the phrase 'a machine starts up' a reference to?

Ans. (i) (c) The tree seems to stir up.
(ii) The goldfinch's baby birds are making the chittering sounds when she arrives.
(iii) The phrase is a reference to the activity and the liveliness that has filled the tree.

Short Answer Type Questions

1. Explain the reason behind the title. 'The Laburnum Top'.

Ans. The poem has been titled 'The Laburnum Top' because the top of the Laburnum tree has been described in detail in the poem. It is on the top of the Laburnum tree that the nest of the goldfinch is located and where all the activity takes place when the goldfinch visits the nest.

2. Interpret the use of the colour 'yellow' in visual imagery by Ted Hughes in the poem 'A Laburnum Top'. Competency Based

Ans. The flowers of the Laburnum tree and its leaves (in autumn) both are yellow in colour. Apart from this, the goldfinch's feathers are also yellow in colour. The poem highlights the high security that the mother bird (goldfinch) ensures for her babies and the colour yellow helps in camouflaging the babies. Hence, they escape being noticed by any predator.

3. Explain how is the tree transformed during the bird's visit.

Ans. After the goldfinch arrives on the tree, the silent and still Laburnum tree suddenly starts trembling and moving. The whole tree comes to life as the chicks of the goldfinch make a lot of noise as they chitter on seeing their mother.

4. The laburnum tree and the goldfinch maintain a mutually beneficial relationship. Explore this theme in relation to the poem 'The Laburnum Top'. Competency Based

Ans. Both the tree and the goldfinch are important for each other's survival. The goldfinch's presence, the sounds of the birds chirping and the branches twitching bring life to the tree. Its dead silence is broken by the bird's arrival. The laburnum tree, in return, provides a safe haven for the goldfinch and its young.

The relationship between the tree and the goldfinch is, thus, similar to the relationship between the body and the soul. The tree is the body and the goldfinch is the soul, and both are essential to each other.

5. How does the Laburnum ensure security for the nestlings?

Ans. According to a popular belief, the bark and the seeds of the Laburnum tree are poisonous. So, predators normally do not come near the tree. Apart from this, its yellow flowers and yellowing leaves in the autumn season complemented by the yellow coloured feathers of the goldfinch help in camouflaging the nestlings from the predators.

6. Explain the line—'And the Laburnum subsides to empty'. Also, elaborate on its importance.

Ans. This is the last line of the poem. It describes that, after the departure of the goldfinch from the Laburnum tree, it falls silent. The tree was noisy and lively when the goldfinch came to feed its chicks but it reverts to its earlier self after its departure from the tree.

This return to the initial image from the start of the poem aligns with the circle of life. It also asserts the importance of the goldfinch.

7. Comment on the tone of the poem and how it reflects the theme. Competency Based

Ans. The tone of the poem is contemplative and observational. It begins with a calm and serene description of the laburnum tree in September, portraying a sense of stillness and calm. As the poem progresses, the tone becomes more vibrant and animated when the goldfinch arrives. There is a sense of excitement and energy in describing the bird's sudden presence and activity within the tree. Towards the poem's end, the tone becomes melancholic as the laburnum tree subsides to emptiness once the goldfinch departs. This shift in tone reflects the transient nature of life and beauty.

8. 'The Laburnum Top' by Ted Hughes is primarily a nature poem with elements of lyricism. Elucidate. Competency Based

Ans. 'The Laburnum Top' by Ted Hughes is primarily a nature poem with elements of lyricism. While it focuses on describing a laburnum tree and the arrival of a goldfinch in a natural setting, it also contains aspects of lyricism in the poet's observations and emotions.

The poem captures a brief moment of liveliness in nature. It expresses the poet's feelings and reflections on that moment, blending nature's and lyric poetry's characteristics.

9. How the free verse structure of the poem impacts it? Competency Based

Ans. **Structure** The poem consists of a single stanza with 15 lines. It doesn't follow a traditional rhyme scheme or meter, which gives it a free-verse structure. The poem's structure mirrors the suddenness and unpredictability of nature, with the goldfinch's arrival and departure disrupting the laburnum tree's initial stillness.

10. Assess how the laburnum tree can be seen as a symbol of the passage of time and the cyclical nature of life.

Ans. The laburnum tree can be seen as a symbol of the passage of time and the cyclical nature of life. Its yellowing leaves and fallen seeds represent ageing and the end of one phase of life. The goldfinch symbolises vitality, transformation and the fleeting moments of vibrancy that punctuate the stillness of life. It represents the unexpected and the beauty that can emerge suddenly and disappear just as quickly. The tree's transformation from stillness to activity symbolises the dynamic and ever-changing nature of the natural world.

11. What do you like most about the poem?

Ans. The aspect that stands out most about the poem is its vivid imagery and how Ted Hughes captures the intricacies of nature's rhythms. The poem immerses the reader in the sensory experience of the scene, from the golden September sunlight to the tremor of wings and trillings of the goldfinch. Hughes skillfully explores themes of life, movement, and emptiness, inviting reflection on the fleeting beauty of existence.

12. How does the goldfinch's departure contribute to the broader themes of impermanence and renewal in 'The Laburnum Top'? Competency Based

Ans. The goldfinch's departure is a poignant reminder of life's impermanence, emphasising the transient nature of vibrant moments. Additionally, its exit hints at the theme of renewal, suggesting that the fading of one moment paves the way for new cycles of growth and vitality within the natural world.

13. What emotions does the goldfinch's departure evoke in the poem? Competency Based

Ans. The goldfinch's departure evokes a sense of longing and nostalgia, highlighting the bittersweet nature of transient experiences. It prompts reflection on the fleeting beauty of existence and the human desire to hold onto fleeting moments of vitality.

Long Answer Type Questions

1. The arrival of the goldfinch on the Laburnum top brings about a change in the poem. Interpret this change. What role does change play in life? Give your views.

Ans. At the start of the poem, the top of the Laburnum tree in the poem is silent and still.

There is hardly any activity on it as the sunlight falls on it on a September afternoon. However, with the arrival of the goldfinch, it suddenly becomes a place of feverish activity. The silence of the place is broken by the twittering and chirruping of the chicks and the goldfinch.

I think that the change brought about by the arrival of the goldfinch on the Laburnum top is good as it breaks the monotony. The tree becomes alive and lively with the movement of the goldfinch and the twitterings and chirrupings of the chicks.

Change can be good or bad in life depending on a situation. However, an important fact is that change is the only constant in life. So, even if a change is bad, we have to accept it and move on in life.

2. The poem 'Laburnum Top' beautifully describes how the goldfinch transforms the tree and makes it come alive. Imagine yourself to be a primary school teacher who has to address the students. Write this address in 120-150 words, elaborating on the values that can be learnt from the goldfinch in the poem.

You may begin like this

Good morning, students!

The goldfinch has its nest on the top of ......

Ans. Good morning students!

The goldfinch has its nest on the top of the Laburnum tree in the poem 'The Laburnum Top'. The mother goldfinch keeps going out at regular intervals to get food to feed her chicks while the chicks stay in the nest. This shows her caring nature and highlights the values of motherly care and affection of a mother towards her offspring.

The other aspect of the goldfinch that is captured in the poem is its movement. She arrives at the Laburnum top in a sudden manner and is alert to her surroundings. The poet has compared her movement with the sleek movement of a lizard.

However, there is a reason for her moving like this (in an alert and sudden manner). She is moving in this manner so as to avoid getting noticed by any predator. She does not want any predator to know that her chicks are resting in her nest on the Laburnum top as then the predators may kill them or harm them. The values of safety and security for her offspring is highlighted in this act of the goldfinch.

Thank you

3. In what ways does Hughes employ figurative language and poetic devices to convey the interconnectedness of nature and the cyclical rhythms of life?

Ans. Hughes uses figurative language and various poetic devices to highlight the interconnectedness of nature and the cyclical rhythms of life in 'The Laburnum Top.' He utilises imagery to paint vivid pictures of the natural world, such as describing the goldfinch's arrival with phrases like 'sleek as a lizard' and 'alert, and abrupt,' creating a sensory experience for the reader. Hughes uses personification to attribute human-like qualities to the natural elements, such as describing the tree as having an 'engine of her family' and trembling with activity.

Furthermore, Hughes utilises symbolism, such as the goldfinch representing vitality and renewal, to convey deeper meanings about the cycles of life and the interconnectedness of all living things.

Hughes weaves a rich tapestry of imagery and symbolism through these poetic devices, illuminating the intricate dance of nature's rhythms.

SELF ASSESSMENT TEST

Extract Based Questions

Read the extract given below and answer the questions that follow.

1. It is the engine of her family.
She stokes it full, then flirts out to a branch-end
Showing her barred face identity mask
Then with eerie delicate whistle-chirrup whisperings
She launches away, towards the infinite
And the laburnum subsides to empty.

(i) Select the phrase that suggests the following.
After feeding and caring for her young, the goldfinch leaves towards the sky.

(ii) Why does the goldfinch flirt out to a branch end?

(iii) Read the Assertion (A) and the Reason (R) below with reference to the given extract.

Assertion (A) The goldfinch feeds her young and then flies away with them.

Reason (R) The laburnum tree restores its initial condition of being dull.

Choose the correct option regarding their relationship

(a) Both A and R are true, and R is the correct explanation for A.
(b) Both A and R are true, but R is not the correct explanation for A.
(c) A is true, but R is false.
(d) A is false, but R is true.

Short Answer Type Questions

1. Give a description of the Laburnum tree as it looks like in September.

2. What do 'thickness' and 'machine' refer to in the poem 'The Laburnum Top'?

3. Describe the entry of the goldfinch in the poem 'The Laburnum Top'.

4. "She stokes it full, then flirts out to a branch-end."
What does she 'stoke'? Why does she stoke it full?

Long Answer Type Questions

1. The poem is about a tree and a bird. Write an article in 120-150 words describing the importance of trees in our life.

2. The poem goes about in a cyclic pattern. For example, the stillness and tranquility of the Laburnum tree is disturbed by the goldfinch which makes it lively, and it becomes still again after the departure of the goldfinch.
Does the cyclic pattern exist in our life as well? What should we learn from it?

03

The Voice of the Rain

About the Poet

Walter Whitman

(1819–1892) was an American poet, essayist, and journalist. He is considered one of the most influential poets in American literature. Whitman has to be credited for inventing the 'Free Verse'. His book 'Leaves of Grass', which he edited and expanded over the course of his life, is a masterpiece of American literature. Whitman's poetry celebrates the beauty of nature and the spirituality found in it. He believed that nature is divine and that all beings are equally perfect. This mindset is reflected in his poem 'The Voice of the Rain'.

▼ YOUR STUDY GOALS

- Central Idea of the Poem
- Explanation of the Poem

▼ YOUR PRACTICE GOAL

- NCERT Folder
- Extract Based Questions
- Short Answer Type Questions
- Long Answer Type Questions

Central Idea of the Poem

The poem 'The Voice of the Rain' by Walt Whitman signifies the eternal role that rain plays in nurturing, healing, rejuvenating and purifying the Earth.

The rain returns the favour to its place of origin from where it rises unseen. The rain itself is explaining to the reader about its origin, work and its cyclic movement. A comparison has also been drawn between rain and music as both of them make the world more lively and return to their place of origin after fulfilling their purpose.

Explanation of the Poem

Stanza 1

And who art thou? said I to the soft-falling shower,
Which, strange to tell, gave me an answer, as here translated:
I am the Poem of Earth, said the voice of the rain,

Exp. The poem begins with the poet asking for the identity of the soft-falling rain shower. Much to his surprise, the rain replies to his question which the poet translates for his readers. The rain tells the poet that she is the poem of Earth. The rain is trying to say that, as music or poetry gives pleasure to human beings, so rain brings happiness to mother Earth.

Stanza 2

Eternal I rise impalpable out of the land and the bottomless sea,
Upward, to heaven, whence, vaguely form'd, altogether changed, and yet the same,

Exp. The poet says that the rain is an eternal process, but it takes different forms at different times. It rises from the land and the deep sea in the form of untouchable or unseen water vapour and goes up to the sky where it takes an indistinct shape in the form of clouds.

Although it changes in its form or shape, its core matter remains the same. The words, 'impalpable' and 'eternal' indicate that nature is not fully understood and some part of it always remains beyond our reach.

Stanza 3

I descend to lave the droughts, atomies, dust-layers of the globe,
And all that in them without me were seeds only, latent, unborn;

Exp. The raindrops pour down from above to wash away droughts and dust layers enveloping Earth. It satisfies the thirst of the dry Earth and heals everything that is degrading and is lying lifeless.

The rain also helps in the germination of seeds which were lying dormant due to a dry spell.

Stanza 4

"And forever, by day and night, I give back life to my own origin, And make pure and beautify it;
(For song, issuing from its birth-place, after fulfilment, wandering Reck'd or unreck'd, duly with love returns.)

Exp. The rain is involved in a continued process of giving life to the Earth. Rain helps in enhancing the beauty of Earth as, in the absence of water, everything turns dull or lifeless and dust accumulates everywhere.

The last two lines are the poet's own words and his reflections upon the answers given by the rain. The poet observes that the life of rain is similar to that of a song. A song or poem is creativity at its best.

It has the power to calm, heal, rejuvenate, transform and thrill. In the same way, repeated evaporation and condensation purifies the Earth. The poet, therefore, draws a parallel between rain and music as both have rhythm and ability to thrill. Both of them rejuvenate and beautify life.

Word-Meaning

thou	—	you
soft-falling	—	dropping softly
eternal	—	everlasting
impalpable	—	unable to be felt by touching
whence	—	from where
form'd	—	made into a specific shape or form
lave	—	wash
atomies	—	very tiny particles
latent	—	dormant, inactive
issuing	—	originating/starting
wandering	—	moving from one place to another
reck'd	—	cared about
unreck'd	—	uncared for
duly	—	properly, rightly

Literary devices used in the Poem

- **Personification** *Stanza 1, Line 3* 'I am the Poem' [rain has been given a voice]
- **Metaphor** *Stanza 1, Line 3* 'I am the Poem of the Earth' [rain compared with a poem]
- **Hyperbole** *Stanza 2, Line 4* 'bottomless sea'
- **Imagery** *Stanza 1, Line 1* 'soft-falling shower' [gives an image of gentle rain or drizzle]

NCERT Folder

I. Think it Out (NCERT Page 35)

1. There are two voices in the poem. Who do they belong to? Which lines indicate this?

Ans. The poem, 'The Voice of the Rain', presents a dialogue between the poet and the rain itself. In this poem, the poet asks rain who it is. The poet gets an answer as the rain itself gives its introduction.

The lines that, the two voices in the poem are those of rain and the poet. *These lines are*

(i) **In the poet's voice** And who art thou? said I to the soft-falling shower.

(ii) **In the voice of the rain** And I am the Poem of the Earth, said the voice of the rain.

2. What does the phrase 'strange to tell' mean?

Ans. The phrase expresses the poet's surprise at the rain's ability to reply and use words. The general belief is that rain cannot speak like living beings. The poet believes that the readers will also find it surprising and weird that the rain should speak and answer the poet's question.

3. There is a parallel drawn between rain and music. Which words indicate this? Explain the similarity between the two.

Ans. The last two lines of the poem (in brackets) indicate the parallel drawn between rain and music (here, it is called 'song', as a song always has music associated with it). In these lines, the poet observes that the life-cycle of rain and a song are alike. The song issues from the singer and travels to reach others. It wanders and, whether heard and enjoyed or not, eventually returns to its creator with all due love.

Similarly, rain originates from the Earth, and after fulfilling its role of spreading beauty and purity, returns to its origin. Both are perpetual in nature. Moreover, the sound of the soft-falling rain is in itself a kind of music.

4. How is the cyclic movement of rain brought out in the poem? Compare it with what you have learnt in science.

Ans. In the poem, it is stated that water rises from the 'land and the bottomless sea' to reach the sky. There, it transforms itself into vague formations of clouds, different in their structure than the water from which they originated. After wandering, these clouds descend to Earth in the form of rain.

In science, we learn this cyclical process of rain using terms like evaporation, condensation, precipitation, flowing rivers, ground water, ocean water, etc. Thus, we can say that, in the poem the same process is made more poetic, interesting and unusual. The rain speaks itself to describe its course.

5. Why are the last two lines put within brackets?

Ans. The last two lines of the poem have been put within brackets as they do not form a part of the conversation between the poet and the rain. The lines in the brackets indicate the reflections, observations and thoughts of the poet. He makes observations about the life course of a song and draws similarities between the life cycle of a song and the rain.

6. List the pairs of opposites found in the poem.

Ans. The pairs of opposites in the poem are rise-descend; day-night; reck'd-unreck'd

II. Notice the following sentence patterns

(a) **And who art thou? *said I* to the soft-falling shower.**

(b) **I am the Poem of Earth, *said the voice of the rain.***

(c) ***Eternal I rise.***

(d) **For song ......*duly with love returns.***

Rewrite the above sentences in prose.

Ans. (a) I enquired the soft-falling shower about its identity.

(b) The voice of the rain answered, saying that it was the Poem of Earth.

(c) The voice of the rain explained its upward movement towards the sky as eternal.

(d) The poet says that, similar to the rain, a song starts from the heart of the singer, travels to reach others and, after fulfilling it purpose (whether cared for or not) returns to the singer with all due love.

III. Look for some more poems on rain and see how this one is different from them.

Ans. Do it yourself

Hint Students can talk about the conversational tone of the poem wherein the rain presents itself as the poem of the Earth. However, many other poems of rain just describe the benefits of rain and how is impacts a reader.

Exam Pattern Questions

Extract Based Questions

Read the extracts given below and answer the questions that follow.

1. And who art thou? said I to the soft-falling shower,
Which, strange to tell, gave me an answer, as here translated:
I am the Poem of Earth, said the voice of the rain,

(i) What is so strange in the above stanza?

(ii) Why does the rain call itself the 'Poem of Earth'?
(a) As it is beautiful
(b) As it has a purpose
(c) As it travels back to its origin
(d) As it beautifies the Earth

(iii) Select the correct option from those given in bracket to fill in the blank.

In the third line of the above stanza, the poet uses the poetic device ………… (metaphor/simile).

Ans. (i) It is so strange in the given stanza that the rain is answering the question.
(ii) (c) As it travels back to its origin
(iii) metaphor

2. Eternal I rise impalpable out of the land and the bottomless sea,
Upward to heaven, whence, vaguely form'd, altogether changed, and yet the same,

(i) Where does the poet say that rain rises from?

(ii) Select the phrase that suggests the following.

The rain is unclear and lacking a clear shape in the sky.

(iii) Read the Assertion (A) and the Reason (R) below, with reference to the given extract.

Assertion (A) The rain has completely changed.

Reason (R) The rain is still the same.

Choose the correct option regarding their relationship.
(a) Both A and R are true, and R is the correct explanation for A.
(b) Both A and R are true, but R is not the correct explanation for A.
(c) A is true, but R is false.
(d) A is false, but R is true.

Ans. (i) The poet says that the rain rises from the land and the sea.
(ii) 'vaguely form'd'
(iii) (b) Both A and R are true, but R is not the correct explanation for A.

Short Answer Type Questions

1. The poem's tone is contemplative, respectful, and almost mystical. Elucidate. **Competency Based**

Ans. The poem's tone is contemplative, respectful, and almost mystical. It's as if the speaker is engaged in a profound conversation with nature itself, specifically with the rain. The tone conveys a sense of awe and wonder at the rain's role in the natural world. The tone is spiritual or ethereal, as the rain is personified and described as eternal and transformative. It evokes a sense of unity with nature and a deep appreciation for its regenerative power.

2. Comment on the structure of the poem. How does it impact our understanding.

Ans. Walt Whitman's poem 'The Voice of the Rain' is a lyric poem, characterised by its expression of personal thoughts and emotions. The poem consists of a single stanza with eleven lines. It is a free-verse poem which lacks a specific rhyme scheme or metrical pattern.

The structure allows for a natural flow of thought and expression, mirroring the unstructured beauty of nature itself. In this case, the speaker engages in a direct conversation with the rain, expressing their wonder and understanding of its role in the cycle of life. The poem is highly subjective, reflecting the speaker's thoughts and emotions as they contemplate the significance of the rain.

3. Explain how the rain justifies its claim that it is the 'Poem of Earth'.

Ans. The rain calls itself the 'Poem of Earth' because of the similarity with the poem written by the poet.

This poem has the task of bringing joy, happiness, life to its readers.

Similarly, when the rain falls down over Earth, a rhythm or music is created. That's why the rain calls itself the 'Poem of Earth'.

4. Describe the never ending cycle of rain.

Ans. Water rises unperceived in the form of vapour from land and water bodies on the Earth.

It goes up, takes the form of a cloud, changes its shape and falls down on Earth in the form of water drops. The water returns through rivers to oceans and seas.

5. The rain calls itself 'impalpable'. Identify the factor(s) that lead(s) to this. **Competency Based**

Ans. 'Impalpable' refers to something that cannot be felt by touching or seeing. When water takes the form of vapour, it is not visible to the human eye and nor can we feel its touch, making it 'impalpable'.

Further, vapour rises to the sky, condenses and forms clouds which cause rain. Though we are aware of its presence, the process remains invisible to us.

6. How does the rain prove beneficial after a long hot spell?

Ans. After a long hot spell, everything is dried up on Earth. When it rains, all the dust that has accumulated on Earth gets washed away, giving a new fresh look to nature. Moreover, the seeds which were lying latent till now, get germinated with the help of rain and new trees and plants start growing.

7. Latent seeds get a life by rain. Explain.

Ans. The seeds lying on Earth require water to germinate and take shape. When it rains, the seeds start germinating and change into the form of saplings. In this way, the seeds which would have dried up or gotten wasted, get a new lease of life by rain.

8. Interpret the poet's use of the phrase 'reck'd or unreck'd. **Competency Based**

Ans. The words have been poetically drafted. Reck'd and unreck'd stand for 'reckoned' and 'unreckoned'. The words literally mean cared and uncared for, respectively. The poet uses these words to emphasise the fact that when the rain falls on the Earth, we sometimes take notice of it or sometimes completely ignore it. But, even if it is left uncared for, it completes its destiny and returns to absorbed where it started from.

9. The poem has a conversational tone throughout. Who are the two participants? Is there any advantage of this method?

Ans. The two participants are the poet and the voice of the rain which answers the poet's questions.

The advantage of this method is to maintain continuity of thoughts and ideas expressed by the poet and to bring about clarity in what he wants to express.

10. Justify the title 'The Voice of the Rain'.

Ans. The poem is about the eternal process of rain and its benefits. Through the conversation between himself and the rain, the poet has tried to bring out the importance of rain for Earth, plants and man. As the poet is translating what the rain is speaking through its own language (the sounds it makes when it falls), the whole poem is about the rain talking to the poet. Thus, the title is justified.

Long Answer Type Questions

1. The poem 'The Voice of the Rain' gives a hidden message that rain is essential for this Earth. Write an article in 120-150 words describing the importance of rain.

Ans.

Importance of Rain

by Ali Jawed

As we all know, the three essentials for survival are water, food and air. The most important element of weather is water. We get water in different forms of precipitation but rain is the most beneficial of all types of precipitation.

Rain helps in harvesting our crops, giving us food to eat. Without rain, no crops would grow and we would perish. It also helps in the removal of dust in air, making our air clean, because we need clean air to breathe. Rain water plays a key role in creating the climate of certain areas. Its presence in the atmosphere provides replenishment of the moisture in cloud systems.

The most well-known and most important effect of rain water is to provide us with water to drink. Without rain, there would be no life.

2. Rain is perennial while human life is ephemeral. Contrast rain with human life and mention if eternal elements of nature should be disturbed.

Ans. The poem 'The Voice of the Rain' beautifully shows the continued process of rain which sounds like music to human ears, as it fulfils our needs. It is an eternal process which sustains human life and provides us with food, pure air and green cover. In contrast, human lives are mortal.

We come on this Earth for a short period and then, depart without leaving any mark on this planet. Moreover, human beings, for their greed and selfish motives, indulge in destructive activities which may disturb these eternal processes of nature.

We must learn a lesson from nature. If we want peaceful co-existence, we need not disturb the balance of nature, otherwise the whole of humanity will be in danger.

We must learn a lesson from such eternal processes and do something good for humanity at large.

3. The poem 'The Voice of the Rain' shows how natural elements such as air and rain make no discrimination and bless everyone equally. Imagine yourself to be a member of an NGO that works against discrimination who has to address university students. Write this address in 120-150 words, elaborating class distinction and inequality, which is an entirely human creation. Competency Based

You may begin like this

Good morning, students!

Man's existence on this Earth is short-lived

but ....

Ans. **Good morning, students!**

Man's existence on this Earth is short-lived but even in this short span, he has been responsible for many wrongdoings against other human beings. God has created everyone as equal. But it is very unfortunate that man has divided this society on the basis of class, caste and other factors.

Man must learn from elements of nature which provide us fresh air, heat or water, without making any distinction. But in human society, class and caste distinctions both exist, and inequality prevails in large numbers.

Human beings should learn from nature and adopt universal brotherhood for the betterment of the society.

Thank you!

4. You have read the following summary of the poem 'The Voice of the Rain'.

In 'The Voice of the Rain,' Walt Whitman personifies rain, revealing it as the 'Poem of Earth,' embodying the planet's essence. Rain's journey from land and sea to the heavens symbolises life's cyclical nature. Its descent back to Earth nurtures growth, cleansing and revitalising. Whitman's metaphor of rain as a song underscores its harmonising role in the eternal cycle. The poet explores nature's interconnectedness through dialogue with rain, emphasising its life-giving properties and cyclical patterns. Rain's significance transcends its physical attributes, becoming a vital link in the life cycle, depicted as purposeful nourishment.

Based on this summary, point out the various themes present in the poem. Competency Based

Ans. The various themes of the poem are discussed below

The Vitality of Nature One of the central themes of this poem is nature's perpetual vitality and regeneration. The rain, personified as a sentient being, describes its eternal cycle of rising from the Earth and the sea, ascending to the heavens, and returning to the Earth to nourish and renew all living things. This theme celebrates nature's life-giving and rejuvenating power.

Connectedness of All Life Whitman's poem emphasises the interconnectedness of all life forms on Earth. The description of how rain descends to 'lave the droughts' and bring life to latent seeds highlights the idea that all living beings are part of a vast, interconnected ecosystem. It underscores the notion that everything in the natural world is interdependent.

The Perpetuity of Art and Creation Through the rain's assertion that it is the 'Poem of Earth', Whitman suggests that art and creativity are inherent aspects of the natural world. The rain's eternal cycle mirrors the cyclical nature of artistic and creative expression. Like the rain, art is continually born, fulfilled and returns to its source, potentially impacting and beautifying the world in the process.

The Transcendence of Time and Change The poem explores the idea that while the rain changes as it rises and falls, it remains fundamentally the same. This theme of continuity amid change reflects Whitman's broader belief in the enduring nature of the human spirit and the timeless aspects of life.

SELF ASSESSMENT TEST

Extract Based Questions

Read the extract given below and answer the questions that follow.

1. I descend to lave the droughts, atomies, dust-layers of the globe,
And all that in them without me were seeds only, latent, unborn;
And forever, by day and night, I give back life to my own origin,
And make pure and beautify it;

(i) With what purpose does the rain descend from the sky?

(ii) How does the rain narrate the story of her birth and functions?

(iii) Complete the following suitably.
The impression the readers can form about the speaker (the rain) is that ....

Short Answer Type Questions

1. How does rain give life to its origin?

2. The rain changes its form but its content remains the same. Elucidate.

04

Childhood

About the Poet

Markus Natten is a renowned Norwegian poet. Natten's poetry often delves into the depths of emotions and the complexities of relationships. Through his introspective and evocative language, he invites readers to explore the intricacies of their own feelings and experiences.

Markus Natten, was 12 years old when he submitted (and was subsequently published) his poem 'Childhood' under the theme – CHILDHOOD for 'CHILDREN AS WRITERS 20th Year'- Winning entries

YOUR STUDY GOALS

- Central Idea of the Poem
- Explanation of the Poem

YOUR PRACTICE GOAL

- NCERT Folder
- Extract Based Questions
- Short Answer Type Questions
- Long Answer Type Questions

Central Idea of the Poem

'Childhood' by Markus Natten revolves around the gradual transition from innocence to experience, as the speaker reflects on key moments that mark the loss of childhood. Through introspection, the protagonist wonders about the disillusionment and self-discovery inherent in growing up, recognising the disparity between childhood idealism and adult reality. The poem highlights the protagonist's realisation that childhood innocence goes away gradually, rather than in a single moment, as they navigate the complexities of life.

The poem also hints at the hypocrisy prevalent in our society where people pretend to be nice to each other but, in reality, do not like each other.

Explanation of the Poem

Stanza 1

When did my childhood go?
Was it the day I ceased to be eleven,
Was it the time I realised that Hell and Heaven,
Could not be found in Geography,
And therefore could not be,
Was that the day !

Exp. The poet wonders when he lost his childhood. He reflects that perhaps it was the day when he crossed the age of eleven. Maybe, it was the time when he realised that the concepts of Hell and Heaven did not exist in reality. Geography textbooks did not give the location of any such places.

The poet realises that he might have lost his childhood when he gained education and thus, a rational outlook.

Stanza 2

When did my childhood go?
Was it the time I realised that adults were not
all they seemed to be,
They talked of love and preached of love,
But did not act so lovingly,
Was that the day!

Exp. In this stanza, the poet reflects that maybe the loss of his childhood occurred when he was able to see through the hypocrisy of adults. These people followed double standards with a difference in what they followed and what they preached.

They told the poet to be loving and caring; however, they themselves were argumentative, violent and discourteous. Their behaviour was a far cry from the love they taught and advocated to the child.

Stanza 3

When did my childhood go?
Was it when I found my mind was really mine,
To use whichever way I choose,
Producing thoughts that were not those of other
people, But my own, and mine alone
Was that the day!

Exp. The poet asks the same question again. This time, he wonders that perhaps he lost his childhood on the day when he realised that his mind could think independently, forming his own opinions and being able to take his own decisions.

He gained a sense of individuality which sets him free from the preconceived opinions of others. His own individual opinions and experiences shape his thoughts now.

Stanza 4

Where did my childhood go?
It went to some forgotten place,
That's hidden in an infant's face,
That's all I know.

Exp. In this stanza, the poet changes his question. The poet now wonders where his childhood has gone. He realises that he has lost his childhood to a forgotten place.

He says that his childhood can only be found by looking at the innocent face of a child who does not have any pretensions and rationality and who trusts others unconditionally. In other words, a small child is full of innocence and there one can find one's own childhood.

Word-Meaning

go	—	end
ceased to be	—	stopped being
really mine	—	when not influenced by others' opinions

Literary devices used in the Poem

- **Alliteration** *Stanza 1, Line 3* 'Heaven and Hell' [repetition of the initial letter 'H']
  Stanza 3, Line 14 'my mind was really mine' [repetition of the initial letter 'm']
- **Antithesis** *Stanza 1, Line 3* 'Heaven and Hell' [Heaven and Hell are opposite ideas]
- **Enjambment** *Stanza 2, Line 8-9* 'Was it the time I realised that adults were not all they seemed to be' [a sentence continued in the next line]

NCERT Folder

Think it Out (NCERT Page 44)

1. Identify the stanza that talks of each of the following.

1. Individuality **2. Rationalism**

3. Hypocrisy

Ans. *Before answering, let us understand these terms.*

Individuality is a person's quality that makes him different from others or thinking for himself without following others' thinking blindly.

Rationalism is a stage when an individual is able to analyse a situation using reason and come to his own conclusions.

Hypocrisy is a practice of engaging in the same behaviour or activity for which one criticises another. The poet has talked about the hypocritical behaviour of adults who preach something else and practise something else.

Individuality stanza 3

Rationalism stanza 1

Hypocrisy stanza 2

2. What according to the poem is involved in the process of growing up?

Ans. According to this poem, the process of growing up involves many stages. Attainment of mental maturity can be seen as an indication of growing up.

When a person becomes logical, rational and is able to maintain individual thoughts, he/she is assumed to be grown up. They can discriminate between reality and fantasy and between reality and hypocrisy.

3. What is the poet's feeling towards childhood?

Ans. The poet grows nostalgic about his childhood. He feels that childhood is full of innocence. A child is neither a hypocrite nor manipulative. He/She is free from all these wrong habits found in adults.

During childhood, the poet is not able to distinguish between truth and imagination or reality and fiction. He seems to suffer from a sense of loss in losing his childhood.

4. What do you think are the most poetic lines? Why?

Ans. *The most poetic lines in the poem are*

Where did my childhood go?
It went to some forgotten place,
That's hidden in an infant's face,

These poignant lines explain beautifully what most adults feel. These lines take us back to the innocent world of an infant where the poet thinks his childhood seems to be lying hidden. Naturally, the pure and unadulterated childhood will never come back to us though we can find it in an infant's face.

Exam Pattern Questions

Extract Based Questions

Read the extracts given below and answer the questions that follow.

1. **When did my childhood go?**
Was it the day I ceased to be eleven,
Was it the time I realised that Hell and Heaven,
Could not be found in Geography,
And therefore could not be,
Was that the day!

(i) Select the correct option from those given in brackets to fill in the blank.

The excerpt tells us that the poet's tone is .... (passionate/nostalgic) as he wonders about his childhood and innocence.

(ii) Read the Assertion (A) and the Reason (R) below with reference to the given extract.

Assertion (A) Heaven and Hell cannot be found in Geography books.

Reason (R) As he matures and acquires reasoning powers, the poet concludes that Heaven and Hell are imaginary places.

Choose the correct option regarding their relationship.

(a) Both A and R are true, and R is the correct explanation for A.
(b) Both A and R are true, but R is not the correct explanation for A.
(c) A is true, but R is false.
(d) A is false, but R is true.

(iii) What does the poet realise about heaven and hell?

(a) They do not exist in reality.
(b) They cannot be found in Geography books.
(c) They still exist in reality.
(d) Both (a) and (b)

Ans. (i) nostalgic
(ii) (a) Both A and R are true, and R is the correct explanation for A.
(iii) (d) Both (a) and (b)

2. When did my childhood go?
Was it the time I realised that adults were not all they seemed to be,
They talked of love and preached of love,
But did not act so lovingly,
Was that the day!

(i) What is the particular quality associated with adults?

(a) They say something and do another thing.
(b) They are liars.
(c) They do not act lovingly.
(d) They do not care for others.

(ii) The poet is continuously asking questions and answering it himself. What does this show?

(iii) Complete the following suitably.

The significance of the given extract is that it highlights ....

Ans. (i) (a) They say something and do another thing.
(ii) The poet's act of continuously asking questions and answering it himself shows that the poet feels that the journey from childhood to adulthood is set in stages.
(iii) the contrast between adulthood and innocence

3. Where did my childhood go?
It went to some forgotten place,
That's hidden in an infant's face,
That's all I know.

(i) Where does the poet think that his childhood is hidden?

(ii) Select the correct option from those given in brackets to fill in the blank.

The excerpt tells us that the poet has become .... (unaware/knowledgeable) about himself.

(iii) Read the Assertion and the Reason below with reference to the given extract.

Assertion (A) The poet has changed his question from 'when' to 'where' his childhood has gone.

Reason (R) The poet has found out when he lost his childhood with certainty.

Choose the correct option regarding their relationship.

(a) Both A and R are true, and R is the correct explanation for A.
(b) Both A and R are true, but R is not the correct explanation for A.
(c) A is true, but R is false.
(d) A is false, but R is true.

Ans. (i) The poet thinks that his childhood is hidden in an infant's face.
(ii) knowledgeable
(iii) (b) Both A and R are true, but R is not the correct explanation for A.

Short Answer Type Questions

1. The poet has discussed two stages of life — childhood and adulthood. How do we differentiate one from another?

Ans. The poet considers childhood as a blissful period in one's life, where a child trusts everyone.

Adulthood, however, is marked by rational and creative thoughts, ability to perceive and differentiate and learn new things. In this stage of life, one also learns to be double faced and crafty.

2. Discuss the realisation that dawned upon the poet when he crossed the age of eleven years.

Ans. When the poet crossed the age of eleven years, he realised that he had lost his childhood and had developed a mind of his own. He also found out the non-existence of Hell and Heaven.

3. Interpret the use of hypocrisy by the poet when he talks about adults.

Ans. As the poet grew up, he could make out the double standards followed by adults.

He realised that though adults preached and talked of love, their behaviour was totally different and full of manipulation.

They were all hypocrites who behaved differently from the way they talked.

4. Express the poet's view about independent thinking. Futher, analyse its importance.

Ans. The poet discovered that he was different from others and could think independently. He could have his own opinions without getting influenced by anyone else. This discovery was very important to him as it revealed to him his abilities for independent thinking and decision taking.

5. Childhood cannot be regained or restored. Present your views. Competency Based

Ans. Childhood, marked by innocence, curiosity and wonder, gradually fades as one matures and confronts the realities of the world. Furthermore, one's childhood is shaped by the ever-changing time and place in which it is experienced. Therefore, childhood can only be remembered and cherished but not relived or recreated.

6. Assess the tone of the poem 'Childhood'.

Ans. The tone of the poem 'Childhood' by Markus Natten is reflective and contemplative. The speaker looks back on their childhood and explores the moments and realisations that marked their transition into adulthood. The poem has a sense of nostalgia and introspection as the speaker ponders the loss of innocence and the passage of time. The tone conveys a mix of curiosity, wistfulness, and a desire to understand the process of growing up.

7. Discuss the symbols used in the poem. Critically examine them.

Ans. The poet Markus Natten had used three symbols in the poem. These are

Age (Eleven) Age is a prominent symbol in the poem, representing the passage of time and the process of growing older. The speaker reflects on specific moments and realisations that marked their transition from childhood to adulthood, highlighting the significance of age as a symbol of change and maturation.

Geography Geography serves as a symbol for the speaker's early understanding of the world. The realisation that Hell and Heaven cannot be found in Geography signifies the speaker's growing awareness of the limitations of their childhood perceptions and beliefs.

Infant's Face The hidden place in an infant's face symbolises the innocence and purity associated with childhood. It represents the essence of childhood that is lost as one grows older. The speaker suggests that this purity is hidden or forgotten as people mature.

Long Answer Type Questions

1. Write an article in about 150 words about childhood and the process of growing up.

Ans.

Childhood

by Manav Singh

When I was a child, the world seemed to be a place of joy and happiness to me. There was nothing worth worrying about. Whenever I cried, somebody consoled me. When I did not like to sit alone, I was always in somebody's arms. My mother always looked after me. These are my most cherished memories and I believe that looking at a child playing and enjoying childhood makes me somewhat nostalgic.

Childhood is free from cares. There are no duties or responsibilities on a child's shoulders. A child only eats, drinks, sleeps and plays. Thus, a child lives in the bliss of ignorance and innocence. As we grow in age, worries about studies, choice of profession, shouldering responsibilities, etc. keep haunting us. Tensions, stress and worries become a part of adult life and the individual forgets to live a carefree life.

2. Is independent thinking a step towards adulthood? If yes, then how? Explain with reference to the poem 'Childhood'.

or Markus Natten, though showing disapproval regarding the behaviour of adults, also raises a very important point, that of independent thinking and individuality. Do you agree that independent thinking and individuality make us what we are? Elaborate in the context of the poem 'Childhood'. Competency Based

Ans. Yes, independent thinking is a step towards adulthood. As a child, one is not able to make one's own decisions and one's thinking is always influenced and directed by adults. A child is so innocent that it is not able to distinguish between truth and imagination.

As a child's thinking is influenced by others, it has no individuality. Moreover, it is prone to manipulations which lead to fickle-mindedness. Independent thinking makes us what we are. It shapes our personality and we are known among people through what our mind thinks and what decisions we take.

If we want to stay away from evil people who try to influence our thoughts for their selfish purposes, then only independent thinking can help us.

We cannot claim to be an individual if we cannot take decisions ourselves.

SELF ASSESSMENT TEST

Extract Based Questions

Read the extract given below and answer the questions that follow.

1. When did my childhood go?
Was it when I found my mind was really mine,
To use whichever way I choose,
Producing thoughts that were not those of other people
But my own, and mine alone
Was that the day!

(i) Complete the following suitably.

The realisation that he could use his mind the way he wanted symbolises ....

(ii) Select the phrase from that suggests the following.

In any manner one wants.

(iii) Read the Assertion (A) and the Reason (R) below with reference to the given extract.

Assertion (A) The poet realised that he could use his mind in the way he wanted.

Reason (R) The poet could not produce his own thoughts.

Choose the correct option regarding their relationship.

(a) Both A and R are true, and R is the correct explanation for A.
(b) Both A and R are true, but R is not the correct explanation for A.
(c) A is true, but R is false.
(d) A is false, but R is true.

Short Answer Type Questions

1. Why does the poet think that he had lost his childhood?

2. Why does the poet mention Hell and Heaven in the poem?

3. What are some positive aspects of the process of growing up?

4. What did the poet discover about his mind? How was that discovery important?

5. The poet asks four questions in the poem but he knows only one answer for sure. What is that? Give reasons to support your answer.

Long Answer Type Question

1. Natten in his poem shows that the loss of childhood is a gradual process. With the passage of time, we transition from childhood to adulthood. How does the poet show this transition?

05

Father to Son

About the Poet

Elizabeth Jennings (1926–2001) was an English poet. She completed her graduation from Oxford University. She finally became a full-time writer for the rest of her life after switching jobs twice. Jennings was greatly influenced by the poetries of Edwin Muir and Robert Frost. In most of Jennings's poems, there has been strong logic, emotional sensitivity, an avoidance of decoration, an absence of vagueness, and an eschewing of any mystification. She had always taken care of the use of rhyme and meter when it came to the form of poetry. Her use of words and sentence structure in the poem is very easy to understand. All her poems were simple and without literary decoration and pretentiousness in literature.

YOUR STUDY GOALS

- Central Idea of the Poem
- Explanation of the Poem

YOUR PRACTICE GOAL

- NCERT Folder
- Extract Based Questions
- Short Answer Type Questions
- Long Answer Type Questions

Central Idea of the Poem

The poem's central idea revolves around parental (lack of affection) and the struggle to understand and connect with one's child. The father in the poem feels emotionally distant from his son, even though they live close to each other. He regrets their lack of communication and understanding.

The poem explores the complex challenges in parent-child relationships, especially the difficulty of forming a deep connection and the pain of seeing a child grow independent.
It addresses themes of forgiveness, longing, and the universal need for families to heal and reconcile.

Explanation of the Poem

Stanza 1

I do not understand this child
Though we have lived together now
In the same house for years. I know
Nothing of him, so try to build
Up a relationship from how
He was when small.

Exp. In these lines, the father unhappily reflects on his inability to understand his own son. They have been staying in the same house for years but due to a lack of communication and understanding, both of them are not able to understand each other. The father does not know much about his son's interests, likes or dislikes.

Thus, he tries to build up the same kind of relationship as he used to have when his son was a little child. The father has now realised that there is a lack of understanding between his son and himself and he wants to take measures so that their relationship improves.

Stanza 2

Yet have I killed
The seed I spent or sown it where
The land is his and none of mine?
We speak like strangers, there's no sign
Of understanding in the air.
This child is built to my design
Yet what he loves I cannot share.

Exp. The father wonders whether it is he himself who is responsible for the failure of the relationship. The father feels that though the child is his son, he lives in a world different from him. Both of them behave like strangers. There is lack of understanding and a communication gap which makes them behave not like father and son but more like strangers. The father says that physically the child resembles him but their likes are different.

Stanza 3

Silence surrounds us. I would have
Him prodigal, returning to
His father's house, the home he knew,
Rather than see him make and move
His world. I would forgive him too,
Shaping from sorrow a new love.

Exp. Silence surrounds their relationship because there is a complete lack of communication between them. The father sees his son as 'prodigal' (a child who foolishly runs away from home) and wants him to return to the home he has always known so that they can rebuild the relationship to have a new start. He does not want the son to start life afresh without him.

He further says that he is willing to forgive his son for going away and growing apart.

Here, the father's tone is somewhat condescending, implying that the father is unable to let his son go despite restricting the son's independence and development.

Stanza 4

Father and son, we both must live
On the same globe and the same land,
He speaks: I cannot understand
Myself, why anger grows from grief.
We each put out an empty hand,
Longing for something to forgive.

Exp. Both of them must learn to live together in spite of their misunderstandings and differences. At this point in the poem, the son speaks for the first time and admits that he too feels the sadness of the broken relationship, but he is angry due to his confusion.

Both of them want to forgive each other but neither is willing to take the first step of asking for forgiveness from the other. However, the situation can improve if they find a way of getting closer to each other.

Word-Meaning

prodigal	—	extravagant, wasteful
move his world	—	shift to newer avenues
shaping from sorrow	—	making something new
put out	—	extend

Literary devices used in the Poem

- **Antithesis** *Stanza 2, Line 9* 'The land is his and none of mine' [contrasting ideas put together]
  Stanza 3, Line 19 'Shaping from sorrow a new love' [contrasting ideas put together]
- **Alliteration** *Stanza 2, Line 8* 'The seed I spent or sown' [repetition of the initial letter 's']
  Stanza 3, Line 14 'Silence surrounds us' [repetition of the initial letter 's']
  Stanza 3, Line 19 'Shaping from sorrow' [repetition of the initial letter 's']
- **Enjambment** In all stanzas

NCERT Folder

Think it Out (NCERT Page 72)

1. Does the poem talk of an exclusively personal experience or is it fairly universal?

Ans. The poem explores a deeply personal experience between a father and his son, but its themes of misunderstanding, distance, and longing for connection are universal, resonating with anyone who has struggled to understand or connect with a loved one. What happens in the poem usually, happens to most fathers and sons. It is very common in every family all over the world.

The generation gap has remained as it is. Moreover, the structure of the society is such that a father expects his son to follow his wishes, leading to individuality clashes.

2. How is the father's helplessness brought out in the poem?

Ans. The father's helplessness is brought out through his inability to understand his son despite their shared history of living together for years. He tries to build a relationship based on memories of his son as a child but finds himself unable to bridge the gap between them. This sense of helplessness is also evident in his desire for his son to return to the familiar, even if it means forgiving him for straying, and in his acknowledgement of his inability to comprehend his son's feelings and motivations.

3. Identify the phrases and lines that indicate distance between father and son.

Ans. The following phrases and lines bring out the deep differences that separate both of them

(i) I do not understand this child

(ii) I know nothing of him

(iii) We speak like strangers

(iv) What he loves I cannot share

(v) Silence surrounds us

(vi) There's no sign of understanding in the air

4. Does the poem have a consistent rhyme scheme?

Ans. No, the poem doesn't follow a consistent rhyme scheme.

Exam Pattern Questions

Extract Based Questions

Read the extracts given below and answer the questions that follow.

1. I do not understand this child
Though we have lived together now
In the same house for years. I know
Nothing of him, so try to build
Up a relationship from how
He was when small.

(i) What does the speaker of the above lines want?

(ii) Select the correct option from those given in bracket to fill in the blank.

The problem highlighted in the given lines is ……… (communication gap/enmity).

(iii) Read the assertion and the reason below with reference to the given extract.

Assertion (A) The poet wants to try to build up a relationship with his son.

Reason (R) The poet doesn't know his son well.

Choose the correct option regarding their relationship

(a) Both A and R are true, and R is the correct explanation for A.

(b) Both A and R are true, but R is not the correct explanation for A.

(c) A is true, but R is false.

(d) A is false, but R is true.

Ans. (i) The speaker of the given lines wanted to build a good relationship with his son.

(ii) communication gap

(iii) (a) Both A and R are true, and R is the correct explanation for A.

2. Yet have I killed
The seed I spent or sown it where
The land is his and none of mine?
We speak like strangers, there's no sign
Of understanding in the air.
This child is built to my design
Yet what he loves I cannot share.

(i) What does the father feel in the given lines?
(a) That his son is responsible for the situation
(b) That he is responsible for the situation
(c) That no one can be blamed for the situation
(d) That he himself should correct the situation

(ii) Which poetic device is used in the following line?
"The seed I spent or sown it where"

(iii) State what the poet means by the last line of the extract.

Ans. (i) (b) That he is responsible for the situation
(ii) The poetic device used in the given line is alliteration.
(iii) By the last line of the extract, the poet means that the father and the son do not have the same interests.

3. Silence surrounds us. I would have
Him prodigal, returning to
His father's house, the home he knew,
Rather than see him make and move
His world. I would forgive him too,
Shaping from sorrow a new love.

(i) What is the tone of the above stanza?
(a) Regret (b) Betrayal
(c) Anger (d) Disappointment

(ii) Why was the father ready to forgive him?

(iii) State, in one sentence, what the son feels when he spoke for the first time.

Ans. (i) (a) Regret
(ii) The father was to ready to forgive him to let go of all the sorrows he had inside.
(iii) The son felt bad about the distance between himself and his father when he spoke for the first time.

Short Answer Type Questions

1. Give reasons why the father knows nothing about his son even though they have lived in the same house.

Ans. The father-son relationship is actually non-functional. The father doesn't understand the aspirations, longings and cravings of the son. They do not communicate with each other and behave like strangers. Therefore, the father doesn't know anything about his son.

2. The father is responsible for the present situation. Do you agree?

Ans. Yes, I think the father is responsible for the present situation.

The father is guilty of allowing continued silence and non-communication between them and also not understanding his son's aspirations and feelings.

3. Interpret the poet's use of 'Silence surrounds us' and its meaning. **Competency Based**

Ans. The father feels helpless as he has no dialogue with his son. They don't understand each other and they are living like strangers with each other. Their outlook and temperament are so different that they remain separated from each other. They have a communication gap along with the generation gap, which causes the silence and, further, stretches it.

4. Describe the father's attitude towards his son in the third stanza. Analyse.

Ans. The father expresses his wish to rectify the situation in the third stanza. The father wants his son to return to the home that he has left. The father is willing to forgive his son and build their relationship.

5. The father is ready to have his prodigal son return. Draw an inference from this.

Ans. 'Prodigal' means wastefully extravagant. Here, the reference is to the story in the Bible in which a father gives his inheritance to his sons. The younger brother leaves, wastes his fortune and returns to his father's home.

Still, the father is ready to take him back and forgive him. In the poem, the father also wants to forgive his son so that they live peacefully together again.

6. The root cause of the generation gap presented in the poem lies in the fact that it is the father only talking to his son rather than hearing or understanding him. Explain. **Competency Based**

Ans. One of the reasons of the generation gap is the absence of understanding and communication. Here, in this poem, we hear only the father's point of view. We do not hear anything from the son's side until the end. This presents that the root cause of the generation gap has been the lack of sharing of interests or not paying attention to a child's emotional needs when he/she is growing up.
The child should be allowed to express his/her opinions freely and adults should not behave like dictators.

7. Write the significance of the words 'an empty hand'.

Ans. The words 'empty hand' signify that both the father and the son want to forgive each other and extend a hand of friendship to each other but neither of them is willing to be the first one to do so. This means that, although they are longing to forgive each other, their ego is coming in the way.

8. How does the poem present the themes of the struggle of parenting?

Ans. 'Father to Son' explores the challenges and complexities of parenting. It portrays the father's struggle to relate to and understand his child, a theme that resonates with parents who may struggle to bridge generational gaps and connect with their children.

9. How is the theme of silence portrayed in the poem?

Ans. The poem highlights the theme of silence in the relationship between the father and son. They speak 'like strangers', and there is no sign of understanding in the air, emphasising their lack of communication and emotional distance.

Long Answer Type Questions

1. Generation gap is a universal problem. Give reason for its existence. How can someone avoid such confrontations? Express your views in 120-150 words.

Ans. Generation gap is a psychological and emotional gap between parents or elder people and the younger ones. This creates misunderstanding and lack of attachment between parents and children. The success of parenting lies in how effectively they avoid the generation gap or manage differences with their children.

Generation gap is the result of the fast-paced development of society. In earlier times, two or three generations lived in the same lifestyle and environment as development was slow. Today, parents do not even know many of the modern technologies and equipment children use.

Being up-to-date and more involved in a child's life are the only ways to cope with generation gap. Moreover, generation gap occurs when there is a difference of opinion. One should be flexible in approach and must try to understand the reason of a particular behaviour.

2. In the fast moving materialistic world of today, parents are busy in earning while their children grow without them giving enough time to them. This is a major factor in creating a generation gap. There should be a balancing act on the part of parents. Discuss.

Ans. In today's materialistic world, parents, especially fathers, are busy with their careers finding very little time for their children.

Childhood is a tender age and a child needs his/ her parents at every stage of his/her growing up. In the pursuit of money or career, children are left at the mercy of caretakers or maids who may provide or fulfill a child's basic need but their emotional and intellectual needs are left unfulfilled. Bonding between parents and children keeps on diminishing until it reaches an alarming level.

Parents need to understand that, between career and children, a balancing act has to be practised. Children need their parents to guide them, to share their likes and dislikes, and to spend quality time with them.

No parent should allow such a situation where they may not understand their children or there may be no communication at all between them. Emotional bonding is a must for a family to stay together.

SELF ASSESSMENT TEST

Extract Based Questions

Read the extract given below and answer the questions that follow.

1. He speaks: I cannot understand
Myself, why anger grows from grief.
We each put out an empty hand,
Longing for something to forgive.

(i) Select the correct option from those given in bracket to fill in the blank.

The poet expresses a sense of mutual .... (longing/hurt) between himself and his son for forgiveness.

(ii) Read the Assertion (A) and the Reason (R) below with reference to the given extract.

Assertion (A) The poet's son accepts that his anger grows from grief of a lost relationship.

Reason (R) The poet and his son hope for a reconciliation.

Choose the correct option regarding their relationship.

(a) Both A and R are true, and R is the correct explanation for A.
(b) Both A and R are true, but R is not the correct explanation for A.
(c) A is true, but R is false.
(d) A is false, but R is true.

(iii) State, in one sentence, what is stopping the poet and his son from seeking each other's forgiveness.

Short Answer Type Questions

1. What is the cause of the problem between the father and the son?

2. "Physically the son resembles his father yet they are strangers to each other." Why?

3. "Communication is an essential part of relationship and bonding." Express your views on this statement.

4. Where did the father fail? How could he have avoided this failure?

5. What do both father and son yearn for?

Long Answer Type Question

1. The poem 'Father to Son' describes the relationship between a father and a son. Imagine yourself to be a teacher who has to address the parents on the occasion of Father's Day. Write a speech in 120-150 words mentioning how a father can be a role model for his son. Also, elaborate on the type of relationship that a father and son should share.

You may begin like this

Good morning, parents and students!

A father's actions and values shapes not only ....

01

The Summer of the Beautiful White Horse

About the Author

William Saroyan (1908-1981) was an internationally renowned Armenian American writer, playwright, and humanitarian.

He achieved great popularity in the thirties, forties, and fifties through his hundreds of short stories, plays, novels, memoirs, and essays. In 1939, Saroyan was the first American writer to win both the New York Drama Critics' Circle Award and the Pulitzer Prize for his play 'The Time of Your Life.'

Saroyan was concerned with the basic goodness of all people, especially the obscure and naive, and the value of life. His mastery of the vernacular makes his characters vibrantly alive. Often his stories portray the world from the perspective of children, whose instinctual embrace of life echoes the author's philosophy.

YOUR STUDY GOALS

- Chapter Sketch
- About the Characters
- Summary of the Chapter

YOUR PRACTICE GOAL

- NCERT Folder
- Extract Based Questions
- Short Answer Type Questions
- Long Answer Type Questions

Chapter Sketch

The story is about two poor Armenian boys who are fond of riding horses. Aram (9 years old) and Mourad (13 years old) belong to the Garoghlanian tribe where people were well-known for honesty, and trust. Mourad is able to steal a horse and, after enjoying riding for one month, he invites his cousin to join him in horse-riding. Finally, they decide to return the horse to its owner as they do not want to bring any shame to their family.

About the Characters

Mourad He is the 13 year old cousin of the narrator (Aram). He is a lively and crazy person but loves his cousin, Aram, whom he offers the horse to ride for some time. He knows how to handle a horse.

Aram (the narrator) He is a 9 year old boy. He and Mourad belong to the Garoghlanian tribe. He justifies Mourad's stealing of the horse for the purpose of horse-riding as they did not intend to sell it off.

John Byro He is a farmer and the owner of the beautiful white horse which was stolen by Mourad. He is sad over the sudden disappearance of his horse a few weeks ago.

Uncle Khosrove He is the narrator's uncle who was considered to be a crazy man. He has been described as a man with a short temper and irritable nature.

Summary of the Chapter

Aram's Memory

Aram was 9 years old when Mourad woke him at four on a summer morning. He was surprised to see that his cousin was sitting on a beautiful white horse and was asking Aram to join him. Aram had always wanted to ride a horse but he was doubtful. He knew that his Garoghlanian tribe was poor and could not afford a horse. Hence, he knew that Mourad couldn't possibly have bought the horse. At the same time, he also knew that his tribe was known for their honesty and integrity. They would never even take advantage of anyone.

Aram's Explanation

Aram was sure that the horse was stolen as they were both very crazy about riding horses. So, he justified Mourad's act by stating that it was not really stealing because they had not sold the horse.

Then, he got ready and joined Mourad to ride the horse. As they lived on the boundary of the town on Walnut Avenue, there was a vast countryside full of orchards, vineyards and irrigation ditches nearby. As a result, both Aram and Mourad were having a wonderful time riding the horse.

The Family's Crazy Streak

Mourad was considered the natural inheritor of the crazy streak of their tribe. Before Mourad, uncle Khosrove was considered crazy in the family. Khosrove was an enormous man with black hair and the largest moustache in the San Joaquin valley. He displayed his crazy streak when he ignored the fact that his house was on fire.

Even though Mourad was considered a crazy boy though his father, Mr. Zorab, was a practical man.

Aram Rides the Horse Alone

After enjoying the horse ride together, Mourad rode the horse alone for five minutes. Now, Aram also wanted to ride the horse alone. Mourad was not sure that Aram could ride the horse alone as he did not know how to control a horse.

At his turn, Aram was a little scared but he jumped on to the back of the horse. Then, he kicked into the muscles of the horse. However, instead of running across the field, the horse ran to the vineyard and leaped over seven vines before Aram fell.

Hiding the Horse

Mourad came running because he was worried about the horse. He also wanted to take the horse before anyone could see him. However, the horse was running away and got lost. It took the boys half an hour to find it.

Then the boys decided to hide the horse, after discussing that they would tell everyone they started riding the horse that very morning, if someone found out. They took the horse to the deserted vineyard of a farmer named Fetvajian and hid it in the barn. Herein, Aram realised that Mourad had been riding the horse for a long time.

John Byro's Sadness

That afternoon uncle Khosrove came to Aram's house for coffee and cigarettes. Just then, John Byro, a farmer, also arrived. John Byro was sad because his white horse was stolen the previous month and has not been found. He explained that his carriage was no good without a horse and he had to walk ten miles to reach there. Uncle Khosrove showed his crazy streak again by stating that it was not a big deal to lose the horse.

Riding the Horse

Aram informed Mourad about John Byro's visit. He also told Mourad that he should not return the horse for a year so that he had learnt riding. Mourad knew that they could not keep a horse for one year as it would amount to stealing. So, they decided to return it after six month. Every morning, for the next two weeks, the boys rode the horse.

Returning the Horse

One morning, the cousins were on their way to the vineyard when they encountered John Byro. He inquired about the name of the horse and observed the horse very keenly. He doubted that the white horse was his stolen horse. However, he knew that their tribe was honest and could not doubt them.

The next morning, the boys took the horse to John Byro's vineyard and left it there. That afternoon, John Byro came to the narrator's house. He was very happy as his horse had become stronger and better tempered.

Word-Meaning

hallmarks	— typical characteristics or features	hind	— back legs of an animal
tapping	— hitting quickly and lightly with fingers	dripping	— extremely
around the corner of the world	— away	reared	— raised
Garoghlanian	— an Armenian tribe	barn	— a large building on a farm in which animals and their feed are kept
bellies	— stomachs	vineyard	— a plantation of grapevines
pious stillness and humour	— innocence and unconcern	hearty	— substantial
trot	— used for horse or similar animal running at its slowest speed	dweller	— resident
streak	— an inherent quality	surrey	— a light four wheeled carriage
trimmed	— made neat or tidy by clipping	stalked	— marched
capricious	— impulsive, unpredictable	slamming	— shutting with force
vagrant	— not fixed	homesick	— acutely longing for one's home
have a way	— have success in dealing	ran into	— met accidentally
Vazire	— a word in Armenian language meaning 'run'	studied	— examined
		swear	— guarantee
		suspicious	— full of mistrust
		whispered	— spoke in a low voice
		patted	— stroked lightly
		better-tempered	— well-behaved

Important Themes of the Chapter

Emotions and Reason Throughout the story, Aram and Mourad are caught between how they feel and what they know.

Importance of Character and Reputation Though they live in extreme poverty, the Garoghlanians do not steal, valuing honesty over wealth and their reputation over whatever they might gain through stealing.

Balancing Adventure and Integrity Another theme prevalent in the story is the conflict between family values and the desire for adventure. The story highlights the importance of honesty, a core value of the Garoghlanian family. Mourad and Aram's adventure with the stolen horse reveals their love for freedom and excitement and tests their integrity. The boys struggle with the morality of keeping the horse versus returning it to its rightful owner. Ultimately, their actions show respect for their family's reputation for honesty and the importance of doing the right thing, even when it's complicated.

NCERT Folder

Reading with Insight (NCERT Page 8-9)

1. You will probably agree that this story does not have breathless adventure and exciting action. Then what, in your opinion, makes it interesting?

Ans. This story may not have breathless adventure and exciting action but its charm lies in its exploration of relationships, values and the inner world of the characters. The dynamic between Aram and his cousin Mourad, the contrast between their adventurous spirit and the family's strong moral code, adds depth to the narrative. The story explores honesty, integrity, and the complexities of right and wrong. Through simple yet vivid storytelling, readers are drawn into the world of these characters, their dilemmas and their adventures, making it compelling despite the lack of conventional action.

2. Did the boys return the horse because they were conscience-stricken or because they were afraid?

Ans. The story does not give any indication that the boys (Mourad and Aram) were afraid of anyone or anything. If they had been afraid, they would not have carried on with horse-riding every day for weeks. They had an intense desire for horse-riding.

To fulfill their intense urge, they had kept the horse for some time but they had the intention of returning the horse to its owner, simultaneously. During their conversation with John Byro, the boys got conscience-stricken as their family and tribe were well-known for their honesty and integrity. So, they decided to return the horse to its owner.

3. **"One day back there in the good old days when I was nine and the world was full of every imaginable kind of magnificence and life was still a delightful and mysterious dream.......". The story begins in a mood of nostalgia. Can you narrate some incident from your childhood that might make an interesting story?**

Ans. Reading these lines, one can recount innumerable memories of childhood. My father had been transferred to Raniganj, a breathtakingly beautiful place. We lived in a palatial bungalow with a massive garden. Since it was close to the forest, I usually found wandering wild animals in my garden in the morning. What was very surprising was that none of them harmed me. One day, I saw a small deer cub. The moment I saw it, I decided to make it my pet. Everybody advised me against it.

But I had taken it as a challenge. Every morning, he would come into my garden. I used to feed it green leaves. Soon, we became good friends. Then, he would stay back in the verandah at night. How the days flew! I started dreaming of keeping this beautiful creature with me. Finally, my dream was shattered when my father was posted back to the city. I had to leave my beautiful friend in its natural habitat.

4. **The story revolves around characters who belong to a tribe in Armenia. Mourad and Aram are members of the Garoghlanian family. Now, locate Armenia and Assyria on the Atlas and prepare a write-up on Garoghlanian tribes. You may write about people, their names, traits, geographical and economic features as suggested in the story.**

Ans. **The Garoghlanian Tribe**

The Garoghlanian tribe, as depicted in 'The Summer of the Beautiful White Horse', is characterised by its strong sense of honesty, pride and modesty. The people of this tribe, residing in Armenia, are known for their humble yet noble demeanour, reflecting their long-standing traditions and values. This tribe used to be prosperous once. However, when they had to leave their lands due to war, they entered the condition of object poverty. Despite their poverty, they prioritise honesty and integrity over material wealth, emphasising the importance of character and moral principles.

Geographically, the Garoghlanian family resides on Walnut Avenue, on the outskirts of a town, surrounded by vineyards, orchards, and countryside. This setting reflects the rural landscape in Armenian regions, characterised by agricultural livelihoods and close-knit communities.

Names within the Garoghlanian family, such as Mourad, Aram, Khosrove and Zorab, reflect Armenian cultural heritage. These names often have historical or religious significance and are passed down through generations, connecting individuals to their ancestry and identity.

Try this Out (NCERT Page 9)

"The horse stood on its hind legs, snorted and burst into a fury of speed that was the loveliest thing I had ever seen." These lines could be an artist's delight. Try to draw a picture as depicted in the above lines.

Ans. Do it yourself.

Exam Pattern Questions

Extract Based Questions

Read the extracts given below and answer the questions that follow.

1. **This was the wonderful part.**
In the second place, we were poor.
This was the part that wouldn't permit me to believe what I saw.
We were poor. We had no money. Our whole tribe was poverty stricken. Every branch of the Garoghlanian family was living in the most amazing and comical poverty in the world. Nobody could understand where we ever got money enough to keep us with food in our bellies, not even the old men of the family.

(i) **"This was the wonderful part."**
What does 'this' refer to?

(ii) **"Nobody could understand where we ever got money enough to keep us with food in our bellies, not even the old men of the family."**
In the above line, what is indicated about the profession of the members of the tribe?

(a) They were honest professionals

(b) Their work/profession is a mystery
(c) They owned land
(d) None of the above

(iii) Complete the sentence appropriately, with reference to the extract.

The narrator couldn't believe what he saw because ....

(iv) Who is the speaker of the above lines?

Ans. (i) 'This' refers to his desire to ride a horse getting fulfilled.

(ii) (d) None of the above

(iii) no one in his family could afford a horse

(iv) The speaker of the given lines is a 9 year old boy of the Garoghlanian tribe, named Aram.

2. Before him was our uncle Khosrove, an enormous man with a powerful head of black hair and the largest moustache in the San Joaquin Valley, a man so furious in temper, so irritable, so impatient that he stopped anyone from talking by roaring. It is no harm; pay no attention to it.
That was all, no matter what anybody happened to be talking about. Once it was his own son Arak running eight blocks to the barber's shop where his father was having his moustache trimmed to tell him their house was on fire.

(i) Complete the following suitably.
In the given extract, the narrator is talking about ....

(ii) When the author says 'roaring', he indicates that
(a) the person who roars is like a tiger.
(b) the person is loud and pompous.
(c) the person is speaking loudly in an angry tone.
(d) the person is short-temperedly when his son told him about the fire?

(iii) How do you think Khosrove reacted to the news of fire?

(iv) How did Khosrove reply when his son told him about the fire?

Ans. (i) the crazy streak that runs in the family.

(ii) (c) the person is speaking loudly in an angry tone.

(iii) Khosrove wasn't affected by the news in the slightest. He simply roared, "Enough, it is no harm, I say."

(iv) Khosrove got angry and started screaming when his son told him about the fire.

3. My mother brought the lonely visitor coffee and tobacco and he rolled a cigarette and sipped and smoked, and then at last, sighing sadly, he said, my white horse which was stolen last month is still gone — I cannot understand it.
My Uncle Khosrove became very irritated and shouted, it's no harm. What is the loss of a horse? Haven't we all lost the homeland? What is this crying over a horse?

(i) Who is the lonely visitor mentioned in the extract?
(a) Mourad (b) Uncle Khosrove
(c) John Byro (d) Fetvajian

(ii) Why was Uncle khosrove irritated?

(iii) Complete the sentence appropriately, with reference to the extract.

Uncle Khosrove's reaction shows that he was ....

(iv) Whose mother brought coffee and tobacco for the lonely visitor?

Ans. (i) (c) John Byro

(ii) Uncle khosrove was irritated because he considered John Byro's troubles about his horse to be inconsequential.

(iii) unneccesarily angry

(iv) Aram's mother brought coffee and tobacco for the lonely visitor.

4. A lovely name, John Byro said, for a lovely horse.
I could swear it is the horse that was stolen from me many weeks ago.
May I look into his mouth?
Of course, Mourad said, the farmer looked into the mouth of the horse.
Tooth for tooth, he said, I would swear it is my horse if I didn't know your parents. The fame of your family for honesty is well known to me. Yet the horse is the twin of my horse. A suspicious man would believe his eyes instead of his heart. Good day, my young friends.

(i) What is the importance of the incident presented in the given extract?

(ii) The horse's owner refused to believe that the boys had stolen his horse because ....

(iii) Why did the boys return the horse?
(a) Because they were conscience stricken.
(b) Because they were afraid.
(c) Because they found it difficult to hide the horse.
(d) Because they were accused of theft.

(iv) John Byro said, "A suspicious man would believe his eyes instead of his heart." What does it tell about him?

Ans. (i) The incident in the given extract made Aram realise that their act would bring shame to their family and tribe that were known for honesty.

(ii) their family was known for honesty

(iii) (a) Because they were conscience stricken.

(iv) The given statement by John Byro indicates that even though he eyes and brain believe that the white horse is his, his heart and his trust in the honesty of the Garoghlanian tribe assure him that it can never be the case. He knows that the boys from the tribe would never steal.

Short Answer Type Questions

1. "...but this was more than even I could believe." Identify the speaker and give reason why he said so.

Ans. Aram said this when he saw Mourad riding a horse. Aram could not believe what he saw. He knew that their tribe was poverty-stricken, so could not afford a horse. He was sure that Mourad would not steal the horse as their tribe was famous for its honesty. However finally he got to know that Mourad had actually stolen the horse.

2. Aram didn't want to return the horse. Substantiate.

Ans. Like his cousin Mourad, Aram was also fond of horse-riding. When Mourad stole a beautiful white horse, Aram at first was shocked but eventually didn't consider it as stealing. Rather, he himself wanted to learn horse-riding. So, Aram wanted Mourad to keep the horse until he could become a perfect horse rider.

3. Give reason for the Garoghlanian tribe's popularity?

Ans. The Garoghlanian tribe was famous for their honesty and integrity for the last eleven centuries. Whatever may be the circumstances, they never compromised with their honesty. They also knew how to differentiate between right and wrong.

4. Assess the mindset of Aram when he justifies his claims that Mourad did not steal the horse. Competency Based

Ans. Aram's justification that Mourad's act of stealing the white horse isn't necessarily stealing shows his innocent mindset. It takes us into a child's psychology which drives him to reach the rationalisation. Aram's deep admiration for Mourad and the magical experience of riding the horse blur the lines between right and wrong in his mind. Thus, Aram views Mourad's actions as less severe and more aligned with their love for horses rather than a breach of their ethical standards.

5. Aram justified that his stealing the horse wasn't actually stealing. Do you agree? Competency Based

Ans. Aram justified the act of keeping the horse, saying that it wasn't stealing until they offered to sell the horse, which they would never do.

In my opinion, the justification is not appropriate. They kept the horse without the consent of its owner for a long time. The owner's work suffered as his carriage was without a horse, and the loss troubled him. Hence, I don't agree with Aram.

6. "Mourad was considered the natural descendant of this man." Whose natural descendant was he considered?

Ans. According to the narrator, every family has a crazy streak. In their family, Uncle Khosrove was the true inheritor of that streak. He was a man of 'ill-temper and impatience.' Mourad resembled his uncle in many ways, so he was also considered to be the descendant of that crazy streak in the family.

7. State some instances that show the crazy streak that was found in Uncle Khosrove.

Ans. The story mentions two instances which show the crazy streak that was found in Uncle Khosrove. First is seen in his reaction on getting the information that his house had caught fire. Second is seen in his reaction when John Byro laments the loss of his horse. In both the cases, he acts indifferently and advises not to pay attention to it.

8. The 'spirit' of his tribe was being capricious and vagrant. Why did the narrator say so?

Ans. The given statement means that the spirits of their tribe had been unsettled and wandering. The narrator's cousin Mourad had a crazy streak, although his father Zorab was practical and nothing else. That's how their tribe was. A man could be the father of his son's flesh, but that did not mean that he was the father of his spirit.

9. "A man could be the father of his son's flesh, but that did not mean that he was the father of his spirit." Do you agree with this statement? Give reasons. Competency Based

Ans. Through this line, the author points out the fact that a man may father a son and may be responsible for his physical features and his looks but that does not mean that he is also responsible for his inner soul. Mourad inherited his Uncle Khosrove's personality traits, although his father was Zorab. Thus, it is true that a son may resemble his father in body but may exhibit quite a different character.

10. Do you think Mourad was selfish in his decision to not let Aram ride the horse initially? Justify your answer.

Ans. I do not think that Mourad was selfish in his decision to not let Aram ride the horse initially. Mourad knew that Aram had never rode a horse also and was not a good rider. Further, he also understood that Aram did not understand the horse's temperament and mood correctly. Hence, for these reasons, he was not keen of letting Aram ride the horse alone.

11. How does Aram feel when riding the horse for the first time?

Ans. Aram feels both excitement and fear when riding the horse for the first time. While exhilarated by the experience and the freedom it represents, he also experiences a sense of apprehension, unsure how to handle the powerful and unfamiliar animal beneath him.

12. What understanding does the cousin claim to have with animals (horses)?

Ans. The cousin Mourad claims to have a unique talent and a deep connection with animals, highlighting his exceptional understanding and empathy. He asserts that he can get horses to want to do anything he desires, which he shows with his effortless control and calming influence over the stolen horse. Mourad's confidence and ease with the horse showcase a deep, intuitive connection with horses, built on mutual respect and communication rather than coercion or force.

13. What does Aram's cousin do to convince the horse to behave nicely?

Ans. To convince the horse to behave nicely, Aram's cousin employs a combination of physical gestures and calming words. He presses his nose against the horse's nose, pats it affectionately and speaks to it reassuringly. This gentle approach helps soothe the horse and gain its co-operation.

14. What suddenly dawned upon Aram while talking to Mourad about the white horse?

Ans. Aram suddenly realised that Mourad had been riding the horse for quite some days as he had learnt to control the horse. If Mourad had been riding the horse the first time that day, he would not have been able to control it as well as he did.

15. Contrast the two people who visited Aram's house that afternoon.

Ans. John Byro, a farmer, visited Aram's house the afternoon after Aram rode the horse. He complained that his white horse which was stolen last month was still not found. He was a gentleman who was sad at the loss of his horse. The second visitor was Aram's Uncle Khosrove, who was irritable and impatient, and did not allow anyone to talk.

16. Identify the quality of Mourad that reveals that he is more than just a 'crazy person'.

Ans. When Aram visited Mourad's house, he found that Mourad was treating the hurt wings of a young Robin. It showed that inspite of a crazy streak, Mourad was kind-hearted and gentle towards every being.

17. "A suspicious man would believe his eyes instead of his heart."
Who said these words? Why?

Ans. John Byro, the farmer, said it to the boys when he saw the horse with them. He became very surprised to see the white horse which was similar to his missing one. However, in his heart he could not doubt the integrity and honesty of the boys due to his faith in their tribe, which was famous for its honesty.

18. John Byro was a happy man in the end. Give reasons.

Ans. It is true to say that John Byro was a happy man at the end because he had gotten his beloved white horse back. Further, now the horse was much stronger and had a better temperament. In addition, now, he could successfully function his business which may have been hampered with the loss of the horse for a few days.

19. Why does the Aram want to keep the horse hidden for a year?

Ans. Aram wants to keep the horse hidden for a year to learn to ride correctly. He believes that it will take approximately a year to acquire the necessary skills, hoping to master horse riding before returning the horse to its rightful owner.

20. How does the setting of the story shape the events and characters' actions? **Competency Based**

Ans. The story's setting, situated in a rural area with vineyards, orchards and country roads, fosters a sense of freedom and possibility. The expansive landscape allows the characters to engage in spontaneous adventures, such as stealing and riding a horse, while reflecting the family's humble origins and close connection to nature.

21. What does the story suggest about the theme of freedom in terms of physical freedom and personal choices?

Ans. The story suggests that true freedom transcends physical constraints and encompasses the ability to make independent choices. While the characters enjoy the freedom of riding the horse and exploring the countryside, they also navigate moral dilemmas and the consequences of their actions, highlighting the complexity of personal liberty and responsibility.

22. Discuss the significance of the horse as a symbol in the story and its impact on the characters' lives. **Competency Based**

Ans. The beautiful white horse plays an important role in the story. It symbolises freedom, adventure, temptation and the extraordinary possibilities of life beyond their impoverished reality. Its unexpected appearance ignites excitement and desire of making their childhood fantasies tangible in the characters, leading them to question their values and moral boundaries. Thus, the horse is a powerful symbol of his aspirations, innocence and the magical moments of childhood. However, its presence disrupts their lives, forcing them to confront their desires, integrity, and the consequences of their actions.

Long Answer Type Questions

1. How does Aram describe his cousin Mourad's personality and how does it contrast with the family's reputation?

Ans. The Aram describes his cousin Mourad as someone who enjoys life more than anyone else, with a zest for adventure and a touch of craziness that sets him apart. Mourad's love for excitement and carefree spirit contrast sharply with the Garoghlanian family's long-standing reputation for honesty and integrity.

While the family is known for their poverty and unwavering moral principles, Mourad's behaviour seems contradictory, mainly his stealing a horse. Despite this, Mourad's actions are portrayed with a sense of innocence and passion for life, highlighting a tension between his individualistic streak and the family's collective values. This contrast adds to Mourad's character and emphasises the story's themes of tradition and individuality.

2. How does Uncle Khosrove's reaction to John Byro's complaints about the stolen horse contribute to the story's humour and themes?

Ans. Uncle Khosrove's exaggerated indifference and comical impatience in response to John Byro's complaints about the stolen horse contribute to the story's humour and themes. His repeated dismissals—'It is no harm; pay no attention to it'—regardless of the seriousness of the situation, create a humorous contrast to the distress felt by John Byro. The reaction highlights the theme of resilience and perspective within the Garoghlanian family, emphasising their prioritisation of more significant existential concerns over material losses.

Khosrove's outbursts and the absurdity of his responses add a layer of fun to the narrative, illustrating how the family's firm, almost stubborn pride and unique outlook on life allow them to navigate their challenges with humour and stoicism.

3. Compare and contrast the two Cousins present in the story.

Ans. The protagonists of the story- Mourad and Aram are cousins. Both of them belong to the Garoghlanian family, wherein the values of honesty and integrity are long-standing family traditions. However, the boys are very different in nature.

Aram is a nine years old boy who is narrator of the story, providing insights into the Garoghlanian family's values and traditions. He is an innocent and naive boy who views the world with wonder and imagination. He shows a keen desire to adventure and thus, is fascinated by the idea of riding a horse. Even when he knows that his mischievous cousin had stolen the horse, he admires and looks up to Mourad. He trusts Mourad's judgment and decisions. However, throughout the story we see him torn between his love for adventure and his family's values. He struggles with the idea of riding a stolen horse.

In contrast stands his cousin Mourad who is the inheritor of the 'crazy streak' of the Garoghlanian family. He is adventurous, brave, passionate and free-spirited. Mourad demonstrates resourcefulness in finding a place to hide and maintain the horse. His skill in handling animals is shown through his ability to tame and control the horse and his rapport with dogs. Mourad's charisma is evident in his interactions, convincing Aram to ride and confidently speaking to John Byro. His persuasive skills help him handle situations, such as when they meet the horse's owner. Despite his mischievous act of taking the horse, Mourad shows a strong moral compass. He ultimately decides to return the horse, respecting his family's reputation for honesty.

4. In today's materialistic world where greed and money are the most important things, the example of the Garoghlanian tribe can teach us many things – to be honest, to discriminate between right and wrong. What values can we learn from the example of this tribe?

Ans. It is truly said that in today's materialistic world where greed and money are the most important things, the example of the Garoghlanian tribe can teach us many things – to be honest, to discriminate between right and wrong. The present day is such that we have become selfish beings, ready to go to any lengths to fulfill our greed and desires. We do not blink an eye while doing an immoral act just for the satisfaction of having something.

In this light, the Garoghlanian tribe comes as a breath of fresh air with its values and characteristics. The tribe is known for its honesty, integrity and hospitality. It's sense of morality if so strong that they are not doubted to done anything wrong even when the circumstances show that they may be the culprits. This is exactly what happened with Mourad and Aram when John Byro believes them. However, their conscience made the boys see their wrongs and they could retain the values ingrained in them. Their example shows us that we should not be immoral in any case and if by chance we commit a wrong act, we should rectify it as soon as possible.

5. Both Aram and Mourad diverted a little bit from their family values for some time. However, they corrected themselves when they realised their mistake. You wish to include a cameo of both in your upcoming blog post. As part of the research, write about the human values reflected in the character of these two young boys in 120-150 words.

[Clue: Include the incidents from the story-desire to ride a horse-delight realisation of the mistake]

Ans. 'The Summer of the Beautiful White Horse' is a story about two boys who belong to the Garoghlanian family, which has been famous for its integrity and honesty for centuries. Both the boys, Aram and Mourad, reflected these qualities in their characters very well. They never let their family down under any condition.

However, for some time, they diverted from their values when Mourad stole the beautiful white horse.

Both Aram and Mourad were crazy for riding a horse so, when Mourad stole a horse, they justified it to be not stealing so, they rode the horse for some time without any guilt.

However, when they met John Byro, they become conscience-stricken. They realised that their act could put a question mark on their tribe's dignity and reputation. So, they decided to return the horse to its rightful owner.

Hence, this incident shows that the two young characters reflect those human values which are quite necessary in today's world.

6. The story 'The Summer of the Beautiful White Horse' beautifully throws light on the statement 'we are nothing but a set of values'. Write an article in 120-150 words discussing this statement with reference to the story.

You may begin like this ....

Human beings are nothing without as set of values. They are ...

Ans.

We are Nothing But a Set of Values

by XYZ

Human beings are nothing without a set of values. They are the very base of any human life. Without principles or a set of values, we cannot lead an honourable life. It is not necessary to have wealth or education but to have good values is of utmost importance. Values lead us to a correct way of life, discriminating between right and wrong. In this chapter, the boys gave importance to the values of honesty and trust which was the hallmark of their tribe.

Though they went astray for some time, it was the value system inherited from their elders which made them realise that they were on the wrong path and needed to correct the situation. In the end, the boys returned the horse to its rightful owner who was really feeling miserable without his horse.

SELF ASSESSMENT TEST

Extract Based Questions

Read the extract given below and answer the questions that follow.

1. I could hear it breathing, so exciting; I couldn't believe the horse had anything to do with my cousin Mourad or with me or with any of the other members of our family, asleep or awake, because I knew my cousin Mourad couldn't have bought the horse, and if he couldn't have bought it he must have stolen it, and I refused to believe he had stolen it.

(i) Why does the narrator say that Mourad couldn't have brought the horse?

(ii) Why does the narrator refuse to believe that Mourad had stolen the horse?

(a) Mourad was too young.

(b) No one in their family could be a thief.

(c) Mourad was considered crazy and could not steal.

(d) Mourad was the most intelligent child of the family.

(iii) What is the relationship between the speaker and Mourad?

(iv) Complete the sentence appropriately, with reference to the extract.

The speaker of the given lines is ....

Short Answer Type Questions

1. The big surprise that Mourad give to Aram led to conflicting thoughts in the latter's head. Elucidate.

2. Where did Mourad and Aram hide the horse and why?

3. Describe Aram's first horse ride.

4. Why did the narrator want to keep the horse for one year?

5. Briefly explain how the cousins convince John Byro that their horse isn't stolen.

6. Explore the theme of family loyality and its complexities as portrayed in the story.

Long Answer Type Questions

1. Can stealing be justified by any reason? Discuss Aram and Mourad's stealing of a horse in the light of this statement.

2. 'Mourad showed special concern for animals.' Discuss Mourad's love for animals in contrast to today's youths who are engaged in thoughtless killing of animals.

3. Discuss the themes of childhood innocence and adventure in the story. How do Aram and Mourad embody these themes through their actions and experiences.

02

About the Author

Marga Minco

(1920–2023), also known as Marga Faes, was a Dutch journalist and writer, and a Holocaust survivor. Most of her books are partly autobiographical; they often relate to the persecution of Jews during World War II and the lack of understanding of the non-Jewish world after the war. They describe the deportation of her family and her own survival in hiding during World War II. It was translated into many languages.

▼ YOUR STUDY GOALS

- Chapter Sketch
- About the Characters
- Summary of the Chapter

▼ YOUR PRACTICE GOAL

- NCERT Folder
- Extract Based Questions
- Short Answer Type Questions
- Long Answer Type Questions

The Address

Chapter Sketch

Marga Minco's 'The Address' tells the story of a daughter from Jewish background who returns to Holland after World War II to retrieve her mother's belongings from a woman named Mrs. Dorling.
During the war, Mrs. Dorling had taken the items for safekeeping. When the daughter visits Mrs. Dorling's house, she feels uneasy seeing her mother's possessions in a different setting. Despite the memories they evoke, she decides not to take anything back, realising that the objects have lost their meaning and connection to her past. She resolves to leave the past behind and move on with her life, forgetting the address and the painful memories associated with it.

About the Characters

The Daughter She is the narrator who returns to Holland to go to the address where her mother's precious belongings were kept.
As normalcy had returned after the Second World War, she wanted to see or perhaps take back all the possessions that represented the bond between her family and herself.

Mrs. S.—The Narrator's Mother In the story, narrator's mother has been called Mrs. S. She was a simpleton who could not see the manipulating and fraudulent nature of Mrs. Dorling, her acquaintance. She trusted Mrs. Dorling and allowed her to keep all her precious belongings for the time being.

Mrs. Dorling She has been described as an old acquaintance of Mrs. S. She possessed a cunning personality. She is reluctant to recognise the daughter and does not allow her to enter the house.

Summary of the Chapter

Mrs. Dorling's Indifference

The narrator knocked at the door of a house and informed the owner that she was Mrs. S's daughter. But the owner of the house, Mrs. Dorling, gave no sign of recognition. This made the narrator think that perhaps she had rung the wrong bell. However, the narrator got a glimpse of her mother's green knitted cardigan which Mrs. Dorling was wearing. This confirmed that she had reached the correct address. However, Mrs. Dorling excused herself and asked the girl to come some other time.

The Narrator's Memory

The narrator stood at the steps even after the door closed and felt that someone was watching her. She assumed it to be someone else and then, walked back to the station, thinking about her mother.

The narrator remembered that her mother had given her Mrs. Dorling's address during the first half of the war. Her mother has informed her that Mrs. Dorling was an old acquaintance and that whenever Mrs. Dorling came, she took something home with her. She had explained that Mrs. Dorling wanted to save all the good things, if they had to leave suddenly. The narrator's mother had accepted the idea and felt obliged towards Mrs. Dorling.

Meeting Mrs. Dorling

The narrator arrived at the station without having paid much attention to things on the way. She didn't want to upset herself with the sight of streets and houses full of memories of the past. In the train, she remembered that she saw Mrs. Dorling for the first time the day after her mother had told her about the lady. Mrs. Dorling was wearing a brown coat and a shapeless hat. Upon enquiry, her mother told her that Mrs. Dorling lived at Number 46, Marconi Street.

The Narrator's Reluctance

The narrator had remembered the address but waited a long time to go there. Initially, after the war was over, she was not interested in them. She was afraid to see the things that had belonged to her dead mother, fearing that they might make her very nostalgic. It was only when her life became normal again that she became curious to know about all the possessions.

The Narrator Visits Again

After her first visit, the narrator decided to visit the address again. This time, a fifteen year old girl, who had a broad back similar to that of Mrs. Dorling, opened the door. She followed the girl inside the house and went into the living-room. The girl was placing teacups and pouring tea from a white teapot which had a gold border on the lid. She also she took out some spoons from the box.

All this crockery and cutlery belonged to the narrator's family but perhaps the girl was not aware of this fact. She cracked a joke about eating dinner in those antique plates which shocked the girl. The narrator also found a burn mark on the table cloth.

The Narrator's Feelings

Seeing the things that belong to her family, the narrator was horrified. She was hurt to see the things lying in a tasteless way with the ugly furniture and muggy smell. She felt oppressed her as her mother's possessions were kept in strange surroundings and in a very tasteless manner.

The Narrator's Resolution

The narrator decided that she could not stay there anymore. The address was correct but the narrator didn't want to remember it anymore. She felt that the objects were linked to a memory of a time which no longer existed. They had lost their value in the strange surroundings. She comforted herself by thinking that her present house was too small to accommodate all the old stuff. Then, she left the house, leaving all her family's belongings behind.

Word-Meaning

poignant	— arousing sadness	crick	— strain
chink	— narrow opening	reprovingly	— with disapproval
cardigan	— sweater with buttons	beckoned	— called
musty	— stale	stored stuff	— belongings kept in a safe place
bay window of a -	— large window sticking out of the wall house	errand	— work involving going out of the house
jamb	— doorpost	hanukkah	— used in the Jewish festival of lights
antique	— a collectable object, old and often valuable	cumbersome	— unmanageable
table silver made	— cutlery (knives, forks and spoons) of silver	still life	— painting of an arrangement of flowers and/or fruits
lugging	— carrying	pewter	— tin alloy
		jingling	— light metallic sound

Important Themes of the Chapter

Nostalgia The narrator's mother's possessions are a reminder of the narrator's past which is why she finally goes to seek them.

Loss The story deals with the loss of one's mother.

Letting Go and Moving on from the Past The story explores themes of memory, loss and moving on. It highlights the emotional impact of the war on survivors as the daughter searches for her mother's belongings. She finds that the objects, once full of personal and sentimental value, no longer hold the same significance when seen in a different setting. This realisation shows how memories and the past can be painful and how clinging to physical objects may not bring comfort. Ultimately, the daughter decides to leave the items behind and move forward with her life, illustrating the theme of letting go and the difficulty of reconciling with a traumatic past.

NCERT Folder

Reading with Insight (NCERT Page 15)

1. "Have you come back?" said the woman. "I thought that no one had come back." Does this statement give some clue about the story? If yes, what is it?

Ans. Yes, this woman's statement suggests a clue about the story's context. It implies that during a significant period, possibly after a war or a difficult time, many people did not return to their homes or were presumed lost. Mrs. Dorling's surprise that someone has returned indicates that the speaker's visit is unexpected and possibly rare. This clue hints at a historical backdrop of upheaval, loss and displacement, where people faced uncertain fates and families were separated.

It sets the stage for exploring themes of resilience, memory and the impact of historical events on personal lives. The statement suggests that the speaker's return to investigate their past is uncommon, highlighting the enduring effects of a challenging period on individuals and communities.

2. The story is divided into pre-war and post-war times. What hardships do you think the girl underwent during these times?

Ans. The girl in the story likely faced many hardships during the pre- and post-war periods. Before the war, the growing tension and fear of what would come might have disrupted her life.

During the war, she and her family probably experienced displacement, losing their home and being separated from loved ones. They may have faced scarcity of food, danger, and the constant threat of persecution, mainly if they were targeted groups like Jews. The author herself mentions through her recollections that the food they ate during the wars was bad (bread was black in colour) and that they could not go out for the fear of being caught.

After the war, returning to find her old life in ruins would have been emotionally challenging. She had to cope with the loss of family members, friends and her home. Rebuilding her life in a new, unfamiliar place would also have been difficult, filled with the pain of memories and the struggle to move on.

3. Why did the narrator of the story want to forget the address?

Ans. The narrator wanted to forget the address because visiting it brought back painful memories. The house at 46 Marconi Street contained belongings that reminded her of her mother and past. However, seeing these familiar items in a strange and oppressive atmosphere made her feel uncomfortable and sad. The objects, which once had happy associations, now felt out of place and upsetting. By forgetting the address, the narrator aims to let go of these painful memories and move on with her life. Forgetting the address symbolised her desire to leave behind the emotional burden of the past and find peace in the present.

4. 'The Address' is a story of human predicament that follows war. Comment.

Ans. Marga Minco's short story 'The Address' describes the human predicament that follows war. It had caused a big change in the lives of the people of Holland as they lost their lives and homes. The war caused loss, displacement and a profound change in the lives of people.

When the narrator visits Mrs. Dorling's house to claim the articles with which her mother's precious memories were associated, Mrs. Dorling was surprised to see her and even pretended not to recognise her. Later, the narrator returns to find her mother's belongings, which were taken for safekeeping during the war. However, these items now evoke painful memories instead of comfort. The war caused loss, displacement and a profound change in people's lives. The narrator's visit to Mrs. Dorling's house shows how even familiar objects can become sources of distress when associated with traumatic events. The story highlights how war affects physical lives, emotional well-being, relationships, and memories. It portrays the challenge of moving forward while dealing with the heavy burden of the past, showing the long-lasting impact of war on individuals.

Exam Pattern Questions

Extract Based Questions

Read the extracts given below and answer the questions that follow.

1. I was home for a few days and it struck me immediately that something or other about the rooms had changed. I missed various things. My mother was surprised I should have noticed so quickly. Then she told me about Mrs. Dorling. I had never heard of her but apparently she was an old acquaintance of my mother, whom she hadn't seen for years.

She had suddenly turned up and renewed their contact. Since, then she had come regularly.

(i) Which of the following aspects was noticed by the narrator?

(a) Her mother was surprised
(b) Various things were missing
(c) Room has changed with different items
(d) Didn't witness anything different

(ii) Why would the narrator's mother have been surprised?

(iii) Complete the sentence appropriately.
Since Mrs. Dorling suddenly turned up and renewed the contact with the narrator's mother, she had come ………………… .

(iv) Who was Mrs. Dorling?

Ans. (i) (b) Various things were missing

(ii) The narrator's mother would have been surprised because her daughter quickly noticed the changes in the house.

(iii) regularly

(iv) Mrs. Dorling was an old acquaintance of the narrator's mother whom she hadn't seen for many years.

2. And one day I noticed I was curious about all the possessions that must still be at that address. I wanted to see them, touch, remember.
After my first visit in vain to Mrs. Dorling's house I decided to try a second time. Now a girl of about fifteen opened the door to me. I asked if her mother was at home.

(i) Here, which possessions are discussed by the author?

(a) Those things which are earned by the author
(b) Things taken away by Mrs. Dorling

(c) Things which were important to her mother
(d) Things which were stolen from the author

(ii) Why did the author feel curious about the possessions?

(iii) Complete the sentence appropriately.

When the narrator visited Mrs. Dorling's house the second time, the door was opened by ....

(iv) Why is the first meeting described by the author as 'in vain'?

Ans. (i) (b) Things taken away by Mrs. Dorling

(ii) The author felt curious about the possessions as they belonged to her mother and she wanted to remember the past through them.

(iii) Mrs. Dorling's daughter

(iv) The first meeting is described by the author as 'in vain' because Mrs. Dorling refused to recognise and help her.

3. I looked up. The girl put cups ready on the tea-table. She had a broad back. Just like her mother. She poured tea from a white pot. All it had was a gold border on the lid. I remembered. She opened a box and took some spoons out.

'That's a nice box.' I heard my own voice. It was a strange voice. As though each sound was different in this room.

'Oh you know about them?' She had turned round and brought me my tea. She laughed. 'My mother says it is antique. We've got lots more.' She pointed round the room. 'See for yourself.'

(i) What similarity did the author notice about the daughter of Mrs. Dorling?

(a) Voice like her mother
(b) Attitude like her mother
(c) Broad back like her mother
(d) Walking style like her mother

(ii) Why was it a 'strange voice'?

(iii) Complete the following suitably.

The narrator said, 'that's a nice box' because ....

(iv) What is the significance of the given lines?

Ans. (i) (c) Broad back like her mother

(ii) It was a 'strange voice' because the author couldn't recognise her feelings.

(iii) the author had recognised it

(iv) The significance of the given lines is that the author realises the meaninglessness of things.

Short Answer Type Questions

1. Describe the events of the narrator's first visit.

Ans. After the war, the narrator visited Mrs. Dorling for the first time at Number 46, Marconi Street. However, Mrs. Dorling denied recognising her and showed no intention of returning the belongings of the narrator's family. Mrs. Dorling did not even talk to her.

2. Explain how the narrator became sure of the address.

Ans. The narrator realised that she had come to the right address when she noticed that Mrs. Dorling was wearing her mother's green knitted cardigan. Its wooden buttons had gone pale from washing.

3. How does the woman at the door react when the protagonist identifies herself?

Ans. The woman at the door reacts with suspicion and wariness when the protagonist identifies herself. She claims not to recognise the protagonist, speaks evasively, and tries to avoid any conversation. Ultimately, she closes the door on the protagonist, indicating a reluctance to engage or acknowledge her identity.

4. What specific item of clothing confirms to the protagonist that she is at the right house?

Ans. The green knitted cardigan the woman is wearing confirms to the protagonist that she is at the right house. The cardigan, with its pale wooden buttons from frequent washing, had belonged to the protagonist's mother, indicating that the woman was Mrs. Dorling.

5. The narrator noticed a few changes at her house when she visited during the first half of the war. Explain.

Ans. During the first half of the war when the narrator was home for a few days, it struck her that something had changed about the rooms. She missed various things like the table cloth, silver, cutlery, the antique plates that hung in the dining room, some large vases, etc.

6. Give the description of Mrs. Dorling as per the narrator's mother.

Ans. The narrator's mother told her that Mrs. Dorling was an old acquaintance. They had not seen each other for many years but now she had renewed the relationship and was a frequent visitor at her mother's place.

7. Mrs. Dorling gave a justified explanation for taking the belongings of Mrs. S. Do you agree? If not, what could be the real reason?

Ans. No, I don't agree that Mrs. Dorling gave a justified explanation for taking the belongings of Mrs. S.

The real reason for Mrs. Dorling's decision to take Mrs. S. stuff can be the fact that she was a selfish and greedy lady. She found the opportunity to get her hands on Mrs. S. expensive collection. Her sudden desire to renew the friendship in the background of war and Mrs. S. vulnerability indicates this. Perhaps, she thought that Mrs. S. family would not survive the war and then, she could own the things.

8. Did the narrator feel convinced that Mrs. Dorling was the right person to keep all their valuables in safe custody?

Ans. No, the narrator was not convinced by Mrs. Dorling's behaviour and activity. The latter appeared to her to be more keen on taking away all their valuables. The narrator did not like Mrs. Dorling's sudden and excessive interest in her mother's precious possessions. The questions put by the narrator to her mother indicate this.

9. The narrator's mother allowed for her possessions to be taken away. Analyse. **Competency Based**

Ans. The narrator's family was Jewish. At the time of occupation by the Nazis during the war, her mother was afraid that either they may have to leave suddenly or be imprisoned. In either case, their most valuable possessions would be lost. So, her mother was happy when Mrs. Dorling suggested that she would safely keep their possessions with her until after the war.

Naturally, the mother assumed that when she returned after the war, she could take back her possessions.

10. Explain why the narrator didn't pay much attention to things on the way.

Ans. When Mrs. Dorling denied entry or talking to the narrator, she returned to the station without having paid much attention to things on the way. Though she passed through all places familiar to her, she did not want to upset herself with the sight of the streets and houses full of memories of earlier times. She fears being overwhelmed by memories.

11. Write a short note on Mrs. S.

Ans. Mrs. S. appears to be a kind-hearted, trustful and generous lady. She was fond of collecting valuables. She trusts Mrs. Dorling and allows her to take away her precious belongings till the war got over. She does not approve of her daughter's suspicious nature.

12. Explain why the narrator visited Mrs. Dorling's house the second time.

Ans. The narrator grew impatient and her curiosity started troubling her. She wanted to see all those belongings that were once possessed by her mother. She wanted to touch them, to feel them and to remember them so she decided to visit Mrs. Dorling's house again.

13. Assess the narrator's feelings of horror after entering the house.

Ans. The narrator is horrified on entering Mrs. Dorling's house. This is so because when the protagonist sees the familiar objects in the house, she feels a mix of recognition and oppression. Her mother's prized possessions are placed in a strange and tasteless setting. The strange atmosphere, tasteless arrangement, and ugly furniture make the objects lose their sentimental value leaving the protagonist distressed and uneasy about seeing them in this unfamiliar setting.

14. "You only notice when something is missing......" What human trait has been brought out by the narrator through these lines?

Ans. The narrator was absolutely correct when she said that we tend to notice things only when they are missing. It is human nature to take things for granted. We seldom ponder over the 'things' lying around us because they are there. Their true worth is realised only when we don't find them in front of our eyes.

15. How does Marga Minco use symbolism, such as the Hanukkah candle holder and the antique silver, to deepen the story's exploration of loss and survival? **Competency Based**

Ans. Marga Minco uses symbolism, such as the Hanukkah candle holder and the antique silver, to deepen the story's exploration of loss and survival. The iron Hanukkah candle holder in Mrs. Dorling's house symbolises continuity and tradition amidst upheaval. It represents a cultural and religious artefact that survives despite wartime hardships, linking the protagonist to her Jewish identity and heritage. Similarly, the antique silver symbolises wealth and heritage, cherished possessions that embody the family's history and culture.

Through these symbols, Minco poignantly portrays how material objects can transcend their physical form as saddening reminders of what was lost and what endures in the face of overwhelming adversity.

16. How does the protagonist's decision to forget the address symbolise her emotional journey in the story? **Competency Based**

Ans. The protagonist's decision to forget the address symbolises her emotional journey of closure and moving forward. It signifies her acceptance that revisiting the past, represented by the objects and memories associated with the address, only brings pain and disconnect. Letting go symbolises her resolve to embrace a new, unburdened future.

17. Describe the significance of the burn mark on the tablecloth to the protagonist.

Ans. The burn mark on the tablecloth holds significance for the protagonist as a tangible reminder of the ordinary yet cherished moments from her past. It represents imperfection and resilience, symbolising how life and memory endure despite hardship and loss, grounding her in a personal history she is reluctant to let go of.

18. What do the events in the story indicate about the challenges of remembering and establishing one's identity after a war?

Ans. The story suggests that memory and identity become complex and intertwined in the aftermath of war. Memories are fragmented and sometimes painful, yet they anchor individuals to their past. Identity is shaped by what is remembered and lost, reflecting the enduring struggle to reconcile personal history with the upheaval of war.

Long Answer Type Questions

1. Betrayal of trust is an evil which may afflict people of any time or any age. Discuss this statement in the context of the chapter 'The Address'.

Ans. Yes, betrayal of trust is an evil which may afflict people of any time or any age. In this materialistic world, 'trustworthiness' has become a rare quality, as everyone wants to achieve maximum material gain. People do not mind cheating others for their own personal greed.

In the present story, Mrs. Dorling is one such character. She is greedy and she could make out how insecure Mrs. S. felt about her personal valuables.

Mrs. Dorling is cunning enough to take advantage of the situation by offering to keep Mrs. S. valuables in her safe custody, though she surely knew that she would never return these possessions. When daughter of Mrs. S (the narrator) comes to Mrs. Dorling's house to have a look at her family's possessions, Mrs. Dorling first denies having recognised her. She refuses to even talk to the girl. This behaviour is really shameful.

2. Imagine you are Mrs. Dorling. You are filled with guilt at what you have done. You are uncomfortable with what had happened. Write a letter to your friend describing your feelings and your desire to make amends.

Ans. Number 46
Marconi Street
Amsterdam

20th September, 1945

Dear Mrs. Jansen

How are you? You must be surprised to get this letter from me as we had just met a week before. Actually, there is something that I wanted to tell you then but couldn't gather the courage to do so. I hope this letter can help me speak my heart out.

Do you remember how you always inquired about the wonderful stuff at my house and I always said that it belongs to me? The truth is, it doesn't. They are the belongings of my deceased friend. Last month, her daughter came to me asking for her stuff back. I refused to even recognise her. What came over me, I don't know!

I feel like a thief now. I have acted selfishly and also treated the child with rudeness. Her mother had made me the guardian of her possessions. I have cheated the departed soul and betrayed her trust.

I have decided to make amends. I am going to return all the stuff to her daughter. I feel very guilty and apologetic. Please help me out. Tell me what more I can do to undo the bad things that I have done.

Yours lovingly
Mrs. Dorling

3. The story 'The Address' is an autobiographical note at one level, while at another it portrays how futile war is. Write an article describing your views about war and whether you believe it is fruitful in 120-150 words.

You may begin like this ....

Undoubtedly, when war comes, it also brings .....

Ans. **The Futility of War**

by XYZ

Undoubtedly, when war comes, it also brings suffering and disasters with it. It takes away innumerable lives, leaving people with nothing in their hands. It changes the lives of the people drastically by affecting their fortunes forever.

After the war is over, everything becomes normal again and people sleep in their beds unthreatened. However, the wounds given by the war do not heal easily or quickly. The crude and cunning nature of human behaviour is brought out in war.

People have to leave their homes, the place where they spend all their cherished moments. They lose many loved ones. Sometimes their life is completely destroyed.

Hence, how can something that causes so much of damage, not only of life and property but also of human emotions and bonds, be called fruitful? War is synonymous with destruction. We must always aim towards establishing peace. There is nothing in this world that cannot be done with peace. Non-violence is the way to form stronger relationships with others.

4. How does the motif of belongings and memory play a pivotal role in the protagonist's journey of self-discovery and closure? Competency Based

Ans. In 'The Address' by Marga Minco, belongings symbolise the protagonist's connection to her past and healing journey. When she visits Mrs. Dorling's house, she confronts objects that belonged to her mother, triggering memories and emotions long buried since the war. These belongings serve as tangible links to her lost family and former life, yet they also represent a painful reminder of the Holocaust's impact.

Ultimately, the protagonist's decision to leave these items behind signifies her resolve to move forward and find closure. Through this exploration of belongings, Minco portrays how memory intertwines with personal history, allowing the protagonist to reconcile her past and forge a path toward emotional healing and self-discovery.

5. Compare and contrast the protagonist's initial reluctance to visit Mrs. Dorling's home with her eventual decision to return. What drives this transformation?

Ans. Initially, the protagonist in 'The Address' shows reluctance to visit Mrs. Dorling's home, fearing the emotional weight of confronting her mother's belongings and the memories they hold from before the Holocaust. The reluctance stems from a mix of fear, grief and the overwhelming nature of revisiting the past.

However, her curiosity and desire to reconnect with her history drives a transformation over time. She returns to Mrs. Dorling's home, motivated to understand and reconcile with her past. This transformation is fuelled by a gradual acceptance of her history and a realisation that facing these memories is essential for her emotional healing and closure. Ultimately, her return signifies a shift from avoidance to acknowledgement, marking a pivotal moment in her journey towards self-discovery and coming to terms with her familial legacy.

SELF ASSESSMENT TEST

Extract Based Questions

Read the extract given below and answer the questions that follow.

1. At the corner of the road I looked up at the name-plate. Marconi Street, it said. I had been at Number 46. The address was correct. But now I didn't want to remember it any more. I wouldn't go back there because the objects that are linked in your memory with the familiar life of former times instantly lose their value when, severed from them, you see them again in strange surroundings.

(i) The name-plate of Marconi Street was put up at

(a) the edge of the road (b) the front of the road

(c) the corner of the road (d) the far-end of the road

(ii) Why did the author not want to remember the address?

(iii) Complete the sentence appropriately.

The address Number 46, Marconi Street belonged to ....

(iv) Why did the author say that she wouldn't go back to that address again?

Short Answer Type Questions

1. Do you think Mrs. Dorling really wanted to help the family at the time of war? Justify your stance.

2. Describe the narrator and her emotional stance in the story.

3. Who has given the address to the narrator and why?

4. Mrs. Dorling is a typical example of betrayal. Discuss.

5. What does the protagonist notice about the tea table during her second visit to Mrs. Dorling's house?

Long Answer Type Questions

1. What is the significance of the title 'The Address'?

2. Trust and honesty are rare to find. Discuss this statement in the context of the chapter 'The Address'.

3. How does the protagonists' decision to leave Mrs. Dorling's home without taking any of her mother's belonging symbolise her emotional resolution in the story?

03

About the Author

John Boynton Priestley OM (1894 -1984) was an English novelist, playwright, screenwriter, broadcaster and social commentator.

Born in 1894 into a working-class family, his experiences profoundly shaped his worldview and literary pursuits. Priestley's works challenge societal norms and address pressing social issues of his time. Many of his plays, in particular, feature skilful depictions of ordinary people in domestic settings. His unique blend of dramatic storytelling and philosophical exploration garnered significant attention, firmly establishing him as a significant literary figure in the 20th century.

YOUR STUDY GOALS

- Chapter Sketch
- About the Characters
- Summary of the Chapter

YOUR PRACTICE GOAL

- NCERT Folder
- Extract Based Questions
- Short Answer Type Questions
- Long Answer Type Questions

Mother's Day

Chapter Sketch

The play 'Mother's Day' revolves around the challenges and dynamics within a family, mainly focusing on the role of mothers in the 1950s. The play revolves around Mrs. Pearson, a hardworking and unappreciated mother, who uses magic to swap personalities with her bold neighbour, Mrs. Fitzgerald. The transformation shocks her family—husband George, daughter Doris, and son Cyril—who are used to her simple nature. Mrs. Pearson, now assertive and confident, demands respect and points out their neglectful behaviour. The family initially reacts with surprise and discomfort but gradually realises their mistakes. By the end of the play, they promise to be more considerate and helpful. Mrs. Pearson and Mrs. Fitzgerald then revert to their original selves.

About the Characters

Mrs. Annie Pearson She is a pleasant but nervous woman whose excessive love and care has spoilt her two children and husband.

Mrs. Fitzgerald She is Mrs. Annie Pearson's neighbour. She is quite strong-willed, knows magic and helps Mrs. Annie Pearson to reform the spoilt members of Mrs. Annie Pearson's family.

Doris Pearson She is Mrs. Annie Pearson's daughter aged around twenty years. She fails to understand her mother's struggle and doesn't help her in household work.

Cyril Pearson He is Mrs. Annie Pearson's son who is equally demanding and never sympathises with his mother.

Mr. George Pearson He is Mrs. Annie Pearson's proud husband who is not as respected in society as expected. He dominates his wife but is ridiculed in the club where he is a member.

Summary of the Chapter

Mrs. Annie Pearson and Mrs. Fitzgerald

Mrs. Annie Pearson and Mrs. Fitzgerald are next door neighbours. Apart from this, there is no similarity between them. Annie is a pleasant and nervous looking woman in her forties. Mrs. Fitzgerald is older and heavier with a strong personality. Annie has a soft voice whereas Mrs. Fitzgerald has a deep, throaty voice.

Mrs. Fitzgerald is a fortune-teller, who has learnt this art from the East. She is reading Annie's fortune and advises Annie to be strict with her family. She knows the Annie is not treated well by her family and has been reduced to the status of an unpaid domestic servant.

The Plan

One day, she suggests that they should temporarily exchange their personalities by using a magic spell to teach the Pearsons a lesson. Then, she takes Annie's hand and speaks some magic words. A transformation takes place and the personality of Mrs. Fitzgerald shifts into the body of Annie and vice-versa.

Annie is scared but Mrs. Fitzgerald assures her that the change is reversible. Mrs. Fitzgerald, now in the body of Annie, stays at Annie's house and sends Annie (in Mrs. Fitzgerald's body) to her house where she can relax.

Doris Gets a Shock

Doris, Annie Pearson's daughter, enters the house. She is shocked on seeing her mother smoking and playing cards alone. When she asks about her yellow dress, Annie does not respond. Later, when she asks for tea, Annie answers rudely tells her to iron her dress herself and make tea if she wants to.

This makes Doris angry. However, Annie scolds her and even makes fun of Doris' boyfriend, Charlie Spence, for having projecting teeth and being stupid. She tells Doris that she would have found somebody better. As a result, Doris leaves the room crying.

Cyril Also Gets a Shock

Cyril, Annie's son, enters the house and asks for tea in a demanding and angry manner. Annie tells him that she has not bothered to get the tea ready. Cyril then enquires about her health, his clothes and then, asks her to make to immediately. When Annie replies not to everything he gets agitated, he asks his mother what will happen if they all talked like she was talking that day. Annie replies that all three of them always talked to her like that, so there is nothing wrong with her talking in the same tone. She says that if he does not want to do anything at home, he doesn't have to. She adds that she has become a member of the Union so that she gets what she deserves.

Agrument Between Doris and Annie

When Doris appears on the scene wearing a shoulder wrap and Annie makes sarcastic remarks, an argument starts between them. Doris blames Annie for making her cry and ruining her looks. When Annie enquires if any strong beer was left, both Doris and Cyril are filled with horror and shock at their mother's behaviour. Both wonder what has happened to their mother. Doris thinks that she got hit on her head by something.

Then, both the siblings start giggling at the thought of what will happen if their mother keeps behaving in this weird manner in front of their father.

Annie's Remarks about her Family

Annie remarks that it was high time that they grew up. She tells them that it is actually her children and her husband's behaviour that bothered her the most. They always came, asked for something and went without bothering to go out or how she and went without bothering to know whether she wanted to go out or how she was feeling. She always does her best to keep everybody happy but all three of them were not bothered about her.

Annie also remarks that while the three of them do a job of eight hours a day with two days off at the weekend, she goes on working seven days round the clock. She warns them that from now on weekends, she will also take off. She adds that she would do some work on Saturday and Sunday only when she is requested for it and thanked for whatever she does. Further, she might go out for weekends also as she was fed up of staying in the house for years as none of them has ever bothered to take her out.

Mr. George Pearson's Reaction

Mr. George Pearson now enters the house. He is about 50 years old and considers himself as a very important person. He gets annoyed at his wife, who is sipping beer when he enters. He tells her that he does not want any tea as he has to go to the club for supper. When Annie tells him that she has not prepared any tea, George gets annoyed. However, Annie rebukes him, telling him that he is not respected in the club where he keeps going every day. She tells him that people at the bar in the club call him 'Pompy-ompy Pearson' due to his self-important behaviour. George cannot believe what Annie says and confirms the truth from his son, Cyril. Annie tells her son that sometimes it does people good to have their feelings hurt.

The Real Mrs. Annie Pearson

Just then there is a knock and Cyril reports that Mrs. Fitzgerald is at the door. Annie tells him to let her come in. Mrs. Fitzgerald (actually Mrs. Annie Pearson) enters and finds Doris in tears.

Her presence does not stop Annie (the real Mrs. Fitzgerald) from scolding Dorix, Cyril and George. When Mr. George Pearson shouts at his wife, she threatens to slap his big, fat silly face.

The Original Personalities

The real Mrs. Annie Pearson (now Mrs. Fitzgerald) gets really disturbed and wants everyone to leave as she wants to talk in private with Annie (the real Mrs. Fitzgerald). She tells Mrs. Fitzgerald that she wants to switch to their real personalities. Soon, they gain their original personalities.

Mrs. Fitzgerald now advises Annie not to be soft on her family and to remain firm. She further warns her not to give any apology or explanation, otherwise they will again start treating her indifferently. Annie replies that she will be able to manage her husband and children now.

The Changed Situation

Now, when Annie smiles, her family members feel very relaxed. As they had cancelled going out, Annie feels that they all as a family should play a game of rummy. She asks her children to prepare supper for the family and also wants to have a talk with George. All three of them readily agree. The play ends on a happy note where the children and husband are willing to do whatever she suggests.

Word-Meaning

suburb — outlying area of a city
muslin-covered — covered with a muslin curtain
settee — sofa
sinister — strong
flurried — nervous and confused due to overwork
Cockney — style of speaking of people living in the East end of London
Irish — style of speaking of people living in Ireland
out East — in the British colonies in Asia
Lieutenant Quartermaster — non-commissioned officer in British Army
put your foot down — be very strict
treating 'em like dirt — showing lack of respect
dubiously — in an unsure manner
have it out — settle it finally
flustered — agitated
gimme — give me
muttering — speaking in a low voice
go lax — looking like they are dead
puffing — smoking
complacently — feeling happy and satisfied
patience — a card game played by a single person
taken anything in — understood what is going on
square meal — full and satisfying meal
the Clarendon — name of a local restaurant
indignantly — with annoyance
be seen dead — like to be seen
buck teeth — upper set of teeth sticking out
masculine counterpart — brother
get cracking — work quickly
put my things out — lay out my clothes
staggered — shocked
laconic and sinister — briefly and meaningfully
wear that face — look so bad
union — association of employees
bar — stop
stout — strong beer
clot — idiot
barmy — insane
fathead — idiot
concussion — serious injury to her head
far-fetched — unlikely
guffaw — laugh loudly
do with — appreciate
a bit thick — unreasonable
airily — carelessly
bulge — stick out
standing jokes — permanent amusements
greyhound races — races run by tall, slender dogs

dirt tracks	— racing courses for motorcycles	eating out of your hand	— completely under your control
ice shows	— entertainment shows performed by ice skaters	crying her eyes out	— crying uncontrollably
old bag	— unpleasant elderly woman	at sixes and sevens	— in total confusion
smacking	— bringing together with force so they make a sound	tiddly	— slightly drunk
piecan	— stupid person	ticking her off	— reprimanding her
glowering	— angry	cos'	— because
putting 'em in their places	— making them behave properly	rummy	— a card game
doing 'em all a world of good	— helping them to learn how to behave properly	cluster round	— surround

Important Themes of the Chapter

Value of the Mother The play revolves around the challenges and dynamics within a family, mainly focusing on the role of mothers. The play satirically explores how societal expectations and traditional gender roles influence family relationships. It critiques the undervaluation of mothers and their often-overlooked contributions to the household.

Familial Conflicts The play expresses that even though everything may look calm and normal on the surface, every family is dealing with some sort of conflict.

Standing up for Oneself The play advocates the importance of standing up and fighting for one's respect and recognition.

Generational Differences and the Impact of External Influences The play also explores generational differences and the impact of external influences, such as neighbours, on family dynamics. 'Mother's Day' offers a humorous yet critical commentary on family life and the evolving roles of women in society during the mid-20th century.

NCERT Folder

Reading with Insight (NCERT Page 36-37)

1. This play, written in the 1950s, is a humorous and satirical depiction of the status of the mother in the family.

(i) What are the issues it raises?

(ii) Do you think it caricatures these issues or do you think that the problems it raises are genuine? How does the play resolve the issues? Do you agree with the resolution?

Ans. (i) The main issue that the play raises is that the lady of the house is just like an axis around which everything revolves. However, she is never given respect especially if she is simple and timid. The play highlights the family's lack of appreciation for mothers, the unequal distribution of household responsibilities and the emotional neglect they face. It critiques the patriarchal attitude in which mothers are taken for granted and their efforts are unacknowledged.

(ii) While the play uses humour and exaggeration, the issues raised are genuine. The characters' exaggerated behaviours emphasise real societal problems, such as the undervaluation of a mother's role and the complacency of other family members.

The play resolves the issues through a role reversal by the means of magic. Mrs. Pearson and Mrs. Fitzgerald interchange roles. This shift prompts the family to realise their neglect and change their attitudes. The resolution, though simplistic, effectively highlights the need for mutual respect and shared responsibilities in families.

I agree with the resolution as it conveys an important message about valuing and respecting every family member's contributions.

2. If you were to write about these issues today, what are some of the incidents, examples and problems that you would think of as relevant?

Ans. If I was to write about these issues today, I would include incidents like a mother balancing work and household duties without any help. For example, many Indian mothers manage careers and still handle all the household chores. I would mention problems like not getting appreciation from the family members and their takes for granted attitude. Another example could be children and spouses expecting mothers to serve them without recognising their needs or desires. Relevant issues today also include the emotional burden on mothers who rarely get time for themselves. I highlight the importance of sharing responsibilities at home and acknowledging the mother's hard work to create a happier and more balanced family life.

3. Is drama a good medium for conveying a social message?

Ans. Yes, drama is a suitable medium for conveying a social message. Through drama, important issues can be presented in a way that is engaging and relatable. Characters and their stories can reflect real-life situations, making it easier for the audience to connect with the message. Drama can evoke emotions and provoke thought, encouraging people to think deeply about social issues. Besides, humour and satire in drama can highlight societal problems, making serious topics more approachable. Watching a play allows people to see different perspectives and understand the impact of certain behaviours and attitudes. This can lead to greater awareness and inspire change in society. Drama effectively combines entertainment with education, making it a powerful tool for social commentary.

4. Read the play out in parts. Enact the play on a suitable occasion.

Ans. Do it yourself.

5. Discuss in groups plays or films with a strong message of social reform that you have watched.

Ans. In our group discussion, we discussed plays and films focusing on social reform of women's status in society. One famous film is 'Thappad' which deals with domestic violence and the importance of self-respect. It shows a woman's journey to stand up against abuse, even when it comes from a loved one. Another film we discussed is 'Dangal', which highlights the struggles and achievements of female wrestlers in a male-dominated sport. These works are influential because they reflect real issues and inspire viewers to consider gender equality and women's rights. They show that change is possible and encourage society to support women's empowerment.

Exam Pattern Questions

Extract Based Questions

Read the extracts given below and answer the questions that follow.

1. MRS. PEARSON: [dubiously] I—keep dropping a hint...

MRS. FITZGERALD: Hint? It's more than hints your family needs, Mrs. Pearson.

Mrs. PEARSON: [dubiously] I suppose it is. But I do hate any unpleasantness. And it's so hard to know where to start. I keep making up my mind to have it out with them but somehow I don't know how to begin. [She glances at her watch or at a clock] Oh — good gracious! Look at the time. Nothing ready and they'll be home any minute and probably all in a hurry to go out again.

(i) In the given extract, whom does 'them' refer to?

(ii) Select the option that describes Mrs. Pearson in the extract.

(a) Dominating (b) Submissive
(c) Short-tempered (d) Illogical

(iii) Why was Mrs. Pearson so worried?

(iv) In what endeavour does Mrs. Fitzgerald help Mrs. Pearson?

Ans. (i) 'Them' in the given extract refers to the family of Mrs. Pearson, her husband, her daughter and her son.

(ii) (b) Submissive

(iii) Mrs. Pearson was so worried because her family would be home soon and she hadn't cooked anything for them.

(iv) Mrs. Fitzgerald helps Mrs. Pearson in making her family treat her well.

2. Mrs. FITZGERALD: How do you know? Ever tried it?

Mrs. PEARSON: No, of course not...
Mrs. FITZGERALD: [coolly] I have. Not for some time but it still ought to work. Won't last long, but long enough for what we want to do. Learnt it out East, of course, where they're up to all these tricks. [She holds her hand out across the table, keeping the cigarette in her mouth] Gimme your hands, dear.

(i) How do Mrs. Fitzgerald and Mrs. Pearson know each other?

(ii) Complete the following suitably.

The question–'How do you know?' refers to ....

(iii) What does the above extract tell us about Mrs. Fitzgerald?

(a) She hates Mr. Pearson.

(b) She is wild and bold.

(c) She wants Mrs. Pearson to become bold.

(d) She is great friend.

(iv) How does Mrs. Fitzgerald plan to help Mrs. Pearson enter the world of supernatural?

Ans. (i) Mrs. Pearson and Mrs. Fitzgerald know each other as they are neighbours.

(ii) changing bodies

(iii) (b) She is wild and bold.

(iv) Mrs. Fitzgerald plans to help Mrs. Pearson by swapping personalities with her.

3. CYRIL: [moving to the table; annoyed] Why not?

MRS. PEARSON: [coolly] I couldn't bother.

CYRIL: Feeling off-colour or something?

MRS. PEARSON: Never felt better in my life.

CYRIL: [aggressively] What's the idea then?

MRS. PEARSON: Just a change.

CYRIL: [briskly] Well, snap out of it, Ma—and get cracking. Haven't too much time.

(i) It can be said about Cyril from the given lines that ....

(ii) According to Mrs. Pearson, where had Cyril been wasting his time and money?

(iii) Why does Cyril act aggressively?

(a) Because his mother insulted him.

(b) Because his mother had not made tea for him.

(c) Because he was getting late.

(d) Because his mother was behaving strangely.

(iv) What is the 'change' as referred to in the extract?

Ans. (i) he takes his mother for granted

(ii) According to Mrs. Pearson, Cyril had been wasting his time and money in races and ice shows.

(iii) (b) Because his mother had not made tea for him

(iv) The 'change' referred is a change in the way Mrs. Pearson is treated by the family.

Short Answer Type Questions

1. Explain how Mrs. Fitzgerald utilised her husband's posting in the East.

Ans. Mrs. Fitzgerald's husband was posted in the East (meaning the British colonies in Asia) for twelve years. She utilised her time there by learning fortune-telling and how to use magic spells to exchange personalities. She used this knowledge in temporarily exchanging her strong personality with the weak personality of Mrs. Annie Pearson to resolve her problem with her family.

2. Assess the advice given by Mrs. Fitzgerald to Annie.

Ans. The advice given by Mrs. Fitzgerald to Annie to bring a change in her household is to teach her family how that she was a important figure in the household. They cannot treat her like a servant. In her advice, Mrs Fitzgerald wants Annie to become bold and make sure that her family respects her.

3. Annie was responsible for her own fate. Explain.

Competency Based

Ans. It is true to say that to a certain level, Annie was herself responsible for her own fate. She was soft, loving and caring. Unfortunately, her children and husband never acknowledged her role and failed to understand her worth. She wanted to correct them but could not do so due to the fear of hurting their feelings.

4. Explain the process of Mrs. Annie Pearson and Mrs. Fitzgerald exchanging their personalities.

Ans. The process wherein Mrs. Annie Pearson and Mrs. Fitzgerald exchange their personalities is quite simple. Mrs. Fitzgerald knew magic and to complete the change she first held Annie's hand. Then, she spoke the magic words to interchange their personalities. The moment this happened, her personality entered into Annie and *vice-versa*.

5. Identify the first person to face Annie's ire.

Ans. Doris, Annie's daughter, is the first one to face her ire. She comes home and asks about her yellow dress. Mrs. Fitzgerald, in the body of Annie, doesn't even pay attention to her. Doris asks her about tea and Mrs. Fitzgerald replies that she should make it herself. She even ridicules her boyfriend and Doris starts crying at her unusual behaviour.

6. Explain why Mrs. Annie Pearson (with Mrs. Fitzgerald's personality) did not like Doris going out with Charlie Spence.

Ans. Mrs. Annie Pearson (with Mrs. Fitzgerald's personality) did not like Doris going out with Charlie Spence. According to her, Charlie Spence did not look smart with his teeth projecting from his mouth and was also not an intelligent boy, whereas Doris looked pretty and was also intelligent.

Thus, Charlie Spence was not the right kind of man with whom Doris should go out. Annie's opinion was that Doris should give up a man like Charlie Spence and look for another decent man to go out with.

7. What is Cyril's reaction to Mrs. Pearson's changed attitude, and what does this indicate about their relationship?

Ans. Cyril is surprised and upset by Mrs. Pearson's changed demeanour. He argues with her, feeling hurt and confused. This indicates that he is not used to her being assertive and strict, highlighting their previous relationship, where he likely took her for granted.

8. Explain how does Mrs. Annie Pearson discipline her children when she finds them giggling.

Ans. When Mrs. Annie Pearson found her children giggling, she asked them in a very stern tone not to behave like children but to behave according to their age. She also told them to explain to her what was making them laugh, although she realised that her changed behaviour was the reason.

9. Doris and Cyril's behaviour with their mother was extremely rude and unheard of. Do you agree? Competency Based

Ans. Yes, Doris and Cyril were extremely rude to their mother. We generally don't see children speaking to their mother in such a rude manner. Their words "Is tea ready?" and "You are going to iron it for me" are rude and demanding. This shows that the children were extremely selfish, badly behaved and self-centred. They ordered their mother as if she was their servant.

10. Describe Annie's plans for weekends in future as informed to her children.

Ans. Annie informs her children that she would also work for only eight hours a day and take two days off every week on Saturday and Sunday. She said that on these days she would do some work only and that also will depend upon how she was treated and requested to do the work.

11. George was angry that there was no tea even though he didn't want any. What does this reflect about his character and Annie's characters?

Ans. The fact that George was angry that there was no tea for him even though he did not want to drink it shows that he was self-centred and egoistic man. He believed that his wife was below him and should do what he desires. He expects her to be servile and obedient. Hence, when the contrary happens, his ego is hurt and he gets angry.

For Annie, we see her shift from being a submissive, taken-for-granted homemaker to someone who asserts her needs and desires. This change shows she no longer accepts being undervalued and demands respect from her family.

12. How does George react to Doris's emotional state, and what does this reveal about his character?

Ans. George is confused and concerned about Doris' crying but doesn't know how to handle it. His reaction shows that he is used to stability and dislikes change. George's bewilderment and lack of sensitivity reveal that he is somewhat detached and does not understand his family's emotions.

13. What is George's attitude toward Mrs. Pearson drinking stout, and what does this signify about her changing behaviour?

Ans. George reacts with surprise and disapproval when he sees Mrs. Pearson drinking stout during the day, indicating her changing behaviour. This signifies that Mrs. Pearson is asserting her independence and breaking away from traditional norms, which George finds unsettling and unexpected in their household dynamics.

14. How does Mrs. Pearson's revelation about the club's nickname for George impact him? How does it highlight Annie's feelings? Competency Based

Ans. Mrs. Pearson reveals that the club calls George 'Pompy-ompy Pearson,' making him realise they laugh at him. This deeply shocks and hurts George, making him feel embarrassed and humiliated. It shatters his belief that he is respected at the club, significantly affecting his self-esteem. The revelation highlights her frustration that George presents himself differently in social settings compared to how he behaves with his family, revealing a lack of authenticity and respect within their relationship.

15. How does George's attitude shift after learning the truth about his reputation at the club? Competency Based

Ans. George is shocked and hurt after learning the truth about his reputation at the club. He becomes quiet and introspective, realising he is not as respected as he thought. The revelation humbles him, making him more open to listening and changing his behaviour at home.

16. Explain George's astonishment when Mrs. Fitzgerald calls him 'George'. How does Mrs. Annie Pearson (in reality Mrs. Fitzgerald) make fun of him?

Ans. George is surprised when Mrs. Fitzgerald calls him by name because he believed that a neighbour should not call him so informally. He does not know that Mrs. Fitzgerald is actually Annie.

Annie makes fun of him by saying that he is not the Duke of Edinburgh (a royal person) and his real name is George only.

17. Why does Mrs. Pearson insist that George address Mrs. Fitzgerald politely, and what does this reveal about her expectations? Competency Based

Ans. Mrs. Pearson (now with Mrs Fitzgerald's personality) insists that George address Mrs. Fitzgerald politely to teach him good manners and respect. It reveals her expectation for better behaviour and decency within the family. She wants everyone to treat others courteously, highlighting her desire for a more respectful household environment.

18. Give reasons why Mrs. Annie Pearson (in the body of Mrs. Fitzgerald) wants Mrs. Fitzgerald (in the body of Annie) to change back to their real personalities.

Ans. Mrs. Annie Pearson wanted to get back in her own body because she did not like that her husband and her children were suffering. As a simple, sincere, loving and caring person, she could not bear to see her family in pain.

19. Explain how the experience was different for both Mrs. Fitzgerald and Mrs. Annie Pearson after the changing of bodies.

Ans. The experience of both Mrs. Fitzgerald and Mrs. Annie Pearson is different after changing the bodies. While the real Mrs. Fitzgerald enjoyed the experience as she had been able to improve the behaviour of Doris, Cyril and George towards Mrs. Annie Pearson, Annie was unhappy as she saw her family being treated harshly.

20. What final advice does Mrs. Fitzgerald give Mrs. Pearson at the end of the play, and why is it significant?

Ans. Mrs. Fitzgerald advises Mrs. Pearson to keep a firm hand and not go soft on her family. This is significant because it emphasises the need for Mrs. Pearson to maintain her newfound assertiveness to ensure lasting respect and better behaviour from her family.

21. Annie's family exhibited some changes in the end. Describe them.

Ans. After being treated very rudely and roughly by Mrs. Fitzgerald, all the family members responded properly to Mrs. Annie Pearson's smile and decided to stay back and spend time with her. They also responded properly to whatever she says.

22. How does the family react to Mrs. Pearson's newfound assertiveness, and what does this indicate about their previous dynamic?

Ans. The family reacts with surprise and discomfort to Mrs. Pearson's newfound assertiveness. It indicates that previously, they were used to taking her for granted and not respecting her. Her assertiveness forces them to reconsider their behaviour and how they treat her.

23. How does the conversation between Mrs. Pearson and Mrs. Fitzgerald after the family leaves highlight the play's central theme?

Ans. In their conversation after the family leaves, Mrs. Pearson and Mrs. Fitzgerald discuss the need for firmness and consistency in managing family dynamics. This highlights the play's central theme of the challenges within family relationships, the underappreciation of mothers and the importance of asserting authority to maintain harmony and respect among family members.

24. How does Doris's response to Mrs. Pearson's critique of Charlie Spence reflect her relationship with her mother? Competency Based

Ans. Doris's defensive response to Mrs. Pearson's critique of Charlie Spence reflects a strained relationship with her mother. It suggests Doris feels criticised and misunderstood, possibly indicating a pattern of tension and miscommunication between them, where Doris reacts defensively to her mother's judgements or advice.

25. What does Mrs. Pearson's final plan for the evening suggest about her intentions for the family's future interactions?

Ans. Mrs. Pearson's final plan for a family game of rummy and joint supper preparation suggests her intention to foster unity and cooperation within the family. By proposing these activities, she aims to improve their interactions and behaviour towards her and create a more harmonious atmosphere at home, moving away from previous conflicts and misunderstandings.

26. How does the family's apprehension at the end of the scene set the stage for future changes in their behaviour?

Ans. At the end of the scene, the family's apprehension suggests they are uncertain yet hopeful about Mrs. Pearson's new approach. Their reactions hint at anticipating changes in their behaviour, reflecting readiness to adapt to her assertiveness. This sets the stage for potential improvements in their interactions and family dynamics.

Long Answer Type Questions

1. Mother is the axis around whom the family revolves. Mother should always be respected. Elaborate.

Ans. A mother is expected to give her whole life to her family. She is someone who holds a family together because it is up to her to provide the love, care, attention and support needed. She is a good listener, problem solver and guide, while always being available for her children.

Unfortunately, in many situations a mother's love is not reciprocated the way it should have been. Some children do not recognise the importance of what their mother is doing for them. They do not take into account the sacrifices she makes so that her children could be reared in the best possible way.

This is aptly presented in the play 'Mother's day' wherein we see Annie Pearson's family completely disregarding her. They feel that they are superior to her and thus, can command her to do things for them. The play, thus, seeks to resolve such a mistreatment and presents that we need to respect and love our mothers.

2. The play 'Mother's Day' is a humorous and satirical depiction of the status of the mother in the family. Express your relationship with your mother.

Ans. The play, 'Mother's Day' very humorously and interestingly depicts the status of the mother in a family. Through the character of Mrs. Annie Pearson, the play very subtly depicts the plight of women, especially housewives.

Playing of magic, exchange of personalities and the shocked behaviour of Mrs. Annie Pearson's family members are all humorous as well as satirical.

My relations with my mother are very healthy and friendly. We are more like friends and enjoy each other's company. I try to help my mother in the kitchen as well as in other household work. I realise that my mother keeps busy the whole day taking care of everyone's needs. I try to help her as much as I can and really appreciate her selfless efforts without demanding anything. I respect my mother and have much regard for her.

3. Imagine a conversation between Mrs. S. from the chapter 'The Address' (before her death) and Mrs. Annie Pearson about the challenges faced by each of them in their families. Write this exchange in 120-150 words.

You may begin the conversation like this...

Mrs. S. You take great care of your family. You must be really fond of them.

Ans. **Mrs. S.** You take great care of your family. You must be really fond of them.

Mrs. Pearson Yes, I am really fond of them even though they are so thoughtless and selfish.

Mrs. S. Do they take you for granted?

Mrs. Pearson They used to but not anymore. Ever since my neighbour, Mrs. Fitzgerald, took my place and taught them a lesson, everything has been great and they treat me with respect.

Mrs. S. That is great, Mrs. Pearson. Congratulations.

Mrs. Pearson Thank you. Also, I am sorry to hear about the war and the problems you had to face.

Mrs. S. It has all been very challenging. At least, I am hoping we will be able to save all our nicest things once the war is over.

Mrs. Pearson How would that be possible?

Mrs. S. Mrs. Dorling has agreed to keep them for us. She has taken many of the things from our house with her to keep them safe.

Mrs. Pearson I see. Who is Mrs. Dorling? Are you both related?

Mrs. S. No, she is just an old acquaintance of mine. We hadn't seen each other for many years until one day, she suddenly came up and we renewed our contact.

Mrs. Pearson Now I understand. She has been really helpful to you, just as Mrs. Fitzgerald has been to me.

Mrs. S. Yes, I do agree.

4. How does the dynamic between Mrs. Pearson and her children, Doris and Cyril, change by the end of the play?

Ans. After the personality swap, Mrs. Fitzgerald assumes Mrs. Pearson's role and the dynamic between her, Doris, and Cyril undergoes a significant transformation. Initially, Doris and Cyril exhibit disrespectful behaviour towards their mother, Mrs. Pearson (Mrs. Fitzgerald in Mrs. Pearson's body), ignoring her feelings and asserting their desires callously.

However, Mrs. Fitzgerald challenges their behaviour directly with assertive guidance and newfound authority. She reproaches Cyril for his dismissive attitude and Doris for her flippant remarks, demanding respect and compliance with household rules. This shift in dynamic forces Doris and Cyril to acknowledge her authority, creating a more disciplined and respectful environment. Ultimately, Mrs. Fitzgerald's intervention helps restore order and respect within the family, illustrating her effective influence in shaping their behaviour and attitudes towards parental authority.

5. How do Doris and Cyril's responses to Mrs. Pearson's assertiveness differ, and what does this indicate about their characters?

Ans. Doris and Cyril's responses to Mrs. Fitzgerald's assertiveness in 'Mother's Day' reflect their contrasting personalities and attitudes towards authority. Doris initially shows defiance and irritation, evidenced by her sarcastic remarks and reluctance to comply with her mother's directives. She openly challenges Mrs. Fitzgerald's authority, suggesting a rebellious streak and tendency to push boundaries.

In contrast, Cyril responds with sulkiness and embarrassment when confronted by Mrs. Fitzgerald. He exhibits a more subdued resistance, indicating a sensitivity to criticism and a desire to avoid conflict.

These differing responses highlight Doris's bold and defiant nature, whereas Cyril appears more compliant yet internally conflicted. Their reactions suggest underlying tensions within the family dynamics, influenced by Mrs Fitzgerald's newfound assertiveness and the disruption caused by the identity swap.

6. How does Mrs. Fitzgerald react to the changes in the Pearson household, and what does this suggest about her role in the play?

Ans. Mrs. Fitzgerald's reaction to the changes in the Pearson household reveals her satisfaction and sense of accomplishment in shaking up their dynamics. Initially, she initiates the swap to assertiveness, intending to teach them a lesson through tough love. As she witnesses Mrs. Pearson (actually herself) taking charge and the family's responses, Mrs. Fitzgerald shows pride and determination. Her insistence on maintaining firmness highlights her belief that the family needs discipline and structure to function better.

The reaction suggests that Mrs. Fitzgerald sees herself as a catalyst for positive change within the Pearson family. Her role extends beyond mere meddling; she actively seeks to improve their relationships and behaviours.

To summarise, Mrs. Fitzgerald's satisfaction indicates her role as a transformative figure, challenging and reshaping the family dynamics for their betterment.

7. Mrs. Pearson undergoes a significant transformation from a submissive and apologetic figure to polite assertiveness influenced by the personality swap with Mrs. Fitzgerald. Comment.

Ans. It is true to say that Mrs. Pearson undergoes a significant transformation from a submissive and apologetic figure to polite assertiveness influenced by the personality swap with Mrs. Fitzgerald. Mrs. Annie Pearson is a homemaker in her forties. She is a pleasant looking lady with a soft and gentle voice which has a touch of suburban Cockney in her accent. As a person, she is shown to be a kind and gentle lady who is often taken for granted by her family. She is initially portrayed as a downtrodden housewife who does everything for her family without receiving much appreciation. Unassertive and accommodating, she rarely stands up for herself and is all about pleasing her family.

However, through the influence of Mrs. Fitzgerald, she becomes more assertive and demands respect from her family. After the swap, she refuses to be a doormat and stands up for herself.

She begins to assert her own needs and desires. Initially characterised by her self-sacrificing nature and reluctance to confront familial issues, she transitions into a confident leader who challenges the status quo and demands respect. Her transformation is crucial to the play's exploration of self-respect and empowerment and the importance of balanced family relationships. It demonstrates the importance of mutual respect within a family and the need for personal boundaries.

SELF ASSESSMENT TEST

Extract Based Questions

Read the extract given below and answer the questions that follow.

1. MRS. PEARSON: I'll try not to, Mrs. Fitzgerald.

MRS. FITZGERALD: They've not had as long as I'd like to have given 'em — another hour or two's rough treatment might have made it certain...

MRS. PEARSON: I'm sure they'll do better now — though I don't know how I'm going to explain...

(i) When Mrs. Pearson says that she will try not to, what is she talking about?

(ii) Complete the following suitably.

The rough treatment was to

(iii) Select the option that mentions the explanation talked about here.

(a) About not making tea
(b) About insulting everyone
(c) About becoming firm with all
(d) All of the above

(iv) When do Mrs. Pearson and Mrs. Fitzgerald get back to their original selves?

Short Answer Type Questions

1. How does Mrs. Pearson's interaction with Mrs. Fitzgerald differ from her interactions with her family?

2. When Mrs. Annie Pearson did not want Mrs. Fitzgerald to help her change her family's behaviour, how did Mrs. Fitzgerald convince her to agree?

3. What does Mrs. Pearson's criticism of Cyril's activities reveal about her perspective on their family life?

4. How does Mrs. Fitzgerald's role in transforming Mrs. Pearson's behaviour contribute to the play's resolution?

5. Mrs. Fitzgerald advises Mrs. Annie Pearson not to get soft with her family members. Why?

6. What are the issues that the play 'Mother's Day' highlights?

Long Answer Type Questions

1. Do you think Mrs. Fitzgerald played fairly in exchanging her personality with Mrs. Annie Pearson? What lesson did Annie teach to her children and husband?

2. What values do you observe in Annie's character in the beginning of the play and right at the end?

3. What role does Mrs. Fitzgerald play in helping Mrs. Pearson assert herself in her family?

04

About the Author

Archibald Joseph Cronin (19th July, 1896–6th January, 1981), known as A. J. Cronin, was a Scottish physician and novelist who wrote around 5000 words a day. His best-known novel is 'The Citadel (1937)', which is about a Scottish physician who serves in a Welsh mining village before achieving success in London, where he becomes disillusioned about the venality and incompetence of some doctors.

▼ **YOUR STUDY GOALS**

- Chapter Sketch
- About the Characters
- Summary of the Chapter

▼ **YOUR PRACTICE GOAL**

- NCERT Folder
- Extract Based Questions
- Short Answer Type Questions
- Long Answer Type Questions

Birth

Chapter Sketch

Birth, an excerpt from 'The Citadel' by A.J. Cronin, is a story about a young doctor Andrew Manson who is called to assist Joe Morgan's wife, Susan, deliver their first child after twenty years of marriage. The tense scene unfolds late at night in their small, humble home. Andrew is troubled by personal issues but he dedicates himself to the difficult task at hand. When the baby is born lifeless, he faces a heartbreaking dilemma: help the child or save the mother. Acting instinctively, Andrew revives Susan and then tries various methods to revive the baby. After half an hour of intense effort, the baby finally takes its first breath. Exhausted yet triumphant, Andrew feels he has done something significant.

About the Characters

Dr. Andrew Manson He is a young medical graduate working in a small mining town. On the call of Joe Morgan, a miner, Dr. Andrew Manson manages to help in a difficult birth and saves the baby's life with his practical knowledge and efforts.

Joe Morgan He is a miner and Susan's husband. He asks Dr. Andrew Manson to help in his wife's delivery and reposes full faith in the doctor.

Susan Morgan's Mother She is a tall, grey-haired woman aged 70 who is concerned about her daughter.

The Midwife She is pessimistic about the child's survival when he is found to be not breathing when born but dutifully assists Dr. Andrew Manson in his work.

Summary of the Chapter

Joe Morgan was Waiting for Dr. Andrew

Dr. Andrew had recently graduated from medical college. One night, he was returning home when he found Joe Morgan waiting for him. Joe informed the doctor that he was needed at their home as his wife was expecting to deliver a baby. Dr. Andrew asked him to wait for a few minutes. He got his medical bag and set out for Joe Morgan's house.

The Demanding Case

Joe Morgan stopped outside the house and requested Dr. Andrew to go inside alone. The doctor reached a small, clean but scantily furnished room and found, Susan Morgan's mother and an elderly midwife beside the patient.

Dr. Andrew sensed that there would be some waiting time and still decided to stay. An hour later, he went to check the patient and came down.

Dr. Andrew's Thoughts

Dr. Andrew was deep in his thoughts about his own personal life. He was worried about his love life with Christine. He wanted to marry her but remembered how unhappy a man becomes in case of betrayal by wife or in case of separation. He was thinking when he heard the voice of the old lady (Susan Morgan's mother). She informed him that her daughter didn't want him to give her chloroform if it would harm the baby. He replied that it would do no harm. Just then, he heard the midwife's voice. It was time for him to start working on the delivery.

The Horrifying Dilemma

After a harsh struggle for an hour, a perfectly formed boy was born. Unfortunately he was not breathing. He wanted to resuscitate the child but the mother herself was in a very bad state. So, he gave the child to the midwife and turned his attention to the mother.

Condition of the Baby

After a few minutes of continuous efforts, he stabilised her by giving her an injection. Then, he asked for the child. The midwife had kept the child under the bed, presuming him to be dead. His head was hanging loosely and the limbs seemed boneless. Dr. Andrew concluded that the child was suffering from *asphyxia pallida* (an abnormal medical condition in a newly born baby).

Effort to Revive the Baby

Dr. Andrew recalled a case he had once seen in the Samaritan (a medical journal) and the treatment that was given. He asked the midwife to quickly get hot water and cold water in two bowls.

He started plunging the child once into the icy water and then into the steaming bath, alternately. Nothing happened but he continued his efforts.

Dr. Andrew started rubbing the child's chest with a rough towel and thumping his little chest, trying to get air into that limp body.

The Miracle

Then, as if by miracle, the child's chest began moving. Dr. Andrew felt weak and nervous at the sight of life under his hands. He doubled his efforts and the child was now breathing. Soon, life came to the baby's limbs, its head became erect and skin started turning pink. Suddenly, the child cried.

Dr. Andrew is Relieved

After so much frantic effort and success, Dr. Andrew felt weak and speechless. Susan's mother was still standing against the wall, praying.

Andrew went downstairs and found Joe Morgan still waiting with an anxious, eager face. He shared the happy news that both the mother and the baby were all right. Andrew was really happy at succesfully practising medicine.

Word-Meaning

mining town	—	a town where most people work in a coal mine
surgery	—	operating room
burly	—	large and strong
driller	—	a miner who uses a drill machine
missus	—	wife (informal)
ye	—	you
contemplation of	—	thinking about
drew up short	—	stopped
stout	—	strongly built
midwife	—	woman trained to help in childbirth
bach	—	dear
leave the case	—	not stay till the delivery was completed
overwrought	—	very tired
lethargy of spirit	—	lack of enthusiasm
cinder	—	partly burnt piece of coal
grate	—	fireplace
muddled	—	mixed up
obsessed him	—	dominated his thinking
idyllic	—	perfect
awful set upon	—	very much wanting
ay	—	yes
fancy	—	believe
top landing	—	top of the stairs
elapsed	—	passed
streaks of dawn	—	light of morning
strayed past	—	came through
blind	—	sunshade
still form	—	lifeless body
resuscitate	—	bring back to life
pulseless	—	not having the pulse of life
not yet out of the ether	—	not become conscious
ebbing	—	receding
glass ampoule	—	sealed glass capsule with liquid medicine
hypodermic syringe	—	needle used to inject liquid medicine in the bloodstream
unsparingly	—	without a break
flaccid	—	lifeless
in his shirt sleeves	—	in only his shirt without a jacket over it
brow	—	forehead
fishing	—	searching
sodden	—	soaked
tallow	—	animal fat
cord	—	umbilical cord connecting the mother to the child in her womb
of a lovely texture	—	with a wonderful feel
lolled	—	hung loosely
haggard frown	—	worried and tried look
asphyxia pallida	—	an abnormal medical condition in a newly born baby who appears pale and limp, temporarily unable to breathe and having a slow heart action
the Samaritan	—	name of a medical journal
threw out	—	spoke quickly
basins	—	large bowls
pallid	—	pale
ewer	—	a large jug with a wide mouth
crazy juggler	—	madman moving the child quickly
consternation	—	feeling of anxiety
dashed away	—	finished
draggled	—	dirty and wet
sopping	—	drenched
stillborn	—	born dead
pigmy	—	small
convulsive	—	jerky
heave	—	gasp
turned giddy	—	became weak
unavailing	—	ineffective
exquisite	—	enjoyable
mucus	—	viscous liquid
iridescent	—	sparkling
spinelessly	—	loosely
blanched	—	pale
hysterically	—	uncontrollably
shuddering litter	—	total mess
soiled	—	dirty
impaled	—	stuck
scullery	—	room for washing dishes
thickly	—	in a hard to understand tone
spent	—	tired
footfalls	—	sounds made by feet while walking

Important Themes of the Chapter

Medical Ethics Medical ethics is an important theme in this excerpt. Dr. Andrew Manson faces a serious ethical dilemma when the baby is born lifeless and the mother, Susan, is in critical condition. He must decide quickly whom to prioritise: the mother or the child. The scene reflects the ethical responsibility of doctors to make fast, difficult choices to protect life, even in extreme situations.

Contrast Between Theory and Real-World Experience The excerpt emphasises how, in medical school, students learn standard procedures and ideal outcomes, but real-life practice often presents unpredictable and complex challenges. Doctors must rely on their knowledge and intuition, adaptability, and perseverance when faced with unique cases or urgent ethical decisions. This theme also highlights that true medical expertise is gained through hands-on experience, where doctors learn the importance of empathy, resilience, and quick decision-making beyond what textbooks can teach.

Dedication and Perseverance Another theme of this excerpt is dedication and perseverance. Dr. Andrew Manson is committed to his work despite being troubled and tired. Despite the difficult situation, he never gives up, trying every possible method to save the mother and the baby. His determination finally brings success, giving life to a lost newborn.

The Value of Life Another theme is the value of life—Andrew's hard work and care give him a renewed sense of purpose as he realises he has made a real difference in someone's life. This excerpt highlights how dedication to helping others can lead to personal fulfillment.

NCERT Folder

Reading with Insight (NCERT Page 43)

1. "I have done something; oh, God! I've done something real at last." Why does Andrew say this? What does it mean?

Ans. Dr. Andrew utters these words after he was able to bring an almost stillborn child back to life, although it seemed impossible in the beginning. The child was born to Sue Morgan with a peculiar breathing problem called *asphyxia pallida* in medical terminology. After feverish efforts to revive the child with the known treatment for this condition, he brought the child to life.

He spoke these words out of a deep satisfaction on achieving the seemingly impossible task. He had been able to apply his medical knowledge and skills to revive a newborn child, which was a great achievement for him. He felt that God had used him as a medium to grant life to the child and Andrew acknowledged this with his words.

2. There lies a great difference between textbook medicine and the world of a practising physician. Discuss.

Ans. For a long time, we have been hearing that there is a lot of difference between theory and practice. This is true. Theoretical information gathered from books does not provide solutions to all problems. The medical textbook provides information about the treatment of various diseases but at times, doctors face a dilemma which cannot be solved by any theory.

In this chapter, Dr. Andrew undergoes the same experience. When the mother and the son both needed his attention, he had to make a decision about who to take care of first. In this decision-making, no medical textbook could have helped him. In this case, Dr. Andrew acted instinctively. He first saved the mother and then the child. He treated the mother with the traditional treatment and the child with a mixture of traditional and intuitive treatment. The net result was that both survived and his efforts were successful.

If Dr. Andrew had gone by the textbook, he might have not been able to save the mother or the child. According to the textbook, the child was born lifeless and couldin't be revived.
However Dr. Andrew was successful in reviving it. Hence, we see that there lies a great difference between textbook medicine and the world of a practising physician.

3. Do you know of any incident when someone has been brought back to life from the brink of death through medical help? Discuss medical procedures such as organ transplant and organ regeneration that are used to save human life.

Ans. Yes, I have witnessed one such incident where my friend was blessed with a new life during his kidney transplantation surgery. Medical advancements have made it possible that organs can be transplanted. Organ donation is the process of surgically removing an organ or tissue from one person (the organ donor) and placing it into another person (the recipient).

Transplantation is necessary because the recipient's organ has failed or has been damaged by disease or injury. Unfortunately the need for organ donors is much greater than the number of people who actually donate.

Organs and tissues that can be transplanted include heart, liver, kidney, pancreas, lung and bone marrow.

Organ regeneration procedure is a step ahead in medicine as it is a new kind of solution seen in medical labs. 'Bioartificial' organs are grown from the patient's own cells. Regenerative medicine itself isn't new — the first bone marrow and solid organ transplants were done decades ago. However, advances in developmental and cell biology, immunology and other fields have unlocked new opportunities to refine existing regenerative therapies and develop new ones to save human life. Regenerative medicine holds the promise of a definitive, affordable healthcare that heals the body from within.

Exam Pattern Questions

Extract Based Questions

Read the extracts given below and answer the questions that follow.

1. **"THOUGH it was nearly midnight when Andrew reached Bryngower, he found Joe Morgan waiting for him, walking up and down with short steps between the closed surgery and the entrance to the house. At the sight of him the burly driller's face expressed relief. "Eh, Doctor, I'm glad to see you. I been back and forward here this last hour. The missus wants ye—before time, too."**

Andrew, abruptly recalled from the contemplation of his own affairs, told Morgan to wait. He went into the house for his bag, then together they set out for Number 12 Blaina Terrace. The night air was cool and deep with quiet mystery. Usually so perceptive, Andrew now felt dull and listless. He had no premonition that this night call would prove unusual, still less that it would influence his whole future in Blaenelly."

(i) Explain: "The missus wants ye—before time, too."

(ii) What does the expression "walking up and down with short steps" signify about Joe Morgan's feelings?

(a) He was stressed out
(b) He was more calm
(c) He was impatient
(d) He was angry

(iii) 'Despite feeling dull, Dr. Andrew decides to take the case'.
What does this statement highlight about him?

(iv) What did the contemplation refer to in the extract?

Ans. (i) The given statement means that the pregnant lady needed assistance before labour as well.

(ii) (a) He was stressed out

(iii) The given statement highlights that Dr. Andrew is dedicated.

(iv) The contemplation referred to in the extract is thoughts about his lover, Christine.

2. **Andrew, abruptly recalled from the contemplation of his own affairs, told Morgan to wait. He went into the house for his bag, then together they set out for Number 12 Blaina Terrace. The night air was cool and deep with quiet mystery. Usually, so perceptive, Andrew now felt dull and listless.**

(i) Complete the sentence appropriately.
Although Andrew was generally very perceptive, that night he felt ....

(ii) Why were they going to 12 Blaina Terrace?

(a) To deliver a baby
(b) For a random health checkup
(c) As Mrs. Morgan was unwell.
(d) As Morgan's mother was unwell

(iii) What does 'his own affairs' here refer to?

(iv) Assess Andrew's need for contemplation of his own affairs.

Ans. (i) dull and listless (ii) (a) To deliver a baby

(iii) 'His own affairs' here refers to his career and his relationship with Christine.

(iv) Andrew's need for contemplation of his own affairs indicates his own personal struggles.

He is worried about his career and his relationship, and how they would go in the future.

3. **Inside, a narrow stair led up to a small bedroom, clean but poorly furnished and lit only by an oil lamp. Here Mrs. Morgan's mother, a tall, grey-haired woman of nearly seventy and the stout, elderly midwife waited beside the patient, watching Andrew's expression as he moved about the room.**

"Let me make you a cup of tea, Doctor, bach," said the former quickly, after a few moments. Andrew smiled

faintly. He saw that the old woman, wise in experience, realised there must be a period of waiting that, she was afraid he would leave the case, saying he would return later. "Don't fret, mother, I'll not run away."

(i) Complete the sentence appropriately.

Dr. Andrew was offered tea by ....

(ii) Why does Dr. Andrew focus on the room more than the pregnant Mrs. Susan Morgan?

(iii) What are the old woman's fears in the passage?

(a) That her daughter would not be healthy.
(b) That her grandchild would die.
(c) That the doctor was not interested in the case.
(d) That the doctor would leave.

(iv) "Don't fret, mother, I'll not run away."

Why did Andrew say this?

Ans. (i) Mrs. Morgan's mother

(ii) Dr. Andrew focusses on the room more than the pregnant Susan Morgan because he is quickly assured that she does not need attention right away.

(iii) (d) That the doctor would leave.

(iv) Andrew said this to reassure Mrs. Morgan's mother.

4. It was a conclusion which, in his present state, made him wince. He wished to consider marriage as an idyllic state; yes, he could not otherwise consider it with the image of Christine before him. Her eyes, shining towards him, admitted no other conclusion. It was the conflict between his level, doubting mind and his overflowing heart which left him resentful and confused. He let his chin sink upon his chest, stretched out his legs, stared broodingly into the fire.

(i) What dilemma did Dr. Andrew face?

(ii) Complete the following suitably.

The conclusion that made Andrew wince was ....

(iii) What does this statement mean – '...stretched out his legs, started broodingly into the fire'?

(a) He was angry about his broken relationship with Christine.
(b) He was deep in thought.
(c) He was considering marrying Christine again.
(d) Christine's eyes were doubting him and making him nervous.

(iv) What instances make Andrew doubt his relationship?

Ans. (i) The dilemma that Dr. Andrew faced was whether he should marry or not.

(ii) failure of marriage

(iii) (b) He was deep in thought.

(iv) Andrew doubts his relationship because he had seen a man being sad and hurt by betrayal and another by separation. He does not want the same for himself and thus, is doubtful of whether he should marry Christine.

Short Answer Type Questions

1. How does Andrew Manson feel when he arrives at the Morgans' house for the birth?

Ans. When he arrives, Andrew feels dull and listless. He is tired and absorbed in his thoughts, particularly about Christine. He does not expect the birth to be unusual and feels mentally distant from the situation, but he decides to stay and help.

2. Identify the quality displayed by the doctor as he accompanied Joe Morgan.

Ans. The doctor accompanied Joe Morgan though he was physically and mentally very tired. This shows that doctor was thoroughly professional. For him, duty came first and no personal problem could come in the way of attending his duty.

3. Dr. Andrew had no idea that this particular night would influence his future career in Blaenelly. How did it do so?

Ans. When Dr. Andrew accompanied Joe Morgan at midnight, he had no idea that this particular night was going to affect his whole future career. The doctor did his best to save Susan Morgan, and he revived the child to give a fresh lease of life to the family. Dr. Andrew's efforts were really commendable and shaped his future.

4. Write a short note on the old lady.

Ans. The old lady was Susan Morgan's mother, a tall, grey-haired woman of nearly seventy. She was wise in experience. She realised that there must be a period of waiting before the delivery.

She was afraid that the doctor might leave the case saying he would return later.

5. What is the significance of the old woman's presence in the room during the birth? Competency Based

Ans. Susan's mother, the old woman, is important because she represents experience and tradition. She silently observes Andrew's actions and is emotionally connected to the birth, showing concern for her daughter and the child. Her presence brings a sense of continuity and care during the difficult moment.

6. Dr. Andrew said, "Don't fret mother, I will not run away?" Give reasons. Competency Based

Ans. When Mrs. Susan Morgan's mother told Dr. Andrew that she would prepare tea for him, the doctor could sense the old woman's anxiety that he may go away as there was still some time for delivery. Sensing her anxiety, the doctor uttered these words.

7. How does Andrew respond to the situation when the baby is born lifeless?

Ans. When the baby is born lifeless, Andrew feels a mix of horror and uncertainty. He is torn between trying to save the baby and focusing on the mother, Susan, who is also in danger. He quickly hands the baby to the nurse and works to save Susan.

8. Analyse Dr. Andrew's state of conflict when the child was born. **Competency Based**

Ans. Dr. Andrew was in a state of conflict as he was torn between two situations. The dilemma before him was whether to save the mother first or her child. The dilemma was so urgent that he couldn't solve it consciously.

9. Explain the elderly midwife's thoughts about the young doctor in the beginning. **Competency Based**

Ans. The midwife in the story remained doubtful about the young doctor's abilities and pessimistic about the child's survival. Her act of keeping the child under the bed shows that she never believed that the doctor would be able to revive the child at any stage.

10. What efforts did Dr. Andrew make to save the lifeless-looking boy at birth?

Ans. When Dr. Andrew saw the lifeless-looking boy, he realised that the boy's whiteness meant that he was suffering from *asphyxia pallida,* which required a particular method of revival. So, he began a special method of respiration. In this regard, he alternatively plunged the child into a basin of icy water followed by plunging him into very hot water repeatedly.
Then, in one last desperate effort, he rubbed the boy, crushing and releasing his chest, trying to get breath into its limp body. Suddenly, the child's chest started going up and down, some mucus came out of its nose and finally, the boy gave a cry.

11. How does Andrew's interaction with the mother differ from his work with the child? **Competency Based**

Ans. Andrew's interaction with the mother, Susan, is focused on saving her life, as she is in a fragile state. His work with the child is more urgent and emotional, trying to bring the lifeless baby back to life—his attention shifts between them, driven by different concerns.

12. How does Andrew's experience with the stillborn child affect his view of his medical career?

Ans. Andrew's experience with the stillborn child makes him realise the importance of his work. After saving the child, he feels he has done something real and meaningful in his medical career. This moment changes how he views his doctor role, giving him a new purpose.

13. What does Andrew's physical exhaustion symbolise at the end of the story? **Competency Based**

Ans. At the end of the story, Andrew's physical exhaustion symbolises his emotional and mental strain. After struggling to save the baby and help the mother, he is drained but feels a sense of accomplishment. His tiredness reflects the intense effort and the emotional toll of the experience.

14. How does the story's setting (time and place) influence Andrew's experience during the birth? **Competency Based**

Ans. The story occurs in a small Welsh mining town at night, creating a quiet, tense atmosphere. The isolation and the late hour add to Andrew's exhaustion and mental fog. The setting also emphasises his sense of duty, as he works alone in a modest, old house.

15. What role does Joe Morgan play in the events of the night?

Ans. Joe Morgan's role is mainly as a concerned, supportive husband. He waits anxiously outside while Andrew works. Joe's presence shows the emotional weight of the situation, and his quiet support adds to the urgency of the birth, especially when he reassures Andrew to do well for them.

16. Describe the condition of the room after Dr. Andrew had saved both the mother and the child.

Ans. After Dr. Andrew had saved both the mother and the child, the room was in a mess, full of soiled newspapers, towels, blankets and soiled instruments. The floor was full of mud and water, as the doctor had used two basins full of water. The hypodermic syringe was stuck in the linoleum on the floor, the jug was knocked over and the kettle was on its side.

Long Answer Type Questions

1. "For doctors, the duty towards the patients is foremost, irrespective of their own personal affairs."
Discuss with reference to the chapter 'Birth'.

Ans. There is a saying that after God, it is only a doctor who can save the life of someone. A patient comes to a doctor with the hope that he would cure his/her illness. Thus, it is a doctor's duty and oath to focus on the patient first. For them, their profession is foremost respective of their own personal affairs.

This is suitably presented in the chapter 'Birth' in how Dr. Andrew made frantic efforts to save the lives of Mrs. Susan Morgan and her child. Dr. Andrew also used his intuition and medical knowledge to save the lifeless child when there was no hope. Though he was really upset before coming to Joe Morgan's house, Dr. Andrew stayed there, as the case demanded all his attention. He could barely see his own future but was diligent enough to realise his call of duty.

Hence, we can say that even though being preoccupied with his own personal affairs, he did not forget his duty and made sincere attempts to succeed.

2. No matter what your profession is, moral values always play an important role in making you a complete human being. Explain with reference to the chapter 'Birth'.

Ans. One of the most challenging and complex areas of life is the realm of moral issues and decisions. Every day of our life, in whatever profession we may be, we make moral choices and decisions that reflect our own moral orientation.

In the chapter 'Birth', Dr. Andrew considered it his moral duty to attend to a patient inspite of his mental agony and tiredness. He spent the whole night in saving two lives.
He used all his knowledge as well as instincts to revive the child and finally succeeded in making the family happy.
In the end, he emerged as a distinct human being who went all out to save lives not out of greed but because he considered it his moral duty to do his best. His efforts were applauded and he himself indulged in self-appraisal 'on doing something really good.' His moral values helped him in achieving this feat.

3. How does the author use physical descriptions of the child to create a sense of tension and urgency?

Ans. The author uses vivid physical descriptions of the child to build tension and urgency. When Andrew first sees the newborn, he notices that the baby is pale, limp, and lifeless, with skin 'white and soft as tallow,' suggesting it isn't breathing. The body appears "boneless," and the head droops, making the child seem very fragile and close to death. These descriptions make the reader feel the seriousness of the situation and emphasise how critical it is for Andrew to act quickly.

By showing the baby's delicate state, Cronin highlights Andrew's desperation and the intense effort required to save the child. The reader shares Andrew's anxiety and hopes for the child's survival, which creates a gripping and urgent atmosphere.

4. How does Cronin use the interactions between the characters to highlight the themes of life, death, and hope?

Ans. Cronin uses interactions between characters to explore life, death, and hope. Joe Morgan's nervous pacing shows his fear and hope for safe delivery, while his trust in Andrew suggests his faith in life's possibilities. Mrs. Morgan's mother watches Andrew closely, praying silently, reflecting her strong hope for her grandchild. When the baby is born lifeless, Andrew faces a difficult choice between saving the mother or reviving the child. His intense efforts to save the baby symbolise his deep respect for life and his unwillingness to give in to despair. Finally, when the child begins to breathe, both the nurse's joy and the grandmother's quiet prayer capture a moment of miraculous hope, celebrating life's power to overcome death.

5. Write a character sketch of Andrew Manson.

Ans. Andrew Manson is the protagonist of AJ Cronin's story 'Birth'. He is young man who had just completed his medical studies and is starting his career in a small town, which reflects his lack of real-world experience. This inexperience is evident as he struggles to handle the challenges of his first real medical case. His enthusiasm to prove himself is tempered by moments of doubt and confusion, especially as he tries to balance his emotions and professional duties.

As a doctor, Andrew shows concern for his patients. He remains compassionate and attentive to Mrs. Morgan's needs despite his emotional distractions. He reassures the elderly woman in the house and ensures that the case gets his full attention, showing his nurturing nature. He also offers kind words to the elderly woman, calming her fears and letting her know he won't leave. His gentle, reassuring attitude reflects his ability to empathise with others in their times of need.

He has a keen sense of duty and professionalism, as seen in his decision to stay and see the case through.
He shows perseverance when the situation seems dire. Andrew's immediate reaction is a desperate attempt to revive the infant. His persistence is crucial in this situation, even when the odds seem stacked against him. His ability to think on his feet and remain calm under pressure showcases his adaptability and resourcefulness. His commitment to his work is evident when he decides to remain despite his exhaustion.

Despite the challenges, Andrew's final success—reviving the baby—marks a significant shift in his confidence and understanding of his role as a doctor, transitioning from doubt to belief in his ability to make a difference.

6. After reading the story 'Birth', you were inspired to write about the situation of marriages in India. Write an article in 120-150 words, discussing the author's view on marriage as given in the chapter as well as your personal opinion about Indian marriages.
You may begin like this ......

The author in the chapter gives some examples of bad marriages and ....

Ans.

Marriages in India
by XYZ

The author in the chapter gives some examples of bad marriages and puts Dr. Andrew in a confused state of mind, as he considered marriage as an ideal state and a peaceful happiness.

Actually, marriage succeeds only due to the efforts of both the partners. It is unsuccessful where there are problems like dishonesty, cheating, mistrust, authoritarian attitude, intolerant partner, etc., a marriage cannot survive.

But in India, we see less marriage failures due to the cultural and moral values incorporated in the people.
Here, people believe in the institution of marriage and respect it.

Through patience, understanding and sympathy, both husband and wife try to continue their married life and do not opt for divorce easily.

There may be several problems due to individual differences but both the partners try to sort them out and keep the relationship alive.

SELF ASSESSMENT TEST

Extract Based Questions

Read the extract given below and answer the questions that follow.

1. He redoubled his efforts feverishly. The child was gasping now, deeper and deeper. A bubble of mucus came from one tiny nostril, a joyful iridescent bubble. The limbs were no longer boneless. The head no longer lay back spinelessly. The blanched skin was slowly turning pink. Then, exquisitely, came the child's cry.

(i) Complete the sentence appropriately.
The efforts were redoubled by ....

(ii) What is the significance of the above extract?

(iii) The word 'feverishly' as used in the extract can be replaced by
(a) madly (b) easily (c) rapidly (d) courageously

(iv) Why has the baby's bubble of mucus been described as 'a joyful iridescent bubble'?

Short Answer Type Questions

1. Dr. Andrew was tired yet he decided to wait at the Morgan's house. Why?

2. What was Dr. Andrew's concept about women? What made him think that way?

3. 'Sometimes instincts play a vital role along with one's bookish knowledge.' Is this statement true in the context of this chapter 'Birth'? Why?

4. What was Susan Morgan's suggestion to Andrew which was informed through her mother and why did she give the suggestion?

5. "Saving the stillborn child was nothing less than a miracle." Discuss.

6. How does Andrew react to the old woman's concern about the chloroform?

Long Answer Type Questions

1. Justify the title 'Birth'.

2. The story 'Birth' brings out how Dr. Andrew managed to perform his duties as a doctor very well even though he was undergoing an emotional crisis.

Imagine you are a doctor who has to address students at a medical university. Write this speech in 120-150 words, elaborating upon the fact that emotional instability should never be a hurdle in one's profession.

You may begin like this ....

Good morning, Students!

Just like Dr. Andrew, all of us go through emotional crisis from time to time. However, it is important to ....

3. How does Cronin create a sense of urgency and tension in the birth scene? **Competency Based**

05

About the Author

Vikram Seth (1952-Present) is an Indian poet, novelist, and travel writer known for his verse novel 'The Golden Gate (1986)' and his epic novel 'A Suitable Boy (1993)'. Seth has been honoured with many prizes like 'Thomas Cook Travel Book Award', the Commonwealth Poetry Prize (Asia) among others.

Vikram Seth's works are characterised by their depth, insight, and exploration of universal themes that resonate with readers across cultures and backgrounds. His writings often include social and political commentary, addressing issues such as class divisions, corruption, and the impact of historical events on society. He offers a critical on the social and political fabric

YOUR STUDY GOALS

- Chapter Sketch
- About the Characters
- Summary of the Chapter

YOUR PRACTICE GOAL

- NCERT Folder
- Extract Based Questions
- Short Answer Type Questions
- Long Answer Type Questions

The Tale of Melon City

Chapter Sketch

'The Tale of Melon City' by Vikram Seth is a poetic satire about a king, his ministers and the kingdom. The king has been ironically called lawful. But, in reality, he stretches justice too far. Due to this quality of his character, one day he himself is hanged. The ministers also are a group of fools who decide an odd way to choose the next king. An idiot announces that a melon should be the king and people unhesitatingly crown a melon as their king. People in the Melon City do not even care who their king is as long as they enjoyed their freedom.

About the Characters

The King He has been portrayed as just and quiet. However, he is not an intelligent person and does not have any decision taking ability. Because of his foolishness, he had to lose his life.

The Architect He is a smart person who is able to frustrate the king. When his turn came to be hanged, he pointed out something which put the king in a tricky situation and made him angry.

The Wisest Man He is an old man who can neither walk properly nor see well. He is picked up by the council of ministers to give a wise decision to the king. But unfortunately, the decision given by him was not wise at all.

The Idiot He is a man of low intelligence and does not act rationally. His advice is asked for choosing the king. Without thinking, he says a melon should be made the king as he was very fond of melons.

Summary of the Chapter

The King's Orders and Angers

This poem is about a city and its king who was lawful and gentle. The king had an arch (curved structure) to be built as a symbol of his accomplishments. The arch was built soon and king rode down the main road to inspire people.

However, the arch was built too low and the king's crown fell as it struck the arch. As a result, the king felt insulted and ordered the chief of builders to be hanged. The arrangements for the hanging were made and the chief of builders was called.

The Blame Game Begins

The chief of builders pleaded that it was not his mistake; it was rather the workmen's fault. So, the king ordered all the workmen to be hanged. The workmen claimed that the bricks used were not of the right size. So, the masons were called who, in turn blamed the architect for the wrong design.

The Tricky Situation

The king now ordered that the architect must be hanged. The architect reminded the king that he himself had changed the original plan sometime back.

The king was trapped and withdrew to consult the wisest man in the country. The wisest man was chosen on the criteria that he should be very old. The person chosen could not walk or see properly and was carried by other people. This man suggested that the culprit should be punished and it was decided that the arch would be hanged.

The King is Hanged

The arch was being taken for the hanging when one of the councillors said that the arch actually touched the royal head with respect. The king agreed but the crowd was getting restless and wanted a hanging. So, he ordered that someone must be hanged, guilty or not.

Now, they decided to hang the man who would reach the loop of the rope which was set up high. Only the king himself was tall enough so he was hanged and the ministers heaved a sigh of relief.

The Dilemma

The ministers now faced the dilemma that the country had no king. They followed their old custom and sent out messengers to proclaim that the next person who would pass the city gate would choose the next king. After some time, an idiot passed the gate and was asked to name the king. The idiot answered with his standard answer to all the questions – 'a melon'.

The Melon King

After the answer, a melon was made the king of the city.

This happened long ago. If you now ask the people why their king appears to be a melon, they reply that it is a customary choice. It makes no difference to them if their king is a melon. They are happy because the king doesn't interfere with their lives. They live in peace and harmony.

Word-Meaning

- placid — even-tempered
- arch — gate structure with a circular top
- span — pass over
- thoroughfare — main road
- edify — enlighten
- he lost his crown — his crown struck the arch and fell down
- gallows — structure on which criminals are hanged
- quivering — trembling
- architect — planner
- do ordain — order
- amendments — changes
- lost his head — lost control over his emotions
- nay — no
- quavering — shaky
- banged — hit
- by and by — one after another
- muttering — talking in low voices
- noose — a loop of rope with a knot used for hanging criminals
- standard — fixed
- decree — order
- unruly — uncontrollable
- crown — ruler
- dilemma — perplexing situation
- heralds — messengers
- enforced — implemented
- with due ceremony — ceremonially
- scaffold — a raised wooden platform used for hanging
- laissez-faire — the policy of leaving things to take their own course

Important Themes of the Chapter

The Absurdity of Power and Justice The poem 'The Tale of Melon City' explores the absurdity and randomness of authority and justice. The king, who starts as a just ruler, ends up blaming everyone but himself for a simple mistake. His decision-making process becomes increasingly irrational, culminating in his accidental hanging. The poem satirises the tendency of those in power to shift blame and make arbitrary/random decisions. Ultimately, the absurdity is further emphasised when a melon is crowned king, showing that leadership is reduced to a meaningless tradition as long as peace is maintained. The poem critiques the idea of justice and leadership, suggesting that power often leads to chaos and foolishness.

The Folly of Authority and Responsibility Another critical theme in 'The Tale of Melon City' is the folly of authority and the failure of leaders to take responsibility for their actions. The king's quick shift in blame—from the builders to the architect–reflects the inability of those in power to accept their own mistakes. His desire to maintain control leads him to make irrational decisions, and in the end, the situation's absurdity is revealed when a melon becomes the ruler. This theme highlights the irresponsibility of leadership and how leaders often prioritise their image over the well-being of their people, leading to chaos, and a breakdown in authority.

NCERT Folder

Reading with Insight (NCERT Page 40)

1. Narrate 'The Tale of Melon City' in your own words.

Ans. The lawful and gentle king of a city once had a desire for building an arch across the main road to enlighten the people. Workmen constructed the arch as the king had ordered it. When the king rode down the main road and passed under the arch, his crown struck the arch and fell down. Furious at his disgrace, the king ordered the chief of builders to be hanged. However, the chief of the builders blamed the workmen for the mistake. The workmen blamed the masons for making the bricks of the wrong size. The masons blamed the architect for making the wrong plans. The architect put the king in dilemma as he reminded the king that he himself had made a change in the plans made by the architect.

The king wanted the wisest man in the city to decide the guilty person. An old man, who could neither see nor walk, was considered the wisest because of his age. He blamed the arch itself for the disgrace. But a Councillor said that something that touched the king's head should not be punished. Meanwhile, the people were getting restless and the king understood that guilty or not, somebody must be hanged.

So, he asked for the loop of rope to be used for the hanging to be set high and anyone whose head reached it would be hanged. One by one all the people were measured but nobody reached its height except the king himself, as he was the tallest. So, according to the royal order, the king himself was hanged.

The ministers heaved a sigh of relief but a new crisis arose: who would be the king? So, the ministers decided that the next man who passed the City Gate would choose the king.

An idiot who was fond of melons happened to pass the gate first. The guards asked him about who should be the king to which his answer was 'a melon'. So, a melon was named the king and was crowned in a proper ceremony. The people were happy to have a melon as king as long as it left them in peace and at liberty.

2. What impression would you form of a state where the king was 'just' and 'placid'?

Ans. A state where the king is 'just and placid' would initially seem peaceful and fair. The king's calm and reasonable nature suggests he would make decisions based on justice, without anger or harsh punishment. People might feel safe and treated fairly because a 'just' ruler would try to solve problems fairly.

However, in the poem, the king's placid/calm nature also makes him easily influenced by others and quick to blame others without considering his own mistakes. The poem highlights that being too calm and not thinking carefully can lead to foolish decisions. So, while the state may seem peaceful, it can also be full of confusion and poor choices if the King doesn't make wise and thoughtful decisions.

3. How, according to you, can peace and liberty be maintained in a state?

Ans. Peace and liberty are the two most important factors for a state to flourish and prosper. Ofcourse, the best method lies in good governance. If this is done properly, it benefits both the citizens as well as the rulers.

Peace and liberty in a state can be maintained when the government treats all citizens fairly and respects their rights. Leaders should make decisions based on justice, considering everyone's needs and opinions. Laws should protect people's freedom, allowing them to express themselves without fear. People should be encouraged to participate in decisions that affect them, promoting a sense of responsibility and cooperation. Education about rights and duties also plays a vital role in maintaining peace. When citizens feel heard and protected, they are more likely to live peacefully and enjoy their liberty without fear of unfair treatment or oppression.

4. Suggest a few instances which highlight humour and irony.

Ans. 'The Tale of Melon City' has a lot of irony and humour.

Some humorous instances are

- The king decides to make an arch across the main road to enlighten the people, but creates a humorous scene when his crown hits the arch and the crown falls.
- The king wants to punish the guilty that made the faulty arch, but their passing the blame to others, finally blaming the king himself.
- When the wisest man is called, his pointing to the arch itself as the culprit and the people's readiness to hang it is a humorous situation.
- When we find that the king is the fittest person for the hanging and he is actually hanged, it is another humorous situation.
- The process of choosing the new king and making a melon as the king is the most humorous of all.

Some instances of irony in this chapter are

- The king who desired a hanging to punish the guilty gets hanged himself.
- The wise man was only selected because he was old. They could not see anything or even walk.
- The ministers chose a king on the basis of a fool's choice.
- All accept the choice for king without bothering whether the king was human or not.

5. 'The Tale of Melon City' has been narrated in verse form. This is a unique style which lends extra charm to an ancient tale. Find similar examples in your language.

Ans. In many languages, ancient stories are often told in verse to make them more exciting and memorable. For example, in Hindi, The Ramayana and Mahabharata are ancient epics traditionally recited in verse form, with rhymes and rhythm to make the stories easier to remember and enjoy. In Tamil, works like Thirukkural by Thiruvalluvar use verse to teach moral lessons, making it poetic and instructional. These examples, like The Tale of Melon City, show how storytelling in verse adds a unique charm and helps pass down stories from generation to generation.

Exam Pattern Questions

Extract Based Questions

Read the extracts given below and answer the questions that follow.

1. The workmen went and built the thing.
They did so since he was the king.
The king rode down the thoroughfare
To edify spectators there.

(i) What does 'the thing' refer to?

(a) A citadel
(b) A stadium
(c) An arch
(d) A statue

(ii) Why did the workmen build it?

(iii) What happened when the king 'rode down the thoroughfare'?

(iv) The literary device used in line 'The king rode down the thoroughfare' is ....

Ans. (i) (c) An arch

(ii) The workmen built the arch because the king had asked them to do so.

(iii) The arch was built too low and the king's crown fell when it struck the arch.

(iv) Alliteration

2. 'Well, architect,' said his majesty.
'I do ordain that you shall be
Hanged.' Said the architect, 'O King,
You have forgotten one small thing.
You made certain amendments to
The plans when I showed them to you.'
The king heard this.

(i) Select the option that mentions the person whom the architect blamed for the mistake.

(a) The brick-maker (b) The ministers
(c) The people (d) The king

(ii) Why was the king blamed?

(iii) What was the punishment for the mistake for which the architect was blamed?

(iv) Who put the blame on the architect?

Ans. (i) (d) The king

(ii) The king was blamed because he made adjustments to the original plan.

(iii) The punishment for the mistake for which the architect was blamed was that he would be hanged.

(iv) The masons, when summoned, put the blame on the architect.

3. **By now the crowd,**
Restless, was muttering aloud.
The king perceived their mood and trembled
And said to all who were assembled —
'Let us postpone consideration
Of finer points like guilt. The nation
Wants a hanging. Hanged must be
Someone, and that immediately.'
The noose was set up somewhat high.
Each man was measured by and by.
But only one man was so tall
He fitted. One man. That was all.

(i) What does the given lines tell us about the crowd?

(ii) Why does the king postpone the punishment?

(a) He wanted to punish the right person.
(b) He knew the entire ordeal was stupid.
(c) He wanted to please the crowd.
(d) None of the above

(iii) In the end, who received the punishment?

(iv) Who was the one man who fit the length?

Ans. (i) The given lines tell us that the crowd wanted justice.

(ii) (d) None of the above

(iii) In the end, the king was hanged as punishment.

(iv) Only the king was tall enough to fit the length.

Short Answer Type Questions

1. Give reason why the king ordered to build an arch.

Ans. The king proclaimed for an arch to be constructed keeping in mind that the arch would be a symbol of his triumphs — a sort of victory monument. He wanted the arch to be extended across the main road of the city.

2. Explain what happened when the king passed under the arch. State his reaction to the event.

Ans. When the king was passing from under the arch, the low height knocked his crown off, leading to a chain of absurd blame and punishment decisions that reflect the poem's satire on justice.

The king was initially displeased and called the incident a disgrace. He ordered the chief of builders to be hanged but later shifted the blame to others, showing his attempt to maintain justice. His reaction highlights the absurdity and arbitrariness of his decisions, adding humour to the poem's satire.

3. Interpret the information provided by the architect when summoned by the king.

Ans. The architect informed the king that he himself had changed the plans of the arch when the architect had shown them to him. Thus, he implied that the blame for the faulty design was with the king himself and that the architect was not to be blamed. This shows the king's lack of self-awareness and inability to recognise his role in the problem.

4. The king was trapped by the architect. Do you agree? What solution was found by the king to avert the situation?

Ans. Yes, the architect trapped the king by blaming him. The king became very furious and was unable to remain calm. He asked for the wisest man to be brought there so that a proper solution could be found to the problem.

5. A blame game started and the king was confused. Who were involved in this?

Ans. People knew that the king could be easily influenced. They started passing the blame from one to another. The chief of builders blamed the workmen. The workmen blamed the masons, who blamed the architect and the architect blamed the king himself. Thus, they finally held the king responsible, which made him confused as to what action to take.

6. What role did the 'wisest man' play in the king's decision?

Ans. The 'wisest man', too old to walk or see, advised that the arch was at fault and should be punished. The ridiculous suggestion, meant to resolve the blame, highlights the satire of misplaced wisdom and justice. It influenced the king's decision, further showcasing the situation's absurdity.

7. The crowd was getting restless by the drama. Explain.

Ans. The crowd had been watching for long the drama of people passing the blame for the disgrace of the king. They expected a hanging to happen soon but it was being averted due to one reason or another. They felt bored and wanted some real action. So, they were getting restless.

8. Assess the king's final decree reading the hanging. Competency Based

Ans. The king's final decree, which demands a hanging to satisfy the crowd, highlights his failure as a ruler. It symbolises his blind adherence to authority and the absurdity of his decisions. The decree emphasises the poem's critique of leadership, where actions are based on appearance and maintaining power, not justice.

9. How did the king end up being hanged?

Ans. The king ended up being hanged because he declared that someone must be punished for the crowd's satisfaction. When measured for the noose, only the king's height fit. Sticking to his decree, he accepted his fate, emphasising the poem's satire on blind justice and absurd leadership.

10. What does the crowd's reaction to the king's punishment reveal about their loyalty? Competency Based

Ans. The crowd's reaction reveals their loyalty is shallow and focused on maintaining peace rather than genuine respect for the king. They seem indifferent to the absurdity of his punishment, showing that their allegiance is more about avoiding chaos than any real attachment to leadership or justice.

11. The people of Melon City were unbothered by their king. Analyse.

Ans. The people of Melon City did not bother at all about who was their king because it did not matter to them as long as they were allowed to enjoy peace and liberty. Even their previous king was idiotic and would change his mind all the time, whereas a melon will not be able to interfere at all in their activities, as it is not a human being.

12. Define Laissez-faire and explain its principles.

Ans. *Laissez-faire* is a french word which means 'to leave alone' or the policy of leaving things to take their own course without interfering. This principle was well-established in 'Melon City' as their king, being a lifeless object, did not interfere in the lives of its subjects.

13. Justify the title of the chapter 'The Tale of Melon City'.

Ans. The title is well justified because it narrates the part of the history of this city when a melon was made the king. That is how the city got its name. It tells the full story of how the foolish king sentenced himself to death and a melon was chosen as king. It also suggests that the chapter is satirical, suggesting the faults of most humans.

14. What is the main message conveyed by the poem's ending?

Ans. The poem's ending conveys a satirical message about governance and people's indifference to their rulers. The citizens are content with a melon as king as long as they enjoy peace and liberty, reflecting a critique of passive acceptance and the absurdity of political customs.

15. How does the king's decision-making process evolve throughout the poem? Competency Based

Ans. The king's decision-making evolves from blaming individuals for the arch's fault to seeking advice from the 'wisest man' and finally succumbing to public pressure. His choices become increasingly absurd, reflecting a satirical take on flawed leadership where decisions are driven by appearances and appeasement rather than logic or fairness.

16. How does the king's placid nature influence his actions in the poem? Competency Based

Ans. The king's placid nature contributes to his passive decision-making, where he avoids confronting the deeper issues. His calm demeanour leads him to make arbitrary, illogical decisions without questioning their fairness. Rather than ensuring wise leadership, this placidity results in absurd consequences and highlights the flaws in his rule.

17. Why is the idea of a melon as king significant in the context of the poem? Competency Based

Ans. The idea of a melon as king is significant because it satirises the absurdity of leadership and governance. The melon, chosen by an idiot, symbolises the randomness of power and the people's passive acceptance of whatever ruler they are given, mocking the importance placed on authority and leadership.

18. What does the phrase 'customary choice' suggest about the people's attitude toward leadership? Competency Based

Ans. The phrase 'customary choice' suggests that the people are indifferent to the qualities of their leader, following tradition without questioning it. Their passive attitude reflects a complacency towards leadership, where choosing a ruler becomes a ritual rather than a meaningful decision, highlighting a lack of critical engagement.

Long Answer Type Questions

1. It is essential to possess intelligence and common sense to rule over others. Comment in the context of the chapter 'The Tale of Melon City'.

Ans. It is a fact that a ruler must have common sense and intelligence to judge things in their correct perspective. Multiple situations and varied people require quick judgement and ability to differentiate between right and wrong. People tend to fool others to save themselves, which is very well-reflected in the chapter 'The Tale of Melon City'.

The king is so foolish that he is not able to see through the excuses of others and pays heavily by losing his life. The architect or the people who set the noose were far more intelligent than the king which is why they could easily trap him in an unavoidable situation.

For a leader, it is essential to be a good administrator who should be intelligent. He should be able to analyse and rationalise the situation; otherwise, he can be in a difficult situation from which it will be difficult to come out.

2. Write a note on the passive subjects of the kingdom in the poem 'The Tale of Melon City'. Competency Based

Ans. The kingdom's subjects in 'The Tale of Melon City' are portrayed as passive and compliant individuals who follow the king's decisions without questioning them. They are depicted as a typical crowd, persuaded by the whims of authority rather than actively participating in governance or decision-making.

When the king orders the hanging of various individuals, including the workmen and the architect, the subjects do not protest but instead accept the outcomes without objection. This reflects their submissiveness and reliance on the king's decisions. They are more concerned with maintaining peace and stability than questioning the absurdity of the king's actions. In the final part of the poem, when a melon is chosen as the new king, the subjects again show no resistance. They accept the melon as their ruler, demonstrating their tendency to follow tradition, even when illogical. The subjects' passive acceptance highlights the poem's critique of blindly following authority, no matter how foolish or unreasonable it may be.

3. The king is initially portrayed as a fair and just ruler, but his lack of insight makes him easily swayed by external opinions and leads to misguided decisions. Elaborate.

Ans. The king is initially portrayed as a fair and just ruler, but his lack of insight makes him easily swayed by external opinions and leads to misguided decisions. The king, despite his self-perception as a wise ruler, ends up being the victim of his unreasonable actions, culminating in his accidental hanging, which highlights the futility of his authority.

Right from the beginning of the poem, we see the king to be vain who wants people to learn from him. Hence, he gets an arch constructed. However, when he feels that he has been disgraced by his crown falling down due to the arch, he becomes angry. Instead of calmly assessing the situation, he quickly blames others for the arch's failure, shifting responsibility without considering his mistakes. His decisions change repeatedly throughout the poem, revealing his inability to make firm, rational judgements. He follows the crowd's demands rather than standing by his reasoning.

Further, throughout the poem, the king remains placid and untroubled, even in the face of ridiculous circumstances, suggesting that he is more concerned with maintaining his image than understanding his errors. Thus, the king becomes a means to satirise the foolishness of absolute power. The king's downfall reflects how authority can lead to chaos when detached from reason and justice.

4. Analyse the concept of justice as portrayed in the poem.

Ans. The poem portrays justice humorously and ironically. The king wants to appear fair, but his decisions are illogical. When the arch knocks off his crown, he blames and punishes others instead of taking responsibility. The king changes his mind repeatedly, blaming builders, masons, and even the arch itself. Justice becomes a joke when the wise man suggests hanging the arch, and the ministers focus on pleasing the crowd instead of finding the real culprit. Finally, the king himself is hanged because he fits the noose, showing how absurd the system is. The poem highlights how, when handled by foolish leaders, justice can become unfair and ridiculous, showing the flaws in authority and decision-making.

5. Mob psychology is beyond any reason. Politicians use this in their favour. A good leader can use the mob to achieve some useful purposes or goals.

Write an article in 120-150 words to express your opinion on the given lines.

You may begin like this ....

The crowd or mob may be very intelligent but ....

Ans. **Use of Mob by Leaders**

by XYZ

The crowd or mob may be very intelligent but when they are excited, they act solely on their emotions and set aside any discretion or reason. Many politicians try to arouse the mob to achieve their personal goals or to damage the good image of an honest party or leader.

A good leader can use the crowd to achieve some visions or goals which may be beneficial to the nation. For example, Gandhiji aroused the passions of the common man to make India free. It was with the help of a large gathering of common people who believed in *satyagraha* and non-violence that the Britishers finally left India.

6. Satire can be an effective tool for social reform. Keeping the chapter 'The Tale of Melon City' in mind, write an article in 120-150 words to express your views on the above statement.

Ans. **Satire as a Tool for Social Reform**

by XYZ

The word 'satire' means conveying a message without using harsh or direct words. The literal meaning of satire is the use of humour to expose and criticise people's stupidity, particularly in the context of contemporary politics. This writing style has been in use for ages. Writers, poets and dramatists have used this style to create an emotional impact on readers.

The writer tries to impress the reader through subtle use of language. In this poem, the poet has used satire to bring out the fact that our leaders should be wise so that they can lead the country in the path of development and prosperity.

The purpose of the writer is to get matters corrected by pointing towards the wrong actions in a humorous manner.

SELF ASSESSMENT TEST

Extract Based Questions

Read the extract given below and answer the questions that follow.

1. 'Well, on
Account of customary choice.
If his majesty rejoice
In being a melon, that's OK
With us, for who are we to say
What he should be as long as he
Leaves us in peace and liberty?'

(i) Why did the people have a melon for their king?

(ii) What do the given lines tell us about the kingdom?

(a) The people hated the old king.
(b) The people wanted peace and liberty.
(c) The melon king is just and placid.
(d) God chose melon to be the king.

(iii) Complete the sentence appropriately.

The word 'customary' in the context of the given extract means ....

(iv) What, according to the people of Melon city, was a benefit of the king being a melon?

Short Answer Type Questions

1. After reading only the first two lines of the chapter, what do you think a just and placid king should be like?

2. What happened when the king rode down the main road?

3. Ultimately, who was held responsible for the king's disgrace and why?

4. What do you learn about the ministers from their behaviour?

5. How does the poem use humour to critique the system of monarchy and justice?

Long Answer Type Questions

1. Write a speech for your student in 120-150 words about how a king should be chosen, according to you. Elaborate on the qualities that the king must possess to rule the kingdom.

You may begin like this ....

Good morning, Students! A leader should be chosen carefully because ....

2. Sometimes, stressing too much on rules and regulations can lead to chaos in running a state. Should such strict implementation be followed, in the context of what happened in 'The Tale of Melon City'.

Assessment of Speaking & Listening Skills (ASL)

Sample Question Papers (1-5)

ASL

Assessment of Speaking and Listening Skills

CBSE has clearly outlined the significance of Speaking and Listening Skills as a part of co-scholastic areas of achievement by every learner. Considering this, CBSE has formally introduced the Assessment of Speaking and Listening Skills with 10 marks allotted to it. Thus, Schools have to conduct ASL themselves as per the guidelines provided by the CBSE.

The ASL comprises two skill sets- Listening and Speaking Skills which are assessed throughout the year in student interactions and participation. Further, teachers can also organise special tasks and activities in the session for assessment purposes. The parameters for assessment are as follows

- Interactive competence (Initiation and turn taking, relevance to the topic)
- Fluency (Cohesion, coherence and speed of delivery)
- Pronunciation
- Language (Grammar and vocabulary)

So, let us prepare ourselves for the ASL properly.

Speaking Skills

Speaking skills have acquired a very important place as a communication skill with a number of sub-skills needed to be consciously developed among students. Some of the sub-skills are as follows

- Speaking intelligibly using appropriate word stress, sentence stress and intonation patterns.
- Narrating incidents and events, real or imaginary, in a logical sequence.
- Presenting oral reports or summaries; making announcements clearly and confidently.
- Expressing and arguing a point of view clearly and effectively.
- Taking active part in group discussions, showing ability to express agreement or disagreement, summarising ideas, eliciting the views of others and presenting own ideas.
- Expressing and responding to personal feelings, opinions and attitudes.
- Participating in spontaneous spoken discourse in familiar social situations.

Assessment Patterns

Generally, teachers assess this skill by organising like debates, extempore, speeches, etc. For the same, teachers would provide you any topic, primarily related to the literature prescribed in the syllabus.

Some of these topics include

- Voting Rights
- Value of the Discipline
- Importance of Education in Developing Character
- Sports are Important in a Student's Life.

- Population Explosion Issue and its Repercussions
- Social Media Morality
- India's Poverty
- India's Changing Face
- Online Gaming- Is it Good or Bad?
- Learning Technology
- Value of Reading Literature
- Role of a Mother in a Family
- Impact of War on Society
- Various Facets of Discrimination
- Technology Addiction, whether it's Good or Bad
- Make in India Initiative
- Travel to India- The Country of Magnificent Individuals
- Increasing adoption of AI
- E-sports
- Value of Mental Wellness
- Yoga's significance in a student's life
- Value of Joint Family
- Importance of Retrospection
- Internet Privacy
- Dependence on Technology is Making Humanity Less Intelligent
- Human Overpopulation
- Importance of Culture and Music
- There are Enough Resources for Everyone's Need but not for Anybody's Greed
- Importance of Kindness and Compassion in Modern Society
- The Double Burden on Modern Woman
- Urban Rural Gap
- Laughter is the Best Medicine
- Stereotypes in the Mass Media
- Peer Pressure
- Current Developments in India's Educational System
- Honesty is the Best Policy
- Importance of Discipline
- Are Uniforms Required or Optional?
- Competitive Test Rat Race

The total administration time for the speaking assessment is approximately 10 minutes.

Speaking Skills Assessment (Sample Tasks)

TASK 1 : Voting Rights (Speech)

Voting rights are one of the most important aspects of democracy. They give citizens the power to choose their leaders and have a say in decisions that shape their country's future. In many countries, people over a certain age are granted the right to vote, ensuring that everyone's voice is heard in the political process. The right to vote is more than just a privilege - it's a way for people to influence the policies that affect their daily lives. In India, for example, every citizen over the age of 18 has the right to vote, which strengthens democracy by reflecting the will of the people.

However, voting is not just about casting a ballot. It comes with responsibility. Voters should take the time to learn about the candidates and the issues before making a choice. An informed vote helps ensure that decisions are made for the good of the country. There's also ongoing discussion in many countries about who should be allowed to vote. Some suggest that younger citizens or even non-citizens should have a voice in elections. These conversations reflect how democracy evolves, and how we consider who should have a say in shaping society.

In conclusion, voting rights are a powerful tool in democracy. They give people a chance to be part of the decision-making process and when used responsibly, they help build a better future for everyone.

TASK 2 : Technology Addiction-Good or Bad? (Debate)

Technology is everywhere in our lives today. From smartphones to computers, it makes things easier and faster. It connects us to people and information like never before. But with all these advantages, there's also a downside-technology addiction.

On the positive side, technology has made our lives more convenient. It helps us stay in touch with loved ones across the world, learn new things online, and get tasks done more quickly. Social media lets us connect with friends, and the internet opens up endless learning opportunities for students.

However, when we use technology too much, it can cause problems. Spending too much time on screens can lead to issues like eye strain, bad posture, and trouble sleeping. It can also make us feel disconnected from the real world, as we focus more on our devices than on face-to-face interactions. In some cases, this can even lead to feelings of isolation.

In the end, technology isn't inherently bad. It's all about how we use it. When used in moderation, it can make our lives better. But like everything, finding a balance is important for our overall well-being.

☑ TASK 3 : Sports are Important in Student's Life (Extempore)

Sports are really important for students, not just for staying healthy, but for growing in many ways. Playing sports helps keep the body fit and strong. It builds stamina, improves coordination, and reduces stress, which is really helpful when balancing schoolwork. But sports aren't just about physical benefits - they teach us important life lessons. Through sports, students learn how to work with others, stay disciplined, and develop leadership skills. These lessons are valuable, not only in sports but also in school and later in life.

Sports also offer a chance to take a break from studying. They're a fun way to relax and refresh, so students can come back to their books feeling more focused and energized. On top of that, sports boost self-confidence and help students deal with both winning and losing in a positive way. They teach the value of persistence and continuous improvement.

In the end, sports are a key part of a student's life. They help in staying healthy, teach important skills, and help students grow both inside and outside the classroom. Balancing sports with academics makes for a healthier and more fulfilling life.

Listening Skills

The Listening skills section tests the student's ability to listen for basic interpersonal, instructional and academic purposes. It includes a number of sub-skills that include the following

- Listening for specific information
- Predictive listening
- Listening for pleasure
- Evaluative listening
- Listening for general understanding
- Inferential listening
- Intensive listening

Assessment Patterns

The listening skill assessment takes places in a language lab, which is the specific lab comprises individual equipments for each students. The equipment comprises a headset and audio recordings. Students are made to listen to those recordings and answer some questions. If there is no such equipment, the teacher would read a piece of literature. The topic of the audio recording can be anything.

General Instructions for Students

- You are not allowed to ask questions or interrupt the Examiner at any point.
- You will hear a set of recordings of the Listening Input.
- Each of the recordings will be played twice.
- You are required to answer a set of questions based on each of the Listening Inputs.
- After you have listened to the input, you will be given specified minutes to answer the questions on your worksheet.
- You may answer the questions on your worksheet while listening.

Listening Skills Assessment (Sample Tasks)

TASK 1

The given bar code or link contains an audio recording. Listen to the recording and answer the following questions.

TO LISTEN THIS TRANSCRIPT

Link https://youtu.be/XwPeKkpkK1s?si=1XUdCKi3EPxHCxBe

OR **Scan the Code**

Questions

1. A68 is a road that...

(a) looks very similar to the other roads.
(b) is made with traditional asphalt.
(c) had a lot of construction problems.

Ans. (a)

2. The plastic material used to make the road...

(a) comes entirely from bottles.
(b) is easy to recycle.
(c) cannot be easily recycled.

Ans. (c)

3. In this region,...

(a) there are a few places that make plastic for roads.
(b) there is only one place that makes plastic for roads.
(c) there are many roads made using plastic waste

Ans. (b)

4. Regarding quality, they think that plastic asphalt is...

(a) better than traditional asphalt.
(b) as good as traditional asphalt.
(c) worse than traditional asphalt.

Ans. (b)

5. For a part of the A689 road, they used...

(a) 60,000 shopping bags.
(b) 6 tons of plastic.
(c) 6,5 tons of plastic.

Ans. (c)

6. In the UK, we...

(a) recycle about 50% of the plastic.
(b) recycle less plastic than other countries.
(c) bring recycled plastic from other countries.

Ans. (a)

TASK 2

The given bar code or like contains an audio recording. Listen to the recording and answer the following questions.

TO LISTEN THIS TRANSCRIPT

Link https://youtu.be/Av-vwHXF6_U OR **Scan the Code**

Questions

1. **Which building is the library?**
   (a) Building A (b) Building B (c) Building C (d) Building D
   (e) Building E
2. **Which building is the pharmacy?**
   (a) Building A (b) Building B (c) Building C (d) Building D
   (e) Building E
3. **Which building is the grocery store?**
   (a) Building A (b) Building B (c) Building C (d) Building D
   (e) Building E
4. **Which building is the bank?**
   (a) Building A (b) Building B (c) Building C (d) Building D
   (e) Building E
5. **Which building is the post office?**
   (a) Building A (b) Building B (c) Building C (d) Building D
   (e) Building E

TASK 3

The given bar code or link contains an audio recording. Listen to the recording and answer the following questions.

TO LISTEN THIS TRANSCRIPT

Link https://youtu.be/Gy69OZP04ws OR **Scan the Code**

Questions

1. **Who would give money to charity?**
2. **Who would stop working?**
3. **Who would buy a big country house?**
4. **Who would study something creative?**
5. **Who would go travelling?**
6. **Who would give the money to family members?**
7. **Who would buy a horse?**
8. **Who would save some of the money for later?**

TASK 4

The given bar code or link contains an audio recording. Listen to the recording and answer the following questions.

TO LISTEN THIS TRANSCRIPT

Link https://youtu.be/WkpHFzegBg8 OR **Scan the Code**

Questions

1. **Someone killed James Carrington with ....**
   (a) a gun (b) a knife (c) poison
2. **Lucille was staying with her .... Joanna at the time of his death.**
   (a) friend (b) aunt (c) daughter
3. **On the afternoon of the 5th June, Lucille was buying ....**
   (a) tea (b) medicine (c) clothes
4. **She spent that afternoon ....**
   (a) with Joanna (b) with James (c) alone
5. **The neighbour, Mrs. Box, saw a woman wearing a ....**
   (a) grey hat (b) coat (c) long dress
6. **According to Mrs. Box, a man and a woman were .... in the house.**
   (a) talking (b) fighting (c) arguing
7. **Lucille ....**
   (a) knew who James' lover was (b) had seen James with his lover once
   (c) didn't know who James' lover was
8. **Lucille thinks that James' lover killed him ....**
   (a) for money (b) because she found something in his pocket (c) because she was jealous

TASK 5

The given bar code or link contains an audio recording. Listen to the recording and answer the following questions.

TO LISTEN THIS TRANSCRIPT

Link https://youtu.be/X2yfUL8uct0 OR **Scan the Code**

Questions

1. **What does the woman in the introduction NOT say they are going to talk about in the video?**
2. **According to James Wyatt, what is the sleep pattern of the people on the US?**
3. **What is the REM Stage?**
4. **List some causes of sleep disorders, according to experts?**
5. **State some of the doctor's recommendations?**
6. **Define Sleep Hygiene.**
7. **According James Wyatt, ...**
   (a) they always give medication to their patients (b) they can treat any sleep disorder
   (c) they never give medication

TASK 6

The given bar code or link contains an audio recording. Listen to the recording and answer the following questions.

TO LISTEN THIS TRANSCRIPT

Link https://youtu.be/p21i15knnT8 OR **Scan the Code**

Questions

1. **A cyberchondriac is a person who ...**
   (a) tries to find what illness they have on the Internet
   (b) reads a lot about medicine
   (c) writes online diagnoses to try to help other people
2. **Doctor David Hilden thinks people ...**
   (a) look for symptoms on the Internet too often
   (b) often reach erroneous conclusions about their symptoms
   (c) are sometimes sicker than they may think
3. **Doctor David Hilden ...**
   (a) has been an expert on cyberchondria for a long time
   (b) has known about cyberchondria only for a short time
   (c) thinks that cyberchondria is becoming less prevalent
4. **He says that cyberchondria causes people ...**
   (a) to ask for medicines they don't need
   (b) to panic and visit their doctor too often
   (c) to be distressed and ask doctors for unnecessary tests
5. **He spends a considerable amount of time ...**
   (a) telling patients that they don't have the illness they think they have
   (b) making sure patients don't pay attention to the internet
   (c) telling patients which websites they can visit
6. **According to the doctor, the Internet is beneficial because ...**
   (a) people get an idea of what illness they have
   (b) people learn about how healthy food, and lifestyle
   (c) people learn about what symptoms they should be worried about
7. **Hilden says the Internet can also ...**
   (a) be a substitute for going to the doctor
   (b) help prevent illnesses
   (c) provide information about medicines

Rubric for ASL

CBSE has also provided a rubric which helps the teacher assess and grade a student's listening and speaking skill.

	1	2	3	4	5
Interaction	• Contributions are mainly unrelated to those of other speakers • Shows hardly any initiative in the development of conversation • Very limited and interaction	• Contributions are often unrelated to those of the other speaker. • Generally passive in the development of conversation.	• Develops interaction adequately makes however minimal effort to initiate conversation • Needs constant prompting to take turns	• Interaction is adequately initiated and developed • Takes turn but needs some prompting	• Initiates and logically develops simple conversation on familiar topics • Takes turns appropriately
Fluency & Coherence	• Noticeably/long pauses; rate of speech is slow • Frequent repetition and/or self-correction this is all right in informal conversation • Links only basic sentences; breakdown of coherence evident	• Usually fluent; produces simple speech fluently, but loses coherence in complex communication • Often hesitates and/ or resorts to slow speech • Topics partly developed; not always concluded logically	• Is willing to speake at length, however repetition is noticeable • Hesitates and/or self corrects; occasionally loses coherence • Topics developed, but usually not logically concluded	• Speaks without noticeable effort, with a little repetition • Demonstrates hesitation to find words or use correct grammatical structures and/or use correct grammatical structures and/or self-correction • Topics not fully developed to merit.	• Speaks fluently almost with no repetition and minimal hesitation • Develops topic fully and coherently
Pronunciation	• Frequent inaccurate pronunciation • Communication is severely affected	• Frequently unintelligible articulation • Frequent phonological errors • Major communication problems	• Largely correct pronunciation and clear articulation except occasional error	• Mostly correct pronunciation and clear articulation • Is clearly understood most of the time; very few phonological errors	• Pronounces correctly and articulated clearly • Is always comprehensible • Uses appropriate intonation
Vocabulary & Grammar	• Demonstrated almost no flexibility, and mostly struggles for appropriate words • Many Grammatical errors impacting communication	• Is able to communicate on some of the topics, with limited vocabulary. • Frequent errors, but self-corrects	• Is able to communicate on most of the topics, with limited vocabulary. • A few grammatical errors	• Is able to communicate on most of the topics with appropriate vocabulary • Minor errors that do not hamper communication	• Is able to communicate on most of the topics using a wide range of appropriate vocabulary, using new words and expressions No grammatical errors

Project Work

Apart from the specific skill test given above, CBSE also allots 10 marks to ASL based project work. This project work involves a project which can include an interview based project, an audio-visual data based project or a one-act play project. These project can be done by students individually or in a group.

Students have to plan and prepare the project throughout the academic session to given a presentation at the end of the year and answer the viva questions. Hence, the project work includes

(a) Project (b) Presentation (c) Viva Questions

Let us learn how to prepare for them to score well.

Themes of Project

CBSE mentions that the project can be inter-disciplinary in theme. The ideas/issues highlighted in the chapters/ poems/ drama given the prescribed books can also be developed in the form of a project. Students can also take up any relevant and age-appropriate theme. Some suggested themes include

- Voting Rights
- Technology Addiction
- Increasing Adoption of AI
- Role of a Mother in a Family
- Various Facets of Discrimination
- Evolving Food Tastes in my Neighbourhood
- Sports as a Career
- Travel to India- The Country of Magnificent Individuals
- Value of Mental Wellness
- Impact of War
- Hobbies-Changing Scenario
- Corona-Impact of Environment and Health Consciousness, etc.

Types of Project

As mentioned, CBSE has suggested 3 types of project that can be made

- Interview-based research
- An audio-visual data based
- One-act play project

1. Interview-Based Research

In this project, students can choose a topic on which to do their research. Then, they can read as much as they can about the topic. Then, they make questionnaire to be filled by at least 5-10 people around them or interview them. After the interviews are taken and the questionnaire are filled. They write an essay/ write up / report etc. up to 1000 words on his/her research and submit it.

Here is a sample of a questionnaire or interview questions and the essay.

Questionnaire: Evolving Food Tastes in My Neighbourhood

Demographics (Optional)

Age

☐ Under 18 ☐ 18-24 ☐ 25-34 ☐ 35-44 ☐ 45-54 ☐ 55+

Gender

☐ Male ☐ Female ☐ Non-binary/Other ☐ Prefer not to say

How long have you lived in this neighbourhood?

☐ Less than 1 year ☐ 1-3 years ☐ 4-10 years ☐ More than 10 years

Food Preferences and Trends

How would you describe the general food preferences in your neighbourhood?

☐ Traditional, home-cooked meals ☐ Modern, fusion cuisine

☐ Health-conscious (e.g., vegan, organic) ☐ Fast food and takeout

☐ Other (Please specify) ________________

Do you feel that food tastes have changed in your neighbourhood over the past 5-10 years?

☐ Yes, significantly ☐ Yes, somewhat ☐ No, not much ☐ Not sure

What factors do you think have influenced food tastes in the neighbourhood the most? (Select all that apply)

☐ Increase in international restaurants ☐ Growing awareness of healthy eating

☐ Popular food trends (e.g., keto, plant-based) ☐ Cultural influences from new residents

☐ Changes in economic factors (e.g., affordability of dining options)

☐ Other (Please specify) ________________

Are there any specific cuisines or types of food that have become more popular in your neighbourhood recently?

☐ Yes (Please specify) ________________ ☐ No ☐ Not sure

In your opinion, what food-related trend is currently most popular in your neighbourhood?

☐ Street food ☐ Plant-based or vegan options ☐ Fast casual dining

☐ International (e.g., Asian, Mediterranean) ☐ Health-conscious and organic options

☐ Other (Please specify) ________________

How often do you eat out or order food from restaurants or cafes in your neighbourhood?

☐ Every day ☐ Several times a week ☐ Once a week ☐ Once a month

☐ Rarely or never

What type of establishments do you prefer for eating out?

☐ Fine dining ☐ Casual dining ☐ Cafes or bakeries ☐ Fast food or takeout

☐ Street food vendors ☐ Other (Please specify) ________________

Local Food Scene and Impact

Do you believe that local restaurants and food businesses reflect the tastes of the community?

☐ Yes ☐ Somewhat ☐ No ☐ Not sure

What are some of the most popular food spots or restaurants in your neighbourhood?

____

Do you think there is a growing demand for more diverse or specific food options in your neighbourhood?

☐ Yes ☐ No ☐ Not sure

How important is sustainability (e.g., eco-friendly packaging, locally sourced ingredients) when choosing where to eat or what to buy?

☐ Very important ☐ Somewhat important ☐ Not important

☐ I don't consider sustainability when making food choices

Final Thoughts

What would you like to see more of in the food offerings in your neighbourhood? (Check all that apply)

☐ More international cuisine ☐ Healthier food options ☐ Vegan/plant-based options

☐ Family-friendly dining ☐ Affordable dining options ☐ Sustainable and locally sourced food

☐ Other (Please specify) ______________

Do you have any other comments or suggestions about food trends or changes in the neighbourhood?

____

____

Interview Questions

1. Can you tell me a little about yourself and how long you've lived in this neighbourhood?
2. How would you describe the general food culture or eating habits in this neighbourhood?
3. Do you feel like the food tastes in this neighbourhood have changed over the years? If yes, how so?
4. What kind of food do you typically enjoy eating in this area? Has that changed over time?
5. Have you noticed any new food trends emerging in your neighbourhood recently? If so, what are they?
6. In your opinion, what are the most popular types of food in the neighbourhood right now? Are there any specific cuisines or dishes that seem to be gaining popularity?
7. Do you think there is more variety in the types of food available now compared to a few years ago?
8. What factors do you think have influenced the evolving food tastes in your neighbourhood? (e.g., cultural influences, new businesses, economic changes)
9. Have you noticed an increase in demand for healthier or more sustainable food options? If so, in what ways?
10. What types of dining establishments or food spots are most popular in this area right now? Do you think the community's food tastes are reflected in the types of restaurants and food businesses here?
11. How has your personal food preference evolved since you've lived in this neighbourhood?
12. What do you think the future of food in this neighbourhood looks like? Are there any emerging trends you expect to see more of in the coming years?
13. What would you like to see more of in terms of food offerings or dining experiences in this neighbourhood?
14. Is there anything else you'd like to share about the food scene or food culture in the neighbourhood?
15. How can the community support or encourage positive changes in food preferences and trends here?

Report on Evolving Food Tastes in My Neighbourhood

Introduction

Food plays a central role in our lives, serving not just as sustenance but also as a key element of socialisation, culture, and identity. Over time, food preferences can change due to various factors such as cultural shifts, economic trends, and global influences. This report examines how food tastes have evolved in my neighbourhood, the factors driving these changes, and the impact these shifts are having on local dining and food culture. By analysing local trends and community responses, this report aims to provide insights into the dynamic food landscape in my area.

The Changing Food Landscape

Over the past decade, food tastes in my neighbourhood have evolved significantly. Historically, the neighbourhood was known for its classic comfort foods, often featuring hearty, traditional dishes passed down through generations. Local eateries typically offered home-cooked meals, with a focus on regional flavours and familiar, well-loved recipes. However, this traditional food culture has gradually given way to a more diverse and dynamic food scene, reflecting broader societal shifts and the influence of global food trends.

One of the most noticeable changes has been the rise of ethnic and international cuisines. Ten years ago, the neighbourhood had only a handful of international restaurants, mostly offering Italian, Chinese, and American fast-food options. Today, however, the culinary landscape has expanded significantly, with new restaurants and food vendors serving Mediterranean, Latin American, Middle Eastern, and Asian fusion dishes. This shift can be attributed to a growing interest in global flavours, as well as an influx of residents from different cultural backgrounds, each bringing their culinary traditions with them.

Key Factors Influencing Changing Food Tastes

Several factors have contributed to the evolving food tastes in my neighbourhood. These include demographic changes, economic influences, the rise of food trends, and increased awareness of health and sustainability.

Demographic Changes and Cultural Diversity One of the key drivers of the shift in food tastes is the changing demographics of the neighbourhood. Over the past few years, there has been an increase in the number of people from diverse cultural backgrounds moving into the area. As these new residents bring their food traditions and culinary preferences, local dining options have had to adapt. For example, the introduction of Mediterranean and Indian restaurants can be directly linked to an influx of people from those regions. This has led to a richer and more diverse culinary environment, where traditional dishes from around the world are now readily available and appreciated by both newcomers and long-time residents.

Economic Factors and the Rise of Food Entrepreneurs The local economy has also played a role in reshaping food tastes. The rise of the 'foodie' culture, supported by social media and food blogs, has created a demand for unique and novel dining experiences. As a result, there has been a boom in food startups and small, independent eateries. Many local entrepreneurs have capitalised on this trend, opening restaurants and food trucks that offer inventive, artisanal, or fusion dishes. This entrepreneurial spirit has not only brought fresh food concepts to the neighbourhood but also encouraged established restaurants to diversify their menus to cater to the changing tastes of consumers.

Health and Wellness Trends In recent years, there has been a noticeable shift towards healthier eating. The growing awareness of issues such as obesity, dietary restrictions, and food allergies has led many residents to prioritise healthier food choices. As a result, there has been an increase in the number of restaurants offering vegetarian, vegan, gluten-free, and low-carb options. Additionally, organic and locally sourced ingredients have become more popular, with consumers increasingly interested in the quality and sustainability of the food they eat. This health-conscious shift has also been fueled by social media influencers and fitness enthusiasts who promote clean eating and healthy lifestyles.

Sustainability and Ethical Eating Alongside the focus on health, sustainability has emerged as a significant factor in the evolving food landscape. Many residents are becoming more conscious of the environmental impact of their food choices. As a result, there has been a noticeable rise in demand for restaurants that serve sustainably sourced, ethically produced food. This includes organic produce, free-range meats, and seafood that is responsibly harvested. In addition, there is a growing trend towards zero-waste dining, with restaurants opting for compostable packaging, reducing food waste, and offering plant-based menu options as a more sustainable alternative to traditional meat-based dishes.

Emerging Food Trends in the Neighbourhood

Several food trends have emerged as particularly influential in my neighbourhood in recent years. Some of the most notable trends include

Plant-Based and Vegan Options Veganism and plant-based eating have moved beyond a niche lifestyle and have become mainstream in my neighborhood. Many local restaurants now offer extensive plant-based menus that cater to the growing demand for meat alternatives. Dishes like vegan burgers, plant-based sushi, and dairy-free desserts have become common offerings, even at non-vegan establishments. This trend is likely driven by both ethical concerns regarding animal welfare and environmental impact, as well as health-conscious consumers looking for cleaner, plant-based options.

Street Food and Casual Dining Street food has gained popularity in the neighbourhood, with food trucks and pop-up vendors offering affordable, quick, and flavourful meals. These vendors often specialise in international cuisines, providing an accessible way for people to try new and exotic dishes. The growing trend toward casual dining, where the focus is on high-quality, flavourful food without the formality of fine dining, has also contributed to this shift.

Health-Conscious Fast Food As traditional fast food chains face growing competition from healthier alternatives, a new wave of 'health-conscious fast food' has emerged in the area. These establishments focus on providing fast, affordable meals that are made with wholesome, minimally processed ingredients. Many of these businesses offer grain bowls, smoothie bowls, salads, and wraps, emphasising fresh vegetables, lean proteins, and nutrient-dense foods.

Fusion Cuisine Fusion cuisine, which combines elements from different culinary traditions, is another growing trend in the neighbourhood. Restaurants that experiment with blending diverse flavours and techniques are attracting attention from adventurous diners. For example, you might find Korean tacos, sushi burritos, or Mediterranean-style pizza. These inventive dishes allow residents to experience the best of multiple culinary worlds in a single meal.

Challenges and Opportunities

While the evolving food tastes in the neighbourhood present many exciting opportunities, there are also challenges to consider. The rapid diversification of food options has led to increased competition among local restaurants, making it difficult for some businesses to stand out. Additionally, as the demand for organic and sustainably sourced ingredients grows, it can be challenging for smaller, independent restaurants to keep up with the rising costs of these products.

On the other hand, the evolving food scene presents a wealth of opportunities for innovation and community engagement. New food trends open the door for creative entrepreneurs to develop niche concepts that cater to emerging consumer preferences. Furthermore, the neighbourhood's growing food diversity can help build stronger connections between residents of different cultural backgrounds, fostering a more inclusive and interconnected community.

Conclusion

The food tastes in my neighbourhood have evolved significantly over the past decade, driven by demographic changes, economic shifts, and global food trends. The rise of international cuisines, health-conscious eating, and sustainability concerns has transformed the local dining scene, offering a wider variety of dining options to cater to diverse tastes and preferences. As the food culture continues to evolve, it is clear that the neighbourhood will continue to embrace innovation while honouring its rich culinary traditions. With increased demand for ethical, healthy, and unique food options, there are many exciting opportunities for both consumers and food businesses in the years to come.

Sample Viva Questions

Some viva-based questions on this report are

1. Can you briefly summarise the main changes in food tastes in your neighbourhood over the past decade?
2. What are some of the key factors that have contributed to the evolution of food tastes in your neighbourhood?
3. How have cultural diversity and demographic changes impacted the food scene in your neighbourhood?
4. What role does social media and food bloggers play in the evolution of food tastes in your area?
5. In your report, you mentioned a rise in plant-based and vegan food options. Why do you think this trend has gained popularity in recent years?
6. Can you discuss any specific examples of restaurants or food establishments in your neighbourhood that focus on sustainable or organic offerings?
7. In your report, you mentioned the rise of street food. Why do you think street food has become so popular, especially in urban areas?
8. Do you think the neighbourhood's shift towards health-conscious fast food will continue to grow, or is it just a passing trend? Why?
9. You mentioned the increased competition among food businesses. How do you think restaurants can differentiate themselves in such a competitive environment?
10. How do you see the future of food tastes in your neighbourhood? Do you think the changes will continue, or will there be a shift back to more traditional food options?
11. Do you think the growing interest in sustainable food choices is driven more by consumer demand or by businesses trying to capitalise on a trend?
12. From your research and observations, which food trend do you think will have the most lasting impact on your neighbourhood in the next decade?

2. An Audio-visual Data Based

In this project, students can listen to podcasts/interviews/radio or TV documentary on a topic and prepare a report countering or agreeing with the speakers.

Here is a list of some podcasts, interviews and documentaries that a student can listen to.

Podcasts

- Ted talks
- Think Fast Talk Smart
- Reducing Human Impact on the Environment-Lauren Pettifer
- The Time of India Podcast
- Think School
- BBC Earth
- The Stories of Mahabharata

Shows, Videos and Documentaries

- Why go to mars- The Economist - https://youtu.be/ticaLyuePjA
- How to fuel the future- The Economist- https://youtu.be/_d325ohXLxE
- Susan Benett- The voice behind Siri- https://youtu.be/QP-iVhdXjPk
- The hidden underground city of Turkey- https://youtu.be/Wc7MgKMYN7s
- How languages become extinct? The Economist- https://youtu.be/Qr8QsNCe3C4
- The Ecocapsule- https://youtu.be/c6jbJwckH7o
- Interview with Lily Singh- https://youtu.be/Fwo7UW7c_8o
- Detox camps for internet addicts- https://youtu.be/YuT_RAugJu0
- Threat of War Between South Korea and North Korea- https://youtu.be/K0oAWBs9Ha0

- Planet Earth (2006) by BBC
- Our Planet (2019)
- The White Tiger
- The True Cost of Fashion
- Writing with Fire (2021)
- Cosmos: A Spacetime Odyssey (2014)
- The Social Dilemma (2020)
- Period, end of sentence
- Cities of Sleep
- The Elephant Whisperers (2022)

SAMPLE

You can access the Podcast titled Transform your fear into strength - Gautam Buddha from the bar code given below.

https://open.spotify.com/episode/0xyMzWaWj2kf75BJy2Uofc?si=cSSttCk8QbOZlBZhNX1KEw

Sample Essay

'Transform Your Fear into Strength' by Gautama Buddha

Fear is a natural human emotion that has been a part of our existence since the dawn of time. While it serves an essential role in survival, fear can often become a hindrance, limiting our growth and preventing us from living our lives to the fullest. Gautama Buddha, the founder of Buddhism, offered profound insights on how to overcome fear and transform it into a source of strength. His teachings emphasise the importance of self-awareness, mindfulness, and inner peace as pathways to conquer fear. This essay explores the essence of transforming fear into strength through the teachings of Buddha and how we can apply his wisdom in our modern lives.

Understanding Fear from a Buddhist Perspective

Buddha viewed fear not as an inherent part of our nature, but as a product of the mind and our attachments to worldly desires. According to him, fear arises from ignorance-the inability to see things as they truly are. This ignorance leads to attachments, expectations, and desires, all of which give birth to anxiety and fear. We fear losing what we love, being judged by others, or failing to meet our own standards. These fears are all connected to our sense of 'self'-an ego that we are desperately trying to protect.

One of Buddha's central teachings is the concept of 'impermanence' (anicca)-the understanding that all things are temporary. Fear often arises from our attachment to things that are fleeting. Buddha taught that by acknowledging impermanence, we can release our attachment to outcomes and the fear of loss. When we realise that all things, including life itself, are temporary, fear loses its power over us.

The Role of Mindfulness in Overcoming Fear

Mindfulness, or sati, is another key Buddhist practice that Buddha proposed as a way to transform fear into strength. Mindfulness is the art of being present in the moment, fully aware of our thoughts, feelings, and sensations without judgement. Fear often arises when we dwell on the past or worry about the future. We become trapped in our anxieties and forget to live in the present.

By practicing mindfulness, we learn to observe our fears without being controlled by them. Instead of reacting impulsively to fear, mindfulness teaches us to pause, breathe, and approach the situation with clarity and wisdom. When we are fully present in the moment, we begin to see fear for what it is-a mental construct, not a reality. This realisation allows us to approach fear not with resistance, but with acceptance, which weakens its grip over us.

Buddha also emphasised the importance of meditation as a tool for cultivating mindfulness. Through meditation, we can develop a deep awareness of our inner world and understand the root causes of our fears. Meditation helps calm the mind, reduce anxiety, and foster a sense of peace. By regularly meditating, we can shift our focus from fear to inner strength, gradually transforming our fearful thoughts into sources of empowerment.

Courage and the Path to Freedom

Buddha taught that fear is an obstacle on the path to enlightenment. To attain freedom from suffering, one must overcome the limitations of the mind, including fear. This requires cultivating courage, which Buddha described not as the absence of fear, but as the ability to act despite it.

In his famous teachings, Buddha emphasised that the 'middle path'-a path of moderation-was key to overcoming fear. This involves balancing our desires and actions, neither overindulging nor suppressing them. Fear often arises from extremes: extreme attachment to pleasure or avoidance of pain. By practicing moderation, we can learn to accept both joy and suffering, and in doing so, reduce the anxiety that arises from trying to control everything.

Buddha's teaching on compassion also plays a crucial role in transforming fear. Fear often comes from isolation, from feeling alone in our struggles. By cultivating compassion for ourselves and others, we can realise that we are not alone in our fear. Everyone experiences fear, and through empathy, we can connect with others and find strength in our shared humanity. Compassion softens the heart, making it less susceptible to fear and more open to love and courage.

Applying Buddha's Teachings in Modern Life

In our modern world, fear continues to manifest in many ways-fear of failure, fear of judgement, fear of loss, and fear of the unknown. Buddha's teachings remain highly relevant today, offering a roadmap for overcoming these fears and transforming them into sources of inner strength.

Embrace Impermanence Understanding that all things are temporary can help us release the grip of fear. Whether it's a difficult situation, a relationship, or a personal challenge, knowing that nothing lasts forever can bring comfort and perspective. This awareness helps us approach life's uncertainties with calm and resilience.

Practice Mindfulness In our fast-paced world, it is easy to become overwhelmed by fear. By practicing mindfulness-whether through meditation, deep breathing, or simply pausing to observe our thoughts, we can cultivate a sense of presence and awareness that weakens the power of fear. Mindfulness helps us confront fear without judgement, allowing us to take conscious, empowered action.

Build Courage Fear is natural, but courage is a choice. Buddha's teachings encourage us to take action despite fear, knowing that we are capable of overcoming obstacles. By embracing the discomfort that fear brings, we can build inner strength and resilience. Each step taken despite fear strengthens our capacity for courage.

Cultivate Compassion Fear often isolates us, making us feel separate from others. By practicing compassion-for ourselves and others–we can create connections that dissolve the barriers fear builds. Compassion nurtures understanding, reduces judgement, and opens the heart to greater courage.

Conclusion

Buddha's teachings offer profound wisdom for transforming fear into strength. By understanding the impermanent nature of life, practicing mindfulness, cultivating courage, and embracing compassion, we can gradually free ourselves from the grip of fear. Fear will always be a part of human existence, but through the lens of Buddha's teachings, we can learn to face it with equanimity and wisdom. In doing so, we transform fear into a powerful force that propels us toward greater growth, inner peace, and freedom. Fear, once a barrier to our potential, becomes a catalyst for our strength and enlightenment.

Sample Viva Questions

Some viva-based questions on this report are

1. Can you explain the Buddhist concept of fear? How does Buddha define fear in relation to the mind?
2. What is the relationship between ignorance and fear, according to Gautama Buddha?
3. Buddha talks about the impermanence of things. How does the understanding of impermanence help in overcoming fear?
4. What is the significance of the 'middle path' in overcoming fear and anxiety?
5. Can you give an example from your own life or current events where understanding impermanence helped reduce fear?
6. Do you think fear is a natural and necessary emotion for personal growth, or do you believe it is purely detrimental? Why?
7. How has your understanding of fear changed after learning about Buddha's teachings?
8. What specific Buddhist practice would you start with if you wanted to work on transforming your own fears into strength?
9. What do you think is the biggest obstacle in applying Buddha's teachings on fear in modern society?

3. One- Act Play Project

Another project that students can do is to create their own video/audio, after writing a script. While planning the one-act play project, a student has to keep the following things in mind

- Theme/topic of the audio/video
- What are the elements that need to be part of the script?
- What would be the duration?
- How would they present the script/report to the teacher, e.g. Can it be in the form of a narrative?

Remember, this is a team-based project. It will involve planning, preparation and presentation. There will be researching, discussion, writing the script, auditioning and ultimately producing the play.

Sample Script

Here is a sample of a script that students can use to make their once act play.

Characters

Aarav A school student, concerned about the environment.

Maya Aarav's friend, focuses on health and hygiene.

Teacher The class teacher, guiding the students.

Doctor A health expert discussing the pandemic's effects.

Environmental Activist A passionate advocate for environmental protection.

SCENE

(The stage is set as a classroom. Aarav and Maya are seated, along with several other students. The Teacher is standing at the front, ready to begin a discussion. There is a doctor and an environmental activist sitting on chairs, facing the children. There is a large poster on the wall that reads "Corona- A Wake-Up Call for Our Planet and Health.")

Teacher (Addressing the class) Good morning, everyone. Today, we are going to discuss something that has affected the entire world-COVID-19. It has not only changed our daily lives but has also impacted our environment and our consciousness about health. Let's start by hearing your thoughts one by one. Aarav, you start.

Aarav (excitedly) Sir, I've been reading about how the environment has actually benefited during the lockdown. With fewer cars on the road and industries temporarily shutting down, the air quality improved in many cities. I've even heard about wildlife returning to urban areas.

Doctor (Smiling warmly) Its true to say that The COVID-19 pandemic has certainly transformed how we think about our health. In the past, many people didn't take basic hygiene seriously. But the virus has shown us how easily diseases can spread if we don't take these precautions.

After seeing and suffering from the devastating impact of the virus, people have become more aware of their health. People are exercising more, eating healthier and being more conscious about their overall well-being. We've seen an increase in mental health awareness as well, as many people have struggled with isolation, stress and anxiety during lockdowns.

Aarav Dr. Gupta, what do you think the future holds for health consciousness after the pandemic? Will people continue to be this careful, or will things go back to how they were?

Doctor (thoughtfully) That's a great question, Aarav. There is hope that some of the habits we've developed during the pandemic-like wearing masks during flu season or regularly washing hands-will stick around. But we also need to stay vigilant, as the temptation to return to old habits can be strong. The key is to make these health-conscious behaviours a part of our everyday life.

Teacher Maya, what do you think about the impact of COVID?

Maya From a health perspective, the pandemic has made us much more conscious of cleanliness and hygiene. People are washing their hands more, wearing masks and sanitising everything. It's like we've realised how important these small actions are for our health.

Environmentalist I agree with you Maya. The pandemic has been a wake-up call for our environment, and we mustn't forget the lessons it's taught us. When human activity slowed down, we saw the environment healing. Air pollution levels dropped, rivers and oceans became cleaner, and wildlife began to reclaim spaces we had taken from them.

Maya (curious) That's amazing! So, you mean the environment benefited from the lockdown?

Environmentalist (nodding) Yes, absolutely! But, we must recognise that these positive effects were temporary. Once restrictions were lifted, pollution and environmental degradation started creeping back. The real question is Can we maintain this balance? Can we adopt habits that protect our planet while also focusing on our health?

Aarav (thoughtful) I think we need to rethink how we live. The pandemic showed us that small changes in our habits, like reducing unnecessary travel or using less plastic, can make a big difference in reducing our impact on the environment.

Environmentalist (smiling) Exactly, Aarav. Small steps make a big difference. If we all choose to live more sustainably-whether it's using public transport, conserving water, or reducing waste-we can protect the environment and our health at the same time.

The pandemic has taught us that we are all interconnected–with each other, with nature and with our health. Let's not wait for another crisis to remind us of this. Let's use what we've learned to build a healthier, more sustainable world.

Doctor (nodding) The journey towards better health and a cleaner environment starts with us. Every small action counts.

Teacher (concluding) So, remember, the lessons from COVID-19 aren't just about surviving a pandemic. They're about living consciously and responsibly. Let's commit to being more aware of our actions, making health-conscious choices, and protecting the planet for the generations to come.

(The students nod in agreement as the lights dim, and the play concludes.)

Sample Viva Questions

Some viva-based questions on this one act play are

1. Maya talks about health and hygiene. How do her concerns represent the shift in people's attitude toward health during the pandemic?
2. Do you think the play successfully addresses the idea of long-term environmental recovery following a global crisis like COVID-19? Why or why not?
3. Do you agree with the view that individual habits like reducing travel or using less plastic could have a significant long-term effect on the environment? Explain your answer.
4. How does the play suggest that young people, like the students in the classroom, can make a difference in shaping a more sustainable and healthy future?
5. What impact do you think this play would have on a young audience in terms of raising awareness about health and environmental issues?
6. If you were to perform this play in front of a large audience, how would you ensure the message about health and environmental consciousness reaches them effectively?
7. How do you think the play handles the theme of responsibility, both individual and collective, when it comes to the pandemic's effects on health and the environment?

Compilation of the Project

Now that we know about how to make the project, students should be aware of how to compile the project. This compilation comprises all the work that the students produce during the process of working on their ALS Project. It includes

- Cover page, with title of project, school details/details of students.
- Statement of purpose/objectives/goals
- Certificate of completion under the guidance of the teacher.
- Students Action Plan for the completion of assigned tasks.
- Materials such as scripts for the theatre/role play, questionnaires for interview, written assignments, essays, survey-reports and other material evidence of learning progress and academic accomplishment.
- The 800-1000 words essay/script/report.
- Student/group reflections.
- If possible, photographs that capture the positive learning experiences of the student(s).
- List of resources/bibliography

Presentation of the Project and Viva

Presenting your Class XI-XII project effectively is crucial to communicating your hard work and ideas clearly. Here are some tips to ensure that your presentation is successful

- **Understand your Project Thoroughly** You should know every detail of your project, from its objectives to the results and conclusions.
- **Anticipate questions** Think about possible questions that might arise during your presentation, and prepare clear, concise answers.
- **Grab attention** Begin with an interesting hook-an intriguing fact, a relevant question, or a personal story related to the project topic. Clearly state the problem or question your project addresses. This will set the context for your audience.
- **Follow a logical flow** Organise your presentation into clear sections-Introduction, Methodology, Results, Discussion, and Conclusion.
    - **Introduction** Briefly explain the topic, objectives, and significance.
    - **Methodology** Explain thc methods or processes you followed to carry out the project.
    - **Results** Present the findings or outcomes in a concise and understandable way.
    - **Discussion/Conclusion** Discuss the implications of your results and summarise your conclusions.
- **Avoid unnecessary details** Focus on the most important aspects of your project. If something is too technical or detailed, explain it briefly or provide supplementary material.
- **Maintain eye contact** Make sure to look at your audience (or camera, if virtual) to establish a connection.
- **Stick to the time limit** Respect the time allotted for your presentation. Plan your content so it fits within the time frame.
- **Rehearse your presentation** Practice delivering your project multiple times. This will help you become familiar with the flow and build confidence. Present in front of friends or family members for feedback.
- **Stay calm during the Viva** Listen to each question carefully and take a moment to think before responding. Don't be afraid to ask for clarification if needed.

Rubrics for Assessment

Remember that CBSE has suggested some parameters and a rubric to assess students on their project. These include the following

- Quality of content of the project
- Adherence to the specified timeline
- Clarity of thoughts and ideas
- Contributions by group members
- Accuracy of information
- Content in respect of (spellings, grammar, punctuation)
- Creativity
- Knowledge and experience gained

Sample Rubric for ALS Project Work (For Theatre/Role Play/Oral presentation/Interview/Podcast)

Category	1	2	3	4	5
Time Limit	• Presentation is less than or more than 5 minutes long	• Presentation exceeded or less than specified time limit by 4 to 5 minutes	• Presentation exceeded or less than specified time limit by 3 to 4 minutes	• Presentation exceeded or less than specified time limit by 2 to 3 minutes	• Students/group adhered to the given time limit
Content/Script/Questionnaire	• Script is not related to topic or issue	• Well written script/ content shows little understanding of parts of topic	• Well written script/ content shows good understanding of parts of topic	• Well written script/ content shows a good understanding of subject topic	• Well written script/ content shows full understanding of subject topic
Creativity	• No props/costumes/ stage presentation lack-lustre	• Some work done, average stage set-up and costumes	• Well organised presentation, could have improved	• Logical use of props, reasonable work done, creative	• Suitable props/honest effort seen/ considerable work done/Creative and relevant costumes
Preparedness	• Student/group seems to be unprepared	• Some preparedness visible, but rehearsal is lacking	• Some what prepared, rehearsal is lacking	• Good preparedness, but need better rehearsal	• Complete preparedness/ rehearsed presentation
Clarity of Speech	• Lack of clarity in presentation many words mispronounced	• Speaks clearly, some words are mispronounced	• Speaks clearly 90% of the time/a few mispronounced words	• Speaks clearly and distinctly 95% of time/ few mispronounced words	• Speaks clearly distinctly 95% of time/fluency in pronunciation
Use of Props (Theatre/Role Play)	• Only 1/no relevant props used	• 1 to 2 relevant props used	• 2 to 3 relevant props used	• 3 to 4 relevant props used	• 4 to 5 relevant props used
Expression/Body Language	• Very little use of facial expressions facial/body language, does not generate much interest	• Little use of facial expressions and body language	• Facial expressions and body language are used to try to generate some enthusiasm	• Facial expression and body language sometimes generate strong enthusiasm with the topic	• Facial expression and body language generate strong enthusiasm with the topic
Portfolio-Presentation	• Inadequate and unimpressive	• Some what suitable and convincing	• Adequate and relevant	• Interesting, enjoyable and relevant	• Brilliant, creative and exceptional

SAMPLE QUESTION PAPER 1

A Highly simulated Sample Question Paper for CBSE Class XI

ENGLISH CORE

GENERAL INSTRUCTIONS

1 This paper is divided into three sections : A, B and C. All sections are compulsory.
2 Separate instructions are given with each part and question wherever necessary.
3 Read these instructions very carefully and follow them faithfully.
4 Do not exceed the prescribed word limit while answering the questions.

TIME : 3 HOURS ***MAX. MARKS : 80***

FULLY SOLVED

SECTION - A

Reading Skills [26 *Marks*]

1. Read the passage given below. (10)

1. There are two types of diabetes, insulin-dependent and non-insulin-dependent. Between 90-95% of the estimated 13-14 million people in the United States with diabetes have non-insulin-dependent, or Type 2 diabetes. Because this form of diabetes usually begins in adults over the age of 40, it is called adult-onset diabetes. Its symptoms often develop gradually and are hard to identify at first; therefore, nearly half of all people with diabetes do not know they have it. This can be particularly dangerous because untreated diabetes can cause damage to the heart, blood vessels, eyes, kidneys and nerves. While the causes, short-term effects and treatments of the two types of diabetes differ, both types can cause the same long-term health problems.
2. What causes Type 2 diabetes? There is no simple answer to this question. While eating sugar, for instance, doesn't cause diabetes, it only causes weight gain. Scientists do not fully understand why obesity increases someone's chances of developing diabetes but they believe obesity is a major factor leading to Type 2 diabetes.
3. Age, sex, weight, physical activity, diet, lifestyle and family health history, all affect someone's chances of developing Type 2 diabetes. Experts now know that diabetes is more common in African Americans, Hispanics, Native Americans, and Native Hawaiians than in whites. While the chances of developing diabetes increase with age, gender isn't a risk factor.
4. Both types affect the body's ability to use digested food for energy. Diabetes does not interfere with digestion but it does prevent the body from using *glucose* (commonly known as sugar), for energy. After a meal, the normal digestive system breaks food down into glucose. The blood carries the glucose or sugar throughout the body, causing blood glucose levels to rise. In response to this rise, the hormone insulin is released into the bloodstream and signals the body tissues to burn the glucose for fuel, which causes blood glucose levels to return to normal. The glucose that the body does not use right away is stored in the liver, muscle or fat.

5. In both types of diabetes, however, this normal process malfunctions. A gland called the *pancreas*, found just behind the stomach, makes *insulin*. In people with insulin-dependent diabetes, the pancreas does not produce insulin at all so they take daily insulin injections to survive. This condition usually begins in childhood and is known as Type 1 diabetes.
6. In some cases people with non-insulin-dependent diabetes usually produce some insulin in their pancreas but their bodies' tissues do not respond well to the insulin signal and therefore do not metabolise the glucose properly, a condition known as insulin resistance. Scientists have identified two causes of insulin resistance.
7. There's no cure for diabetes yet. However, there are ways to alleviate its symptoms. In 1986, a National Institute of Health panel of experts recommended that the best treatment for non-insulin-dependent diabetes is a diet that helps one maintain a normal weight and pays particular attention to a proper balance of the different food groups. Many experts, including those in the American Diabetes Association, recommend a diet wherein 50-60% of daily calories come from carbohydrates, 12-20% from protein, and no more than 30% from fat.

Based on your understanding of the passage, answer of the following questions. $(1 \times 10 = 10)$

(i) According to paragraph 5, what do you think is common between both types of diabetes? (1)

(ii) Insulin resistance is a problem commonly found in non-insulin dependent diabetes. Justify. (1)

(iii) Read and complete the following sentence suitably. (1)

Choose the correct response from the two options to complete the sentence.

In both types of diabetes, however, this normal process malfunctions. A gland called the *pancreas*, found just behind the stomach, makes *insulin*. In people with insulin-dependent diabetes, the pancreas does not produce insulin at all so they take daily insulin injections to survive. This condition usually begins in childhood and is known as Type 1 diabetes.

People suffering from Type 1 diabetes ....

(a) may take insulin injections daily to survive
(b) must take insulin injections daily to survive

(iv) Complete the following suitably with an appropriate inference with respect to the following. (1)

The best way for treating non-insulin diabetes focuses on maintaining a normal weight and eating a ....

(v) The writer would not agree with the following statement EXCEPT (1)

(a) Both types of diabetes affect the body's ability to use digested food for energy.
(b) Pancreas does not make insulin.
(c) Type 1 diabetes is more common.
(d) There exists a cure for diabetes. (1)

(vi) State the correlation between Type-II diabetes and age. (1)

(vii) Comment on writer's reference to the major functions of insulin as mentioned in the passage. (1)

(viii) Complete the analogy with one word.

disease : diabetes :: cure : .... (1)

(a) gland secretion (b) glucose
(c) balanced diet (d) low calories

FULLY SOLVED

(ix) Which of the following, as stated in the last paragraph, plays a central role in preventing and managing Diabetes? (1)

(a) Calories intake (b) Exercise

(c) Sugar intake (d) Both (a) and (b)

(x) Assess the treatment suggested for diabetes. What kind of diet is recommended. (1)

2. Read the passage given below. (8)

1. Social media addiction is an emerging health problem in India, especially among the young population. Nowadays, irrespective of their socioeconomic background, adolescents have greater exposure to electronic gadgets like smartphones at a much younger age. The introduction of internet and the launch of low-cost data packages in 2016/2017 has put India on the global map for large-scale consumption of mobile data with active social media users going up to 197 million (14% of the population).
2. For adolescents, phone-based communication is an important way to maintain their social relationships. The use of social media websites then is one of the most common activities that has become an integral part of their day-to-day lives. Hence, making them more prone to social media overuse or addiction which may have a deleterious effect on the physical, and psychological health. Hence, it became important to study the pattern of social media usage and associated physical and mental health issues among Pre-University (PU) college students as they are the vulnerable group.
3. A cross-sectional study was conducted in Government and Private PU colleges situated in Urban Bengaluru city, Karnataka, India, during July to December 2016.The objectives of the study were to assess and compare the prevalence of social media addiction in different organisations, to assess the health problems related to social media usage, and to assess the various factors associated with social media addiction.
4. A total of 1870 study participants were recruited from both Government and Private PU colleges. Each participant was administered a pretest and semi-structured questionnaire as the study tool. They were asked to answer about the non-academic usage of social media. Scale comprised 10 questions, each given a score ranging from 0 to 4 (0-never, 1-seldom, 2-occasionally, 3-often, and 4-always), with a minimum score of 0 and a maximum score of 40. Participants were classified based on the scores as: Normal (<12), mild addiction (13–20), moderate addiction (21–32) and severe addiction (≥33).

Distribution of Study Subjects According to Grading of Social Media Addiction*

Grading	Government	Private	Total
Mild	182 (80.8)	191 (66.3)	373 (72.7)
Moderate	39 (17.3)	93 (32.2)	132 (25.7)
Severe	4 (1.9)	4 (1.5)	8 (1.6)
Total	225 (100)	288 (100)	513 (100)

**Figures in parenthesis indicate percentages*

5. There was no difference in the prevalence of Social Media Addiction between Government and Private PU college study subjects contrary to the assumption that Private college subjects will be more prone to social media addiction due to higher social status and purchasing capacity.

Based on your understanding of the passage, answer of the following questions. (1 × 8 = 8)

(i) Complete the following suitably. (1)

It was assumed that private college students will be more prone to social media addiction. This was because of their ....

FULLY SOLVED

(ii) Which of the following was not an objective for the study? (1)

(a) To assess the health problems associated with social media usage

(b) To assess and compare the prevalence of social media in a particular organisation

(c) To assess the various factors related to social media usage

(d) To assess and compare the prevalence of social media in different organisations

(iii) Give two reasons for the rise in active social media users in India. (1)

(iv) Classify the following statements as 'cause' and 'effect'. (1)

Statement I It is important to study the pattern of social media usage among Pre-University (PU) students.

Statement II Social media is becoming an integral part of students' day-to-day life for both academic and non-academic usage.

(v) Read the following. (1)

A social media addiction study was conducted in a school where it was found out that Shalini, Class IX student scored 38 in the same. Her friend, Akshat's score was 10, while their other friends Saksham and Priya scored 15 and 25 respectively.

Select the option that identifies the correct category Shalini, Akshat, Saksham and Priya belong to.

(a) Shalini – severe; Akshat – normal; Saksham – mild; Priya – moderate

(b) Shalini – moderate; Akshat – mild; Saksham – normal; Priya – severe

(c) Shalini – severe; Akshat – moderate; Saksham – normal ; Priya – mild

(d) Shalini – severe; Akshat – mild; Saksham – moderate; Priya – normal

(vi) What, according to you, makes the adolescents susceptible to social media overuse? (1)

(vii) Based on the reading of the text, state a point to challenge the given statement. (1)

Higher social status and purchasing capacity is directly linked to Social media addiction.

(viii) The study tool used in the survey comprised of (1)

(a) yes-no questions (b) a scale based questionnaire

(c) some physical and IQ based tests (d) Both (b) and (c)

3. Read the passage given below. (8)

Good decoration reflects the personality of the people who live in the home. It should, first of all, be distinctive, just as each person is distinct. A home should have unity not only within each room but also throughout the house. Rooms should, to some degree, harmonise with each other. The colour and styling of each room, particularly, should fit into the colour and styling of the rooms which run out of it. Attractive home furnishings set the stage for pleasant living. If they are an expression of yourself, you will have a feeling of satisfaction every time you enter your home, and friends will share your enjoyment.

However, furnishings and surroundings expressive of just the right note of restfulness, gay informality, or elegant simplicity are not often assembled by accident. Even enthusiasm alone is not enough. For most home decorators, it takes poring over plans, trying colour schemes, finding ingenious ways to make the best of what you have, and shopping around to search out just the right purchases at prices you can afford to pay. But there is keen pleasure in striving for the perfect result, and great satisfaction in achieving it.

FULLY SOLVED

Work and plan to enjoy life in your house. Limit the expenditures of time, effort and money to the extent of your abilities, so that just running the house doesn't dominate your life. Elegance and delicate things may be a drain you can afford only in a limited way. If you can't afford outside help, select a house and furnishings that require less care. Plan your activities so that tumult and upset are limited to a few rooms – an activity room or a bedroom, or a corner of the dining room.

You can select a pleasing combination of colours from a wallpaper, a fabric, an oriental mug, a flower or scene, or even a picture in a magazine. If you don't already have the furniture or mugs, it is a good idea to make up a colour scheme in this way. Let one colour predominate. Limit a colour scheme to two or three colours, with white or gray tones.

(i) On the basis of your reading of the above passage, make notes on it using headings and sub-headings. Use recognisable abbreviations wherever necessary (minimum 4). Supply an appropriate title to it. (5)

(ii) Write a summary of the above passage in 80-100 words. (3)

SECTION - B

Grammar

[7 *Marks*]

4. I. Choose the correct option. Answer any three. (1 × 3 = 3)

(i) The room .... is extremely tiny is mine.
(a) that (b) what (c) which (d) Both (a) and (b)

(ii) I will see you next .... it snows in Manali.
(a) where (b) when (c) then (d) why

(iii) Delhi .... on the bank of river Yamuna.
(a) stands (b) stood (c) has been standing (d) is standing

(iv) When I visited him in Mumbai, he .... there for five years.
(a) have been teaching (b) is teaching
(c) had been teaching (d) has been teaching

5. Transform the following sentences. (1 × 4 = 4)

(i) Transform the given sentence into Past Perfect Tense.
Every boy and girl was present in the class today.
(a) Every boy and girl are present in the class today.
(b) Every boy and girl had been present in the class today.
(c) Every boy and girl have been present in the class today.
(d) Every boy and girl had present in the class today.

(ii) Transform the given sentence into Present Perfect Tense.
I had not found the ring yet.
(a) I didn't found the ring yet.
(b) I will not found the ring yet.
(c) I has not found the ring yet.
(d) I have not found the ring yet.

(iii) Transform the given sentence into Future Continuous Tense.
I will read various kinds of book this summer.
(a) I will be reading various kinds of book this summer.
(b) I am going to read various kinds of book this summer.
(c) I will have read various kinds of book this summer.
(d) I will have been reading various kinds of book this summer.

(iv) Transform the given sentence into Simple Future Tense.
We will have been engaged in June of next year.
(a) We have been engaged in June of next year.
(b) We will be engaged in June of next year.
(c) We will have engaged in June of next year.
(d) We are going to be engaged in June of next year.

Creative Writing Skills

[16 *Marks*]

6. Draft an advertisement to be published in a local daily about German coaching classes. *(50 words)* (3)

Or

Your school, Akash Public School, Agra needs a canteen manager. On behalf of the Principal, draft an advertisement in 50 words to be published in the classified columns of a local daily.

7. Recently the Prime Minister has appealed to the citizens of India to conserve water and go in for rainwater harvesting on a mass scale. Design a poster for making the people aware of this important concept. *(50 words)* (3)

Or

Design a poster for promoting cleanliness in the surroundings of your colony. *(50 words)*

8. Write a speech in 120-150 words on 'Exam Stress on Students' to be delivered in the morning assembly. You are Rohan/Ruhi of Class XI-A. (5)

Or

Write a speech in 120-150 words on 'Hazards of Global Warming' to be delivered in the special weekly assembly held on Saturday.

9. "Bottled Water should be banned." Write a debate in about 120-150 words, in either for or against the topic. (5)

Or

"Online smart slasses are the future of education style". Write a debate either for or against the motion. *(120-150 words)*.

FULLY SOLVED

SECTION - C

Literature Textbooks

[31 Marks]

10. Read the extracts given below and answer the questions that follow. ***(Do any one)***. (1 × 3 = 3)

"Some twenty- thirty- years later
She'd laugh at the snapshot. "See Betty
And Dolly," she'd say, "and look how they
Dressed us for the beach." The sea holiday
was her past, mine is her laughter. Both wry
With the laboured ease of loss"

(i) Who is 'she' in the extract?

(ii) "The sea holiday was her past, mine is her laughter" these lines indicate

(a) the poet is remembering her childhood

(b) the poet is remembering her mother's childhood

(c) the poet is grieving at the absence of her mother

(d) the poet is missing the sea holiday

(iii) Select the correct option from those given in the brackets, to fill in the blanks.

The phrase "laboured case of loss" suggests that both the speaker and the woman in the photo feel a mix of fondness and .... (ecstasy/melancholy).

Or

When did my childhood go?
Was it when I found my mind was really mine,
To use whichever way I choose,
Producing thoughts that were not those of other people
But my own and mine alone.
Was that the day!

(i) Select the line that suggests the following.

The poet developed a sense of individuality and independent thinking.

(ii) What is the significance of the line "my own and mine alone"?

(a) It indicates that he is an adult now.

(b) It indicates that his opinions had always been influenced by others.

(c) It indicates that his opinions are now free from the influence of others.

(d) None of the above

(iii) What does this stanza reflect about childhood?

11. Read the extracts given below and answer the questions that follow. ***(Do any one)***. (1 × 3 = 3)

Although we shared the same room, my grandmother no longer came to school with me. I used to go to an English school in a motor bus. There were no dogs in the streets and she took to feeding sparrows in the courtyard of our city house. As the years rolled by we saw less of each other. For some time she continued to wake me up and get me ready for school. When I came back she would ask me what the teacher had taught me. I would tell her English words and little things of western science and learning, the law of gravity, Archimedes' Principle, the world being round, etc. This made her unhappy.

(i) What changes occurred in the relationship of the author and his grandmother in the city?
 (a) Grandmother didn't accompany him to school.
 (b) She couldn't help him with his studies.
 (c) She was unhappy with the things being taught to him in school.
 (d) All of the above

(ii) Read the assertion and reason based on the extract.

Assertion (A) The narrator's English school had little connection with the grandmother's traditional beliefs.

Reason (R) The grandmother was knowledgeable about western science and English but did not like it.
 (a) Both (A) and (R) are true and (R) is the correct explanation of (A).
 (b) Both (A) and (R) are true, but (R) is not the correct explanation of (A).
 (c) (A) is true, but (R) is false.
 (d) (A) is false, but (R) is true.

(iii) Why was grandmother unhappy with author's new school?

Or

Water, Water, Everywhere. I could feel that the ship had water below, but I dared not abandon the wheel to investigate. Suddenly, the front batch was thrown open and Mary appeared. 'We're sinking', she screamed. "The decks are smashed; we're full of water'. "Take the wheel", I shouted as I scrambled for the hatch.

(i) 'Water, Water, Everywhere' includes the use of which of the following literary devices?

(ii) Choose the statement that is not true with reference to the given extract.
 (a) The author and his family were saved by another sailor.
 (b) The ship was badly damaged by the wave.
 (c) The author and his daughter was badly injured.
 (d) None of the above

(iii) How does Mary's reaction contribute to the tension in the passage?

12. Read the extracts given below and answer the questions that follow. ***(Do any one)*** (4 × 1 = 4)

One day back there in the good old days when I was nine and the world was full of every imaginable kind of magnificence, and life was still a delightful and mysterious dream, my cousin Mourad, who was considered crazy by everybody who knew him except me, came to my house at four in the morning and woke me up tapping on the window of my room. Aram, he said. I jumped out of bed and looked out of the window. I couldn't believe what I saw. It wasn't morning yet, but it was summer and with daybreak not many minutes around the corner of the world it was light enough for me to know I wasn't dreaming. My cousin Mourad was sitting on a beautiful white horse. I stuck my head out of the window and rubbed my eyes.

(i) Select the textual option that indicates that the author is referring to his positive childhood.

(a) 'good old days'

(b) 'delightful and mysterious dream'

(c) 'beautiful white horse'

(d) None of the above

(ii) Select the suitable option to complete the following.

The opening lines of the extract depict ....

(a) the beauty of white horse

(b) the beauty of life

(c) the beauty of childhood

(d) the beauty of summer morning

(iii) Complete the following suitably.

The narrator says that everyone thought Mourad was crazy except him, means that the narrator ....

(iv) Why couldn't Aram believe that Mourad was riding a horse?

Or

"Mrs. Pearson I might. Who d'you think?

Doris [Staring at her] Mum—what's the matter with you?

Mrs. Pearson Don't be silly.

Doris [Indignantly] It's not me that's being silly— and I must say it's a bit much when I've been working hard all day and you can't even bother to get my tea ready. Did you hear what I said about my yellow silk?

Mrs. Pearson No. Don't you like it now? I never did.

Doris [Indignantly] Of course I like it. And I'm going to wear it tonight. So I want it ironed.

Mrs. Pearson Want it ironed? What d'you think it's going to do—iron itself?"

(i) Identify the tone in which Mrs. Pearson talks.

(a) Cool and Incisive
(b) Flattering and Apologetic
(c) Brave and Strong
(d) Taunting and Angry

(ii) Why is Doris consistently reacting 'indignantly' towards her mother Mrs. Pearson?

(a) The mother is not listening to her
(b) The mother is angry at her as well
(c) The mother is acting unusual
(d) All of these

(iii) What does the passage reflect upon the relationship between Doris and Mrs. Pearson?

(iv) What does Mrs. Pearson do with Doris for being over dependent on her?

13. Answer *any two* of the following questions in 40-50 words. **(3 × 2 = 6)**

(i) Which is the 'most beautiful island in the world'?

(ii) Describe the scene when goldfinch with her family starts chirruping to the maximum.

(iii) Elaborate why the author was disappointed with Darchen.

(iv) What can you say about the childhood of poet's mother in the poem 'A Photograph'?

FULLY SOLVED

14. Answer *any one* of the following questions in 40-50 words. **(3 × 1 = 3)**

Interpret what was wrong in the Pearson family in the chapter 'Mother's Day'?

Or What did Mrs. S. ask her daughter to rememeber?

15. Answer *any one* of the following questions in 120-150 words. **(1 × 6 = 6)**

How was the author's experience in Hor different from the accounts he had read?

or What impression do you form of the poetess and her mother after reading the poem 'A Photograph'?

16. Answer *any one* of the following questions in 120-150 words. **(1 × 6 = 6)**

Theoretical knowledge is very different from practical observation and experience. Do you agree? Answer in reference to 'Birth'.

Or What qualities did the two boys Aram and Mourad have which are reflected by their actions? Explain by citing instances from the story.

ANSWERS

1. (i) Both types of diabetes, i.e. Type-I and Type-II diabetes can cause the same long term health problems.

(ii) It is true that insulin resistance is a problem commonly in non-insulin dependent diabetes. In some cases of non-insulin dependent diabetes the pancreas does not respond to the insulin signal. At a result, glucose is not property metabolised. This condition is called insulin resistance.

(iii) (b) must take insulin injections daily to survive

(iv) proper balanced diet containing different food groups

(v) (a) Both types of diabetes affect the body's ability to use digested food for energy.

(vi) There exists a correlation between Type-II diabetes and age. The chances of developing Type-II diabetes increase as the age of a person increases. Gender of a person doesn't play a role in it.

(vii) As per the information given in the passage, the major function of insulin is to signal the body tissues to burn the glucose for fuel.

(viii) (c) Balanced diet

(ix) (d) Both (a) and (b)

(x) The recommended treatment for diabetes includes a diet that helps maintain a healthy weight while ensuring a proper balance of different food groups. The suggested diet consists of 50-60% of daily calories from carbohydrates, 12-20% from protein, and 30% from fat.

2. (i) higher social status and purchasing capacity

(ii) (b) To assess and compare the prevalence of social media in a particular organisation.

(iii) Phone based communication is an important way to maintain the relationships for youngsters. The launch of low-cost data packages in 2016/17 has led to the rise of active social media users in India.

(iv) Statement 1 : effect, Statement 2 : Clause

(v) (a) Shalini – moderate ; Akshat – mild ; Saksham – mild ; Priya – moderate

(vi) Adolescents use phone-based communication as an important way to maintain their social relationships. Therefore, social media websites are used by them and have become an integral part of their lines. This makes them susceptible to social media overuse.

(vii) The given statement is untrue as the data revealed by the survey indicates that despite higher social status and purchasing capacity of private PU students, there is not much difference between government and Private PU college students as far as social Media relevance is concerned.

(viii) (b) a scale based questionnaire

3. (i) **Title** Decorating One's Home

I. Reflects prsnlty

(i) Distinctive

(ii) Unity and harmny

(iii) Colour and styling shuld match

(iv) Exprsn of yourself

(v) Give satisfaction

FULLY SOLVED

II. Dfclt task
   (i) Restfulness, simplicity and informality- accident
   (ii) Requires-
      - Plans
      - Mking the bst out wht you have
      - Trying colour schemes
      - Shpng for right purchases
   (iii) Perfect result satisfaction

III. Enjoy life in house
   (i) Limit-
      - Expend – time, effort and money
   (ii) Get house with less furnishing
   (iii) Hectic activities to be limited to few rooms
   (iv) Get pleasing combination of colours

Key to Abbreviations

Abbreviations	Words
prsnlty	personality
harmny	harmony
shuld	should
exprsn	expression
dfclt	difficult
mking	making
bst	best
wht	what
shpng	shopping

(ii) **Summary** A house reflects the personality of its residents. A house must be an expression of its residents which in turn pleases and provides satisfaction to them. Hence, good decoration of a house is important. This task requires hard work as a number of things must be sorted. After its construction, the way we enjoy our lives in the house depends upon us. We must limit our expenditure and only decorate it in a manner that does not upset us. A perfect colour scheme then acts as an added bonus.

4. (i) (d) Both (a) and (b)
(ii) (b) when
(iii) (a) stands
(iv) (c) had been teaching

5. (i) (b) Every boy and girl had been present in the class today.
(ii) (d) I have not found the ring yet.
(iii) (a) I will be reading various kinds of book this summer.
(iv) (b) We will be engaged in June of next year.

6.

Learn German in 6 Months
Contact Director,
Institute of Foreign Languages,
B-21, South Extension Part 2, New Delhi.
Phone: 011-2647XXXX

Or

Situation Vacant

Applications are invited by Akash Public School, Agra for the post of Canteen Manager. Applicant should be around 35 years of age, minimum Class X pass with at least of ten years of experience in running a canteen in a school. Apply within a week with full particulars and documents expected, to the Principal, Akash Public School, 12, Besant Road, Agra.

7.

Water is the Essence of Life

SAVE WATER SAVE LIFE !

Apply

Rainwater Harvesting

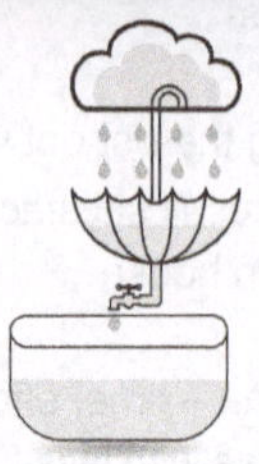

- Don't let rainwater go waste
- Preserve it in tanks and ponds
- Save this gift of nature for your coming generation

Issued by **Ministry of Information and Broadcasting Government of India**

Or

A CLEANLINESS DRIVE

CHARITY BEGINS AT HOME

Lets Begin with Neat and Clean Colony, Join this Drive

Date *: Sunday, 5th October, 20XX*

Time *: 9 : 00 AM*

Venue *: Community Centre, Janakpuri*

Tasks to do

- *Remove Filth*
- *Clean Environment*
- *Each One, Clear One Patch*
- *Make Janakpuri Spick and Span*
- *Keep Delhi Green and Clean*

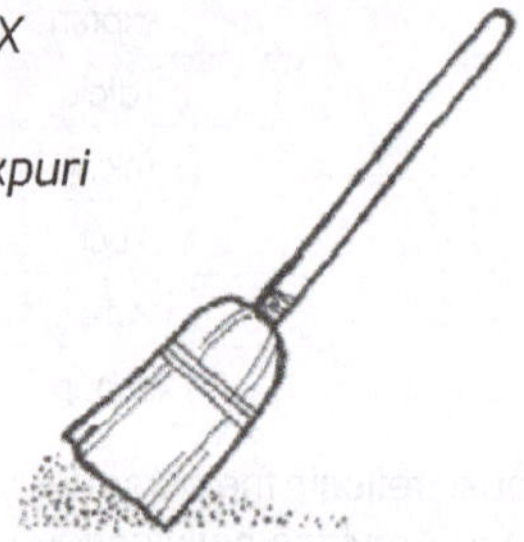

For More Details Contact Mr Deepak (923266XXXX)

8. Good Morning, everyone. I am Rohan of Class XI-A and today I will express my views on the topic 'Exam Stress on Students'.

Examination stress is defined as heightened anxiety affecting a student before, during and after an examination. It is a common problem faced by students throughout their academic life. Symptoms of stress vary from person to person. Some students are mildly affected and exhibit a few symptoms, while others experience severe reactions. Examination stress can be a real problem, especially when nervousness takes over and the candidate cannot even focus on the exams.

However, there are steps you can take to keep stress at a manageable level. In dealing with stress, there are Do's and Don'ts.

The many Don'ts include not to be negative or rushed or be influenced by those more stressed than you. The Do's include positive statements, natural breathing techniques and believing in yourself. After all, it is just an examination!

A little stress helps one to achieve one's objective, however too much stress adversely affects one's performance. One can have no stress, too little or too much stress. In the first instance, the candidate is overly confident. In the second instance, the candidate is spared much stress. In the third instance, the candidate is a bundle of nervousness and anxiety.

Thank you

Or Respected Principal, teachers and my dear friends.

This morning, I wish to draw your attention to the catastrophe that is slowly and surely coming towards us. I am talking about the 'Hazards of Global Warming'.

Some of my friends may not be aware of 'global warming'. This term means the rise of the temperature of the atmosphere surrounding our planet. This is happening because of over industrialisation, large-scale pollution and deforestation. Hot emissions from industry and release of chemicals in the air are making the atmosphere of the earth warmer day by day.

What are the hazards of global warming? Already, the polar ice caps have started melting. This can bring disaster to the world. Huge glaciers in the Himalayas and other mountains are shrinking. This will cause a rise in the sea level and will eventually lead to the flooding of coastal areas. Global warming will also bring about changes in the world climate.

There will be excess rains, floods, unbearable heat and cold. These changes will surely bring disaster to the flora and fauna of our planet.

What can we do about this problem? Effective measures to control pollution can be taken by all. The manufacturing companies can make sure to only use eco-friendly products and avoid using harmful substances in their products.

Simultaneously, we can make sure to keep a clean and healthy environment and stop overuse of equipments like AC, cars, etc, that aid in the continuously rising temperature.

With such steps and more, the problem of 'Global Warming' and its adverse effects on our planet can be dealt with.

Thank you

9.

For the Motion

By just taking a look around our environment; we can see that there is too much plastic that is scattered every where such as dumping areas and even at shores or by the roadside. Bottled water is drinking water packaged in plastic or glass water bottles. They have become a part of our lives.

Proponents of the ban on bottled water say that it would reduce waste and protect the environment by preventing the manufacture, purchase, use, and discarding of up to 68 billion plastic water bottles a year. They also say that banning bottled water is good for our health because of reduced exposure to potentially contaminated sources of water and to the toxic chemicals emitted from the bottles themselves and the plastic bottle manufacturing plants.

A ban would save consumers and local governments money, and protect local communities from the threat of depleted or contaminated municipal tap water supplies.

Against the Motion

Bottled water is perceived by many as being a safer alternative to other sources of water such as tap water. Bottled water usage has increased even in countries where clean tap water is present.

Opponents of the ban on bottled water say that it would remove a healthy beverage choice for consumers, leading to increased consumption of unhealthy sugary drinks. They also say that the ban is misguided as a waste- saving measure as other beverages are sold in containers that are more harmful than plastic water bottles.

A ban would remove a practical option for water storage and dissemination during times when municipal tap water supplies are contaminated, as well as removing a beverage choice that the majority of the consumers want, negatively harming small business profits.

Or

For the Motion

Honourable judges and worthy listeners,

"If you are so old minded and think that computers will be distracting children from studies, with a sincere sorry for you, let me tell you that the young generation has gone a long way with computers!"

Thus, I am here to talk about the endless possibilities of computer and internet based teaching methods.

When most parents think of learning from computers, socializing websites like facebook appear before their eyes. It is the biggest cyber tragedy. There are definitely a large number of sites beyond just facebook.

Udemy, Coursera, Khan academy, Byju's teaching app, the list of online teaching platforms is endless and ever growing. There are millions of students and teachers who use these websites and apps for their exam-preparation.

They are mostly free and it is what makes one turn away from traditional paper-guides. With a smartphone in every hand, city and village alike, these online libraries are within everyone's reach.

Google has already replaced the word Guru to become the greatest knowledge-provider.

With seven hundred billion population and six hundred trees, it is the need of the century to go paperless. In this context you can find no better solution than eLearning.

Rather than living the life of a consumer, let's be contributors. Instead of buying paper books, let's buy eBooks. Instead of collecting a thousand books in our shelves, let's convert our phones or computers into virtual libraries and learn.

Thank you

Against the Motion

Good morning, ladies and gentlemen! My topic for the day is 'Online Classes are the Future of Education Style' and I choose to speak against the motion.

Online learning or e-learning refers to learning conducted via electronic media, typically on the Internet. There is no face-to-face interaction between the teacher and the student. It decreases the scope of adjusting and modifying the language or the concept according to various audiences. Moreover, humans are known to be social animals and are thus, more interested in direct tuition than virtual tuition.

There is lack of proper guidance and self-assessment mechanisms. Not only this, it would also reduce employment among teachers.

Since it involves only brain work and not physical work, they tend to get lethargic resulting in altered physiology. Also, it leads to lack of discipline. Attending a school makes one have a time schedule in a day. This helps them learn some good habits like, bathing, breakfast, going to bed at the right time, etc. Physical school helps children adopt a discipline.

Not to forget the excellent interactions involved in physical learning. People tend to make friends who support them and mentors who guide them. Thus, no matter how fast technological developments are taking place, the traditional way of learning should not be displaced.

Thank you

10. (i) She is 'poet's mother in the extract.
(ii) (c) the poet is grieving at the absence of her mother
(iii) melancholy

Or (i) Producing thoughts that were not those of other people.
(ii) (c) It indicates that his opinions are now free from the influence of others.
(iii) The given stanza reflects that children's opinions are often influenced by others.

11. (i) (d) All of the above
(ii) (c) (A) is true, but (R) is false.
(iii) Grandmother was unhappy with author's new school because she couldn't help the author in his studies anymore.

Or (i) (c) It uses two leterary devcees – allusion and repclition.
(ii) (a) The author and his family were saved by another sailor.
(iii) Mary's reaction, appearing suddenly and screaming, heightens the sense of urgency and fear. It conveys that severe and immediate action is needed.

12. (i) (a) 'good old days'
(ii) (c) the beauty of childhood
(iii) understood Mourad better than others
(iv) Aram couldn't believe that Mourad was riding a horse because his Garoghlanian family and the entire tribe had no money and were poverty-stricken.

FULLY SOLVED

Or (i) (a) Cool and Incisive

(ii) (c) The mother is acting unusual

(iii) Doris is a selfish child, who only talks to her mother to get her work done. She takes her mother for granted and the passage reflects that.

(iv) Mrs. Pearson (actually Mrs. Fitzgerald) wants Doris and other family members to treat Mrs. Pearson with respect. For the same, she scolds and berates everyone so that they understand how they had taken Annie for granted.

13. (i) The most beautiful island in the world is Ile Amsterdam, a piece of volcanic rock with little vegetation. It is a French scientific base, as mentioned by the narrator in 'We're Not Afraid to Die...If We Can All Be Together'. After a long suffering in the storm, the family and the crew finally reached land on this island.

(ii) When the goldfinch starts chirruping to the maximum, the scene becomes musical. Chitterling and trilling is heard all round. The whole tree that was silent few moments ago now seems to be trembling and thrilling because the tree has become like a live engine of great power.

(iii) The author was indeed disappointed in Darchen as the place was dusty, partially derelict and punctuated by heaps of rubble and rubbish left behind by tourists. Further, even though the place was full of people, there were no tourists or pilgrims in whose company he could complete his kora.

(iv) The childhood of poet's mother seems to have been filled with fun and happiness.This is clear from the snapshot of a sea holiday from her childhood. All the three girls are smiling in the photograph which means that they were enjoying their holiday.

Also, years later, the poet's mother laughs while looking at the photograph which means it has pleasant memories attached to it.

14. The Pearson family consisted of Mrs Pearson's husband, George and their two children, Doris and Cyril, who were self-centered and demanding. The Pearson family wrongly behave with Mrs Annie Pearson who took care of all their needs without demanding anything. She was taken for granted and was not respected by her family members.

Or One day, when the narrator noticed that most of the items from their house were missing, she asked her mother about it. The narrator's mother told her that she had handed over all her precious items to Mrs Dorling for safekeeping. Further, she gave the narrator the address as Number 46, Marconi Street and told her to remember it.

15. Hor was a small town placed in the back on the main East-West highway that followed the old trade route from Lhasa to Kashmir. The author found the place very grim and miserable. There was no vegetation whatsoever, just dust and rocks, scattered all around along with heaps of garbage left behind by people. The town sat on the shore of lake Manasarovar, Tibet's holiest stretch of water. Ancient Hindu and Buddhist scriptures tell that Lake Manasarovar was the source of four great Indian rivers: Indus, Ganges, Sutlej and Brahmaputra. Actually only the Sutlej flows from the lake, the headwaters of the others rise nearby on the slopes of Mount Kailash.

His experience in Hor came as a stark contrast to accounts he had read of earlier travellers' first encounters with Lake Manasarovar. Ekai Kawaguchi, a Japanese monk who had arrived there in 1900, was so moved by the sanctity of the lake that he burst into tears. Similarly, in 1902, Sven Hedin from Sweden was also moved by the vision of the lake. However, now you could only find open-air dumps of rubbish in the town.

Or The poem 'A Photograph' presents the poet as a very sensitive person who is quite attached to her mother and remembers her every day. She remembers all the incidents connected with her life including her laughter on looking at an old photograph. She finds it very hard to cope with the death of her mother. The separation from her mother has left her speechless and sad.

The poetess mother appears as a physically well-formed person with a sweet smiling face. She has a friendly temperament and a free mixing nature. She has great affection for her two girl cousins and goes with them for a sea-holiday where they wear strange dresses. She poses with them smilingly for a snap. Her laughter in the photograph indicates that she is a very lively person and enjoys every moment and incident of her life.

16. It is a fact that books provide us information and knowledge in a particular area. But practical knowledge and observation provide a platform to test that knowledge. It has been observed many times that a person gains insight into that bookish knowledge through practice and keen observation.

Dr Andrew used this knowledge as well as his observation to revive the stillborn child. He made sincere efforts and acted on his instincts. This practice he would not have gained in any book of medicine.

After practicising it in reality, he was successful in giving a family new hope and lots of happiness. This would have not happened if Dr Andrew would have stuck to bookish knowledge only. Practice develops a better understanding of the situation.

Or Both Aram and Mourad, in the story 'The Summer of the Beautiful White Horse', have a number of good qualities which are reflected by their actions. These two boys in the story belong to the Garoghlanian family which had been famous for its integrity and honesty for centuries. Both the boys, reflected these qualities in their actions very well.

Their tribe was poverty-stricken, but they never indulged themselves in bad deeds to fulfill their desires. They never let their family down for anything. Undoubtedly, for some time, they got diverted from their principles of life when Mourad temporarily stole the beautiful white horse. Both Aram and Mourad were passionate about riding a horse, so it wasn't stealing to them. But soon, as per their character, they became conscience-stricken. They were overpowered by their conscience and realised that this step could put a question mark on their tribe's dignity and reputation. They finally decided to return the horse to its rightful owner.

Hence, their action shows that the two young characters reflect the human qualities of integrity and honesty which are very necessary in today's world. They were the true representatives of their tribe.

SAMPLE QUESTION PAPER 2

A Highly simulated Sample Question Paper for CBSE Class XI

ENGLISH CORE

GENERAL INSTRUCTIONS

1 This paper is divided into three sections : A, B and C. All sections are compulsory.
2 Separate instructions are given with each part and question wherever necessary.
3 Read these instructions very carefully and follow them faithfully.
4 Do not exceed the prescribed word limit while answering the questions.

TIME : 3 HOURS ***MAX. MARKS : 80***

FULLY SOLVED

SECTION - A

Reading Skills [26 *Marks*]

1. Read the passage given below. (10)

1. While there is no denying that the world loves a winner, it is important that you recognise the signs of stress in your behaviour and be healthy enough to enjoy your success. Stress can strike anytime, in a fashion that may leave you unaware of its presence in your life. While a certain amount of pressure is necessary for performance, it is important to be able to recognise your individual limit.
2. Stress is a body reaction to any demands or changes in its internal and external environment. Whenever there is a change in the external environment such as temperature, pollutants, humidity and working conditions, it leads to stress. In these days of competition, when a person makes up his mind to surpass what has been achieved by others, there is an imbalance between demands and resources, which causes psycho-social stress.
3. Stress reduces productivity and pressure to the management of organisations. Today companies prefer women to men as employees because of the hope that they bring additional qualities such as innovation, patience and dedication in the workplace. But due to increased pressure for women both at the workplace and at home, they face stress. Thus, any employee will make the maximum effort and give the maximum contribution when kept happy and without any stress. Hence, to increase productivity, it is the responsibility of the employer to keep the employees free from stress. Hence, it is essential to take steps to minimise the effects of determinants of stress and help individuals and organisations evolve newer and more effective coping strategies.
4. Stress takes a different meaning, depending on the stage of life you are in. The loss of a toy or a reprimand from the parents might create a stress shock in a child. An adolescent who fails in examination may feel as if everything has been lost and life has no further meaning. In an adult, the loss of his or her companion, job or professional failure may appear as if there is nothing more to be achieved.

5. Such signs appear, in the attitude and behaviour of the individual, as muscle tension in various parts of the body, palpitation and high blood pressure, indigestion and hyperacidity. Ultimately the result is self-destructive behaviour such as eating and drinking too much, smoking excessively or relying on tranquilisers. There are other signs of stress such as trembling, shaking, nervous blinking, dryness of throat and mouth and difficulty in swallowing. The professional under stress behaves as if he is a perfectionist.
6. A person under stress reacts in different ways and the common ones are flight, fight or flee depending upon the nature of the stress and capabilities of the person. The three responses can be elegantly chosen to cope with stress so that stress does not damage the system and become distress.
7. When a stress crosses the limit peculiar to an individual, it lowers his performance capacity. Frequent crossings of the limit may result in chronic fatigue, in which a person feels lethargic, disinterested and is not easily motivated to achieve anything. This may make the person mentally undecided, confused and accident prone as well. Diet, massage, food supplements, herbal medicines, hobbies, relaxation techniques and dance movements are excellent stress busters.

Based on your understanding of the passage, answer of the following questions. (1 × 10 = 10)

(i) What causes psycho-social stress? (1)

(ii) When does 'chronic fatigue' occur? How does it affect a person? (1)

(iii) Complete the sentence by choosing an appropriate option. (1)

A certain amount of pressure is ....

(a) necessary for under performance
(b) necessary for performance

(iv) Complete the given sentence with an inference with respect to the following. (1)

The writer quotes the example of a child, an adolescent and an adult in Paragraph 5 in order to highlight that ....

(v) Select the option that conveys the opposite of 'praise', from words used in Paragraph 5. (1)

(a) Stage (b) Loss
(c) Shock (d) Reprimand

(vi) How would you define stress? (1)

(vii) List the ways in which a person under stress behaves. (1)

(viii) Complete the analogy with one word. (1)

Stress : Chronic fatigue :: Relaxation : ....

(a) Healthy wind (b) Palpitation
(c) High Blood Pressure (d) Confusion

(ix) The writer would not agree with the given statements based on paragraph three EXCEPT (1)

(a) Stress increases productivity.
(b) Women face stress only due to increased pressure at home.
(c) An employee will give an average contribution when kept happy and without stress.
(d) To increases productivity the employer should keep his/her employees free from stress.

(x) List the symptoms of stress in individuals. (1)

2. Read the passage given below. (8)

The average age of India will be just 27 in 2020, which means that the majority of the country will comprise young students and youth. But even now with the clock ticking, the unemployment crisis is raging the country and the main reason behind this problem is that there are a huge number of

FULLY SOLVED

youth passing out from schools and colleges every year and there are many new career options and job roles being added to various industries as well.

However, the youth do not have the kind of skills the new industries want which results in a wide skill gap. A recent survey by Mindler, an online career-counseling platform, has proved that the majority of Indian students are aware of just seven career paths, even though there are 250 career options that can be pursued in India - most new and in-demand.

The survey on the awareness of career options among Indian students in the age group of 14-20 was conducted among 10,000 participants. The responses collected in the survey showed that a staggering 93% of the students who participated in the survey were aware of just seven career options law, engineering, medicine, accounts and finance, design, computer applications and IT and management.

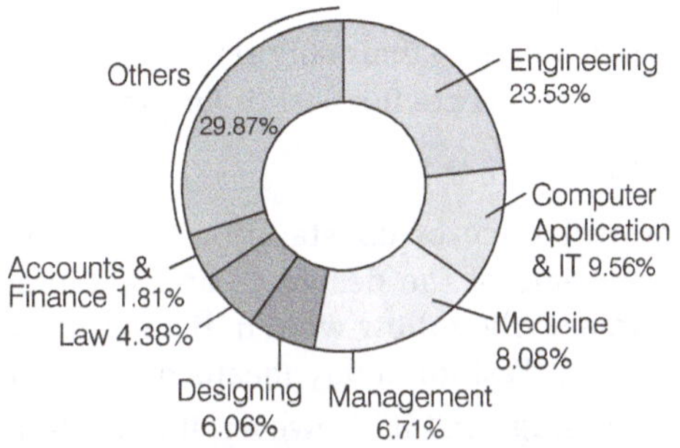

Common Career Options Considered by Students

According to researchers, India has a variety of 250 career options available across 40 domains covering 5,000 job types. This shocking lack of awareness among Indian students regarding their future career options can spell a death knell for the economic bonus that could have come to India due to its demographic dividend the time period where its population is young and earning.

Thus, if parents and teachers can build their own awareness regarding new career options coming up, then they can be a very helpful part in their child's career decisions rather than being one of those parents who push their child into one of the most common careers simply because they are unable to understand which area would be the perfect fit for their child.

If parents utilise the available technology and tools available, they can become more aware of which careers will help their children grow the most and career counselling can help both parties get the desired satisfaction.

Based on your understanding of the passage, answer of the following questions. (1 × 8 = 8)

(i) Complete the following suitably.

Most of the parents push their child into one of the most common careers. (1)

This happens simply because ....

(ii) Do you think the researchers of the study aimed to change the students outlook towards the new career options? Support your answer with reference to the text. (1)

(iii) What is the main essence of the passage? (1)

(a) There is a huge gap between education and employment opportunities.

(b) There is a lack of awareness regarding new professions available.

(c) Parents must be involved in the process of career selection.

(d) Only 7 professional field are popular in India.

(iv) Which two fields, according to the survey, was most popular among students? (1)

(v) According to the passage, the lack of awareness regarding various career options results in (1)

(a) unemployment
(b) frustration and depression
(c) economic stagnation with any bonus
(d) lack of economic bonus

(vi) Based on the reading of the text, state a point to challenge the given statement. (1)

Parents need not be aware of the upcoming career options.

(vii) How, according to you, is lack of awareness regarding various career options is affecting our country? (1)

(viii) How can parents become more aware? (1)

(a) By using the available tools and technology
(b) By talking to their children
(c) By providing career counselling to their children
(d) By finding which career options are the best fit for their children.

3. Read the passage given below. (8)

Fashion is a force – a powerful force of constantly altering patterns of change and growth. Its constant movement affects the fate of the designers and manufacturers who distribute it, and of course, the lives of the consumers who follow what it dictates. All of its facets taken together add up to a multi-million dollar industry. Fashion today means mega bucks.

Fashion is also a science. Surprising, isn't it? However, it is well-known that it involves known facts and basic principles and its actions and reactions can be predicted, as these are based on those facts and principles. Fashion is one of those distinct and unique trades that is highly dependent on the environment and the changes that are continuously taking place in it. These have to be understood by the designers if they want to become successful.

For one to make it to the top in the fashion business and stay there, one has to continue to discover and innovate to fulfil the needs and wants of the customers. For this, most of the top designers such as Yves Saint Laurent, Karl Lagerfeld, Claiborne etc., all rely upon their creativity backed by years of invaluable experience. In this line of work, instinct and intuition play a very major role besides the knowledge of past successes and failures.

As the power of fashion to influence our lives grows, a number of misconceptions about it continue to abound. The most common of these is that designers and retailers dictate what the fashion will be, by accepting or rejecting the styles and trends that are offered. They are truly, as one 'fashion guru' once said, 'Variety vultures'. However, it is not so – actually customers dictate the trends.

The second misconception is that fashion acts as an influence on women only. However, actually, men today are as much influenced by, and responsive to, fashion as women. In point of fact, the male fashion industry has been growing at a dizzying rate. Yes, there was a time when menswear was not exactly worth talking about. It was staid and unimaginative. But that does not mean that men did not dress up according to the latest trends of the day.

Fashion today is more lifestyle oriented and quite practical. The modern male and female want to dress differently for office and leisure. Designers are becoming more daring so that the women as well as the men have a wide choice. There are different designs for every moment of a busy social schedule - from work, lunch to afternoon tea, cocktails, dinner and gala banquets.

(i) On the basis of your reading of the above passage, make notes on it using headings and sub-headings. Use recognisable abbreviations, wherever necessary (minimum 4). Supply an appropriate title to it. (5)

(ii) Write a summary of the given passage in 80-100 words. (3)

FULLY SOLVED

SECTION - B

Grammar

[7 *Marks*]

4. Choose the correct option. Answer any three. (1 × 3 = 3)

(i) .... I wasn't feeling well, I went to school.

(a) When (b) Hence
(c) Although (d) Whether

(ii) I wonder .... she doesn't want to go to the picnic.

(a) why (b) how (c) where (d) when

(iii) Before I got the end of his article I felt that I knew everything there and eagerly .... about the North America Free Trade Agreement.

(a) is known (b) was to know (c) has been known (d) has to be known

(iv) In recent decades, the efficiency of the United Nations .... by a growing number of countries.

(a) have been questioned (b) was questioned
(c) had been questioned (d) has been questioned

5. Choose the correct option. (1 × 4 = 4)

(i) P: he wants to
Q: is a party
R: learn whether there
S: today or not

(a) PRQS (b) RPSQ (c) RPQS (d) SQPR

(ii) P: daughter been
Q: had her
R: eating anything
S: at all

(a) PQSR (b) RPSQ (c) QPRS (d) SQPR

(iii) P: that you
Q: won't always
R: I can understand
S: be with me

(a) PQRS (b) RPSQ (c) RPQS (d) SQPR

(iv) P: weather forecast
Q: raining tomorrow
R: according to the
S: it will be

(a) PQSR (b) RPSQ (c) QPRS (d) SQPR

FULLY SOLVED

Creative Writing Skills

[16 *Marks*]

6. You are the Director of Eco-centre, Bangalore. Draft an advertisement in 50 words about diploma courses in waste water management. (3)

Or

You are Harish/Harshita of 12, Seva Nagar, Pune. You want to sell your flat as you are shifting to another city for work. Draft a suitable advertisement in not more than 50 words to be published in The Pune Times under the classified columns.

7. You are Secretary of the Best Friends Animal Society. Prepare a poster on kindness to animals to be displayed in the city at public places appealing to people to join the society and show kindness towards animals. *(50 words)* (3)

Or

Design a poster for promoting space saving furniture. (*50 words*)

8. Write a speech in 120-150 words on 'The Problem of Terrorism in India'. Use the clues given in the box below. (5)

Terrorism a cowardly act disturbs the peace – creates a state of panic – major impact on tourism and economy – loss of life and property

Or

Manish has to speak in debate supporting the motion that life in the country (a village) is preferable to life in the city. Use the clues given below to develop Manish's speech in 120-150 words.

Country (a village) peace and quiet–soothing air–fresh and pure green fields all around–lovely sight helpful neighbours

City

vehicles–smoke

industries–smoke-pollution

crowded streets

people hurry–never relax

9. "Video games promoting violence should be banned." Write a debate in about 120-150 words, in either for or against the topic. (5)

FULLY SOLVED

Or

Are celebs responsible for the products they endorse? Taking a cue from the headlines given below and using your own ideas, write a debate for or against the topic. (120-150words)

- Amitabh Bachchan steps back from promoting Pepsi after a school girl questions the health impact of the drink.
- Brief ban on Maggi noodles causes trouble for its celebrity brand ambassadors.

SECTION - C

Literature Textbooks

[31 *Marks*]

10. *Read the extracts given below and answer the questions that follow.* ***(Do any one)*** (1 × 3 = 3)

"When did my childhood go?
Was it the day I ceased to be eleven
Was it the time I realised that
Hell and Heaven
Could not be found in Geography
And therefore could not be
Was that the day!"

(i) Select the correct option from those given in bracket to fill in the blank.

The tone of the given lines is .... (matter–of–fact/hopeful).

(ii) What did he realise about Hell and Heaven?

(a) They were near his house.
(b) They were in some other country.
(c) They were imaginary.
(d) They were difficult to find.

(iii) Complete the following suitably.

The poet realised that Hell and Heaven were imaginary when ....

Or

Eternal I rise impalpable out of the land and the bottomless sea, upward to heaven, whence, vaguely form'd altogether changed, and yet the same,

(i) Select the phrase that suggests the following.

The speaker is indicating continuity and timelessness.

(ii) The word 'impalpable' in the extract means

(a) something that can be touched. (b) something that cannot be heard.
(c) something that can be heard. (d) something that cannot be touched.

(iii) How is 'I' altogether changed and yet the same?

FULLY SOLVED

11. Read the extracts given below and answer the questions that follow. ***(Do any one)*** (1 × 3 = 3)

Although we shared the same room, my grandmother no longer came to school with me. I used to go to an English school in a motor bus. There were no dogs in the streets and she took to feeding sparrows in the courtyard of our city house. As the years rolled by we saw less of each other. For some time she continued to wake me up and get me ready for school. When I came back she would ask me what the teacher had taught me. I would tell her. English words and little things of Western science and learning, the Law of Gravity, Archimedes' Principle, the world being round, etc. This made her unhappy.

(i) What do the changes in the narrator's routine suggest about the passage of time and growing up?

(ii) Choose the option that gives the correct significance of the given lines.

(a) It talks about the orthodox views of the grandmother.

(b) It talks about the lack of Indian scriptural education.

(c) It talks about the gradually changing relationship between the author and the grandmother.

(d) It talks of the effects of city life on the grandmother.

(iii) What made the grandmother unhappy?

Or

Regardless of his fame and the speculations about his fate. Tut is one mummy among many in Egypt. How many? No one knows. The Egyptian Mummy Project, which began an inventory in late 2003, has recorded almost 600 so far and is still counting. The next phase : scanning the mummies with a portable CT machine donated by the National Geographic Society and siemens, its manufactures. King Tut is one of the first mummies to be scanned in death, as in life, moving regally ahead of his countrymen.

(i) Read the assertion and the reason given below. choose the correct option.

Assertion (A) King Tut was one of the first mummies to be scanned using the portable CT machine.

Reason (R) His fame and the speculations about his fate made him a priority for the Egyption Mummy Project.

(a) Both (A) and (R) are true and (R) is the correct explanation of (A).

(b) Both (A) and (R) are true, but (R) is not the correct explanation of (A).

(c) (A) is true, but (R) is false.

(d) (A) is false, but (R) is true.

(ii) The given extract does not talk about

(a) the new advanced CT scanner discoveries about Tut

(b) the Egyptain tradition of mummifying

(c) speculations of Tut's death

(d) the inaccuracy of the data presented prior to the CT

(*iii*) Complete the sentence appropriately.

The CT scan done on King Tut was significant because ....

FULLY SOLVED

12. Read the extracts given below and answer the questions that follow. (***Do any one***) (4 × 1 = 4)

I wouldn't go back there because the objects that are linked in your memory with the familiar life of former times instantly lose their value when, severed from them, you see them again in strange surroundings. And what should I have done with them in a small rented room where the shreds of black-out paper still hung along the windows and no more than a handful of cutlery fitted in the narrow table drawer? I resolved to forget the address. Of all the things I had to forget, that would be the easiest.

(i) Why did she not claim her mother's belongings?

(ii) Select the textual option that is closest to indicating the sufferting brought by the war.
- (a) 'Linked in your memory'
- (b) 'Shreds of black-out paper still hung along'
- (c) 'Resolved to forget'
- (d) 'Of all the things I had to forget, that would be the easiest'

(iii) Why did the narrator not want to go back?

(iv) What is the depiction of the author's room symbolic of?
- (a) Realisation of war
- (b) Consequence of war
- (c) Affermation of war
- (d) Neglect of war

Or

Andrew, abruptly recalled from the contemplation of his own affairs, told Morgan to wait. He went into the house for his bag, then together they set out for Number 12 Blaina Terrace. The night air was cool and deep with quiet mystery. Usually so perceptive, Andrew now felt dull and listless. He had no premonition that this night call would prove unusual, still less that it would influence his whole future in Blaenelly. The two men walked in silence until they reached the door of Number 12, then Joe drew up short.

"I'll not come in," he said, and his voice showed signs of strain. "But, man, I know he'll do well for us."

(i) What was odd about Andrew that night?

(ii) Why did Joe refuse to go in?
- (a) Because he was nervous
- (b) Because he was not needed inside
- (c) Because he had to go somewhere else
- (d) Because he had some work to do

(iii) "He had no premonition that this night call would prove unusual". Did the night turn out to be unusual?
- (a) Yes
- (b) No
- (c) Not mentioned in the story
- (d) None of these

(iv) Complete the following with a suitable reason.

Joe refuses to enter the house because ....

13. Answer *any two* of the following questions in 40-50 words. (3 × 2 = 6)

(i) Identify the movement of the goldfinch that compared with lizard? What is the basis for this comparison? *(The laburnum Top)*

(ii) Interpret how the sparrows expressed their grief over grandmother's death in the chapter 'The Portrait of a lady?

(iii) What preparations did the narrator and his wife make for their round-the world sea voyage in the chapter 'We're not Afraid to Die'?

(iv) What is the poet's feeling towards his childhood in the poem 'Childhood'? Elaborate.

FULLY SOLVED

14. Answer *any one* of the following questions in 40-50 words. **(3 × 1 = 3)**

What did people say about Mourad? From whom had he inherited those traits?

Or

Who is the first person to face Mrs Pearson's anger and what happens to the person?

15. Answer *any one* of the following questions in 120-150 words. **(1 × 6 = 6)**

What according to the poem 'Childhood' is involved in the process of growing up?

Or

Justify the title 'Silk Road'.

16. Answer *any one* of the following questions in 120-150 words. **(1 × 6 = 6)**

Who stole the beautiful white horse and why? How did they use the horse and what made them return the horse to its true owner?

Or

The chapter is about an autobiographical note at one level, while at another it portrays how futile the war is. What are your views regarding war? Is it fruitful? Base your views on the chapter 'The Address'.

ANSWERS

1. (i) The increasing competition and the desire to surpass what had already been achieved results in psycho-social stress.

(ii) 'Chronic fatigue' occurs when stress frequently crosses a limit that a person can handle effectively. Such a person may feel lethargic, disinterested and is not easily motivated to achieve anything.

(iii) (b) necessary for performance

(iv) stress takes a different meaning, depending on the stage of life you are in

(v) (d) Reprimand

(vi) Stress can be defined as the body's reaction to any demands or changes in its internal and external environment.

(vii) A person under stress behaves in different ways. The reaction of an individual depends upon the nature of the stress and capabilities of the person it can be flight, fight or flee.

(viii) (a) Healthy wind

(ix) (d) To increase productivity, the employer should keep his/her employees free from stress

(x) Symptoms of stress are found in the attitude and behaviour of the individual. It includes muscle tension, palpitation, high blood pressure, indigestion, hyper acidity, trembling, shaking, nervous blinking, dryness of throat and mouth and difficulty in swallowing.

2. (i) they are unaware which area would be a perfect fit for their child

(ii) Yes, the researchers if the study aimed to change the students' outlook towards the new career options. It is mentioned in the last paragraph about how parents and teachers can play a helpful part in their child's career decisions by making the student choose a career that fits him/her best.

(iii) (a) There is a huge gap between education and employment opportunities.

(iv) Engineering and computer application and IT were the most popular among the students.

(v) (d) lack of economic bonus

(vi) The given statement is wrong. Parents should be aware of the upcoming career options so that they can help their child in choosing the best career for them.

(vii) Lack of awareness among Indian students regarding their future career options is affecting our country badly since it is unable to reap the economic benefits that could have come to India due to its demographic dividend.

(viii) (a) By using the available tools and technology

3. (i) **Title** Fashion

I. Multi-million dollars industry
  (i) Pwrfl frc
  (ii) Cnstntly changing
  (iii) Affects
    - Designers
    - Manufacturers and distributers
    - Consumers

II. A science
  (i) Invlvs facts and basic principles
  (ii) Actions and reactions- predicted
  (iii) Dpndnt on envrnt and its changes

III. To stay at top
  (i) Discvr and innovate
    - Exprnce
    - Intuition
  (ii) Top designer bckd by
    - Instinct.

IV. Misconceptions
  (i) Designers and retailers dictate industry
    - In reality- consumers do
  (ii) Influence only women
    - In reality, it influence men as well

V. In the present world
  - Lifestyle oriented
  - Practical
  - Different dress for different occasion
  - Designer- daring

Key to Abbreviations

Abbreviations	Words
pwrfl	powerful
frc	force
cnstntly	constantly
invlvs	involves
dpndnt	dependent
envrnt	environment
discvr	discover
bckd	backed
exprnce	experience

(ii) **Summary** Fashion is a multi-million dollar industry that keeps on changing and altering. It is a science based on facts and basic principles which must be followed by the designers. To be a top designer, one must follow instinct and intuition that fulfills the basic needs and wants of people. The fashion industry is full of many misconceptions. First is that it is dictated by designers and the second that it influences women. Today, fashion is a lifestyle oriented and a practical industry where designers have become more daring.

4. (i) (c) Although
(ii) (a) why
(iii) (b) was to know
(iv) (d) has been questioned

5. (i) (a) PRQS
(ii) (c) QPRS
(iii) (c) RPQS
(iv) (b) RPSQ

6. (i)

Courses-Diploma in Waste Water Management– duration one year – practicals arranged–minimum qualification SSCE, first division – prospectus free Contact- The Director, Eco-centre, Post Box-1037, Bengaluru-560019

Or

FOR SALE

Flat No. 12, Seva Nagar, Pune. Ground floor with two bedrooms having attached bathrooms, car parking available, park facing, best location, friendly neighbours, 24 hour power and water supply, low maintenance charges and reasonable price. For further details, contact: Harish/Harshita 98100XXXXX

7.

JOIN JOIN JOIN

BEST FRIENDS ANIMAL SOCIETY

A nationwide animal rescue and advocacy organisation in India.

BE KIND TO ANIMALS

- Do a kind act daily to animals
- Be gentle
- Show concern for animals

Pets give us

- Company
- Love and affection
- Warmth
- Security

ADOPT ANIMALS & SAVE A LIFE

Issued by **Secretary, Best Friends Animal Society**
E-mail: secybfas@gmail.com

Or

LOTUS SPACE SAVING FURNITURE

Furniture of Third Millennium

Do Come Today &
Buy Lotus Space Saving Furniture

Special Features

- *Light but Sturdy*
- *Easy to Pack, Cheap to Buy*
- *Durable, Economical and Space Saving*
- *Ideal for One or Two Room Flats*
- *Fancy Designs Multiple Uses*
- *Caters to Every Pocket*

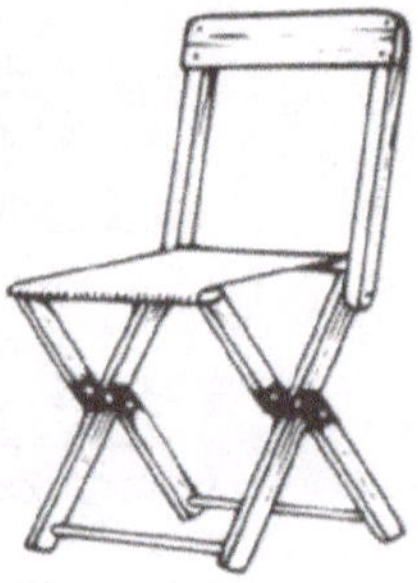

Contact : Lotus Stone, F-18, New Market, Kolkata

8. Respected Principal, teachers and my dear friends. Today, I Kamna Biswas, stand before you to speak on the topic 'The Problem of Terrorism in India'.

Terrorism in India has a long history. It is a cowardly act by the terrorist groups who wish to disturb the peace of the country. It aims to create a state of panic amongst the people. The terrorists want to keep the people in a constant state of fear to stop the country from prospering.

Moreover, terrorism has a major impact on the tourism industry. As tourists avoid visiting places that are vulnerable to terrorist attacks, the tourism industry faces a blow. India is a country that earns a lot of its revenue from tourism. When these attacks happen, they cause fear amongst the tourists as well. The ones planning to visit cancel their trips. Similarly, the ones staying presently shorten their trip and leave.

Furthermore, terrorist attacks create a sense of doubt in the foreign investors of India. They avoid the risk of investing in India and instead opt for safer alternatives. This causes a huge blow to the business of India. Thus, it damages the economy. As terrorist attacks cause loss of life and property, the replenishment takes up a lot of capital.

Thus, terrorism in India needs to be eradicated to safeguard the country and help it prosper.

Thank you

Or

Respected Chairperson, Members of faculty and my dear friends.

I stand before you to express my view on the 'Life in the country side is preferable to life in the city'. First, I would like to remind the audience about the numerous advantages that the villages offer. In fact life in the country has so many advantages over life in the city that I don't think anyone present would disagree with me. The atmosphere is peaceful and quiet and has a soothing effect. The air is fresh and pure. Green fields which can be seen all around are a lovely sight. In the country people are friendly and the neighbours are helpful. On the other hand, cities are full of vehicles giving out smoke and creating atmospheric pollution. There is also air pollution from the chimneys of industries spewing off smoke. Moreover, the streets in the city are always crowded with people. Everyone is in a hurry and never finds time to relax. Village life is tension free. There is no undue hurry and excitement. The villagers may be poor in terms of income but they live a far happier life than the city dwellers. Hence I conclude that life in the countryside is preferable to life in the city.

Thank you

9.

For the Motion

Video games are a common form of entertainment among today's children and youth, and playing them is exciting and entertaining they have a darker side that parents, teachers and health professionals can no longer ignore. Violent video games have been blamed for school shootings, increase in bullying, and violence towards women. Critics argue that these games desensitise the players to violence, reward players for simulating violence, and teach children that violence is an acceptable way to resolve conflicts.

There is broad consensus among medical associations, pediatricians, parents, and researchers that violent video games increase aggressive behaviour among children. Violent video games require active participation and identification with violent characters, which reinforces violent behaviour. Young children are more likely to confuse fantasy violence with real world violence, and without a framework for ethical decision making, they may mimic the actions they see in violent video games. Exposure to violent video games is linked to lower empathy and decreased kindness. Video games that portray violence against women lead to more harmful attitudes and sexually violent actions towards women.

Thus, video games promoting violence should be banned.

Against the Motion

Video game advocates contend that a majority of the research on the topic is deeply flawed and that no causal relationship has been found between video games and social violence. They argue that violent video games may provide a safe outlet for aggressive and angry feelings and may reduce crime.

Studies claiming a casual link between video game violence and real life violence are flawed. Many studies failed to control for factors that contribute to children becoming violent, such as family history and mental health, plus most studies do not follow children over long periods of time.

Violent video games allow players to release their stress and anger (catharsis) in the game, leading to less real world aggression. By age seven, children can distinguish fantasy from reality, and can tell the difference between video game violence and real-world violence. Video game players understand they are playing a game. Therefore, imposing a ban on video games is not going to be helpful in lowering violence among youth.

Or

For the Motion

Respected judges and my worthy opponents. Today, I stand before you all to accentuate why celebrities are responsible for the products they endorse.

Advertising agencies often pick celebrities because their fan following ensures more eyeballs. The celebrities are the present-day gods. They are adored, venerated, and worshipped by many. Given the fan base and the celebrity power of influence, many questions come up. Are they accountable for what the endorser does? Do they at least have the moral responsibility to understand the product better?

It becomes a misleading advertisement if it is found that the product does not have the attributes that the manufacturer professed. And if the brand ambassador has promoted that product and said specifically that the product has those attributes, they are also certainly liable for action.

The brief ban on Maggi noodles had an implication for its celebrity endorsers. Not so long ago, Amitabh Bachchan stepped back from promoting Pepsi after a school girl questioned the health impact of the drink. Celebrities vouch for the performance of a product; they should first use it before endorsing it.

Public figures have an ethical obligation towards those who follow them and this necessitates a framework that guides them to take responsibility for their public image, which includes the products they endorse. Moving in and out of paid contracts might be a solution for the celebrity endorser but it doesn't erase the impact of their previously branded image.

Thank you

Against the Motion

Respected judges and my worthy opponents. Today, I stand before you all to accentuate why celebs should not be held responsible for the products they endorse. Advertising agencies often pick celebrities because their fan following ensures more eyeballs. No doubt the advertisement will attract you, but it's unlikely that you will buy the product unless you have seen it and tested it. Buying financial products and real estate is more nuanced and, hence, advertisements alone shouldn't be your guiding light. Consumers need to be more discerning in such cases.

Take for instance, the case of Mahendra Singh Dhoni. He did end his contract with the real estate firm but how would he have known that the company would fail to honour its commitment? If it was so easy to determine the intention of the company then the first to exit the deal would have been the home buyers. Or take the case of celebrity tourism mascots for states. Would you blame a celebrity if the state government ends up doing something ridiculous?

Many celebrities endorse multiple brands and it is not possible for them to use all. Celebs endorse brands for money. Don't make them responsible for the efficacy of the product. There are government agencies to ensure quality for the products sold in their countries and it is justified to make only those people accountable whose job is to certify products.

Thank you

10. (i) matter-of-fact
(ii) (c) They were imaginary.
(iii) he could not find them in Geography books

Or (i) 'Eternal I rise'
(ii) (d) Something that cannot be touched
(iii) In the given extract, 'I refers to the cloud. It changes and yet remains the same because it only changes its form while the core matter, i.e., water, remains the same.

11. (i) The changes suggest that as the narrator grew older, his life became more independent and as he was exposed to new ideas that created a gap between him and his grandmother. This highlights how growing up often brings about shifts in relationship.
(ii) (c) It talks about the gradually changing relationship between the author and the grandmother.
(iii) The grandmother was unhappy because she couldn't help the author in his studies anymore, his new school didn't teach about God and his scriptures and the school taught music.

Or (i) (a) Both (A) and (R) are true and (R) is the correct explanation of (A).
(ii) (d) the inaccuracy of the data presented prior to the CT
(iii) It revealed his breast bone and front ribs missing.

12. (i) She did not claim her mother's belongings because it brought back painful memories.
(ii) (d) 'of all the things I had to forget, that would be the easiest'
(iii) The narrator did not want to go back because she felt that her belongings had lost their value in the absence of her family and home.
(iv) (b) Consequence of war

Or (i) (a) It was odd that Andrew felt dull and listless that night.
(ii) (a) Because he was nervous
(iii) (a) Yes
(iv) he feeling very anxious

FULLY SOLVED

13. (i) The movement of the goldfinch is compared with that of a lizard, which moves with sleek and sudden movements. The basis of comparison with a lizard is because the goldfinch makes similar kinds of movements when it arrives in the Laburnum tree to avoid being noticed by any predator.

(ii) In the evening, when the author and his family members went where grandmother's body was lying, they saw thousands of sparrows sitting scattered on the floor near the grandmother's body. They expressed their grief by being silent and not chirping. They didn't even eat the bread that was offered to them by the author's mother.

(iii) For the journey first of all they got a boat especially designed and professionally built for that purpose. They tested it for months in the roughest weather. They spent all their leisure time in strengthening their seafaring skills in British waters. They prepared themselves both mentally and physically to undertake their exceptionally long and challenging sea voyage.

(iv) In the poem 'Childhood', the poet regards childhood as a period of innocence. Childhood only knows the language of love and care. A child is unaware of hypocrisy. There is no difference between his thoughts and actions. In short, the poet feels that childhood is a state of innocence and purity of heart.

14. People said that Mourad also had a crazy streak in him. He enjoyed being alive. He was fond of adventures. He had inherited this craziness traits from his Uncle Khosrove. He said boastfully that he had a way with horses, dogs and farmers.

Or

Doris, Mrs Pearson's daughter, is the first person to face her anger. When Doris comes home and asked her mother about her yellow dress, Mrs Fitzgerald who is in Mrs Pearson's body, ignores her she not only refuses to acknowledge her but also insults her boyfriend bringing Doris into tears.

15. According to the poem 'Childhood', during the process of growing up, the child is undergoing the process of attaining mental maturity. The poet puts a question again and again, which is 'Where did my childhood go?'. He makes his own guesses that whether it was the time when he found out that hell and heaven do not lie on the geographical map and hence do not exist or when he found out that adults are not what they pretend to be or when he found out that he could produce his own thoughts.

During this process the child is able to distinguish between reality and fantasy. The child is also able to see the hypocrisies practiced by the adults. Moreover, the child is also able to use his thoughts as these are his original ideas and not copied from anywhere.

Or

The 'Silk Road' is not single highway, but a network of overland routes linking Europe with Asia, making trade possible between those with a passion for silk, horses and exotic fauna and flora. Just about every transaction imaginable has occurred along its many trails over the centuries. It's a thread that links East and West, a network of veins that pumped new lifeblood into mighty empires, a fabled route trodden by innumerable adventurers through the ages.

Yet, underlying this romantic trail is one of the most extraordinary tracts of land on this planet, a vast region separating China from the Mediterranean world that rates as one of the least hospitable areas on Earth. It was the difficulty of crossing such unforgiving territory that kept East and West apart for so long, allowing them to develop in their own distinct ways.

The author records the challenges and hardships he faced in the Silk Road regions as they are now. The reader finds it refreshing to traverse such vast tracts of the natural world that remain largely unchanged from earlier days.

16. 'The Summer of The Beautiful White Horse' is a simple but interesting story about stealing of a horse by two Armenian boys Mourad and Aram, and later how they returned it to its rightful owner. Mourad had a passion and love for horse riding. Due to his passion for riding and fun once, he stole a beautiful white horse.

Actually, the poverty of the tribe forced them to fulfil his desire for riding by stealing the horse. His cousin Aram too loved riding and in their childish innocence, they justified that stealing a horse for a fun and riding was not the same as stealing and selling it for money. The two boys enjoyed riding the horse early every morning and hide it in the barn of the deserted vineyard.

The boys belonged to the Garoghlanian family which was known for its integrity and honesty. One day when the boys met John Byro, true owner of the horse and heard his confidence in the honesty of their family, the boys became conscience – stricken.

Soon the pride and honesty which they inherited from their tribe overpowered their childish pranks and they realised that what they did was wrong as this could bring disgrace to their family. Thus, conscience-stricken, they eventually returned the horse to its rightful owner.

Or

My view about war is that it is not fruitful at all. War brings suffering and disasters with it. It takes away so many lives, leaving people with nothing in their hands. It changes the lives of the people drastically by affecting their fortunes forever.

After the war is over, everything becomes normal again after some time. But the wounds given by the war do not heal easily or quickly. The crude and cunning nature of human behaviour is brought out in war. In war people have to leave their homes, the place where they have spent all their cherished moments. They lose many loved ones. Sometimes, their life is completely destroyed.

Hence, how can something that causes so much of damage, not only of life and property, but also of human emotions and bonds, be called fruitful? War is synonymous with destruction. We must always aim towards establishing peace. There is nothing in this world that cannot be done with peace. Non-violence is the way to form stronger relationships with others. So, we must shun war and promote non-violent ways for resolving conflicts.

FULLY SOLVED

SAMPLE QUESTION PAPER 3

A Highly simulated Sample Question Paper for CBSE Class XI

ENGLISH CORE

GENERAL INSTRUCTIONS

1 This paper is divided into three sections : A, B and C. All sections are compulsory.

2 Separate instructions are given with each part and question wherever necessary.

3 Read these instructions very carefully and follow them faithfully.

4 Do not exceed the prescribed word limit while answering the questions.

TIME : 3 HOURS ***MAX. MARKS : 80***

UNSOLVED

SECTION - A

Reading Skills [26 *Marks*]

1. Read the passage given below. (10)

1. Given the standing of some of its institutions of higher learning, the IITs and IIMs, India is a potential knowledge power. Realising the potential, however, is not going to be easy. The impressive strides made by Sarva Shiksha Abhiyan (SSA) notwithstanding, universal access to quality school education- a minimum necessary condition for any progress towards making India a knowledge society', as the 2006 report of the National Knowledge Commission (NKC) puts it-remains a distant goal.
2. There is as yet no legislation at the national level to affirm the right to education, a fundamental right under the Constitution. The number of school buildings for elementary and secondary education falls far short of requirements and so does the number of qualified teachers. The pressure on government budgets, which forces governments to hire teachers on contract paying a pittance of a salary, is playing havoc with quality. While the incursion of the private sector in the field is providing some competition, mechanisms to enforce the required standards are lacking.
3. Not that there are no national standards or standards-enforcing agencies. We have the National Council for Educational Research and Training (NCERT) to bring out textbooks in various subjects for school education. The Central Board of Secondary Education (CBSE) conducts examinations for schools affiliated to it across the country. The states too have their school boards to conduct exams and enforce minimum standards. How even the standards vary widely. In their anxiety to show spectacular performance, some states are overly lenient-in marking answer papers.
4. Questions arise even over the standards applied by CBSE. Going by the number of students securing 90% or more in their higher secondary exam, it would appear India is on the brink of a knowledge revolution. The numbers are so large that the cut-off point for admission to top colleges is now above 90%. However, admissions to IITs and medical colleges are not based only on CBSE or State Board Exam results. Leading undergraduate colleges offering non-professional degree courses hold their own admission tests. Obviously, Higher Secondary School results are not taken to be a reliable index of the quality of a student's learning capability or potential.

5. The numbers seem to be growing every year. The standards applied by Higher Secondary Boards like CBSE seem to have been diluted to the point that leaves a big gap between what students learn at school and what they have to face on entering institutions of higher learning.
6. In an attempt to remedy the situation, NCERT had recently commissioned experts to rewrite textbooks on economics. Though not entirely free from blemishes, these new texts should go some way in helping beginners get acquainted with the basic concepts in the subject and their applications.
7. Not surprisingly, their introduction is facing roadblocks. Teachers do not like to be compelled to look at textbooks they are not familiar with. Those who revel in seeing students score 90% are reluctant of ushering in something that may stop the rush of such scores.

Based on your understanding of the passage, answer of the following questions. (1 × 10 = 10)

(i) Why do leading undergraduate colleges hold their own admission tests? (1)

(ii) Based on the information given in the last paragraph, why do you think that teachers are opposing the introduction of new textbooks? (1)

(iii) Choose the correct response from the two options to complete the sentences. The word 'roadblocks' in the last paragraph indicates (1)
(a) obstacles in teaching-learning procedures
(b) inability to understand the curriculum

(iv) Complete the given sentence with an appropriate inferences with respect to the following.
The main factor that has affected the quality of education is .... (1)

(v) The writer would not agree with the following statements based on Paragraph 4, EXCEPT. (1)
(a) a large number of students score more than 90% in their higher secondary school exams
(b) the cut-off point for admission to top colleges is above 85%
(c) admissions to IITs are based only on CBSE or state board results
(d) higher secondary school exam results are taken to be a reliable index of the quality of a student's learning capabilities

(vi) List the reason as to why India is referred as a potential knowledge power. (1)

(vii) Why is making India a knowledge society a distant goal? (1)

(viii) Complete the analogy with one word. (1)
Remedy : Solution :: Roadblock : ....
(a) Optimisation (b) Problem
(c) Growth (d) Reluctancy

(ix) What is the tone of writer when he remarks "India is on the brink of a knowledge revolution?" (1)
(a) Sarcastic (b) Optimistic
(c) Imaginative (d) Presumptuous

(x) Why do the governments hire teachers on contract basis? Elaborate. (1)

2. Read the passage given below. (8)

1. In recent years India has seen manifold increase in crimes committed by minors. While analysing the factors responsible for the spurt in crime rate the experts believe that the rural-urban conflict is at the core of these crimes in cities especially underage crimes. The largely rural and semi-urban background of most of the offenders point to that direction. According to the researchers, these young people are not benefitting from the economic reforms in comparison to the educated and professional counterparts in the cities. They feel neglected, frustrated and distressed which leads to crimes such as murder etc.

2. An increase in number of rural people migrating to cities in search of better life opportunities however do not prepare them for the urban value system. The children are often neglected, as both parents are working and unable to spend time with them. The children do not get the attention and right values essential for upbringing.

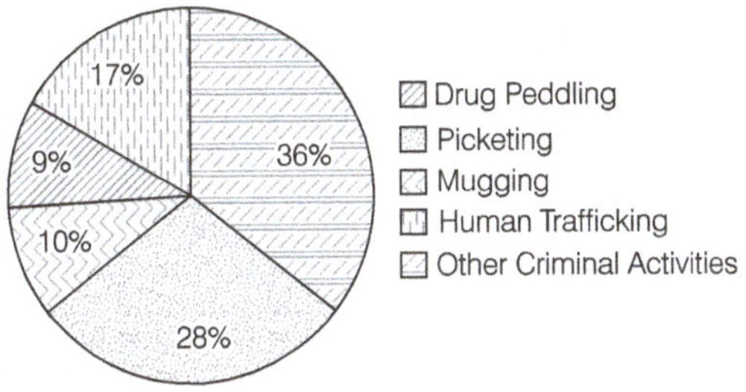

Incidence of Juvenile Crime

3. The report 'Why Children Commit Offences' published by Delhi Commission for Protection of Child Rights (DCPCR) in June, 2015, focused on children in conflict with the law in Delhi. The report looks at multiple issues like the socio-economic profile of children with a criminal record, the nature of offence that these children were accused of and analysed the factors that push children towards deviant behaviour. The report highlighted the role of the family, the community, the school and education as well the peer influence. The report after studying 182 children in observation homes, special homes found that poverty is one of the biggest contributing factors in children taken to crimes. Most of the children had undergone multiple deprivations with low economic households, uneducated parents; disrupted families. The children were dropouts and working independently to support their families.
4. A first step would be for the government to support those families that have poor economic status. In addition, universal education among children is absolutely necessary to eradicate crime among teens. However, only passing legislation is not enough. Society has to ensure that every family sends its children to school, rather than making them work at home or outside, or simply neglecting them. The problem has to be nipped in the bud. A good family atmosphere and proper counselling are needed at all stages for children belonging to vulnerable social groups.

Based on your understanding of the passage, answer of the following questions. **(1 × 8 = 8)**

(i) Complete the following suitably. **(1)**

As a result of the neglection of children, they do not inculcate ....

(ii) How can the solutions, suggested in the last paragraph, be described? **(1)**

(a) Practical
(b) Presentable
(c) Popular
(d) Prejudiced

(iii) What do you understand by the term 'peer influence' mentioned in the third paragraph of the passage? **(1)**

(iv) Classify the following sentences as 'solution' and 'problem'. **(1)**

Sentence 1 The rate of juvenile crime is increasing because children are often neglected and they do not know how to prepare for urban value system.

Sentence 2 The problem has to be nipped in but by introducing measures such as universal education and proper counselling.

(v) Arrange the given illegal activities into their prevalence. **(1)**

1. Picketing
2. Drug peddling
3. Mugging
4. Human trafficking

UNSOLVED

Codes

(a) 1, 2, 3, 4 (b) 4, 2, 3, 1

(c) 3, 2, 1, 4 (d) 1, 4, 3, 2

(vi) What was the conclusion of the survey conducted by the DCPCR? (1)

(vii) What was the common characteristic of the children found in special homes? (1)

(viii) What can be done to eradicate crimes? (1)

(a) A good family atmosphere (b) Proper counselling

(c) Universal education (d) Passing legislation

3. Read the passage given below. (8)

In Indian homes, the floor of the house is always the best maintained element, cleaned twice a day and wiped down to a sparkling state. In front of the threshold of the home, the floor is often decorated with *Rangoli* and other ritual diagrams. This is true in rural as well as in many urban homes in metropolitan cities. When building a new home, people spend as much money per square foot for a beautiful floor as they would spend on the entire structure. Yet, this pride and obsession for a clean floor suddenly vanish as we step out into the street: the floor of the city.

In Delhi, where 80% of the people are pedestrians in some stage of their commuting, the least attention is paid to pedestrian paths. Delhi's sidewalks are too narrow, very poorly maintained and full of potholes, poles, junction boxes and dangerous electrical installations, not to speak of the garbage dumps that stink and stare at the pedestrian.

Delhi's citizens leave home and want to get to their destination as fast as they can. No one wants to linger on the road, no leisure walks, no one looks at a stranger in the eye. It is on the pedestrian path that the citizen encounters head-on the poor pubic management and the excuse called 'multiplicity of authorities'. One agency makes the road, another digs it up to lay cables, a third one comes after months to clear up the mess and the cycle of unaccountability goes on. Meanwhile, crores are spent in repairing the carriageway for vehicles and in construction of flyovers without a care for the pedestrians below. The solution offered is to make an expensive underpass or an ugly foot overbridge, ostensibly for facilitating the pedestrian, while in reality, it only facilitates the cars to move faster at the expense of the pedestrians.

In modern cities across the world, the pedestrian is king. The floor of the city is designed and maintained as an inclusive environment, helping the physically challenged, the old and the infirm, children and the ordinary citizen to move joyfully across the city. Delhi aspires to be a 'world class city'. Hopefully, the authorities would look once again at the floor of Delhi. The pleasure of strolling on the road is deeply connected to our sense of citizenship and sense of belonging. Pride in the city grows only on a well designed floor of the city.

(i) On the basis of your reading of the above passage, make notes on it using headings and sub-headings. Use recognisable abbreviations, wherever necessary (minimum 4). Supply an appropriate title to it. (5)

(ii) Write a summary of the given passage in 80-100 words. (3)

SECTION - B

Grammar

[7 Marks]

4. Choose the correct option. Answer any three. (1 × 3 = 3)

(i) He knows .... I won't come to school tomorrow.

(a) what (b) when (c) this (d) that

(ii) You haven't told me .... care this is.

(a) whose (b) whom (c) where (d) how

(iii) The river Thames .... through London.
(a) is flowing (b) has been flowing (c) flows (d) has flowed

(iv) There is something wrong with her car so she .... to work by bus.
(a) has been going (b) goes (c) went (d) is going

5. Choose the correct option. (1 × 4 = 4)

(i) Transform the given sentence into Future Continuous Tense.
He is waiting for us.
(a) He will being wait for us. (b) He will wait for us.
(c) He will be waiting for us. (d) No change needed

(ii) Transform the given sentence into Present Perfect Tense.
I always wanted to be a scientist.
(a) I has always wanted to be a scientist. (b) I have always wanted to be a scientist.
(c) I have always want to be a scientist. (d) I has always want to be a scientist.

(iii) Transform the given sentence into Past Perfect Continuous Tense.
I have worked all afternoon and have just finished the assignment.
(a) I have been working all afternoon and have just finished the assignment.
(b) I had been working all afternoon and have just finished the assignment.
(c) I shall be working all afternoon and have just finished the assignment.
(d) I am working all afternoon and have just finished the assignment.

(iv) Transform the given sentence into Simple Past Tense.
He wants to know more about the job.
(a) He wanted to know more about the job.
(b) He has wanted to know more about the job.
(c) He had wanted to know more about the job.
(d) He did want to know more about the job.

UNSOLVED

Creative Writing Skills [16 *Marks*]

6. You are Karan Kumar/Karuna Bajaj, a leading lawyer practising in Surat. You want to buy an independent house at City Light Road to be used as office-cum-residence. Draft an advertisement in about 50 words for the classified columns of a local newspaper. You can be contacted at 45645678. (3)

Or

You are Vikram/Sonia, an Hon's graduate in history with specialisation in Medieval India. You are well acquainted with places of historical interest in Delhi, Agra and Jaipur. You are looking for the job of tourist guide. Write an advertisement in about 50 words for the situations wanted column of a local newspaper. Your contact no. 999751234.

7. National Book Trust is organising an exhibition displaying books on yoga on the occasion of International Yoga Day on 21st June. Design a poster highlighting the advantages of developing the habit of yoga for the occasion. (*50 words*) (3)

Or

Design an attractive and instructive poster on behalf of the Delhi Police to educate and warn the people against any suspicious or unclaimed objects in public places/trains/ buses to avert bomb blasts. (*50 words*)

8. The recent rise in incidents of violent behaviour of students is a matter of concern for all. The problem can be cured if students learn how to manage anger. Write a speech on the topic in 120-150 words to be delivered in the school's morning assembly. **(5)**

Or

You are the Class Representative, Class XI of Gandhi Memorial School, Pushp Vihar. You have been asked to prepare a speech on the need to imbibe principles of truthfulness, gentleness and cooperation to counter the growing violence in today's world. Write this speech in 120-150 words.

9. "Introduction of Common Eligibility Test is a step in right direction." Give your views for or against the motion. (*120-150 words*) **(5)**

For the Motion: No more multiple exam fees – one application form is enough – single window procedure – one exam – saving time – saving resources Against the Motion: If disqualified, have to wait a year - no more waiting list – single window method selections – no chance of redemption if failed in the CET as against the present system where a candidate can appear in other exams

Or

"Rising prices can be controlled only by the Government". Write a debate in 120 – 150 words either for or against the motion.

SECTION - C

Literature Textbooks

[31 *Marks*]

10. Read the extracts given below and answer the questions that follow. ***(Do any one)*** **(1 × 3 = 3)**

Then sleek as a lizard, and alert and abrupt,
She enters the thickness,and a machine starts up
Of chitterings, and of tremor of wings,and trillings
The whole tree trembles and thrills
It is the engine of her family.

UNSOLVED

(i) Read the given assertion and reason, based on the extract.

Assertion (A) The creature's movements are described as sleek and alert, indicating she is well-suited to her environment.

Reason (R) The combination of 'sleek as a lizard' and 'alert' implies agility and awareness, qualities important for survival.

Choose the correct option regarding their relationship.
(a) Both (A) and (R) are true and (R) is the correct explanation of (A).
(b) Both (A) and (R) are true, but (R) is not the correct explanation of (A).
(c) (A) is true, but (R) is false.
(d) (A) is false, but (R) is true.

(ii) What is the 'machine'?
(a) The Laburnum tree
(b) Sound of goldfinch's chicks
(c) The goldfinch
(d) None of these

(iii) Complete the following suitably.

The movement of goldfinch compared to that of lizard because ....

Or

"All three stood still to smile through their hair
At the uncle with the camera. A sweet face,
My mother's, that was before I was born
And the sea, which appears to have changed less,
Washed their terribly transient feet."

(i) Which figure of speech is used in last line?
(a) Alliteration (b) Metaphor (c) Simile (d) Personification

(ii) Select the phrase that suggests the following.

Life is fleeting and temporary. It is subject to change and time.

(iii) Complete the sentence appropriately.

All three people stood still and smiled because ....

11. Read the extracts given below and answer the questions that follow. ***(Do any one)*** (1 × 3 = 3)

Hor was a grim, miserable place. There was no vegetation whatsoever, just dust and rocks, liberally scattered with years of accumulated refuse, which was unfortunate given that the town sat on the shore of Lake Mansarovar, Tibet's most venerated stretch of water. Ancient Hindu and Buddhist cosmology pinpoints Mansarovar as the source of four great Indian rivers: the Indus, the Ganges, the Sutlej and the Brahmaputra. Actually only the Sutlej flows from the lake, but the headwaters of the others all rise nearby on the flanks of Mount Kailash.

(i) What did the town of Hor seem to the narrator?

(ii) Which river actually flows from Lake Mansarovar?
(a) The Ganges (b) The Indus (c) The Brahmaputra (d) The Sutlej

(iii) Why did narrator feel that Hor's misery was unfortunate?

Or

All over the verandah and in her room right up to where she lay dead and stiffwrapped in the red shroud, thousands of sparrows sat scattered on the floor. There was no chirruping. We felt sorry for the birds and my mother fetched some bread for them. She broke it into little crumbs, the way my grandmother used to and threw it to them. The sparrows took no notice of the bread.

(i) Complete the following suitably.

The birds were not chirping because ....

(ii) The phrase 'took no notice' used in the above extract means

(a) didn't worry (b) it did matter

(c) didn't pay any attention (d) None of these

(iii) Why did the author's mother bring some bread?

12. Read the extracts given below and answer the questions that follow. ***(Do any one)*** (1 × 4 = 4)

"For mercy's sake, Doctor," whimpered the midwife. "It's still born." Andrew did not heed her. Beaten, despairing, having laboured in vain for half an hour, he still persisted in one last effort, rubbing the child with a rough towel, crushing and releasing the little chest with both his hands, trying to get breath into that limp body.

And then, as by a miracle, the pigmy chest, which his hands enclosed, gave a short, convulsive heave, another... and another... Andrew turned giddy. The sense of life, springing beneath his fingers after all that unavailing striving, was so exquisite it almost made him faint.

(i) What does the given lines tell us about the doctor?

(a) Dedicated (b) Cruel

(c) Self-centered (d) Unwavering

(ii) What was the miracle brought by Andrew's efforts?

(a) He infused life in lifeless baby.

(b) He made the baby cry.

(c) He performed a difficult operation.

(d) He delivered the baby without proper facilities.

(iii) What can we say about Andrew as a person?

(iv) Select the textual option that is closest to indicating the fragelity of the baby.

(a) 'Laboured in vain' (b) 'Beaten, despairing'

(c) 'So exquisite' (d) 'Pigmy chest'

Or

MRS PEARSON: Of course they do. You ought to have found that out by this time. Anybody else would have done. You're one of their standing jokes. They call you Pompy-ompy Pearson because they think you're so slow and pompous.

GEORGE: [horrified] Never!

MRS PEARSON: It's always beaten me why you should want to spend so much time at a place where they're always laughing at you behind your back and calling you names. Leaving your wife at home, night after night. Instead of going out with her, who doesn't make you look a fool...

(i) Complete the following with a suitable reason.

George was called 'Pompy-ompy Pearson' at the bar because ....

(ii) What is Mrs Pearson complaining?

(a) George doesn't give her money.

(b) George doesn't love her.

(c) George spends more time with others than with her.

(d) None of the above

(iii) What do we come to know about George as a person?

(iv) Describe George's behaviour towards his wife.

UNSOLVED

13. Answer *any two* of the following questions in 40-50 words. (3 × 2 = 6)

(i) Interpret what happened in the Third Battle of Panipat in the parallel world.

(ii) Explain the significance of the yellow colour in the poem 'The Laburnum Top'.

(iii) In 'Discovering Tut: The Saga Continues', how can the CT scan prove more effective than X-rays?

(iv) What moment does the photograph depict in the poem 'A Photograph'?

14. Answer *any one* of the following questions in 40-50 words. (3 × 1 = 3)

In the story 'The Address', when did the author realise that she was at the correct address?

Or In 'Mother's Day', what was wrong with George's attitude towards his wife, Annie?

15. Answer *any one* of the following questions in 120-150 words. (1 × 6 = 6)

What does the rain do to things day and night? What is the result of rainfall on things at Earth. Answer with reference to poem 'The Voice of Rain'?

Or The love of a mother or grandmother cannot be compared to any other love. Discuss with reference to 'The Portrait of a Lady'.

16. Answer *any one* of the following questions in 120-150 words. (1 × 6 = 6)

Why was a melon crowned king? How was this coronation beneficial to the people of melon city?

Or Could Aram learn to ride the white horse? Describe his first ride on it.

UNSOLVED

ANSWERS

1. (i) The leading undergraduate colleges hold their own admission tests because they distrust the school results.

(ii) Teachers are opposing the introduction of the new textbooks as they are not familiar with them.

(iii) (a) obstacles in teaching-learning process

(iv) shortage of well-qualified teachers.

(v) (a) a large number of students score more than 90% in their higher secondary school exams

(vi) India is referred as a potential knowledge power due to the excellent rankings of its institutions of higher learnings like the IITs and IIMs.

(vii) Making India a knowledge society is a distant goal because universal access to quality school education, as per the 2006 report of NKC, hasn't been accomplished.

(viii) (b) Problem

(ix) (a) Sarcastic

(x) The governments hire teachers on contract basis because of the pressure on government budgets. With contractual teachers, they can get off by paying pittiance of a salary.

2. (i) human values

(ii) (a) Practical

(iii) 'Peer influence' means when you are influenced by other people (year peers) to act in a certain way.

(iv) Sentence 1 : problem, Sentence 2 : Solution

(v) (d) 1, 4, 3, 2

(vi) The conclusion of the survey conducted by the DCPCR was that most minor criminals came from deprived backgrounds.

(vii) The common characteristic of the children found in special homes was that they earned for their family.

(viii) (c) Universal education

SAMPLE QUESTION PAPER 4

A Highly simulated Sample Question Paper for CBSE Class XI

ENGLISH CORE

GENERAL INSTRUCTIONS

1 This paper is divided into three sections : A, B and C. All sections are compulsory.
2 Separate instructions are given with each part and question wherever necessary.
3 Read these instructions very carefully and follow them faithfully.
4 Do not exceed the prescribed word limit while answering the questions.

TIME : 3 HOURS **MAX. MARKS : 80**

UNSOLVED

SECTION - A

Reading Skills

[26 Makrs]

1. Read the passage given below. **(10)**

1. My father, the late Dr Gustav Bucky, was the physician to Einstein's two stepdaughters and this relationship had prompted the professor to invite us to dinner once. My father and he became friends and from then onwards I spent my summer vacations at his home for the next eight years.
2. To a boy, Einstein was a God. Even his appearance had a God-like distinctiveness – the massive head with its unruly mane of hair; the ragged moustache; the deep, gentle eyes that could twinkle with amusement; the droopy upper lids; and the soft, expressive wrinkles that creased his face.
3. One time, after I had known him for several years, I impulsively remarked that it might be time for him to abandon a frayed stretched sweater that was part of his daily uniform. His sudden, cool silence told me that I had stepped across the line.
4. Yet he had a good sense of humour. His only reading for fun was Emily Post's book on etiquette. He read the book in his bedroom and study in the evening and his sharp laugh rattled through the house.
5. Einstein's friends never expected him to behave in the conventional manner. Yet his regard for others often prompted him to do the conventional thing. When I was ill with tuberculosis at a veteran's hospital in the Bronx, Einstein created a sensation there by visiting me. I was tremendously moved. I knew how much he disliked to leave his work, how much he was bored by the two-and-a-half hour automobile trip and how pained he felt under public scrutiny.
6. Since we knew how Einstein was tortured by formal occasions, we didn't invite him to my wedding in 1953 at the Plaza in New York. He showed up without being invited. He was dressed in a dark suit, with white shirt and tie – the perfect attire for the proceedings, according to his standards.

7. The problem of keeping an important secret may produce a sweaty conflict in most people, but not in Einstein. I was hardly a hundred feet from him during one of the most important meetings of this century and I never knew about it. During the summer of 1939, I was staying at Einstein's vacation house near Southold on the tip of Long Island. On 1st August, the housekeeper told me that a group of scientists were coming to visit the professor. When the visitors left, Einstein made no reference to the meeting. I only remember his expressing a vague fear in late 1944 that Germany might be making progress towards a new and terrible weapon.
8. After the United States exploded the first atomic bomb, the bits and pieces of the story behind its development began to sift out. Only then did I realise what had happened during the meeting on that August day. Fermi, Szilard and a few other physicists had persuaded Einstein to write to Roosevelt, the famous letter, now in the Library of Congress, that prompted the President to launch the Manhattan Project for the production of the atomic bomb.
9. He won the Nobel Prize for his Photoelectric Theory – a series of equations that he considered relatively minor in importance – but he didn't have any curiosity in observing how his theory made television possible.
10. One puzzle that Einstein could never understand was his own fame. He had developed theories that were quite esoteric and capable of exciting comparatively few scientists. Yet his name was a household word across the civilised world. He was baffled by the phenomenon of himself. 'I've had good ideas and so have other men," he once said. "But it's been my good fortune that my ideas have been accepted." He was bewildered by the deluge of public attention; people wanted to meet him, strangers stopped on the street to stare and smile at him, scientists, statesmen, students and housewives wrote him letters. He could never understand why he received this attention, why he was singled out as something special.

UNSOLVED

Based on your understanding of the passage, answer of the following questions. (1 × 10 = 10)

(i) What was a part of Einstein's dress? What promoted the author to comment on it? (1)

(ii) What are some of the characteristics of Einstein. (1)

(iii) Complete the following sentence by choosing an appropriate option. (1)

The author was well-known to the professor because ....

(a) he was his classmate

(b) his father was the physician to his two stepdaughters

(iv) Complete the following suitably. (1)

'Bits and pieces' in the first line of Paragraph 8 means ....

(v) The writer would not agree with the given statements based on the passage EXCEPT (1)

(a) Einstein knew why he was so famous.

(b) Einstein did not have a sense of humour.

(c) Einstein did not go to the author's wedding as he was not invited.

(d) Einstein's friends never expected him to behave in the usual manner.

(vi) What important 'secret' was kept by Einstein in the summer of 1939? (1)

(vii) List two things that the professor disliked. (1)

(viii) The famous scientists mentioned in the passage are (1)

1. Fermi 2. Szilard

3. Dr Bucky 4. Roosevelt

Codes

(a) 1 and 3 (b) 2 and 4
(c) 1 and 2 (d) 3 and 4

(ix) Select the option that conveys the opposite of 'familiar', from words used in Paragraph 10. (1)

(a) civilised (b) baffled
(c) deluge (d) esoteric

(x) How can you say that Einstein disliked his fame? (1)

2. Read the passage given below. (8)

1. India is a major producer of several agricultural/food items in the world but only less than 10 per cent of that is processed. Demand for processed food items is set to increase in India in the coming years providing opportunities for greater value addition, lower wastages and alternative employment opportunities. Analysis of corporate data shows that food processing firms have been profitable, but the value addition component needs to increase significantly.
2. India has made vast progress overtime in providing food security for its people and has become largely self-reliant in agriculture. Accordingly, the policy focus has shifted from attaining self-sufficiency to generating higher and stable income for the farming population. Food Processing Industry (FPI) is one area which has the potential to add value to farm output, create alternate employment opportunities, improve exports and strengthen the domestic supply chain.
3. India, with about 11.2 per cent of total arable land in the world, is ranked first in the production of milk, pulses and jute, second in fruits and vegetables and third in cereals (Government of India, 2019). It is also the sixth largest food and grocery market in the world (Law, et al., 2019). Recognising the immense potential of FPI in promoting inclusive growth, it has been identified as one of the key thrust areas under the 'Make in India' programme.
4. Food processing is defined as transforming agricultural products into food that are in consumable form or transforming one food item into another by adding value to it (Government of India, 2019). Based on physical properties of the final product, the Ministry of Food Processing Industries categorises food processing under two sub-categories, *viz.* (i) manufactured processes, whereby the original physical properties of the product undergo a change through a process involving employees, power, machines or money and the transformed product is edible and has a commercial value and (ii) other value-added processes where the product does not undergo any manufacturing process, but gains significant value addition like increased shelf life, shelled and ready for consumption, etc.
5. Depending on the type and extent of value addition, it is categorised as primary and secondary processing. Primary processing relates to conversion of raw commodity to one that is fit for consumption. It involves steps such as drying, threshing, cleaning, grading, sorting, packing, etc. Secondary processing involves creation of value added products like bread, wine, sausages, etc.
6. The importance of processed food items in the consumer basket has increased globally over time. With higher income, urbanisation, demographic shifts, improved transportation and changed consumer perceptions regarding quality and safety, food consumption patterns have changed over the years. Further, advertising through mass media/social media is also found to have resulted in a higher demand-led Food Processing Industry (FPI) growth in India.

UNSOLVED

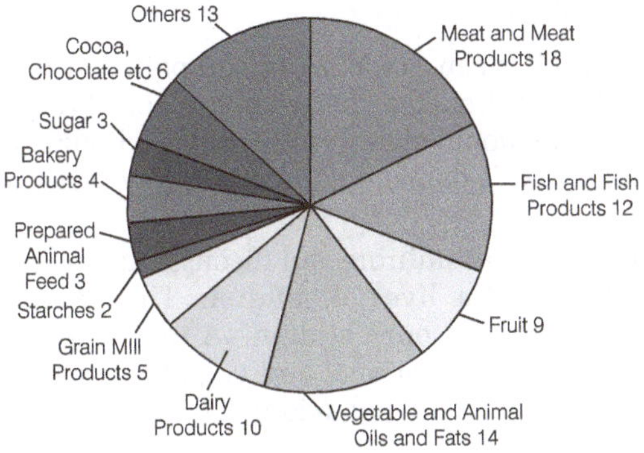

Pattern of Processed Food Trade

7. The share of processed food in world especially Indian exports in value terms has remained stable over the years. In 2018, it accounted for 6.5 per cent of total world processed exports and 5.7 per cent of total world exports.
8. With the increasing importance of processed food in consumers' food basket, quality standards have also emerged as an important factor with new regulations. The food system is being regulated through a mix of private-public standards which provide the basis of competitive strategies while also proving to be entry barriers. The implementation of quality standards has been an issue of contention between developed and developing countries.

Based on your understanding of the passage, answer of the following questions. (1 × 8 = 8)

(i) Complete the following suitably. (1)

'Arable' land mentioned in Paragraph 3 means ....

(ii) Which of the following leads to a change in the food consumption pattern? (1)

(a) Urbanisation (b) Demographic shifts
(c) Improved transportation (d) All of these

(iii) List two advantages of processed food as mentioned in the passage. (1)

(iv) Complete the sentence based on the following statement. (1)

FPI has been identified as one of the key thrust areas under the 'Make in India' programme.

This has happened because of ....

(v) According to the passage, India has become self-reliant because of (1)

(a) agriculture (b) stable income
(c) employment opportunities (d) import business

(vi) What does the passage highlight? (1)

(vii) What are drying threshing and grading a part of? (1)

(viii) Complete the sentence appropriately. (1)

Manufactured processing of food involves ....

(a) no change
(b) mixing of spices to increase shelf life
(c) drying and spicing
(d) a change in the properties of raw materials

UNSOLVED

3. Read the passage given below. **(8)**

Are your children toxic? I don't mean 'toxic' as in the pain-in-the neck teenager state that occurs between the ages of 12 and 16 and makes you wish you could flush them down the toilet because they grunt instead of talk and loll about sighing endlessly for hours on end. I mean, are your children having the kind of childhood that is damaging them in a way that will debilitate them for the rest of their lives?

All around the world, teachers are examining and discussing how the cultural and lifestyle changes of the past 25 years, are affecting the lives of children. They know that many of the changes that benefit adults are far from healthy for our children. "A toxic cocktail of the side effects of cultural change is now damaging the social, emotional and cognitive development of a growing number of children with knock-on effects on their behaviour", is how educationist and author Sue Palmer explains it.

Over a hundred teachers, psychologists, childrens authors and leading childcare experts called on the Government of Great Britain to act to prevent childhood being killed off altogether. According to them, processed food, computer games and over-competitive education are poisoning today's children and increasingly children are being forced "to act and dress like mini adults".

Research backs what these childcare experts are saying. Changes in diet, childcare patterns, parenting, family structures, play, bed times, family interaction, education, marketing, peer pressure, technology, electronics and the way we communicate with our children are creating a 'toxic mix' that is damaging them. Children are becoming increasingly unhealthy and depressed and are experiencing growing levels of behavioural and developmental problems. Not only this, the experts also point out that children lack first-hand experience of the world and regular interaction with their parents.

So before you answer the question, "Are your children toxic?", take a good long look at them and their lifestyle. And remember, parents don't usually poison their children on purpose. Adults too are susceptible to 'market forces' and peer pressure. It is almost natural when other people's kids are eating junk and living toxic lives to look at your own child and think: mine must too. But it doesn't have to be that way. Luckily, for all of us there are plenty of changes we can make to detoxify our children's childhood. All it needs is a little thought and some common sense. In the process, we can help detoxify ourselves.

(a) On the basis of your reading of the given passage, make notes on it using headings and sub-headings. Use recognisable abbreviations, wherever necessary (minimum 4). Supply an appropriate title to it. **(5)**

(b) Write a summary of the given passage in 80-100 words. **(3)**

UNSOLVED

SECTION - B

Grammar

[7 *Marks*]

4. Choose the correct option. Answer any three. **(1 × 3 = 3)**

(i) .... you were sleeping, our puppy knocked over the table.

(a) Whether (b) Whenever
(c) While (d) Because

(ii) My cousin finally finished the project, ... months of research.

(a) before (b) after
(c) because (d) while

(iii) Thomas is an author. He .... mystery novels and travel memoirs.

(a) writes (b) is writing
(c) write (d) has been writing

(iv) I .... for this company for more than 30 years, and I intend to stay here till I retire.
(a) have been working (b) had been working
(c) has been working (d) have worked

5. Choose the correct option. (1 × 4 = 4)

(i) P: did was not
Q: very useful
R: what that boy
S: for her
(a) PRQS (b) RPSQ (c) RPQS (d) SQPR

(ii) P: to buy a car until
Q: I will wait to
R: I have saved
S: more money
(a) PQSR (b) RPSQ (c) QPRS (d) SQPR

(iii) P: during our
Q: vacation we still
R: even though it rained
S: had a good time
(a) PQRS (b) RPSQ (c) RPQS (d) SQPR

(iv) P: her with a
Q: will suprise
R: birthday party
S: when she visits, we
(a) PQSR (b) RPSQ (c) QPRS (d) SQPR

Creative Writing Skills [16 *Marks*]

6. You have lost your leather wallet containing your Examination Entry Ticket for Class XII while travelling by bus from Banashankari to M.G. Road in Bangalore. Write a notice in not more than 50 words, to be published in 'Deccan Herald'. You are Pranav/Parveen, 12 Gandhi Road, Bengaluru. (3)

Or

You possess an acre of land in the heart of the city. You want to dispose of this property since you have decided to buy a flat. Write an advertisement to be published in a national daily, giving all the necessary details. You are Krishan of Moti Nagar, Delhi.

7. Design a poster for the 'No Tobacco Day' to create awareness among the masses about the harms of smoking. (*50 words*) (3)

Or

You are Ratna Pathak, a female activist. Design a poster highlighting the 'Evils of Dowry'. (*50 words*)

8. Rapid economic reforms to boost MSMEs is the need of the hour. Write a speech on the given topic in about 120-150 words. (5)

Or

The actions and behaviour of senior college and university students are a far cry from the normal, decent and civilised. It's all the more reprehensible because even girls are subjected to indecency and vulgarity. Write a speech on the topic 'Ragging' in 120-150 words for your school's morning assembly.

9. Nepotism has ruined the talent in film industry. Give your views for or against the motion. (*120-150 words*) **(5)**

For the Motion: New actors belonging in to bollywood families launched easily – outsiders struggle – work at low fees – forced into depression – many examples of injustice

Against the Motion: Exists in every field – another form of favouritism – not all star children are successful – many good actors are self made – add examples

Or

The government has banned the use of animals in the laboratories for the purpose of dissection. Write a debate in 120-150 words either for or against this decision.

SECTION - C

Literature Textbooks

[31 *Marks*]

10. Read the extracts given below and answer the questions that follow. ***(Do any one)*** **(1 × 3 = 3)**

The cardboard shows me how it was
When the two girl cousins went paddling
Each one holding one of my mother's hands,
And she the big girl – some twelve years or so

(i) What is the 'cardboard'?

(a) A piece of cardboard
(b) A photograph
(c) A display board
(d) A piece of craft

(ii) Who is the 'Big Girl'?

(iii) Select the phrase from the extract, that suggests the following.

The photo shows the poet's mother as a young child.

Or

I descend to lave the droughts, atomies, dust-layers of the globe,
And all that in them without me were seeds only, latent, unborn;
And forever, by day and night, I give back life to my own origin,
And make pure and beautify it;

(i) What does the rain claim to do?

(a) End droughts
(b) Remove dust
(c) Give life to the seeds
(d) All of these

(ii) Complete the following suitably.

"I give back life to my origin." The origin refers to ....

(iii) Read the following assertion and reason.

Assertion (A) The passage suggests the speaker is connected to the Earth and its natural processes.

Reason (R) The speaker ''descends to lave the droughts' and purifies the Earth, indicating an deep relationship with the planet's renewal and life cycles.

Choose the correct option for their relationship.

(a) Both (A) and (R) are true, and (R) is the correct explanation of (A).
(b) Both (A) and (R) are true, but (R) is not the correct explanation of (A).
(c) (A) is true, but (R) is false.
(d) (R) is true, but (A) is false.

UNSOLVED

11. Read the extracts given below and answer the questions that follow. ***(Do any one)*** (1 × 3 = 3)

After months of carefully recording the pharaoh's funerary treasures, Carter began investigating his three nested coffins. Opening the first, he found a shroud adorned with garlands of willow and olive leaves, wild celery, lotus petals, and cornflowers, the faded evidence of a burial in March or April. When he finally reached the mummy, though, he ran into trouble. The ritual resins had hardened, cementing Tut to the bottom of his solid gold coffin. "No amount of legitimate force could move them," Carter wrote later. "What was to be done?"

(i) Complete the following suitably.

The phrase 'cementing Tut to the bottom' means ....

(ii) How can we say that the burial took place in March or April?

(iii) What was found in first coffin?

(a) Treasure
(b) Board games
(c) Elements of a burial
(d) None of these

Or

When I went in to comfort the children, Jon asked, 'Daddy, are we going to die?' I tried to assure him that we could make it. But, Daddy, 'he went on,' we aren't afraid of dying if we can all be together - you and mummy, Sue and I.

(i) What is true regarding the given extract?

(a) It shows resignation to the circumstances.
(b) It shows the unity felt by the family.
(c) It shows the courage shown by Sue and Jon
(d) All of the above

(ii) Select the correct option from those given in bracket to fill in the blank.

The use of the phrase, 'we aren't afraid of dying, indicates a sense of .... about death (acceptance/terror).

(iii) What effect did Jon's statement have upon the author?

12. Read the extracts given below and answer the questions that follow. ***(Do any one)*** (1 × 4 = 4)

One day back there in the good old days when I was nine and the world was full of every imaginable kind of magnificence, and life was still a delightful and mysterious dream, my cousin Mourad, who was considered crazy by everybody who knew him except me, came to my house at four in the morning and woke me up tapping on the window of my room. Aram, he said. I jumped out of bed and looked out of the window. I couldn't believe what I saw. It wasn't morning yet, but it was summer and with daybreak not many minutes around the corner of the world it was light enough for me to know I wasn't dreaming. My cousin Mourad was sitting on a beautiful white horse. I stuck my head out of the window and rubbed my eyes.

(i) Complete the following suitably.

The opening lines of the extract depict ....

(ii) Select the textual option that is closest to indicating that the narrator viewed life with a sense of mystery and joy.

(a) 'Good old days'
(b) 'Life was still a delightful and mysterious dream'
(c) 'The world was full of every imaginable kind of magnificence'
(d) None of the above

(iii) Why does the narrator call his childhood 'good old days'?

(iv) Why did the narrator rub his eyes?

Or

Perhaps I was mistaken, I thought, perhaps it isn't her. I had seen her only once, fleetingly, and that was years ago. It was most probable that I had rung the wrong bell. The woman let go of the door and stepped to the side. She was wearing my mother's green knitted cardigan. The wooden buttons were rather pale from washing. She saw that I was looking at the cardigan and half hid herself again behind the door. But I knew now that I was right.

'Well, you knew my mother?' I asked.

'Have you come back?' said the woman. 'I thought that no one had come back.'

(i) How did the narrator ensure that she was talking to the right woman?

(a) She had recognised her.
(b) The lady was wearing her mother's cardigan.
(c) The lady told her that she was at the right place.
(d) She had her photograph with her.

(ii) 'I thought that no one had come back.' What does this convey?

(a) Destruction and sadness brought about by the war.
(b) Selfishness of the lady.
(c) Social conditions of the time.
(d) None of these

(iii) Why did the lady hide behind the door?

(iv) Why has the narrator come to visit this woman?

UNSOLVED

13. Answer *any two* of the following questions in 40-50 words. (3 × 2 = 6)

(i) Interpret what happens when the narrator returns from his five year education in abroad? Answer in reference to 'The Portrait of a Lady'.

(ii) Explain why Tsetan left the author alone at Darchen and go back to Lhasa?

(iii) Why, do you think, does the poetess say nothing about her mother's death?

(iv) Explain how Laburnum tree ensures safety for the goldfinch and its chicks?

14. Answer *any one* of the following questions in 40-50 words. (3 × 1 = 3)

Did the boy Aram succeed in learning horse riding?

Or

Describe the impact of the war on the narrator and Mrs. S.

15. Answer *any one* of the following questions in 120-150 words. (1 × 6 = 6)

"Knowledge of the past is useful to complete our knowledge of the world we live in." Discuss with reference to the chapter 'Discovering Tut: the Saga Continues'.

Or

Explain the three stages in life described by Shirley Toulson in the poem 'A Photograph'.

16. Answer *any one* of the following questions in 120-150 words. (1 × 6 = 6)

"For doctors, the duty towards the patients is foremost, irrespective of their own personal affairs." Discuss with reference to 'Birth'.

Or

Describe the narrators's second visit to Mrs. Dorling's house.

UNSOLVED

ANSWERS

1. (i) A stretched sweater was a part of Einstein's dress.
The author was prompted to ask Einstein to replace it was frayed.

(ii) Einstein according to the author, was a studious man with a good sense of humour. He never behaved in an unconventional manner, was very peculiar about his look, was antisocial and never understood his fame.

(iii) (b) his father was the physician to his two step daughters

(iv) details

(v) (d) Einstein's friend never expected him to behave in the usual manner.

(vi) The 'secret' that Einstein kept in the summer of 1939 was that he had written a letter to Roosevelt urging him to develop an atomic bomb.

(vii) The two things that the professor disliked were
(a) The professor disliked to leave his work.
(b) He also did not like getting a lot of public attention.

(viii) (c) 1 and 2

(ix) (d) esoteric

(x) It can be said that Einstein disliked his fame because he couldn't understand why he was singled out or why he received this attention.

2. (i) cultivable

(ii) (d) All of these

(iii) Processed food provide for greater value addition and reduced food wastage.

(iv) recognition of the immense potential of FPI in inclusive growth

(v) (a) agriculture

(vi) The passage highlights the growing demand of processed food.

(vii) Drying, threshing and grading are a part of primary food processing.

(viii) (d) a change in the properties of raw material

SAMPLE QUESTION PAPER 5

A Highly simulated Sample Question Paper for CBSE Class XI

ENGLISH CORE

GENERAL INSTRUCTIONS

1 This paper is divided into three sections : A, B and C. All sections are compulsory.
2 Separate instructions are given with each part and question wherever necessary.
3 Read these instructions very carefully and follow them faithfully.
4 Do not exceed the prescribed word limit while answering the questions.

TIME : 3 HOURS ***MAX. MARKS : 80***

UNSOLVED

SECTION - A

Reading Skills

[26 *Marks*]

1. Read the passage given below. **(10)**

1. Today, we have a generation of people who, after having lived in a joint family system, have taken the initiative to break out and start a nuclear family. This generation today has come of age and very well appreciates the strengths and weaknesses of both the systems.
2. The generation that broke out of the old joint family system did so when individualistic thinking began to gain predominance in society. It was exciting to explore, experiment and establish a living setup on one's own. The nuclear family gave immense freedom from the traditions and ways of life that the old system was ridden with. Hence, whenever and wherever the parents and the grown up adult children could not get along well and when the adult children could afford to build a house to call their own, nuclear families began to be formed. As it happens with most changes in society, initially the people from the old system did not take this change very well. They were saddened to see the disintegration of family values and system and emergence of individualistic nuclear families.

   However, gradually when nuclear families became the order of the day, the old generation slowly began to accept the realities and became comfortable with it.
3. The other factor that gave rise to nuclear families was industrialisation. The industrial revolution brought with it increase in job opportunities in and around major industrialised and commercial cities and towns. This forced men and women to move out of their family home and away from the parents. In this case, often the parents, who remained emotionally attached to the place where they spent most of their life, preferred to continue staying in their family home and accepted with some sadness their children starting out a new life away from them.
4. One of the major reasons why my generation was desperate to break out of the joint family was the attitude of the older generation to impose their views and thoughts on us. In some families, the father's words would be final and nobody could dare say or do anything against

it. Such an autocratic style of leading a family leads to repression and suppression, giving rise to feelings of discontentment and unhappiness.

5. If the joint family system is laid on the founding stone of mutual and genuine love and respect for each and every member (including children), then the system is guaranteed to be a success. It helps to keep in mind that love, respect and affection are things that can be only commanded and not demanded. We command these precious things by giving them first. Further, family members need to communicate openly and honestly with one another. The elders in the family must encourage and create an environment conducive to open communication. In the absence of such an environment, family members can feel repressed and suppressed that can lead to discontentment. Non-judgemental listening and demonstrating mutual trust are necessary to help family members open upto one another.
6. One of the things that disintegrated the old joint family system was the constant interference and meddling by elders in the matters of youngsters. Learning from past mistakes, another important aspect of communication is knowing when NOT to communicate. In other words, it is important to give one another space and respect the boundaries of each other.
7. It is important that members in a joint family system feel accepted for who they are and as they are. The crucial part of acceptance of one another is acceptance of our own weaknesses and limitations and that of others. Realistic expectations help us to be more tolerant of the weaknesses of one another. Having unrealistic expectations of others is often the root cause of disappointments and discontentment with others.

Based on your understanding of the passage, answer of the following questions. (1×10 = 10)

(i) What would be the immediate consequence of a father's word being final in a joint family setup? (1)

(ii) What role does 'acceptance' play in a joint family system? (1)

(iii) Complete the following sentence by choosing an appropriate option. (1)

The need to form nuclear families was felt due to ....

(a) immense freedom from traditions and old styles of joint family system
(b) members in joint family could not live peacefully
(c) it was economical to form an individual set up
(d) advent of industrialisation and more job opportunities

(iv) Complete the given sentence based on the information given in the extract. (1)

.... is the root cause of disappointments and discontent with others in a family.

(v) The writer would not agree with the given statements based on the passage EXCEPT (1)

(a) It is not important to give one another space.
(b) The elders in a family must create an environment conducive to open communication.
(c) Judgemental listening is necessary to help family members open up to one another.
(d) The old generation was happy to see the disintegration of joint family system.

(vi) Which word in the 12th paragraph means 'the opportunity to take a step? (1)

(vii) List a few reasons for how a joint family system can succeed. (1)

(viii) Select the option that conveys the opposite of 'satisfaction', from words used in Paragraph 4. (1)

(a) desperate
(b) impose
(c) discontentment
(d) repression

UNSOLVED

(ix) Select the most appropriate title of the passage. (1)

(a) Joint Family System
(b) Changing Family System
(c) The New Family of Nuclears
(d) Importance of Family

(x) What led to the desintegration of the family system? Give one reason. (1)

2. Read the passage given below. (8)

1. With the enormous amount of information potentially available to travellers, the internet constitutes an important platform for information exchange between the consumer and industry suppliers (e.g. hotels, transportation sectors, attractions), intermediaries (e.g. travel agents), controllers (e.g. governments and administrative bodies), as well as many non-profit organisations such as destination marketing organisations.
2. Different technological interfaces, such as search engines, online travel booking sites and websites of destination marketing organisations facilitate the information exchange between online travellers and the so-called 'online tourism domain'.
3. Particularly, it has been argued that understanding the nature of the online tourism domain, i.e. the composition of online tourism related information potentially available to travellers, provides an important stepping-stone for the development of successful marketing programs and better information systems in tourism.
4. The importance of social media is identified by Xiang & Gretzel (2010). Their analysis showed that social media constitute a substantial part of the search results, indicating that search engines linked the travellers directly to social media sites. Since more and more travellers seem to tap into this 'collective intelligence' available on the web, this will challenge the established marketing practices of many tourism businesses and destinations.
5. The relation between social interaction, communication media and content can provide various supplementary advantages. It is more convenient and efficient way of spreading information compared to traditional media and thus, more and more companies are utilising it as a marketing channel. Furthermore, through media visibility companies are able to create more approachable image and possibly bring awareness among new customers as well as retain existing consumer relationships.
6. One of the popular travel social media site Expedia Media Solutions partnered with ComScore, shed some insightful details of how travellers consume and share content prior to, during and after a trip.
7. It shows that the field of online content consumption is growing at a rapid pace. Another interesting point was that content is available and being accessed by consumers across more platforms and channels than ever before. Not surprisingly coming from an Expedia Solutions study, online travel agencies were found to be an important source across all platforms and throughout all stages of the booking process.

UNSOLVED

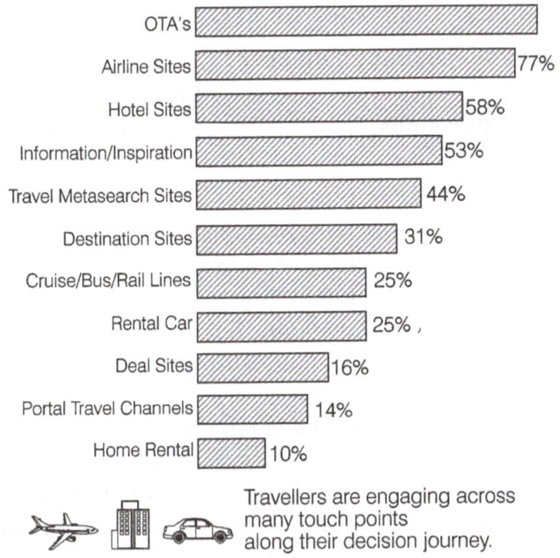

Travel Buyer Reach

8. It is no wonder that destinations, airlines, hotels and most travel marketers are embracing social networks such as pinterest, photo/video applications such as Instagram and Vine, as part of their storytelling toolkit, reaching out to growing crowds of travellers.

Based on your understanding of the passage, answer of the following questions. (1 × 8 = 8)

(i) Complete the following suitably. (1)
The given passage focuses on ....

(ii) Which of the following statements is not substantiated by information in Paragraph 4? (1)
(a) The established marketing practices of many tourism businesses and destinations are challenged by the online media.
(b) Social media constitute a substantial part of the travel search results.
(c) Search engines link the travellers directly to social media sites.
(d) None of the above

(iii) In what way do social media sites given supplementary advantage? (1)

(iv) Based on the given graphical representation of data in the passage, choose the option that lists the statements that are TRUE with respect to the usage of social media networks. (1)
1. Online travel agencies are an important source across all platforms and throughout all stages of the booking process.
2. Through media visibility companies are able to complicate their market standing.
3. Different technological interfaces facilitate the information exchange between online travellers.
4. Travellers seem to move away from the 'collective intelligence' available on the web.

Codes

(a) 1 and 3 (b) 2 and 4
(c) 1 and 4 (d) 2 and 3

(v) According to the given data graph, which marketing field shows the greatest influence of tourists? (1)
(a) Travel Metasearch Sites (b) Portal Travel Channels
(c) Online Travel Agencies (d) Airline Sites

(vi) Who, as per the information given in the passage, are the controllers in the field of tourism? (1)

(vii) Why are more and more companies are utilising social media as a marketing channel? (1)

(viii) What is called the collective intelligence? (1)

(a) Search engines
(b) Social media sites
(c) Online tourism applications
(d) All of these

3. Read the passage given below. (8)

Smoking is the major cause of mortality with bronchogenic carcinoma of the lungs and is one of the factors causing death due to malignancies of the larynx, oral cavity, oesophagus, bladder, kidney, pancreas, stomach and uterine cervix, along with coronary heart disease.

Nicotine is the major substance present in smoke that causes physical dependence. The additives do produce damage to the body, e.g. ammonia can result in a 100-fold increase in the ability of nicotine to enter into the smoke.

Levulinic acid, added to cigarettes to mask the harsh taste of the nicotine, can increase the binding of nicotine to brain receptors, which increases the 'kick' of nicotine.

Smoke from the burning end of a cigarette contains over 4000 chemicals and 40 carcinogens. It has long been known that tobacco smoke is carcinogenic or cancer-causing.

Our brain is made up of billions of nerve cells. They communicate with each other by chemical messengers called neurotransmitters. Nicotine is one of the most powerful nerve poisons and binds stereo-selectively to nicotinic receptors located in the brain, autonomic ganglia, the medulla and neuro-muscular junctions. Located throughout the brain, they play a critical role in cognitive processes and memory.

Recent research studies suggest that acute nicotine administration would result in increased dopamine release from the brain, producing perceptions of pleasure and happiness, increased energy and motivation, increased alertness and increased feeling of vigour during the early phase of smoking.

However, notwithstanding these superficial effects, research shows that the relationship between smoking and memory loss is strongest in people who smoke more than 20 cigarettes each day and this is not specific to the socio-economic status, gender or a range of associated medical conditions. Smoking may speed up age-related memory loss and the details are not yet clear. Some studies suggest that repeated exposure to high nicotine smoke related to the 'brain-wiring' is nothing but neuron-biochemistry that deals with complex interaction among genetic experiences and bio-chemistry of brain cells.

(i) On the basis of your reading of the above passage, make notes on it using headings and sub-headings. Use recognisable abbreviations, wherever necessary (minimum 4). Supply an appropriate title to it. (5)

(ii) Write a summary of the given passage in 80-100 words. (3)

UNSOLVED

SECTION - B

Grammar

[7 *Marks*]

4. Choose the correct option. Answer any three. (1 × 3 = 3)

(i) I met my childhood friend in Dehradun .... I used to live before.

(a) When (b) Where (c) Whereas (d) Why

(ii) He will wait for his sister .... she has her operation.

(a) When (b) If (c) While (d) Then

(iii) The olympic games .... place every four years.

(a) have taken (b) are taking (c) take (d) took

(iv) Look! That man .... to open the door of your car.

(a) tries (b) has been trying (c) tried (d) is trying

5. Choose the correct option. (1 × 4 = 4)

(i) Transform the given sentence into Past Continuous Tense.
The artist has finished the painting.
(a) The artist were finishing the painting.
(b) The artist is finishing the painting.
(c) The artist did finishing the painting.
(d) The artist had finishing the painting.

(ii) Transform the given sentence into Present Perfect Continuous Tense.
Those boys made noise in the library.
(a) Those boys has been making noise in the library.
(b) Those boys will have been making noise in the library.
(c) Those boys have made noise in the library.
(d) Those boys have making noise in the library.

(iii) Transform the given sentence into Future Continuous Tense.
The children will blow up these balloons.
(a) The children will be blowing up these balloons.
(b) The children will be blow up these balloons.
(c) The children will blow up these balloons.
(d) The children will blowing up these balloons.

(iv) Transform the given sentence into Past Perfect Tense.
He will dismiss them from service for carelessness.
(a) He had dismissed them from service for carelessness.
(b) He did dismissed them from service for carelessness.
(c) He had dismiss them from service for carelessness.
(d) He dismissed them from service for carelessness.

Creative Writing Skills [16 *Marks*]

6. You are a manager of ABC Ltd. Sector 30 Gurgaon. You need an efficient data entry operator for your office. Write an advertisement for the 'Situation Vacant' column of a local daily. (3)

Or You are Nayan of WZ-4976 Moti Nagar, New Delhi. Your youger brother, Sahil, aged 15, 145 cms tall, fair coloured, dressed in blue shirt and black pants is missing for the past two days. Draft a suitable advertisement in the 'Missing Persons' column of a daily newspaper in not more than 50 words.

7. You are Praveen / Pari, Secretary of the NGO 'Help the Needy'. Design a poster to be displayed at prominent places in the city asking for people to donate their organs after death. Give details of which organs are to be donated and whom to contact for registering. *(50 words)* (3)

Or As the President, Environmental Club, DAV Sr. Sec. School, Ashok Vihar, Delhi, you want to educate people about the harm done by plastics. You have organised a campaign against plastics. Prepare a suitable poster highlighting the issue. *(50 words)*

UNSOLVED

8. The Prime Minister's campaign 'Swachh Bharat' has become popular throughout India. Inspired by this, you, the Principal of a reputed school decide to address the students on 'The value of cleanliness'. Write your speech in 120-150 words with the help of the following visual. (5)

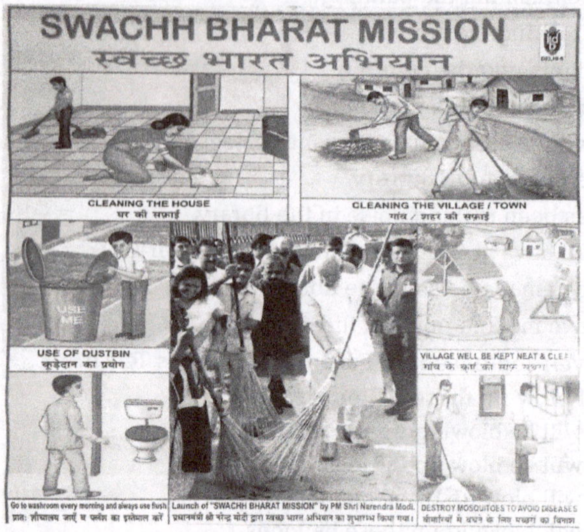

Or Media has a stronghold on society. Write a speech in 120-150 words, on how media influences public opinion, to be delivered in the school assembly.

9. Reality shows are a waste of time and talent. Give your views for or against the motion. *(120-150 words)* (5)

> For the Motion: Nothing real – everything is scripted – more focus on drama than on talent – most winners faded into oblivion – TRP games – play on emotions than on talent
>
> Against the Motion: Many talents have come up through reality shows – provide easy access to industry – provide name and fame – various talents are showcased and acknowledged.

Or Migration from villages to cities has led to the spread of urban slums. People living %in these slums lead a miserable life. Economic disparity leads to the problems of law and order. Write a debate in 120-150 words on 'Solution to the problem of misery in the urban slums lies in creating jobs in the villages'. You are Navtej/Navita.

SECTION - C

Literature Textbooks

[31 *Marks*]

10. Read the extracts given below and answer the questions that follow. ***(Do any one)*** (1 × 3 = 3)

And who art thou? said I to the soft-falling shower,
Which, strange to tell, gave me an answer, as here translated:
I am the Poem of Earth, said the voice of the rain,

(i) What poetic device is used in the last line?

(a) Simile
(b) Personification
(c) Metaphor
(d) Alliteration

(ii) Complete the following suitably.

The rain calls itself ....

(iii) What did the poet find strange?

Or

Now she's been dead nearly as many years
As that girl lived. And of this circumstance
There is nothing to say at all
Its silence silences.

(i) Name the poetic device used in the last line.

(a) Oxymoron (b) Alliteration
(c) Simile (d) Metaphor

(ii) Select the correct option from those given in bracket to fill in the blank.

The theme of the poem is .... (mortality/childhood).

(iii) Select the phrase that suggests the following.

It is emphasised that power of silence is overwhelming.

11. Read the extracts given below and answer the questions that follow. ***(Do any one)*** (1 × 3 = 3)

"Now that we were leaving Ravu, Lhamo said she wanted to give me a farewell present. One evening I'd told her through Daniel that I was heading towards Mount Kailash to complete the kora and she'd said that I ought to get some warmer clothes. After ducking back into her tent, she emerged carrying one of the long-sleeved sheepskin coats that all the men wore. Tsetan sized me up as we clambered into his car. "Ah, yes," he declared, "drokba, sir." We took a short cut to get off the Changtang. Tsetan knew a route that would take us South-West, almost directly towards Mount Kailash. It involved crossing several fairly high mountain passes, he said. "But no problem, sir", he assured us, "if there is no snow." What was the likelihood of that I asked. "Not knowing, sir, until we get there."

(i) Complete the following suitably.

It can be inferred from the passage that Lhamo was .... to travellers.

(ii) Tsetan says that there will be no problem in their journey if there is no snow.

He means that snow ....

(a) can hasten their movement
(b) determines the smoothness of their journey
(c) can tell if they can reach Mount Kailash
(d) will increase their difficulties in the journey

(iii) Why does the author communicate via Daniel as can be understood by when he says "I'd told her through Daniel"?

Or

She searched through the telephone list, the staff list and then through the directory of employees of all the branches of the firm. She shook her head and said, "I am afraid I can't find anyone of that name either here or in any of our branches. Are you sure he works here?"

This was a blow, not totally unexpected. If he himself were dead in this world, what guarantee had he that his son would be alive? Indeed, he may not even have been born!

(i) Complete the following suitably.

In the first line, 'she' refers to ....

(ii) What shocked Professor Gaitonde the most?
(a) His son had lied to him
(b) His son was an absconder
(c) There was no trace of his son
(d) None of these

(iii) Read the assertion and reason given below.

Assertion (A) The speaker feels a sense of uncertainity and despair about finding the person they are searching for.

Reason (R) The failure to find the name in the directory leads the speaker to doubt the person's existence.

(a) Both (A) and (R) are true and (R) is the correct explanation of (A).
(b) Both (A) and (R) are tue, but (R) is not the correct explanation of (A).
(c) (A) is true, but (R) is false.
(d) (R) is true, but (A) is fale.

12. Read the extracts given below and answer the questions that follow. ***(Do any one)*** (1 × 4 = 4)

"[As she is about to rise, Mrs. Fitzgerald reaches out across the table and pulls her down.]

Mrs. Fitzgerald Let 'em wait or look after themselves for once. This is where your foot goes down. Start now. [She lights a cigarette from the one she has just finished.]

Mrs. Pearson [Embarrassed] Mrs. Fitzgerald—I know you mean well—in fact, I agree with you— but I just can't—and it's no use you trying to make me. If I promise you I'd really have it out with them, I know I wouldn't be able to keep my promise.

Mrs. Fitzgerald Then let me do it.

Mrs. Pearson [Flustered] Oh no—thank you very much, Mrs Fitzgerald—but that wouldn't do at all.

It couldn't possibly be somebody else— they'd resent it at once and wouldn't listen— and really I couldn't blame them. I know I ought to do it—but you see how it is? [She looks apologetically across the table, smiling rather miserably.]

Mrs. Fitzgerald [Coolly] You haven't got the idea."

UNSOLVED

(i) What is the contrast in the personalities of the two women?
(a) Polite vs Assertive
(b) Gentle vs Sensible
(c) Scared vs Brave
(d) They have nothing to contrast

(ii) Which of the following explains "This is where your foot goes down"?
(a) To physically fix your foot down to the floor
(b) To restraint yourself against a strong person
(c) To adopt a firm policy when faced with opposition or disobedience
(d) To give into what is expected

(iii) Who are the women talking about in the passage above?

(iv) Why does Mrs. Fitzgerald's idea embarrass Mrs. Pearson?

Or

Then another visitor arrived, a farmer named John Byro, an Assyrian who, out of loneliness, had learned to speak Armenian. My mother brought the lonely visitor coffee and tobacco and he rolled a cigarette and sipped and smoked, and then at last, sighing sadly, he said, My white horse which was stolen last month is still gone — I cannot understand it.

My uncle Khosrove became very irritated and shouted, It's no harm. What is the loss of a horse? Haven't we all lost the homeland? What is this crying over a horse?

(i) Complete the following suitably.

"Haven't we all lost the homeland? What is this crying over a horse?"This statement shows the plight of .... easily and shout at others.

(ii) Why was John Byro sad?
  (a) Because he was lonely.
  (b) Because his white horse had been stolen.
  (c) Because Uncle Khosrove had scolded him.
  (d) None of the above

(iii) Select the correct option from those given in bracket to fill in the blanks.

John Byro learnt to speak Armenian because of .... (loneliness/curiosity).

(iv) For how long did Mourad have the horse before Aram got to know about it?

Literature Textbooks [16 *Marks*]

13. Answer *any two* of the following questions in 40-50 words. (3 × 2 = 6)

(i) What was the farewell present given by Lhamo to the author when he told her that he was going to Mount Kailash?

(ii) Interpret how the rain becomes the voice of Earth?

(iii) Explain why you think scientific discoveries are significant? Discuss it in reference to the chapter 'Discovering Tut: the Saga Continues'.

(iv) The poem 'A Photograph' is a tribute to poet's mother. Explain

14. Answer *any one* of the following questions in 40-50 words. (3 × 1 = 3)

Why was Andrew disturbed that night?

Or What change could be seen in Mrs Pearson's family in the end on 'Mother's Day'?

15. Answer *any one* of the following questions in 120-150 words. (1 × 6 = 6)

Describe the scene that transported Professor Gaitonde to the alternative universe.

Or What are some of the hallmarks of growing up according to Markus Natten with reference to the poem 'Childhood'?

16. Answer *any one* of the following questions in 120-150 words. (1 × 6 = 6)

How does war harm lives? What feelings does war bring with it? Discuss with reference to the story 'The Address'.

Or How did the 'just and placid king' get executed?

ANSWERS

1. (i) The consequence of a father's word being final in a joint family system would be that nobody could dare to say anything against it.

(ii) 'Acceptance' plays an important role in a joint family system.The members of a joint family system should feel accepted for who they are and as they are. Moreover, one should accept one's own weaknesses and limitations and that of others.

(iii) (d) advent of industrialisation and more job opportunities

(iv) Having unrealistic expectations from others

(v) (c) Judgemental listening is necessary to help family members open up to one another.

(vi) 'Initiate' in the 1st Paragraph means 'the opportunity to take a step'.

(vii) A joint family can succeed if there is mutual trust among the members of the family. The members should be tolerant of each other's weaknesses. Moreover, an environment that is conducive to open communication helps in making a joint family system succeed.

(viii) (c) discontentment

(ix) (b) Changing Family System

(x) The constant interference and meddling by elders in youngsters' matters led to the disintegration of the family system.

2. (i) the increasing role of social media in tourism

(ii) (d) None of the above

(iii) Social media sites give supplementary advantage because of the system of communication and interactions.

(iv) (a) 1 and 3

(v) (c) Online Travel Agencies

(vi) The government and administrative bodies are the controllers in the field of tourism.

(vii) More and more companies are utilising social media as a marketing channel because it is a more convenient and efficient way of spreading information.

(viii) Enormous

(viii) (d) All of these

UNSOLVED